# THE DICKENS
# ENCYCLOPÆDIA

# THE DICKENS ENCYCLOPÆDIA

AN ALPHABETICAL DICTIONARY OF REFERENCES
TO EVERY CHARACTER AND PLACE MENTIONED IN
THE WORKS OF FICTION, WITH EXPLANATORY
NOTES ON OBSCURE ALLUSIONS AND PHRASES

ARTHUR L. HAYWARD

LONDON
ROUTLEDGE & KEGAN PAUL

*First published 1924*
*by George Routledge & Sons Limited*

*Reprinted twice 1969*
*by Routledge & Kegan Paul Limited*
*Broadway House, 68-74 Carter Lane*
*London E.C.4*

*Printed in Great Britain*
*by Compton Printing Limited*
*London & Aylesbury*

*SBN 7100 6317 2*

DEDICATED

TO

MY WIFE

# PREFACE

THIS volume needs little introduction. It is intended to be a reference book to the fiction of Charles Dickens, of especial interest to the increasing number of readers to whom many allusions in his novels must, in these days, be almost unintelligible. Dr. Johnson observed that all books describing manners require annotation within sixty years or less. Nearly a century has elapsed since Mr. Pickwick and his friends set out on their travels, and much of the world with which they were familiar has, at the touch of " Time's effacing fingers," altered beyond recognition.

The last hundred years have wrought more changes in our manner of life than any two preceding centuries. Articles which were in everyday use with Mr. Pickwick's contemporaries are now finding places in our museums ; inventions such as then seemed the summit of scientific attainment are considered by later generations as the crude forerunners of modern civilisation ; allusions once on everybody's lips can now be traced only with difficulty, if at all, in rare and expensive works of reference.

With every year that elapses it becomes increasingly hard for new readers to appreciate Dickens to the full, to understand his allusions to contemporary events and people, to visualise the vanished London in which his creatures moved. It has been my object to throw light on these obscurities before Time buries them in yet deeper darkness. I have, therefore, explained every reference which might appear strange or difficult. I have described such topographical changes as have taken place since the books were written, and have done my best to show Dickens's readers something of the world in which their great grandfathers lived and flourished.

I have only dealt with those works which are commonly read. For this reason I have left alone the *American and Italian Notes*, the *Child's History of England* and the *Miscellaneous Papers* so diligently collected by Mr. B. W. Matz, as they are apart from my purpose, and their inclusion would have enlarged this book beyond reasonable bounds. The *Life, Letters and Speeches* are chiefly in the hands of students, and would require even more exhaustive and spacious treatment.

The identification of originals has been a matter of much deliberation, for I have done my best to avoid a pitfall into which their very zeal has beguiled many worthy Dickensians—I mean trying to find more in Dickens's works than he ever put into them. Tracing originals is a fascinating hobby which should be ridden with a very tight rein.

One of the most difficult yet gratifying tasks in writing the preface to a reference book such as this is making suitable acknowledgment to those whose work has smoothed the path of the compiler. There are two names to which every Dickensian instinctively bows with homage and admiration. I allude to the late Mr. F. G. Kitton and to Mr. B. W. Matz.  The prodigious labours and erudition of the latter place every lover of Dickens under an obligation of gratitude he can never hope to discharge.  Messrs. R. Allbut, Snowden Ward, Edwin Pugh, Walter Dexter and C. Van Noorden are others in the hierarchy of Dickensians whose works have been invaluable.  *Notes and Queries* has furnished the solutions to several problems, and I need hardly add that I have delved deep into that mine of lore, *The Dickensian*, by the able editorship of which Mr. Matz heaps yet another obligation upon us.  Mr. J. T. Lightwood's *Charles Dickens and Music* has been of use in identifying some of the quotations.  I am indebted to Mr. T. W. Tyrrell for most of the illustrations and for much useful advice and help.  Finally, I would express my gratitude to Mr. Archibald Hunter for assistance in many ways.

# CHRONOLOGICAL LIST OF THE WORKS DEALT WITH IN THIS ENCYCLOPÆDIA

| Work. | When it Appeared. | Abbreviated Title used in this Book. |
|---|---|---|
| Sketches by Boz. | 1836. | *Boz.* |
| The Strange Gentleman. | St. James's Theatre, 1836. | *Strange Gentleman.* |
| The Village Coquettes. | St. James's Theatre, 1836. | *Village Coquettes.* |
| Is She His Wife ? | St. James's Theatre, 1837. | *Is She His Wife ?* |
| Pickwick Papers. | Monthly parts, Mar., 1836, to Oct., 1837. | *Pickwick.* |
| Public Life of Mr. Tulrumble. | Bentley's Miscellany, Jan., 1837. | *Tulrumble.* |
| Pantomime of Life. | Bentley's Miscellany, Mar., 1837. | *Pantomime of Life.* |
| Mudfog Papers. | Bentley's Miscellany, 1837–8. | *Mudfog.* |
| Oliver Twist. | Bentley's Miscellany, Jan., 1837, to Mar., 1839. | *Twist.* |
| Robert Bolton. | Bentley's Miscellany, Aug., 1838. | *Bolton.* |
| Sketches of Young Gentlemen. | 1838. | *Sketches of Gentlemen.* |
| Nicholas Nickleby. | Monthly parts, April, 1838, to Oct., 1839. | *Nickleby.* |
| Sketches of Young Couples. | 1840. | *Sketches of Couples.* |
| Master Humphrey's Clock. | Weekly parts, April 4, 1840, to Nov. 27, 1841. | *Humphrey.* |
| The Old Curiosity Shop. | Master Humphrey's Clock, April, 1840, to Jan., 1841. | *Curiosity Shop.* |
| Barnaby Rudge. | Master Humphrey's Clock, Jan. to Nov., 1841. | *Barnaby.* |
| A Christmas Carol. | Christmas, 1843. | *Christmas Carol.* |
| Martin Chuzzlewit. | Monthly parts, Jan., 1843, to July, 1844. | *Chuzzlewit.* |
| The Chimes. | Christmas, 1844. | *Chimes.* |
| The Cricket on the Hearth. | Christmas, 1845. | *Cricket on the Hearth.* |
| The Battle of Life. | Christmas, 1846. | *Battle of Life.* |
| Dombey and Son. | Monthly parts, Oct., 1846, to April, 1848. | *Dombey.* |
| The Haunted Man. | Christmas, 1848. | *Haunted Man.* |
| David Copperfield. | Monthly parts, May, 1849, to Nov., 1850. | *Copperfield.* |
| Bleak House. | Monthly parts, Mar., 1852, to Sept., 1853. | *Bleak House.* |

| Work. | When it Appeared. | Abbreviated Title used in this Book. |
|---|---|---|
| Hard Times. | Household Words, April to Aug., 1854. | *Hard Times.* |
| Seven Poor Travellers. | Household Words, Christmas, 1854. | *Seven Poor Travellers.* |
| Little Dorrit. | Monthly parts, Dec., 1855, to June, 1857. | *Dorrit.* |
| The Holly Tree. | Household Words, Christmas, 1855. | *Holly Tree.* |
| The Wreck of the Golden Mary. | Household Words, Christmas, 1856. | *Golden Mary.* |
| The Perils of Certain English Prisoners. | Household Words, Christmas, 1857. | *English Prisoners.* |
| Going into Society. | Household Words, Christmas, 1858. | *Going into Society.* |
| Reprinted Pieces. | 1858. | *Reprinted* (followed by name of Piece). |
| A Tale of Two Cities. | All the Year Round, April to Nov., 1859. | *Two Cities.* |
| The Haunted House. | All the Year Round, Christmas, 1859. | *Haunted House.* |
| Great Expectations. | All the Year Round, Dec., 1860, to Aug., 1861. | *Expectations.* |
| A Message from the Sea. | All the Year Round, Christmas, 1860. | *Message from the Sea.* |
| Hunted Down. | All the Year Round, 1860. | *Hunted Down.* |
| Uncommercial Traveller. | All the Year Round, 1860–8. | *Uncommercial.* |
| Tom Tiddler's Ground. | All the Year Round, Christmas, 1861. | *Tom Tiddler.* |
| Somebody's Luggage. | All the Year Round, Christmas, 1862. | *Somebody's Luggage.* |
| Mrs. Lirriper's Lodgings and Legacy. | All the Year Round, Christmas, 1863–4. | *Mrs. Lirriper.* |
| Our Mutual Friend. | Monthly parts, May, 1864, to Nov., 1865. | *Mutual Friend.* |
| Dr. Marigold's Prescriptions. | All the Year Round, Christmas, 1865. | *Dr. Marigold.* |
| Mugby Junction. | All the Year Round, Christmas, 1866. | *Mugby.* |
| No Thoroughfare. | All the Year Round, Christmas, 1867. | *No Thoroughfare.* |
| A Holiday Romance. | All the Year Round, Jan. to May, 1868. | *Holiday Romance.* |
| George Silverman's Explanation. | All the Year Round, Jan. to Mar., 1868. | *Silverman.* |
| Edwin Drood. | Monthly parts, April to Sept., 1870. | *Drood.* |

# LIST OF ILLUSTRATIONS

*The following plates will be found at the end of the text*

# THE DICKENS ENCYCLOPÆDIA

## A

**AARON, MR.** The name given by Eugene Wrayburn to Riah, the Jew. (*q.v.*)

**ACADEMY.** The old custom of styling the most insignificant school an academy is exemplified in :—

1. Mr. Turveydrop's Academy in Newman Street, Oxford Street. No. 26 is probably the original house. *Bleak House*, 14, 23, 30, 38, 50.

2. Mr. Cripples's Academy in the neighbourhood of the Marshalsea, probably in Lant Street. *Dorrit*, I, 9.

3. Signor Billsmethi's Dancing Academy "in the neighbourhood of Gray's Inn Lane," where Augustus Cooper met his misadventure. *Boz, Characters*, 9.

**ADAM AND EVE COURT.** A small court on the N. side of Oxford Street, next to Wells Street, and the residence of Mr. Sluffen. *Boz, Scenes*, 20.

**ADAMS.** 1. Head boy at Dr. Strong's school at Canterbury. *Copperfield*, 16, 18.

2. Clerk to Mr. Sampson, in the Life Assurance Office. *Hunted Down*.

3. An Army captain who acted as second to Lord Frederick Verisopht in his fatal duel with Sir Mulberry Hawk. *Nickleby*, 50.

4. Jack, "man with a cast in his eye," the hero of one of Cousin Feenix's anecdotes. *Dombey*, 36.

5. Jane, housemaid to the Young Couple and confidential servant to the Old Couple. *Sketches of Couples*.

**ADELPHI.** There have been few changes in the Adelphi since it was built in 1768. It is less residential than of yore, but there is still " the sudden pause to the roar of the great thoroughfare . . . like putting cotton-wool in the ears." Here it was that Arthur Clennam saw Miss Wade and Blandois deep in conversation (*Dorrit*, II, 9), while in the "humble region of the Adelphi" Martin Chuzzlewit found lodgings in a poor public-house (*Chuzzlewit*, 13). It was the residence of Cornelius Brook Dingwall, M.P. (*Boz, Tales, Sentiment*). Mrs. Edson attempted to commit suicide from the Adelphi Terrace (there was no Embankment in those days) (*Lirriper's Lodgings*). The main interest in the Adelphi, however, centres round Osborne's Hotel (*q.v.*) at the corner of John and Adam Streets, where the closing scenes of Pickwick were enacted (*Pickwick*, 54, 56). In intervals of drudgery at Murdstone and Grinby's little David Copperfield liked to wander about the Adelphi, fascinated by the mystery of its gloomy arches ; while at York House, No. 15 Buckingham Street (since demolished), lived Mrs. Crupp with whom he lodged in happier years (*Copperfield*, 11, 23-6, 28, 34, 35, 37, 40). Dickens himself occupied rooms in this house in 1834.

**ADMIRAL BENBOW INN.** The hotel at the empty watering place. *Reprinted, Out of the Season*.

**ADMIRALTY.** One of Mr. Merdle's guests, a Magnate at the Admiralty. *Dorrit*, I, 21.

**AFFERY.** Christian name of Mrs. Flintwinch. (*q.v.*)

**AFRICAN KNIFE SWALLOWER.** A member of the theatrical company, who took the vice-chair at the farewell dinner to the Crummleses on their departure for America. *Nickleby*, 48.

**AGED, THE.** John Wemmick's pet name for his old father. *See* Wemmick.

**AGGERAWATOR.** 1. This was the old name for the long quiff of hair, curling back from the forehead towards the ear, formerly in fashion among gentry of the coster class. *Boz, Characters*, 4.

2. Jerry Cruncher's name for his wife. *Two Cities*, II, 1.

**AGNES.** 1. Maidservant and toady to Mrs. Bloss, who inspired old Tibbs with maudlin affection. *Boz, Tales, Boarding House*.

2. David Copperfield's life-long friend and second wife. *See* Wickfield, Agnes.

**AH SING, GEORGE.** Original of Jack Chinaman. (*q.v.*)

**AKERMAN, MR.** This was one of the keepers of Newgate Prison and an exceedingly humane man who had assisted Howard in his visitation of the prison some time previous to the Gordon Riots. Akerman's adventures in the Riots are accurately narrated in *Barnaby*, 64, 77. Akerman was a friend of James Boswell.

**AKERSHEM, SOPHRONIA.** A friend of the Veneerings, who married Alfred Lammle. (*q.v.*)

**ALBANY, THE.** These chambers, situated on the north side of Piccadilly, between Sackville Street and Burlington House, have been occupied by men of fashion since the beginning of the 19th century. According to the *Uncommercial Traveller* (10) the north wall between the Burlington Arcade and the Albany was the rendezvous of blind beggars. It was one of Mr. Edward Malderton's claims to be a man of fashion that he had actually had an intimate friend who once knew a gentleman who formerly lived in the Albany (*Boz, Tales, Sparkins*). The Albany was the residence of Fascination Fledgeby and the scene of his richly deserved thrashing at the hands of Lammle. *Mutual Friend*, III, 1, 8.

**ALBION, LITTLE RUSSELL STREET.** This popular tavern, where Messrs. Potter and Smithers used to spend their convivial evenings, was a favourite meeting place of actors and one of the centres of Bohemian London until the making of New Oxford Street in 1846. *Boz, Characters*, 11.

**ALDERSGATE STREET.** This thoroughfare was formerly called thus only from St. Martins le Grand to Long Lane, beyond which it became Goswell Street. Arthur Clennam was walking down this street towards St. Paul's when he encountered the crowd escorting Cavaletto to the hospital after he had been knocked down by a Mail Coach (*Dorrit*, I, 13). During his furtive visits to London, John Jasper put up at a "hybrid hotel, boarding house or lodging house," in a little square at the back of Aldersgate Street (*Drood*, 23). The firm of Anthony Chuzzlewit and Son had their warehouse in or near this street (*Chuzzlewit*, 11).

**ALDGATE HIGH STREET** formerly ran eastward from the Pump to the corner of Petticoat Lane, now Middlesex Street, where it became Whitechapel High Street. It is memorable as the residence of Mr. Pickwick's inveterate critic, Blotton (*Pickwick*, I, 11). The Gentleman in Small Clothes had information that the Statue from Charing Cross had been seen arm in arm with the Pump (*Nickleby*, 41). Poor Toots, frantic at the open lovemaking going on between Walter Gay and Florence Dombey, took a walk from Leadenhall Street to the Pump and back to cool himself (*Dombey*, 56). In earlier days Mark Gilbert's master, Thomas Curzon, was a hosier, at the sign of the Golden Fleece, Aldgate (*Barnaby*, 8).

**ALICE.** 1. The bowyer's daughter and heroine of Magog's tale. *Humphrey*.
2. Youngest of the Five Sisters of York. *Nickleby*, 6.

**ALICIA.** Heroine of Miss Alice Rainbird's story. *Holiday Romance*.

**ALICK.** "A damp, earthy child in red worsted socks," encountered in the Gravesend steam packet. *Boz, Scenes*, 10.

**ALICUMPANE, MRS.** A friend of the Oranges. *Holiday Romance*.

**ALLEN.** Arabella Allen was a "black-eyes young lady in a very nice little pair of boots with fur round the tops," who was a guest at Isabella Wardle's wedding and at the Christmas party which followed, when she and Mr. Winkle fell in love with one another. Her brother sent her to their aunt at Clifton, and while staying there she had an interview with Winkle, chaperoned by Mr. Pickwick. A few months later the couple were secretly married, and it was partly through her entreaty that he would break the news to old Mr. Winkle that Mr. Pickwick consented to quit the Fleet prison. Her own winsome ways, however, really won the old man's forgiveness. *Pickwick*, 28, 30, 38, 39, 47, 53, 54, 56, 57.

Benjamin Allen, her brother, was a drunken medical student and bosom friend of Bob Sawyer, whom he intended that Arabella should marry.

While assisting Bob at the chemist's shop at Bristol he heard of his sister's marriage to Winkle, but being reconciled to the event by Mr. Pickwick, accompanied that gentleman on his mission to Birmingham. Eventually Ben Allen and Bob Sawyer went to Bengal, tried abstinence and prospered (*Pickwick*, 30, 32, 38, 48, 50–2, 54, 57). The Allens' Aunt was a rather prim old lady, living at Clifton, to whom Ben sent his sister when he found that she did not favour the idea of becoming Mrs. Bob Sawyer. *Pickwick*, 38, 39, 48.

**"ALLEYBI."** It was Mr. Tony Weller's firm conviction that the verdict would never have gone against Mr. Pickwick if only he had proved an "alleybi." *Pickwick*, 33, 43.

**ALLEY TOR.** This was an extra fine or large marble, possibly originally made of alabaster, hence the name. It was in contrast to the "commoney" or plain marble. *Pickwick*, 34.

**"ALL IN THE DOWNS."** From Gay's "Black-Eyed Susan," beginning, "All in the Downs the fleet was moored." *Pickwick*, 3.

**"ALL ROUND MY HAT."** This song was first sung by W. H. Williams in 1835 and attained extraordinary popularity; "round my hat" developing into a catch phrase as used in *Boz, Scenes*, 23, which was current until the late 50's. The song, which is supposed to be sung by a coster whose sweetheart has been transported for thieving, has a chorus :—

> All round my hat I vears a green villow.
> All round my hat for a twelvemonth and a day.
> If anyone should ax it, the reason vy I wears it,
> Tell them that my true love is far, far away.
> *Boz, Scenes*, 17.

**"ALL'S WELL."** The refrain, with a roll, from a song in Dibdin's "The English Fleet," set to music by Braham. *See also* "Deserted by the waning Moon." *Curiosity Shop*, 56.

**"ALONG THE LINE."** From the first verse of "The Death of Nelson." *Mutual Friend*, IV, 3.

**ALPHONSE.** Mrs. Wittitterley's page, "if ever an Alphonse carried plain Bill in his face and figure, that page was the boy." *Nickleby*, 21, 28, 33.

**ALTRO.** Name given by Pancks to Cavaletto (*q.v.*). It is an Italian word used with a somewhat general sense of affirmation, "certainly," "by all means," and was much in the mouth of the little Italian exile.

**AMELIA.** 1. The wife of Bill, a criminal whose defence had been undertaken by Mr. Jaggers. *Expectations*, 20.

2. A girl who helped her sister Jane to preside over a game of chance in the Ramsgate Library. *Boz, Tales, Tuggs*.

**AMERICA JUNIOR.** Nom de plume of Putnam Smif. (*q.v.*)

**AMERICA SQUARE.** This is situated behind Fenchurch Street Station. In it were the offices of Dringworth Brothers. *Message from Sea*.

**AMIENS.** One of the French towns where Our Missis found to her disgust that the railways refreshment rooms were conducted efficiently. *Mugby Junction*.

**AMSTERDAM.** After the crash, financially and actually, of the house of Clennam, Jeremiah Flintwinch took refuge in Holland and was known in the drinking shops of Amsterdam as Mynheer van Flyntevynge. *Dorrit*, II, 31.

**ANALYTICAL CHEMIST, THE.** The Veneerings' butler who went round at dinner "like a gloomy analytical chemist, always seeming to say after ' Chablis, Sir ? '— ' You wouldn't if you knew what it's made of.' " *Mutual Friend*, I, 2, 10, 17 ; II, 3, 16 ; III, 17.

**ANDERSON, JOHN.** A tramp encountered in the country bearing a spade on which was chalked the word HUNGRY. *Uncommercial*, 11.

**" AND YOU NEEDN'T BE YOUR BLACK BOTTLE."** This is a truly Weggian version of the last verse of Auld Lang Syne :—

> And surely you'll be your pint stoup,
> And surely I'll be mine !
> And we'll tak' a cup o' kindness yet,
> For auld lang syne.
> *Mutual Friend*, III, 6.

**ANGEL INN.** 1. At Bury St. Edmunds. Few changes have taken place in the appearance of this inn since Mr. Pickwick and Sam Weller arrived here in their search for Jingle. Here it was that Sam first met Job Trotter, the "melan-cholly chap with the black hair," and in its parlour Mr. Pickwick received the letter from Dodson and Fogg intimating that Mrs. Bardell was sueing him for breach of promise (*Pickwick*, 15–18). Dickens stayed at the Angel while reporting the Parliamentary election of 1835, and is said to have occupied Room No. 11.

2. The famous Islington tavern, at the corner of Pentonville Road and High Street, was one of the old posting and coaching inns. The premises were rebuilt in 1880 and much altered in more recent years when it became one of Messrs. J. Lyons's establishments. Oliver Twist and Jack Dawkins passed the Angel when they entered London. Mr. Brownlow drove Oliver to his home in Pentonville by way of the inn, and later Noah Claypole and Charlotte passed it when making their way to the City. *Twist*, 8, 12, 42.

**ANGELICA.** An old sweetheart of the Traveller with whom he took shelter from a shower in a church in Huggin Lane. *Uncommercial*, 9.

**ANGLERS' INN.** The river-side tavern where Eugene Wrayburn put up when seeking Lizzie Hexam. She carried him thither after Headstone's murderous attack ; and there they were eventually married. It has been identified as the Red Lion Hotel, Henley-on-Thames. *Mutual Friend*, IV, 6, 10, 11.

**ANGLO - BENGALEE DISINTERESTED LIFE AND LOAN ASSURANCE COMPANY.** The bogus concern engineered by Tigg Montague and David Crimple, with a paid-up capital of " a two and as many noughts after it as the printer can get in the line." The Anglo-Bengalee was typical of the many fraudulent companies which robbed the public before the introduction of adequate legislation. *Chuzzlewit*, 27, 38, 41, 44, 49.

**ANKWORKS PACKAGE.** Mrs. Gamp's rendering of the Antwerp Packet. *Chuzzlewit*, 40.

**ANNE.** 1. One of Mr. Dombey's housemaids who married Towlinson, the butler. *Dombey*, 31, 35, 39.

2. A friend of Jane Adams and housemaid at " No. 26." *Sketches of Couples*.

**ANNUAL REGISTER.** "This is the Annual Register, Wegg, in a cabful of wollumes. Do you know him ? " " Know the Animal Register, Sir ? " returned the Impostor, who had caught the name imperfectly. " For a trifling wager, I think I could find any Animal in him, blindfold, Mr. Boffin." The *Annual Register* is a yearly review of public events at home and abroad. It first appeared, published by Dodsley, in 1758 and came into the hands of Messrs. Longmans in 1890. *Mutual Friend*, III, 6.

**ANNY.** An old pauper woman who was instrumental in unravelling the mystery of Oliver Twist's parentage. *Twist*, 24, 51.

**ANTONIO.** A swarthy Spanish youth who played the guitar in Megisson's lodging house. *Uncommercial*, 5.

**ANTWERP.** Jeremiah Flintwinch's twin brother Ephraim was waiting for the tide to go to Antwerp when he was entrusted with the iron box containing the papers comprising Mrs. Clennam (*Dorrit*, II, 30). It was to a fifth floor, up a narrow back street in Antwerp, that Nickits, the former owner of Josiah Bounderby's country estate, retired after his bankruptcy. *Hard Times*, II, 7.

**APOTHECARY.** In the early nineteenth century the apothecary was not only a chemist, but also acted as a medical man, being called in to attend the poor or practising in country places where better advice was unobtainable. Among such were :—

1. The calm apothecary who was summoned to attend little Paul Dombey at Dr. Blimber's. *Dombey*, 14.

2. The attendant at the deathbed of Nicholas Nickleby, Senior. *Nickleby*, 1.

3. The apothecary's apprentice who attended the workhouse when old Sally died. *Twist*, 24.

**APPARITOR.** The officer of the Court of Arches. *Boz, Scenes*, 8.

**APPRENTICE, THE BONY.** A thin-legged lad who was serving his time with old Lobbs, the sadler. *Pickwick*, 17.

**ARABIN, SERGEANT.** Original of Sergeant Snubbin. (*q.v.*)

**"ARAB STEED."** Dick Swiveller was singing T. H. Bayley's song :—

O give me but my Arab Steed, my prince defends his right,
And I will to the battle speed, to guard him in the fight.
*Curiosity Shop*, 2.

**ARCHBISHOP OF GREENWICH.** Waiter at the inn where Rokesmith and Bella Wilfer celebrated their wedding breakfast. "A solemn gentleman who looked more like a clergyman than *the* clergyman, and seemed to have mounted a great deal higher in the Church : not to say scaled the steeple." *Mutual Friend*, IV, 4.

**ARTFUL DODGER, THE.** Nickname of Jack Dawkins, the young pickpocket. *See* Dawkins.

**ARTHUR.** Surname adopted by Arthur Havisham. (*q.v.*)

**ASHES.** Name of one of Miss Flite's captive birds. *Bleak House*, 14.

**ASHFORD, NETTIE.** A young lady "aged half-past six," the bride of William Tinkling. She wrote the romance of Mrs. Orange and Mrs. Alicumpane. *Holiday Romance*.

**ASSEMBLY.** In the eighteenth and early nineteenth centuries the inconvenience of travel made social intercourse in country parts a matter of difficulty. The country gentry and well-to-do farmers accordingly met at stated times in a fairly central town and held an Assembly, where they danced, played cards, exchanged gossip and made their matches. These Assemblies were usually held in the principal inn of the town, where a large apartment was set aside as an Assembly room.

**ASTLEY'S.** This famous place of amusement, of which the full name was Astley's Royal Equestrian Amphitheatre, was in the Westminster Bridge Road, at the corner of Lambeth Palace Road, and was several times rebuilt after damage by fire, on the last occasion being re-opened by William Batty, on Easter Monday, 1843. The performances consisted of melodramatic spectacles in which a stud of horses was introduced, some of them singly, with riders, others harnessed to carriages or chariots, while realistic battle scenes were much in vogue. The prices were low—from 4s. to 6d.—and Astley's was one of the most popular entertainments of old London. A vivid description is given in *Boz, Scenes*, 11. Kit Nubbles took his mother and little Jacob, with Barbara and her mother to Astley's to celebrate the receipt of his first quarter's wages, and after he had married Barbara, took the whole family party there every quarter (*Curiosity Shop*, 39, 72). After one of his visits to Grandfather Smallweed, Mr. George raised his spirits by a visit to the equestrian show, being much edified to see the Emperor of Tartary get into a cart and bless the united lovers by hovering over them with the Union Jack. *Bleak House*, 21.

**ASTLEY-COOPERISH.** A reference to Sir Astley Cooper (1768-1841), who was one of the most skilful surgeons of his time. He was noted for the vivacity and humour of the remarks he addressed to his patients while operating, for there were no anæsthetics in those days. *Boz, Tales, Excursion*.

**ATHERFIELD, MRS.** A passenger on the *Golden Mary*, who, with her only child Lucy, was put in the long boat when the vessel foundered. Lucy, who died of exposure, was probably founded on Lucy Stroughill, a friend of Dickens's childhood. *Golden Mary*.

**ATKINSON'S.** The famous perfumer in Bond Street. *Uncommercial*, 16.

**ATTORNEY - GENERAL.** Prosecuting counsel against Charles Darnay when he was tried for treason at the Old Bailey. *Two Cities*, II, 2, 3.

**AUNT, MR. F'S.** A crazy old lady who lived with Flora Finching. "Her major characteristics were extreme severity and grim taciturnity, sometimes interrupted by a propensity to offer remarks in a deep warning voice, which, being totally uncalled for by anything said by anybody, and traceable to no association of ideas, confounded and terrified the mind." The most famous and baffling of her sayings was, "There's milestone on the Dover road." *Dorrit*, I, 13, 23, 24, 35 ; II, 9, 34.

**AUSTIN FRIARS.** A winding street, leading from Throgmorton Street, where lived old Martin Chuzzlewit's solicitor, Mr. Fips. *Chuzzlewit*, 39.

**AUSTRALIA.** In the times of the Dickens novels colonization was beginning in Australia and New South Wales was still a penal settlement. It was thither that Abel Magwitch was transported (*Expectations*, 40), as was also Mr. Pratchett (*Somebody's Luggage*, 1). Captain Cuttle wished it to be supposed by Mrs. MacStinger that he had emigrated there (*Dombey*, 25). Its chief interest lies in association with Daniel Peggotty and the

Micawbers, for whom something really did turn up in that colony. *Copperfield*, 57, 63.

**AVENGER, THE.** Name given to Pip's servant, Pepper, who proved an avenging phantom and harassed his master's existence. *Expectations*, 27, 30, 34.

**AVIGNON.** This French city, situated some fifty miles N.W. of Marseilles, was the country of Hortense, the murderess of Mr. Tulkinghorn (*Bleak House*, 12). After his discharge from the dungeon at Marseilles, Cavaletto made his way to Avignon, where he did odds and ends of work (*Dorrit*, I, 11), and it was nearby that Captain Richard Doubledick lived for six months while recovering from his Waterloo wounds (7 *Poor Travellers*).

**"AWAY WITH MELANCHOLY."** This is a song set to an air from Mozart's "Magic Flute." The words, as quoted by Eugene Wrayburn, are :—

> Away with melancholy,
> Nor doleful changes ring
> On life and human folly,
> But merrily, merrily sing
>            Fal la !

*Pickw.*, 44 ; *Curi. Shop*, 58 ; *Mut. Friend*, II, 6 ; *Copper.*, 8.

**AYRESLEIGH.** A haggard debtor whom Mr. Pickwick met in Namby's sponging house. *Pickwick*, 40.

## B

**B., MASTER.** Former occupant of one of the rooms in the Poplars. He appears in this short story as the ghost of the narrator's long dead youth. *The Haunted House.*

**BABLEY, RICHARD.** The full name of Miss Trotwood's protégé, Mr. Dick. (*q.v.*)

**BACHELOR, THE.** A kindly old gentleman who lived in the parsonage house in the village where Little Nell and her Grandfather finally came to rest after their wanderings. He was a brother of Mr. Garland, and had passed many years with his old college friend the Clergyman. It was through a letter from the Bachelor to Mr. Garland that the wandering couple's whereabouts was discovered. *Curiosity Shop*, 52–5, 68, 69, 73.

**BADAJOZ,** where Major Taunton received his mortal wound, was besieged by the British, March–April, 1812, and fell, after a bloody assault, on the 6th of the latter month. 7 *Poor Travellers.*

**BADGER, BAYHAM.** A cousin of Mr. Kenge and a physician with a good practice at Chelsea, to whom Richard Carstone was sent to study medicine. He admired his wife exceedingly, "principally on the curious ground of her having had three husbands." The chief topics of conversation with this curiously complacent couple were Mrs. Badger's previous husbands, Captain Swosser of the Royal Navy, and Professor Dingo. *Bleak House*, 13, 17, 30, 50.

**BAGMAN.** This was the old name for a commercial traveller. The original "commercial" proceeded from town to town on horseback, his samples packed in capacious saddlebags. In later times he would drive his own gig or dog-cart, often a very smart vehicle drawn by a very smart nag.

**BAGMAN, THE.** A loquacious commercial traveller staying at the Peacock, Eatanswill, where he told the story of Tom Smart. He reappeared in the travellers' room of the Bush Inn, Bristol, where he related the tale of The Bagman's Uncle. *Pickwick*, 14, 48, 49.

**BAGNET, MATTHEW,** was an ex-artilleryman and friend of Mr. George, who played the bassoon in the theatre and kept a musical instrument shop near the Elephant and Castle. He stood security for the bill of George's which had fallen into the hands of Grandfather Smallweed. An honest old soldier, with a stolid face which had won him the nickname of Lignum Vitæ, he left the management of everything to his wife— "She has the head, but I don't own to it before her. Discipline must be maintained ; whatever the girl says, do—do it."

Mrs. Bagnet, his wife, was "a strong, busy, active, honest-faced woman of from forty-five to fifty." According to Mr. George, "I never saw her, except on a baggage wagon, when she wasn't washing greens." She had seen service with her husband in all parts of the world and had once made her way home from a distant quarter of the globe with nothing but a grey cloak and an umbrella. "The old girl," said her husband, "is like a thoroughly fine day. Gets finer as she gets on."

The three Bagnet children were known as Woolwich, Quebec and Malta from the places where the family was stationed when they were born. *Bleak House*, 27, 34, 49, 52, 66.

**BAGNIGGE WELLS.** This was an old London pleasure resort in what is now King's Cross Road. It was almost opposite where the Clerkenwell Police Court now stands. The Wells were closed in 1841. *Boz, Char.*, 1.

**BAGSTOCK, MAJOR JOSEPH.** A retired soldier who occupied lodgings in Princess's Place, opposite Miss Tox. He "found an immense fund of satisfaction in little jocularities of which old Joe Bagstock, Old Joey Bagstock, Old J. Bagstock, Joey B. and the like, was the perpetual theme ; it being, as it were, the Major's stronghold of light humour to be on the most familiar terms with his own name." The essence of selfish ambition, he wormed his way into Mr. Dombey's friendship, was his companion at Leamington where he introduced the city merchant to Edith Granger, accompanied him abroad in the search for Carker, and was among the first to desert him when the crash came. His favourite expression was, "Old Joe is tough, Sir, tough and devilish sly." The Major kept an Indian servant, known as the Native, upon whom he vented his anger when stricken by gout or crossed in his designs. *Dombey*, 7, 10, 20, 21, 26, 27, 29, 31, 36, 40, 51, 58, 59.

**BAILEY, CAPTAIN.** A friend of David Copperfield's first love, the eldest Miss Larkins. *Copperfield*, 18.

**BAILEY, JUNIOR.** "A small boy with a large red head and no nose to speak of," who first appeared as bootboy at Todgers's. His real name was supposed to be Benjamin, but among the commercial gentlemen he was known by a variety of names, but principally as Bailey, Junior, in contradistinction to the Old Bailey. He was a good specimen of the Cockney lad, with his gutter wit and repartee. When he left Todgers's he became " tiger " or groom to Tigg Montague, and was nearly killed in the carriage accident which occurred on the fatal visit to Salisbury. He was eventually taken into partnership by his friend and admirer, Poll Sweedlepipe, the barber. *Chuzzlewit*, 8, 9, 11, 26–9, 32, 38, 41, 42, 49, 52.

**BAILLIE.** A friend of the Bagman's Uncle, " Baillie Mac something and four syllables after it." *Pickwick*, 49.

**BAINES, OF LEEDS, MR.** Sir Edward Baines (1800–90) was the editor of the *Leeds Mercury* and a prominent Dissenter. He was a staunch advocate of total abstinence, and well known as an educational philanthropist. He was M.P. for Leeds from 1859 to 1874 and was an active liberal. He was knighted in 1881. *Reprinted, Out of the Season.*

**BAKER'S TRAP.** A swing bridge over " some dark locks and some dirty water." It was a favourite spot for suicides, hence its name, Mr. Baker being the local coroner who investigated the tragedies. The original of Baker's Trap was the bridge in Old Gravel Lane, leading from Ratcliff Highway to Wapping High Street. *Uncommercial*, 3.

**BALDERSTONE, THOMAS.** Brother of Mrs. Gattleton and commonly called Uncle Tom. He prided himself on remembering the lines of all the principal plays of Shakespeare from beginning to end, and Mrs. Joseph Porter meanly took advantage of this knowledge to bring to grief the Gattleton's representation of Othello. *Boz, Tales, Porter.*

**BALDWIN, ROBERT.** One of the characters in the Wonderful Museum whose will created a surprise among his children. *Mutual Friend*, III, 6.

**BALIM.** The young ladies' *Young Gentleman. Sketches of Gentlemen.*

**BALLS POND.** A district of Kingsland, North London, and situated at the upper end of Essex Road, which was formerly known as Lower Road. Balls Pond was practically in the fields in the 40's and 50's. Mr. and Mrs. Theodosius Butler settled there, in a small cottage situated in the immediate vicinity of a brickfield (*Boz, Tales, Sentiment*), and it was the home of Mr. and Mrs. Perch, with their ever-increasing family. *Dombey*, 18.

**BAMBER, JACK.** An old attorney's clerk whom Mr. Pickwick met at the Magpie and Stump. According to Lowten he was never heard to talk of anything but the Inns of Court and had lived alone in them until he was half crazy. He related various stories of these Inns and eventually told the Tale of the Queer Client. *Pickwick*, 20, 21.

Jack Bamber reappears in *Humphrey*, where Mr. Pickwick obtains permission to introduce him to the company.

**BANDOLINE.** This was a sticky, scented preparation applied to the hair to make it glossy and retain its curls. " You should see our Bandolining room at Mugby Junction. It is led to by the door behind the counter, which you will notice usually stands ajar, and it's the room where Our Missis and our young ladies bandolines their hair. You should see 'em at it, betwixt trains, Bandolining away, as if they was anointing themselves for the combat." *Mugby Junction.*

**BANGER, CAPTAIN.** A member of Our Vestry and a resident of Wilderness Walk, who maintained that only one pint of water *per diem* for every adult of the lower classes was necessary for purposes of ablution and refreshment. *Reprinted, Our Vestry.*

**BANGHAM, MRS.** Charwoman and messenger in the Marshalsea Prison, who attended Mrs. Dorrit in her confinement. *Dorrit*, I, 6, 7, 14 ; II, 19.

**BANJO BONES.** A professional entertainer. *See* Bones, Banjo.

**BANK OF ENGLAND.** The present building is the work of Sir John Soane, appointed architect in 1788. He incorporated in it the old offices which the Gordon Rioters, led by Hugh, vainly attacked in 1780 (*Barnaby*, 67). An omnibus ride from the top of Oxford Street to the Bank is described in *Boz, Scenes*, 16. Mr. Charles Cheeryble and Nicholas alighted from their omnibus at the Bank, when the latter was being taken to the business for the first time (*Nickleby*, 35). It was in one of the " grave, old-fashioned city streets, lying not far from the Bank of England by London Wall " that Clennam and Daniel Doyce lived (*Dorrit*, I, 26). Every Wednesday evening Mr. Morfin resorted to " a clubroom hard by the Bank, where quartettes of the most tormenting and excruciating nature were executed " (*Dombey*, 13). During his night prowls the Uncommercial Traveller (13) would make a circuit of the Bank, giving a thought to the treasure within.

**BANKS, MAJOR.** The name adopted by Meltham when, disguised as a crippled old East India Director, he succeeded in rescuing Margaret Niner from the murderous clutches of Julius Slinkton. *Reprinted, Hunted Down.*

**BANTAM, ANGELO CYRUS.** Master of Ceremonies at Bath, " a charming young man of not much more than fifty," and altogether a sumptuously dressed creature. He carried " a pliant ebony cane with a heavy gold top " ; one of the few cases where Dickens was caught napping, as ebony is not a pliant wood. The original of Bantam's house was No. 12 Queen's Square, Bath. *Pickwick*, 35, 37.

**BAPS, MR.** Dancing master at Doctor Blimber's school. With his wife he attended the breaking up party, enquiring of several gentlemen present, " What you were to do with your raw materials when they came into your ports in return for your drain of gold," a question which Toots could only answer by the suggestion, " Cook 'em." *Dombey*, 14.

**BAPTISTE.** A soldier billetted on the Poor Water-carrier, who sat in the Grande Place. *Somebody's Luggage.*

**BAR.** A barrister guest of Mr. Merdle, a talkative, opinionated man with a little insinuating jury droop and a persuasive double eyeglass, which eventually made him Attorney-General. *Dorrit*, I, 21 ; II, 12, 16, 25.

**BARBARA.** The Garland's pretty little servant girl, " very tidy, modest and demure." She was very jealous of Kit Nubbles's devotion to the memory of Little Nell, but after his release from his wrongful imprisonment and the discovery of Nell's death, found that her love was returned and they were eventually married. *Curiosity Shop*, 22, 38–40, 68, 69, 73.

Barbara's mother became friendly with Mrs. Nubbles when Kit took them all to Astley's, and accompanied her to see Kit in prison. *Curiosity Shop*, 39, 40, 61, 63, 68, 73.

**BARBARY.** 1. Miss Barbary was the aunt of Esther Summerson and sister to Lady Dedlock. She lived at Windsor, where she brought the child up with a cold and stern severity. She died when Esther was fourteen, and " to the very last, even afterwards, her frown remained unsoftened." *Bleak House*, 3, 29, 43.

2. Mrs. Captain Barbary of Cheltenham was the owner of a horse which Captain Maroon tried to sell. *Dorrit*, I, 12.

**BARBICAN.** In a courtyard near this old London thoroughfare which leads eastward from Aldersgate Street, was the low tavern where Simon Tappertit and the Prentice Knights held their meetings and where Rudge, the murderer, first ran across the blind villain Stagg (*Barnaby*, 8, 18). Bill Sikes and Oliver Twist passed through Barbican on their way from Bethnal Green to the scene of the burglary (*Twist*, 21). It was in this street that Tom Pinch lost his bearings on the way to Furnival's Inn (*Chuzzlewit*, 37), and at the corner of Aldersgate Street and Barbican Arthur Clennam parted from Pancks after his first visit to the Patriarch Casby. *Dorrit*, I, 13.

**BARBOX BROTHERS.** A house of bill-brokers with a reputation for griping, in a court off Lombard Street. When it came into the hands of Young Jackson (*q.v.*) he closed down the business and " obliterated the firm of Barbox Brothers from the pages of the Post Office Directory and the face of the earth, leaving nothing of it but its name on two portmanteaus." *Mugby Junction.*

**BARDELL, MRS. MARTHA.** The landlady of the rooms in Goswell Street, where Mr. Pickwick lived. " She was a comely woman of bustling manner and agreeable appearance, with a natural genius for cooking, improved by study and long practice, into an exquisite talent." She had one child, Tommy, a spoiled, greedy boy of ten or twelve. When Mr. Pickwick was thinking of engaging Sam Weller as his servant, he remarked to Mrs. Bardell that it would be nice for her to have a companion, which she took as a proposal of marriage. Importuned by the rascally lawyers, Dodson and Fogg, to sue Mr. Pickwick for breach of promise, she won her case through the eloquence of Sergeant Buzfuz, but after Mr. Pickwick's refusal to pay, she was arrested at the instance of Dodson and Fogg and was committed to the Fleet, whence she was only released by Mr. Pickwick paying her costs and his own. *Pickwick*, 12, 18, 20, 22, 26, 31, 34, 46, 47, 57.

**BARGEES.** Some boisterous, uncouth men who gave Little Nell and her Grandfather a lift on their boat. *Curiosity Shop*, 43.

**BARGEMAN, THE.** The character adopted by Bradley Headstone in his murderous pursuit of Eugene Wrayburn. *Mutual Friend*, IV, 1, 7, 15.

**BARK.** A lodging-house keeper and receiver of stolen goods whose house in Whitechapel was visited by Inspector Field and his men. *Reprinted, Inspector Field.*

**BARKER.** 1. Bill Barker, or Boorker, was assistant waterman at the Hackney coach stand at the corner of Haymarket, and later became an omnibus cad, or conductor. *Boz, Scenes*, 17.

2. Phil Barker was a drunken thief at the Three Cripples Inn. *Twist*, 26.

**BARKIS.** The carrier between Blunderstone and Yarmouth, whose courtship of Clara Peggotty was effected through little David Copperfield to whom he entrusted the message, " Barkis is willin'." As Barkis was dying, Daniel Peggotty remarked, " People can't die along the coast except when the tide is pretty nigh out . . . he's a going out with the tide." And true enough " after saying with a pleasant smile, ' Barkis is willin', it being low water, he went out with the tide." The original of this character was a carrier named Barker, who lived at Blundestone. *Copperfield*, 2–5, 8, 10, 17, 21–3, 28, 30, 31, 51.

**BARLEY, CLARA.** Herbert Pocket's fiancée, who took care of her testy old father at their house on Mill Pond Bank, below London Bridge. At Herbert's suggestion she arranged that Magwitch, the convict, under the name of Campbell, should occupy two rooms at the top of the house until he could be smuggled abroad. Despite her father's tyranny Clara refused to leave him when Herbert took his situation abroad, but as soon as the old man was dead, Herbert returned to marry her.

Old Bill Barley, Clara's father, was a retired and bedridden purser, " totally unequal to the consideration of any subject more psychological than Gout, Rum and Purser's Stores." *Expectations*, 30, 46, 55, 58.

**BARLOW, MR.** The pedantic tutor of Sandford and Merton (*q.v.*). *Uncommercial*, 33.

**BARMAID.** 1. The maid at the Town Arms, Eatanswill, who " hocussed the brandy and water of fourteen unpolled electors." *Pickwick*, 13.

2. The young lady at the George and Vulture. *Pickwick*, 31.

3. She of the Blue Boar, who knew Mr. Weller, Senior's, habits in the matter of drink. *Pickwick*, 33.

4. The barmaid of the Saracen's Head, susceptible to the flattery of Frank Cheeryble. *Nickleby*, 43.

5. Two showily dressed damsels in the gin palace. *Boz, Scenes*, 22.

**BARNABY RUDGE.** This novel was begun at the end of 1838 in pursuance of a contract with the publisher Bentley, and was to follow *Oliver Twist* in *Bentley's Miscellany*. Much of the book had been written when, by mutual arrangement, the agreement was transferred to Chapman and Hall, May, 1840. Publication was begun in *Master Humphrey's Clock* in January, 1841, and concluded in November of the same year, when the novel was issued in book form, with illustrations by H. K. Browne.

*Principal Characters.* Barnaby Rudge, a half-witted lad, his mother, and fugitive father ; Old Willett, host of the Maypole Inn, and his son Joe ; Gabriel Varden the locksmith, his wife and daughter Dolly, his apprentice Sim Tappertit, and his maid Miggs ; Geoffrey Haredale, a squire, and his daughter Emma ; Lord George Gordon and his secretary, Gashford ; Sir John Chester and his son Edward ; Hugh, ostler at the Maypole ; Dennis, the hangman.

In the opening chapter some cronies at the Maypole relate the story of Geoffrey Haredale, a Catholic squire, whose elder brother Reuben, together with his faithful steward Rudge, had been murdered. This tragedy casts its shadow throughout the story. Young Joe Willett is in love with Dolly Varden, and one day, after a quarrel with his stupid old father, he goes to London, sees Dolly, who laughs at his lovemaking, and

in despair enlists. A contemporary love story is that of Emma Haredale and young Edward Chester, who are kept apart by their parents and can only communicate furtively, Dolly Varden acting as go-between. Sir John Chester taxes his son with carrying on a clandestine courtship and disowns him entirely when the boy refuses to give it up. Through these scenes Barnaby and his raven Grip pass to and fro with little relation to the plot of the story.

Meanwhile, events have begun to move in London, where Lord George Gordon has started the No Popery agitation. Sim Tappertit, Varden's apprentice and a silly bombastic lad, enters into the movement, where he is soon joined by Hugh the Maypole ostler and Barnaby Rudge, who is excited at the noise and commotion, and leaves his mother to follow the rioters. The Gordon Riots are described with considerable detail and great accuracy ; Hugh, Barnaby and Tappertit, set on by Lord George's rascally secretary, Gashford, playing prominent parts. The rioters go out to Chigwell, sack the Maypole Inn and burn the house of Geoffrey Haredale the Catholic. Emma and Dolly fall into the rioters' hands and are carried to an obscure hiding-place by Sim Tappertit and Maypole Hugh. But the troops have been called out by this time, and the ringleaders are caught. Joe Willett, now a soldier home wounded from the Savannahs, rescues Dolly and Emma.

Throughout the story Mrs. Rudge has been blackmailed and harried from one home to another by the sinister figure of her husband, the steward who was supposed to have been killed in defence of his master, but who was really his murderer. After the burning of his house Geoffrey Haredale discovers this man and hands him over to justice. Hugh and Dennis are hanged, but through the exertions of Gabriel Varden, Barnaby is reprieved, while in due course Dolly and Joe Willett, Emma and Edward Chester are married.

**BARNACLE.** Name of a family that " for some time had helped to administer the Circumlocution Office." The family is described at length in *Dorrit*, I, 34.

1. Clarence, also called Barnacle Junior, son of Tite Barnacle and " the born idiot of the family—most agreeable and most endearing blockhead." I, 10, 17, 26, 34.

2. Lord Decimus Tite Barnacle, uncle of Mr. Tite and a master of the art of How not to do it. I, 17, 34 ; II, 12, 24.

3. Ferdinand, private secretary to Lord Decimus, an airy young fellow. I, 10, 34 ; II, 12, 28.

4. Mr. Tite Barnacle, a permanent civil servant who lived in snobbish state in Mews Street, near Grosvenor Square. I, 9, 10, 34 ; II, 12.

5. William, a parliamentary Barnacle,

who always kept ready his own particular recipe for How not to do it. I, 34.

**BARNARD CASTLE.** This market town in Durham was in the neighbourhood where Newman Noggs had lived before his ruin, and when Nicholas Nickleby went to Yorkshire Newman recommended him to call at the King's Head, " where there is good ale " (*Nickleby*, 7). Dickens and H. K. Browne stayed at this inn when they made a journey together in 1838 to investigate the Yorkshire school scandals.

**BARNARD'S INN.** A former inn of Chancery, situated on the S. side of Holborn and W. of Fetter Lane. The Hall is now occupied by the Mercers' School. Herbert Pocket's chambers, when Pip joined him, were in the Inn, " the dingiest collection of shabby buildings ever squeezed together in a rank corner as a club for Tom Cats " (*Expectations*, 21). The premises of Langdale, the distiller, destroyed by the Gordon Rioters, were next to Barnard's Inn, with an entrance from Fetter Lane, and the flames from the blazing vats nearly burned the old inn. *Barnaby*, 66, 67.

**BARNET.** This Hertfordshire town, some eleven miles north of London, was an important coaching stage on the Great North Road. Oliver Twist was passing through it on his way to London when he met the Artful Dodger (*Twist*, 8). Esther, Ada and Richard changed horses there on their way to their new home with Mr. John Jarndyce, as did Esther and Inspector Bucket in their vain pursuit of Lady Dedlock. *Bleak House*, 6, 57.

**BARNEY.** The Jewish waiter at the Three Cripples public-house, who assisted Sikes and his accomplice in planning the Chertsey burglary. *Twist*, 15, 22, 26, 42, 45.

**BARNSTAPLE.** The North Devon seaport, where Captain Jorgan and the Raybrocks went to visit the lawyer and clear up the mystery solved by *A Message from the Sea*.

**BARNWELL, CASE IN.** Perker was referring to a well-known law book, *Reports of Cases argued and determined in the court of King's Bench*, by R. V. Barnewall, 1818–22. *Pickwick*, 10.

**BARNWELL, GEORGE.** Hero of a tragedy entitled *The Merchant*, or the *History of George Barnwell*, written by George Lillo and produced at Drury Lane Theatre, June 22, 1730. The play was an immediate success and for over a century retained possession of the British stage. In 1796 it was produced at Covent Garden Theatre with Charles Kemble as Barnwell and Mrs. Siddons as Sarah Millwood.

The story relates that George Barnwell, a London apprentice, was induced by Sarah Millwood, a light o' love who lived at Shoreditch, to steal £200 of his master's money. When more money was needed Millwood

prompted her paramour to murder his uncle, who lived at Camberwell. As soon as his wealth had been squandered, they gave evidence against each other and both were hanged.

**BARRONNEAU, MADAME.** The young widow of an old innkeeper of Marseilles, whom Rigaud married and murdered for her money. *Dorrit*, I, 1.

**BARROW, JANET.** Original of Miss La Creevy. (*q.v.*)

**BARSAD, JOHN.** Name assumed by Solomon Pross. (*q.v.*)

**BARTELLOT.** A fashionable peruquier of Regent Street ; branch of a business at 22 Hatton Garden. *Boz, Tales, Boarding House.*

**BARTHOLOMEW CLOSE.** A byway in the vicinity of Little Britain, where Pip saw some of Mr. Jaggers's clients pacing up and down while waiting for that astute solicitor. *Expectations*, 20.

**BARTON, JACOB.** A grocer friend of the Maldertons' who poked fun at their pretensions to quality, and " was so lost to all sense of feeling that he actually never scrupled to avow that he was not above his business." *Boz, Tales, Sparkins.*

**BASTILLE.** This ancient and infamous Parisian prison, notorious for the many State offenders who had there been incarcerated, never to be heard of again, became a symbol of the tyranny of the old monarchical government, and its capture, July 14, 1789, was the first event of importance in the French Revolution. The incident is described in *Two Cities*, II, 21.

**BATES.** 1. Charley, a sprightly lad, one of Fagin's apprentices at pocket-picking. After the break-up of the gang Bates repaired to the rendezvous on Jacobs' Island, and was largely instrumental in the capture of Sikes, whom he hated for the murder of Nancy. Horrified and disgusted with the life of crime he had hitherto led, the lad went into the country and became " the merriest young grazier in all Northamptonshire." *Twist*, 8, 9, 10, 12, 13, 16, 18, 25, 39, 43, 50, 53.

2. Belinda Bates was one of the guests at the Haunted House, " who went in for Woman's Rights and Woman's Wrongs and everything that is Woman's with a capital W." *Haunted House.*

**BATH.** Little can be added to the description of Bath given in *Pickwick*, which was written when the town's importance as a fashionable centre had already begun to wane. The White Hart Hotel, kept by Moses Pickwick, the coach proprietor whose name Dickens adopted for his hero, stood on the site now occupied by the Grand Pump Room Hotel. The older building was demolished in 1867. Tradition still points out Mrs. Craddock's house in Royal Crescent, while the shop of Harris, the greengrocer, where Sam Weller attended the " leg o' mutton swarry," is said to be the Beaufort Arms, near Queen's Square, where, at No. 12, lived Mr. Angelo Cyrus Bantam, M.C. (*Pickwick*, 35–37). The place is only mentioned otherwise as the residence of Volumnia Dedlock. *Bleak House*, 28.

**BATTENS.** The oldest resident of Titbull's Almshouses, a virulent old man full of complaints. *Uncommercial*, 27.

**BATTERSEA.** There are few references to this part of London lying on the south side of the river to Chelsea. Only the bridge is mentioned, and in those times it was a rickety and ancient wooden structure which acted rather as an obstacle to navigation than as a means of crossing the river. The new bridge was built in 1890.

**BATTERY, THE.** An old disused fort on the marshes, where Pip took food to the convict Magwitch. *Expectations*, 1, 3.

**BATTLE BRIDGE.** This was the old name for King's Cross and the place was so called from being the site of a bridge over the Fleet river, where a fierce battle took place between the Romans and Britons under Boadicea. In the early part of the nineteenth century Battle Bridge had a bad reputation as a criminal haunt. In 1830 a curious octagonal structure, the lower part of which was used as a police station, was erected by the architect Bray, who called it King's Cross. This was demolished in 1845. The neighbourhood was famous for its huge unsightly heaps of dust and refuse. The little sweep of Boz's early days settled near Battle Bridge (*Boz, Scenes*, 20). There Conkey Chickweed, the redoubtable burglar, kept a public-house to which young lords went for cockfights and badger drawing (*Twist*, 31). R. Wilfer was crossing the desert of rubbish which lay between Battle Bridge and his home in Holloway when he remarked, "Ah, what might have been is not what is ! " (*Mutual Friend*, I, 4), while Mr. Boffin gave it as a direction to help Wegg reach the Bower (*Mutual Friend*, I, 5). Finally, the men who played the handbells at Mr. Dombey's wedding practised in a back settlement near Battle Bridge. *Dombey*, 31.

**BATTLE OF LIFE, THE.** This was the fourth of the Christmas Books, and appeared in December, 1846.

*Principal Characters.* Dr. Jeddler, a philosopher who looks on the world as a gigantic practical joke ; his daughters Grace and Marion ; Alfred Heathfield, engaged to Marion ; Michael Warden, a spendthrift landowner ; Snitchey and Craggs, lawyers ; Benjamin Britain and Clemency Newcome, Dr. Jeddler's servants.

The story opens on the birthday of Marion and of Alfred Heathfield, when the latter, having come of age, is leaving for a foreign tour. After his departure Michael Warden, who has been a wastrel, during a business conversation with Snitchey and Craggs, tells them that he has fallen in love with Marion, although he knows that she is affianced to Heathfield. On the night of Heathfield's return, Marion and Michael Warden disappear and for six years nothing is heard of either. During that time Benjamin Britain and Clemency Newcome marry and take over the village inn. One day Michael Warden enters the inn to rest, and learns that Grace and Heathfield are married and living happily in the midst of a growing family. Craggs, the lawyer, then prepares Grace for receiving her long lost sister, Marion, who returns to her father's roof. It transpires that she had perceived that Grace had fallen in love with Heathfield and, in a spirit of loving self-abnegation had gone away, apparently with Michael Warden, though in reality to live with an aunt. There she had remained in seclusion ever since. In the end Marion marries Michael Warden. The principal interest of the story centres round the quaint characters of Benjamin Britain and Clemency Newcome, and in the dry wit of the lawyers Snitchey and Craggs.

**BAYTON.** A poor man in the parish of Bumble the Beadle, whose wife died and was given a " porochial " funeral. *Twist*, 5.

**BAZZARD.** Confidential clerk of Mr. Grewgious who seemed possessed of some strange power over his master. His melancholy demeanour and sense of superiority arose from having written a tragedy which nobody would, on any account, hear of bringing out. *Drood*, 11, 20.

**BEADLE.** There can be no better description of this happily extinct functionary than that supplied in sundry passages of Dickens' works. Of these the principal is in *Boz, Our Parish*, while Bumble, the beadle in *Oliver Twist* is, of course, the classic example. According to Mr. G. K. Chesterton, Dickens " stepped up to the grave official of the vestry, really trusted by the rulers, really feared like a god by the poor, and he tied round his neck a name that choked him ; never again now can he be anything but Bumble." Mr. Meagles' sentiments on the subject are worth reading in *Dorrit*, I, 2. Mention should also be made of Mooney, beadle of the parish where Nemo was found dead (*Bleak House*, 11), and of the beadle whom Sam " spiled " in a single combat (*Pickwick*, 19). A final example of this much detested functionary may be found in *Uncommercial*, 18.

**BEADLE, HARRIET.** Actual name of Tattycoram. (*q.v.*)

**BEADNELL, MARIA.** This lady was the original of Dolly Varden, Bella Wilfer, Dora Spenlow and, as an older woman, of Flora Finching. She was the daughter of George Beadnell of 2 Lombard Street, a manager of Smith, Payne and Smith's bank, who was portrayed as Casby and Spenlow. Dickens met and fell in love with Maria in 1830, when she was a pretty coquette of nineteen. While she was "finishing off" in Paris mischief was made between them, and they ceased corresponding in 1833. Later, she married a Mr. Winter. In 1855 Mrs. Winter wrote to Dickens and renewed the friendship, but by that time she had developed from the charming original of Dora to the garrulous prototype of Flora Finching.

**BEADWOOD, NED.** Mentioned by Miss Mowcher. "When they took him to church to marry him to somebody, they left the bride behind." *Copperfield,* 22.

**BEAR, PRINCE.** The enemy of Prince Bull, representing Russia in the allegorical fairy tale. *Reprinted, Prince Bull.*

**"BEARINGS OF THIS OBSERVATION LAYS IN THE APPLICATION ON IT."** An explanatory remark which Captain Jack Bunsby habitually uttered when propounding his more abstruse words of wisdom. *Dombey,* 23, 39.

**BEARS AND BARBERS.** Sam Weller's story of Jinkinson the barber seems one of the most improbable of his anecdotes, but it would appear that bears were actually kept and killed for the sake of their grease. The following advertisement appeared in *The Times* of February 7, 1793 :—

"Just killed, an extra fine Fat Russian Bear, at Ross's Ornamental Hair and Perfumery Warehouse, No. 119 Bishopsgate Street (late Vickery's) three doors from the London Tavern.

"The excellent virtue which the fat of bears possesses has been experienced by thousands of both sexes and of all ages in this Metropolis. . . . It is sold at 1s. per ounce or 16s. the pound, to be seen cut off the animal in the presence of the purchaser."

This shop was, within living memory, adorned outside with pictures of raging bears. *Humphrey ; Nickleby,* 35 ; *Robert Bolton.*

**BEAUVAIS.** The birthplace of Dr. Manette, and one of the halting places of Charles Darnay when he was being taken to Paris. *Two Cities,* III, 1, 10.

**BEAVER, NAT.** A guest in the Haunted House. He was the captain of a merchantman, "with a thick-set wooden face and figure . . . and a world of watery experience in him." *Haunted House.*

**BEBELLE.** Pet name of Gabrielle, the little orphan girl befriended by Corporal Theophile and later adopted by Mr. Langley. *Somebody's Luggage.*

**BECKHAMPTON.** Possible original of the Marlborough Downs inn. *See* Inn (1).

**BECKWITH, ALFRED.** Name adopted by Meltham in order to entrap Julius Slinkton. *See* Meltham. *Hunted Down.*

**BECKY.** Barmaid at the Hampton public-house where Bill Sikes and Oliver Twist rested on their way to commit the burglary. *Twist,* 21.

**BEDFORD, PAUL.** One of the favourite comedians of the '30s–'50s, who for many years acted with Edward Wright at the Adelphi. His greatest hit was in "The Flowers of the Forest," and his favourite phrase, "I believe you my bo-o-oy," became a catch word of the time. Bedford was born in 1792 and died in 1871. *Sketches of Gentlemen (Theatrical).*

**BEDFORD HOTEL, BRIGHTON.** One of the oldest and best hotels in this seaside town. Dickens and his wife stayed there in 1848, 1849 and 1861, and it was there that he made Mr. Dombey put up when he visited little Paul. *Dombey,* 10.

**BEDFORD ROW.** This fine Bloomsbury street is little altered in outward appearance since its erection in the early eighteenth century, and is still a lawyers' haunt. *Boz, Scenes,* 16 ; *Uncommercial,* 14.

**BEDFORD SQUARE.** One of the finest of the Bloomsbury squares ; it was long noted as a residence of judges. It only concerns us as being the residence of a certain Mr. Delafontaine, a friend of Flamwell. *Boz, Tales, Sparkins.*

**BEDLAM.** The popular name for the Bethlehem Hospital, the most famous of all lunatic asylums. The original building was in Moorfields, on the site of an ancient priory, now covered by Liverpool Street Station. In 1812 a new building was begun in Lambeth, on the site of the Dog and Duck Tea Gardens, notorious as the resort of all kinds of low characters, and two years later the inmates were moved to their new quarters. The term Bedlam has long been synonymous with madhouses and lunacy in general. *Uncommercial,* 13.

**BEDWIN, MRS.** Housekeeper to Mr. Brownlow. She was "a motherly old lady, very neatly and precisely dressed," and was a staunch believer in Oliver Twist, whose innocence she championed in face of Mr. Grimwig's most triumphant accusations. *Twist,* 12, 14, 15, 17, 41, 51.

**BEGGING LETTER WRITER, THE.** An amusing sketch which appeared in *Household Words,* May 18, 1850, and was published among the Reprinted Pieces of the Library Edition, 1858. It recounts some of the plausible and ingenious stories resorted to by the writers of begging letters.

**BEGGS, MRS. RIDGER.** One of the Micawber girls who married in Australia. *Copperfield,* 63.

**"BEGONE! DULL CARE."** A seventeenth-century song beginning, "Begone ! dull care, I prithee begone from me." *Curiosity Shop,* 7 ; *Drood,* 2.

**BELGRAVE SQUARE.** Formerly one of the most fashionable residential quarters in London, this square was built in 1825, after the plans of George Basevi. Dickens remarks that the inhabitants of Cadogan Place look on the high folks of Belgrave Square in some such manner as the illegitimate children of the great boast of their connections, although their connections disavow them (*Nickleby*, 21). The dreamer in *Out of Town* imagined he saw the last man in London, an ostler, sitting on a post in Belgrave Square eating straw and mildewing away. Lady Tippins lived over a staymaker's somewhere in the Belgravian borders. *Mutual Friend*, II, 3.

**BELINDA.** A love-lorn correspondent of Master Humphrey, who wrote from Bath. *Humphrey*.

**BELIZE.** A seaport and the capital of British Honduras, where Gill Davis and Harry Charker had been quartered before they were sent to Silver Store Island. *English Prisoners*.

**BELL, BERKELEY HEATH.** This old inn, about a mile out of Berkeley town, yet flourishes as it did on the day when Mr. Pickwick and his companions alighted there for lunch on their way to Birmingham. *Pickwick*, 50.

**BELLA.** 1. The younger of the two girls in the prisoners' van. *Boz, Characters*, 12.

2. Miss Pupford's housemaid, who left Kitty Kimmeens alone in the house. *Tom Tiddler*.

**BELL ALLEY, COLEMAN STREET.** This should really be Great Bell Alley. Here was situated the lock-up of Namby, the sheriff's officer who arrested Mr. Pickwick. The sheriff's offices were actually at 25 Coleman Street. *Pickwick*, 40.

**BELLAMY'S.** In 1773 John Bellamy, deputy housekeeper to the House of Commons, fitted up two rooms in the old Houses of Parliament for providing refreshment to members. A meal of cold meat, bread, cheese and beer was provided for 2s. 6d., rather meagre sandwiches cost 1s. each and other prices were proportionately high. On the completion of the present Houses of Parliament the catering was relegated to a Kitchen Committee, and Bellamy's ceased to exist in 1848. A story of doubtful authority says that the last words of William Pitt the younger, usually recorded as, "Oh, my country, in what a state I leave thee," were really, "Oh, for one of Bellamy's pies." *Boz, Scenes*, 18.

**BELLE.** The spirit of Scrooge's early love, whom he had lost by his greed for money. *Christmas Carol*.

**BELLER, HENRY.** A drunken toast-master mentioned in the report of the Brick Lane Ebenezer Temperance Association as a convert to teetotalism. *Pickwick*, 33.

**BELLE SAUVAGE INN.** The site of this large and important coaching inn is now occupied by the publishing house of Cassell, but the yard bears the old name. It is the first turning on the left going up Ludgate Hill from Farringdon Street. La Belle Sauvage was closed as an inn in 1873, and

there are now no signs of the old building. It was at one time the headquarters of Mr. Weller, Senior. *Pickwick*, 10.

**BELLING.** A boy from Taunton, who accompanied Squeers and Nicholas as a pupil to Dotheboys Hall. *Nickleby*, 4, 5.

**BELLOWS.** A barrister guest at one of the Merdle dinners. *Dorrit*, I, 21.

**BELLS, GOBLINS OF.** Phantom figures seen by Trotty Veck when he climbed the belfry on New Year's Eve. *Chimes*.

**BELLTOTT.** Name commonly given to Mrs. Isabella Tott, widow of a N.C.O. on Silver Store Island. She played a gallant part in the flight from the island. *English Prisoners*.

**BELL YARD, FLEET STREET.** In this narrow lane running up from Fleet Street to Carey Street, entirely altered when the Law Courts were built, was the home of Mrs. Blinder, who took care of the Neckett children. *Bleak House*, 15.

**BELVAWNEY, MISS.** A member of the Crummles theatrical company. "She seldom aspired to speaking parts, but usually went on as a page in white silk hose, to stand with one leg bent and contemplate the audience." *Nickleby*, 23, 24, 29.

**BELZONI-LIKE.** This reference is to G. B. Belzoni, the Italian traveller and archæologist, who excavated the temple of Abu Simbel and explored the second great pyramid at Ghizeh. *Boz, Scenes*, 5.

**BEN.** 1. Guard of the mail coach, whom Sikes heard telling about Nancy's murder. *Twist*, 48.

2. Waiter at the Rochester Inn who served the *Seven Poor Travellers*.

**BENCH.** One of Mr. Merdle's magnate guests. *Dorrit*, I, 21.

**BENJAMIN.** 1, A member of the Prentice Knights and a follower of Sim Tappertit. *Barnaby*, 8.

2. Thomas Benjamin was the principal in a divorce-suit. *Copperfield*, 33.

**BENNETT, GEORGE.** (1800–79.) A well-known actor at Covent Garden and Drury Lane. He usually acted with Macready. *Sketches of Gentlemen (Theatrical)*.

**BENSON.** Name of three characters in the comic burletta entitled *The Village Coquette*. Old Benson was a small farmer, with two children—Young Benson and Lucy. The latter flirted for a while with Squire Norton, but perceived his snares in time to save herself and married her village sweetheart, George Edmunds.

**BENTLEY'S MISCELLANY.** The first number of this monthly magazine, founded by Richard Bentley, appeared January 2, 1837, under the editorship of Boz, who vacated the chair in February, 1839. The *Miscellany* continued until 1868, when it was incorporated with *Temple Bar*. *Mudfog*, *Twist* and *Pantomime of Life* appeared in it.

**BENTON, MISS.** Master Humphrey's housekeeper, who inspired a momentary passion in the bosom of the susceptible Tony Weller, but eventually married Slithers, the barber. *Humphrey.*

**BERINTHIA, or BERRY.** Mrs. Pipchin's niece, middle aged, good natured and a devoted slave to that austere woman. *Dombey,* 8, 11, 59.

**BERNERS STREET.** Running north out of Oxford Street, this was a favourite residential street for artists, but, perhaps achieved greater notoriety by reason of the famous Berners Street hoax perpetrated in 1809 by Theodore Hook. *Boz, Characters,* 9.

**BERRY.** Short for Berinthia. *(q.v.)*

**"BESIDE THAT COTTAGE PORCH."** This is from the second verse of Alexander Lee's "The Soldier's Tear," and, minus Wegg's complimentary additions, is practically as quoted by that worthy. *Mutual Friend,* I, 5.

**"BEST OF ALL WAYS, THE."** Skimpole was singing Moore's "Young May Moon," the first verse of which contains these words. *Bleak House,* 6.

**BETHLEHEM HOSPITAL.** The full name for Bedlam. *(q.v.)*

**BETHNAL GREEN.** Now one of the most crowded parts of the East End of London, a hundred years ago Bethnal Green was a large and densely populated village on the outskirts of London. It was, however, even at that time, tainted with the squalor of Whitechapel, and it was in a mean and dirty street that Bill Sikes and Nancy first kept house (*Twist,* 19). Into the "difficult country" round Bethnal Green Eugene Wrayburn and his friend Mortimer led Bradley Headstone a weary chase when he was playing the spy on Eugene (*Mutual Friend,* III, 10). There is a curious speculation on the fowls at Bethnal Green in *Uncommercial Traveller,* 10.

**BETLEY.** One of Mrs. Lirriper's first lodgers. *Lirriper's Lodgings.*

**BET or BETSY.** Nancy's friend, sweetheart of Tom Chitling and one of Fagin's thieves. Being called upon to identify Nancy's body, the horror of the scene drove her mad. *Twist,* 9, 13, 16, 18, 25, 50.

**BETSEY.** Nurse to the Britain children. *Battle of Life.*

**BETSEY JANE.** Mrs. Wickam's cousin who, as a child, had been endowed with a kind of ghostly influence which was reputed to bring those whom she liked to an early end. *Dombey,* 8, 58.

**BETSY.** Mrs. Raddle's dirty, slipshod maid, "who might have passed for the neglected daughter of a superannuated dustman in very reduced circumstances." *Pickwick,* 32.

**BETTY, MASTER.** William Henry Betty (1791–1874) was a popular actor who achieved fame on the Dublin stage at the age of twelve. In 1804 he went to London, by that time having already gained the name of The Young Roscius, and caused such a sensation that troops were ordered out to cope with the crowds besieging Covent Garden Theatre for admittance. On another occasion the House of Commons adjourned to see him play Hamlet. Betty left the stage for three years (1808–11) to study at Cambridge and finally retired, with great wealth, in 1824. *Boz, Characters,* 7.

**BETTY MARTIN.** The phrase, "All my eye and Betty Martin," meaning "all nonsense," was much in vogue during the first half of the nineteenth century and the first three words are still sometimes used with the same meaning. In one of the Joe Miller jest books the story is told of a sailor who was looking round a foreign church and overheard a suppliant at one of the altars murmuring, "Ah! mihi, beate Martine! (Ah! grant me, blessed Martin). Recording the incident later he said that as far as he could make out she was saying, "All my eye and Betty Martin." The real origin of the phrase is unknown.

**BEULAH SPA.** This once fashionable resort in Upper Norwood came into prominence in 1831, when the proprietor of the grounds, in which rose a spring whose water was impregnated with sulphate of magnesia, spent a considerable sum of money in erecting pump rooms and their attendant amenities. Its popularity was transient and all that remains at the present time is the Beulah Spa Hotel. At the height of its fashion the Spa was the favourite objective of such excursions as that planned by Mr. Gabriel Parsons. *Boz, Scenes,* 5; *Tales, Tottle.*

**BEVAN.** 1. A kindly man from Massachusetts, whose acquaintance Martin Chuzzlewit made at the Pawkins boarding house. He took Martin to visit the Norrises, and when Martin and Mark were at the end of their resources at Eden, sent them money to enable them to return to New York. *Chuzzlewit,* 16, 17, 21, 33, 34, 43.

2. An old friend of Mrs. Nickleby, with whom she once dined off roast pig. *Nickleby,* 41.

**BEVIS MARKS.** This is a short street leading out of St. Mary Axe and is rendered immortal by having contained the house (No. 10) of Mr. Sampson Brass, which was the scene of Dick Swiveller's games of cards with the Marchioness, of the Single Gentleman's adventures with the Punch and Judy shows and of Brass's cunning plot to incriminate Kit Nubbles. Dick discovered "a mild porter" at the Red Lion publichouse. *Curiosity Shop,* 11, 33–7, 50, 51, 56–60.

**BIB, JULIUS WASHINGTON MERRYWEATHER.** A member of the deputation to welcome Elijah Pogram. *Chuzzlewit,* 34.

**BIDDY.** The orphan girl who taught Pip to read. She was Mr. Wopsle's great-aunt's granddaughter and, like Pip, had been brought up by hand. She went to look after the Gargery's home after Orlick's brutal attack on Pip's sister, and there proved the best friend Pip ever had. But he was blinded by his own grandeur and snobbishness, and was unable to perceive Biddy's simple and pure love for himself, parting from her in priggish condescension when he finally left for London. On the death of Pip's sister Biddy went to live with the Hubbles and became schoolmistress. After his loss of fortune Pip decided to return and ask her to marry him, but he arrived on the very day of her wedding to Joe Gargery. *Expectations*, 7, 10, 12, 15–19, 35, 57–9.

**"BID ME DISCOURSE."** Bishop's setting of a song taken from Shakespeare's *Venus and Adonis*. *Boz, Tales, Tuggs's.*

**BIFFIN, MISS SARAH.** (1784–1850.) A celebrity in her day, Miss Biffin was a miniature painter who was born without arms or legs, and was only 3 ft. 1 in. in height. She taught herself to draw and paint by holding a pencil or brush in her mouth, and in 1812 was exhibited in the principal towns of England by her teacher, a Mr. Dukes. Her excellent work attracted the attention of the Earl of Morton and reached the notice of Royalty. Miss Biffin died, October 2, 1850. *Nickleby*, 37; *Chuzzlewit*, 28; *Reprinted, Plated Article*.

**BIGBY, MRS.** Mrs. Meek's mother, "never known to yield any point whatever to mortal man." Assisted by Mrs. Prodgit, the monthly nurse, she made Mr. Meek's life a burden. *Reprinted, Births, Mrs. Meek.*

**BIGWIG FAMILY.** The stateliest and noisiest people in the neighbourhood, who took upon themselves to manage all poor people's affairs. *Reprinted, Nobody's Story.*

**BILBERRY, LADY JEMIMA.** Daughter of the fifteenth Earl of Stiltstalking and wife of Lord Decimus Tite Barnacle. *Dorrit* I, 17.

**BILER.** Nickname of Robin Tootle, also known as Rob the Grinder. (*q.v.*)

**BILKINS.** "The only authority on Taste." *Reprinted, French Watering Place.*

**BILL.** 1. Uncle Bill, who ordered "tea for four; bread and butter for forty." *Boz, Scenes.*

2. Driver of the Oxford Street City omnibus. *Boz, Scenes*, 16.

3. Ostler at the Flower Pot Inn. *Boz, Tales, Minns.*

4. Former turnkey at the Fleet prison. *Pickwick*, 41.

5. Gravedigger who buried Mrs. Bayton. *Twist*, 5.

6. Husband of Amelia and a criminal whose defence was undertaken by Jaggers. *Expectations*, 20.

7. Black Bill, a criminal in Newgate. *Expectations*, 32.

**BILLICKIN, MRS.** A lodging-house keeper of Southampton Street, Bloomsbury Square, from whom Mr. Grewgious took rooms for Miss Twinkleton and Rosa Bud. She never signed her christian name—" so long as this 'ouse is known indefinite as Billickins's, I feel safe, but commit myself to a solitary female statement, no." She considered Miss Twinkleton as her natural enemy and waged fierce warfare with her through the medium of Rosa. *Drood*, 22.

**BILLINGSGATE.** References to the famous London fish market are but casual. "Tip" Dorrit was in the Billingsgate trade during one of his brief fits of industry (*Dorrit*, I, 7). Pip and Herbert Pocket used to look at the old market as they rowed down river to see Magwitch. (*Expectations*, 54), and the *Uncommercial Traveller* (13) visited it during one of his night walks.

**BILLSMETHI, SIGNOR.** The proprietor of a dancing academy near Gray's Inn Lane, whose daughter proved an attraction to the impressionable young oil and colourman, Augustus Cooper, from whom by the threat of a breach of promise action the Billsmethi's extorted £20. *Boz, Characters*, 9.

**BILLSTICKERS, KING OF THE.** "A good-looking little man of about fifty, with a shining face, a tight head, a bright eye, a moist wink and a ready air." *Reprinted, Bill Sticking.*

**BILL-STICKING.** A sketch which appeared in *Household Words*, March 22, 1851, and was published again in *Reprinted Pieces*, 1858. It is interesting as giving some idea of London at the time when Trafalgar Square had just been completed, and was looked upon as a doubtful improvement.

**"BILL STUMPS HIS MARK."** Mr. Blotton's malicious rendering of the inscription upon the ancient stone found by Mr. Pickwick at Cobham. *See* Stumps, *Pickwick*, 11.

**BILSON AND SLUMP.** The wholesale business house of Cateaton Street, Gresham Street, City, for whom Tom Smart travelled. *Pickwick*, 14.

**BINTREY.** Solicitor of Walter Wilding, "a cautious man with twinkling beads of eyes in a large overhanging bald head, who inwardly but intensely enjoyed the comicality of openness of speech or hand or heart." He helped to track down Obenreizer in his villany, was a loyal friend to Marguerite, and eventually succeeded in proving Vendale's identity. *No Thoroughfare.*

**BIRD WALTZ.** This was a popular piano piece by F. Panormo, published about 1825. *Dombey*, 29, 38.

**BIRMINGHAM, MR. and MRS.** Host and hostess of the Lord Warden Hotel, Dover, from *c*. 1851–*c*. 1874. *Uncommercial*, 17.

**BIRMINGHAM.** The great Midland capital was visited by Dickens several times. He made a speech on education to the Birmingham Polytechnic Institution in 1844, and in January, 1853, received a great ovation at the room of the Society of Artists, being presented with a salver and a diamond ring. His most important connection with the city, however, lies in the fact that there he gave his first public readings, December 27, 29 and 30, 1853. Other readings were given in later years, and in 1870, being President of the Institute, he distributed the prizes at the Town Hall. The first reference to Birmingham is rather mysterious, being contained in the original announcement of the *Pickwick Papers*, where it is said that the great man's "fondness for the useful arts prompted his celebrated journey to Birmingham in the depth of winter." This evidently had no reference to the visit he paid in company with Bob Sawyer and Ben Allen. On that occasion he went to see Mr. Winkle, Senior, whose house was pointed out in Easy Row, near the Old Wharf. The travellers stayed at the Old Royal Hotel, of which nothing now remains (*Pickwick*, 50). It was reported that Bill Sikes had fled thither after Nancy's murder (*Twist*, 48). Mr. Weller, Senior, instanced his disapproval of railways by describing a journey to Birmingham in which he was locked into the carriage with a "living widder" (*Humphrey*). Soon after her marriage Mrs. Nickleby visited Stratford in a postchaise from Birmingham (*Nickleby*, 27). Mr. Dombey and Major Bagstock travelled down to Leamington by the Birmingham mail train (*Dombey*, 20). A tightrope accident in the People's Park is mentioned in *Uncommercial*, 23. John, the unfortunate inventor, had worked there all his life. (*Reprinted, Poor Man's Patent*). Finally, Birmingham is mentioned as the place where Lord George Gordon made his public profession of the Jewish faith. *Barnaby*, 82.

**BIRTHS, MRS. MEEK OF A SON.** This sketch appeared in *Household Words*, February 22, 1851, and was published in the bound volume of *Reprinted Pieces* in 1858. It is an amusing account of the slights put upon Mr. Meek by his mother-in-law, Mrs. Bigby, at the birth of his son.

**BISHOP.** 1. One of Mr. Merdle's guests, a magnate of the Church, "with a strong and rapid step as if he wanted . . . to go round the world and see that everybody was in a satisfactory state." *Dorrit*, I, 21; II, 12, 16, 25.

2. A hot drink compounded of red wine poured warm upon oranges, the mixture being sugared and spiced to taste. *Christmas Carol*.

**BISHOP AND WILLIAMS.** John Bishop and Thomas Head, alias Williams, were the English counterparts of Burke and Hare, the Resurrectionist men. Assisted by a certain May they committed dozens of murders in London and sold the bodies to the hospitals for 8–10 guineas apiece. Their procedure was to give the victim rum or beer con-

taining a strong dose of laudanum and then immerse him in a well until dead. On November 3, 1831, they murdered an Italian boy named Carlo Ferrari, but Mr. Partridge, the surgeon to whom they took the body, became suspicious and summoned the police. The murderers were arrested and tried at the Old Bailey, December 2, 1831. May was transported for life, Bishop and Williams were sentenced to death and executed, December 5, 1831. *Boz, Scenes*, 25.

**BISHOPSGATE STREET.** In the early part of the nineteenth century this busy thoroughfare contained many old houses which have since been swept away in the improvement of London. It was a busy headquarters for coaches for the Eastern counties, while the London Tavern (*q.v.*), at its Citywards extremity, was a famous resort of business men. From the Flowerpot Inn (*q.v.*), one of the busiest coaching houses, Mr. Minns set out to visit his cousin at Stamford Hill (*Boz, Tales, Minns*). In this street lived Brogley, the broker, who was put in possession at the Wooden Midshipman (*Dombey*, 9). One of the Gordon Rioters was hanged in Bishopsgate Street. *Barnaby*, 77.

**BITHERSTONE, MASTER.** A boarder at Mrs. Pipchin's Castle. His father was in India, whither the boy had desperate ideas of following him. Major Bagstock made his friendship with Bitherstone's father, "Bill Bitherstone of ours," a useful pretext for obtaining an introduction to Mr. Dombey. *Dombey*, 8, 10, 11, 41, 60.

**BITZER.** One of the promising pupils in Mr. Gradgrind's school. An inveterate sneak, as soon as he had entered the service of Bounderby's Bank as light porter he spied on young Tom Gradgrind. And when Tom, after his theft, took refuge with Sleary's Circus, Bitzer appeared to take him back, "for I have no doubt whatever that Mr. Bounderby will then promote me to young Mr. Tom's situation." "Bitzer, have you a heart ? " said Mr. Gradgrind. "No man, sir, acquainted with the facts established by Harvey relating to the circulation of the blood, can doubt that I have a heart." Such was the fruit of Mr. Gradgrind's teaching of utilitarianism. Sleary, however, with the aid of a performing horse and a dog which pinned Bitzer for some hours to the road, enabled Tom to make his escape. *Hard Times*, I, 2, 5 ; II, 1, 4, 6, 8, 9, 11 ; III, 7–9.

**BLACK.** 1. A constable who met Inspector Field at Whitechapel. *Reprinted, Inspector Field*.

2. Mrs. Black was one of Mrs. Lemon's pupils. *Holiday Romance*.

**BLACK BADGER INN.** The headquarters of the Game Chicken, Mr. Toots' instructor in the noble art of self-defence. *Dombey*, 22.

**BLACKBOY, MR.** This was the name painted by Barkis on the box in which he kept his money. *Copperfield*, 31.

**BLACK BOY INN, CHELMSFORD.** The inn where Mr. Weller, Senior, picked up Jingle and Job Trotter after the trick they had played on Mr. Pickwick at Bury St. Edmunds. The inn was demolished in 1857. *Pickwick*, 20.

**BLACK BOY AND STOMACH ACHE INN.** The house at Oldcastle where some members of the Mudfog Association put up at the second meeting.

**BLACKEY.** A beggar who stood near London Bridge " for twenty-five years with his skin painted to represent disease. *Reprinted, Inspector Field.*

**BLACKFRIARS BRIDGE AND ROAD.** Since 1760, when the original bridge was built, this has been one of the principal thoroughfares across the river, despite the fact that until 1785 a halfpenny toll was charged. It was partly in exasperation at this tax that the Gordon Rioters destroyed the toll houses (*Barnaby*, 47, 67). The bridge was first called Pitt Bridge, after Lord Chatham. Alterations and repairs were constantly required from 1830 onwards until, in 1864, the bridge was demolished and a new one built, 1865–69. This in its turn was widened in 1907–8. As a child Dickens used to cross the bridge daily on his way between Warren's Blacking Factory, and his temporary home in the Marshalsea. Two of his landmarks yet exist at the corners of Union Street—Rowland Hill's Chapel, now the Boxing Ring, and the shop with the "likeness of a golden dog licking a golden pot." The Blackfriars shore is mentioned in *Boz, Scenes*, 10 ; and Mr Gabriel Parsons was followed by small boys from the bridge on his way into the City (*Boz, Tales, Tottle*). It was near Blackfriars Bridge that Mr. Peggotty and David saw Martha, when they were looking for Little Em'ly (*Copperfield*, 46). Poor Jo, after his lecture from Chadband, "moved on " to the bridge where he settled in a baking, stony corner (*Bleak House*, 19) ; while Mr. George went swinging over Blackfriars Bridge and along Blackfriars Road to visit the Bagnets (*Bleak House*, 27). Pip rowed above the bridge when training for the rescue of Magwitch (*Expectations*, 46). Clennam and Plornish drove over the bridge on their way to see the Dorrits in the Marshalsea (*Dorrit*, I, 12). Finally the bridge is mentioned among others in *Reprinted, Down with the Tide*.

**BLACKHEATH.** Until fifty years ago this was little more than a pleasant village, just the sort of place where one would expect to find " the modest little cottage " where John Rokesmith and Bella began married life (*Mutual Friend*, IV, 4). Salem House was in the vicinity (*Copperfield*, 5), and David passed it again when running away to his aunt (*Chapter* 13). The entertainer of the *Seven Poor Travellers* passed it on his way back to London, and the *Un-commercial Traveller* (7) passed through Blackheath on his journey to France.

**BLACK LION INN.** The Whitechapel Inn, where Joe Willett took his dinner when sent to London on his father's errands. Only the yard of this inn remains, at No. 75, Whitechapel Road (*Barnaby*, 13, 31, 72). The host of the inn was called by the same name, because he had instructed the artist who painted the inn sign to give the animal a face as like his own as possible.

**BLACKMORE.** This was an American who performed at Vauxhall Gardens in 1823 and for some years afterwards. His show consisted of ascending a rope amid a blaze of fireworks, carrying out various evolutions whilst wearing a cap embellished with flaming fireworks, and other turns of a like nature. *Boz, Scenes*, 14.

**BLACKPOOL, STEPHEN.** A power-loom operative in Bounderby's mill. Rendered desperate by his drunken wife he asked advice of Bounderby as to whether there was no law which would release him from this creature, and enable him to marry Rachel, the honest, true girl who was the one bright spot in his life. Bounderby explained that there was such a law, but not for the poor, so Stephen returned to his misery. Refusing to join the union which was being formed by the mill hands, Stephen was hounded out of his job and left Coketown. He was on his way back to clear himself from the suspicion of the bank robbery when he fell down an abandoned coal pit shaft and died shortly after his rescue. *Hard Times*, I, 10–13 ; II, 4–6, 8 ; III, 4–7, 9.

**BLACKWALL.** An East London district on the Thames. It was passed by the Margate steam packet, described in *Boz, Scenes*, 10. It is best known from the Blackwall Railway which received its Act in 1836. The terminus was at first in the Minories, but was later moved to Fenchurch Street. This railway was peculiar, in that the power was derived from a stationary engine at either end, which in turn wound or unwound a single rope to which all the carriages were attached. From *Uncommercial*, 9, it would appear to have been used by pleasure trippers. Sergeant Dornton tracked Mesheck, with his carpet bag, to London by this railway. *Reprinted, The Detective Police.*

**BLADUD, PRINCE.** The mythical founder of Bath, whose story is told in *Pickwick*, 36.

**BLAKE, WARMINT.** An out-and-out young gentleman. *Sketches of Young Gentlemen.*

**" BLAME NOT THE BARD."** One of Moore's Irish Melodies. *Curiosity Shop*, 35.

**BLANDOIS.** Name adopted by Rigaud in his negotiations with Mrs. Clennam. *See* Rigaud.

**BLANK.** Member of the Mudfog Association.

**BLATHERS.** A Bow Street detective sent to investigate the burglary at Mrs. Maylie's house. He and his colleague Duff had many theories and waxed enthusiastic over their powers in solving other crimes, but failed to make anything of the case in question. *Twist*, 31.

**BLAZE AND SPARKLE.** The jewellers who knew " where to have the fashionable people." *Bleak House*, 2, 58.

**BLAZO, SIR THOMAS.** A West Indian friend of Jingle, with whom he played a single-wicket cricket match in terrific heat— " bat in blisters, ball scorched brown." *Pickwick*, 7, 53.

**BLEAK HOUSE.** This book was issued in monthly parts, the first appearing in March, 1852, and the last in September, 1853, in which year it was published in book form. It was illustrated by Phiz and dedicated to Carlyle.

*Principal Characters.* Esther Summerson, Ada Clare and Richard Carstone, the three young people who live with John Jarndyce, a benevolent elderly gentleman ; Lawrence Boythorn, a country squire ; Mrs. Jellyby, a philanthropist ; Harold Skimpole, an agreeable rascal ; Mr. Guppy, a lawyer's clerk enamoured of Esther ; Sir Leicester Dedlock and his lady ; Mr. Tulkinghorn, the family solicitor ; Bucket, the detective ; Jo, the street waif ; Snagsby, a law stationer ; Allan Woodcourt, a surgeon.

The story is told partly in narrative form and partly in the autobiographical style which the author had used to such advantage in *David Copperfield*. The plot hinges on an interminable Chancery suit—Jarndyce and Jarndyce—to which the principal characters are parties. John Jarndyce adopts two Chancery wards, Ada Clare and Richard Carstone, taking Esther Summerson into his household as companion to the former, and it is Esther who relates that portion of the story which deals with John Jarndyce and his wards. Ada and Richard soon fall in love with each other, and Richard, after various attempts at a profession, settles down to the study of law. He becomes absorbed entirely in the Jarndyce suit and begins to distrust his guardian, eventually sinking into a decline through worry and overwork. It is then that Ada secretly marries him. At last, when a new will is found, finally settling the great Chancery suit, it is discovered that the whole estate has been swallowed up in costs, and Richard Carstone dies of despair and mortification. The other strand of the story deals with Lady Dedlock, the beautiful and stately wife of Sir Leicester. In her early life she had had a liaison with Captain Hawdon, who, in the early chapters of the book, dies in extreme poverty. For years Lady Dedlock has thought her secret safe, but Guppy, the law clerk, gives her certain information proving that Esther Summerson is her natural daughter by Hawdon. Heartbroken and terrified, Lady Dedlock makes herself known to Esther and soon afterwards discovers that Mr. Tulkinghorn has also divined her secret. He threatens her with exposure, but before he can carry out this menace he is mysteriously murdered. Suspicion falls on Lady Dedlock, who flies from home. She is followed by Inspector Bucket and Esther, but is found dead near Hawdon's grave. There are various subsidiary interests centring round John Jarndyce and his proposal of marriage to Esther, followed by his renunciation in favour of Allan Woodcourt ; round Mrs. Jellyby and her daughter Caddy ; round Jo, the crossing sweeper, and his persecution by the authorities; round George, the scapegrace son of Mrs. Rouncewell, the Dedlock housekeeper. All these are worked into the theme which concludes with Esther's married happiness in the new Bleak House which John Jarndyce has given her and her husband.

**BLEAK HOUSE.** Much discussion has raged around the identity of Bleak House. If Dickens had any particular place in his mind it was probably a house (since christened Bleak House) at the top of Gombard's Road, to the north of St. Albans. *Bleak House*, 3, 6, 8.

**BLEEDING HEART YARD.** This yard, which takes its name from a public-house bearing the pre-reformation sign of the Bleeding Heart of Our Lady, is reached from Charles Street, Hatton Garden. It is now entirely different in character and appearance. Much of the property belonged to Casby, whose collector, Pancks, had the task of collecting the rents of the Yarders. There, also, were the works of Doyce and Clennam. *Dorrit*, I, 9, 12, 23 ; II, 33.

" **BLESS THE BABE** and save the mother is my mortar, sir ; but I makes so free as to add to that, Don't try no impogician with the Nuss, for she will not abear it." One of Mrs. Gamp's apothegms. *Chuzzlewit*, 40.

**BLIGH, CAPTAIN.** The reference is to Admiral William Bligh (1754–1817), who was in command of the *Bounty* when her crew mutinied and set him adrift with eighteen men in the Indian Ocean, April 28, 1789. After seven weeks in an open boat they reached the island of Timor, near Java. The mutiny was caused by Bligh's harsh treatment of his men, and although his naval record was creditable, he was clearly a man of unbearable temper. *Golden Mary ; Long Voyage*.

**BLIGHT, YOUNG.** Eugene Wrayburn's office boy. *See* Young Blight.

**BLIMBER, DOCTOR.** Principal of the school at Brighton to which Paul Dombey was sent. His establishment was " a great hothouse in which all the boys blew before their time. Mental green peas were produced at Christmas, and every description of Greek and Latin vegetable was got off the driest twigs of boys under the frostiest circumstances." In his pompous way he was kind enough to his pupils. He eventually resigned in favour of his son-in-law, Feeder, B.A. The original of Dr. Blimber was possibly a Dr. Everard, who kept a similar school at Brighton. It has been suggested that this school was Chichester House, Chichester Terrace. Mrs. Blimber was not learned, " but pretended to be, and that did quite as well." She said at evening parties that if she could have known Cicero she thought she could have died content. *Dombey*, 11, 12, 14, 24, 28, 41, 60.

Cornelia Blimber was their daughter. "None of your live languages for Miss Blimber. They must be dead—stone dead— and then Miss Blimber dug them up like a ghoul." She married her father's assistant, Feeder, B.A. *Dombey*, 11, 12, 14, 41, 60.

**BLINDER.** 1. Mrs., the motherly old woman in Bell Yard who took care of the Neckett children. *Bleak House*, 15, 47.

2. Bill, was an old hostler who died in a stable and left his lantern to Mr. Tony Weller. *Humphrey*.

**BLINKINS.** Latin master at Our School, whom the headmaster caught asleep one day while taking a class. *Reprinted, Our School*.

**BLOCKADE MEN.** These were the forerunners of the coastguards and were organised at the conclusion of the Napoleonic wars, in 1815. To prevent smuggling a coast blockade system was introduced in Kent and Sussex, and it was the blockade men, patrolling the coast, that passed Cymon Tuggs and Belinda Waters as they were making platonic love. *Boz, Tales, Tuggs. Reprinted, Our Watering Place.*

**BLOCKITT, MRS.** Mrs. Dombey's nurse, " a simpering piece of faded gentility, who did not presume to state her name as a fact, but merely offered it as a mild suggestion." *Dombey*, 1.

**BLOCKSON, MRS.** Charwoman to the Knags, who gave notice on account of having too much work and too little pay. *Nickleby*, 18.

**BLOGG.** The Beadle who permitted Betty Higden to adopt Sloppy. *Mutual Friend*, I, 16.

**BLOOMSBURY SQUARE.** This was formerly called Southampton Square, and was built in the latter half of the seventeenth century. Once a fashionable place of residence it has passed through various descending grades until it is now almost entirely devoted to offices. One of Master Humphrey's correspondents had a friend who had six times carried away every bell-handle in the Square (*Humphrey*). Its historical association with Lord Mansfield's house, situated in the north-eastern corner

of the square, is well described in *Barnaby*, 66, 77.

**BLOSS, MRS.** A wealthy, fat, red-faced, vulgar widow who became a boarder at Mrs. Tibbs's. " I am constantly attended by a medical man," she remarked, " I have been a shocking unitarian for some time." She, or rather her money, became the object of much scheming in the boarding house, and she ended by marrying Gobler, another invalid, with whom she went to live in Newington Butts. *Boz, Tales, Boarding House.*

**BLOSSOM, LITTLE.** Miss Trotwood's pet name for David Copperfield's wife, Dora.

**BLOTTON, MR.,** of Aldgate. He was the member of the Pickwick Club who called Mr. Pickwick a humbug, only using that opprobrious term, however, in its Pickwickian sense. Later he took considerable pains to discredit Mr. Pickwick's discovery of the ancient stone at Cobham. *Pickwick*, 1, 11.

**BLOWERS.** An eminent barrister. *Bleak House*, 1.

**BLUBB.** Member of the Mudfog Association.

**BLUE BOAR INN.** 1. The inn where Pip and Joe, with sundry friends, celebrated the signing of the indentures, and where Pip stayed on subsequent occasions when he went down to visit Miss Havisham. The original was the Bull at Rochester. (*q.v.*) *Expectations*, 13, 19, 28, 30, 43.

2. The Blue Boar, Leadenhall Market, was one of Mr. Tony Weller's resorts, and while waiting for him there on the day before the trial, Sam wrote his famous valentine to Mary. It has been suggested that the original was the Green Dragon, in Bull's Head Passage, Gracechurch Street. There was, moreover, the Blue Boar in Aldgate (where David Copperfield alighted on his first visit to London, *Copperfield*, 5), a few doors on the left from Leadenhall Street. Slow coaches and waggons went from here to Ipswich three days a week. *Pickwick*, 33.

**BLUE DRAGON, THE.** Village alehouse near Salisbury, kept by Mrs. Lupin, where old Martin Chuzzlewit was besieged by his rapacious relatives. When Mark Tapley married Mrs. Lupin he announced that the sign would be changed to the Jolly Tapley. The George at Amesbury and the Green Dragon at Alderbury, 8 m. N. and 3 m. S., respectively, of Salisbury, have been identified as the original of this inn, but the description is more likely composite of these houses, also recalling the Lion's Head at Winterslow, which lies 6 m. N.E. of the city. *Chuzzlewit*, 3, 53.

**BLUE LION INN, MUGGLETON.** This was the scene of the dinner after the great All Muggleton v. Dingley Dell cricket match, and it was from here that Jingle hired a postchaise for the elopement with Miss Rachel Wardle. *Pickwick*, 7, 9.

**BLUE LION AND STOMACH WARMER INN.** The Buff Hotel at Great Winglebury where Horace Hunter put up. *Boz, Tales, Winglebury.*

**BLUES AND BUFFS.** Political parties at Eatanswill and violent opponents on every question. The *Gazette* was the organ of the Blues, the *Independent* that of the Buffs. " There were Blue shops and Buff shops, Blue inns and Buff inns—there was a Blue aisle and a Buff aisle in the very church itself." Blue and Buff were the colours adopted by the Conservative and Liberal parties respectively. *Pickwick*, 13, 51. *Boz, Tales, Winglebury.*

**BLUFFY.** The name given by the young Bagnets to George, the trooper. (*q.v.*)

**BLUNDERBORE, CAPTAIN.** An officer of the Horse Marines and an authority on equine matters. *Mudfog Papers.*

**BLUNDERSTONE.** The little Suffolk village where David Copperfield was born and passed his early years. The name is a thin disguise for the village of Blundestone, which Dickens visited in 1848 while staying at Somerleyton Hall, near Lowestoft. The name, seen on a signpost, attracted his attention, and he adapted it for the novel he was then contemplating. Blundestone Hall was probably the original of the " Rookery," and the Plough Inn was " our little village alehouse " from which Barkis drove to Yarmouth. *Copperfield*, 1–4, 8–10.

**BLUNDERUM.** Member of the Mudfog Association who contributed a paper " On the Last Moments of the Learned Pig."

**BOB.** 1. Hostler at the Golden Cross. *Boz, Scenes*, 15.

2. Turnkey of the Marshalsea Prison, who was Little Dorrit's godfather and earliest friend. He wished to leave her his money, but could find no means of tying it up, and so died intestate. *Dorrit*, I, 6, 7 ; II, 19.

**BOBBO.** " The most generous of all the friends that ever were," a schoolboy in Jemmy Lirriper's story. *Lirriper's Lodgings.*

**BOBBY, LORD.** A nobleman, the true circumstances of whose difference with the Marquis of Mizzler were known to Mr. Chuckster. *Curiosity Shop*, 40.

**BOBSTER, CECILIA.** The pretty young lady whom Newman Noggs mistook for Madeleine Bray. He contrived a clandestine meeting, but at the very moment that Nicholas discovered the mistake, her father arrived, and Nicholas and Newman had only just time to make their escape. *Nickleby*, 40, 51.

**BOCKER, TOM.** The nice orphan, " quite nineteen," whom Frank Milvey suggested that the Boffins might adopt. *Mutual Friend*, I, 9.

**BODGERS.** Name on a tomb in Blunderstone Church. *Copperfield*, 2.

**BOFFER.** A bankrupt on the Stock Exchange whose probable suicide was the subject of a bet between Wilkins Flasher and Frank Simmery. *Pickwick*, 55.

**BOFFIN, NICODEMUS or NODDY.** " A broad, round-shouldered, one-sided old fellow " who had been confidential servant and foreman of the wealthy dust contractor, Harmon. On the supposed death of Harmon's son, Boffin had come into the property, some £100,000, hence his nickname of the Golden Dustman. He and his wife adopted Bella Wilfer, the girl whom the dead miser had destined to be his son's bride. Under the assumed name of Rokesmith, John Harmon, the son, entered Boffin's service as secretary, but the old couple soon recognised the lad whom they had befriended years before, and finally enable him to win Bella's love. An illiterate and unsuspecting old fellow, Boffin was imposed upon by Silas Wegg, who eventually tried to blackmail him by producing a later will than that by which Boffin benefited. But Wegg and his schemes were routed by John Harmon, who finally came into his own. The original of Noddy Boffin was probably Henry Dodd, a well-known dust contractor of Hoxton. *Mutual Friend*, I, 5, 8, 9, 15–17 ; II, 7, 8, 10, 14, 16 ; III, 4–7, 9, 12, 14, 15 ; IV, 2, 3, 12–14, 16.

Mrs. Henrietta Boffin, his wife, was " a stout lady of rubicund and cheerful aspect," described by her husband as a high-flyer at Fashion. She was a simple, sweet old lady, who proved a true friend to Bella Wilfer. *Mutual Friend*, I, 5, 8, 9, 15–17 ; II, 8–10, 14 ; III, 4, 5, 7, 9, 12, 15, 16 ; IV, 2, 3, 12–14, 16.

**BOFFIN'S BOWER.** This was the poetical name given by Mrs. Boffin to the house among the dustheaps where they lived before they came into the property, and where Wegg afterwards resided. It was situated about a mile and a quarter up Maiden Lane, now York Road. *Mutual Friend*, I, 5, 7, 8, 9, 15 ; II, 7, 14 ; III, 6, 7, 14, 15 ; IV, 3, 14.

**BOGLE, MRS.** A boarding-house keeper, visited by bailiffs. *Uncommercial*, 6.

**BOGSBY, JAMES GEORGE.** Landlord of the Sol's Arms. *Bleak House*, 33.

**BOILER, REV. BOANERGES.** A powerful preacher who, with his fifthly, his sixthly, and his seventhly, appeared in the light of dismal and oppressive charade. *Uncommercial*, 9.

**BOKUM, MRS.** The dearest friend of Mrs. MacStinger, who considered it her duty at that lady's wedding to see that Captain Bunsby did not escape. *Dombey*, 60.

**BOLDER.** One of Squeers's pupils, who was caned soundly because his father was £2 10s. short in his payments to Squeers. *Nickleby*, 7, 8.

**BOLDHEART, CAPTAIN.** Pirate captain of the schooner *The Beauty* and hero of Robin Redforth's story of stirring deeds in China seas. *Holiday Romance.*

**BOLDWIG, CAPTAIN.** "A little fierce man in a stiff black neckerchief and blue surtout," bursting with self-importance. Mr. Pickwick fell asleep in his grounds after the shooting party with Wardle, and as, on being awakened, he could say nothing but "Cold punch," the captain had him taken to the village pound. *Pickwick*, 19.

**BOLO, MISS.** A maiden lady "of an ancient and whistlike appearance" who was Mr. Pickwick's partner in a rubber at the Bath Pump Room. Owing to his bad play "Miss Bolo rose from the table considerably agitated and went straight home, in a flood of tears and a sedan chair." *Pickwick*, 35.

**BOLTER, MORRIS.** Name assumed by Noah Claypole. (*q.v.*)

**BOLTON, ROBERT.** "A gentleman connected with the Press . . . with a somewhat sickly and very dissipated expression of countenance." He laid down the law nightly to a circle of admirers at the Green Dragon, Westminster. *Robert Bolton*.

**ROMPAS, SERGEANT.** Original of Sergeant Buzfuz. (*q.v.*)

**BOND, MRS.** Possibly a reference to the beauty practitioners of Bond Street who, at that time, had attained notoriety by using arsenic and other poisons in their concoctions. *Copperfield*, 22.

**BOND STREET.** Since the middle of the eighteenth century this street has been the most fashionable shopping street in London, which explains why a family like the Maldertons should go there to shop (*Boz, Tales, Sparkins*). It was not far from Bond Street that Nicholas Nickleby had his tussle with Sir Mulberry Hawk (*Nickleby*, 32). Jenny Wren had an appointment in the street with two of her dolls on the morning when Lammle thrashed Fascination Fledgeby (*Mutual Friend*, III, 8). Cousin Feenix put up at Long's Hotel, at the corner of Clifford Street, when he came to England for his cousin's wedding to Mr. Dombey (*Dombey*, 31). *See also Uncommercial*, 16.

**BONES, MR. AND MRS. BANJO.** A couple of comic favourites who entertained Mercantile Jack at Mr. Licensed Victualler's house. *Uncommercial Traveller*, 5.

**BONNEY.** The promoter of The United Metropolitan Hot Muffin and Crumpet Baking and Punctual Delivery Company, capital five million pounds. *Nickleby*, 2.

**BOODLE, LORD.** An eminent guest of Sir Leicester Dedlock. *Bleak House*, 12, 28.

**"BOOFER LADY."** The name given by little Johnny, Mrs. Higden's orphan, to Bella Wilfer when she went to visit him in the hospital. *Mutual Friend*, II, 9.

**BOOKSTALL KEEPER.** Proprietor of the stall where Mr. Brownlow was standing when his pocket was picked. He insisted on Mr. Fang listening to his evidence in Oliver Twist's favour. *Oliver Twist*, 11.

**BOOT, ALFRED.** Original of Cheeryble's butler, David. (*q.v.*)

**BOOT INN, THE.** At the time of the Gordon Riots this old alehouse was situated among the fields and was already of bad repute. It was the headquarters of the rioters. The district was built over in the early nineteenth century, and the present Boot, 116 Cromer Street, stands on or near the site of the earlier house. *Barnaby*, 38, 49, 52, 60.

**BOOTJACK AND COUNTENANCE INN.** One of the houses at Oldcastle where certain members of the Mudfog Association put up.

**BOOTS.** The servant at the Holly Tree Inn. *See* Cobbs.

**BOOTS AND BREWER.** Two toadies of the Veneerings who were guests at all their functions. They served as a kind of foolish chorus to everything said at the table. *Mutual Friend*, I, 2, 10; II, 3, 16; III, 17; IV, 17.

**BOOZEY, WILLIAM.** Captain of the foretop on the pirate schooner *The Beauty*. *Holiday Romance*.

**BOOZLE.** An actor who declined a part in one of the Surrey Theatre melodramas. *Sketches of Gentlemen* (*Theatrical*).

**BORE, OUR.** Subject of the sketch of the same name, who "may put fifty people out of temper, but he keeps his own." *Reprinted, Our Bore*.

**BOROUGH, THE.** This part of London was so closely associated with the early days of Charles Dickens that in one way or another it is frequently mentioned in his writings. It was at the old White Hart Inn, Borough, that Mr. Pickwick first met Sam Weller (*Pickwick*, 10); while later he visited Bob Sawyer in Lant Street (*Chapter* 32). The earlier portion of Little Dorrit centres round the Marshalsea Prison, Borough. The various localities are treated separately under their respective headings.

**BOROUGHBRIDGE.** The Yorkshire town, on the main road N.W. of Knaresborough, through which Nicholas passed on his way to London after having thrashed Squeers. *Nickleby*, 13.

**BORRIOBOOLA GHA.** A spot on the left bank of the Niger, whither Mrs. Jellyby and her society were sending families to cultivate the coffee and educate the natives. *Bleak House*, 4.

**BORUM, MRS.** A patroness of the stage who, with her husband and six children, usually took a box to see the Crummles plays. *Nickleby*, 24.

**BOSWELL COURT.** One of the Fleet Street courts, and the residence of Mr. Loggins, the solicitor who was invited to the Steam Excursion. *Boz, Tales, Steam Excursion*.

**BOTTLE.** "Leave the bottle on the chimley piece, and don't ask me to take none, but let me put my lips to it when I am so disposed." A condition laid down by Mrs.

Gamp before undertaking a case. *Chuzzle-wit*, 19.

**BOTTLE-NOSED NED.** The nickname of Edward Twigger. (*q.v.*) *Tulrumble.*

**BOTTLES.** A deaf stableman, " kept as a phenomenon of moroseness not to be matched in England." *The Haunted House.*

**BOUCLET, MADAME.** Landlady of Langley, the Englishman who adopted little Bebelle. *Somebody's Luggage.*

**BOULOGNE.** This French seaport was a favourite residence of such as fled from the importunities of their creditors ; hence it became the home of Mrs. Maplesone and her daughter after the disappearance of Mr. Septimus Hicks (*Boz, Tales, Boarding House*). The arrival of the packet at Boulogne is well described in *Reprinted, A Flight.* Roger Cly swore to having seen Charles Darnay show certain lists to other suspects at Boulogne. *Two Cities*, II, 3.

**BOUNDERBY, JOSIAH.** Banker and manufacturer of Coketown who prided himself on having risen from the gutter. " A man made out of coarse material," he had neither refinement of mind nor manners. He married Louisa Gradgrind, a high-spirited girl much his junior, and when she fled from his home to escape the attentions of Harthouse, cast her off forever. Towards the end of the novel it transpires that, far from being self-made and risen from the gutter, Bounderby was the son of a hard-working woman, Mrs. Pegler, who had scraped and saved to give him an education and whom he conveniently forgot, when he rose in the world, except for paying her a small annuity to keep out of the way. *Hard Times,* I, 3-9, 11, 12, 14-16 ; II, 1-12 ; III, 2-9.

Louisa, his wife, was a pretty girl, of a strong character which had been repressed and soured by her father's stern training. Her whole life was mellowed, however, by love for her graceless brother Tom, for whose sake she sacrificed herself to Bounderby. A stranger to all girlish sentiments and experiences, she was easily carried away by the consideration and attentions paid her by James Harthouse, but when he actually declared his love her better feelings gained the day, and she fled to her father for the protection which her husband was too selfish and callous to afford. Her return had the effect of softening Mr. Gradgrind, and showing him that there are other things in life than common sense. Bounderby refusing to have his wife back except on the most humiliating terms, Louisa remained with her father. *Hard Times,* I, 3, 4, 7-9, 14-16 ; II, 1-3, 5-12 ; III, 1-9.

**BOW.** Until well on into the 50's Bow or Stratford at Bow was little more than a large village clustered round the Mile End Road. Here it was that the Nickleby's settled down in the nice little cottage rented

to them by the Cheerybles, and next door to the amorous old gentleman in Small Clothes. *Nickleby*, 35.

**BOWES.** Original of Dotheboys Hall. (*q.v.*)

**BOWLEY, SIR JOSEPH.** A violent philanthropist who said to Trotty Veck, " I am the Poor Man's Friend. I am your perpetual parent. Feel the dignity of labour. Go forth erect into the cheerful morning air— and stop there." His lady was of similar bountiful nature, having introduced pinking and eyelet-hole making as an evening pastime for the men and boys of the village. *Chimes.*

**BOW STREET.** The associations of this street centre round the police court, which is the chief of the Metropolitan courts. The present building was erected in 1881, and replaced the old court which had been established in 1749. It was, therefore, to the old court that the following references point. At the time of the Gordon Riots the blind magistrate, Sir John Fielding, presided over the courts (*Barnaby*, 58, 77). The removal of prisoners is described in *Boz, Characters,* 12, and the best picture of the court is that given in the account of the Dodger's appearance before the magistrate (*Twist*, 43). Mr. Snevellicci lived in Broad Court, by the side of the police station. *Nickleby*, 30.

**BOW STREET RUNNERS.** Commonly known as Robin Redbreasts, on account of the scarlet waistcoats they wore, these officials attached to the central police court were the only detectives in existence until the formation of the present police force in 1829, though it was not until 1842 that the Criminal Investigation Department was established. Although competent and brave men, the Bow Street runners were too few in number to be really effective, while the lack of any kind of police organisation to assist them seriously hampered their investigations. Messrs. Blathers and Duff (*Twist*, 31) can hardly be taken as fair examples of such a force, and it must be confessed that considerable difficulties lay in the path of the runners sent down to investigate the attack on Pip's sister (*Expectations*, 16.

**" BOW-WOWS."** " Gone to the demnition bow-wows," was one of Mr. Mantalini's phrases. *Nickleby*, 64.

**BOWYER, SAM'L.** A former inmate of the workhouse. *Reprinted, Walk in the Workhouse.*

**BOXER.** John Peerybingle's dog. *Cricket on the Hearth.*

**BOY AT MUGBY.** The precocious lad who served in the Refreshment Room at Mugby Junction. He related the endeavours of the staff to keep up the reputation of the Refreshment Room for " never having yet refreshed a mortal being." His name was Ezekiel. *Mugby Junction,*

**BOYTHORN, LAWRENCE.** The friend and old schoolfellow of John Jarndyce, " a handsome old gentleman, with a massive grey head, a fine composure of face and a smile of much sweetness and tenderness. He was always in extremes, always in the superlative degree." He was a neighbour of Sir Leicester Dedlock, with whom he waged continual warfare over rights of way. For all his exaggeration and ferocity, Boythorn was tender-hearted and gentle as a woman. The character was founded upon Walter Savage Landor, an old and esteemed friend of Dickens and the godfather of his second son. *Bleak House*, 9, 12, 13, 15, 18, 23, 35, 36, 43, 66.

**BOZ.** The pen-name by which Dickens first attained fame. " Boz was a very familiar household word to me, long before I was an author, and so I came to adopt it." According to the preface to *Pickwick* it was the pet name of his youngest brother, Augustus, whom, in honour of the Vicar of Wakefield, he had dubbed Moses, which, being facetiously pronounced through the nose became Boses, and being shortened, Boz. Dickens first used it for a signature to the second part of the Boarding House, which appeared in the *Monthly Magazine*, August, 1834 ; most of the sketches as they appeared periodically bore the signature which was eventually applied to the bound volume. The monthly parts of *Pickwick* were also published under the name of Boz.

**BRADFORD, JONATHAN.** The subject of a book which acquired great popularity in its time, " Jonathan Bradford, or the Murder at the Roadside Inn, a romance by the author of *The Hebrew Maiden*." It appeared in 1851. *Holly Tree*.

**BRAHAM, JOHN.** (1774–1856.) He was a noter of some repute, who sang at Covent Garden and Drury Lane. He played Squire Norton in *The Village Coquettes* at the St. James's, December, 1836. *Sketches of Gentlemen* (*Theatrical*).

**BRANDLEY, MRS.** The widow with whom Estella boarded at Richmond. She was an old friend of Miss Havisham and had a daughter a few years older than Estella. *Expectations*, 38.

**BRASS.** Sampson was " an attorney of no very good repute . . . with a cringing manner, whose blandest smiles were so extremely forbidding that to have had his company under the least repulsive circumstances, one would have wished him to scowl." He was Quilp's legal adviser and tool, employed by him to carry out his designs on Nell and the Grandfather, on Dick Swiveller and Kit Nubbles. Unlike his sister he was secretly terrified of Quilp, whose boisterous bullying eventually goaded Brass into turning evidence against him. For his part in the plot against Kit Sampson he was sent to penal servitude, and finally

appears with his sister as a pariah of the London streets. The Brasses lived in Bevis Marks (probably No. 10), and let rooms to the Single Gentleman (*Curiosity Shop*, 11–13, 33–8, 49, 51, 56–60, 62–4, 66, 67, 73). Sally, his sister, " clerk, assistant, housekeeper, confidential plotter, adviser, intriguer . . . and a kind of Amazon at common law," was a lady of thirty-five or thereabouts. She was the better partner of the shady firm, bold and unscrupulous where her brother was cringing and cunning. She had a little drudge called by Dick Swiveller the Marchioness, who, it is inferred was her natural child by Quilp. When her brother turned evidence against the latter Sally stood out to the last and gave Quilp warning of what had happened. *Curiosity Shop*, 33, 37, 50, 51, 56–60, 62–4, 66, 67, 73.

**BRASS AND COPPER FOUNDER.** Ruth Pinch's employer, a middle-aged gentleman with a pompous voice and manner who treated his daughter's governess as a servant. *Chuzzlewit*, 9, 36.

**BRAVASSA, MISS.** A member of the Crummles company, " who had once had her likeness taken in character by an engraver's apprentice. *Nickleby*, 23–5, 29.

**BRAY, MADELEINE.** The beautiful girl with whom Nicholas Nickleby fell in love when he first saw her at an employment agency. Some time later he was employed by the Cheerybles to render her certain financial aid, her mother having been an old friend of Charles Cheeryble. Unknown to any but old Gride, the miser, Madeleine was heiress to a considerable fortune, and with the assistance of Ralph Nickleby the old rogue persuaded Madeleine's father to consent to his marriage with the young girl. On the wedding day, however, Bray fell down dead, and in spite of Gride's opposition, Nicholas took Madeleine to the shelter of his mother's home, and eventually married her. Madeleine Bray is one of the somewhat colourless heroines founded upon Maria Hogarth (*q.v.*). *Nickleby*, 16, 40, 46–8, 51–7, 61, 63–5.

Walter Bray, her invalid father, was an utterly selfish unscrupulous bankrupt, who lived in the Rules of the King's Bench Prison. Nickleby and Gride were his principal creditors, and to gain his freedom he agreed to the monstrous plan of making Madeleine marry the latter. His timely death saved her from this awful fate. *Nickleby*, 46, 47, 53, 54.

**BREAK-NECK-STAIRS.** Riverside steps leading from " a courtyard diverging from a steep, a slippery and a winding street connecting Tower Street with the Middlesex shore of the Thames." *No Thoroughfare*.

**BREAK OF DAY INN.** The obscure cabaret in Chalons-sur-Saone, where Rigaud took shelter on his way from Marseilles. *Dorrit*, I, 11.

**BRENTFORD.** Now the county town of Middlesex and a busy manufacturing place, there is little to show that Brentford was once a favourite resort of Londoners. Oliver Twist and Bill Sikes passed through it on their weary tramp to the scene of the burglary (*Twist*, 21); Compeyson, the swindler who led Magwitch into crime, had a house near there (*Expectations*, 42). In one of "the complicated back settlements of muddy Brentford" lived Betty Higden, and there she was visited by Mrs. Boffin, Bella Wilfer and the Secretary, who left their carriage at the Three Magpies Inn, an obvious reference to the famous Three Pigeons Inn, closed in 1916. *Mutual Friend*, I, 16 ; II, 9.

**BREWER.** A toady of the Veneerings. *See* Boots.

**BRICK, JEFFERSON.** War correspondent of the New York Rowdy Journal, a very self-important young man, who was perfectly convinced "that the aristocratic circles of England quailed before the name of Jefferson Brick." His wife, "a sickly little girl with tight round eyes," was of an intellectual turn of mind and despite the care of her two small children, found time to attend lectures on the Philosophy of the Soul, the Philosophy of Crime ; the Philosophy of Vegetables, etc. *Chuzzlewit*, 16, 17.

**BRICK LANE.** The meeting-place of the United Grand Junction Ebenezer Temperance Association has been identified at the back of No. 160 Brick Lane, Whitechapel, and is now a Mission Hall, still reached by a wooden ladder. *Pickwick*, 33.

**BRICKMAKER, THE.** A sullen labourer and the husband of Jenny, whom he ill-treated. It was to his hovel that Lady Dedlock went in her flight. *Bleak House*, 8, 22, 31, 57.

**BRIEG.** This Swiss town, at the foot of the Simplon Pass, was the starting-place for Vendale and Obenreizer in their fateful journey across the mountains. Vendale and Marguerite were subsequently married there. *No Thoroughfare*.

**BRIGGS.** 1. Mr. and Mrs. Briggs, friends of the Egotistical *Young Couple*.

2. Mrs. Briggs "was a widow with three daughters and two sons ; Mr. Samuel, the eldest, was an attorney ; and Mr. Alexander, the youngest, was under articles to his brother. They lived in Portland Street and moved in the same orbit as the Tauntons, hence their mutual dislike." The whole family were invited to the Steam Excursion, and the daughters, Miss Julia and Kate, did their utmost to outshine the Misses Taunton. *Boz, Tales, Excursion.*

3. Master Briggs was a pupil at Dr. Blimber's school. *Dombey*, 12, 14, 41, 60.

**BRIGHTON.** This town has many associations with Dickens, beginning with a visit in 1837, when he was busy on *Oliver Twist.*

Four years later he went there again and put up at the Old Ship Hotel, in the King's Road, where he worked on *Barnaby Rudge*. He returned in 1847, 1848, when he stayed at the Bedford Hotel, 1849, 1850, 1853, when he was working at *Bleak House*, and again in 1861. The Tuggs contemplated going to Brighton, but were deterred by the number of accidents to Brighton coaches (*Boz, Tales, Tuggs*). After the fatal duel, Sir Mulberry Hawk and Westwood sped to Brighton and thence crossed to France (*Nickleby*, 50). Old Mr. Turveydrop had been noticed by the Prince Regent when that august being had driven out of the Pavilion (*Bleak House*, 14). Our chief interest in the place lies, however, in its connection with the Dombeys. *See* Bedford Hotel. *Dombey*, 8, 10–12, 14, 41, 59, 60.

**BRIGHTON TIPPER.** Mrs. Gamp's favourite ale was made at the brewery of Thomas Tipper, of Newhaven. It was a very strong ale. *Chuzzlewit*, 25.

**BRIG PLACE.** "On the brink of a little canal near the India Docks," Brig Place was the residence of Captain Cuttle, who lived in Mrs. MacStinger's first floor. *Dombey*, 9, 15, 23, 25, 60.

**BRIMER.** Fifth mate of the East Indiaman *Halsewell* (*q.v.*). *Reprinted, Long Voyage.*

**BRISTOL.** Dickens's personal connection with this city dated from 1835, when he was sent thither to report Lord John Russell's election speeches. He lodged at the Bush Tavern (demolished in 1864), which stood in Corn Street, on the site now occupied by Lloyd's Bank. It was to this same Bush Tavern that Mr. Winkle fled from Dowler's vengeance, and there Mr. Pickwick stayed when he went to break the news of Arabella Allen's marriage to Winkle. Nearby was that most wonderful of all surgeries, "Sawyer late Nockemorf." *Pickwick*, 38, 39, 48, 50.

**BRITAIN, BENJAMIN.** The manservant of Dr. Jeddler, "a small man with an uncommonly sour and discontented face." His view of life may be summed up in his own words : "I don't know anything ; I don't care for anything ; I don't make out anything ; I don't believe anything ; and I don't want anything." He married Clemency Newcome and became host of "The Nutmeg Grater" Inn, where he was known as Little Britain. *The Battle of Life.*

**BRITANNIA THEATRE, HOXTON.** This is now a variety house, but it was for many years the home of melodrama of a very lurid description. It was visited and described in *Uncommercial*, 4.

**BRITISH MUSEUM LIBRARY.** The present Reading Room, beneath its magnificent dome, was built in the then Quadrangle in 1857. Before then the reading-room was what is now known as the Long Room, at the N.E. corner, approached through the

King's Library. It then had an entrance from Montague Street. It was wholly inadequate for housing the books, and there was little accommodation for students. Dickens was a constant reader in the old reading-room, which is mentioned in *Boz, Characters*, 10.

**BRITTLES.** Man-of-all-work at Mrs. Maylie's, "who entered her service a mere child and was treated as a promising young boy, though he was something past thirty." *Twist*, 28–31, 53.

**BRIXTON.** In the early nineteenth century this was a country suburb, where resided the "comfortably-off" middle class business men, who kept their carriages and were proud of their flower gardens. Typical of such establishments was that of Wilkins Flasher, Esq. (*Pickwick*, 55). Mr. Pickwick carried out researches in Brixton, though of what nature we are not told (*Chapter* 1). In Brixton is the tomb of Dr. Jobling's unfortunate friend who died of shock on learning the actual position of his stomach (*Chuzzlewit*, 27), while it was among the eligible bachelors of Brixton that the Misses Malderton hoped to secure husbands. *Boz, Tales, Sparkins*.

**BROBITY, MISS.** The lady who kept a school at Cloisterham and was so overcome by admiration of Mr. Sapsea that she consented to become his wife. When he proposed, she could only say, "Oh, Thou!" The inscription on her tomb will be found in the article on Sapsea. *Drood*, 4.

**BROGLEY.** Broker and appraiser, of Bishopsgate Street Without, who entered into possession at the Wooden Midshipman. On his return from abroad Walter Gay put up at Brogley's, while Florence was living at the Midshipman. *Dombey*, 9, 48, 49.

**BROGSON.** A guest of Octavius Budden. *Boz, Tales, Minns*.

**BROOK DINGWALL, CORNELIUS.** A pompous M.P. who lived in the Adelphi. He put his daughter Lavinia to school with the Misses Crumpton, whence she eloped with Theodosius Butler. *Boz, Tales, Sentiment*.

**BROOKER.** A former clerk and confidant of Ralph Nickleby, who, after serving a sentence of transportation, returned a beggar and attempted to extract money from his old master. Years previously he had been entrusted with Ralph's only child, and, taking him to a Yorkshire school, had there left him under the name of Smike, though reporting to Ralph that the child was dead. *Nickleby*, 44, 58, 60, 61.

**BROOKS.** 1. Friend of Sam Weller's and a pieman who kept a number of cats which he made into pies. "I seasons 'em for beefsteak, weal, or kidney 'cordin' to the demand." *Pickwick*, 19.

2. One of the five occupants of a bed at Dotheboys Hall. *Nickleby*, 7.

3. Brooks, of Sheffield, was the name by which Murdstone alluded to David Copperfield when discussing him with his friends. The allusion is to a well-known Sheffield cutler named Brooks. *Copperfield*, 2, 10.

**BROOKS'S CLUB.** This fashionable club, to which Cousin Feenix belonged (*Dombey*, 41), was founded in 1764, and still occupies its original home at 60 St. James's Street. From its earliest days it has been associated with the Liberal party.

**BROOK STREET.** In this fashionable street, running from New Bond Street to Grosvenor Square, lived Mrs. Skewton in a house borrowed from the Feenix family (*Dombey*, 30); and in the same house Florence went to see Edith and received her last message to Mr. Dombey (*Chapter* 61). On his brief visit to England Mr. Dorrit stayed at an hotel in Brook Street (*Dorrit*, II, 16). The *Uncommercial Traveller* (16) remarked that in Arcadian London's summer the hotels in Brook Street were empty.

**BROUGHAM, LORD.** Original of Pott. (*q.v.*)

**BROWDIE, JOHN.** A corn factor near Dotheboys Hall, and a big, burly Yorkshireman with an enormous appetite. After a passing fit of jealousy occasioned by Nicholas's thoughtless attentions to Matilda Price, Browdie's fiancée, he proved a good friend to the young man and helped him get away from Dotheboys after the thrashing of Squeers. On his wedding trip to London, John Browdie contrived the escape of Smike, who had fallen into the schoolmaster's hands, and after his engagement to Madeleine, Nicholas went down to Yorkshire to tell his old friend the good news. It was Browdie who saved Mrs. Squeers and her family from the vengeance of the boys when the school was broken up. *Nickleby*, 9, 13, 39, 42, 43, 45, 64.

**BROWN.** 1. Good Mrs. Brown was the name adopted by the mother of Alice Marwood, when she kidnapped Florence Dombey. With an indefinite idea of blackmailing her daughter's betrayer, James Carker, she spied on him through Rob the Grinder, and after his flight was able to direct Mr. Dombey to the trysting-place at Dijon. *Dombey*, 6, 27, 34, 40, 46, 52, 58.

2. Mrs. Brown was landlady of one of the paupers. *Boz, Our Parish*, 1.

3. Three Miss Browns laid in wait for the curate. *Boz, Our Parish*, 2, 6.

4. The near-sighted violoncello player in the amateur orchestra at the Gattleton's theatricals. *Boz, Tales, Porter*.

5. The beau of a young lady on the Margate boat. *Boz, Scenes*, 10.

6. Emily, the cause of the Great Winglebury duel, triumphantly carried off by Horace Hunter. *Boz, Tales, Winglebury Duel*.

7. Member of the Mudfog Association.

8. Brown of Muggleton was the maker of Miss Rachel Wardle's shoes. *Pickwick*, 10.

9. A corporal in the East Indies and friend of Mrs. Nubbles. *Curiosity Shop*, 21.

10. Conversation Brown was a friend of Cousin Feenix and a four bottle man at the Treasury Board. *Dombey*, 61.

11. One of Mrs. Lemon's pupils. *Holiday Romance*.

**BROWNDOCK, MISS.** Mr. Nickleby's cousin's sister-in-law, who won a ten thousand pound prize in a lottery. *Nickleby*, 17.

**BROWNE, HABLOT KNIGHT.** (1815–82.) Better known under his name of Phiz, this artist succeeded Seymour in the illustration of *Pickwick Papers*, his first work appearing in Part III. In turn he illustrated *Nickleby, Curiosity Shop* (part), *Barnaby* (part), *Chuzzlewit, Dombey, Copperfield, Bleak House, Dorrit* and *Two Cities*.

**BROWNLOW, MR.** The benefactor and unfailing friend of Oliver Twist. When Oliver was accused of picking his pocket, Mr. Brownlow believed the child's story, and after a remarkable scene with Mr. Fang, the magistrate, took the boy to his home. Despite the bad impression created by Oliver's disappearance and discovery again on the night of the attempted burglary at Mrs. Maylie's, Brownlow maintained his belief in the lad and devoted himself to establishing his identity as Leeford's brother and Rose Maylie's nephew. Mr. Brownlow eventually adopted Oliver Twist as his son. *Twist*, 10–12, 14, 15, 17, 32, 41, 46, 49, 51–3.

**BROWNRIGG.** Young Brownrigg, to whom the facetious boarders at Todgers's likened Bailey, Junior (*Chuzzlewit*, 9), was the son of the infamous Elizabeth Brownrigg, who was hanged for the ill-treatment and murder of her girl apprentice, Mary Clifford. The husband and son were both implicated in the charge, and all three were tried at the Old Bailey, September 2, 1767. The mother was executed a few days later.

**BRYANSTONE SQUARE.** The somewhat vague direction of Mr. Dombey's house is given as being in a "dreadfully genteel street in the region between Portland Place and Bryanstone Square." *Dombey* 3.

**BUCKET, INSPECTOR.** A detective officer employed by Mr. Tulkinghorn to unravel the mystery of Lady Dedlock's secret visit with Jo to Hawdon's grave. Placed in charge of the investigation following Mr. Tulkinghorn's murder, with the aid of his wife, a lady of natural detective genius, he built up the evidence against Hortense. On Lady Dedlock's flight Sir Leicester employed Bucket to trace her, and this he did, taking Esther with him. Finally he wrested the fateful Jarndyce will from Grandfather Smallweed, and was thus instrumental in settling for ever the great case of Jarndyce and Jarndyce. Inspector Bucket was based

upon Inspector Field (*q.v.*). *Bleak House*, 22, 24, 25, 46, 47, 49, 53, 54, 56, 57, 59, 61, 62.

**BUCKINGHAM STREET.** This is one of the streets by the Adelphi, and is ever-memorable on account of Mrs. Crupp, David's landlady, who lived at York House, No. 15, since demolished. Dickens had rooms here about 1834. *Copperfield*, 23–6, 28, 34, 35, 37.

**BUCKLERSBURY.** This short street, running out of Cheapside, almost opposite Old Jewry, was long noted for its eating-houses, one of which is graphically described in *Boz, Characters*, 1.

**BUCKSTONE, J. B.** This popular comedian and playwright first appeared at the Surrey in 1823, and was an immediate success. He managed the Haymarket, 1853–76, and wrote several famous pieces, notably *Green Bushes* and *The Flowers of the Forest*. He invented the one time popular comic way of speaking out of the corner of the mouth. *Sketches of Gentlemen (Theatrical)*.

**BUD, ROSA.** A girl at Miss Twinkleton's school. Her father and Edwin Drood's father had been close friends for many years, and by her father's will she was to marry Edwin as soon as she came of age. Before that time, however, both had realised that they did not truly love each other, and they parted on the understanding that henceforward they would be no more than brother and sister. The next day Edwin disappeared. John Jasper, who had long terrified Rosa by his evil attentions, made a passionate appeal to the girl :—

"There is my peace ; there is my despair. Stamp them into the dust ; so that you take me, were it even mortally hating me." Horrified at the man's passion and violence, Rosa fled to her guardian, Mr. Grewgious, who saw to her safety in London. Where the story closes there is the suggestion that she and Bob Tartar are falling in love. *Drood*, 2, 3, 7–9, 11, 13, 15, 19–23.

**BUDDEN, OCTAVIUS.** The cousin of Mr. Minns, who "having realised a moderate fortune by exercising the trade of a corn chandler, had purchased a cottage in the vicinity of Stamford Hill, whither he had retired with the wife of his bosom and his only son, Master Alexander Augustus Budden." His visit from his cousin Minns forms the subject of Dickens's first story. *Boz, Tales, Minns*.

**BUDGER, MRS.** A little old widow to whom Dr. Slammer was paying his addresses at the Rochester Ball when Jingle came along and cut him out. *Pickwick*, 2.

**BUFFER, DR.** A Member of the Mudfog Association.

**BUFFERS.** Certain nameless guests of the Veneerings. *Mutual Friend*, I, 2, 10 ; III, 17.

**BUFFLE.** The tax-collector whose business manner enraged Major Jackman. When

Buffle's house was burned to the ground the Major rescued him from the flames, and a firm friendship was cemented between them. Mrs. Buffle assumed unwarranted airs on account of keeping a one-horse " pheayton." *Lirriper's Legacy.*

**BUFFS.** One of the political parties at Eatanswill. *See* Blues.

**BUFFUM, OSCAR.** Spokesman of the deputation which arranged the lev-ee in Elijah Pogram's honour. *Chuzzlewit*, 34.

**BUFFY, WILLIAM.** A friend of Sir Leicester Dedlock and a member of the Government. *Bleak House*, 12, 28, 53, 58, 66.

**BULDER, COLONEL.** Head of the Rochester garrison. With his wife and daughter he was present at the ball held at the Bull, and later commanded the troops at the review. *Pickwick*, 2, 4.

**BULE, MISS.** The young lady of eight or nine who took the lead in society at Miss Griffin's school. *The Haunted House.*

**BULL, PRINCE.** The antagonist of Prince Bear, and typifying England in the Crimean War allegory. *Reprinted, Prince Bear and Prince Bull.*

**BULL INN.** 1. Mrs. Gamp's " Bull in Holborn " was an old-established inn and coach office at 121 Holborn, on the right-hand side of the street going from Farringdon Street. The site is now occupied by Messrs. Gamage's premises. *Chuzzlewit*, 25, 29.

2. The Bull and Victoria Inn, Rochester, more commonly known as the Bull, was the first place the Pickwickians put up at on their journey, and the scene of the ball where Jingle brought such disgrace on the Club coat. The house is full of Pickwickian memories, that great man's room being No. 17, Tupman's No. 13, and Winkle's No. 19 (*Pickwick*, 2). The Bull is also the original of the Blue Boar of *Expectations* (*q.v.*) and of the Winglebury Arms in *Boz.* (*q.v.*)

3. The Bull, Whitechapel, was a principal starting-place for the East Anglican coaches, and thence it was that Mr. Weller, Senior, drove the Pickwickians and Mr. Peter Magnus on their fateful journey to Ipswich. It was demolished in 1868, and the site is now occupied by Aldgate Avenue. *Pickwick*, 0, 22.

**BULLAMY.** Porter employed by the Anglo-Bengalee Assurance Company. He was " a wonderful creature, in a vast red waistcoat and a short-tailed pepper-and-salt coat." When the crash came after Tigg Montague's murder, Bullamy and Crimple decamped with all the available money. *Chuzzlewit*, 27, 51.

**BULLDOGS, THE UNITED.** The name taken by the Society of Prentice Knights when the indentures of the older members expired. *Barnaby*, 36.

**BULLFINCH.** The friend with whom the Uncommercial Traveller visited Namelesston

and partook of an " ill-served, ill-appointed, ill-cooked, nasty little dinner." *Uncommercial Traveller*, 32.

**BULLMAN.** Plaintiff in the case of Bullman and Ramsey. *Pickwick*, 20.

**BULLOCK.** Defendant in a Doctors' Commons case. *Copperfield*, 29.

**BULL'S-EYE.** " A white shaggy dog, with his face scratched and torn in twenty different places," belonging to Bill Sikes. *Twist*, 13, 15, 16, 18, 19, 39, 48, 50.

**BULPH.** A pilot at whose house, in St. Thomas Street, Vincent Crummles and his family put up during their visit to Portsmouth. It is supposed that Bulph's house, which " sported a boat-green door, with window frames of the same colour," was No. 78. *Nickleby*, 23, 30.

**BUMBLE.** Beadle of the workhouse where Oliver Twist was born, and a character which proved one of the most potent of Dickens's weapons for the destruction of certain social evils. Ever since the description was first published the name Bumble has been synonymous with officious officialdom. Having neglected and ill-treated Oliver until the lad ran away, Bumble was officially anxious for his recovery. Enamoured of Mrs. Corney's " six teaspoons, a pair of sugar-tongs, and a milk-pot, with a small quantity of second-hand furniture and twenty pounds in ready money," he married that lady, then the matron of the workhouse. But she immediately took command of affairs, and although Bumble became master of the workhouse, he was never master of his own house. Bumble and his wife were eventually disgraced by the efforts of Mr. Brownlow and ended their days in the workhouse of which they had once had charge. *Twist*, 2–5, 7, 17, 23, 27, 37, 38, 51, 53.

**BUMPLE, MICHAEL.** Promoter in the case at Doctors' Commons of Bumple against Sludberry, Bumple being summoned for brawling by saying at a vestry meeting, " You be blowed " to Sludberry. *Boz, Scenes*, 8.

**BUNG.** Formerly a broker's man and eventually the successful candidate for the office of beadle. *Boz, Our Parish*, 4, 5.

**BUN HOUSE, CHELSEA.** The old Bun House, next door but two to which lived Mr. Bucket's aunt (*Bleak House*, 53), stood at the end of Jews' Row, now Pimlico Road, opposite the barracks. It was demolished in 1839. In command of his section of the Royal East London Volunteers, Gabriel Varden marched to the Bun House during the regimental evolutions. *Barnaby*, 42.

**BUNKIN, MRS.** A friend of Mrs. Sanders and " a lady which clear starched." *Pickwick*, 34.

**BUNSBY, CAPTAIN JACK.** Skipper of the *Cautious Clara*, a " bulkhead—human and very large—with one stationary eye in the mahogany face, and one revolving one, on the principle of some lighthouses." He was considered a fount of wisdom by his friend Cuttle, but his sagacity expressed itself after the following style : " My name's Jack Bunsby. And what I says I stands to. Whereby, why not ? If so, what odds ? Can any man say otherwise ? No. Avast then." He left to his hearers the responsibility of interpreting his meaning, remarking, " The bearings of this observation lays in the application on it." Bunsby rescued Captain Cuttle from Mrs. MacStinger, but at the cost of his own liberty, for that masterful woman ended by marrying him. *Dombey,* 15, 23, 39, 60.

**BURGESS AND CO.** Tailors to Mr. Toots, " fash'nable but very dear." *Dombey,* 12, 18, 41, 48.

**BURKE.** William Burke and William Hare were murderers and body-snatchers who carried on their vile trade in Edinburgh. After killing at least fifteen persons and selling their bodies, Hare turned evidence against Burke, who was hanged, January 28, 1829. Hare died in London, a blind beggar, about 1860.

**BURNETT.** 1. Fanny, Dickens's sister, original of Fanny Dorrit. (*q.v.*)

2. Harry, her son, original of little Paul Dombey. (*q.v.*)

3. Henry, her husband, original of Nicholas Nickleby. (*q.v.*)

**BURTON, THOMAS.** Convert to teetotalism whose case was mentioned at the Brick Lane temperance meeting. *Pickwick,* 33.

**BURY ST. EDMUNDS.** Described as " a handsome little town of thriving appearance," this ancient West Suffolk town has changed but little since the days when Mr. Pickwick and Sam Weller alighted at the Angel from the Eatanswill coach. It was there that Job Trotter first appeared upon the scene and sent Mr. Pickwick on a fool's errand to Westgate House, the young ladies' seminary kept by Miss Tomkins, and since identified as Southgate House (*Pickwick,* 15, 16). Little Mr. Chillip, the doctor, settled down near Bury, where he had for neighbours Mr. and Miss Murdstone (*Copperfield,* 60). The never-finished story of Mr. Gabriel Parsons centred round an adventure of his at Bury (*Boz, Tales, Tottle*) ; finally the *Uncommercial Traveller* (23) considered London dull beside a " bright little town like Bury St. Edmunds."

**BUSH INN, BRISTOL.** This was where Mr. Winkle put up after his precipitate flight from Bath, and where Mr. Pickwick stayed on his subsequent visits to the town. The inn, which belonged to the coach proprietor, Moses Pickwick, stood in Corn Street, near the Guildhall. It was demolished in 1864, and the Wiltshire Bank (now absorbed in Lloyds) was built on its site. *Pickwick,* 38, 39, 48, 50.

**BUSS, ROBERT WILLIAM.** On the death of Seymour this painter was commissioned to illustrate Pickwick, and he contributed two plates to Part III. His work was not liked, and he was succeeded by H. K. Browne, who supplied two drawings to replace Buss's in the bound edition.

**" BUT BEEF IS RARE."** From *Don Juan,* Canto II, Stanza, 154. *Boz, Tales, Boarding House.*

**BUTCHER, THE YOUNG.** The terror of the youth of Canterbury and especially bully of Dr. Strong's boys. *Copperf.,* 18, 60.

**BUTCHER, WILLIAM.** The Chartist, who explained to William the laws of society governing the poor. *Reprinted, Poor Man's Patent.*

**BUTLER.** 1. The Veneering's servant, known as the Analytical Chemist. (*q.v.*)

2. The staid old butler of the Cheeryble Brothers, named David. (*q.v.*)

3. Dr. Blimbers's butler, " in a blue coat and bright buttons, who gave quite a winey flavour to the table beer ; he poured it out so superbly." *Dombey,* 12.

4. Mrs. Skewton's " silver-headed butler, who was charged extra on that account as having the appearance of an ancient family retainer." *Dombey,* 30.

5. The Chief Butler in Mr. Merdle's establishment, who was " the stateliest man in company. He did nothing, but he looked on as few other men could have done." When told of Mr. Merdle's suicide he remarked, " Mr. Merdle never was the gentleman, and no ungentlemanly act on Mr. Merdle's part would surprise me." *Dorrit,* I, 21, 33 ; II, 12, 16, 25.

**BUTLER, THEODOSIUS.** Cousin of the Misses Crumpton, and the author of " Considerations on the Policy of Removing the Duty on Beeswax," under the name of Edward McNeville Walter. He eloped with Lavinia Dingwall. *Boz, Tales, Sentiment.*

**BUTTON, WILLIAM.** The tailor of Tooley Street, acted by Jupe, the clown, in " the hippo-comedietta of 'The Tailor's Journey to Brentford.' " *Hard Times,* I, 3.

**BUZFUZ, SERJEANT.** Counsel for Mrs. Bardell and a lawyer " with a fat body and a red face." Typical of the browbeating, bullying counsel of the period, he made an impassioned speech for his client, dwelling on the concealed expressions of tenderness in Mr. Pickwick's message of " Chops and Tomata Sauce," and extracted with deadly effect Winkle's story of the adventure with the lady in curl papers. The prototype of Buzfuz was Sergeant Bompas, a prominent member of the Bar. *Pickwick,* 34.

# C

**CABBURN.** In the 40's and 50's Cabburn's Oil and Pills were widely advertised as specifics for rheumatism, general debility, etc. Cabburn's dispensary was at 1 King's Cross. *Reprinted, Bill Sticking.*

**CAB - DRIVER, THE.** " A brown - whiskered, white-haired, no-coated cabman," who drove a gorgeously painted red cab which seemed ubiquitous. He was always getting into trouble with the police, and was last seen in the Middlesex House of Correction. *Boz, Scenes,* 17.

**CABRIOLET,** later abbreviated to Cab. This was a public conveyance which plied for hire in the London streets and was the ancestor of the Hansom cab. It was a light two-wheeled, hooded carriage, built to hold two persons in addition to the driver, who was partitioned off from his fares, sitting on a little dickey on the off side. In the Hansom cab the driver's seat was high up, behind the body of the cab. The fare was eightpence a mile. The best account of these old vehicles, illustrated by Cruikshank, is in *Boz, Scenes,* 17.

**CAD.** This was the old term applied to omnibus conductors, and had no opprobrious meaning. *Boz, Scenes,* 16.

**CADOGAN PLACE.** Here lived Mrs. Wittitterley; it is described as the connecting link between the aristocratic pavements of Belgrave Square and the barbarism of Chelsea. *Nickleby,* 21.

**CAEN WOOD OR KEN WOOD.** This estate on the Hampstead to Highgate Road, and now public property, belonged to the Earl of Mansfield, and would have been destroyed by the Gordon Rioters had they not been diverted thence by troops (*Barnaby,* 66). In his flight after the murder Bill Sikes skirted Caen Wood on his way to Hampstead. *Twist,* 48.

**CAG MAGGERS,** or Cag-mag, was a curious old English dialect word applied to worthless scraps of meat and hence to the small butchers who sold such pieces. The excited little Jew who made a sort of chant of, " Oh, Jaggerth, Jaggerth, Jaggerth ! All otherth ith Cag-Maggerth, give me Jaggerth," evidently used the term in a slighting sense as meaning paltry, inefficient, worthless. *Expectations,* 20.

**CALAIS.** It was at this French seaport that Roger Cly saw Charles Darnay show incriminating lists to French gentlemen (*Two Cities,* II, 3). After their bankruptcy the Veneerings retired thither to live on Mrs. Veneering's diamonds (*Mutual Friend,* IV, 17). For similar motives of economy the late Mr. Sparsit lived and died there (*Hard Times,* I, 7). The *Uncommercial Traveller's* emotions on reaching Calais after an indifferent passage are described in Chapter 17. Flora Finching spent her honeymoon there (*Dorrit,* I, 24) and thither it was that Clennam, and later Meagles, undertook fruitless visits to enquire of Miss Wade about Blandois. *Dorrit,* II, 20, 33.

**CALLOW, DR.** " One of the most eminent physicians in London " consulted by *Our Bore, Reprinted.*

**CALTON, MR.** " A superannuated beau whose face it was impossible to look upon without being reminded of a chubby street door knocker—half lion, half monkey." He was one of Mrs. Tibbs's first boarders and fell a victim to Mrs. Maplesone, to the tune of £1000, damages for breach of promise to marry. *Boz, Tales, Boarding House.*

**CAMBERWELL.** This was long a pleasant and rather countrified suburb of London, much favoured by city men of the Malderton type (*Boz, Tales, Sparkins*). Mr. Pickwick had conducted some important researches there (*Pickwick,* 1). The brass and copper-founder who employed Ruth Pinch lived at Camberwell, in a house " so big and fierce that its mere outside made bold persons quail " (*Chuzzlewit,* 9, 36). It was near Camberwell Green that Wemmick remarked, " Hullo ! Here's a church . . . and here's Miss Skiffins: let's have a wedding" (*Expectations,* 55). A young lady of this place, inspired by Queen Victoria's official announcement of her marriage, " informed her papa that ' she intended to ally herself in marriage ' with Mr. Smith of Stepney " (*Sketches of Couples*). It was a delicately minded gentleman from Camberwell who made a very tactful presentation of flowers to Mr. Dorrit, enclosing two guineas in the wrappings (*Dorrit,* I, 8). Camberwell, it may be added, was the scene of the Barnwell murder. *Chuzzlewit,* 9. *Expectations,* 15.

**CAMBRIDGE.** After his acquittal at the Old Bailey, Charles Darnay went to Cambridge, where he read with undergraduates (*Two Cities,* II, 10). Matthew Pocket was a Cambridge man (*Expectations,* 23), as was also George Silverman (*Silverman*). Sally Rairyganoo represented herself as coming from Cambridge, though Mrs. Lirriper always suspected an Irish extraction. *Lirriper's Legacy.*

**CAMDEN TOWN.** During the first half of the nineteenth century this was the N.W. extremity of London, being separated by fields from Holloway, Kentish Town and Hampstead. Dickens had many personal associations with the place. In 1822-3 the family settled at 141 Bayham Street, one of the poorest parts of the London suburbs, and a few years later, while his father was in the Marshalsea, Charles was " handed over as lodger to a reduced old lady . . . in Little College Street, who took children in to board . . . and who began to sit for Mrs. Pipchin in Dombey when she took me in." This was Mrs. Roylance (*q.v.*). City clerks would walk to their work from Camden Town (*Boz, Scenes,* 1), though in the 30's it was still considered a rural district (*Boz, Scenes,* 20). Miss Ivins resided in the most secluded portion of Camden Town (*Boz, Characters,* 4), while the shabby-genteel, drunken engraver lived there, in a new row of houses near the Canal (*Boz, Characters*, 10). Heyling hunted down his father-in-law to a wretched lodging in Camden Town, as narrated in the Old Man's Tale about the Queer Client (*Pickwick*, 21); and it was among the poor children of the place that Fagin suggested Noah Claypole should do a little easy pilfering (*Twist*, 42). Near the Veterinary College (Great College Street) was the Micawber house, where Traddles lodged (*Copperfield*, 27, 28). In " Camberling Town" was Staggs Gardens (*q.v.*), where the Toodles at one time lived. *Dombey*, 6.

Finally, at Camden Town lived that immortal family, the Cratchits. *Christmas Carol.*

**CAMILLA.** A sister of Matthew Pocket and wife of Cousin Raymond. She was one of Miss Havisham's toadies. *Expectations*, 11, 25.

**CAMPBELL.** 1. The name adopted by Magwitch when hiding in Mrs. Whimple's house. *Expectations*, 46.

2. Original of Mrs. Skewton. (*q.v.*)

**CANDLESTICK, FLAT.** Better known in modern times as a bedroom candlestick in distinction to the upright candlestick used in sitting-rooms. Candles used in these sticks were known as flat candles.

**CANNON STREET.** Before its extension in 1854 Cannon Street only ran from the junction of Walbrook and Budge Row (practically Cannon Street Station) to Eastcheap. In it was apparently a rival boarding house to Todgers's, of which Mr. Jinkins had not much opinion. *Chuzzlewit*, 9.

**CANONGATE.** This was the scene of the story of the Bagman's Uncle, and the coach yard where the vehicles were stored belonged to a Mr. Croall. *Pickwick*, 49.

**CANTERBURY.** The years which have elapsed since Dickens described this old cathedral city have wrought comparatively few changes, and no great imagination is required to see it now as it appeared in the eyes of David Copperfield. Dr. Strong's school still exists as King's School, in the cathedral precincts, while his house has been identified as No. 1 Lady Wootton's Green. David lived with Mr. Wickfield at the house now numbered 71, St. Dunstan's Street, and when Mr. Dick came to see him every alternate Wednesday, he put up at the Fountain Hotel, called by Dickens the County Hotel. The little inn where the Micawbers stayed (*Chapter* 17) was probably the Sun Hotel, in Sun Street, unchanged in appearance since those days; and the Heep's house, where he and David met, was possibly in North Lane. *Copperfield*, 13, 15–19, 39, 52, 54, 61, 62.

**CAPE.** The violin accompanist in the Malderton's orchestra. *Boz, Tales, Porter.*

**CAPE HORN.** It was near Cape Horn that the *Golden Mary* struck an iceberg (*Golden Mary*), while on an island near Cape Horn Captain Jorgan found the bottle containing *The Message from the Sea.*

**CAPPER, MR. AND MRS.** Host and hostess of Mr. Mincin, the very friendly Young Gentleman. *Sketches of Gentlemen.*

**CAPRICORN AND CAULIFLOWER.** Uncle and brother of the high-trotting horse driven by Bailey Junior in the service of Tigg Montague. *Chuzzlewit*, 26, 27.

**CAPTAIN.** 1. " A spare, squeaking old man who invokes damnation on his own eyes or somebody else's at the commencement of every sentence he utters." He was a frequenter of Bellamy's. *Boz, Scenes*, 18.

2. The half-pay captain, who played strange jokes on the old lady next door. *Boz, Our Parish*, 2.

3. The Yankee captain of the *Screw*. *Chuzzlewit*, 16.

4. Captain or Capting of the *Esau Slodge*, the Mississippi steamer. *Chuzzlewit*, 33.

**CARKER.** James, the manager for Dombey and Son and Mr. Dombey's confidential assistant. He was a particularly heartless scoundrel, especially where his sister and elder brother were concerned, and was zealous in poisoning Mr. Dombey's mind against Florence and young Walter Gay. When employed to humiliate Edith Dombey by carrying messages, he abused his master's confidence by eloping with her. By the treachery of Rob the Grinder and Mrs. Brown, whose daughter Alice had been seduced by Carker, the whereabouts of the rendezvous with Edith was communicated to Mr. Dombey, who followed the couple thither. Carker eluded him, however, and fled back to England, pursued by the injured husband. They finally met on the platform of a railway station, and in an attempt to evade his master, Carker was run down and killed by a passing train. *Dombey*, 10, 13, 17, 18, 22, 24, 26–8, 31–4, 36, 37, 40, 42, 43, 45–7, 51–5.

John Carker was James's elder brother, but was always known as Mr. Carker the Junior, because, in his youth, he had robbed the firm and had been given a humble post from which he was never to rise. On the death of his brother, John came into his wealth, but devoted the interest to the use of his ruined master, Mr. Dombey. *Dombey*, 6, 13, 19, 22, 33, 34, 46, 53, 58, 62.

Harriet, sister of the Carker brothers, was " a slight, small, patient figure . . . who of all the world went over to her brother in his shame, put her hand in his, and, with a sweet composure and determination, led him hopefully upon his barren way." She befriended Alice Marwood and succeeded in touching the girl's embittered heart. Eventually she married Morfin, once one of Mr. Dombey's managers. *Dombey*, 22, 33, 34, 53, 58, 62.

**CARLAVERO, GIOVANNI.** Keeper of an Italian wineshop, who had been rescued from the galleys, to which he had been consigned as a political prisoner. *Uncommercial Traveller*, 28.

**CARLISLE.** On his way from Lancaster to Carlisle Doctor Marigold first noticed the deaf and dumb young man who courted Sophy. *Doctor Marigold.*

**CARLO.** One of Jerry's performing dogs. *Curiosity Shop*, 18.

**CAROLINE.** Wife of one Scrooge's debtors who rejoiced in the thought of his approaching death. *Christmas Carol.*

**CARSTONE RICHARD.** A ward of Chancery and a party to the suit of Jarndyce and Jarndyce. He and his cousin, Ada Clare, had not long been together in the house of John Jarndyce, their guardian, before they fell in love with one another. Richard was given several starts in life, but he took finally to the law and devoted himself to the study of the suit. He fell into the hands of Vholes, the lawyer, who poisoned his mind against his benefactor and friend, John Jarndyce. The worry and disappointments of the Chancery suit destroyed Richard's health, and Ada Clare, after secretly marrying him, went to nurse him in his chambers, but the sudden ending of the case by the absorption of all the estate in costs, fairly broke Richard's heart and he died, leaving his widow and unborn child to the care of Mr. Jarndyce. *Bleak House*, 1-6, 8, 9, 13, 14, 17, 18, 20, 23, 24, 35, 37, 39, 43, 51, 59-62, 64, 65.

**CARTER.** Member of the Mudfog Association.

**CARTON, CAPTAIN GEORGE.** A sailor, "with bright eyes, brown face and an easy figure," who led the expedition against the pirates on Silver Store Island. He married Miss Marion Maryon. *English Prisoners.*

**CARTON, SYDNEY.** A good-hearted, dissolute barrister who acted as Stryver's devil in working up law cases. "I am a disappointed drudge. I care for no man on earth, and no man on earth cares for me," were the words in which he described himself. His extraordinary resemblance to Charles Darnay was used effectively by the defence when the latter was being tried at the Old Bailey, and the incident served to introduce Carton to Lucy Manette, with whom he fell in love. Going over to Paris at the time that Darnay was awaiting execution, Sydney Carton contrived to introduce himself into the prison and substitute himself for Lucy's husband. The resemblance between the two men prevented the discovery of this deception, and Sydney Carton ascended the scaffold and was guillotined in place of Charles Darnay. *Two Cities*, II, 2-6, 11, 13, 20, 21 ; III, 8, 9, 11-13, 15.

**CASBY, CHRISTOPHER.** The father of Flora Finching and a former town agent of Lord Decimus Tite Barnacle. He had a " shining bald head ; long grey hair at its side and back, which looked so benevolent . . . that various old ladies spoke of him as the ' Last of the Patriarchs.' " He was, however, a hard, griping landlord of some slum property, including Bleeding Heart Yard, and employed Pancks to extort the money from his poor tenants, himself posing as a model of humanity and kindness. Eventually Pancks showed up the Patriarch to the Bleeding Heart Yarders in his true colours. The original of this character was George Beadnell. *Dorrit*, I, 12, 13, 23, 24, 35 ; II, 9, 23, 32.

**CASTLE, THE.** 1. Mr. Wemmick called his little moated house at Walworth the Castle. *Expectations*, 25.
2. Mrs. Pipchin's house was the ogress's castle in a steep by-street at Brighton. *Dombey*, 8.
3. Coavinses lock-up in Cursitor Street was familiarly known as the Castle. *Bleak House*, 14.

**CASTLE STREET, HOLBORN.** This is now called Furnival Street, in memory of the inn which stood on the other side of Holborn. Traddles lodged there when studying law, and it was in his chambers that Mr. Dick was first introduced to the art of engrossing. *Copperfield*, 36.

**CATEATON STREET.** That portion of the present Gresham Street which lies between Milk Street and Old Jewry was, until 1845, called Cateaton Street. Here was the warehouse of Tom Smart's employers, Messrs. Bilson and Slum. *Pickwick*, 49.

**CATECHISM.** "Walk fast, Wal'r my lad, and walk the same all the days of your life. Overhaul the catechism for that advice, and keep it. ' Love ! Honour ! And obey ! ' Overhaul your catechism till you find that passage, and when found turn the leaf down." Words of wisdom from Captain Cuttle. *Dombey*, 4, 9.

**CATHERINE STREET, STRAND.** The lower end of this street was demolished when Aldwych was made, 1899–1905. Boz describes a private theatre of a type at that time found in Catherine Street. *Boz, Scenes*, 13.

**CATLIN, GEORGE.** (1796–1872.) An American painter and writer who spent seven years (1832–9) among the North American Indians. His work *Illustrations of the Manners, etc., of the North American Indians* (1857) is still an authority. Catlin exhibited some Ojibway Indians in London in 1843. On December 20 he presented them to the Queen and Prince Consort when, greatly to the royal amazement, they performed some of their medicine dances. *Reprinted, The Noble Savage.*

**CATNACH AND PITTS.** These were two publishers of ballads, songs, broadsides and " last dying speeches " of murderers. Their

printing offices were both in the neighbourhood of Seven Dials. *Boz, Scenes,* 5.

**CAUDLE.** This was a warm drink, much
in vogue in confinement cases, containing
wine and other suitable ingredients.

**CAULIFLOWER.**  Brother  of  Mr.
Montague's prancing steed, driven by Mr.
Bailey, Junior. *Chuzzlewit,* 26, 27.

**CAUTIOUS CLARA.**  Captain  Jack
Bunsby's vessel. *Dombey,* 23.

**CAVALETTO, JOHN BAPTIST.** An Italian
refugee who shared Rigaud's cell in the
Marseilles prison, and eventually made his
way to London, where he was befriended by
Arthur Clennam, and made the acquaintance
of Pancks, who called him " Altro," from his
constant repetition of that word.  He was
instrumental in tracking down Rigaud in
London, and helped to nurse Clennam in the
Marshalsea.  *Dorrit,* I, 1, 11, 13, 23, 25 ;
II, 9, 13, 22, 23, 28, 30, 33.

**CAVENDISH SQUARE.**  Near this square,
probably in Wigmore Street, was Madame
Mantalini's place of business (*Nickleby,* 10),
while the corner house outside which Wegg
had his stall, and where the Boffins moved
later, was also in the vicinity. *Mutual
Friend,* I, 5 ; II, 7.

**CAVETON.** The throwing-off young gentleman. *Sketches of Young Gentlemen.*

**CECIL STREET.** In this little street off
the Strand lived Mr. Watkins Tottle in the
happy days when he pictured the pleasures
of married life. *Boz, Tales, Tottle.*

**CELIA.** One of the charity children who
made love in the grim City church. *Uncommercial,* 21.

**CERTAINPERSONIO, PRINCE.**  Alicia's
bridegroom, provided by the good fairy
Grandmarina. *Holiday Romance.*

**CHADBAND.** " A large yellow man, with
a fat smile and a general appearance of having
too much train oil in his system . . . who
never speaks without putting up his great
hand, as delivering a token to his hearers
that he is going to edify them . . . he is,
as he expresses it, in the ministry."  Chadband will, for all time to come, serve as the
portrait of hypocrisy and cant.  His remarks
on the subject of "Terewth " are the words
of the religious humbug at his best.  After
imposing on the Snagsbys, Chadband and
his wife were induced by the Smallweeds to
assist in a scheme for blackmailing Sir
Leicester Dedlock, in which they were
thwarted by Inspector Bucket.

Mrs. Chadband was originally Mrs. Rachael,
the hard and unsympathetic nurse of Esther
Summerson's childhood. *Bleak House,* 3,
19, 22, 24, 25, 44, 54.

**CHAISE.**  This was a light two- or four-
wheeled travelling carriage drawn by one
or more horses.  The chaise had no shafts
and there was no driver's seat, the horses
being driven by postilions.  It was the
quickest vehicle on the roads and was used

largely for posting, and making such expeditious journeys as that of Mr. Jingle and
Miss Rachael Wardle.

**CHALONS.** In the Break of Day Inn, near
Chalons sur Saone, Rigaud and Cavaletto
met unexpectedly when the former was in
flight from Marseilles. *Dorrit,* I, 11.

**CHANCERY, COURT OF.**  Previous to
the erection of the present Law Courts (1874)
the Chancellor's court was held at Westminster Hall or at Lincoln's Inn Hall.  In
*Bleak House,* 1, the case of Jarndyce and
Jarndyce was being heard in Lincoln's Inn,
but the conclusion of the case was at Westminster (65).

**CHANCERY LANE.**  This legal highway
is so frequently mentioned that it is difficult
to deal with each instance separately.  Large
parts of the story of *Bleak House* are enacted
in the Lane or its vicinity (*Chapters* 1, 4, 10,
14, 19, 20, 32, 33, 39, 59) ; the courtyard in
which stood old Krook's shop and the Sols
Arms, being Chichester Rents, opposite
Breams' Buildings.  Mr. Gabriel Parsons
went up Chancery Lane on his way to
Cursitor Street, where Tottle was imprisoned
for debt (*Boz, Tales, Tottle*).  Rokesmith
followed Mr. Boffin down the Lane before he
first approached him with the offer of his
services (*Mutual Friend,* I, 8).  The old
Serjeant's Inn, where Mr. Pickwick was
accosted by a bail tout, was four houses up
on the right-hand side from Fleet Street.
It was closed as an inn of law in 1877 and
demolished shortly afterwards. *Pickwick,* 40.

**CHANCERY PRISONER.**  " A tall, gaunt,
cadaverous man, with sunken cheeks and a
restless, eager eye.  God help him ! the iron
teeth of confinement and privation had been
slowly filing him down for twenty years."
For a small sum he let his room at the Fleet
to Mr. Pickwick. *Pickwick,* 42, 44.

**CHANDLER.**  This was the old term for
a general dealer, originally one who sold
candles.  An oil shop or village all-sorts shop
are fair equivalents of the old chandler.

**" CHARGE, CHESTER, CHARGE."** Silas
Wegg was quoting from Scott's *Marmion,*
Canto IV, Stanza 32. *Mutual Friend,* III, 6.

**CHARING CROSS.** Few parts of London
have changed more in the last century than
Charing Cross and its vicinity.  Trafalgar
Square was not begun until 1829, its site
being a slum.  The Nelson column was
erected in 1842-3, approximately on the
site of the Golden Cross Hotel (*q.v.*).  On
the south-east side of the square stood
Northumberland House, surmounted by its
huge lion.  The house was demolished in
1874, and its site is commemorated by
Northumberland Avenue.  Where Charing
Cross Station now stands was Hungerford
Market, which was pulled down in 1862.

There are innumerable mentions of Charing
Cross in the novels.  It was outside the
Golden Cross that Mr. Pickwick had his

encounter with the cabman, while from the same inn he and his friends started on their first journey (*Pickwick*, 2). On his arrival in town from Canterbury, David Copperfield put up at the Golden Cross, and considered Charing Cross " a stuffy neighbourhood " (*Copperfield*, 19). While lounging round Charing Cross, Eugene Wrayburn saw Mr. Dolls staggering across the road (*Mutual Friend*, III, 10). According to the Gentleman in Small Clothes the statue of King Charles, looking down Charing Cross, had been seen at the Stock Exchange, arm in arm with Aldgate Pump. *Nickleby*, 41.

**CHARITABLE GRINDERS.** A charitable institution to which Polly Toodle's eldest boy was sent on Mr. Dombey's presentation. " The dress is a nice warm blue baize tailed coat and cap, turned up orange-coloured binding ; red worsted stockings ; and very strong leather small clothes." Rob the Grinder was but typical of the charity boys of London. All the charities, most of which dated from the middle eighteenth century, dressed their children in distinguishing garments, features of which were the " muffin " cap, leather breeches and buckled shoes. Charity girls usually wore a crimped cap and Quaker-like dress. *Dombey*, 5.

**CHARKER, HARRY.** A comrade of Gill Davis, and a corporal in the Royal Marines. *English Prisoners.*

**CHARLES.** 1. The well-bred, easy-going husband in the Cool Couple. *Sketches of Couples.*

2. Old Charles, once a waiter at a west-country hotel and by some considered the father of the waitering. *Somebody's Luggage.*

**CHARLEY.** 1. Charlotte Neckett, in-variably called Charley, was the daughter of a bailiff who died, leaving her, a mere child, to support the family. She was engaged by Mr. John Jarndyce as servant to Esther Summerson, and eventually married a well-to-do miller near Esther's home in the country. *Bleak House*, 15, 21, 23, 30, 31, 35–7, 44, 45, 51, 57, 61, 62, 64, 67.

2. The marine store dealer at Chatham to whom David Copperfield sold some clothes on his way to Dover. *Copperfield*, 13.

3. Potboy at the Magpie and Stump. *Pickwick*, 20.

4. The narrator of the *Holly Tree*, who thinking himself jilted by Angela Leath, left London to go to America, but was snowed up on his way to Liverpool at the Holly Tree Inn.

**CHARLOTTE.** 1. Sowerberry's servant girl who sided with Noah Claypole against Oliver Twist and eventually ran away to London with Noah. *Twist*, 4–7, 27, 42, 45, 53.

2. One of the Contradictory Couple. *Sketches of Couples.*

3. A treacherous schoolfellow of Miss Wade. *Dorrit*, II, 21.

4. The daughter of John the inventor. *Reprinted, Poor Man's Patent.*

**CHARTISTS.** In 1838 the London Working Men's Association drew up the People's Charter of six demands for reform. A monster petition was signed the next year, but was ignored, and for some years there was considerable unrest in London and the provinces. Finally, in 1848, a petition with 7,000,000 signatures was prepared, the intention being to take it to the Commons with a large force. Every preparation was made to preserve order, many special constables being sworn in, but the firm handling of the situation by the Duke of Wellington discouraged the leaders and the whole affair proved a fiasco.

**CHATHAM.** This town was associated with the early years of Dickens and finds frequent mention in his writings. The family lived at (now No. 11) Ordnance Terrace from 1817–21, when they moved to 18, St. Mary's Place, remaining there until 1823, and during these happy years of his childhood Dickens became intimate with the whole neighbourhood. Chatham first appears in his writings under the name of Mudfog. It next occurs in *Pickwick*, 2, 4, Winkle's duel with Dr. Slammer taking place near Fort Pitt, where Dickens had often played as a lad. Little David toiled through the town on his way to his aunt, and there disposed of some of his clothes to old Charley (*Copperfield*, 13). Richard Doubledick tramped into Rochester or Chatham (" because if anybody knows to a nicety where Rochester ends and Chatham begins it is more than I do ") in the year 1799 (*Seven Poor Travellers*). The town is described as Dullborough in *Uncommercial*, 12, while another chapter (24) deals with the dockyard. Serjeant Dornton relates his search at Chatham for Mesheck, the Jew, in 1847. *Reprinted, Detective Police.*

**CHEAPSIDE.** It was a hot summer Sunday when Mr. Minns toiled up the shady side of Cheapside on his way to the Flowerpot, whence he was to take coach to the Buddens (*Boz, Tales, Minns*), whereas Mr. Dumps, on his way to the Bloomsbury christening found that everybody in Cheapside looked wet, cold and dirty (*Boz, Tales, Christening*). While walking up Cheapside with Sam, after his interview with Dodson and Fogg, Mr. Pickwick expressed a wish for a glass of brandy and water warm. Sam replied without hesitation, " Second court on the right-hand side, last house but vun on the same side the vay," and there they met Mr. Weller Senior for the first time (*Pickwick*, 20). A certain slipper and dog's collar man had his portrait screwed on an artist's door in Cheapside (*Dombey*, 13), and after his day's work Mr. Carker was wont to ride up Cheapside (*Dombey*, 22). Pip was strolling there, undecided where to dine, when he was overtaken by Mr. Jaggers and carried off to Gerrard Street (*Expectations*, 48). Sitting in his pleasant parlour in the vicinity, Mr. Mould, the undertaker, listened to the distant hum of traffic in Cheapside. *Chuzzlewit*, 25.

**CHEERYBLE, CHARLES AND EDWIN.** The twin brothers who gave Nicholas Nickleby employment, and were charitable and kind to all who crossed their path. They had come to London as penniless lads, but succeeded in building up a prosperous business as German merchants. Among the many objects of their benevolence was Madeleine Bray, the daughter of the woman who had rejected Charles to marry a wastrel, and it was in their service that Nicholas saw Madeleine and fell in love with her. The Cheerybles established Nicholas and his family in a cottage at Bow, performed numberless other kind actions, and having finally joined the hands of Nicholas and Madeleine, of their nephew Frank and Kate Nickleby, they handed the business over to Frank and Nicholas and retired. The Cheeryble brothers were founded on William and Daniel Grant, wealthy calico printers of Manchester, whose acquaintance Dickens made in 1838. William (brother Ned) died in 1842, and Daniel (brother Charles) in 1855. *Nickleby*, 35, 37, 40, 43, 46, 49, 55, 59–61, 63, 65.

Frank Cheeryble was the nephew of the twin brothers—"a sprightly, good-humoured, pleasant fellow with much, both in his countenance and disposition, that reminded Nicholas very strongly of the kind-hearted brothers." He fell in love with Kate Nickleby, and after their marriage became a partner with Nicholas in the firm of Cheeryble Brothers. *Nickleby*, 43, 46, 48, 49, 55, 57, 61, 63, 65.

**CHEESEMAN, OLD.** The hero of the *Schoolboy's Story*, who was unpopular at the school and had only one friend, Jane Pitt the wardrobe woman, whom he eventually married. *Reprinted, The Schoolboy's Story.*

**CHEGGS, ALICK.** The market gardener, "shy in the presence of ladies" who cut out Dick Swiveller and won Sophy Wackles for his bride. *Curiosity Shop*, 8, 21, 50.

**CHELMSFORD.** This town is on the main road to Ipswich, and was thus on Mr. Weller's route when he picked up Jingle and Job Trotter at the Black Boy (demolished in 1857) and heard them laughing at having "done old Fireworks." *Pickwick*, 20.

**CHELSEA.** Described in 1831 as a large and populous village, its position on the river has always made Chelsea a favourite resort of Londoners. The place has a personal association with Dickens, whose marriage took place in the new parish church of St. Luke, in 1836. The Royal East London Volunteers, with Gabriel Varden as a sergeant, marched in glittering order to the

Bun House (*q.v.*) (*Barnaby*, 42) next door but two to which lived Mr. Bucket's aunt (*Bleak House*, 53). The polite folk of Cadogan Place considered Chelsea barbarous (*Nickleby*, 21), but it had its compensations, for there lived the Wackles family when visited by Dick Swiveller (*Curiosity Shop*, 8). Mr. Bayham Badger had a good practice there (*Bleak House*, 13). Thomas Joy, the carpenter with whom John lodged when he came to patent his invention, lived near Chelsea Church (*Reprinted, Poor Man's Patent*). Sergeant Witchem, when tracking her husband, watched Mrs. Tally-Ho Thompson, who resided in the neighbourhood (*Reprinted, Detective Police*). Silas Wegg identified his father with Dibdin's poetic Chelsea ferryman (*Mutual Friend*, I, 15). Battersea Bridge marks the sight of old Chelsea Ferry, though there was a later ferry near the present Victoria Bridge. Chelsea Waterworks, to which Sam Weller likened the lachrymose Job Trotter, were on the E. side of the Grosvenor Canal, now railway yards. *Pickwick*, 23.

**CHELTENHAM.** Mrs. Captain Barbary, who "was not up to the courage" of a certain fine grey gelding, in dealing with which Tip Dorrit had found himself imprisoned for debt, lived at Cheltenham (*Dorrit*, I, 12). The only other mention of the place that possesses any interest refers to Miss Knaggs's cousin, a tobacconist who lived there, and who had such small feet that they were no bigger than those usually joined to wooden legs. *Nickleby*, 17.

**CHERTSEY.** This was the scene of the attempted burglary by Bill Sikes and Toby Crackit, in which Oliver Twist was injured. Mrs. Maylie's house, which they broke into, has been identified in Pycroft Road (*Twist*, 19, 22, 28–32, 53). Chertsey was one of the places Betty Higden visited when wandering about the River towns. *Mutual Friend*, III, 8.

**CHERUB, THE.** Bella Wilfer's pet name for her father, R. Wilfer. (*q.v.*)

**CHESNEY WOLD.** This was the Lincolnshire mansion of the Dedlocks, with its Ghost Walk and ancient memories. The original was Rockingham Castle, in Northamptonshire, from which the picture has been faithfully drawn, the fine old Yew Walk at the end of the terrace being the original of the Ghost's Walk. *Bleak House*, 2, 7, 12, 16, 28, 36, 40, 41, 56, 66.

**CHESTER.** Sir John, was a cynical, courtly, unprincipled rogue, indifferent to any but his own interests in pursuance of which he was determined to prevent the match between his son and Emma Haredale. His chief tool was Hugh, the wild hostler of the Maypole, who turned out to be his natural son. During the riots Sir John played for safety, but soon afterwards he met his lifelong enemy, Geoffrey Haredale, in a duel and was killed. The character of Sir John Chester is obviously an exaggerated picture of Lord Chesterfield (*Barnaby*, 5, 10–12, 14, 15, 23, 24, 26–30, 32, 40, 43, 53, 75, 81, 82). Edward Chester, his son, was the lover of Emma Haredale. As he persisted in his intention of marrying her, in face of his father's and her uncle's objection, Sir John disowned him, and he went away to the West Indies. After five years he returned at the time of the riots and was able to save Emma from the clutches of Gashford. After their marriage he took her to live abroad. 1, 3–6, 12, 14, 15, 19, 20, 24, 27, 29, 32, 67, 71, 72, 78, 79, 82.

**CHESTLE.** The elderly hop-grower, who married the eldest Miss Larkins. *Copperfield*, 18.

**CHIB, MR.** The father of the vestry, a hale old man of eighty-two, who ordered the removal of the contentious vestrymen, Banger and Tiddypot. *Reprinted, Our Vestry.*

**CHICK.** Mr. John, "a stout, bald gentleman, with a very large face, and his hands continually in his pockets, who had a tendency in his nature to whistle and hum tunes" which he did at most inopportune moments. *Dombey*, 2, 5, 8, 29, 31, 36.

Mrs. Louisa Chick, his wife and sister of Mr. Dombey, was embued with the spirit of the Dombeys and always felt convinced that if the first Mrs. Dombey had only made an effort she would not have died in childbed. With her friend Miss Tox she took charge of little Paul, but she renounced that lady with great vigour when it became apparent that she had hoped to become the second Mrs. Dombey. When the house of Dombey fell, Mrs. Chick could find no other cause for the disaster than that her brother had not made an effort. 1, 2, 5–8, 10, 14, 16, 18, 19, 31, 36, 51, 58, 59.

**CHICKEN, THE GAME.** Mr. Toot's pugilistic friend. *See* Game Chicken.

**CHICKENSTALKER, MRS. ANNE.** A stout lady who kept a shop in the general line and was one of Trotty Veck's creditors. Later she married Tugby, Sir Joseph Bowley's porter, who joined her in the business. *Chimes.*

**CHICKSEY, VENEERING AND STOBBLES.** The name of the firm of drug dealers, near Mincing Lane, of which Veneering was sole partner and in which R. Wilfer was a clerk. It has been suggested that the house next Dunster Court was the office of this firm. *Mutual Friend*, 1, 4, 11; II, 8; III, 16.

**CHICKWEED, CONKEY.** The Battle Bridge publican who committed a fake burglary on himself, which was detected by Jem Spyers, the Bow Street runner. The tale was narrated with much gusto by Mr. Blathers. *Twist*, 31.

**CHIGGLE.** The immortal sculptor who carved "the Pogram statter in marble which

rose so much con-test and pre-judice in Europe." *Chuzzlewit*, 34.

**CHIGWELL.** This was a favourite resort of Dickens about the time he was working on *Barnaby*. In 1841 he wrote to Forster, "Chigwell is the greatest place in the world," and it was the good fare and bright welcome that he received at the King's Head Inn that made him immortalise it as the Maypole and centre his story round the place.

**CHILDERS, E. W. B.** A member of Sleary's circus, who spoke his mind plainly to Messrs. Gradgrind and Bounderby when they came to adopt Sissy Jupe, but did good work when Gradgrind was in trouble, and smuggled young Tom away to Liverpool. Childers married Sleary's daughter, Josephine, and their little boy, at three years of age, was named The Little Wonder of Scholastic Equitation. *Hard Times*, I, 6; III, 7, 8.

**CHILDREN'S HOSPITAL.** The hospital to which Mrs. Boffin took little Johnny to die was no doubt the Children's Hospital in Great Ormonde Street. *Mutual Friend*, II, 9.

**CHILD'S DREAM OF A STAR.** A short sketch which first appeared in *Household Words*, April 6, 1850, and was included in *Reprinted Pieces* in 1858.

**CHILD'S STORY, THE.** This little story first appeared in the Christmas Number of *Household Words*, 1852; being one of the tales in *A Round of Stories by the Christmas Fire*. It was published in *Reprinted Pieces*, 1858.

**CHILL, UNCLE.** The avaricious old uncle of Michael. *Reprinted, Poor Relations Story.*

**CHILLIP, DR.** The mild, little medical man who attended Mrs. Copperfield when David was born. "He carried his head on one side, partly in modest depreciation of himself, partly in modest propitiation of everybody else." On marrying his second wife, a woman with some property, he moved to near Bury St. Edmunds. *Copperfield*, 1, 2, 9, 10, 22, 30, 59.

**CHIMES, THE.** This was the second of the Christmas Books, and was published in 1844. It was written at Genoa, and on its completion Dickens started for London, where, on the 2nd of December, he read the story to a select audience, including Forster, Jerrold, Blanchard, Carlyle and Maclise.

*Principal Characters.* Trotty Veck, a ticket porter; Meg, his daughter; her sweetheart, Richard; Alderman Cute, a practical man who thinks he understands the "common people"; Will Fern, a poor man with a bad name; Lilian, his niece.

The moral of *The Chimes* is practically the same as that of *A Christmas Carol*. Trotty Veck, a cheerful, honest old man who delights to believe that he is worth his salt, falls asleep at his fireside on New Year's Eve and dreams that he goes into the neighbouring belfry (St. Dunstan's, Fleet Street) which is full of the elfin spirits of the bells. At the order of the Goblin of the Great Bell Trotty follows a little child, the Spirit of the Chimes, and is shown scenes of the future, all sorrowful and some of them concerning his own daughter and others he loves. When he awakes with a start, Trotty is overjoyed to hear the chimes pealing in the New Year, and to find that all the sorrow he has felt is but that of a dream. Nevertheless he learns his lesson and applies it in the New Year that has dawned.

**CHIMNEY SWEEPS.** It is easy to understand Oliver Twist's terror of being apprenticed to Gamfield, the sweep. Before the Act of 1842 chimneys were swept by little boys, who clambered up, sweeping as they went. The cruelty of master-sweeps was notorious, cases were familiar of fires being lit beneath the lads to make them more expeditious, while there were many instances of boys being smothered or sticking fast in the flues. All this was abolished by the Act which made employment of such boys illegal. May Day was the London chimney sweep's festival. Forming small parties they paraded the City streets dressed up in paper hats and fancy clothes, their faces coloured with brick dust. One of their number, called Jack-in-the-Green, was placed within a sort of movable bower of branches and leaves, where he danced and cracked jokes while the coins were being collected from the onlookers. *Boz, Scenes*, 20.

**CHINAMAN, JACK.** Keeper of an opium den in opposition to that run by Princess Puffer. The original was George Ah Sing, who had an opium den in Cornwall Road, St. George's-in-the-East. *Drood*, 1, 23.

**CHINK'S BASIN.** Mrs. Whimple's house, where old Bill Barley lodged, was in Mill Pond Bank, Chink's Basin, near the Old Green Copper Rope Walk. The description might apply to many places on either side of the river thereabouts, but none of the above names are real. *Expectations*, 46, 47.

**CHIN MUSIC.** This accomplishment of Mr. Hardy was popular in the 20's and 30's, and had been introduced by Michael Boai. It was produced by striking the chin with the fist, at the same time making rapid movements of the mouth to modulate the sounds caused. *Boz, Tales, Excursion*.

**CHIPS.** The principal character in one of the nurse's stories. All the Chips men sold themselves to the Devil, and the hero of the tale tried in vain to escape the family bargain. *Uncommercial*, 15.

**CHIRRUP, MR. AND MRS.** The nice little couple. *Sketches of Couples*.

**CHISWICK.** Bill Sikes and Oliver Twist passed through this village on their way to Chertsey (*Twist*, 21). Gaffer Hexam pushed up as far as Chiswick on his gruesome quests, and waited there until after the turn of the tide. *Mutual Friend*, I, 6.

**CHITLING, TOM.** A member of Fagin's gang of thieves who, after a term of imprisonment, returned to the Jew and took up with Betsy. When the gang was dispersed at Fagin's capture, Chitling repaired to Jacob's Island with Toby Crackit, and was there when Bill Sikes met his end. *Twist*, 18, 25, 39, 50.

**CHIVERY.** A non-resident turnkey at the Marshalsea Prison. "There was a native delicacy in Mr. Chivery—true politeness; though his exterior had very much of a turnkey about it, and not the least of a gentleman." His wife "was a comfortable-looking woman, much respected for her feelings and her conversation." She had a small tobacco shop in Horsemonger Lane (now Union Street). *Dorrit*, I, 18, 19, 22, 25, 31, 35, 36; II, 26, 27, 29, 31, 34.

Young John Chivery was the son of the turnkey and a sentimental lad "of small stature . . . but great of soul; poetical, expansive, faithful." As a boy he fell in love with Little Dorrit and composed touching epitaphs for himself when he realised the hopelessness of his passion. Young John helped Prancks to search out the facts which established the Dorrits' right to their fortune, and when Arthur Clennam was imprisoned in the Marshalsea, went to comfort him and, breaking his heart in the effort, told him how truly Little Dorrit loved him. *Dorrit*, I, 18, 19, 22, 25, 31, 35, 36; II, 18, 26, 27, 29, 31, 33, 34.

**CHOKE, GENERAL CYRUS.** A general in the American militia and "one of the most remarkable men in the country." He recommended Martin Chuzzlewit to purchase land from the Eden Corporation. *Chuzzlewit*, 21.

**CHOLLOP, MAJOR HANNIBAL.** "A splendid example of our na-tive raw material," in other words a lawless rascal who called on Martin Chuzzlewit at Eden. *Chuzzlewit*, 33, 34.

**CHOPPER.** 1. Mrs. Chopper was the mother of Mrs. Merrywinkle, one of the couple who coddled themselves. *Sketches of Couples*.

2. Mr. Chopper was a great-uncle of Master William Tinkling. *Holiday Romance*.

**CHOPS.** A dwarf in Toby Magsman's show. His real name was Stakes, and his professional name Major Tpschoffki, but he was always known as Chops. He won £12,000 in a lottery and went into society, but lost all his money and came to the conclusion that "it ain't so much that a person goes into Society, as that Society goes into a person." *Going into Society*.

**CHORDS.** "There *are* chords in the human mind——" such was the unfinished sentence with which Mr. Guppy deprecated allusion to the "unrequited image imprinted on his art." *Bleak House*, 20, 32.

**CHOWSER, COLONEL.** This gentleman, of the Militia and the racecourses, was one of the shady guests at Ralph Nickleby's dinner party. *Nickleby*, 19, 50.

**CHRISTIAN, FLETCHER.** He was the mate of the *Bounty* and ringleader of the mutineers against Captain Bligh. He and his son, Thursday October Christian, are real characters. *Reprinted, A Long Voyage.*

**CHRISTIANA.** The beautiful girl who had once been the sweetheart of Michael, the Poor Relation. *Reprinted, Poor Relations Story.*

**CHRISTINA, DONNA.** One of Jingle's Spanish conquests, daughter of Don Bolaro Fizzgig. " Splendid creature—loved me to distraction—jealous father—high-souled daughter—handsome Englishman—Donna Christina in despair—prussic acid—stomach pump in my portmanteau—operation performed—old Bolaro in ecstasies—consent to our union—join hands and floods of tears." Unfortunately Donna Christina did not survive the excitement. *Pickwick*, 2.

**CHRISTMAS CAROL, A.** This, the most popular of Dickens's Christmas Books, and perhaps of all his writings, was written in October and November and published in December, 1843. It was the outcome of much emotion and excitement on his part ; and it is recorded that " he walked thinking of it fifteen and twenty miles about the black streets of London, many and many a night after all sober folks had gone to bed."

*Principal Characters.* Ebenezer Scrooge, a tightfisted old curmudgeon ; Bob Cratchit, his clerk and father of a family ; Fred, Scrooge's nephew ; the Fezziwigs, Scrooge's old master and his family.

One Christmas Eve Scrooge is brooding over the fire, in his lodgings, when he sees the ghost of his old partner, Marley, dead these seven years. Marley tells him that he is fettered by a chain forged by selfishness in his lifetime, and advises Scrooge to take timely warning. Scrooge then casts himself on his bed, and is visited by the spirits of Christmas Past, Christmas Present and Christmas Yet to Come, all of whom reveal the folly and cruelty of his present selfish life, and show him what happiness might be his if he would but open his heart to others. Scrooge repents and determines to make amends for his past selfishness and surliness ; he sends a turkey to the Cratchits ; goes to dinner with his nephew, whose invitation he had refused ; and " became as good a friend, as good a master, and as good a man, as the good old city knew, or any other good old city, town, or borough in the good old world."

**CHRISTMAS TREE, A.** This rather pretty sketch first appeared in the 1850 Christmas Number of *Household Words* and was published in *Reprinted Pieces*, 1858.

**CHRISTOPHER.** A head waiter with strong views as to a head waiter's position in society. " A head waiter must be either head or tail ; he must be at one extremity

or the other of the social scale ; he cannot be at the waist of it." He narrates the story of *Somebody's Luggage*.

**" CHRISTOPHER COLUMBUS " SLOOP.** This was the British armed vessel which took part in the exciting adventures on Silver Store Island. *English Prisoners.*

**CHUCKSTER.** Mr. Witherden's clerk, a friend of Dick Swiveller and one of the " Glorious Apollers." He had a very hearty contempt for Kit Nubbles, whom he designated a snob ; and when Kit was cleared of the charge of theft, was rather disgusted than otherwise, as it showed that " Snobby " had not even the spirit to steal. *Curiosity Shop*, 14, 20, 38, 40, 56, 60, 64, 65, 69, 73.

**CHUFFEY.** The old clerk of Chuzzlewit and Son, a faithful half-crazy old man whose whole life was bound up in his old master, Anthony Chuzzlewit. After the death of the latter and Jonas's marriage to Mercy Pecksniff, Chuffey devoted himself to the bride, but having awakened Jonas's suspicions, he was handed over to the tender care of Mrs. Gamp. At the final exposure of Jonas, Chuffey narrated the story of that villain's attempt to poison old Anthony. *Chuzzlewit*, 11, 18, 19, 25, 26, 46, 48, 49, 51, 52, 54.

**CHUZZLEWIT.** It is difficult to follow the ramifications of this family, but apart from the main characters, who are dealt with separately, the following are mentioned :—

1. Diggory, a remote ancestor in the habit of dining with Duke Humphrey. *Chuzzlewit*, 1.

2. George, a gay bachelor cousin of old Martin. 4, 54.

3. Mrs. Ned, widow of a deceased brother of old Martin and mother of three spinster daughters. 4, 54.

4. Toby, an ancestor who, being asked on his death-bed who was his grandfather, replied, " The Lord No Zoo." 1.

5. A grandnephew of old Martin, " very dark and very hairy." 4, 54.

6. Mrs. Spottletoe (*q.v.*), once Martin's favourite niece.

7. Chevy Slyme (*q.v.*), a nephew.

**CHUZZLEWIT, ANTHONY.** A brother of old Martin and father of Jonas, a Manchester warehouseman, who lived in a very narrow street behind the Post Office (probably Foster Lane). Accompanied by Jonas he attended the family party held in Pecksniff's house when old Martin was lying sick, and on that occasion, to his unfading satisfaction, called Pecksniff a hypocrite. Later he summoned Pecksniff to London in order to arrange a match between Jonas and one of his cousins, but before he could come to any definite terms with Pecksniff he died. *Chuzzlewit*, 4, 8, 11, 18, 19, 48, 51.

**CHUZZLEWIT, JONAS.** The only son of Anthony, with " all the inclination to be a profligate of the first water. He only lacked the one good trait in the common catalogue of debauched vices—open-handedness—to be a notable vagabond." Impatient at his father's longevity and for the sake of his insurance money, Jonas tried to poison the old man and, as he thought, succeeded. But Anthony's death was from grief at finding out his son's plot. Soon after his father's death Jonas married Mercy Pecksniff, whose spirit he broke by cruelty and neglect. After entering the bogus insurance business run by Tigg, his designs on his father were discovered by Nadgett, and Jonas was compelled, by the threat of exposure, to plunge deeper into Tigg's dishonest schemes. Goaded to despair, Jonas finally murdered him, the crime was discovered by Nadgett and Jonas was arrested, but eluded justice by poisoning himself. The original of this character was Thomas Griffiths Wainewright, art critic and author, who poisoned his wife's father and sister for the sake of their insurance money. He was never brought to justice for these crimes, to which he confessed, but was transported in 1838 on a charge of forgery, and died in Hobart in 1852. *Chuzzlewit*, 4, 8, 11, 18–20, 24–8, 38, 40–4, 46–8, 51.

**CHUZZLEWIT, MARTIN, THE ELDER.** A rich and suspicious old man who distrusted all his family and quarrelled with his grandson, the younger Martin. He adopted a girl, Mary Graham, and thereby aroused the anger of the whole family, who thought she had designs on his money. After his grandson had gone to America, Martin went to live with Pecksniff and deliberately lured that individual into thinking that he was to receive a handsome inheritance. When Tom Pinch was turned away by Pecksniff, Martin secretly helped him by giving him employment in the Temple ; finally, when his grandson had returned, improved by his hardships in America, the elder Martin had a great day of reckoning, when Pecksniff was degraded and young Martin and Mary were given to each other. *Chuzzlewit*, 3, 4, 6, 10, 14, 24, 30, 31, 43, 44, 50–4.

**CHUZZLEWIT, MARTIN, THE YOUNGER.** The character after whom the novel is named, and an unlovable, selfish young man who, even when improved by hardship, awakens little interest or sympathy from the reader. Having fallen in love with Mary Graham, and on that account being turned out of the house by his grandfather, Martin went to Pecksniff as a pupil, but at a suggestion from the old man, was ejected thence with contumely. After suffering poverty in London young Martin met Mark Tapley, and they both went to America, where Martin was beguiled into purchasing a worthless estate in Eden (probably Cairo, Ill.). There they suffered many hardships, culminating in fever, but they contrived to get back to New York, whence Mark Tapley worked a passage for both of them to England. On the final exposure of Pecksniff, Martin was reinstated in his grandfather's

favour and married Mary Graham. *Chuzzlewit*, 2, 5–7, 10, 12–17, 21–3, 31, 33–5, 43, 48–50, 52, 53.

**CICERO.** A negro truckman who had bought his own liberty and was saving up to buy that of his daughter. *Chuzzlewit*, 17.

**CICERO.** Mrs. Blimber used to say that if she could have known Cicero she thought she could have died contented. *Dombey*, 11, 24, 60.

**CIDER CELLARS.** This haunt of the "salaried law clerk" . . . was on the south side of Maiden Lane, Covent Garden, a little to the west of the present Catholic Church of Corpus Christi. It was a place of low repute, being conducted somewhat on the lines of the old Coal Hole. *Pickwick*, 31.

**CIRCUMLOCUTION OFFICE.** An admirable satire on the dilatory and red-tape-bound methods of government. It was "the most important department under Government . . . no public business of any kind could possibly be done at any time without the acquiescence of the Circumlocution Office. Whatever was required to be done, the Circumlocution Office was beforehand with all the public departments in the art of perceiving—How Not to Do It." *Dorrit*, I, 10, 34 ; II, 28.

**CITY ROAD.** Described in 1831 as a wide and handsome thoroughfare ; the City Road was far from being the acme of desolation that it has now become, when Mr. Micawber honoured it with his residence. Windsor Terrace (*q.v.*), where he was living when David first lodged with him, is on the right-hand side, beyond St. Luke's Workhouse. *Copperfield*, 11.

**CITY THEATRE.** The City of London Theatre was in Norton Folgate, and from its location may be imagined the character of its patrons. There it was that Messrs. Smithers and Potter created such a disturbance. *Boz, Characters*, 11.

**CLAPHAM.** In the early years of the nineteenth century Clapham Rise was famous for its "seminaries" for young ladies, but it was also a favourite habitat of the well-to-do City man, such as Mr. Gattleton, who lived at Rose Villa (*Boz, Tales, Porter*). Less aristocratic was the residence of the cook's sister in the Haunted House, though her address of 2 Tuppinstock's Gardens, Liggs's Walk, Clapham Rise, is not to be found in Kelly (*The Haunted House*). In the Clapham Road lived the Poor Relation, who passed some sad reflections on the place. *Reprinted, Poor Relations Story*.

**CLARE, ADA.** A ward in Chancery who was committed to the guardianship of Mr. John Jarndyce, Esther Summerson being adopted by that gentleman as her companion. Ada was "a beautiful girl with such rich golden hair, such soft blue eyes, and such a bright innocent trusting face," that her cousin and fellow-ward, Richard

Carstone, fell in love with her immediately. She was constantly troubled about her lover's restlessness, but she would not allow him to shake her loyalty and trust in her guardian. When, at last overcome with worry and disappointment, Richard fell ill in his chambers, Ada married him, and went to take care of him, and there he died in her arms. With her baby boy she was provided for by her cousin and guardian, John Jarndyce. Ada Clare is one of the Maria Hogarth heroines. *Bleak House*, 1, 3–6, 8, 9, 13–15, 17, 18, 23, 24, 30, 31, 35–7, 43, 45, 50, 51, 59–62, 64, 65, 67.

**CLARE MARKET.** Although there is still a street bearing this name, between the Law Courts and Kingsway, the old Clare Market was demolished when Kingsway and the Aldwych were made, 1899–1905. The site of the market, in the midst of disreputable slums, was approximately the lower end of Kingsway. The reconstruction of all that district of London makes it difficult to designate the actual sites of many old places. Boz remarks that the ginshops of Clare Market were among the handsomest in London (*Boz, Scenes*, 22). The Magpie and Stump, favourite resort of Lowten and other legal lights, was in the vicinity of the Market. There was never a tavern of that name in Clare Market, but the original was probably the Old Black Jack, or the George the Fourth, both of which were in Portugal Street. *Pickwick*, 20.

**CLARK.** 1. Betsy, a housemaid. *Boz, Scenes*, 1.

2. A stout man in a wharfinger's office, who, when Florence Dombey was lost, gave her into the charge of Walter Gay. *Dombey*, 6.

3. Mrs. Clark was a lady to whom the registry office sent Madeleine Bray—"she'll have a nice life of it if she goes there," remarked the proprietress. *Nickleby*, 16.

**CLARKE, SUSAN.** The widow whom Mr. Weller Senior was inveigled into marrying by the touts at Doctors' Commons. *See* Weller, Mrs. *Pickwick*, 10.

**CLARKSON.** The counsel for some thieves arrested by Sergeant Mith. Mr. Clarkson was a very well-known barrister at the Old Bailey in the 40's and 50's. *Reprinted, Detective Police.*

**CLARRIKER.** A shipping broker introduced by Wemmick to Pip, who purchased a partnership in the business for Herbert Pocket. Eventually Pip himself obtained employment in the firm. *Expectations*, 37, 52, 58.

**CLATFORD.** *See* Inn (1).

**CLATTER, DR.** One of Our Bore's medical men. *Reprinted, Our Bore.*

**CLAYPOLE, NOAH.** "A large-headed small-eyed youth of lumbering make and heavy countenance," who was Sowerberry's assistant and neglected no opportunity of bullying Oliver Twist. Accompanied by Charlotte he made his way to London, having previously emptied his master's till, and there fell into the hands of Fagin, assuming the name of Morris Bolter. Fagin set him to spy on Nancy, after whose murder Noah turned evidence against the Jew. He finally set up on his own account as an informer. *Twist*, 5–7, 27, 42, 43, 45–7, 53.

**CLEAVER, FANNY.** This was the real name of the little doll's dressmaker, always known as Jenny Wren. (*q.v.*)

**CLEM, OLD.** St. Clement is the patron saint of blacksmiths, his festival being on the 23rd November. The song of Old Clem which Pip records has not been traced, though there were many similar chants sung by smiths at their work. *Expectations*, 12.

**CLENNAM.** Arthur, was the adopted son of Mrs. Clennam. On his return from China, where he had buried his father, he met Little Dorrit at his mother's house and immediately took an interest in her and her imprisoned father. His enquiries into their affairs brought him into contact with Flora Finching, whom he had loved as a young man. Despite her garrulity and inconsequence Flora proved a true and loyal friend, and at Arthur's request gave employment to Little Dorrit. Entering into partnership with Daniel Doyce, Arthur unwisely embarked all the firm's money in one of Merdle's ventures, and on that rogue's bankruptcy and suicide found himself ruined and became a prisoner in the Marshalsea. While lying there ill he was lovingly tended by Little Dorrit, herself ruined in the Merdle crash. Arthur was eventually released through Doyce and married Little Dorrit. *Dorrit*, I, 2, 3, 5, 7–10, 12–17, 22–8, 31–6; II, 3, 4, 8–11, 13, 17, 20, 22, 23, 26–34.

Mrs. Clennam was an austere woman, for many years confined to her bedroom. "She was always balancing her bargain with the Majesty of Heaven; posting up the entries to her credit; strictly keeping her set off; and claiming her due." In her youth she had married Arthur's father, only to discover that he had a liaison. Mrs. Clennam forced his mistress to give up her child, which was brought up, coldly and sternly, as her own. On the death of Gilbert Clennam, her husband's uncle, a codicil was found to his will bequeathing a thousand guineas to Frederick Dorrit, or his youngest niece. The suppression of this codicil forms the theme for the part Mrs. Clennam plays in the story. Obtaining the incriminating papers through some underhand means, Rigaud attempted to blackmail her. After a final interview with him she took the papers to Little Dorrit. The two women then made their way back, arriving in time to see the old Clennam house collapse, killing Rigaud in its fall. *Dorrit*, I, 3–5, 8, 14, 15, 29, 30; II, 10, 17, 20, 23, 28, 30, 31.

**CLEOPATRA.** This was the name given by her admirers to Mrs. Skewton (*q.v.*) on account of a published sketch of herself which had appeared some fifty years before, bearing the name of Cleopatra. *Dombey*, 21.

**CLERGYMAN.** 1. Our Curate, "a young gentleman of prepossessing appearance and fascinating manners." *Boz, Our Parish*, 2.

2. The benevolent clergyman of Dingley Dell, who recited the poem of "The Ivy Green" and told the tale of the Convict's Return. *Pickwick*, 6, 18, 28.

3. The clergyman of the parish where Little Nell and her grandfather finally settled and died. *Curiosity Shop*, 52, 73.

4. The gentleman who attended Mr. Nickleby's death-bed. *Nickleby*, 1.

5. "A mild-looking young curate, obviously afraid of the baby," who christened Paul Dombey. *Dombey*, 5.

**CLERKENWELL.** There is a good description of the district, when it was little more than a suburb, in *Barnaby*, for it was there that Gabriel Varden lived at the sign of the Golden Key (*Barnaby*, 4, 63). About the same period Mr. Jarvis Lorry lived there (*Two Cities*, II, 6). Phil Squod plied his tinker's trade in Clerkenwell (*Bleak House*, 26). Near Clerkenwell Green, which is now close to the junction of Farringdon Road and Clerkenwell Road, was the bookstall where Mr. Brownlow was standing when his pocket was picked by Charley Bates and the Artful Dodger, and it was at the same spot that Oliver Twist was later recaptured by Nancy (*Twist*, 10, 15). All interest in the place must centre, however, in its association as the residence of Mr. Venus, where he carried on his grisly business with stuffed animals, birds, and "human warious." *Mutual Friend*, I, 7 ; II, 7 ; III, 7, 14 ; IV, 3, 14.

**CLEVERLY, WILLIAM AND SUSANNAH.** Mormon emigrants for Salt Lake City. *Uncommercial*, 20.

**CLICK.** 1. A friend of Tom, the pavement artist, of a theatrical turn by taste and a gas-fitter by trade. *Somebody's Luggage*.

2. A slum rat of St. Giles. *Reprinted, Inspector Field*.

**CLICKETT.** Mrs. Micawber's maid and "a dark-complexioned young woman with a habit of snorting . . . who informed me that she was a 'Orfling' and came from St. Luke's Workhouse." *Copperfield*, 11, 12.

**CLICKIT, MR. AND MRS.** Friends of the Bobtail Widgers. *Sketches of Couples*.

**CLIFFORD'S INN.** This is the most ancient of the inns of Chancery, and though part had been demolished, the hall and several houses were still intact in 1924. The inn occurs in Mr. Bamber's reminiscences (*Pickwick*, 21); it was the residence of Melchisidek, the lawyer (*Bleak House*, 34, 47). When applying for his post as secretary to Mr. Boffin, Rokesmith took that gentleman aside out of the noise of Chancery Lane into Clifford's Inn to discuss the matter (*Mutual Friend*, I, 8). For six months "Tip" Dorrit worked with a solicitor there. *Dorrit*, I, 7.

**CLIFTON.** A residential suburb of Bristol, which was considered by Ben Allen as "a nice dull place" in which to break the high spirits of his sister Arabella. She was sent to her aunt, on Clifton Downs, and there was discovered by Sam Weller through the medium of Mary, the pretty housemaid, who was in service next door. *Pickwick*, 38, 39.

**CLIP.** A hairdresser who wanted to borrow £10 of Mr. Thicknesse. *Robert Bolton*.

**CLISSOLD, LAWRENCE.** The clerk in Dringworth Brothers who stole five hundred pounds, and by a successful forgery contrived to put the blame on his fellow clerk, Tregarthen. *Message from the Sea*.

**CLIVE.** A clerk at the Circumlocution Office. *Dorrit*, I, 10.

**CLOCKER.** A grocer in the seaside resort (Folkestone) described in *Reprinted, Out of the Season*.

**CLOISTERHAM.** The cathedral town where most of the scene of *Drood* is laid. It is a thinly veiled disguise for Rochester.

**CLUBBER, SIR THOMAS.** The head of Chatham Dockyard. He, with his wife and daughters, were guests at the Bull Inn ball. *Pickwick*, 2.

**CLUPPINS, MRS. ELIZABETH.** "A little, brisk, busy-looking woman" who was one of Mrs. Bardell's most intimate friends, and sister to Mrs. Raddle. *Pickwick*, 26, 34, 46.

**CLY, ROGER.** A former servant of Charles Darnay, who gave evidence against his master at the Old Bailey. Fearing the anger of the mob he later feigned death and was given a sham burial, to the disgust of Jerry Cruncher, the Resurrection man. Proceeding to France, Cly acted as a spy and informer, and eventually found his way to the guillotine. *Two Cities*, II, 3, 14 ; III, 8, 15.

**CO, MR.** Martin Chuzzlewit and Mark Tapley established themselves in Eden under the name of Chuzzlewit and Co. Mark called himself Co. and was commonly known thus to the inhabitants. *Chuzzlewit*, 21.

**COACH AND HORSES INN.** This inn is at Isleworth, near which Bill Sikes and Oliver alighted from the cart which had brought them from Kensington. Its actual name is the Old Coach and Horses, and it stands to-day, little changed by passing years. *Oliver Twist*, 21.

**COACH.** There were two types of fast coach on the English roads immediately previous to the introduction of railways. These were the Mail Coach and the Stage Coach. In both the body consisted of a closed carriage holding four passengers, with a flat roof for outside seats, a front seat for the driver and two passengers and a back seat for the guard and two passengers. Each coach accommodated four inside and from ten to twelve outside passengers. At both ends were large receptacles, called boots, in which luggage and parcels were carried. Mail coaches carried the mail bags on the top of the carriage.

Mail coaches were uniform in appearance. The lower part of the body was a chocolate or mauve in colour ; the upper part and the fore and hind boots were black ; the wheels and under-carriage, vivid scarlet. On the door panels were emblazoned the royal arms ; on the fore boot, the royal cipher in gold ; on the hind boot, the number of the vehicle ; on the upper quarters, on either side of the window, were painted various devices, such as the badge of the garter, the rose, shamrock and thistle, etc.

Stage coaches were painted in brilliant colours, and each had its own name, such as Defiance, Express, Rapid, Comet. They were labelled with the names of the principal towns they passed as well as others for which they made connection.

The mails, subsidised by the Post Office, were obliged by contract to run to time and, travelling day and night, were the terror of smaller vehicles upon the road. Horses were changed every six or eight miles, the average speed maintained being twelve miles an hour on most roads. On its outward journey from London the Mail coach loaded passengers at its own inn early in the evening and then, with the exception of certain West Country coaches which started from the White Horse Cellar in Piccadilly (which at that time stood on the site now occupied by the Ritz Hotel), repaired to St. Martin's-le-Grand to collect the mail bags. At 8 p.m. precisely, all the mails started. "They come racing out of Lad Lane and Wood Street at twelve and fourteen miles an hour, them Mails do ! The only wonder is that people ain't killed oftener by them Mails. They're a public nuisance, them Mails is." *Dorrit*, 13.

In-coming mails reached London at various times of the early morning, but all had arrived by 7 a.m., except on Sundays when, there being no delivery of letters, the up-coachmen usually took their own time on the journey, spending a few hours of Saturday night with any convivial whips they chanced to meet at their favourite inns.

Stage coaches were run by private enterprise and were under no obligation to keep time. For long distances there were day and night coaches, the former starting very early in the morning and the latter late at night. The discomfort of the early morning start, together with the scene in a coach booking office, is graphically described in *Boz, Scenes*, 15.

In length of stage and average speed the stages ran much the same as the mails, but they were usually better maintained and did more to attract custom. The coachmen,

originally of the Tony Weller type, latterly became ostentatious as they tried to ape the " swells " and young noblemen who took up coaching as a hobby.

Seats by coach had to be secured several days in advance, when at least half the fare was paid, the name of the passenger being entered in a book, whence arising the term Booking Office. The fares worked out at about 5d. a mile for inside and 3d. a mile for outside passengers. Meals on the journey were taken at inns where the horses were being changed.

Short stages, within a radius of some twenty miles of London, were performed by two-horse coaches, starting from various smaller inns. They made several journeys a day and charged moderate fares.

**COACHMAN.** The following are the principal members of this ancient profession who are not mentioned by name.

1. The driver of the early coach. *Boz, Scenes*, 15.

2. The friend of Mr. Whiffers, who announced that gentleman's resignation at the Bath " swarry." *Pickwick*, 37.

3. Tony Weller's friends. *Pickwick*, 43, 55.

4. The driver of the Yorkshire coach which took Nicholas to Dotheboys Hall. *Nickleby*, 5.

5. The coachman who took David to London for the first time. *Copperfield*, 5.

6. The coachmen with whom Jonas Chuzzlewit came into contact on the journey which ended in the murder of Montague. *Chuzzlewit*, 47.

7. The driver of the coach which carried Charley to Yorkshire. *The Holly Tree.*

**COAVINSES.** Described by Mr. Neckett as " a 'ouse." Coavinses was the sheriff's office in Cursitor Street by whom Neckett was employed. In his airy way Mr. Skimpole called Neckett himself, Coavinses. The original was Sloman's spunging house, 2, Cursitor Street. *Bleak House*, 6.

**COBB, TOM.** General chandler and post office keeper at Chigwell, and one of old John Willett's cronies, " beyond all question the dullest dog in the party." *Barnaby*, 1, 30, 33, 54, 56, 82.

**COBBEY.** One of Squeers's wretched pupils, whose pocket money of eighteenpence was appropriated by Mrs. Squeers. *Nickleby*, 8.

**COBBLER, THE.** A prisoner in the Fleet who rented a small room in which Sam Weller hired a bed. Having been always accustomed to a four-post bed, he made up his mattress under the table, finding the legs quite as good as bed posts. *Pickwick*, 44.

**"COBBLER THERE WAS, A."** This was a song in the 1728 edition of *The Beggar's Opera*, appearing also in the *Fashionable Lady* of 1730. It begins :—

A cobbler there was and he lived in a stall,
Which served him for parlour, for kitchen and hall.
*Dombey*. 2.

**COBBS.** The boots at the Holly Tree Inn, who told Charley the story of the elopement of Master Harry and Miss Norah. *Holly Tree.*

**COBBY.** The giant who was partaking of a meal with the white-haired lady beneath a Kentish hedgerow. *Uncommercial*, 11.

**COBHAM.** This Kentish village has changed little since Mr. Tupman arrived there to soothe his wounded heart in solitude. The Leather Bottle is unaltered, and proud of its Pickwickian associations, while if there are no stones of antiquarian interest in the village street, it must be because so many thousands of Pickwick devotees have ransacked the place. *Pickwick*, 11.

**COBOURG THEATRE.** This was the original name of the Royal Victoria Hall, better known as the Old Vic. The Cobourg Theatre was built in 1817, and was so named after the Prince Regent's daughter, Princess Charlotte, who was married to Prince Leopold of Saxe-Cobourg, afterwards King of the Belgians. In 1833 the name was changed to the Victoria Theatre, in honour of Princess Victoria, later Queen. Always a home of melodrama, it passed through many vicissitudes until 1880, when it became famous for grand opera and its Shakespeare productions. *Boz, Scenes*, 21. *Nickleby*, 30.

**COCKER, MR. INDIGNATION.** This was the name given to a discontented guest at the Temeraire Inn, at Namelesston. The name is taken from Edward Cocker (1631–75), who wrote a standard arithmetic book which was so well-known that " According to Cocker " became a synonym for mathematically Correct. *Uncommercial*, 32.

**COCK LANE GHOST.** Cock Lane runs out of Snow Hill into Giltspur Street, and here it was that in 1762 occurred the famous imposture of the Cock Lane Ghost. Noises and various manifestations were reported from the house of a certain Parsons, and many famous men, including Dr. Johnson, interesting themselves in the phenomenon, watched and made careful observations. It was then discovered that a hoax had been perpetrated by the daughter Elizabeth, who moved a board concealed in her bed, and simulated various ghostly doings. Although the exposure was complete and final, many continued to believe in the supernatural cause of the noises. *Nickleby*, 49. *Two Cities*, I, 1.

**CODGER, MISS.** One of the literary ladies presented to Elijah Pogram. " Codger's the lady so often mentioned in the English newspapers," whispered Mark. " The oldest inhabitant who never remembers anything." *Chuzzlewit*, 34.

**CODLIN, THOMAS.** A Punch and Judy showman, partner of Harris, or Short, with whom Little Nell and her Grandfather travelled a short way. Codlin had a surly, grumbling manner, but he tried to insinuate himself into Nell's confidence with a view to selling her secret to anyone prepared to pay a suitable reward. *Curiosity Shop*, 16–19, 37, 73.

**COILER, MRS.** A toady neighbour of the Matthew Pockets, " who agreed with everybody, blessed everybody, shed smiles and tears on everybody, according to circumstances." *Expectations*, 23.

**COKETOWN.** The scene of the novel *Hard Times*, and, there is very little doubt, a pseudonym for Manchester.

**COLDBATH FIELDS.** This was one of the strictest of London prisons, and, a year before *The Prisoner's Van* was written the discipline had been made yet more rigid by the introduction of compulsory silence among the prisoners. Its site is now occupied by part of the Mount Pleasant Post Office buildings. *See* Silent System. *Boz, Scenes*, 17. *Characters*, 12.

**COLE, KING.** The father of Prince Bladud, whose story Mr. Pickwick read at Bath. *Pickwick*, 36.

**COLESHAW, MISS.** One of the *Golden Mary's* passengers. *Golden Mary.*

**COLLEGE HORNPIPE.** This is an old and well-known tune of uncertain origin, though probably dating from the early eighteenth century. *Dombey*, 2. *Copperfield*, 12.

**COLLEGIANS.** Debtors in the Marshalsea prison. *Dorrit*, I, 19.

**COLLINS.** A constable who ejected an insistent member of the public from the precincts of the House of Commons. *Boz, Scenes*, 18.

**" COLLINS'S ODE."** Mr. Wopsle's recitation was " The Passions, an Ode for Music," by W. Collins. *Expectations*, 7, 13.

**COLONEL.** An ex-soldier in Newgate who was awaiting execution for coining. *Expectations*, 32.

**COLOSSEUM.** This once famous place of amusement stood at the south-east corner of Regent's Park, a few yards up from Cambridge Gate, on the site now occupied by Cambridge Terrace. Originally planned by Thomas Horner, it was designed by Decimus Burton and built in 1824. In the interior was a remarkable panorama of London, taken from the top of St. Paul's, and covering more than 46,000 sq. ft. This panorama was popular from 1829–54, though at times others were exhibited. The Colosseum also contained various collections, artistic and otherwise, and in 1844 a form of roller skating was introduced. The Colosseum ceased to be a place of amusement in 1855, and after various vicissitudes was demolished in 1875. *Boz, Scenes*, 12.

**COMMERCIAL ROAD.** This was visited on several occasions by the *Uncommercial Traveller*, 3, 23, 34.

**COMPACT ENCHANTRESS.** A French actress in the train to Paris. *Reprinted, A Flight.*

**"COMPAGNON DE LA MAJOLAINE."**
This is from an old French roundelay called
"Le Chevalier du Guet" (police officer). It
should really be "Marjolaine." *Dorrit*,
I, 1 ; II, 10, 28.

**COMPEYSON.** The gentlemanly scoundrel
who was responsible for leading Magwitch
into crime, and the man who had deserted
Miss Havisham on the morning they were to
have been married. He was the object
of Magwitch's implacable hatred, and when
the latter returned to England to see Pip,
Compeyson informed against him and
assisted in his capture, but at the cost of
his own life, for in the desperate struggle
that ensued, Magwitch drowned him. *Expectations*, 3, 5, 42, 45, 47, 50, 53–5.

**COMPORT, JANE.** The name in a prayer
book in one of the City churches. *Uncommercial*, 9.

**CONCIERGERIE.** This is an ancient
prison in Paris, situated on the island and
forming part of the Palais de Justice.
During the Revolution it was largely used for
political prisoners, among others Danton,
Robespierre and Marie Antoinette. It was
in the Conciergerie that Sydney Carton
substituted himself for Darnay. *Two
Cities*, III, 13.

**CONKEY CHICKWEED.** An accomplished burglar. *See* Chickweed.

**CONSEQUENCE.** "It's of no consequence." A favourite remark of Mr. Toots.
(*q.v.*)

**CONSTABLE'S MISCELLANY.** This work
was brought out by Archibald Constable,
Scott's publisher, in 1827, and acquired considerable popularity. *Pickwick*, 42.

**CONWAY, GENERAL.** The character who
appears in *Barnaby*, 49, was Marshal Henry
Seymour Conway, a distinguished soldier
and politician. He was (1720–95) com-
mander-in-chief in 1782, and was a strong
opponent of the war against the American
colonists.

**COOK.** 1. The cook at Mr. Nupkins's
house, engaged to Mr. Muzzle. *Pickwick*,
23, 25, 39.
2. The buxom-looking lady who sought to
console Mr. Tony Weller for the loss of his
wife. *Pickwick*, 52.
3. The cook at Westgate House. *Pickwick*, 16.
4. Mrs. Jellyby's cook, who skirmished
with the housemaid. *Bleak House*, 4.
5. The Cheeryble's cook. *Nickleby*, 37.
6. Mr. Dombey's cook, and leader of the
kitchen society at that august house. On
each succeeding event of importance she
produced something special in the way of
food, and incurred the special enmity of
Mrs. Pipchin. *Dombey*, 18, 31, 35, 51, 59.
7. Mrs. Maylie's servant who was terror-
stricken at Brittles's story of the attempted
burglary. *Twist*, 28.
8. The cook of The Haunted House,

amiable, but of a weak turn of intellect.
*The Haunted House.*

**COOK'S COURT, CURSITOR STREET.**
This was the court where Snagsby kept his
law stationery shop. It is a thin disguise for
Took's Court, in the same street. *Bleak
House*, 10, 16, 19, 22, 25.

**COOLING.** This village, about four miles
N.E. of Rochester and separated from the
Thames by a long stretch of bleak marsh, was
the scene of the opening chapters of *Great
Expectations*, in which the wild loneliness of
the Marshes are graphically described.
Cooling churchyard is much the same as
when Pip met his convict there for the first
time ; Joe's forge is not far distant, and the
Horseshoe and Castle (Three Jolly Bargemen)
is still the village house of refreshment.

**COOPER, AUGUSTUS.** A young gentleman in the oil and colour line "with a little
money ; a little business ; and a little
mother" who managed him and his affairs.
He succumbed to the charms of Miss Billsmethi, daughter of his dancing master, and
fell an easy prey to her father who extorted
£20 from him for breach of promise. *Boz,
Characters*, 9.

**COPENHAGEN HOUSE.** This was a
favourite Cockney resort, being an inn and
tea gardens situated among the fields which
then separated Holloway from Camden
Town. Copenhagen Fields were the scene
of many popular demonstrations. The
House was pulled down in 1853, and on its
site and the adjoining fields was built the
Caledonian Cattle Market, opened in 1855.
*Boz, Scenes*, 20.

**COPPERFIELD, DAVID,** is the central
figure and narrator of the novel of the same
name. The little boy and his widowed
mother, with Clara Peggotty the nurse, were
living happily together at Blunderstone in
Suffolk, when Mrs. Copperfield married
again. Mutual hatred between David and
his step-father, Edward Murdstone, induced
the latter to send him to school at Salem
House, where he learned nothing, but formed
a close friendship with James Steerforth.
On his mother's death David was put to
work in Murdstone and Grinby's wine vaults,
cleaning bottles and consorting with lads of
the lowest type, his existence only made
bearable by the friendship of the Micawbers.
At last the child ran away to his aunt,
Betsey Trotwood, who adopted him, gave
him a proper education and eventually
articled him to a proctor of Doctors' Commons. On losing all her money his aunt
came to London, and to support the household David learned shorthand reporting.
He was by this time in love with Dora
Spenlow, and soon after her father's sudden
death he married her. Their life was little
the less happy that Dora was impracticable
and just a child wife, and when she died
after little more than a year's married life,

David went abroad, brokenhearted. After some time he returned to England and married his life-long friend, Agnes Wickfield. The original of David Copperfield was Dickens himself, who in the story of David's wretched boyhood depicts his own sufferings in Warren's Blacking Warehouse.

Mrs. Clara Copperfield, David's mother, was barely twenty years of age when he was born. Her husband was double her age when they married and only lived a year afterwards. By her second marriage, to Edward Murdstone, she ruined her own happiness, was separated from her boy and soon succumbed to the cold and spirit-breaking regime of her husband and his sister. 1–4, 8, 9, 13, 14.

**COPPERNOSE.** A member of the Mudfog Association.

**CORNBERRY, MR.** A former suitor of Miss Julia Manners. *Boz, Tales, Winglebury.*

**CORNEY, MRS.** Matron of the workhouse where Oliver Twist was born. The locket and ring which were stolen from his mother's corpse came into her possession and she sold them to Monks, Oliver's half-brother, who was anxious to destroy all means of identifying the lad. Wooed and won by Bumble the beadle, she soon gained complete ascendency over her second husband. Finally her dealings with Monks being discovered by Mr. Brownlow, she and Bumble lost their posts and eventually became inmates of the workhouse they had once ruled. *Twist,* 23, 24, 27, 37, 38, 51, 53.

**CORNHILL.** This thoroughfare is closely associated with Mr. Pickwick, as in Freeman's Court (now covered by the Royal Exchange) was the office of Dodson and Fogg, the rascally attorneys of Mrs. Bardell (*Pickwick,* 20), while the George and Vulture, although actually opening from Lombard Street, is equally accessible from Cornhill (*Pickwick,* 26). The secretive Nadgett, when on the track of Jonas Chuzzlewit, forsook his usual route to business by way of Cornhill (*Chuzzlewit,* 38). Bradley Headstone made his impassioned appeal to Lizzie Hexam in the churchyard of St. Peter, Cornhill (*Mutual Friend,* II, 15). Captain Ravender, when considering whether he should take command of the *Golden Mary,* walked up and down at the back of the Royal Exchange, occasionally looking into Cornhill (*Golden Mary*). On a certain fateful Christmas Eve, Bob Cratchit took a slide down that street when he left Scrooge's office for home (*Christmas Carol*). It was in Cornhill that the queer Bill Stickers' procession was seen (*Reprinted, Bill Sticking*). The Standard in Cornhill, from which distances were frequently measured, was at the junction of Cornhill, Gracechurch Street, Bishopsgate Street and Leadenhall Street.

**CORONER.** The official who presided over the inquests of Nemo and Krook.

"The Coroner frequents more public-houses than any man alive. The smell of sawdust, beer, tobacco-smoke, and spirits is inseparable in his vocation from death in its most awful shapes." *Bleak House,* 11, 33.

**COUNTESS, THE.** The name by which Eliza Grimwood was usually known. *See* Grimwood, Eliza.

**COUNTY FIRE INSURANCE CO.** This was established in 1807, and its offices, 50 Regent Street, are still (1924) one of the familiar landmarks of Piccadilly Circus. *Boz, Tales, Winglebury.*

**COUNTY INN.** This Canterbury Inn where Mr. Dick stayed on his fortnightly visits to David Copperfield was the Royal Fountain Hotel in St. Margaret's Street. *Copperfield,* 17.

**COUR, CAPITAINE DE LA.** Commanding officer in the French town where Langley found little Bebelle. *Somebody's Luggage.*

**COVENT GARDEN.** There is hardly any part of London so often mentioned by Dickens, and it is only possible to name the most frequent references. Covent Garden Market in the early morning is described in *Humphrey* and *Boz, Scenes,* 1, and a typical gin shop there in *Scenes* 22. The arrest and conveyance of a pickpocket from Covent Garden to Bow Street is related in *Boz, Characters,* 6, while it should not be forgotten that Mr. Augustus Minns lived in Tavistock Street, Covent Garden (*Boz, Tales, Minns*). Having summoned Mr. Perker to attend Mr. Pickwick with a view to liberating that gentleman from the Fleet, Job Trotter betook himself to Covent Garden to spend the night in a vegetable basket (*Pickwick,* 47). Little David Copperfield used to wander about there of an evening looking at the pineapples (*Copperfield,* 12). Later, on arriving in town as a young man, he spent his first night at the Covent Garden Theatre (19), and when giving his first dinner party went thither in search of dessert (24). There, too, Tom Pinch and Ruth had many a pleasant stroll (*Chuzzlewit,* 40). Herbert Pocket, as a fit welcome to Pip, had bought a little fruit at the Garden (*Expectations,* 21). It was at an hotel there (the Hummums) that the Finches of the Grove "spent their money foolishly" on dining together (34), while, when warned by Wemmick to keep away from his chambers in the Temple, Pip spent the night in the same hotel (45). In a doorway in Covent Garden Market Mr. Dolls was attacked with his last fit of the horrors and, pelted by the urchins of the place, made his way thence to the Temple (*Mutual Friend,* IV, 9). Arthur Clennam was lodging in Covent Garden when Little Dorrit and Maggie went to see him (*Dorrit,* I, 13, 14). The *Uncommercial Traveller* also had rooms in Covent Garden (1), and in *Chapter* 13 he describes the children who prowl about among the market refuse.

**COVENTRY.** On his return from the fruitless visit to Mr. Winkle, Senior, Mr. Pickwick and his companions changed horses at Coventry in a deluge of rain (*Pickwick*, 51). It is probable that Coventry was the scene of Mrs. Jarley's exhibition immediately after she met Nell, and consequently the place where the child was terrified by a sight of Quilp. *Curiosity Shop*, 27, 28.

**COWER.** Mr. Joseph Tuggs's solicitor, in the Temple, whose clerk brought tidings of the inheritance. *Boz, Tales, Tuggs.*

**CRACKIT, TOBY.** One of Fagin's gang of thieves and accomplice of Bill Sikes in the attempt to break into Mrs. Maylie's house. He occupied a rickety old house on Jacob's Island, to which Sikes was finally tracked by his pursuers. *Twist*, 19, 22, 25, 26, 28, 39, 50.

**CRADDOCK, MRS.** Landlady of the house in Royal Crescent, Bath, where the Pickwickians and Dowlers took lodgings. *Pickwick*, 36, 37.

**CRAGGS, THOMAS.** One of the partners of Snitchey and Craggs, Dr. Jeddler's solicitors. He was " a cold, hard, dry man, dressed in grey, and white, like a flint ; with small twinkles in his eyes as if something struck sparks out of them." He was reticent and usually left the conversation to his partner, who expressed the opinion of " self and Craggs." *Battle of Life.*

**CRATCHIT.** Bob, the father of the family, was Scrooge's clerk, who, with his meagre pay of fifteen shillings a week, lived in a four-roomed house in Camden Town. Amidst all his poverty and troubles he was happy and cheerful, and was one of the first to benefit by Scrooge's change of spirit. The same happiness and content were found in his wife and daughters, Martha and Belinda, and their brother Peter, but the main interest of the story conjured up for Scrooge by the Christmas spirits centres round the cripple child, Tiny Tim, the idea of whose death created a tenderness which softened Scrooge's heart. *Christmas Carol.*

**CRAVAT.** This was the term formerly applied to a necktie, and took its name from the wrap or scarf worn by a regiment of Croats quartered in Paris in 1636. The Parisians adopted the mode and the fashion passed over to England. The original manner of tying was in a bow, with long ends, but various fashions have been prevalent at different times.

**CRAWLEY.** A visitor at the Bath Assembly Rooms, whose father had eight hundred a year. *Pickwick*, 35.

**CREAKLE.** The headmaster of Salem House. " I should think there can never have been a man who enjoyed his profession more. He had a delight in cutting at the boys . . . I am confident that he couldn't resist a chubby boy especially . . . I was chubby myself and ought to know." He kept his wife and daughter in a state of terror, and only respected James Steerforth, at whose instance he dismissed the usher, Mr. Mell. In his later years Creakle became a Middlesex magistrate. The original of Creakle was William Jones, headmaster of Wellington House Academy, at the corner of Hampstead and Granby Street, Camden Town, which Dickens attended from 1824–6. The same school is described in *Reprinted, Our School*. The greater part of the schoolhouse was demolished in 1835. *Copperfield*, 5–7, 9, 13, 27, 61.

**CREWLER, SOPHY.** Fiancée of Thomas Traddles and " the dearest girl in the world." She was the daughter of an ill-paid country curate, the Rev. Horace Crewler, whose household consisted of himself ; his invalid wife ; his eldest daughter, a beauty ; Sarah, weak in the spine ; Louisa, Margaret, and Lucy. They were all mothered and cared for by Sophy. After a long engagement she and Traddles were married " on a Britannia metal footing," the silver to follow with his rise in the profession. *Copperfield*, 27, 28, 34, 41, 43, 59, 61, 64.

**CRIBB, TOM.** A champion English pugilist (1781–1848) who was only once beaten—by George Nicholls in July, 1809. He beat Jem Belcher, February 1, 1809, and held the championship until his death, May 11, 1848. *Chuzzlewit*, 9.

**CRICKET ON THE HEARTH, THE.** This was one of the most successful of the Christmas Books, and appeared in 1845. It was dedicated to Lord Jeffrey and illustrated by Maclise, Doyle, Leech, Stanfield and Landseer. It later formed a popular " reading," and was translated into almost every European language.

*Principal Characters.* John Peerybingle, a carrier, and his wife Dot ; Caleb Plummer, a toymaker, and his blind daughter Bertha ; Edward Plummer, Caleb's son, and his fiancée May Fielding ; Tackleton, the toy merchant.

Edward Plummer, who has been away to the Golden South Americas, is returning to claim his bride, May Fielding, when he hears that she is about to marry Tackleton, the surly old toy merchant. Upon this Edward disguises himself as an old man and comes to stay with the Peerybingles. Dot Peerybingle soon penetrates his disguise, but keeps the secret from her husband, who is much concerned to find her carrying on furtive conversations with a stranger. Dot sees this, but though it nearly breaks her heart to realise that her husband is mistrusting her, does not set him right until she has brought Edward Plummer and May Fielding together again.

Another interest of the story lies in Caleb Plummer and his blind daughter. Caleb has never told Bertha of their poverty. She " never knew that ceilings were discoloured, walls blotched and bare of plaster . . . that sorrow and faint-heartedness were in the house ; that Caleb's scanty hairs were turning greyer and more grey before her sightless eyes. She never knew they had a master—cold, exacting and uninterested—that Tackleton was Tackleton, in short," and so she grows to love the ideal master whom Caleb describes as the Guardian Angel of their lives. When the truth is told her, and she realises that the master whom she idolises is a heartless boor, she turns to her father with renewed love and thankfulness for his innocent deceit.

**CRIMPLE, DAVID.** Originally a pawnbroker's clerk (when his name was Crimp), he became Secretary and resident Director of Tigg Montague's bogus insurance company. In the general confusion which followed the murder of Montague, Crimple and the porter Bullamy made off with all the available funds. *Chuzzlewit*, 13, 27, 28, 49, 51.

**CRINKLES.** Member of the Mudfog Association and inventor of a pocket-picking contrivance.

**CRIPPLE CORNER.** The courtyard in which was situated Wilding's house, office and warehouse. "All Cripple Corner belonged to Wilding and Co., Wine merchants. Their cellars burrowed under it, their mansions towered over it." *No Thoroughfare*.

**CRIPPLER, THE.** Captain Swosser's vessel, on the quarter-deck of which he fell in love with (the future) Mrs. Bayham Badger. *Bleak House*, 13.

**CRIPPLES.** Proprietor of a night school, above which lived Frederick Dorrit and his niece Fanny. *Dorrit*, I, 9.

**CRIPPS, TOM.** Errand boy to the firm of Sawyer, late Nockemorf, whose principal duty was to leave bottles of medicine at the wrong addresses. *Pickwick*, 38, 48, 50.

**CRISPARKLE, REV. SEPTIMUS.** A minor canon of Cloisterham, "fair, rosy . . . an early riser, musical, cheerful, classical, kind, good-natured, social, contented, and boy-like." He lived with his old mother—a pretty old lady whose " dress is as the dress of a china shepherdess, so dainty in its colours." The Reverend Septimus took in Neville Landless as a pupil and did his utmost to tame that lad's wild spirit. He was thoroughly perturbed at the disappearance of Edwin Drood, but was convinced of the innocence of Neville and took counsel with Mr. Grewgious how they might clear him of suspicion. *Drood*, 2, 6–8, 10, 12–17, 19, 21–3.

**CROCKFORD'S.** This gaming house in St. James's Street (now the Devonshire Club) was notorious in the early nineteenth century for the high play which was there carried on. It was closed in 1844. *Nickleby*, 2.

**CROFTS.** The young barber who shaved old Mr. Harvey. *Sketches of Couples* (*Old Couple*).

**CROOKEY.** The waiter at Namby's lock-up house in Bell Yard, " he looked something between a bankrupt grazier and a drover in a state of insolvency." *Pickwick*, 40.

**CROPLEY, MISS,** of Exeter, was a friend of Mrs. Nickleby, whose brother had a place at Court. *Nickleby*, 33.

**CROSS KEYS INN, WOOD STREET.** This was a well-known inn whence coaches for many parts started, among others those for Rochester (*Expectations*, 20. *Uncommercial*, 12). The inn was on the left-hand side from Cheapside, on the site now occupied by Nos. 129/130 Wood Street.

**CROWL.** " A hard-featured, square-faced man, elderly and shabby " and incredibly selfish, who occupied the next lodging to Newman Noggs. *Nickleby*, 14, 15, 32.

**CROWN INN.** 1. There was an inn of this name at Muggleton, where Mr. Jingle stayed. *Pickwick*, 7.

2. The Miss Ivinses were persuaded to taste some shrub at the Crown, Pentonville. *Boz, Characters*, 4.

3. The Crown, at the corner of Silver Street and James's Street, Golden Square, was a favourite resort of Newman Noggs. These streets are now called Beak Street and Upper James Street respectively, and a new Crown occupies the site of the old tavern. *Nickleby*, 7.

**CROZIER INN, CLOISTERHAM.** This was the inn where Mr. Datchery put up on his arrival at the cathedral city. It is another name for the Crown Inn, Rochester, the same house as that patronised by Mr. Jingle under the name of Wright's. It was at one time called Wright's, after its proprietor. The house was rebuilt in 1864. *Drood*, 18.

**CRUMMLES.** Vincent Crummles was manager of a touring theatrical company. " He had a very full underlip, a hoarse voice, as though he were in the habit of shouting very much, and very short black hair, shaved off nearly to the crown of his head—to admit (as Nicholas afterwards learnt) of his more easily wearing character wigs of any shape or pattern." During his stay with the actors, Nicholas received great kindness of the heavy father sort from Vincent Crummles, and some time afterwards was privileged to attend a farewell dinner to the family on their departure for America. Mrs. Crummles, " a stout portly female, apparently between forty and fifty," was a woman of great genius and had originally won Mr. Crummles's heart in a piece in which she " stood upon her head on the butt end of a spear, surrounded by blazing fireworks." Ninetta Crummles, better known as the Infant Phenomenon, the daughter had been ten years of age for the last five years. She was " a little girl in a dirty white frock, with tucks up to the knees, short trousers, sandalled shoes, white spencer, pink gauze bonnet, green veil and curl papers." She was the star of every piece the Crummles produced. The family was completed by Percy and Charles, the Phenomenon's two brothers. *Nickleby*, 22–5, 29, 30, 48.

**CRUMPTON, THE MISSES.** Amelia and Mary by name, they kept a ladies' seminary at Minerva House, Hammersmith, to which Miss Lavinia Brook Dingwall was sent to "finish," and from which she eloped with Theodosius Butler. *Boz, Tales, Sentiment.*

**CRUNCHER, JERRY.** Outdoor messenger of Tellson's Bank and a Resurrection Man, in which capacity he took an unholy interest in funerals. This midnight work aroused the curiosity of his son, Young Jerry, but caused the utmost horror and detestation in his wife, "a woman of orderly and industrious appearance," whose piety was a constant source of annoyance to her husband. "You're a nice woman ! What do you mean by flopping yourself down and praying agin me ? I won't put up with it, Aggerawayter." He accompanied Mr. Lorry and Miss Pross to Paris during the height of the Terror, and there gained such a horror of death and murder that he resolved to forswear the Resurrectionist business and treat his wife properly in future. *Two Cities*, I, 2, 3 ; II, 1–3, 14, 24 ; III, 3, 7–9, 14.

**CRUPP, MRS.** Landlady of the rooms where David Copperfield set up as a bachelor. She was "a short lady with a flounce of flannel petticoat below a nankeen gown. . . . Mrs. Crupp expressly intimated that she should always yearn towards me as a son . . . and said, 'thank Heaven she had now found summun she could care for.'" A martyr to a peculiar disorder called "the spazzums," she helped herself liberally to David's spirits, and deeply resented the arrival of Peggotty. She was eventually routed by Miss Betsy Trotwood, when that lady went to live with David. Mrs. Crupp's house, since demolished, was York House, No. 15 Buckingham Street, Adelphi, where Dickens himself lodged in 1834. *Copperfield*, 23–6, 28, 34, 35, 37, 44.

**CRUSHTON, THE HON. MR.** The bosom friend of Lord Mutanhed, who accompanied him to Bath. *Pickwick*, 35, 36.

**CUMMINS, TOM.** The gentleman in the chair at a convivial evening spent by one of Dodson and Fogg's clerks. *Pickwick*, 20.

**CUNNING.** One of Miss Flite's captive birds. *Bleak House*, 14.

**CUPIDON.** Fanciful name given by Lady Tippins to her ledger of lovers. *Mut. Fr.* I, 2.

**CURDLE, MR. AND MRS.** Dramatic patrons of Portsmouth who gave their support to Miss Snevellicci's benefit. Mr. Curdle had written a pamphlet of sixty-four pages on the character of the Nurse's deceased husband in *Romeo and Juliet*. *Nickleby*, 24.

**CURSITOR STREET.** In this street was the residence of Mr. John Dounce, the susceptible glove and braces maker (*Boz, Characters*, 7). The lock-up establishment of Mr. Solomon Jacobs, where Watkins Tottle was detained (*Boz, Tales, Tottle*) was the same as Coavinses Castle in *Bleak House*, 15, and both were in reality Sloman's spunging house, No. 2 Cursitor Street. Out of this street was Cook's Court (*q.v.*), where Mr. Snagsby lived.

**CURZON, THOMAS.** Hozier at the sign of the Golden Fleece, Aldgate, and master of Mark Gilbert, initiate of the Prentice Knights. *Barnaby*, 8.

**CUTE, ALDERMAN.** A magistrate who was determined to "put down" any nonsense on the part of the poor, such as the nonsense talked about want, and the cant about starvation. Poverty, sick persons and young children, were all to be put down, and there was to be no more nonsense of suicide. The character was founded on Sir Peter Laurie, a prominent City alderman, Lord Mayor, 1832–3, and a very zealous magistrate. Like Alderman Cute, he was determined to "put down" suicide. *Chimes.*

**CUTLER, MR. AND MRS.** Friends and neighbours of the Kenwigses. *Nickleby*, 14.

**CUTTLE, CAPTAIN EDWARD.** "A gentleman in a wide suit of blue, with a hook instead of a hand attached to his right wrist ; very bushy black eyebrows ; and a very thick stick in his left hand, covered all over, like his nose, with knobs." A retired pilot-skipper, he was a friend of Sol Gills, and when that old man departed in search of Walter Gay, Cuttle made a valiant escape from his landlady, Mrs. Macstinger, and took charge of the Wooden Midshipman. He was there when Florence Dombey ran away from her father, and took care of her until Walter Gay returned. Finally, with the reappearance of Sol Gills, Captain Cuttle became his partner in the instrument business. His sailor simplicity and childlike credulity make Cuttle one of the most lovable characters Dickens ever drew, while some of his quaint sayings have become proverbial. Of these the most famous is, "When found, make a note of." *Dombey*, 4, 9, 10, 15, 17, 19, 23, 25, 31, 32, 38, 39, 48–50, 56, 57, 60, 62.

# D

**DABBER, SIR DINGLEBY.** The author, existing only in Mrs. Nickleby's imagination, of lines to Kate in the event of her becoming Lady Mulberry Hawk. *Nickleby*, 27.

**DADSON, MR.** The writing master at Minerva House. *Boz, Tales, Sentiment.*

**DAFFY.** Daffy's "Elixir Salutis" was a well-known soothing syrup which maintained its popularity for about two hundred years, the original Daffy dying in 1680. *Twist*, 2.

**DAISY, SOLOMON.** Parish clerk of Chigwell and one of old John Willet's cronies. He related the story of Reuben Haredale's murder, as he was the only person who ever heard the bell which the murdered man rang to give the alarm. *Barnaby*, 1–3, 11, 30, 33, 54, 56, 82.

**DAISY.** Steerforth's nickname for David Copperfield. "My dear young Davy, you are a very Daisy. The daisy of the field at sunrise is not fresher than you are." *Copperfield*, 19, 20.

**DAME DURDEN.** John Jarndyce's pet name for Esther Summerson. *Bleak House*, 8.

**DANCER, DANIEL.** A famous miser whose biography was studied by Mr. Boffin. He was born at Weald, Harrow, in 1716, and inherited a moderate estate which, by horrible penuriousness and almost incredible self-denial, he increased to a fortune. He died in 1794, and large sums of money were found concealed in various parts of the premises he had occupied for many years. *Mutual Friend*, III, 6.

**DANDO.** 1. A boatman at Searle's Yard.
2. Between 1830 and 1840 John Dando, a Jew, was so well known that his name became a byword for one who ran up a bill at a restaurant and went away without paying. Dando was, according to Macaulay, "a bouncing seedy swell who was at least twice in every month brought before the magistrates for having refused to settle his bill after over-eating himself in an oyster-shop." On one of these many occasions (*vide Times*, August 20, 1830), he was summoned for eating eleven dozen oysters at a stall and going away without paying a halfpenny. Dando was the subject of a play by Edward Stirling, produced at Norton Folgate Theatre in 1838, and there were several caricatures, of the penny plain and twopence coloured style, to the effect that "Dando Astonishes the Natives." He ended his days in Clerkenwell gaol. *Boz, Scenes*, 10.

**DANTON.** A friend of the Kitterbell's who "had acquired, somehow or other the reputation of being a great wit; and accordingly, whenever he opened his mouth, everybody who knew him laughed very heartily." *Boz, Tales, Christening*.

**DARBY.** 1. A police constable who accompanied Bucket and Snagsby on their search of Tom-all-Alones. *Bleak House*, 22.
2. Keeper of a disreputable Liverpool lodging house frequented by merchant seamen. *Uncommercial*, 5.

**DARNAY, CHARLES.** This was the name adopted in England by Charles St. Evre-monde, nephew of the Marquis of that name. Disgusted with the whole system of French society he renounced his claim to the property and title and went to live in England. Having been tried for high treason at the Old Bailey and acquitted, mainly through the extraordinary resem-blance between himself and Sydney Carton, he became intimate with the Manette

family, and eventually married Lucy. Soon after the Revolution broke out he returned to France, was imprisoned as a *ci-devant* aristocrat, and, chiefly on the testimony of a statement written by Dr. Manette and found in his cell in the Bastille, was sentenced to death. Sydney Carton, however, for love of Lucy, contrived to make his way into the prison, and substituted himself for Darnay who escaped, with his wife and child, to England. *Two Cities*, II, 2–4, 6, 9, 10, 16–18, 20, 21, 24 ; III, 1, 3–13.

**DARTLE, ROSA.** A distant relative and companion of Mrs. Steerforth. "She never said anything she wanted to say outright ; but hinted it, and made a good deal more of it by the practice." Infuriated by Steer-forth's elopement with Little Em'ly, Rosa Dartle devoted all her energies to wreaking her revenge on the girl after Steerforth had abandoned her, and tracking her to a lodging in London, poured contempt and vituperation on the object of her hatred. After Steerforth's death Rosa remained with Mrs. Steerforth, consoling yet quarrelling with her. *Copperfield*, 20, 21, 24, 29, 32, 36, 46, 50, 56, 64.

**"DASHING WHITE SERGEANT."** This is a song by General Burgoyne, set to music by Bishop. It begins :—

If I had a beau for a soldier would go,
Do you think I'd say no ? No, no, not I !
When his red coat I saw, not a tear would it draw,
But I'd give him éclat for his bravery.
If an army of Amazons e'er came in play,
As a dashing white sergeant I'd march away.
*Copperfield*, 28.

**DATCHERY, DICK.** "A white-haired personage with black eyebrows. He had something of a military air ; but he an-nounced himself at the Crozier as an idle dog who lived upon his means." He took lodgings with the Topes, where he could keep Jasper constantly under observation, eventually eliciting particulars about him from the Princess Puffer. The identity of Datchery has puzzled all the writers of "conclusions" to *Drood*, and various sug-gestions have been made that he was Edwin Drood, Bazzard, Helena Landless, or Tartar. *Drood*, 18, 23.

**DAVENTRY.** This town was one of the stages on the route followed by Mr. Pickwick and his friends when returning from their vain visit to Mr. Winkle, Senior, at Bir-mingham. *Pickwick*, 51.

**DAVID.** 1. The Cheeryble's butler "of apoplectic appearance and with very short legs. . . . When Tim Linkinwater's health was to be drunk, David "by a feat of dexterity which was the admiration of all the company, bringing his left hand from behind the small of his back, produced the bottle with the corkscrew already inserted ; uncorked it at a jerk ; and placed the magnum and the cork before his master with the dignity of conscious cleverness." David was a real character, his original being

Alfred Boot, for many years butler of the Grants, prototypes of the Cheeryble twins. *Nickleby*, 37, 63.

2. Old David was the sexton of the parish where Little Nell and her grandfather ended their days. *Curiosity Shop*, 54.

**DAVID COPPERFIELD.** This book was published in monthly parts, illustrated by Phiz, the first appearing May 1, 1849, the last in November, 1850, when the work also appeared in book form. The original title was "*The Personal History, Adventures, Experiences, and Observations of David Copperfield the Younger, of Blunderstone Rookery* (*which he never meant to be published on any account*)." In his preface Dickens wrote, "Of all my books I like this the best . . . like many fond parents I have in my heart of hearts a favourite child, and his name is David Copperfield."

*Principal Characters.* David Copperfield, the narrator; his nurse, Clara Peggotty; his aunt, Miss Betsey Trotwood, and her protégé, Mr. Dick; Daniel Peggotty, a Yarmouth fisherman; his niece, Little Em'ly, and her cousin Ham; David's stepfather, Edward Murdstone, and his sister Jane; Steerforth, David's schoolboy hero and friend; the Micawber family; Agnes Wickfield, eventually David's second wife; her father, Mr. Wickfield, and his rascally clerk and partner, Uriah Heep; Dora Spenlow, David's child wife; Dr. Strong and his wife; Traddles, David's schoolfellow and faithful friend of after years.

In addition to the actual adventures of David himself (*see* Copperfield, David) the principal theme of the story is the betrayal of Little Em'ly by Steerforth and her uncle's search for the girl. There is also the story of Uriah Heep's deception of Mr. Wickfield and his subsequent exposure through Micawber, interwoven with which is the misunderstanding between Dr. Strong and his wife. Mr. and Mrs. Micawber, with their remarkable financial difficulties, are, perhaps, among the best known of all Dickens's characters.

**DAVIS, GILL.** A private in the Royal Marines and the narrator and real hero of the adventures at Silver Store Island. *English Prisoners.*

**DAWES, MARY.** The nurse in the nobleman's family where Miss Wade acted as governess. *Dorrit*, II, 21.

**DAWKINS, JACK.** Also known as the Artful Dodger, Dawkins was one of Fagin's most promising young thieves. "He was a snub-nosed, flat-browed, common-faced boy enough, and as dirty a juvenile as one would wish to see; but he had about him all the airs and manners of a man." He found Oliver Twist at Barnet, and took him to Fagin's den, where he was, in his own way, a friend to the child. A deft pickpocket, the Dodger was cut off in his prime, for having

been arrested with a stolen snuff-box on him, was tried and sentenced to transportation for life. At his appearance at Bow Street, Dawkins upheld his reputation as a "fly one," and was game to the end. *Twist*, 8–10, 12, 13, 16, 18, 19, 25, 39, 43.

**DAWS, MARY.** Mr. Dombey's kitchenmaid who, at the servants' discussion of the bankruptcy, "having sat with her mouth open for a long time, unexpectedly discharged words from it to this effect : "Suppose the wages shouldn't be paid." *Dombey*, 59.

**DAWSON.** The surgeon of Our Parish. *Boz.*

**DEAF GENTLEMAN, THE.** A friend of Master Humphrey, whom he met in a tavern. *Humphrey.*

**DEAL.** Richard Carstone, during his brief army career, was stationed at Deal, and thither Esther Summerson went to visit him. Among the many ships lying in the Downs was the Indiaman which had brought Allan Woodcourt back to England, and at the Deal Inn he and Esther met. *Bleak House*, 45.

**DEAN, THE.** Dignitary of Cloisterham Cathedral, a modest and worthy gentleman on whom Mr. Sapsea founded himself. *Drood*, 2, 4, 12, 16.

**DEATH.** One of Miss Flite's captive birds. *Bleak House*, 14.

**DEBILITATED COUSIN, THE.** A weak and foolish connection of the Dedlock family. *Bleak House*, 40.

**"DECLINE AND FALL OFF THE ROOSHAN EMPIRE."** This was Mr. Boffin's rendering of the title of Gibbon's immortal history, which he engaged Silas Wegg to read aloud. When that arch imposter discovered it was Roman and not "Rooshan," he was asked by Boffin what was the difference. "The Difference, Sir ? There you place me in a difficulty, Mr. Boffin. Suffice it to observe, that the difference is best postponed to some other occasion when Mrs. Boffin does not honour us with her company. In Mrs. Boffin's presence, sir, we had better drop it." *Mutual Friend*, I, 5.

**DEDLOCK.** Sir Leicester, was the owner of Chesney Wold and head of an influential family. "He is only a baronet, but there is no mightier baronet than he; his family is as old as the hills, and infinitely more respectable ; he has a general opinion that the world might get on without the hills, but would be done up without the Dedlocks." He had married Lady Dedlock for love and proved a gallant husband ; after her flight and his knowledge of the disgrace she had brought on his honourable name, sending Bucket to tell her she was forgiven. The shock of her death brought on paralysis, from which he never recovered (*Bleak House*, 2, 7, 9, 12, 16, 18, 27–9, 40, 41, 43, 48, 49, 53–6, 58, 63, 66). Lady Honoria, Sir Leicester's wife, was a beautiful and proud woman who, though of no family herself, had proved worthy of the station to which her marriage had raised her. She was Esther Summerson's mother, and for her tragic story see the article *Bleak House*. (2, 7, 9, 12, 16, 18, 23, 28, 29, 33, 36, 37, 40, 41, 43, 48, 53–9.) Volumnia Dedlock was an elderly cousin of Sir Leicester, who went to keep house for him after Lady Dedlock's death. (28, 40, 53, 56, 58, 66.)

**DEDLOCK ARMS.** The inn, kept by W. Grubble, at Chesney Wold village, where Richard and Skimpole stayed when they visited Esther after her illness. The original was the Sondes Arms, Rockingham. *Bleak House*, 37.

**DEEDLES.** A banker and friend of Alderman Cute and Sir Joseph Bowley, who committed suicide in his counting house. *Chimes*.

**DEFARGE, ERNEST.** A Parisian wineshop keeper, who having in his youth been servant to Doctor Manette, took charge of him after his release from the Bastille. He and his wife played a prominent part in the Revolution. On the taking of the Bastille Defarge made his way to the cell once occupied by Dr. Manette, and recovered a written statement which the prisoner had concealed. This statement, implicating the St. Evremonde family, Defarge produced when Charles Darnay was on trial, and thus secured his condemnation. *Two Cities*, I, 5, 6; II, 7, 15, 16, 21, 22; III, 1, 3, 6, 7, 9, 10, 12, 14.

Therese Defarge, his wife, was a typical woman of the Revolution. Sitting in the wineshop she kept an eager eye for spies, and was one of the famous knitting women who thus made a record of those to be devoted to the guillotine. The fact of his being an aristocrat induced her to compass the death of Darnay at all costs, and in pursuance of this idea she made her way to his apartments soon after their escape. There she encountered Miss Pross, and in the struggle which ensued Madame Defarge was shot by her own pistol. *Two Cities*, I, 5, 6; II, 7, 15, 16, 21, 22: III, 3, 5, 6, 8–10, 12, 14.

**DEFRESNIER AND CIE.** The Neuchatel firm of wine merchants for whom Obenreizer acted as London Agent. *No Thoroughfare*.

**DE LA FONTAINE.** A gentleman of Bedford Square whose acquaintance was claimed by Horatio Sparkins. *Boz, Tales, Sparkins*.

**DEMENTED TRAVELLER.** A passenger of the fast Paris Express who was continually making mistakes and in constant danger of being left behind. *Reprinted, A Flight*.

**DEMERARA.** Mr. Jingle and Job Trotter, thanks to the munificence of Mr. Pickwick, were sent to Demerara to start their lives afresh. *Pickwick*, 53.

**DEMPLE, GEORGE.** Son of a doctor and a pupil at Salem House. *Copperfield*, 5, 7.

**DENHAM, EDMUND.** The name assumed by Edward Longford. (*q.v.*)

**DENNIS, EDWARD.** The common hangman and one of the ringleaders of the Gordon rioters. He carefully kept his trade a secret, though openly boasting that every article of his clothing had been left him by dead men. He was arrested as a ringleader and sentenced to death, awaiting, in a state of pitiful panic, the fate he had so often meted out to others. Dennis was an actual person, but in reality he was reprieved and did not suffer the capital penalty for his share in the disorders. *Barnaby*, 36–40, 44, 49, 50, 52–4, 59, 60, 63–5, 69–71, 74–7.

**DENTIST'S SERVANT.** The wonderful man who "knows what is done with the extracted teeth." *Uncommercial*, 16.

**DEPORTMENT.** This was the forte of old Mr. Turveydrop (*q.v.*), who, on all occasions and under all circumstances, was a model of Deportment. *Bleak House*, 14.

**DEPTFORD.** Although chiefly famous for its docks, there were once market gardens "down Deptford way," where Mr. Jobling sought a refuge from his difficulties (*Bleak House*, 20). In these same market gardens, "among the marsh lands near the river's level," Mr. Toby Magsman was interviewed and told the story of *Going into Society*.

**DEPUTY.** "Man-servant up at the Travellers' Twopenny in Gasworks Garding. . . . When we are chock full, and the Travellers is all abed, I come out for my 'elth." He was also known as Winks. His night walks were made profitable by Durdles, who paid him a halfpenny to pelt him home with stones when he stayed out too late. On sight of Durdles, Deputy would begin his chant :—

> Widdy widdy wen!
> I-Ket-ches-Im-Out-arter-ten,
> Widdy widdy w'y!
> Then-E-don't-go-then-I-shy—
> Widdy Widdy Wake-cock warning!
>                 *Drood*, 5, 12, 18, 23.

**DERRICK, JOHN.** Valet of the juryman who relates the first of the *Two Ghost Stories*.

**"DESERTED, AS YOU WILL REMEMBER."** Putting aside his interpolations, Wegg's quotation of the opening lines of "All's Well" (*q.v.*) was fairly correct. *Mutual Friend*, III, 7.

**DESPAIR.** One of Miss Flite's captive birds. *Bleak House*, 14.

**DETECTIVE POLICE, THE.** These detective stories were first published in *Household Words*, July 27 and August 10, 1850, making a reappearance in *Reprinted Pieces*, 1858. Detective stories had not at that time attained the popularity they acquired later, and the detective force was but little known to the general public. The crudity of these detective tales compares strangely with the baffling stories of mystery which have since become current. The narrators of the stories were prominent detectives of the time, their names being thinly disguised : Wield, Field;

Stalker, Walker; Witchem, Whicher; Fendall, Kendall; Dornton, Thornton; Mith, Smith; Straw, either Shaw or Haynes.

**DEVASSEUR, LOYAL.** Landlord at the French Watering Place. *See* Loyal.

**DEVIL'S PUNCH BOWL.** This is a curious depression on the north side of Gibbet Hill on Hindhead Common. Here stands the memorial stone commemorating the murder of a sailor in 1786, which Nicholas read to Smike, when they passed it on their way to Portsmouth. *Nickleby*, 22.

**DIBABS, JANE.** A former acquaintance of Mrs. Nickleby. "She married a man who was a great deal older than herself, and *would* marry him, notwithstanding all that could be said to the contrary." *Nickleby*, 55.

**DIBBLE.** A blind Mormon emigrant and his family, bound for Salt Lake City. *Uncommercial*, 20.

**DICK, MR.** This was the name by which Mr. Richard Babley was always known. He was an amiable old gentleman who boarded with Miss Trotwood, rather shortwitted, though she would never admit it, and generally occupied in memorialising the Lord Chancellor about his affairs. Unfortunately he could never keep out of his memorial some reference to Charles the First losing his head. Miss Trotwood always averred that he had sound common sense, and he proved himself a model of tact in restoring harmony between Dr. Strong and his wife. *Copperfield*, 13–15, 17–19, 23, 34–8, 40–3, 45, 49, 52, 54, 59, 60, 62, 64.

**DICK.** 1. One of the pauper orphans brought up by Mrs. Mann. *Twist*, 7, 17, 51.

2. The guard of the coach which took Nicholas and Squeers to Greta Bridge. *Nickleby*, 5.

3. The hostler at the Salisbury Inn where Tom Pinch was wont to put up. *Chuzzlewit*, 5.

4. Joram's youngest apprentice. *Copperfield*, 51.

5. The sweetheart of Sally, nurse at the Foundling Hospital. *No Thoroughfare.*

6. Tim Linkinwater's blind blackbird. *Nickleby*, 37.

**DICKENS, CHARLES JOHN HUFFHAM.** Born at Portsmouth, February 7, 1812. Lived at Chatham, 1816–23, then moved to London. Warren's Blacking Warehouse, *c.* 1823–24. Wellington House School, 1824–26. Ellis and Blackmore's law offices, 1827–28. Newspaper reporter, 1829–36. First sketch published, December, 1833. *Pickwick*, 1837. (For dates of novels see list at beginning of this book.) Married Catherine Hogarth, April, 1836. First visit to America, 1842. Founded *Daily News*, January, 1846. Founded *Household Words*, March, 1849. Bought Gadshill, 1856. First Reading Tour, 1858–59. Founded *All the Year Round*, 1859. Second Reading Tour, 1861–63. Third Reading Tour, 1866–67.

Second visit to America, 1867–68. Fourth Reading Tour, 1868–70. Last Reading, at St. James's Hall, March 1, 1870. Died at Gadshill, June 9, 1870. Buried Westminster Abbey, June 14.

**DICKENS, JOHN.** The father of Charles, and original of Wilkins Micawber (*q.v.*). Aspects of the character of his wife, the novelist's mother, are portrayed in Mrs. Nickleby and Mrs. Wilfer.

**DIDDLER, JEREMY.** A typical swindler, one of the characters in Kenney's popular farce, *Raising the Wind*. *Nickleby*, 23.

**DIEGO, DON.** The inventor of a flying machine. *Reprinted, A Flight.*

**DIGBY.** Stage name given to Smike in the Crummles company. *Nickleby*, 30.

**DIJON.** This French town was the rendezvous of Edith Dombey and James Carker. An apartment had been taken for Edith, dinner had been sent over from the Golden Head, and Carker arrived, only to find that Edith had used him merely as a tool to injure her husband. *Dombey*, 52, 54.

**DILBER, MRS.** A laundress who disposed of stolen goods to Old Joe. *Christmas Carol.*

**DILWORTH, REV.** Thomas Dilworth was the author of *A New Guide to the English Tongue*, published in 1812. On the title-page there was a picture of the author wearing a kind of nightcap. *Boz, Scenes*, 10.

**DINGLEY DELL.** There have been innumerable attempts to identify the village whose Manor Farm was the residence of Mr. Wardle. The most likely claimant to the honour is Sandling. The identification of the place, however, depends largely on the identification of Muggleton, and if Muggleton and Maidstone be the same, Dingley Dell is certainly Sandling. On the authority of Mr. F. G. Kitton, Cob Tree Hall, near Sandling, was the Manor Farm. *Pickwick*, 4–9, 28, 30.

**DINGO, PROFESSOR.** Second husband of Mrs. Bayham Badger and a botanist of European reputation. *Bleak House*, 13.

**DINGWALL, CORNELIUS BROOK.** *See* Brook Dingwall.

**DIOGENES.** Dr. Blimber's dog, and a pet of little Paul Dombey. After the child's death Toots secured Diogenes and gave him to Florence. *Dombey*, 14, 18, 22, 23, 28, 30, 31, 35, 41, 44, 48–50, 56.

**"DI PIACER."** This is a once popular air from Rossini's opera, *La Gazza Ladra*. *Boz, Tales, Boarding House.*

**DISMAL JEMMY.** This was the nickname of the strolling player, Jem Hutley. (*q.v.*)

**DIVER, COLONEL.** The editor of the *New York Rowdy Journal*, whom Martin encountered on his arrival at New York, and who introduced him to the Pawkins boarding house. *Chuzzlewit*, 16.

**DOBBLE.** The host of the party held at the house with green blinds on New Year's Eve. *Boz, Characters*, 3.

**DOBBLETON, THE DOWAGER DUCHESS OF.** A mysterious member of the aristocracy whom Mrs. Tuggs was supposed to resemble. *Boz, Tales, Tuggs.*

**DOBBS, JULIA.** The heroine of the comic burletta *The Strange Gentleman*, and the same character as Julia Manners in *Boz, Tales, Winglebury.*

**DOCHE, MADAME.** A dealer at Poissy Calf Market. *Reprinted, Monument of French Folly.*

**DOCTOR MARIGOLD.** This appeared in the Christmas number of *All the Year Round* for 1865. It proved one of the most successful subjects for the Readings, especially in New York, where at the conclusion of the first reading the audience almost stormed the platform in their enthusiasm. Dickens's own account of its origin was this : " Tired with *Our Mutual* (which he had just concluded), I sat down to cast about for an idea, with a depressing notion that I was, for the moment, overworked. Suddenly, the little character that you will see, and all belonging to it, came flashing up in the most cheerful manner, and I had only to look on and leisurely describe it."

**DOCTORS' COMMONS.** A society or college of English lawyers, founded in 1768, with its headquarters near St. Paul's Cathedral. Its members, called fellows, had the sole right of appearing in Ecclesiastical (which included divorce) Probate and Admiralty courts. Proctors, equivalent to solicitors, were attached to the Commons. The college was dissolved in 1857, and the buildings were pulled down in 1867. The entrance was, according to Sam Weller, in " Paul's Churchyard, sir ; low archway on the carriage-side, bookseller's at one corner, hot-el on the other, and two porters in the middle as touts for licences." Doctors' Commons is admirably described in *Boz, Scenes*, 8. Sam Weller's description of his father's matrimonial adventure at the Commons has already been mentioned (*Pickwick*, 10) ; the old gentleman paid another visit there in connection with proving his wife's will (55). David Copperfield was articled to Mr. Spenlow, a proctor at the Commons, and describes some of his experiences (*Copperfield*, 23, 26, 33, 35, 39). Mr. Boffin described to Mortimer Lightwood his proceedings at " Doctor Scommons " when he came into possession of the Harmon fortune (*Mutual Friend*, I, 8). William Blinder the hostler, having chalked his last will and testament on the lid of a corn chest, the lid had to be sent up to Doctors' Commons to be proved. *Humphrey.*

**DODD, HENRY.** Original of " Noddy " Boffin. (*q.v.*)

**DODGER, THE ARTFUL.** Nickname of Jack Dawkins. (*q.v.*)

**DODSON AND FOGG.** The firm of speculative attorneys who took up Mrs. Bardell's case against Mr. Pickwick, reckoning on that gentleman paying damages and costs without much demur. Dodson was a plump, portly, stern-looking man, who always took upon himself the rôle of spokesman. The offices of the firm were in Freeman's Court, Cornhill, now covered by the Royal Exchange. When Mr. Pickwick refused to pay the damages, Dodson and Fogg arrested Mrs. Bardell and threw her into the Fleet prison. *Pickwick*, 18, 20, 22, 26, 31, 34, 35, 46, 47, 53, 57.

**DOE AND ROE.** The names of John Doe and Richard Roe were formerly used in English legal procedure for fictitious personages introduced for purposes of convenience in law suits. For example, if John Brown wished to claim freehold land in the possession of Henry Thompson, in view of the fact that an ejectment could only be brought by a leaseholder, Brown would grant a fictitious lease to John Doe, and Doe, as a tenant of Brown, could obtain an ejectment against Thompson. This legal fiction was done away with in 1852. *Curiosity Shop*, 33.

**DO'EM.** Accomplice of Captain Fitz-Whisker Fiercy, who dressed as his manservant to inspire confidence in their dupes. *Pantomime of Life.*

**DOGGINSON.** A member of the vestry, considered as a regular John Bull in consequence of his having already made up his mind on every subject without knowing anything about it. *Reprinted, Our Vestry.*

**DOG'S NOSE.** A beverage which, according to the committee of the Ebenezer Temperance Association, confirmed by one of its lady members, was compounded of warm porter, moist sugar, gin and nutmeg. *Pickwick*, 33.

**DOLLOBY.** An old-clothes dealer in the Kent Road, to whom David Copperfield sold his waistcoat when making his way to Dover. *Copperfield*, 13.

**DOLLS, MR.** This was the name given by Eugene Wrayburn to Jenny Wren's drunken father. She herself called him her bad child, and really seemed to have almost a motherly care and love for him. At the cost of sundry " threepennyworths o' rum," Eugene extracted from him the address of Lizzie Hexam, and it was in hopes of getting more three pennyworth that he made his final visit to the Temple, when he was overcome with delirium and died on a police stretcher. *Mutual Friend*, II, 1, 2 ; III, 10, 17 ; IV, 9.

**DOLPHIN'S HEAD INN.** An old stage coach-house, kept by J. Mellows, and sadly reduced by the advent of the railway. *Uncommercial*, 22.

**DOMBEY.** Mr. Paul Dombey was a pompous City merchant of great wealth. The firm had always been Dombey and Son, and accordingly the birth of Little Paul inspired his ambition and consoled him for the unwanted daughter—his first child. When the boy died, Mr. Dombey was overcome with jealousy of his daughter, to whom the child had given all his love. Urged on by old Joe Bagstock, Mr. Dombey made a second marriage, but his bride, Edith Granger, was as proud as himself, and their married life soon became unhappy. Blind in his conceit, Dombey made Carker, his business manager, the bearer of humiliating messages, with the result that Edith, to spite her husband, eloped with Carker. Mr. Dombey followed the couple to their meeting-place at Dijon, pursued Carker back to England, only in time to see him killed on the railway. Broken by his domestic troubles, and the obstinate hatred which had made him drive Florence from the house, Mr. Dombey was unable to weather a severe financial crisis, and the great house of Dombey and Son went bankrupt. The Carkers devoted their brother's money to relieve their old master, and Mr. Dombey ended his days in reconcilement with Florence and her husband. *Dombey*, 1–6, 8–11, 13–16, 18, 20, 21, 23, 26–31, 35–7, 40–5, 47, 51–5, 58, 59, 61, 62.

Florence was the neglected, unwanted daughter of Mr. Dombey and the heroine of the novel. It was little Paul's love for her that first turned her father's indifference into active dislike. When her father brought home his second wife a great friendship sprang up between her and Florence, and this was another cause of displeasure to Mr. Dombey, who again found himself put aside for his unwanted daughter. On Edith's flight Mr. Dombey turned Florence from his house, and she took refuge with Captain Cuttle, whom she knew through Walter Gay, whom she had long liked and whose friendship with her had been yet another cause of dissension with her father. Florence was staying with Captain Cuttle at the Wooden Midshipman when Walter, whom all thought had been drowned, returned alive and well. In due course Florence and he were married, and eventually her father, broken in fortune and spirit, was glad to yield to his daughter's unfailing love. Throughout her sad youth Florence was cheered by the devoted service of Susan Nipper, and the hopeless love of Mr. Toots. She is one of the Maria Hogarth heroines. 1, 3–6, 8–12, 14, 16–20, 22–4, 26, 28–32, 35–7, 39–45, 47–50, 56, 57, 59–62.

Little Paul was Mr. Dombey's long hoped-for son and the heir to the House's fame and fortune. His mother died at his birth and he was cared for by Polly Toodle and the doleful Mrs. Wickam, when old enough being sent, in company with his devoted sister Florence, to Mrs. Pipchin at Brighton. From there Paul was sent to Dr. Blimber, but his always failing health made a marked turn for the worse, and after a term at that educational forcing house, he was taken seriously ill. Removed to London, and constantly tended by his fond sister, the only being whom he loved, little Paul gradually sank and died. The original of Little Paul was Dickens's cripple nephew, Harry Burnett. 1–3, 5–8, 10–12, 14–16.

Mrs. Fanny Dombey was the merchant's first wife and the mother of Paul and Florence. Despite Mrs. Chick's admonitions she failed to make an effort and died when little Paul was born. 1, 3, 16, 31.

Edith Dombey was Paul Dombey's second wife, " very handsome, very haughty, very wilful, who tossed her head and drooped her eyelids, as though, if there were anything in all the world worth looking into, save a mirror, it certainly was not the earth or sky," had been married at eighteen to Colonel Granger, who died two years later. She then accompanied her mother, Mrs. Skewton, to the fashionable watering places and at that veteran matchmaker's instigation, married Mr. Dombey. When she was established in the great London mansion she devoted her whole affection to Florence and thus angered her husband. To humiliate his proud young wife, and break her spirit, Mr. Dombey made James Carker his go-between, sending by his means messages and orders which infuriated Edith to the point of eloping with Carker. Though losing her fair name she kept her honour, however, and merely used Carker as an instrument for making her escape. She eventually made her home with her Cousin Feenix. 21, 26–31, 35–7, 40–3, 45–7, 54, 61.

**DOMBEY AND SON.** This novel appeared in monthly parts, between October 1, 1846, and April, 1848, when it was issued in volume form. The full title of the book is *Dealings with the Firm of Dombey and Son, Wholesale, Retail and for Exportation.*

*Principal Characters.* The Dombeys ; Sol Gills and his nephew, Walter Gay ; their friend Captain Cuttle, a retired mariner ; Mrs. Chick and her friend Miss Tox ; Major Joe Bagstock, an old army man ; the Blimbers, of Brighton ; Mrs. Pipchin, a stern widow ; Toots, in love with Florence Dombey ; Mrs. Skewton, mother of Edith Dombey ; James Carker, Dombey's business manager ; Susan Nipper, Florence's maid ; Rob the Grinder, son of Mrs. Toodle, Little Paul's nurse ; Alice Marwood.

The first part of the story centres round little Paul, the hope of the Firm, who, after a few years of sickly childhood, dies and leaves his father a disappointed man. Dombey marries again and his part in the novel will be found in the entry under his name. While he is following out his own schemes and ambitions, the story turns to Sol Gills, the old instrument maker and his nephew, Walter Gay. Walter is despatched by Mr. Dombey to the West Indies, but the ship founders on the voyage and he is presumed to be lost. Sol Gills, however, does not believe this, and one day vanishes in search of his nephew, leaving the shop to the care of their friend, Captain Cuttle. Meanwhile things go badly with Mr. Dombey, his second wife elopes, Florence is driven out, and eventually the great firm goes bankrupt. Walter Gay returns and marries Florence, and together they give Mr. Dombey a home, where, broken by grief and disappointment, he learns to value his daughter's love. Toots, the most amiable character in the book, albeit rather short-witted, marries Susan Nipper, Florence's maid; Harriet Carker marries Morfin, and the faithful Miss Tox is left trying to reform Rob the Grinder.

**DONKEY, A DEAD.** Sam Weller's "gen'l'm'n in black silk smalls as know'd the young 'ooman as kep' a goat" referred to Sterne's *Sentimental Journey*, in which the narrator encounters the corpse of a dead ass at Nampont. The "young 'ooman" was Maria, who appears at Moulins towards the end of that book. Her story is told in *Tristram Shandy*, Vol. IX, Chap. 24. *Pickwick*, 51.

**DONKEYS.** "Janet, Donkeys!" was Miss Trotwood's indignant call to hostilities on seeing donkey boys driving their beasts over the little green in front of her house. *Copperfield*, 13, 14.

**DONNY, MISSES.** The proprietors of Greenleaf, the boarding school near Reading, where Esther Summerson was educated. *Bleak House*, 3.

**DOR, MADAME.** Jules Obenreizer's Swiss housekeeper and a true friend to Marguerite. "That speechless matron was never seen in a front view, from the moment of her arrival to that of her departure—except at dinner. And from the instant of her retirement to the drawing-room, after a hearty participation in that meal, she turned her face to the wall again." *No Thoroughfare*.

**DORA.** The name of David Copperfield's first wife. *See* Spenlow, Dora.

**DORKER.** One of the pupils at Dotheboys Hall, who succumbed to the Squeers' regime. *Nickleby*, 4.

**DORKING.** The interest in this quiet Surrey town centres round Mr. Weller's home at the Marquis of Granby, the identity of which inn is discussed under its own entry.

**DORNTON, SERGEANT.** A detective in the London police force, who told the story of the Adventures of a Carpet Bag. The original was Serj. Thornton, of Bow Street. *Reprinted, Detective Police*.

**DORRIT.** Amy, or Little Dorrit, the title character of the novel, was the daughter of William Dorrit and was born in the Marshalsea Prison. The only member of the family with any pride, she worked hard to keep her father from accepting "testimonials," and although their junior, put both her brother and sister out into the world. She was working as a seamstress at Mrs. Clennam's when she met Arthur Clennam and inspired him with a new interest in life. When the family came into their money, she continued to tend her father, now spoiled by fortune as he had previously been by adversity, and tried to make him a better man. After his death and the loss of their money, Amy returned to England and nursed Arthur Clennam in the Marshalsea Prison, eventually marrying him at St. George's Church, where, as the child of the Marshalsea, she had been christened. It has been suggested, on slender grounds, that the original of Little Dorrit was Miss Mary Ann Mitton, later Mrs. Cooper, who lived at Southgate and was a friend of Dickens. She died in 1910, *vide Evening Times*, November 26th, 1910. *Dorrit*, I, 3, 5–9, 12–15, 18–20, 22–5, 27, 29, 31, 32, 35, 36; II, 1, 3–8, 11, 14, 15, 17–19, 24, 27, 29–31, 33, 34.

William Dorrit, father of the family, was a weak, irresolute man who, after twenty-five years' imprisonment in the Marshalsea for debt, proudly answered to the title of Father of the Marshalsea. "If he had been a man with strength of purpose to face his troubles and fight them, he might have broken the net which held him—or broken his heart; but, being what he was, he languidly slipped into this smooth descent, and never more took one step upward." He was lovingly tended by his daughter Amy, who tried to shield him from the results of his weakness and false pride. When, through the industry of Pancks, it was found that he was heir to a large fortune, William Dorrit left the Marshalsea with ridiculous grandeur and took the family abroad. He employed a Mrs. General to chaperon his daughters, and was about to suggest matrimony to that lady when he was stricken ill. The blow fell at a dinner-party given by Mrs. Merdle, and Dorrit imagining himself back in the Marshalsea, called on Bob the turnkey to come to his help. After his death it was found that he had embarked his whole fortune in one of Merdle's wild schemes, the failure of which reduced the family to ruin. I, 6–10, 12, 18–20, 22, 23, 31, 32, 35, 36; II, 1–3, 5–7, 12, 15–19.

Edward, or "Tip" Dorrit, Amy's brother, was a ne'er-do-weel, ruined in early life by the spirit of the Marshalsea. When the family came into their fortune Tip became a very grand young man, but his weak character was unable to bear prosperity, and by the time their fortune was lost, drink had made him a hopeless invalid. I, 6–8, 12, 20, 22, 24, 31, 35, 36; II, 1, 3, 5, 7, 11, 14, 15, 19, 24, 29, 33, 34.

Fanny, Little Dorrit's elder sister, was a vain, frivolous girl. Through her sister's exertions she had been taught dancing. While in the ballet of the Surrey Theatre she attracted the attention of Mr. Edmund Sparkler, Mrs. Merdle's son, but was bought off by Mrs. Merdle. After the Dorrits had become rich, Fanny and Edmund met again in Italy and were eventually married. Fanny proved as vain and heartless a wife as she had been a daughter and sister, and it eventually fell to Little Dorrit's lot to look after her neglected children. There is reason to suppose that the original of Fanny Dorrit was, in some degree, Dickens's own sister, Fanny Burnett, though the prototype was in no way so heartless as the character in the story. I, 6–9, 14, 20, 31, 33, 35, 36 ; II, 1, 3, 5–7, 11, 12, 14–16, 18, 19, 24, 33, 34.

Frederick Dorrit was William's brother and a down-at-heels clarionet player (at the Surrey Theatre). Long before this he had befriended the girl who was Arthur Clennam's mother, and by a codicil to Gilbert Clennam's will, he, or his youngest niece, was left £1000. This codicil was suppressed, however, by Mrs. Clennam (q.v.). Frederick Dorrit was taken abroad by his brother when the former came into his inheritance, and, despised by the rest of the family, found his only friend in his niece, Little Dorrit. I, 7–9, 19, 20, 35, 36 ; II, 1, 3, 5, 19, 30.

**DOTHEBOYS HALL.** " A long, cold-looking house, one story high, with a few straggling out-buildings behind, and a barn and stable adjoining." This was the home of Squeers and the scene of his disgraceful cruelty to the boys in his charge. The original was William Shaw's school at Bowes, which until recent years was a long low building of two stories. " The pump at which Shaw's pupils used to wash, is still in the yard at the back of the house." (Kitton.) *Nickleby*, 7–9, 12, 13, 64.

**DOUBLE DIAMOND.** This special port which the Cheeryble's butler served with such ceremony was Dixon's Double Diamond, which has been shipped for over 100 years, being the property of Morgan Bros., Oporto. *Nickleby*, 37.

**DOUBLEDICK, RICHARD.** The hero of a tale told to the *Seven Poor Travellers*. Dick Doubledick was a good-hearted wastrel who enlisted and turned over a new leaf. He rose to be major, was badly wounded at Waterloo and eventually married the girl of his heart, Mary Marshall. (*q.v.*)

**DOUNCE, JOHN.** A retired glove and braces maker who lived in Cursitor Street, and became infatuated with a young lady at an oyster bar. He began to ape the manners of a young man, alienated his family and friends, and when he had been jilted by the oyster lady, married his cook, who ever after henpecked him. *Boz, Characters*, 7.

**DOVER.** Although so near Broadstairs, Dickens seldom visited Dover. In 1852 he said, " It is not quite to my taste, being too bandy (I mean musical ; no reference to its

legs) and infinitely too genteel." In that year he stayed for three months at No. 10 Camden Crescent, and in 1861 he was at the Lord Warden Hotel. The place figures fairly frequently in his stories, however, and descriptions are given in *Two Cities*, I, 4, and in *Uncommercial*, 7, 11, 17. It will best be remembered as the home of Miss Betsey Trotwood, whose cottage was on the cliffs above Dover (*Copperfield*, 13, 39). It was under a feint of going to Dover that Magwitch was smuggled from his first lodgings by Herbert Pocket and Wemmick (*Expectations*, 45). Arthur Clennam, on his return to England, travelled from Dover to London by the Blue Eyed Maid coach. *Dorrit*, I, 3.

Of the Dover Road, David gave a good idea when recounting his tramp to find his aunt (*Copperfield*, 13) ; the effect of travelling over it at night by coach is graphically described in *Two Cities*, I, 2. In *Pickwick*, 43, mention is made of two coachmen, twin brothers, who passed each other on the Dover Road every day for twenty-four years, never exchanging any other greeting than the coachman's salutation of a jerk round of the right wrist and a tossing of the little finger into the air at the same time. Finally, Mr. F.'s aunt made the following inexorable and awful statement : " There's milestones on the Dover road ! " *Dorrit*, I, 23.

**DOWDLES, THE MISSES.** According to Mrs. Nickleby " the most accomplished, elegant, fascinating creatures," who kept the school in Devonshire where Kate was educated. *Nickleby*, 26.

**DOWGATE.** An ancient City family whose prayer books the Uncommercial Traveller found in the ancient City Church. *Uncommercial*, 9.

**DOWLER, MR. AND MRS.** An army officer and his wife who travelled with Mr. Pickwick and his friends to Bath. He was a " stern-eyed man of about five and forty . . . with a good deal of black hair at the sides and back of his head, and large black whiskers," who posed as a great fire-eater. The Dowlers shared the Pickwickians' lodgings at Royal Crescent, Bath, and it was while admitting Mrs. Dowler late one night that Mr. Winkle became involved in the affair of the sedan chair. Dowler threatened to cut Mr. Winkle's throat, but next day they both met at Bristol, whither each had fled from the other's wrath. *Pickwick*, 35–38.

**DOWN WITH THE TIDE.** This account of a tour of inspection with the river police first appeared in *Household Words*, February 5, 1853, and was collected in *Reprinted Pieces*, 1858. It forms one of the series of police studies for which Dickens always had a penchant.

**DOYCE, DANIEL.** A friend of Meagles and an inventor who had expended most of his energies in trying to induce the Government to take up a useful invention. At Meagles' suggestion Arthur Clennam became his partner, with works in Bleeding Heart Yard, but, embarking the firm's money in one of Merdle's schemes, lost it all. Meanwhile, Doyce had taken his invention abroad and sold it to advantage. He returned to clear Clennam from the difficulties which had landed him in the Marshalsea, and reinstated him in his position. *Dorrit*, I, 10, 12, 16, 17, 23, 26, 28, 34 ; II, 8, 13, 22, 26, 33, 34.

**DOYLANCE, OLD.** Master B.'s former schoolmaster. *Haunted House.*

**DOZE, PROFESSOR.** A member of the Mudfog Association.

**DRAWLEY, MR.** A member of the Mudfog Association.

**DRINGWORTH BROS.** A firm in America Square, London, with whom Lawrence Clissold was a clerk. *Message from the Sea.*

**DROOCE, SERGEANT.** "The most tyrannical non-commissioned officer in Her Majesty's service." He was a sergeant of Marines on the *Christopher Columbus* Sloop, and by his stern discipline helped to organise resistance to the pirates. *English Prisoners.*

**DROOD, EDWIN.** The title character of the unfinished novel. He was the nephew of John Jasper, and by a condition of his father's will was betrothed to Rosa Bud, a schoolgirl at the Nun's House. They did not love each other, but were prepared to carry out the destiny marked out for them when the arrival of the Landless brother and sister created a new situation. Neville Landless was obviously attracted by Rosa and deeply resented the air of proprietorship adopted by Edwin Drood. This led to a quarrel, fomented by Jasper, but the young men agreed to a reconciliation. On the day this was to take place Edwin and Rosa came to the understanding that they would consider their betrothal at an end, and remain brother and sister. They gave one another a final kiss, which was observed by Jasper, and parted. Shortly afterwards Edwin disappeared and was never seen again, though his watch was found in the river. *Drood*, 2, 3, 7–11, 13–16, 19, 23.

**DROWVEY, MISS.** Miss Grimmer's partner in the girls' school. *Holiday Romance.*

**DRUMMLE, BENTLEY.** Pip's fellow-pupil at Matthew Pocket's, and, from the first his tacit enemy. Mr. Jaggers found him an interesting criminal study and called him the Spider. Estella married him for the sake of his position and wealth, but he beat and otherwise ill-used her, at last meeting his death by kicks from a horse he had cruelly used. *Expectations*, 23, 25, 26, 34, 38, 43, 44, 48, 59.

**DRUMMOND, MISS R. M.** Original of Miss La Creevy. (*q.v.*)

**DRUNKARD, THE.** Subject of the last tale of *Boz*, entitled *The Drunkard's Death.*

**DRURY LANE.** The squalid district, centring round this street, made famous by its theatre, naturally occasions passing mention in almost any story relating to London. Such references will be found in *Boz, Scenes*, 11, 21–23 ; *Characters*, 10 ; *Uncommercial*, 4, 10, 23, 35. Dick Swiveller lodged over a tobacconist's shop in the neighbourhood (*Curiosity Shop*, 7, 8). David Copperfield occasionally patronised a famous *à la mode* beef house in the vicinity (*Copperfield*, 11). This was in Clare Court, opening out of the Lane, which vanished in the making of Aldwych, 1905. Kean Street is approximately on its site.

**DUBBLEY.** Grummer's second-in-command in the hazardous undertaking of the arrest of Mr. Pickwick at Ipswich. *Pickwick*, 24, 25.

**DUBLIN.** The chief mention of the Irish capital is in connection with Mr. Frederick O'Bleary, who never allowed Ireland to be outdone on any point, and could always match London with something better in Dublin, even if it were only a broken chimney pot. *Boz, Tales, Boarding House.*

**DUCROW.** Andrew Ducrow (1793–1842) was an equestrian performer and mimic. In 1808 he was chief equestrian and rope dancer at Astley's, and five years later became famous in pantomime. He toured the Continent for a time and then returned to Astley's, of which, in the 20's, he took over the management. The total destruction of the amphitheatre by fire in June 8, 1841, so affected him that he went out of his mind and died, January 27, 1842. *Boz, Scenes*, 11, 15.

**DUFF.** A Bow Street runner and colleague of Blathers in the investigation of the attempted burglary at Mrs. Maylie's house. *Twist*, 31.

**DUKE STREET.** 1. Over a livery stable in this quiet street off Piccadilly lived Mr. Twemlow. *Mutual Friend*, I, 2.

2. In Duke Street, Lincoln's Inn Fields, stood the Sardinian Chapel which was destroyed by the Gordon Rioters. Duke Street exists no longer ; it opened out of the west side of the Fields under a gloomy archway and extended into Great Wild Street. The cutting of Kingsway has entirely altered the topography of this part. *Barnaby*, 50.

**DULL.** Vice-President of the Umbugology and Ditchwateristics section of the Mudfog Association.

**DULLBOROUGH.** In the description of this town the *Uncommercial Traveller* (12) gives a vivid description of Chatham.

**DULWICH.** This was the village honoured by Mr. Pickwick with his last residence. "It has a large garden and is situated in one of the most pleasant spots near London." Dulwich village is little altered since that time, but there is no identifying Mr. Pickwick's house, for, according to Charles Dickens, Junior, his father had no particular place in his mind when settling Mr. Pickwick there. *Pickwick*, 57.

**DUMBLEDON.** "An idiotic goggle-eyed boy with a big head and half-crowns without end, who suddenly appeared as a parlour boarder." *Reprinted, Our School.*

**DUMKINS.** One of the most renowned members of the All-Muggleton Cricket Club, eventually caught out after a fine innings. *Pickwick*, 7.

**DUMMINS.** An "out and out" individual described in *Sketches of Gentlemen.*

**DUMMY.** A member of the Mudfog Association.

**DUMPS, NICODEMUS.** "A bachelor; six feet high, and fifty years old; cross, cadaverous, odd and ill-natured. He was never happy but when he was miserable; and always miserable when he had the best reason to be happy." He was Charles Kitterbell's uncle, and reluctantly agreed to be godfather to young Master Kitterbell. On his way to the christening his pocket was picked of the mug which he was presenting to his godchild. *Boz, Tales, Christening.*

**DUNCHURCH.** This is on the main Birmingham to London road, some 11 miles beyond Coventry. Here Mr. Pickwick and his friends, Ben Allen and Bob Sawyer, obtained a dry postboy and fresh horses. *Pickwick*, 51.

**DUNDEY, DOCTOR.** An Irish bank robber who escaped to America. *Reprinted, Detective Police.*

**DUNKLE, DOCTOR GINERY.** A shrill boy and the self-appointed spokesman of the committee which welcomed Elijah Pogram. *Chuzzlewit*, 34.

**DUNSTABLE.** The butcher in Pip's village. *Expectations*, 4.

**DUNSTABLE.** Pancks despatched Mr. Rugg thither to interview an old seafaring man about one of the clues relating to the Dorrit legacy. *Dorrit*, I, 25.

**DURDLES.** A drunken stonemason at Cloisterham who spent most of his time in tapping the cathedral walls to find concealed recesses containing ancient tombs. He was employed by John Jasper to show him some of the secret nooks of the old building, and was no doubt destined to play a more important part in the development of the story. *Drood*, 4, 5, 12, 14, 18.

**DURHAM.** John Chivery went to Durham to see a parish clerk who held one of the clues in the Dorrit claim to a fortune. *Dorrit*, I, 25.

**DUST.** One of Miss Flite's captive birds. *Bleak House*, 14.

**DUSTMAN, THE GOLDEN.** This was the nickname commonly applied to Mr. Boffin. (*q.v.*)

**E**

**EAGLE, THE.** This famous tavern in the City Road was one of the ancestors of the modern music-hall. A good entertainment was provided, in what was later known as the Grecian Saloon, and it was famous for its comic singers. Miss Jemima Ivins and her friend were taken there by their respective swains. *Boz, Characters*, 4.

**EATANSWILL.** There is probably no identification which has aroused so much controversy as that of Eatanswill (eat an' swill). Ipswich, Bury St. Edmunds and Norwich have been named as its prototypes, but there can be little doubt that Sudbury was the town Dickens had in his mind. He had been present at an election there, July 25–26, 1834, and doubtless thus obtained his impressions of the place. *Pickwick*, 13.

**EATANSWILL NEWSPAPERS.** The two great political parties, Blues and Buffs, had each their newspaper, the *Gazette* and the *Independent* respectively. "Fine newspapers they were. Such leading articles, and such spirited attacks! 'Our worthless contemporary, the *Gazette*'—'That disgraceful and dastardly journal, the *Independent*'— 'That vile and slanderous calumniator, the *Gazette*.'" The *Gazette* was edited by Mr. Pott, the *Independent* by Mr. Slurk, and these worthies came to fisticuffs in the kitchen of the Saracen's Head, Towcester. *Pickwick*, 13–15, 18, 51.

**EATON SOCON.** Original of Eton Slocomb (*q.v.*). It was formerly suggested by a few Dickensians that this was the original of Eatanswill, but this view has now been abandoned.

**EATON SQUARE.** Boz took a walk round Eaton Square when it was building, and to his surprise found that bells were replacing knockers on the front doors. *Boz, Our Parish*, 7.

**EDDARD.** The intelligent donkey who knew Mr. Boffin and Harmony Jail. *Mutual Friend*, I, 5.

**EDEN.** This was "the flourishing city . . . with banks, churches, cathedrals, market-place" in which Martin Chuzzlewit was persuaded to buy land, only to find, on arriving there, that it was "choked with slime and matted growth," merely a dismal swamp. The original of this was Cairo, Illinois, since become the ideal city foreseen by Mr. Scadder! *Chuzzlewit*, 21–3, 33, 34.

**EDGWARE ROAD.** In the neighbourhood of the Edgware Road, at that time entirely residential, lived Miss Cecilia Bobster, the young lady with whom Newman Noggs arranged an interview for Nicholas, mistaking her for Madeleine Bray. *Nickleby*, 40.

**EDINBURGH.** Dickens went to Edinburgh in 1834 as a reporter for the *Morning Chronicle*, proceeding thither by sea to Leith. He subsequently visited the city in 1841, 1858, 1861 and 1868, the last three occasions being connected with readings. His impressions of Edinburgh in 1834 enabled him to place there the scene of the story of the Bagman's Uncle. *Pickwick*, 49.

**EDKINS.** One of the steam excursion party, " a pale young gentleman in a green stock and spectacles of the same, a member of the Honourable Society of the Inner Temple." *Boz, Tales, Excursion.*

**EDMUNDS.** 1. John Edmunds was the subject of the Dingley Dell clergyman's story of *The Returned Convict*. *Pickwick*, 6.

2. George Edmunds was a character in the play of *The Village Coquettes*.

**EDSON.** A lodger at Mrs. Lirriper's who, after a few months of married life, deserted his wife. Years later Mrs. Lirriper was informed that she was wanted at Sens, in France. She went there with Major Jackman and their adopted son, and there found Edson on his death-bed.

His wife, Peggy, broken-hearted at his desertion and shortly expecting a child, was prevented from drowning herself by Mrs. Lirriper. She died, however, in giving birth to a little son, who was adopted by Mrs. Lirriper. *Lirriper's Lodgings and Legacy.*

**EDWARD.** The husband of Charlotte and one of the Contradictory Couple. *Sketches of Couples.*

**EDWARDS, MISS.** A pupil teacher in Miss Monflathers's establishment. " Being motherless and poor she was apprenticed at the school—taught for nothing—teaching others what she learnt, for nothing—boarded for nothing—and rated as something immeasurably less than nothing." *Curiosity Shop*, 31, 32.

**EDWIN.** Charley's schoolfellow and supposed rival in the affections of Angela. He appeared at the *Holly Tree Inn* on his way to Gretna Green with Emmeline, Angela's cousin.

**EDWIN DROOD.** This, the last and unfinished work of Dickens was begun at Gad's Hill in the autumn of 1869, and he was working on it during the afternoon of his last day of consciousness, Wednesday, June 8, 1870. The next evening he died. The book was to have appeared in twelve monthly parts, of which the first was published April 1, 1870. The third appeared a few days before his death, but there were three parts in MS., thus completing half the novel. Dickens left no clue as to what his intentions were with regard to the plot.

*Principal Characters.* Edwin Drood ; his uncle, John Jasper ; Edwin's betrothed bride, Rosa Bud ; Neville and Helena Landless ; Septimus Crisparkle, a Minor Canon ; Mr. Grewgious, Rosa's trustee ; Mr. Sapsea, Mayor of Cloisterham ; Durdles, a stonemason ; Datchery, a mysterious visitor to the city ; Miss Twinkleton, Rosa's schoolmistress and friend.

John Jasper, Edwin Drood's uncle and

guardian, is choirmaster at Cloisterham, and secretly an opium eater. Another secret of his life is his passionate love for Rosa Bud, his nephew's affianced bride. When Helena Landless and her brother Neville come to Cloisterham, the latter deeply resents the air of proprietorship which Edwin adopts towards Rosa, with the result that the two young men quarrel, while John Jasper, pretending to be a peacemaker, fans their ill-feeling to furnace heat. On the intervention of Crisparkle Edwin and Neville agree to a reconciliation and meet at Jasper's rooms on Christmas Eve. Meanwhile, unknown to Jasper, Edwin and Rosa have come to an understanding that henceforward they will be only brother and sister. After the meeting of Edwin and Neville at Jasper's rooms, the former disappears and Neville is arrested on suspicion of having murdered him. He is, however, released for want of evidence and goes with his sister to London. To escape Jasper's attention Rosa also flies to London and takes refuge with her lawyer, old Mr. Grewgious, who establishes her and Miss Twinkleton, who has followed from Cloisterham, in rooms with Mrs. Billickin. With the advent of two new characters, Lieutenant Tartar, and Datchery, the unsolved riddle of the plot is further complicated.

**EFFORT.** " Make an effort ! " This was Mrs. Chick's sovereign cure for the ills of life. She attributed the first Mrs. Dombey's death to her failure to make an effort, and considered her brother's domestic and business misfortunes arose from the same cause. *Dombey*, 1, 60.

**EGG-HOT.** This is another name for Egg Flip. A contemporary recipe for making it is : Make warm 1 pint of ale. Beat 2 or 3 eggs with 3 oz. sugar. Throw the eggs into a jug containing the ale and then throw all back into an empty jug. Do this 5 or 6 times until the whole is thoroughly mixed, then grate ginger and nutmeg over the top. *Copperfield*, 11.

**EGHAM.** At Egham races Chops the Dwarf learned that he had drawn a lottery prize of twelve thousand pounds. *Going into Society.*

**ELEPHANT AND CASTLE INN.** One of the best known taverns in London, this inn finds surprisingly little mention by Dickens. The Bagnets lived in " a street of little shops, lying somewhere in that ganglion of roads from Kent and Surrey, and of streets from the bridges of London, centring in the farfamed Elephant who has lost his castle formed of a thousand four-horse coaches, to a stronger iron monster than he." *Bleak House*, 27.

**ELIZABETH, MISS.** One of the inmates of what Mr. Wegg called Our House. " He knew so little about them that he gave them names of his own invention, as Miss Elizabeth, Master George, Aunt Jane, Uncle Parker; having no authority whatever for any such designations." *Mutual Friend*, I, 5; II, 7, 10; III, 6, 7; IV, 1, 14.

**"ELIZABETH, OR THE EXILES OF SIBERIA."** A once popular story founded on fact, translated from the French of Madame S. Cottin. *Reprinted, Christmas Tree.*

**ELLIS.** 1. "A sharp-nosed, light-haired man, in a brown surtout reaching nearly to his heels," who formed one of the company in the City Road public-house. *Boz, Characters,* 5.

2. Original of Perker. (*q.v.*)

**ELTON, MISS ESTHER.** Original of Esther Summerson. (*q.v.*)

**ELWES.** John Elwes, the miser whose life Mr. Boffin professed to read with such enjoyment, was one of the least offensive of this class of human beings. He was born in 1714 and succeeded to a much encumbered estate in Suffolk which, by dint of almost incredible self-sacrifice and penury, he not only cleared, but, on his death in 1789, left a fortune of over £500,000. He was good-hearted, honest and kindly to all but himself, a character rare enough under the circumstances. *Mutual Friend*, III, 5.

**ELY PLACE.** This quiet backwater of City life is little changed since Mr. Waterbrook lived there. In those days it turned off Holborn Hill (the third turning on the right, going up from Farringdon Street) and was largely a residence of lawyers. Thither David Copperfield went to make his excuses to Agnes after his drunken behaviour at the theatre. *Copperfield*, 25.

**EMANUEL CHAPEL.** The place of worship at Dorking where Mr. Stiggins helped to officiate. *Pickwick*, 22, 27, 52.

**EMILE.** One of the soldiers in the French town, billeted upon the clockmaker. *Somebody's Luggage.*

**EMILIA.** Mrs. Orange's baby, with eight teeth. *Holiday Romance.*

**EMILY.** One of the girls removed in the prison van. *Boz, Characters*, 12.

**EM'LY, LITTLE.** Peggotty's orphan niece who lived with him in the boat on Yarmouth beach. When she grew up she became a seamstress at Omer's shop and was engaged to marry her cousin Ham, but in an evil day David took Steerforth down to Yarmouth, and, on the eve of her marriage, Little Em'ly eloped with him. After her disappearance Daniel Peggotty gave up his home and devoted his whole life to finding his niece. After a long search Little Em'ly was discovered by Martha Endell and restored to her uncle. It appeared that Steerforth had taken her abroad and, tiring of her after a while, had suggested passing her on to his servant Littimer. Em'ly had indignantly refused this, and with great difficulty had made her way back to England. Having found his lost niece, Peggotty

emigrated to Australia with her, Mrs. Gummidge, and Martha. *Copperfield*, 3, 7, 10, 17, 21–3, 30, 31, 40, 46, 47, 50, 51, 55, 57, 63.

**EMMA.** 1. One of the buxom maidservants at the Manor Farm, Dingley Dell. *Pickwick*, 5, 8, 9, 11, 28.

2. A waitress at an Angler's Inn. *Holly Tree.*

**EMMELINE.** The cousin of Angela Leath, "She was wrapped in snow-white fur, like the snowy landscape, but was warm and young and lovely." She eloped with Charley's friend Edwin. *Holly Tree.*

**ENCYCLOPAEDIA BRITANNICA.** The first edition of this appeared in 1771. Mr. Pott's assistant probably studied Chinese metaphysics in the 6th edition of 1824. *Pickwick*, 51.

**ENDELL, MARTHA.** An unfortunate girl who at one time worked at Omer's shop and had been a friend of Little Em'ly. Disgraced in Yarmouth, she went to London, where she helped Peggotty in his search for Em'ly. It was Martha who found the girl, and gave her shelter. She emigrated with Peggotty and his family, and married a farm labourer. *Copperfield*, 22, 40, 46, 47, 50, 51, 57, 63.

**EPPING FOREST.** Chigwell stands on the edge of the forest, hence some of the action of *Barnaby* takes place in the vicinity. One of the old inmates of Titbull's Almshouses was taken to Epping for a day's outing (*Uncommercial*, 27), and the young ladies' young gentleman was the principal figure at a picnic there. *Sketches of Gentleman.*

**EPSOM.** It was at Epsom races that Abel Magwitch first met Compeyson (*Expectations*, 42). One Derby Day Inspector Wield and Sergeant Witchem went down to Epsom on the track of the Swell Mob. *Reprinted, Three Detective Stories.*

**ESAU SLODGE.** The large river steamer which carried Martin's appeal for help to Mr. Bevan. *Chuzzlewit*, 33.

**ESSEX STREET, STRAND.** Pip found a lodging for Magwitch in a house on the left-hand side going down from the Strand. *Expectations*, 40.

**ESTELLA.** Miss Havisham's adopted daughter and a beautiful girl whom that eccentric woman brought up to hate and break the hearts of all the men she met. As a girl Estella treated Pip cruelly, jeering at his ignorance and poverty. But even then Pip loved her and when, as a young man with "great expectations," he met her again his love grew deeper and truer. She married Bentley Drummle for his money and position, and lived a life of misery with him—ill-treated and neglected—until they were separated. Some time after her husband's death Pip again on the spot where Satis House used to stand, and there the sorrows of the past were forgotten and there was "no shadow of another parting from her." During the course of the story

Pip discovered that Estella was really the daughter of Magwitch the convict, her mother being Jaggers's servant, Molly. *Expectations*, 7, 8, 11–15, 22, 29, 30, 32, 33, 38, 44, 48–51, 56, 59.

**ETON SLOCOMB.** This is a thin disguise for Eaton Socon, about 10 miles north of Biggleswade on the Great North Road. At Eton Slocomb Nicholas and his fellow-travellers stopped for a good coach dinner. *Nickleby*, 5.

**EUGENE.** A soldier billeted at the Tinman's. *Somebody's Luggage*.

**EUSTACE, MR.** John Chetwode Eustace (d. 1815) was a classical scholar of some repute who, among other books, wrote *A Tour through Italy, exhibiting a View of its Scenery, Antiquities and Monuments*, 1813. This was the book upon which Mrs. General founded her opinions. *Dorrit*, II, 5, 7, 15.

**EUSTON.** Euston Square had no huge railway terminus when Miss Amelia Martin lived at No. 47 Drummond Street, George Street. Drummond Street runs in front of the gigantic entrance archway. Euston Station was the first railway terminus in London, dating from 1838. *Boz, Characters*, 8.

**EVANS.** 1. Miss Jemima Evans, " or Ivins, to adopt the pronunciation most in vogue with her circle of acquaintance," was the heroine of the scene at the Eagle, City Road, in which Mr. Samuel Wilkins and his friend had a fight with a gentleman in a plaid waistcoat. *Boz, Characters*, 4.

2. "A tall, thin, pale young gentleman with extensive whiskers . . . pronounced by all his lady friends to be a dear," who played Roderigo in the Gattleton's theatricals. *Boz, Tales, Porter*.

3. Richard Evans was one of Mr. Marton's pupils. *Curiosity Shop*, 52.

4. Superintendant Evans was a former Thames Police officer. *Reprinted, Down with the Tide*.

**"EVENING BELLS."** Julia Mills might have sung either Moore's "Those evening Bells " or a somewhat doleful song by Alexander Lee, beginning :—

Come away, come away, evening bells are ringing
Sweetly, sweetly, 'tis the vesper hour.
*Copperfield*, 38.

**EVENSON, JOHN.** A boarder at Mrs. Tibbs's house, " very morose and discontented. He was a thorough radical and used to attend a great variety of public meetings, for the express purpose of finding fault with everything that was proposed." *Boz, Tales, Boarding House*.

**EVERARD, DR.** Original of Doctor Blimber. (*q.v.*)

**EXCHEQUER COFFEE HOUSE.** This was the address given by Harmon, as Julius Handford. The coffee house was at the N.W. angle of Westminster Hall, in New Palace Yard, and was originally called Oliver's Coffee House. *Mutual Friend*, I, 3 ; II, 13.

**EXETER.** The chief interest in Exeter for us lies in the fact that Mrs. Wittitterley danced with the baronet's nephew at an election ball at Exeter (*Nickleby*, 21). Doctor Marigold's wife drowned herself in the river Exe. *Doctor Marigold*.

**EXETER CHANGE.** This building, demolished in 1829, stood on the north side of the Strand, almost opposite Wellington Street. It was for many years a menagerie, the roar of the lions sometimes alarming the horse traffic in the Strand. *Boz, Characters*, 1.

**EXETER HALL, STRAND,** was built in 1830–31 and was long a centre for religious meetings, attended, according to Miss La Creevy, by all sorts of people with flat noses (*Nickleby*, 5). It was demolished in 1907 and the Strand Palace Hotel built on its site.

**EZEKIEL.** The actual name of the Boy at Mugby. (*q.v.*)

## F

**F., MR.** This was the abbreviation invariably used by Flora Finching when speaking of her late husband. *See* Finching.

**FACE-MAKER, THE.** " A corpulent little man in a large red waistcoat," who impersonated various characters in one of the booths at a Flemish country fair. *Uncommercial*, 25.

**FAGIN.** The receiver of stolen goods and master thief into whose hands Oliver Twist fell on coming to London. Bribed by Monks and perceiving in the child's innocence and good looks a valuable asset to his vile trade, Fagin determined to make Oliver a pickpocket. Though unsuccessful in this, he lent him to Bill Sikes to assist in carrying out a burglary. This failed and Oliver was left in the hands of Mrs. Maylie and Mr. Brownlow. Fagin's suspicions were aroused by Nancy's secret meetings with Mr. Brownlow, and he told Sikes that the girl was turning informer, thus being largely responsible for her murder. The crime broke up the gang, but Fagin would have escaped had it not been for Noah Claypole's turning evidence against him. He was arrested, tried, condemned to death and hung, raving and shrieking for mercy. The name was taken from Bob Fagin, one of Dickens's fellow-slaves in the blacking factory. *Twist*, 8–10, 12, 13, 15, 16, 18–20, 25, 26, 34, 39, 42–7, 50, 52.

**FAIR, THE.** The basement of the Fleet Prison was called the Fair, or Bartholomew Fair. This cellar floor was leased to a tapster who kept his stock of liquor there, and at the same time housed the very poorest of the debtors. *Pickwick*, 41.

**FAIRBURN'S COMIC SONGSTER.** There were a number of comic song books brought out by John Fairburn in the 20's–40's. Little Warblers were similar productions. *Reprinted, Out of Season*.

**FAIRFAX, MR.** The censorious young gentleman reputed to be " a remarkably clever person." *Sketches of Gentlemen.*

**"FALL OF PARIS."** This was a popular piano piece which appeared about 1822. *Boz, Tales, Sparkins.*

**FALSTAFF INN, GAD'S HILL.** Though not mentioned by name, this was probably the "little road-side public-house with two elm trees, a horse trough, and a sign-post in front," where Mr. Pickwick and his friends vainly sought help from the red-headed man after their spill on the way to Dingley Dell. The Falstaff stands opposite Gad's Hill Place. *Pickwick,* 5.

**FAN.** Scrooge's little sister " who always had a large heart." *Christmas Carol.*

**FANCHETTE.** The daughter of a Swiss innkeeper. *Reprinted, Our Bore.*

**FANG, MR.** The magistrate before whom Oliver Twist was haled on the charge of picking Mr. Brownlow's pocket. A rude and intolerable bully, whose court was a mere travesty of justice, he treated Mr. Brownlow with incredible insolence and sentenced Oliver to three months' hard labour without so much as knowing the facts of the case. When the bookstall-keeper made his appearance this sentence was annulled and the case dismissed, every ignominy being heaped upon Mr. Brownlow. The original of Fang was a Metropolitan magistrate named Allan Stewart Laing, of Hatton Garden Police Court. He was removed on account of the disgraceful manner in which he conducted his court. *Twist,* 11.

**FANNY.** A pretty little guest at the Christmas Party. *Reprinted, Child's Story.*

**"FARE THEE WELL."** A quotation from Lord Byron's well-known poem. *Curiosity Shop,* 58.

**FAREWAY.** The family in whose patronage was the living granted to George Silverman. Lady Fareway, a managing woman, presented Silverman to the living on condition that he acted as tutor to her daughter, Adelina. For officiating at this girl's secret wedding to Granville Wharton, Lady Fareway demanded Silverman's resignation. *George Silverman.*

**FARM-HOUSE, THE OLD.** A common lodging house in the Borough, visited by Dickens and Inspector Field. " It is the old Manor House of these parts and stood in the country once." Its remains are in Harrow Street, Marshalsea Road. *Reprinted, Inspector Field.*

**FARRINGDON STREET.** Until 1829 this street was largely occupied by the Fleet Market (*q.v.*), and until the late 40's did not extend further than the corners of Snow and Holborn Hills, the continuation, now called the Farringdon Road, being made about 1848 and originally christened Victoria Street. The Gordon Rioters made Fleet Market a convenient camping ground

(*Barnaby,* 60). The Fleet Prison stood on the east side of the street on the site now partly occupied by the Memorial Hall, the painted ground abutting on the street itself (*Pickwick,* 41). The Fleet Prison was jocularly known as the Farringdon Hotel.

**FASCINATION FLEDGEBY.** Sobriquet of Fledgeby. (*q.v.*)

**FAT BOY, THE.** Mr. Wardle's remarkable servant. *See* Joe.

**FATHER OF THE MARSHALSEA.** The name proudly accepted in the prison by Mr. William Dorrit. (*q.v.*)

**FAUCIT, MISS HELENA.** A famous English actress who made her debut at Covent Garden in 1836, and next year became Macready's leading lady. She married Sir Theodore Martin in 1851. Miss Faucit died in 1898. *Sketches of Gentlemen* (*Theatrical*).

**FEE, DR. W. R.** A member of the medical section of the Mudfog Association.

**FEEDER, B. A.** Dr. Blimber's assistant, " a kind of human barrel organ, with a little list of tunes at which he was continually working over and over again." He had a kindly nature and was good to little Paul Dombey. He finally realised his ambition and succeeded to Dr. Blimber's school and to the hand of his daughter, Cornelia, to whom he was married by his brother, the Rev. Alfred Feeder. *Dombey,* 11, 12, 14, 41, 60.

**FEENIX, LORD.** Generally known as Cousin Feenix, he had been " a man about town forty years ago," and still retained a youthful air. He had a way of mentioning in his conversation all sorts of society people with whom he presumed his hearers to be acquainted. After her flight from Mr. Dombey, Cousin Feenix gave Edith shelter in his town house. *Dombey,* 21, 31, 36, 41, 51, 61.

**FENCHURCH STREET.** It was at the corner of Fenchurch Street and Mincing Lane that Bella Wilfer waited in the great Boffin equipage for her father, when she visited him in the City. *Mutual Friend,* II, 8.

**FENDALL, SERGEANT.** " A prodigious hand at pursuing private inquiries of a delicate nature." This is clearly meant for Inspector Edward Kendall, a well-known detective of the 50's. *Reprinted, Detective Police.*

**FERDINAND, MISS.** A high-spirited girl at Miss Twinkleton's school. *Drood,* 9, 13.

**"FERGUSON!"** This was a curious slang expression in the 30's–50's. " It's all very well, Mr. Ferguson, but—you can't come here, or you mustn't do that," or similar prohibitions was the original formula. " Ferguson " was the name given by the young bloods when they were haled before the magistrate for upsetting watchmen, wrenching off knockers or other deeds at that time considered the height of humour. *Nickleby,* 2.

"**FERGUSON'S FIRST.**" This is a somewhat obscure remark, but it probably refers to a clock made by the Scottish astronomer, J. Ferguson (1710–76). This instrument had wooden wheels and was something of a marvel in its day. *Boz, Scenes*, 23.

**FERN, WILL.** A poor man who came to London seeking work, bringing with him his niece, Lilian. Being found asleep in a shed, he was taken before Alderman Cute, who determined to "put him down." Trotty Veck gave the couple shelter and they played a part in his New Year vision. It turned out that they were relatives of Mrs. Chickenstalker, who took them into her charge. *Chimes*.

**FEROCE.** A polite bathing machine proprietor at *Our French Watering Place*. *Reprinted Pieces*.

**FETTER LANE.** This was the residence of Mr. Augustus Cooper, the victim of the Billsmethis' wiles. *Boz, Characters*, 9.

**FEZZIWIG.** Scrooge's old master when he was an apprentice. He was "an old gentleman in a Welsh wig," and Christmas Past conjured up before Scrooge's eyes a jolly Christmas when he was but a simple, good-hearted lad, and old Fezziwig gave a dance to his family and servants. "In came Mrs. Fezziwig, one vast, substantial smile. In came the three Miss Fezziwigs, beaming and lovable." This scene is one of the most delightful incidents of the *Christmas Carol*.

**FIBBITSON, MRS.** An old inmate in the almshouse where Mrs. Mell lived. *Copperfield*, 5.

**FIELD, INSPECTOR.** This was Charles F. Field, who was promoted to inspector in the R Division (Greenwich) in 1833 and subsequently became a well-known member of the Detective Force. Under the name of Charley Wield some of his adventures are related in *Reprinted, Detective Police* and *Three Detective Anecdotes*. He conducted Dickens through some of the worst London slums, vividly described in *Reprinted, Inspector Field*. He was the original of Inspector Bucket (*q.v.*), though he had nothing to do with the Manning Case.

**FIELDING.** 1. Sir John was a well-known magistrate who was blind from birth. He succeeded his half-brother, Henry Fielding the novelist, as magistrate at Bow Street in 1754 and administered justice there until his death, September 4, 1780. He was an energetic, capable magistrate of whom it was said that he knew three thousand thieves by their voices alone. *Barnaby*, 58, 66.

2. Emma, the young lady engaged to that "angel of a gentleman," Mr. Harvey. *Sketches of Couples*.

3. May, a pretty young girl who, after the long absence of her lover, Edward Plummer, agreed to marry the surly old curmudgeon Tackleton. When Edward returned in disguise Dot Peerybingle brought about the reunion of the lovers. *Cricket on the Hearth*.

**FIELD LANE.** That portion of Great Saffron Hill lying between Charles Street and Holborn was formerly called Field Lane, and was one of the most disreputable slums of London. It was demolished with the construction of Holborn Viaduct in 1863–69. The place is well described in *Twist*, 26.

**FIERCY, HON. CAPTAIN FITZWHISKER.** A blustering, swaggering swindler who aped the airs of a military man and duped his tradesmen. *Pantomime of Life*.

**FIERY-FACE.** Name given to John Westlock's charwoman, "a fiery-faced matron in a crunched bonnet." *Chuzzlewit*, 45, 53.

**FIKEY.** A forger who was arrested by Inspector Wield. *Reprinted, Detective Police*.

**FILER.** A friend of Alderman Cute—"a low-spirited gentleman of middle age, of a meagre habit, and a disconsolate face, who was a great man for statistics and much upset at the improvidence of the poor." *Chimes*.

**FILLETOVILLE, MARQUESS OF.** Father of the young man in sky blue who abducted the lady rescued by the Bagman's Uncle. *Pickwick*, 49.

**FINCHBURY, LADY JANE.** "Woman with tight stays" and, according to Cousin Feenix, something of an artist. *Dombey*, 41.

**FINCHES OF THE GROVE.** A club to which Herbert Pocket, Pip, Startop and Drummle belonged. Its only apparent object was that members should dine expensively once a fortnight in a Covent Garden hotel (Hummums) and quarrel amongst themselves as much as possible after dinner. *Expectations*, 34, 38.

**FINCHING, FLORA.** The daughter of Christopher Casby and the object of Arthur Clennam's boyish affections. She married Mr. Finching (always referred to as Mr. F.), and when he came back from China Arthur found that "Flora, always tall, had grown to be very broad, too, and short of breath; but that was not much. Flora, who had seemed enchanting in all she said and thought, was diffuse and silly. That was much. Flora who had been spoiled and, artless long ago, was determined to be spoiled and artless now. That was a fatal blow." Despite her incoherence and inconsequence, Flora was a good-hearted, kind woman, with a very tender place in her heart for her old lover. For his sake she befriended Little Dorrit, and there was something very touching in her final resignation of all hopes of winning back Arthur's love. Flora Finching was Dora Spenlow grown older—both characters being founded on Maria Beadnell, the description of Flora being written after Dickens had met his first love in after years, when she was Mrs. Winter. *Dorrit*, I, 13, 23, 24, 35; II, 9, 17, 23, 34.

**FINCHING, MRS.** One of the Bobtail Widgers' friends. *Sketches of Couples.*

**FINCHLEY.** While writing *Martin Chuzzlewit* (1843) Dickens lodged for a time in Finchley, and there conceived the idea of Mrs. Gamp. The Garlands lived in Abel Cottage, "a beautiful little cottage with a thatched roof and little spires at the gable ends and pieces of stained glass in some of the windows" (*Curiosity Shop*, 21, 22). After the burning of Newgate, Barnaby Rudge and his father made their way out to a deserted shed in the fields near Finchley (*Barnaby*, 68). A less tragic connection with the Finchley fields is Mr. Toots, who went "to get some uncommonly fine chickweed that grows there, for Miss Dombey's bird." *Dombey*, 32.

**FIPS, MR.** The solicitor of Austin Friars who was employed by old Martin Chuzzlewit to befriend Tom Pinch by giving him some books to arrange. *Chuzzlewit*, 39, 40, 53.

**FISH.** "A not very stately gentleman in black," who was Sir Joseph Bowley's confidential secretary. *Chimes.*

**FISHER, MR. AND MRS.** Residents on Silver Store Island. The husband was one of the defenders of the fort ; his wife, who had been Fanny Venning, was "a fair, slight thing . . . quite a child she looked, with a little copy of herself holding to her dress." *English Prisoners.*

**FITHERS, MR.** An artist friend of the Bobtail Widgers. *Sketches of Couples.*

**FITZ BALL, EDWARD.** (1792–1873.) A well-known dramatist of his time who wrote many plays and supplied librettos to a good many operas. *Sketches of Gentlemen (Theatrical).*

**FITZBINKLE, LORD AND LADY.** Patrons of the Indigent Orphans' Friends' Benevolent Society. *Boz, Scenes,* 19.

**FITZ-MARSHALL, CAPTAIN CHARLES.** The name adopted by Jingle at Eatanswill and Ipswich. *Pickwick,* 15, 25.

**FITZ-OSBORNE.** Mr. Flamwell thought that possibly the mysterious Horatio Sparkins was the Honourable Augustus Fitz-Edward Fitz-John Fitz-Osborne living under disguise. *Boz, Tales, Sparkins.*

**FIXEM.** A broker who employed Bung before that worthy became parish beadle. *Boz, Our Parish,* 5.

**FIZKIN, HORATIO.** The Buff candidate for Eatanswill defeated by the Hon. Samuel Slumkey. *Pickwick,* 13, 18.

**FIZZGIG, DON BOLARO.** A grandee of Spain, whose only daughter, Donna Christina, fell a victim to Jingle's charms. After his daughter's death from the use of a stomach pump, Don Bolaro disappeared and was eventually found in the public fountain in the great square "with a full confession in his right boot." *Pickwick,* 2.

**FLABELLA, LADY.** A character in a fashionable novel read aloud by Kate Nickleby to Mrs. Wittitterley. *Nickleby,* 28.

**FLADDOCK, GENERAL.** A fellow passenger of Martin Chuzzlewit in the *Screw* and a friend of the Norrises. *Chuzzlewit,* 15, 17.

**FLAM, HON. SPARKINS.** A friend of Squire Norton and an admirer of Rose, one of *The Village Coquettes.*

**FLAMWELL.** A friend of the Maldertons ; "one of those gentlemen of remarkably extensive information, whom one occasionally meets in society, who pretend to know everybody, but in reality know nobody." *Boz, Tales, Sparkins.*

**FLANDERS, SALLY.** An old servant, at the funeral of whose husband the Uncommercial Traveller was present when a child. *Uncommercial,* 26.

**FLASHER, WILKINS.** A stockbroker who transferred the stock left by the late Mrs. Weller to her relict. *Pickwick,* 55.

**FLEDGEBY, "FASCINATION."** A malicious, boorish young man who owned the moneylending business of Pubsey and Co., though it was ostensibly carried on by Riah the Jew. He promised Lammle a thousand pounds if he could arrange for him a match with Georgiana Podsnap. On Lammle's failure to do this he found himself at the moneylender's mercy, for Fledgeby had bought up many of his bills. Calling at his chambers at the Albany Lammle gave the young rogue a sound thrashing. Shortly afterwards Mortimer Lightwood got on Fledgeby's track and rescued Eugene Wrayburn, Twemlow and several others from his clutches. *Mutual Friend,* II, 4, 5, 16 ; III, 1, 12, 13, 17 ; IV, 8, 9, 16.

**FLEET MARKET.** When the Fleet River was converted into a sewer, it was bridged over at the part now called Farringdon Street, and the Fleet Market opened on the site. This was in 1737, and a market for meat, fish and vegetables it remained for many years, finally developing into a vegetable market only which, in 1829, was moved to one side in order to allow of the widening of Farringdon Street. The Market was finally closed in 1892, and Farringdon Avenue built on its site. The Gordon Rioters took shelter in the Fleet Market (*Barnaby*, 8, 60). Sam Weller related to Mr. Pickwick the story of the prisoner at the Fleet, "number twenty" who, looking out of the prison gates, had a sudden longing to go and see Fleet Market. *Pickwick,* 41.

**FLEET PRISON, THE.** This famous debtors' prison stood in Farringdon Street, between Fleet Lane and the corner of Ludgate Hill, part of its site being now occupied by the Memorial Hall. After its destruction in the Gordon Riots (*Barnaby*, 67) the prison was rebuilt and continued in use until 1842, when the debtors were removed to the Queen's Bench Prison. The Fleet was built in four floors, called Galleries, with a cellar floor, known as the Fair, or Bartholomew Fair. To the left of the entrance lodge was the Painted Ground, so called from crude paintings on the wall, separated from Farringdon Street by a high wall; behind the prison, now covered by the railway viaduct, was the Racket Ground. There is, however, little need to supplement the description of the prison given in *Pickwick*, 40–2, 44, 45, 47. In 1844 the building was purchased by the City Corporation and most of the materials sold; twenty years later it became the property of the L.C. and D. Rly., and the ruins were finally demolished. In 1874 the Memorial Hall was erected on part of the site.

**FLEET STREET.** Innumerable are the references in Dickens to this, the most famous and one of the most important of London thoroughfares. Considerable changes have taken place in the street in the last hundred years. Temple Bar, at the western extremity, was removed in 1878, and the Law Courts erected, 1874–82; old St. Dunstan's Church was replaced by the present edifice in 1831, the famous clock, with its giants which struck the hours, being removed to Lord Hertford's villa in Regent's Park, now the well-known Institution for the Blind. Most of the south side has been rebuilt, while Ludgate Circus, at the City end of Fleet Street, was made in 1864. The obelisk to Waithman, in the centre of the entrance to Farringdon Street, was erected on the site of his first shop, then the corner of Fleet Street and Fleet Market. Tellson's Bank, by Temple Bar, was Child's Bank, which stands on the same site, though the building is new (*Two Cities*, II, 1, 4, 14). On his way to relieve Mr. Watkins Tottle, Gabriel Parsons was held up by a block of the traffic in Fleet Street (*Boz*, *Tales*, *Tottle*). Down Fleet Street drove Mr. Pickwick and Perker in a hackney cab on their way to the Fleet Prison (*Pickwick*, 40), while a little later, when Sam Weller was escorted to the prison by a contingent of coachmen "some little commotion was occasioned in Fleet Street, by the pleasantry of the eight gentlemen . . . who persevered in walking four abreast" (43). At the corner of Middle Temple Lane and Fleet Street Mr. Fips met Tom Pinch and John Westlock, to instal the former in his new work (*Chuzzlewit*, 39). After his mysterious warning from Wemmick—"Don't go home"—Pip made his way from Whitefriars to Fleet Street and took a hackney coach to the Hummums in Covent Garden (*Expectations*, 45). In the broiling days of summer "Temple Bar got so hot that it was, to the adjacent Strand and Fleet Street, what a heater is in an urn, and kept them simmering all night" (*Bleak House*, 19). After instructing Mortimer Lightwood to offer a reward for discovery of the Harmon murderer, Mr. Boffin was jogging along Fleet Street when he became aware of being

followed by Rokesmith (*Mutual Friend*, I, 8). During the dreadful days at Murdstone's and Grinby's little David Copperfield used to look with longing eyes at a venison shop in Fleet Street (*Copperfield*, 11). In later days, when going with his aunt to be articled to Spenlow and Jorkins, David and she stood and watched the giants striking the time on St. Dunstan's clock (23), while when Peggotty came to London, among the other sights David took her to the "perspiring waxwork in Fleet Street." This was Mrs. Salmon's Waxwork, exhibited in the ancient building opposite Chancery Lane, now known as Prince Henry's Room (33). Lastly, Fleet Street at five o'clock on a winter morning is well described in the opening passages of *The Holly Tree Inn*.

**FLEETWOOD.** A family who went on the *Steam Excursion*. *Boz*, *Tales*.

**FLEMING, AGNES.** Oliver Twist's mother, a girl who had been seduced by Edwin Leeford, the father of Monks and an old friend of Mr. Brownlow. Leeford had wished to make some reparation for the wrong he had done her, but the confession he wrote and the money he bequeathed were kept by his wife, the mother of Monks. *Twist*, I, 49, 51, 53.

Agnes's sister, Rose, had been adopted as a child by Mrs. Maylie, who called her Rose Maylie. (*q.v.*)

**FLIGHT, A.** This little sketch of a trip to Paris by the express service of the South Eastern Railway first appeared in *Household Words*, August 30, 1851, and was published in *Reprinted Pieces*, 1858. This express service was run in connection with the Great Exhibition. It will be noticed that the South Eastern main line to Folkestone at that time ran through Croydon and Reigate.

**FLIMKINS, MR. AND MRS.** Actors in the Surrey Theatre melodramas. *Sketches of Gentlemen* (*Theatrical*).

**FLINTWINCH, JEREMIAH.** Mrs. Clennam's confidential clerk and partner. In his long service with Mrs. Clennam he had acquired an intimate knowledge of her private as well as her business affairs, and thus came to know of the suppressed legacy to Little Dorrit. When Arthur Clennam came back from China Flintwinch put the papers relating to this legacy in a box, which he entrusted to his brother Ephraim to carry out of the country. Rigaud obtained possession of this box and began to blackmail Mrs. Clennam. On the day the final settlement between Rigaud, Flintwinch and Mrs. Clennam was to have been made the Clennam house collapsed, and in the confusion Jeremiah made his escape to Holland (*Dorrit*, I, 3–5, 14, 15, 29, 30; II, 10, 17, 23, 28, 30, 31). Affery, Jeremiah's wife, was an old and trusted servant of the Clennam family and had been Arthur's nurse. When he returned he found her married to Jeremiah, through no wish of her own, but as the result of an arrangement between " the clever ones," as she called Mrs. Clennam and Jeremiah, whose doings kept her in a constant state of bewilderment. *Dorrit*, I, 3–5, 14, 15, 29, 30 ; II, 10, 17, 23, 30, 31.

**FLIP.** This was a compound of ale, beer, cider, etc., sweetened and spiced and heated, often by the immersion of a hot iron. *See also* Egg-Hot.

**FLIPFIELD.** One of the Uncommercial Traveller's friends whose birthday party is described in *Uncommercial*, 19.

**FLITE, MISS.** " A little mad old woman in a squeezed bonnet, who is always in court, from its sitting to its rising, and always expecting some incomprehensible judgment to be given in her favour." She took a liking to Esther and her friends, calling the former Fitz Jarndyce, and showed them her lodging at old Krooks, where she kept some captive birds, to be liberated when her judgment was given " on the day of Judgment." Upon the settlement of the Jarndyce case, she liberated her birds. The original of Miss Flite was a Miss Little-wood, who lived in Chichester Rents and laboured under delusions similar to those of the poor little Chancery victim. *Bleak House*, 1, 3, 5, 11, 14, 20, 23, 24, 33, 35, 45, 47, 50, 60, 65.

**FLOPSON.** One of Mrs. Pocket's maids who took charge of the children. *Great Expectations*, 22, 23.

**FLOWERPOT INN.** This was a well-known coaching house, and the starting-place of many of the East Anglian coaches. It stood near the junction of Threadneedle Street and Bishopsgate Street. Local coaches also ran from the inn, there being a half-hourly one to Stamford Hill, which Mr. Augustus Minns took to reach the Budden's villa. *Boz, Tales, Minns.*

**FLOWERS.** Mrs. Skewton's attendant, skilful in all the intricacies of that lady's wonderful make-up. *Dombey*, 27, 30, 36, 37, 40.

**" FLOW ON, THOU SHINING RIVER."** One of Moore's National Airs. *Boz, Tales, Boarding House.*

**FLUGGERS.** The elderly member of Mr. Crummles's theatrical party, who did the heavy business. *Nickleby*, 30.

**FLUMMERY.** A member of the Mudfog Association.

**" FLY, FLY FROM THE WORLD."** This is a song, words and music by Moore, beginning, " Fly from the world, O Bessy, to me." *Boz, Scenes*, 2.

**FLYING THE GARTER.** A street game based on jumping over a string which is being continually raised higher. *Pickwick*, 38.

**FOGG.** The more silent member of the firm of Dodson and Fogg, " an elderly, pimply-faced vegetable-diet sort of man in a black coat, dark mixture trousers, and small black gaiters." *See* Dodson and Fogg.

**FOLAIR, TOMMY OR AUGUSTUS.** A pantomimist and member of the Crummles company. He was of a malicious, spiteful turn of mind, carried Lenville's ridiculous challenge to Nicholas and was perfectly ready to turn against his friend when Nicholas showed his anger at the impertin-ence. *Nickleby*, 23–5, 29, 30.

**FOLEY.** A friend of Cousin Feenix, seen at Brighton riding a blood mare. *Dombey*, 41.

**FOLLY.** One of Miss Flite's captive birds. *Bleak House*, 14.

**FOLLY DITCH.** Jacob's Island and Folly Ditch have been cleaned up and rebuilt since the days of Oliver Twist. The ditch was filled in 1851. *Twist*, 50.

**FOOTMAN.** The principal unnamed domestics of this description are :—

1. The various members of the profession who attended the " swarry " at Bath. *Pickwick*, 37.

2. Mrs. Mantalini's liveried footman. *Nickleby*, 10.

3. Mrs. Wititterley's big servant. *Nickleby*, 21.

4. The brass and copperfounder's footman, " with such great tags upon his liveried shoulder that he was perpetually entangling and hooking himself among the chairs and tables." *Chuzzlewit*, 9.

5. Dr. Blimber's weak-eyed young man, who was always falling foul of Mrs. Pipchin. *Dombey*, 11.

6. Mr. Tite Barnacle's servant, whose gorgeousness was not unmixed with dirt. *Dorrit*, I, 10.

7. Mr. Boffin's footman, summoned by Mrs. Wilfer as " The male domestic of Mrs. Boffin." *Mutual Friend*, II, 8.

**FOREIGN GENTLEMAN, THE.** One of the Podsnap's guests at Georgiana's birth-day dinner. " There was a droll disposition to treat him as if he were a child who was hard of hearing." *Mutual Friend*, I, 11.

**FORSTER, JOHN.** Dickens's most in-timate friend and biographer. Practically all the novels were submitted to him in proof for his suggestions, and he exercised a great influence on his friend. Forster was a man of somewhat overbearing manner, which was merely the mask of a very tender and sympathetic character. This manner is caricatured in Podsnap. Forster's house, 58 Lincoln's Inn Fields, was the original of Mr. Tulkinghorn's chambers.

**" FOR THE PORT OF BARBADOS."** Although a typical sea song the original of this has not been traced, and it is presumably Dickens's own composition. *Dombey*, 15.

**FORT PITT.** A deserted fortification in the vicinity of Chatham, where, as a lad, Dickens and his sister had many a childish game. He made it the scene of the duel between Mr. Winkle and Dr. Slammer (*Pickwick*, 2) and referred to the place again in *Reprinted, The Child's Story.*

**FOULON.** This man was one of the last props of French monarchy, and, according to Carlyle, " a man grown grey in treachery, in griping, projecting, intriguing and iniquity, who once when it was objected to some finance scheme of his, ' What will the people do ? ' made answer . . . ' The people may eat grass.' " He was massacred July 22, 1789. *Two Cities*, II, 22.

**FOUNDLING HOSPITAL.** In the days of *Barnaby* (38) the Foundling was in the fields, though a sea of houses was soon to surround it. The present building, in Guilford Street, Bloomsbury, was erected in 1754, and was at first open for the indiscriminate admission of foundlings. Since 1760, however, it has been restricted to the illegitimate children of women of previously good character who have been deserted by the father. It was formerly fashionable to go to the Foundling on Sunday mornings when the children's singing, assisted by a trained choir, was as good as could be had in London. It was on such an occasion that the Meagles decided to adopt one of the Foundling girls (*Dorrit*, I, 2). The plot of *No Thoroughfare* rests, to a large extent, on a somewhat similar adoption of a Foundling child. The slowness of the Foundling Clock is remarked upon in *Boz, Tales, Boarding House.*

**FOUNTAIN COURT, TEMPLE.** This is one of the pleasantest spots in the Temple and has changed little these two hundred years. " There is still the plash of falling water in fair Fountain Court " as there was when Sir John Chester lived in Paper Buildings, near by (*Barnaby*, 15), and there are still lovers who make it a trysting-place, even as Ruth Pinch and John Westlock did, so many years ago. *Chuzzlewit*, 45, 53.

**FOUNTAIN HOTEL, CANTERBURY.** Original of the County Inn. (*q.v.*)

**FOXEY.** 1. A member of the Mudfog Association.

2. The father of Sampson and Sally Brass, whose maxim was " always suspect everybody." *Curiosity Shop*, 66.

**FOX UNDER THE HILL INN.** This was a little riverside alehouse which stood at the foot of Ivy Bridge Lane and near to Salisbury Stairs, whence boats plied to London Bridge. The whole neighbourhood was entirely changed when the Embankment was made, and the Hotel Cecil now stands on the site of Salisbury Street and the above-mentioned localities, including the Fox under the Hill. This public-house was one of Dickens's resorts when a lad in Warren's warehouse, and in *Copperfield*, 11, he relates how he would go there to watch the coalheavers dancing. *See also Pickwick*, 42.

**FRANCOIS.** 1. Waiter at the Golden Head Restaurant, Dijon. *Dombey*, 54.

2. A butcher at the Poissy Calf Market. *Reprinted, Monument of French Folly.*

**FRANK, LITTLE.** A friend of Michael, the Poor Relation. " We talk but little, still we understand each other." *Reprinted, Poor Relation's Story.*

**FRED.** Scrooge's nephew, who asked him to dinner on Christmas Day and was harshly rebuked. The Spirit of Christmas Present showed Scrooge Fred and his wife—" pretty, exceedingly pretty, with a ripe little mouth that seemed made to be kissed—as no doubt it was," passing a merry Christmas and pitying their miserly old uncle. When he awoke from his vision Scrooge went to Fred to eat his Christmas dinner after all. *Christmas Carol.*

**FREEMAN'S COURT.** This court, which has since disappeared, was on the north side of Cornhill, and opened out about six houses up from the old Royal Exchange. The site is now covered by the new Exchange. There were the offices of Dodson and Fogg, attorneys for the plaintiff in the case of Bardell v. Pickwick. *Pickwick*, 18, 20.

**FRENCH PRISONERS.** The unfortunates referred to by Mr. Lillyvick were prisoners taken in the Napoleonic Wars and confined in prisons in various parts of England. *Nickleby*, 16.

**FROME.** Dick Doubledick went to this quiet Somerset town to break to Mrs. Taunton the news of her son's death at Badajoz. *Seven Poor Travellers.*

**" FROM SPORT TO SPORT."** This is from the first verse of, " Oh, no, we never mention her," by T. H. Baily, set to music by Bishop, beginning :—

Oh, no, we never mention her, her name is never heard ;
  My lips are now forbid to speak that once familiar word.
From sport to sport they hurry me, to banish my regret,
  And when they win a smile from me, they think that I
    forget.             *Curiosity Shop*, 58.

**FROST, MISS.** A mistress at Our School. *Reprinted, Our School.*

**F.'S AUNT, MR.** The old lady whom Flora Finching considered as a legacy from her late husband. *See* Aunt, Mr. F.'s.

**FULHAM.** Sir Barnet and Lady Skettles lived " in a pretty villa at Fulham, on the banks of the Thames ; which was one of the most desirable residences in the world when a rowing match happened to be going past, but had its little inconveniences at other times, among which may be enumerated the occasional appearance of the river in the drawing-room." With these kindly but pompous folk Florence went to stay while her father was at Leamington (*Dombey*, 24). Arthur Clennam walked out to see the Meagles at their Twickenham home, by way of Fulham and Putney. *Dorrit*, I, 16.

**FURNACE FIRE, THE MAN WHO FED.** A kindly labourer in a smelting works who sheltered Little Nell and her grandfather by his furnace, giving them a bed of warm ashes to sleep on. *Curiosity Shop*, 44, 73.

**FURNIVAL'S INN.** This was one of the inns of Chancery, and stood on the north side of Holborn, between Leather Lane and Brooke Street, on part of the site now occupied by the offices of the Prudential Assurance Company. It ceased to be a Chancery Inn in 1818, when it was rebuilt and let out in chambers. The last part of this new building was demolished in 1898 to make room for an extension of the insurance offices. Dickens's associations with Furnival's Inn were very intimate. He rented a 3-pair back at No. 13 in 1834, and the next year moved to No. 15, to which in 1836 he brought his bride. At No. 15 he began and wrote the greater part of *Pickwick*. Mr. Samuel Briggs was a solicitor of Furnival's Inn (*Boz, Tales, Excursion*). The genteel young man who assisted Mr. Nicodemus Dumps to cross Hatton Garden, helped himself at Furnival's Inn to the christening cup that gentleman was carrying (*Boz, Tales, Christening*). John Westlock's chambers, whither Tom Pinch went to find him on arriving in London, were two stories up, in the inn (*Chuzzlewit*, 36). The hotel in Furnival's Inn which supplied the dinner with which Mr. Grewgious entertained Edwin Drood and Bazzard, and where, later, he arranged lodgings for Rosa Bud was Wood's Hotel, which disappeared with the rest of the building. *Drood*, 11, 20.

# G

**G.** The gentleman whom her pupils took to be in love with Miss Pupford. *Tom Tiddler*.

**GABELLE, THEOPHILE.** Postmaster at the village belonging to the St. Evremonde estate. When the Revolution broke out he wrote to Charles Darnay, beseeching him to return to France and rescue him from prison. Darnay went thither, to his cost, for Gabelle purchased his own safety by denouncing the man who had come to rescue him. *Two Cities*, II, 8, 9, 23, 24 ; III, 1, 6.

**GABRIELLE.** The full name of the little orphan girl, Bebelle, adopted by Mr. Langley. *See* Bebelle.

**GAD'S HILL.** This was the last residence of Dickens, and the scene of some of his happiest days. It is situated on the Dover Road, between Gravesend and Rochester, some two miles from the latter. The Place stands on the brow of the hill and commands a splendid view. The house was built in 1779 and, after passing through many hands, fell into the market in 1855. Dickens had long known the place, and desired it for his own. In 1856 he bought it for £1790, but did not enter into continued residence until 1860. From then until his death, ten years later, it was his constant home and the scene of much entertaining. There he wrote the conclusion of *Dorrit, Two Cities, Expectations, Mutual Friend, Uncommercial*, and was working on *Drood* the day before he died,

June 8, 1870. After his death Gad's Hill Place was occupied for a time by his son, Charles, who disposed of it in 1879.

**GAFFER.** This was the nickname by which Hexam, Lizzie's father, was usually known by the waterside characters. *See* Hexam.

**GALLANBILE.** The M.P. whose wife needed a cook : " Fifteen guineas, tea and sugar, and servants allowed to see male cousins if godly." *Nickleby*, 16.

**GAME CHICKEN, THE.** A pugilist employed by Toots to teach him the noble art, " knocking him about the head three times a week for the small consideration of ten and six a visit." Disgusted at last with his pupil's pusillanimity in failing " to go in and win " Miss Dombey, the Chicken demanded a " fi'typunnote " and gave up the job as a slur upon his game reputation. About 1830 there was a pugilist named Hen Pearce bearing this sobriquet whom Dickens probably had in mind. *Dombey*, 22, 28, 31, 32, 41, 44, 56.

**GAMFIELD.** A chimney sweep " whose villainous face was a regular stamped receipt for cruelty." Despite his notorious illtreatment of his boys, the guardians would have apprenticed Oliver to him had not the magistrates refused to sanction the indentures. *Twist*, 3, 51.

**GAMMON.** One of Miss Flite's captive birds. *Bleak House*, 14.

**GAMP, SARAH.** Midwife and nurse who " went to a laying-out or a lying-in with equal zest and relish. . . . She was a fat old woman with a husky voice and a moist eye . . . and it was difficult to enjoy her society without becoming conscious of a smell of spirits." Summoned to perform the last rites for Anthony Chuzzlewit, she was later employed to look after old Chuffey and, by piecing together his half-crazy remarks and the feverish ramblings of another patient, Lewsome, was one of the instruments in bringing about the exposure of Jonas Chuzzlewit. Her quarrel with Betsey Prig is famous among Dickens's scenes, while her " gig umbrella, in colour like a faded leaf, except where a circular patch of a lively blue had been dexterously let in at the top " has added the word gamp to the English language. Equally famous was her mythical friend, Mrs. Harris, whose complimentary remarks furnished Mrs. Gamp was unfailingly apposite testimonials. Mrs. Gamp lived in Kingsgate Street, High Holborn, since demolished and absorbed into Southampton Row. Sarah Gamp and Betsey Prig accurately portrayed the appalling character of the professional nurses of the time. Dickens's exposure of the cruelty, drunkenness and ignorance of these women had much to do with their final disappearance. According to Lockhart, Mrs. Gamp was drawn from the attendant of an invalid lady, and the common habit of this nurse in the sickroom, among other Gampish peculiarities, was to rub her nose along the top of a tall fender. Mrs. Gamp's best-known sayings will be found set forth on page 175. *Chuzzlewit*, 19, 25, 26, 29, 38, 40, 46, 48, 49, 51, 52.

**GANDER, MR.** One of Mrs. Todgers's boarders and a gentleman of a witty turn. *Chuzzlewit*, 9.

**GANZ, DR.** A physician of Neuchatel, whose evidence helped to prove the identity of George Vendale. *No Thoroughfare.*

**GARDEN COURT.** A green court in the Temple, reached by a flight of steps descending from Fountain Court. There Ruth Pinch would wait to meet her brother Tom, and surprisingly often see Mr. John Westlock (*Chuzzlewit*, 45). Herbert Pocket and Pip had chambers in Garden Court. *Expectations*, 39.

**GARGERY, JOE.** The blacksmith who brought up Pip and was his constant and true friend. He was " a mild, good-natured, sweet-tempered, easy-going fellow," much bullied by his wife, Pip's sister. Before he came into his " Expectations " Pip was apprenticed to Joe, but after he had gone to London he became ashamed of his brother-in-law's awkward ways and lack of polite manners. When he fell ill, Joe came up to nurse him, paid his debts, and went away again, feeling that he was not wanted. After his wife's death Joe married Biddy, and found the happiness in life he so richly deserved. *Expectations*, 2, 4–7, 9, 10, 12, 16, 18, 19, 27, 35, 57–9.

Joe's wife, Pip's sister, Georgiana Maria, was a veritable tartar who made life at the forge a burden. She had brought up Pip " by hand " and kept him in order with her cane, Tickler. She was eventually the object of a brutal attack by Orlick, and never recovered her speech nor the use of her limbs. 2, 4–7, 9, 10, 12, 13, 15–18.

**GARLAND, MR. AND MRS.** A kindly couple who befriended and took Kit Nubbles into their service to look after the fat pony the old gentleman usually drove. They were devoted to their only son, Abel, and were friendly with Witherden, the notary who helped them to defend Kit when Quilp and Brass hatched a conspiracy to brand him a thief. Mr. Garland accompanied the single gentleman on his journey to find Little Nell and her grandfather. They are supposed to have been founded on a couple with whom Dickens lodged in Lant Street when his father was in the Marshalsea. *Curiosity Shop*, 14, 20–2, 38–40, 57, 60, 63, 66, 68–71, 73.

Abel Garland, the son, had " a quaint, old-fashioned air about him, looked nearly the same age as his father, and bore a wonderful resemblance to him in face and figure." He was articled to Mr. Witherden, eventually

entered into partnership with him, and married the most bashful young lady that ever was seen. 14, 20, 21, 38–41, 57, 60, 63–6, 68, 69, 73.

**GARRAWAY'S** was one of the oldest coffee houses in the city. It stood in Change Alley, where its site is marked by a tablet, and was a common meeting-place for business men. Latterly it was practically an auction mart for landed property, reversionary interests and securities not in the market. Garraway's was originally famous for its tea, but for the last fifty years of its existence it was noted for its sherry and sandwiches. It was demolished in 1874. It was from Garraway's that Mr. Pickwick dated his compromising note to Mrs. Bardell—"Chops and tomata sauce " (*Pickwick*, 34). There, too, the mysterious Nadgett kept a watch on Jonas Chuzzlewit, while waiting for the man who never appeared (*Chuzzlewit*, 27). Some of Jeremiah Flintwinch's business was transacted at Garraway's (*Dorrit*, I, 29), while the *Uncommercial Traveller* (21) in one of his Sunday rambles found its shutters barred and wondered if the man who cut the sandwiches was lying on his back in a hayfield.

**"GAS AND GAITERS."** An ecstatic remark of the Gentleman in Small Clothes on seeing Miss La Creevy. " My love, my life, my bride, my peerless beauty. She is come at last—at last—and all is gas and gaiters ! " *Nickleby*, 49.

**GASHFORD.** Lord George Gordon's hypocritical secretary and the instigator of most of his extravagances. He was a renegade Catholic, formerly acquainted with Geoffrey Haredale, and it was his intention to avail himself of the excesses committed by the rioters to obtain possession of Emma Haredale, but in this he was defeated by young Chester and Joe Willett. After the suppression of the riots Gashford saved his life and tried to further his own ends by turning evidence and selling Lord George's secrets. He finally poisoned himself. The original of Gashford was Robert Watson, a Scotsman born in 1746. Although an adventurer and somewhat of a rogue, he was not such a villain as Gashford. He committed suicide in a Thames Street tavern in 1838. *Barnaby*, 35–8, 43, 44, 48–50, 52, 53, 57, 71, 81, 82.

**GAS MICROSCOPE.** This was a sort of forerunner of the magic lantern, and was worked with oxygen and hydrogen lamps. In his "Topical" Edition of *Pickwick* (Chapman and Hall), Mr. Van Noorden reproduces the advertisement of one of these apparatus, which claims that it magnifies to three million diameters. This advertisement is dated 1837, nine years subsequent to Sam's allusion ! *Pickwick*, 34. *Humphrey.*

**GASPARD.** A Parisian whose child was run over and killed in the street by the Marquis St. Evremonde. When the Marquis returned to his country seat, Gaspard followed behind his carriage and eventually murdered him, suffering, in turn, for his crime on a forty-foot gallows. *Two Cities,* I, 5 ; II, 7, 15, 16.

**GATTLETON, MR.** "A stockbroker in especially comfortable circumstances" who lived at Rose Villa, Clapham Rise. He and his whole family were "infected with the mania for private theatricals," and got up the performance of *Othello* which was so utterly spoiled by the machinations of Mrs. Joseph Porter. *Boz, Tales, Porter.*

**GAY, WALTER.** The nephew of old Sol Gills who entered the house of Dombey as a junior clerk. When Florence was lost Gay was instrumental in taking her home, and, furthermore, winning the affection of little Paul Dombey incurred the displeasure of the pompous father, who sent him away to the West Indies. The *Son and Heir* on which he sailed was wrecked, and Walter Gay was given up for lost, although his old uncle would never believe him drowned, but set off to find him. Walter made his way back to London and found Florence living at the old instrument shop, under the care of Captain Cuttle. Florence and Walter were married and went abroad, on their return taking Mr. Dombey to live with them. *Dombey,* 4, 6, 9, 10, 13, 15–17, 19, 22, 23, 32, 35, 49, 50, 56, 57, 59, 61, 62.

**"GAY, THE FESTIVE SCENE."** Wegg's adaptation of the opening lines of the "Light Guitar" (*q.v.*). The actual words are :—
    Oh! leave the gay and festive scene,
    The halls, the halls of dazzling light.
          *Mutual Friend,* I, 15 ; *Curiosity Shop,* 3.

**GAZELEE, SIR STEPHEN.** Original of Mr. Justice Stareleigh. (*q.v.*)

**GAZINGI, MISS.** One of the actresses in Mr. Vincent Crummles' company. *Nickleby,* 23.

**"GEE HO DOBBIN."** This is a song in the old play *Love in a Village,* beginning :—
    As I was a driving my waggon one day,
    I met a young damsel, light, buxom and gay;
    I kindly accosted her with a low bow,
    And I felt my whole body I cannot tell how.
    Gee ho Dobbin, Hi ho Dobbin, Gee ho Dobbin,
          Gee up and Gee ho.    *Copperfield,* 12.

**GENERAL, MRS.** The genteel chaperon engaged by Mr. Dorrit to look after his daughters. "She was the daughter of a clerical dignitary . . . and was a model of accurate dressing. . . . If her eyes had no expression it was because they had nothing to express." She accompanied the family to Italy and sought to impart to Fanny and Amy a ladylike demeanour. "You will find it serviceable in the formation of a demeanour, if you sometimes say to yourself in company—Papa, potatoes, poultry, prunes and prism, all very good words for the lips ; especially prunes and prism." Mrs. General had designs on Mr. Dorrit, and would doubtless in time have captured him for her second husband. *Dorrit,* II, 1–7, 11, 15, 19, 24, 33.

**GENTLEMAN IN SMALL CLOTHES, THE.** A madman who lived with his keeper next door to the Nickleby's cottage at Bow. He made violent protestations of love to Mrs. Nickleby, expressing his sentiments by throwing vegetable marrows and other garden produce over the wall. Convinced of the seriousness of his intentions Mrs. Nickleby's vanity was agreeably flattered until, on his appearance one day down the parlour chimney, he deserted her in favour of Miss La Creevy. *Nickleby,* 37, 41, 49.

**GEORGE, TROOPER.** This was the name adopted by George Rouncewell when he ran away from home. Having left the army he opened a shooting-range near Leicester Square. He was an object of interest to Mr. Tulkinghorn, as he possessed some handwriting of his old officer, Captain Hawdon, whose connection with Lady Dedlock the old lawyer made it his business to discover. Thanks to his faithful friends the Bagnets, he was eventually restored to his old mother, Mrs. Rouncewell, and became Sir Leicester Dedlock's companion and attendant. *Bleak House,* 7, 21, 24, 26, 27, 34, 47, 49, 52, 54–6, 58, 63, 66.

**GEORGE.** 1. A lad of fourteen years who accompanied his family to Astley's and tried to look as if he did not belong to them. *Boz, Scenes,* 11.

2. A lovesick swain at Greenwich Fair. *Boz, Scenes,* 12.

3. Uncle and Aunt George who entertained a jolly Christmas Eve party. *Boz, Characters,* 2.

4. A friend of the Kenwigs and "much esteemed by the ladies as bearing the reputation of a rake." *Nickleby,* 14, 15.

5. Master George was one of Wegg's mythical patrons. *See* Elizabeth, Miss. *Mutual Friend,* I, 5 ; II, 7, 10 ; III, 6, 7 ; IV, 3, 14.

6. Two coach guards were named George (*Copperfield,* 5, and *Holly Tree*), as was also Mr. Tony Weller's insolvent coachman friend. *Pickwick,* 43.

7. The driver of Mrs. Jarley's van, and eventually that lady's husband. *Curiosity Shop,* 26, 28, 47.

8. Mrs. George was one of Mrs. Quilp's friends and sympathisers. *Curiosity Shop,* 4.

9. Clerk of Buffles, the tax collector. *Lirriper's Legacy.*

10. Assistant to Christopher, the waiter. *Somebody's Luggage.*

**GEORGE INN, GRANTHAM.** Described as "one of the best inns in England," this excellent hostelry still maintains its reputation. It is at the north end of the High Street. Dickens and H. K. Browne put up at the George, January 30, 1838, on their visit to Yorkshire in search of material for *Nickleby. Nickleby,* 5.

**GEORGE AND NEW INN, GRETA BRIDGE.** The inn where the coach deposited Squeers and his party on their arrival from London. There were two inns at Greta, the George and the New, but Mr. T. P. Cooper has recently discovered that in the Nickleby days the George was closed and the landlord had transferred the sign to the New, which was thus called the George and New Inn. Both have been turned into private residences, the latter being now known as Thorpe Grange. *Nickleby*, 6.

**GEORGE AND VULTURE INN.** This is one of the few comparatively untouched Dickens's inns in London, and is the resort of many pilgrims. It stands between Cornhill and Lombard Street, being approached from the latter by George Yard and from the former by St. Michael's Alley. Mr. Pickwick took up his residence there on coming up to attend to the business connected with Mrs. Bardell's action. On his return there from Bath, he was arrested in his room by the sheriff's officers and thither he repaired after his release from the Fleet. Mr. Winkle and his bride were staying there after their marriage when old Mr. Winkle came up to see what his new daughter-in-law was like. *Pickwick*, 26, 40, 47, 50, 54–6.

**GEORGE IV INN.** *See* Magpie and Stump.

**GEORGE SILVERMAN'S EXPLANATION.** This story was written for the *Atlantic Monthly*, in which publication it appeared, January–March, 1868. It was published the same year in *All the Year Round*. According to Forster, Dickens received £1000 for this and *Holiday Romance*, at that time an unprecedented price for short stories.

**GEORGIANA.** A cousin of Miss Havisham, "who called her rigidity religion, and her liver love." She was one of that lady's toady relatives and received £20 by her will. *Expectations*, 11, 25, 57.

**GERRARD STREET, SOHO.** Mr. Jaggers, the Old Bailey lawyer, lived in this street, in " rather a stately house " on the south side. This has not been identified, but the description " dolefully in want of painting and with dirty windows " is applicable to most of the old houses in the street. Dickens's uncle, Thomas Barrow, lived at No. 10, and this may have been the original. *Expectations*, 26.

**GHOST OF ART, THE.** This amusing satire on the conventionality of contemporary art first appeared in *Household Words*, July 20, 1850, and was republished in *Reprinted Pieces*, 1858.

**GHOSTS OF CHRISTMAS.** The Ghosts of Christmas Past, Present and Yet To Come showed Scrooge the visions which made him turn from his old life of meanness and converted him into a jolly, generous man. *Christmas Carol*.

**GIBBS, VILLIAM.** The impressionable young hairdresser whose story Sam Weller related to the assembled company in Master Humphrey's kitchen. *Humphrey*.

**GIGGLES, MISS.** One of Miss Twinkleton's pupils, unhappily deficient in sentiment. *Drood*, 9, 13.

**GILBERT, MARK.** " An ill-looking, one-sided, shambling lad," who was initiated into the secret society of the Prentice Knights and later became Sim Tappertit's lieutenant. *Barnaby*, 8, 39.

**GILES.** Steward and butler at Mrs. Maylie's house in Chertsey. When Sikes and Crackit attempted their burglary, Giles gave the alarm and fired the pistol which wounded Oliver Twist. *Twist*, 28–31, 34–6, 53.

**GILL, MR. AND MRS.** Clients of Mrs. Gamp, the lady being notable for her skill in forecasting family events. Mr. Gill " would back his wife agen *Moore's Almanack*, to name the very day and hour for ninepence farden." *Chuzzlewit*, 29.

**GILLS, SOLOMON.** Walter Gay's uncle and the proprietor of the ships' instrument shop, The Wooden Midshipman. His whole life was bound up in his nephew Walter, and when the ship in which the lad sailed was reported as missing, old Sol refused to believe the boy drowned, but set off to find him, leaving the shop in charge of his friend, Captain Cuttle. For long nothing was heard of him, but soon after Walter's return he reappeared and, on the marriage of Walter Gay and Florence Dombey, took Captain Cuttle into partnership. The original of Sol Gills's shop, with its sign of the Wooden Midshipman, was No. 157 Leadenhall Street. When Messrs. Norie and Wilson moved their business to 156 Minories, they took the Midshipman with them. *Dombey*, 4, 6, 9, 10, 15, 17, 19, 22, 23, 25, 39, 50, 56, 57, 62.

**GIMBLET, BROTHER.** A drysalter and expounder, who acted as a kind of echo to Verity Hawkyard. *George Silverman*.

**GIOVANNI.** The operatic form of *Don Juan*, from Mozart's opera. *Boz, Tales, Boarding House*.

**GLAMOUR, BOB.** One of the regular customers at the Six Jolly Fellowship Porters. *Mutual Friend*, I, 6 ; III, 3.

**GLASGOW.** The Bagman's uncle made the return journey from Edinburgh to Glasgow on his annual visit to the North (*Pickwick*, 49). Dickens's first connection with the city was in 1847, when he opened The Athenæum on December 28, in presence of a huge assemblage of people. The Lord Provost entertained him to a state lunch with the Town Council, which was followed by a great dinner party at night. Some of his most successful readings were in Glasgow, on the first occasion (1858) £600 being taken for three evenings and one morning.

**GLAVORMELLY.** A former actor at the Cobourg Theatre (The Old Vic) and a deceased friend of Mr. Snevellicci. *Nickleby*, 30.

**GLIDDERY OR GLIBBERY, BOB.** The potboy at the Six Jolly Fellowship Porters. He is introduced under the name of Glibbery, but after chapter VI is called Gliddery. *Mutual Friend*, I, 6, 13 ; III, 2, 3.

**GLOBES, USE OF THE.** The study of the terrestrial and celestial globes was formerly an important part of the education of young ladies. *Tom Tiddler.*

**GLOBSON, BULLY.** A lad who bullied the Uncommercial Traveller when he was a boy at school. *Uncommercial*, 19.

**GLOGWOG, SIR CHIPKINS.** An aristocratic friend of the Egotistical Couple, who told a capital story about mashed potatoes. *Sketches of Couples.*

**GLORIOUS APOLLERS.** "A select, convivial circle," of which Dick Swiveller and Chuckster were members, the former having the honour to be Perpetual Grand. *Curiosity Shop*, 13, 38.

**GLUBB, OLD.** A Brighton sailor, who used to wheel Paul Dombey's chair along the Parade and tell him stories of the deep seas. *Dombey*, 8, 12.

**GLUMPER, SIR THOMAS.** A friend of the Gattleton's, who "had been knighted . . . for carrying up an address on somebody's escaping from nothing." *Boz, Tales, Porter.*

**GOBLER.** A hypochondriacal guest at Mrs. Tibbs's boarding house. According to Mrs. Tibbs "he had no stomach," and the lack of this essential organ immediately invested him with interest in the eyes of Mrs. Bloss, the wealthy and vulgar widow whom he eventually married. *Boz, Tales, Boarding House.*

**GOBLIN OF THE BELLS.** The spirit of the Great Bell which Trotty Veck encountered during his New Year's Eve visit to the belfry. This goblin put him in charge of the Spirit of the Chimes, who showed Trotty scenes of the future. *Chimes.*

**GODALMING.** It was at this quiet country town on the Portsmouth road that Nicholas Nickleby and Smike "bargained for two humble beds and slept soundly." *Nickleby*, 22.

**"GO, DECEIVER, GO."** From Moore's "When first I met thee," of which the second verse concludes :—

> But go, deceiver, go,
> Some day perhaps thou'lt waken
> From pleasure's dream to know
> The grief of hearts forsaken.
> *Curiosity Shop*, 23.

**GOG AND MAGOG.** These are two huge carved figures, 14 ft. 6 in. high, which stand in the Guildhall, London. They date from 1708, but represent much older characters associated with the traditional history of the City. Each tells a story in *Humphrey*. They were invoked by the Gentleman in Small Clothes. *Nickleby*, 41.

**GOING INTO SOCIETY.** This story originally appeared in a series written by various hands, entitled, *A House to Let*, published in the Christmas number of *Household Words*, 1858. It is now included in the *Christmas Stories*.

**GOLDEN CROSS HOTEL, CHARING CROSS.** The old coaching inn whence Mr. Pickwick started on his travels on the 13th of May, 1827 (*Pickwick*, 2), was a Gothic-fronted building which stood immediately facing King Charles's statue, almost on the spot where the Nelson column was afterwards erected. It was demolished when the whole neighbourhood was pulled down to make Trafalgar Square, and the present hotel, facing the station, was built in 1831–32. From the Golden Cross ran coaches to Blandford, Dorchester, Exeter, Cheltenham, Salisbury, Portsmouth, Hastings, Dover, Norwich, Brighton and other towns. The booking office with the start of an early coach is graphically described in *Boz, Scenes*, 15. David Copperfield put up here when he first came to London as a young man, and here he met his old schoolfellow, Steerforth. At that time St. Martin's Lane ran down to the Strand between houses, and a side entrance of the Golden Cross opened into the Lane. There it was that David and Peggotty saw Martha Endell, the unfortunate who later befriended Little Em'ly. *Copperfield*, 19, 20, 30, 40.

**GOLDEN DUSTMAN, THE.** Popular nickname for Mr. Boffin. (*q.v.*)

**"GOLDEN MARY."** The sailing vessel commanded by Captain Ravender and chartered to carry out diggers and emigrants to California. She was sunk after colliding with an iceberg in the vicinity of Cape Horn. *Golden Mary.*

**GOLDEN SQUARE.** Once a fashionable residential square, now mostly devoted to offices and warehouses, Golden Square was already well on its downward path when Ralph Nickleby resided there. "It is one of the squares that have been ; a quarter of the town that has gone down in the world, and taken to letting lodgings" (*Nickleby*, 2). It was in one of the streets in the vicinity (probably Carnaby Street) that the Kenwigs resided (*Nickleby*, 14), and thereabouts Little Em'ly was at last found by her uncle. *Copperfield*, 50.

**GOLDING, MARY.** A friend of the Waters', whom they saw bathing at Ramsgate. *Boz, Tales, Tuggs.*

**GOLDSMITHS' ARMS.** See Huggin Lane, Pickwick Club.

**GOLDSMITH'S BUILDINGS.** See Lightwood, Mortimer.

**GOLDSTRAW, SARAH.** A nurse at the Foundling Hospital, who later became housekeeper to Mr. Wilding. It was she who told him of the mistake which had been made in his identification. *No Thoroughfare.*

**GOODWIN.** "A young lady, whose ostensible employment was to preside over Mrs. Pott's toilet, but who rendered herself useful in a variety of ways, and in none more so than in the particular department of constantly aiding and abetting her mistress in every wish and inclination opposed to the desires of the unhappy Pott." *Pickwick*, 18, 51.

**GOODY, MRS.** An elderly parishioner of Mr. Milvey, who at a Christmas Eve party " drank eleven cups of tea and grumbled all the time." *Mutual Friend*, I, 9.

**GORDON, EMMA.** The tightrope dancer in Sleary's Circus, who took care of Cissy Jupe as a child. In later years Emma Gordon, according to Mr. Sleary, " married a cheethemonger ath fell in love with her from the front." *Hard Times*, I, 6 ; III, 7.

**GORDON, LORD GEORGE.** This fanatic, the third son of the Duke of Gordon, was born in London, December 26, 1751. After serving in the navy he entered Parliament in 1774. As President of the Protestant Association, on June 2, 1780, he led some 60,000 men to present a petition to Parliament for the repeal of the Catholic Relief Act. The mob thus assembled soon got out of hand and committed the series of outrages so accurately described in *Barnaby*, 35–7, 43, 48–51, 57, 73, 82.

**GORDON PLACE.** The select part of Our Parish in which the Miss Willises took a house, No. 25. *Boz, Our Parish*, 3.

**GORDON RIOTS, THE.** No description of the riots of 1780 can better that given in *Barnaby*. The agitation was caused by a bill introduced by Sir George Savile, which was to lighten the burdens at that time resting on Roman Catholics. The bill was duly passed as regards England, but it met with fanatical opposition in Scotland, where it never became law. A certain section of English Protestants formed an association for the purpose of repealing the Act ; Lord George Gordon put himself at the head of these extremists ; a rabble soon collected at his heels and a series of disgraceful outrages, burning and pillage ensued. On the personal orders of George III the military were at last called out and the rioting was suppressed.

**GOSWELL STREET.** In Mr. Pickwick's time Goswell Street began where Long Lane and Barbican cross Aldersgate Street, and became Goswell Street Road at the crossing of Percival Street and Wellington Street (now Lever Street). Practically the whole length of this is now called Goswell Road. It was from his lodgings in Goswell Street that Mr. Pickwick looked forth, May 13, 1827. " Goswell Street was at his feet, Goswell Street was on his right hand—as far as the eye could see Goswell Street extended on his left ; and the opposite side of Goswell Street was over the way." It may be remarked that Mrs. Bardell's house, where the great man lodged, had a red door ; no other clue for its identification is given. *Pickwick*, 2, 12, 26, 37, 46.

**GOVERNOR, JACK.** " A portly, cheery, well-built figure of a broad-shouldered man

. . . unmistakably a naval officer." He was a guest at the Haunted House. *Haunted House*.

**GOWAN, HENRY.** An indolent, well-connected young man who, for lack of better to do, decided to become a painter. To the secret grief of the Meagles he won the heart of their daughter, Pet, and married her. After spending their honeymoon on the Continent they returned to England, and before long Gowan decided that his wife's relatives were not to be known, except for the trifling matter of receiving Pet's yearly allowance. *Dorrit*, I, 17, 26–8, 33, 34 ; II, 1, 3–9, 11, 14, 20, 21, 28, 33.

Mrs. Gowan, the mother of the above, by virtue of her husband having been " a commissioner of nothing in particular, and having died at his post with his drawn salary in his hand," had rooms in Hampton Court Palace. I, 17, 26, 33 ; II, 5, 8.

**GRADGRIND, THOMAS.** Gradgrind was a retired mill-owner, living at Stone Lodge, Coketown, who had become obsessed with the doctrine of facts. He brought up a large family on facts, carefully checking any imaginativeness or youthful tendencies. As a result, his eldest son went astray, while his favourite daughter, Louisa, was sacrificed in marriage to Josiah Bounderby. These two failures of his pet theories induced him to change his views, and, softened by unhappiness and a sense of his own responsibility for what had occurred, he took a new and more lenient aspect of the realities of life. *Hard Times*, I, 1–9, 14–16 ; II, 1, 2, 11, 12 ; III, 1–9. *See also* Bounderby, Louisa.

Mrs. Gradgrind, his invalid wife, was " a little, thin, white, pink-eyed bundle of shawls, of surpassing feebleness mentally and bodily." I, 4, 8, 9, 15 ; II, 9, 11.

His son Thomas, otherwise called "The Whelp," was a victim of his father's upbringing. Mean, cringing, dishonest and selfish, he traded on his sister's sacrifice on his behalf in marrying Bounderby. Involved in debt by his dissipation, he robbed Bounderby's bank, and having succeeded in casting suspicion on Stephen Blackpool, made his escape. With the assistance of Sleary he was eventually smuggled out of the country. I, 3, 4, 7–9, 14, 16 ; II, 1–3, 6–8, 10–12 ; III, 2, 4–9.

**GRAHAM.** 1. Mary, the companion of old Martin Chuzzlewit, and the object of young Martin's love. Faithful to her lover during his absence in America, her position with old Martin left her at the mercy of Pecksniff, who, thinking that she would inherit the old man's money, forced upon her his disagreeable attentions. This was discovered by Tom Pinch, who was himself deeply in love with the beautiful girl. When the day of reckoning arrived between old Martin and Pecksniff, she was reunited to her lover with old Martin's blessing. Mary

Graham is another of the Mary Hogarth heroines. *Chuzzlewit*, 3–6, 12, 14, 24, 30, 31, 33, 35, 43, 48, 52, 53.

2. Hugh, the bold, young London apprentice who loved his master's daughter, Alice, befriended her after the desertion of her lover, and was eventually killed when he had avenged her. *Humphrey*.

**GRAINGER.** A friend of Steerforth, and one of the guests at David Copperfield's first bachelor dinner. *Copperfield*, 24.

**GRANDFATHER, LITTLE NELL'S.** The proprietor of the Old Curiosity Shop and a weak, self-deluded gambler who was determined to make a fortune by the cards for his grandchild, Little Nell. She was his good angel, and rescuing him from the clutches of Quilp, fled with him far into the country. There, in the quiet village where they settled, he was removed from temptation, but the death of Little Nell broke his heart, and he soon followed her to the grave. The Grandfather was the elder brother of Master Humphrey. *Curiosity Shop*, 1–3, 6, 7, 9–13, 15–19, 24–32, 40, 42–6, 52, 54, 55, 69, 71, 72.

**GRANDMARINA.** An all-powerful fairy "dressed in shot silk of the richest quality," who befriended the Princess Alicia. *Holiday Romance*.

**GRANGER, EDITH.** The name, before her marriage, of Edith Dombey. (*q.v.*)

**GRANNETT.** Parish overseer, attached to the workhouse where Oliver Twist was born. "He relieved an outdoor dying pauper with the offer of a pound of potatoes and half a pint of oatmeal." *Twist*, 23.

**GRANT, W. AND D.** Originals of the Cheeryble twins. (*q.v.*)

**GRAPES INN.** Original of Six Jolly Fellowship Porters. (*q.v.*)

**GRAVESEND.** After his enlistment Joe Willett was taken by boat from London to Gravesend, whence he and his fellows were to march to Chatham (*Barnaby*, 31). The scenes on the Gravesend steam packet are described in *Boz, Scenes*, 10. The Tuggs family voted Gravesend "low" (*Boz, Tales, Tuggs*). David Copperfield and Peggotty went thither to bid farewell to the emigrants for Australia (*Copperfield*, 57). Pip and his companions rowed Magwitch down below Gravesend in their vain attempt to smuggle him abroad (*Expectations*, 54). Caddy Jellyby and Prince Turveydrop went there in a coach and pair to spend their honeymoon. *Bleak House*, 30.

**GRAYMARSH.** A pupil at Dotheboys Hall, whose maternal aunt thought Mrs. Squeers an angel. *Nickleby*, 7, 8.

**GRAYPER, MR. AND MRS.** Neighbours and friends of the Copperfields at Blunderstone. It was at their house that Mrs. Copperfield first met Murdstone. They eventually went to South America. *Copperfield*, 2, 9, 22.

**GRAY'S INN.** This is one of the London Inns of Court which has changed but little during the last hundred years. Early in his career (May, 1827–Nov., 1828) Dickens was a clerk in the offices of Ellis and Blackmore, 1 Raymond Building, Gray's Inn, but originally of Gray's Inn Square and in the Square he placed the chambers of Mr. Perker (*Pickwick*, 10, 20, 47, 53); there also resided Mr. Percy Noakes (*Boz, Tales, Excursion*). In South Square, until 1829 known as Holborn Court, were Mr. Phunky's chambers (*Pickwick*, 31), and in No. 2 were the rooms where Traddles began his married life (*Copperfield*, 59). Flora Finching archly led Arthur Clennam to understand that she would be on the north-west side of Gray's Inn Gardens at exactly four in the afternoon (*Dorrit*, I, 13). Life in the inn is vividly and somewhat depressingly described in *Uncommercial*, 14. Gray's Inn is approached from Holborn by a low archway, beneath which Sam Weller and his master passed on their way to Perker's chambers. Gray's Inn Coffee House was in Holborn, turning from this gateway Citywards. There David Copperfield put up on his return to England, occupying a room over the archway. *Copperfield*, 59.

**GRAY'S INN ROAD.** This was formerly called Gray's Inn Lane between Holborn and Guilford Street, and Gray's Inn Road beyond. Signor Billsmethi's dancing academy was in that neighbourhood (*Boz, Characters*, 9). Near the Lane were some of the worst parts of the city, as mentioned in *Twist*, 42, and *Reprinted, Inspector Field*. Near the top of Gray's Inn Road Mr. Micawber, while under one of his financial clouds, occupied lodgings under the name of Mortimer (*Copperfield*, 36), while in a side street at about the same part lived Mr. Casby. *Dorrit*, I, 13; II, 9.

**GRAZINGLANDS, MR.** A gentleman of comfortable property visiting London from the Midlands. *Uncommercial*, 6.

**GREAT CORAM STREET.** Mrs. Tibbs opened her boarding establishment in the neatest house in this street, which is now known as Coram Street. It runs from Brunswick Square to Woburn Place. *Boz, Tales, Boarding House.*

**GREAT EXPECTATIONS.** This novel, considered by many the best of Dickens's works, began in the December 1 issue of *All the Year Round*. The following year it was published in book form, with illustrations by Marcus Stone. It may be remarked that the author's original intention was to leave Pip unmarried, but at Bulwer Lytton's suggestion he finished the novel in its present form.

*Principal Characters.* Pip, the narrator of the story, who has been brought up by his brother-in-law, Joe Gargery, the village blacksmith; Uncle Pumblechook, a mouthy hypocrite ; Miss Havisham, a half-demented old woman ; Estella, her protégée ; Jaggers, an Old Bailey lawyer ; Wemmick, his clerk ; Magwitch, a convict ; Herbert Pocket, Pip's friend.

Pip begins with an incident in his early childhood when he gave food to an escaped convict, Magwitch, who was, however, caught the next day. Some time later Pip is hired by Miss Havisham to wheel her about and amuse her. When he grows older Miss Havisham apprentices Pip to his brother-in-law, Joe Gargery. One day Pip is informed by Mr. Jaggers that an unknown friend has arranged to pay him an annuity of £500 with "Great Expectations" for the future. Pip goes to London, lives with Herbert Pocket and becomes educated, all the time thinking that he owes his good fortune to Miss Havisham's generosity, an opinion which is confirmed when she throws Estella in his way. One day, however, Magwitch, the convict he once befriended as a child, arrives from Australia, and Pip learns that his wealth and expectations are due to the gratitude of this man who had been transported, made a fortune, and was now returned at the risk of his life to see his " dear boy." While relating his past life Magwitch unconsciously reveals the fact that Estella is his daughter by Molly, a woman in Jaggers's employ, and that the lawyer had taken her away when an infant and given her to Miss Havisham to adopt. For a time Pip keeps his benefactor in hiding, but an old accomplice informs on the returned convict, who is arrested as Pip is smuggling him out of the country. In pursuance of the law Magwitch is sentenced to death, but he dies in the hospital. Pip, no longer rich and robbed of his " Great Expectations," takes employment in a business house. He eventually marries Estella, who has herself had many sad adventures and is, by this time, a widow.

**GREAT MARLBOROUGH STREET.** This street, running east from the upper end of Regent Street, was the residence of the Taunton family, who occupied the upper part of a house (*Boz, Tales, Excursion*). The owner of *Somebody's Luggage* vainly endeavoured to dispose of his writings to a bookseller there.

**GREAT QUEEN STREET** is best known for containing Freemasons' Hall (*Boz, Scenes*, 19). Dick Swiveller " bought a pair of boots in Great Queen Street last week, and made that no thoroughfare," i.e. one of the streets down which he could not pass while the shops were open. *Curiosity Shop*, 8.

**GREAT RUSSELL STREET.** Mr. Charles Kitterbell lived at No. 14, near the Tottenham Court Road end of this street (*Boz, Tales, Christening*). There was a famous pipe shop in this street, mentioned by the *Uncommercial Traveller*, 4.

**GREAT WHITE HORSE, IPSWICH,** the large inn where Mr. Pickwick encountered his adventure with Miss Witherfield, " the middle-aged lady in the yellow curl papers." Formerly the White Hart Tavern, it is little changed since Mr. Pickwick and Peter Magnus alighted at its door from the London coach. The sign, " distantly resembling an insane carthorse," still stands over the main entrance in Tavern Street, while Room 16 is pointed out as the scene of Mr. Pickwick's dilemma. Dickens stayed at this " overgrown tavern " when reporting the election of 1835 for the *Suffolk Chronicle*. He was already working on *Pickwick* and took the opportunity of recording his unfavourable impressions of the inn. *Pickwick*, 22.

**GREAT WINGLEBURY.** "The little town of Great Winglebury " was intended for Rochester, and the Winglebury Arms, where Alexander Trott put up, was the Bull Hotel, Rochester. *Boz, Tales, Winglebury*.

**GREEN.** 1. Charles Green, a well-known aeronaut, was the first to ascend in a gas balloon. He made many famous ascents from Vauxhall, in 1838 reaching a height of 27,146 ft. His last ascent was in 1852. One of his journeys is described in the *Ingoldsby Legends* (The Monstre Balloon). *Boz, Scenes*, 14.

2. Miss Green, a friend of the Kenwigses. *Nickleby*, 14.

3. Tom Green was the name taken by Joe Willett, when in the army. *Barnaby*, 58.

4. A Whitechapel constable. *Reprinted, Inspector Field*.

5. A friend of Mrs. Nubbles, who lodged at the cheesemonger's round the corner. *Curiosity Shop*, 21.

6. A law writer who knew Nemo. *Bleak House*, 11.

7. Lucy Green, the child sweetheart of The Uncommercial Traveller, whom he meets again as the wife of Dr. Specks. The original of this character was probably Lucy Stroughill, the sister of Dickens's friend. *Uncommercial*, 12.

**GREENACRE.** James Greenacre (1785–1837) was a London grocer who, having married and ill-treated four wives here and in New York, murdered a charwoman named Hannah Brown, December 24, 1836. He and his mistress, Sarah Gale, were arrested, March 25, 1837, and tried. Greenacre was hanged at Newgate on May 2, over 20,000 persons watching the execution ; Gale was transported and died in Australia so late as 1888. *Mudfog*.

**GREEN DRAGON, WESTMINSTER.** The public-house " in the immediate neighbourhood of Westminster Bridge," where Mr. Robert Bolton held forth to an admiring circle. *Robert Bolton*.

**GREEN LANES.** At the time of the Gordon Riots this name was given to the district now traversed by Cleveland Street, the northern continuation of Newman Street, Oxford Street. The rioters were assembled in Green Lanes when Gashford arrived to instigate Hugh and Dennis to further mischief. *Barnaby*, 44.

**GREENLEAF.** Miss Donny's house, where Esther Summerson was educated. *Bleak House*, 3.

**GREEN PARK.** Beneath the railings separating Green Park from Piccadilly, Tom drew some of his pavement pictures. *Somebody's Luggage.*

**"GREENS."** "Wait till the Greens is off her mind. Then we'll consult. Whatever the old girl says, do—do it." Matthew Bagnet's advice to George the Trooper. *Bleak House*, 27.

**GREENWICH.** In the early nineteenth century Greenwich was a favourite resort of Londoners, and one of the most vivid Sketches is that describing Greenwich Fair (*Boz, Scenes*, 12). There were two annual fairs, at Easter and Whitsun, but these were abolished in 1857. Bella Wilfer and her father made their innocent elopement there, and dined at the Ship, revisited again for the wedding dinner (*Mutual Friend*, II, 8; IV, 4). The wedding itself took place in Greenwich Church.

**GREENWOOD.** 1. A friend of the censorious young gentleman. *Sketches of Gentlemen.*

2. A one-eyed tramp, reported by Ikey to have seen the hooded woman in the Haunted House. *Haunted House.*

**GREGORY.** Foreman of the packers at Murdstone and Grinby's warehouse. *Copperfield*, 11.

**GREGSBURY.** A pompous member of Parliament to whom Nicholas Nickleby applied for a secretary's post. He gave a long and utterly preposterous list of duties he expected his secretary to perform for fifteen shillings a week. *Nickleby*, 16.

**GRETA BRIDGE.** This North Riding town was visited by Dickens and H. K. Browne in 1838 when collecting material for *Nickleby*. They probably put up at the New Inn (now a private dwelling called Thorpe Grange). Squeers and his party alighted there from London and proceeded thence to Dotheboys Hall (Bowes), over three miles distant. *Nickleby*, 6, 7.

**GRETNA GREEN.** The famous goal of runaway couples, is situated just over the Scottish border, nine miles from Carlisle. Advantage could there be taken of the Scottish marriage laws, and the ceremony was usually performed by the blacksmith or innkeeper. Such marriages flourished until 1856, when an Act was passed making it compulsory for one of the parties to reside in Scotland twenty-one days before marriage could be performed. Master Harry and Norah were on their way thither to be married, when they put up at the *Holly Tree Inn*, where, too, Edwin and Emmeline changed horses, when bound for Gretna on the same errand. The two couples from Great Winglebury were married by the blacksmith of Gretna Green. *Boz, Tales, Winglebury.*

**GREWGIOUS, HIRAM.** Rosa Bud's guardian, to whom she fled from the persecution of John Jasper. Grewgious already had his suspicions of Jasper's intimate connection with Edwin Drood's disappearance, and, having settled Rosa and Miss Twinkleton at Billickin's, he decided to devote himself to unravelling the mystery. Mr. Grewgious's chambers were in the second courtyard of Staple Inn, through the doorway still inscribed
$$\text{P.}$$
$$\text{J. T.}$$
$$1747.$$
This refers to President John Taylor during whose term of office the house was built. *See* Staple Inn. *Drood*, 9, 11, 14–17, 20, 23.

**GREY, THE MISSES.** A family of young ladies with whom the Domestic Young Gentleman was on the best of terms. *Sketches of Gentlemen.*

**GRIDE, ARTHUR.** An old money-lender, friend of Ralph Nickleby and his accomplice in various underhand deeds. He was a little old man of about seventy or seventy-five years of age, the whole expression of whose face was " concentrated in a wrinkled leer, compounded of cunning, lecherousness, slyness and avarice." He had acquired dishonestly a deed by which Madeleine Bray should inherit a large sum of money, and with Ralph's assistance he arranged with the girl's wastrel father to marry her. On the wedding day, however, Bray fell dead, Nicholas carried away the bride, and Gride's housekeeper, Peg Sliderskew, disappeared with all his valuable papers. Gride was eventually murdered in his bed by burglars. *Nickleby*, 47, 51–4, 56, 59, 65.

**GRIDLEY.** A victim of the Court of Chancery, commonly known as "The Man from Shropshire." He was continually being imprisoned for contempt of court, incurred in vain and violent efforts to make his grievances known to the Lord Chancellor. He died while evading arrest, in George's Shooting Gallery. *Bleak House*, 1, 15, 24, 27.

**GRIEVANCE, A.** Name given to one of the Veneering's guests. *Mutual Friend*, I, 2.

**GRIFFIN, MISS.** "A model of propriety" and principal of the school in which Master B. was a young pupil. *Haunted House.*

**GRIGGINS, MR.** The funny Young Gentleman. *Sketches of Gentlemen.*

**GRIGGS.** A family at Ipswich who belonged to the Nupkins's circle of acquaintance. *Pickwick*, 25.

**GRIMBLE, SIR THOMAS.** "A very proud man of Grimble Hall, somewhere in.

the North Riding," an old acquaintance of Mrs. Nickleby. *Nickleby*, 35.

**GRIME, PROFESSOR.** A prominent member of the Mudfog Association.

**GRIMMER, MISS.** Partner with Miss Drowvey in the school where Nettie Ashford was a pupil. *Holiday Romance.*

**GRIMWIG, MR.** A lawyer friend of Mr. Brownlow, " a stout old gentleman with a manner of screwing his head on one side when he spoke, and of looking out of the corners of his eyes at the same time, which irresistibly reminded the beholder of a parrot." From the first he distrusted Oliver Twist, and was delighted to find his suspicions justified when the lad failed to return with the books and money entrusted to him by his benefactor. He always backed his most violent assertions with the phrase, " Or I'll eat my head." *Twist*, 14, 15, 17, 41, 51, 53.

**GRIMWOOD, ELIZA.** Commonly called "The Countess," she was an unfortunate, the circumstances of whose murder were related by Inspector Field, who had charge of the case. The crime was committed May 26, 1838, but the culprit was never found. *Reprinted, Detective Anecdotes, Bill Sticking.*

**" GRIND."** " My life is one demd horrid grind." A pathetic outburst from Mr. Mantalini. *Nickleby*, 64.

**GRINDER.** A travelling showman whose party consisted of " a young gentleman and a young lady on stilts." Little Nell and her grandfather encountered them when travelling with Codlin and Short. *Curiosity Shop*, 17.

**GRIP.** The raven which accompanied Barnaby Rudge in all his adventures. " Balancing himself on tiptoe, as it were, and moving his body up and down in a sort of grave dance, rejoined, ' I'm a devil ! I'm a devil ! I'm a devil ! ' " Dickens's own ravens, which died in 1841 and 1845, were the originals for Grip. *Barnaby*, 5, 6, 10, 17, 25, 45–7, 57, 58, 62, 68, 73, 76, 77, 79, 82.

**GROFFIN, THOMAS.** A chemist who was summoned on the jury which tried the Bardell-Pickwick case. *Pickwick*, 34.

**GROGUS.** " The great ironmonger " who lived in a white house opposite the Swan, Stamford Hill. *Boz, Tales, Minns.*

**GROGZWIG, BARON OF.** This was the title of Baron von Koeldwithout, hero of the merryfaced gentleman's story. *Nickleby*, 6.

**GROMPUS.** One of Mr. Podsnap's guests at Georgiana's birthday party. *Mutual Friend*, I, 11.

**GROOMBRIDGE WELLS.** Mrs. Jane Miller, of Groombridge Wells, was commissioned to secure the Foundling to be adopted by the Wildings. The name is, of course, a composite of Groombridge and Tunbridge Wells. *No Thoroughfare.*

**GROPER, COLONEL.** A member of the deputation to welcome Mr. Elijah Pogram. *Chuzzlewit*, 34.

**GROSVENOR.** An East Indiaman, homeward bound, which went ashore on the coast of Caffraria, August 4, 1782. On board was a little child who was looked after by the steward until both died of exhaustion. *Reprinted, Long Voyage.*

**GROSVENOR SQUARE.** This has always been an aristocratic neighbourhood ; during the Gordon Riots Lord Rockingham's house was barricaded and armed against the rabble (*Barnaby*, 67). Mr. Tite Barnacle lived at No. 24 Mews Street, Grosvenor Square, " a hideous little street of dead walls, stables and dunghills," but with two or three airless houses, " abject hangers-on to a fashionable situation." *Dorrit*, I, 9, 10; II, 16.

**GROVES, JAMES.** Landlord of the Valiant Soldier public-house, and a villain who, under the cloak of an irreproachable reputation, connived at the nefarious schemes of a party of gamblers. Their confederacy was eventually broke up by the detection of their accomplice, young Fred Trent. *Curiosity Shop*, 29, 30, 73.

**GROWLERY, THE.** The name given by Mr. John Jarndyce to his study, where he went to growl when out of humour. *Bleak House*, 8, 67.

**GRUB.** 1. Gabriel Grub was a drunken sexton whose adventures in the churchyard, when befuddled with liquor, formed the subject of Mr. Wardle's Christmas Eve story. *Pickwick*, 29.

2. A member of the Mudfog Association.

**GRUBBLE, W.** Landlord of the Dedlock Arms. " A pleasant-looking, middle-aged man, who never seemed to consider himself cosily dressed for his own fireside without his hat and top-boots, but who never wore a coat except at church." *Bleak House*, 37.

**GRUDDEN, MRS.** One of the Crummles Theatrical Company "who assisted Mrs. Crummles in her domestic affairs ; and took money at the doors ; and dressed the ladies ; and swept the house ; and acted any kind of part on any emergency, without ever learning it, and was put down in the bills under any name or names whatever that occurred to Mr. Crummles as looking well in print." *Nickleby*, 23–5, 29, 30, 48.

**GRUEBY, JOHN.** Lord George Gordon's faithful manservant, who did his utmost to save his master from the folly and excess to which his fanatic adherents goaded him. *Barnaby*, 35, 37, 38, 43, 57, 66, 67, 82.

**GRUFF AND GLUM.** An old, wooden-legged Greenwich pensioner, who was present at the wedding of John Rokesmith and Bella Wilfer. *Mutual Friend*, IV, 4.

**GRUFF AND GRIM.** This was the nickname given by Herbert Pocket to Old Bill Barley. *Expectations*, 46.

**GRUFF AND TACKLETON.** The name of the firm of toymakers which employed Caleb Plummer. *See* Tackleton.

**GRUMMER, DANIEL.** Constable at Ipswich and " an elderly gentleman in top boots who had been a peace officer, man and boy, for half a century." With the assistance of a posse of special constables he effected the arrest of Messrs. Pickwick and Tupman. *Pickwick*, 24, 25.

**GRUMMIDGE, DR.** A medical member of the Mudfog Association.

**GRUNDY.** A law clerk and one of the choice spirits who frequented the Magpie and Stump. *Pickwick*, 20.

**GUARDIAN.** The name by which Esther Summerson addressed Mr. John Jarndyce. (*q.v.*)

**GUBBINS.** The ex-churchwarden who presented the inkstand to the curate as a mark of the parish's esteem. *Boz, Our Parish*, 2.

**GUBBLETON, LORD.** An aristocratic friend of Mr. Flamwell. *Boz, Tales, Sparkins.*

**GUILDFORD.** Mr. Crummles was on his way back from Guildford, where he had fulfilled an engagement with the greatest applause, when he met Nicholas Nickleby (*Nickleby*, 22). It was somewhere near that town that Dora's birthday picnic was held. *Copperfield*, 33.

**GUILDHALL.** The court of common pleas, where the great Bardell-Pickwick trial took place, was on the right of the yard, where the Picture Gallery now stands (*Pickwick*, 34). The two giants, Gog and Magog, are described in *Humphrey*.

**GULPIDGE, MR. AND MRS.** Guests of the Waterbrook's. Mr. Gulpidge had something to do at second hand with the law business of the Bank. *Copperfield*, 25.

**GUMMIDGE, MRS.** The widow of Daniel Peggotty's partner, and housekeeper of the boat on the beach. She was subject to fits of great depression, when she would say, " I'm a lone, lorn creetur, and everythink goes contrairy with me." When Peggotty left to search for Little Em'ly, Mrs. Gummidge remained in the boat against the time they should come back, and finally she emigrated to Australia with the re-united couple, becoming a cheerful and happy companion. *Copperfield*, 3, 7, 10, 17, 21, 22, 31, 32, 40, 51, 57, 63.

**GUNTER.** A quarrelsome young medical student, who formed one of the party at Bob Sawyer's party in Lant Street. *Pickwick*, 32.

**GUPPY, WILLIAM.** Clerk to Kenge and Carboy, and a vulgar young man who fell in love with Esther Summerson, whom he was sent to meet on her arrival from the country. Having proposed to her and been refused, he took it into his head to make investigations into the mystery of her birth, and thus became acquainted with Lady Dedlock's secret. After Esther's illness Guppy's admiration waned, but later he changed his mind and with great magnanimity renewed his pro-posal, which was unhesitatingly refused on Esther's behalf by Mr. Jarndyce. *Bleak House*, 3, 4, 7, 9, 13, 14, 19, 20, 24, 29, 32, 33, 38, 39, 44, 55, 62, 64.

Mr. Guppy's mother was an excitable old lady, highly delighted at her son's courtship and highly indignant when it was rejected. " She has her failings—as who has not—but I never knew her do it when company was present, at which time you may freely trust her with wines, spirits or malt liquors," was the handsome tribute paid by her son. *Bleak House*, 9, 38, 64.

**GUSHER.** One of Mrs. Pardiggle's missionary friends. *Bleak House*, 8, 15.

**GUSTER.** The Snagsbys' servant, " by some supposed to have been christened Augusta," who was brought up in a work-house, but developed fits, for which the parish could not account. *Bleak House*, 10, 11, 19, 25, 42, 59.

**GWYNN, MISS.** One of the teachers at Westgate House. *Pickwick*, 16.

# H

**HACKNEY COACH.** This was a heavy two-horse vehicle, like a small coach, let out for public hire at the rate of a shilling for the first and sixpence for each subsequent mile. By the 30's it was being superseded by the cab, but sufficient description of the dirty and clumsy equipage is given in *Boz, Scenes*, 7, to picture what the hackney coach was like.

**" HAD I A HEART FOR FALSEHOOD FRAMED."** This is a song from R. B. Sheridan's *The Duenna*, Act I, Scene 5. *Dombey*, 14.

**HAGGAGE, DR.** A drunken debtor in the Marshalsea, who was summoned to usher Little Dorrit into the world. " Childbed ? " said he. " I'm the boy." *Dorrit*, I, 6, 7.

**HAGUE, THE.** Jeremiah Flintwinch was reported to be consorting with Dutchmen on the banks of the canals at the Hague after his disappearance from England. *Dorrit*, II, 31.

**HALF MOON AND SEVEN STARS.** An obscure alehouse at Mr. Pecksniff's village. *Chuzzlewit*, 4.

**HALL, SAMUEL CARTER.** Possible original of Pecksniff. (*q.v.*)

**HALLIDAY, BROTHER.** A Mormon agent in Bristol. *Uncommercial*, 20.

**HALLIFORD.** Bill Sikes and Oliver Twist got a lift on a cart going to Lower Halliford, when making their way to Chertsey. *Twist*, 21.

**HALSEWELL, THE.** An outward bound East Indiaman lost on the rocks near Sea-combe, on the island of Purbeck. *Reprinted, Long Voyage.*

**HAM HOUSE.** In the fields near this fine old mansion occurred the fatal duel between Sir Mulberry Hawk and Lord Frederick

Verisopht. Ham House is across the river from Twickenham, about half a mile from Petersham village. *Nickleby*, 50.

**HAMLET'S AUNT.** Name given by David Copperfield to Mrs. Henry Spiker. (*q.v.*)

**HAMMERSMITH.** Minerva House, the " finishing establishment for young ladies," kept by the Misses Crumpton, was at Hammersmith (*Boz, Tales, Sentiment*). There also was the school in which the fortunate Miss Browndock, Mrs. Nickleby's husband's cousin's sister-in-law, had a partnership (*Nickleby*, 17). The Matthew Pocket family lived there in a house by the riverside ; hence Herbert Pocket meeting Clara Barley when she was completing her education at Hammersmith (*Expectations*, 21, 22, 46). Oliver Twist was dragged through the town in his weary journey to Chertsey (*Twist*, 21). The Suspension Bridge, near which the market gardener picked up the coquettish serving maid to give her a lift (*Boz, Scenes*, 6), was erected in 1827, being the first suspension bridge near London. It was replaced in 1887 by the present structure.

**HAMPSTEAD.** Pre-eminent among the Dickens associations of Hampstead are the Ponds (near the Hampstead Heath Station of the N.L.Rly.), which engaged Mr. Pickwick's research and inspired his " Speculations on the Source of the Hampstead Ponds with Some Observations on the Theory of Tittlebats." *Pickwick*, 1.

Near these same ponds was Miss Griffin's establishment, consisting of eight ladies and two young gentlemen, who were paraded up and down the Hampstead Road (*Haunted House*). Gabriel Parsons spent his wedding day strolling about the Heath, execrating his father-in-law (*Boz, Tales, Tottle*). David Copperfield, after a plunge in the Roman bath in the Strand, used to walk to Hampstead, getting some breakfast on the Heath (*Copperfield*, 35). In the fields near by Walter Gay would walk and think on his future life in the Barbados (*Dombey*, 15). Bill Sikes crossed up the Heath from the Vale of Health in his flight after murdering Nancy (*Twist*, 48). After his marriage to the Marchioness, Dick Swiveller settled down there in a little cottage (*Curiosity Shop*, 73). Hampstead was, at one time, a favourite resort of Dickens, who would ride out there from Doughty Street with Forster and have a chop and glass of wine at Jack Straw's Castle. At Wylde's Farm, near North End, he wrote a portion of *Bleak House*.

**HAMPTON.** It was at this river town that Bill Sikes and Oliver Twist stayed some hours at " an old public-house with a defaced sign-board " when making their way to Chertsey (*Twist*, 21). Near Hampton was the bachelor cottage " on the brink of the Thames," where Lightwood and Wrayburn set up a joint establishment (*Mutual Friend*, I, 12) ; while at the " little racecourse at Hampton," vividly described in *Nickleby*, 50, began the fatal quarrel between Sir Mulberry Hawk and Lord Frederick Verisopht.

**HAMPTON COURT.** The Palace has for many years been the residence of royal pensioners. Here it was that Mrs. Gowan lived by virtue of her husband having been in a British Embassy, where he died at his post with his drawn salary in his hand. *Dorrit*, I, 17, 26.

**HANDEL.** Herbert Pocket's name for Pip, " We are so Harmonious, and you have been a Blacksmith, would you mind Handel for a familiar name ? " *Expectations*, 22.

**HANDFORD, JULIUS.** The name adopted by John Harmon when he went to see the drowned body supposed to be his own. *Mutual Friend*, I, 3, 16 ; II, 13 ; IV, 12.

**HANGING SWORD ALLEY.** This is a narrow little alley opening out of Whitefriars Street (formerly Water Lane), Fleet Street, in which Mr. Jerry Cruncher had his apartments (*Two Cities*, II, 1). On his tramp to the Bagnets, near the Elephant, George the Trooper cast a glance at the alley, which would seem to be something in his way. *Bleak House*, 27.

**HANNAH.** Miss La Creevy's servant girl "with an uncommonly dirty face." *Nickleby*, 3.

**HARD TIMES.** This book, written as " a satire against those who see figures and averages, and nothing else—the representatives of the wickedest and most enormous vice of the times," was the first story written by Dickens for *Household Words*, in which it appeared, April–August, 1854, being published in book form later in the same year.

*Principal Characters.* Thomas Gradgrind, a man of facts, and his children, Louisa and Thomas ; Josiah Bounderby, a self-made man ; Stephen Blackpool, a mill hand ; Sleary, a circus proprietor ; Cissy Jupe, an orphan adopted by Gradgrind ; Mrs. Sparsit, Bounderby's housekeeper ; James Harthouse, an aristocratic trifler.

Thomas Gradgrind professes to rule his life and bring up his family by a strict adherence to facts. Louisa is married to the impossible upstart Bounderby and young Tom is placed in Bounderby's bank. Being a wastrel, Tom soon gets into debt and steals from the bank, successfully casting suspicion of the theft upon Stephen Blackpool, a mill hand whose life has been ruined by a drunken wife from whom he can get no release. Tom makes use of his sister both before and after her marriage to serve his own ends, but he is watched by Mrs. Sparsit and a lad named Bitzer. When Harthouse comes to Coketown on political business he falls in love with Louisa, and for the moment she is carried away by the novelty of receiving attentions instead of dry facts. When it comes to an elopement, however, she flies to her father and opens his eyes to the knowledge that life contains sentiments as powerful as facts. Bounderby refuses to take her back. Mr. Gradgrind is finally converted from facts by the flight of his son Tom, whose guilt has been brought to light by the accidental death of Blackpool. The father tracks him to Sleary's circus, where he is acting in disguise, and finally, by the help of the once despised circus owner, succeeds in getting his lad out of the country. Gradgrind's conversion is now complete, but the tragic sequels to his facts remain in the ruined life of his daughter, and the wasted career of his fugitive son.

**HARDY.** A friend of Percy Noakes and one of the promoters of the Steam Excursion, "a practical joker; immensely popular with married ladies and a general favourite with young men." *Boz, Tales, Excursion.*

**HAREDALE.** Geoffrey Haredale was a Catholic squire, uncle of Emma Haredale and heir to his murdered brother Reuben. His whole life was embittered by a popular suspicion that he was himself responsible for his brother's death, and by a blind hatred of Sir John Chester and his son Edward. Among the smoking ruins of his house, burned by the rioters, Haredale discovered Rudge, whose guilt of Reuben's murder he had established, and handed him over to justice. Finally, he met Sir John Chester in a duel and killed him, whereupon he fled abroad and entered a monastery, where he spent the remainder of his life. *Barnaby,* 1, 10–12, 14, 15, 20, 25–7, 29, 34, 42–4, 56, 61, 66, 67, 71, 76, 79, 81, 82.

Emma Haredale was the daughter of the murdered Reuben and niece of Mr. Geoffrey, with whom she lived. She was Dolly Varden's foster-sister, and the locksmith's daughter enabled her to keep up a correspondence with her lover, Edward Chester, whose attentions were discouraged by Geoffrey Haredale. When the riots broke out Emma and Dolly fell into the hands of Hugh and Sim Tappertit and were taken to a low resort, whence Gashford tried to inveigle Emma away. Both girls were rescued by their respective lovers; Emma and Edward Chester were married, and went abroad. 1, 4, 12–15, 20, 25, 27–9, 32, 41, 59, 70, 71, 79, 82.

**HARKER.** 1. The Rev. John was a clergyman of Groombridge Wells, who acted as reference for Mrs. Miller when she adopted a Foundling orphan. *No Thoroughfare.*

2. The officer in charge of the jury in The Trial for Murder. *Two Ghost Stories.*

**HARLEIGH.** A musical friend of the Gattletons, who took part in the performance of *Masaniello. Boz, Tales, Porter.*

**HARLEY, JOHN P.** A comic actor of considerable ability, who was well known on the Drury Lane boards. He took the title rôle in *The Strange Gentleman* and was Felix Tapkins in *Is She His Wife?* He died in 1858. *Sketches of Gentlemen (Theatrical).*

**HARLEY STREET.** In the handsomest house in Harley Street lived the Merdles. *Dorrit,* I, 20.

**HARMON, JOHN.** The son of Old Harmon, the Dust Contractor, and central character of *Mutual Friend.* Having been turned out of doors by his father, he went to the Cape, returning thence on news of the old man's death. By his father's will, John was to marry Bella Wilfer. On his arrival at the docks he was robbed and thrown overboard as dead. He swam ashore, however, and assuming the name of Julius Handford, went to see the body which had been found and identified as his own. Henceforth John Harmon was dead and John Rokesmith, as he now called himself, was alive. In this new name he took service with his father's old servant, Boffin, and at the same time went to lodge with the Wilfers and saw the girl who was to have been his bride. He fell in love with her when she went to live at the Boffins, and aided by the old people, who had soon discovered his identity, he beat down the selfishness in her heart and won her love. For a year after their marriage he kept up the Rokesmith pretence, but eventually resumed his real name and entered into his father's property. *Mutual Friend,* I, 2, 3, 4, 6, 8, 9, 12, 15–17; II, 7–10, 12–14; III, 4, 5, 9, 15, 16; IV, 4, 5, 11–14, 16.

**HARMONIC MEETING.** The modern music-hall is a development of the old harmonic meetings held in various public-houses such as are described in *Boz, Scenes,* 2, and in *Bleak House,* 11, 32, 33. Refreshments were served during the programme, and below the platform, which served as a stage, was a large table where the proprietor, or a chairman employed for the purpose, sat surrounded by his friends and announced each item. A seat at the chairman's table was much sought after by the young "bloods," and the chairman's friendship, with a consequent invitation to the table, was usually procurable for an unlimited supply of liquor.

**HARMONY JAIL.** The popular name of Boffin's Bower. (*q.v.*)

**HARRIS.** 1. The real name of Short, the Punch and Judy showman. (*q.v.*)

2. The greengrocer at whose shop the Bath footman held their "swarry." This shop is now the Beaufort Arms. *Pickwick,* 37.

3. A law-stationer friend of Mr. John Dounce. *Boz, Characters,* 7.

**HARRIS, MRS.** A mythical friend of Mrs. Gamp, and one of Dickens's most remarkable creations. "A fearful mystery surrounded this lady of the name of Harris, whom no one in the circle of Mrs. Gamp's acquaintance had ever seen; neither did any human being know her place of residence, though Mrs. Gamp appeared to be in constant communication with her. . . . The prevalent opinion was that she was a phantom of Mrs. Gamp's brain . . . created for the express purpose of holding visionary dialogues with her on all manner of subjects and invariably winding up with a compliment." It was the culminating point in the quarrel between Betsey Prig and Mrs. Gamp when the former, referring to Mrs. Harris, uttered the heresy, " I don't believe there's no sich a person." *Chuzzlewit*, 19, 25, 29, 40, 46, 49, 51, 52.

**HARRISON.** A little orphan whom the Rev. Frank Milvey suggested as being suitable for adoption by the Boffins. *Mutual Friend*, I, 9.

**HARROW.** Matthew Pocket was an old Harrovian. *Expectations*, 23.

**HARRY.** 1. The ostler at the Golden Cross Hotel. *Boz, Scenes*, 15.

2. A debtor in Solomon Jacobs's lock-up. *Boz, Tales, Tottle*.

3. Mr. Marton's favourite scholar. *Curiosity Shop*, 24, 25.

4. The pedlar who offered to remove the blood stains from Bill Sikes's clothes. *Twist*, 48.

**HARTHOUSE, JAMES.** A good-looking, well-dressed, easy-mannered man of the world, who, having been bored with every kind of career, went to Coketown as a Parliamentary candidate. By cunning insinuation and well-assumed sympathy he worked his way into Louisa Bounderby's affections, furthering his progress in her favour by a simulated friendship for young Tom. At last Harthouse seized the opportunity of Bounderby's absence to ask Louisa to run away with him, but the girl, horrified at the trap into which she had nearly fallen, ran away to her father for shelter. Unknown to anyone, Cissy Jupe went to Harthouse and induced him to leave Coketown. *Hard Times*, II, 1–3, 5, 7–12 ; III, 2, 3.

**HART STREET, BLOOMSBURY.** In the parish church of St. George, Hart Street, Frederick Charles William Kitterbell was christened, Mr. Nicodemus Dumps standing sponsor. *Boz, Tales, Christening*.

**HARVEY.** The young gentleman who was to marry Miss Emma Fielding. *Sketches of Couples*.

**" HAS SHE THEN FAILED."** The Gentleman in Small Clothes was quoting from a popular song, set to music by Bishop, running :—

> Has she then failed in her truth,
> The beautiful maid I adore ;
> Shall I never again hear her voice,
> Nor see her loved form any more ?
> *Nickleby.* 49.

**HATFIELD.** After the murder of Nancy Bill Sikes made for Hatfield, where he " crept into a small public-house," probably the Eight Bells in the main street (*Twist*, 48). The town had a sentimental interest for Mrs. Lirriper, for she spent her honeymoon there at the Salisbury Arms (where Dickens himself had put up in 1838), while her husband's brother also spent a fortnight in the same place, at the good lady's expense. Finally,

Mr. Lirriper was laid to rest in the rural churchyard. *Lirriper's Legacy*.

**HATTON GARDEN.** While crossing the corner of Holborn and Hatton Garden Mr. Dumps was assisted by a very genteel young man, who in turn assisted himself to the christening mug Dumps was carrying to the Kitterbells (*Boz, Tales, Christening*). At No. 54 was probably the police court where Mr. Fang presided (*Twist*, 11). Hatton Garden formed part of Phil Squod's beat as a tinker (*Bleak House*, 26), and there, after having " gone through the *Gazette*," Mr. Jellyby and his family took a furnished lodging. *Bleak House*, 30.

**HAUNTED HOUSE, THE.** This was a short story in eight chapters, published in the Christmas number of *All the Year Round*, 1859. Only the two chapters written by Dickens—The Mortals in the House and The Ghost in Master B's Room—are dealt with in this book. The former described how the house was hired and the company invited by John to investigate the ghost ; the latter is a vision of John's own youth.

**HAUNTED MAN, THE.** *The Haunted Man and The Ghost's Bargain* was the full title of the Christmas Book published in 1848. The frontispiece and title-page were from drawings by Tenniel, while Stanfield, Leech and Stone supplied other illustrations.

The story is of a learned chemist, Redlaw, who after a fit of melancholy is visited by a malign spirit which gives him the power to forget the past with its wrongs and troubles, and to communicate this forgetfulness to those whom he meets. The result of this is that he has no memory of the past to soften him. Others are soon infected by the evil he radiates, but Milly Swidger is proof against the workings of this malign influence, and through her, Redlaw is brought back to the memory of the past, and the evil he has disseminated is undone. The burden of the story is, " Lord, keep my memory green."

**HAVISHAM, MISS.** The eccentric old lady who lived in seclusion at Satis House and employed Pip, as a lad, to amuse her. Many years before she had been a beautiful heiress, engaged to be married to a man named Compeyson. On the wedding morning, when she was dressed for the altar, she discovered that Compeyson had deserted her, and the shock unhinged her mind. She passed the remainder of her days in her bridal dress, her only pastime being to adopt young girls and train them up to break men's hearts. Her last protégée was Estella. Miss Havisham paid for Pip's indentures to Joe Gargery, and for many years Pip looked upon her as the secret author of his Great Expectations. When Miss Havisham died she left the bulk of her fortune to Estella, and only small sums to the relatives who had long been cringing to her. *Expectations*, 8, 9, 11–13, 17, 19, 22, 29, 38, 44, 49, 57.

Arthur Havisham, her brother, was a ne'er-do-well who fell into the clutches of Compeyson and died of drink. 42.

**HAWDON, CAPTAIN.** The retired military officer who, under the name of Nemo, lived in abject poverty as a law writer and died in the rooms over old Krook's shop, lamented by no one but Jo, the crossing sweeper. He had, before her marriage, been the lover of Lady Dedlock and was the father of her child, Esther Summerson. This was the secret discovered by Tulkinghorn and Guppy. After her flight Lady Dedlock made her way to the squalid and filthy cemetery (that of St. Mary-le-Strand, now covered by York Street, running between Drury Lane and Catherine Street) where Nemo had been buried. There she was found dead. *Bleak House*, 5, 10–12, 16, 21, 26, 27, 29, 32, 40.

**HAWK, SIR MULBERRY.** A swaggering, bullying man-about-town, who lived by fleecing young noblemen. In this capacity he was helping Ralph Nickleby despoil Lord Frederick Verisopht when he met Kate Nickleby, whom he determined to ruin. He was thwarted in his designs, however, by Nicholas, who gave him a sound thrashing and disfigured him for life. Hawk eventually killed his patron, Lord Verisopht, in a duel, and was compelled to fly the country. *Nickleby*, 19, 26–8, 32, 38, 50, 65.

**HAWKINS.** 1. A middle-aged baker whom Miss Rugg had successfully sued for breach of promise. *Dorrit*, I, 25.

2. A new M.P. severely criticised by the political young gentleman. *Sketches of Gentlemen*.

**HAWKINSES.** An aristocratic family, of Taunton Vale, with whom Mrs. Nickleby used to stay when a girl. *Nickleby*, 35.

**HAWKINSON.** An aunt of Georgiana Podsnap, who left her a necklace. *Mutual Friend*, IV, 2.

**HAWKYARD, VERITY.** "A yellow-faced, peak-nosed gentleman, clad all in iron grey to his gaiters." He was a self-righteous, religious man, accustomed to think that the Almighty thought well of him and valued him as a good servant. He tried to bring up George Silverman, to whom he was trustee, in his own narrow path of religious humbug, but finally washed his hands of him. *George Silverman*.

**HAYDON, R. B.** Part original of Harold Skimpole. (*q.v.*)

**HAYES, MRS.** Suggested original of Polly Toodle. (*q.v.*)

**HAYNES.** A police inspector in the Borough. *Reprinted, Inspector Field*.

**HEADSTONE, BRADLEY.** Charlie Hexam's schoolmaster, and the head of the boys' section in a school on the borders of Kent and Surrey. Falling violently in love with Lizzie Hexam he vainly pressed his suit, and finding her friendly with Eugene Wrayburn, conceived a consuming

hatred for him. Following Wrayburn to the river town where Lizzie had taken refuge, Headstone made a murderous attack on his rival, and left him for dead. The only person aware of his guilt was Rogue Riderhood, who demanded the price of his silence. Desperate and exasperated at the knowledge that Wrayburn was alive after all, and married to Lizzie, Headstone kept an appointment with Riderhood and dragged his enemy into a lock, where both were drowned. *Mutual Friend*, II, 1, 6, 11, 14, 15; III, 9–11; IV, 1, 6, 7, 10, 11, 15.

**HEART'S DELIGHT.** Captain Cuttle's pet name for Florence Dombey. *Dombey*, 23.

**HEATHFIELD, ALFRED.** Dr. Jeddler's ward and a bright young man in love with Marion Jeddler. On coming of age he went on his travels, returning after three years to claim his bride. Marion had, however, learned that her sister Grace loved him, and for her sake she disappeared. In due time Alfred Heathfield fell in love with Grace and married her, settling down as the village doctor, and a real benefactor to the poor and those in need. *Battle of Life*.

**HEEP, URIAH.** Mr. Wickfield's clerk and eventual partner, "a red-haired person, whose hair was cropped as close as the closest stubble, who had hardly any eyebrows, and no eyelashes, and eyes of a red-brown, so unsheltered and unshaded that I remember wondering how he went to sleep." By always being "'umble," the hypocritical young man worked his way into Mr. Wickfield's confidence and partnership, on the tacit understanding that Agnes should become his wife. In his position of trust, Uriah Heep embezzled and forged deeds by which he defrauded various of Wickfield's partners, but his schemes were closely watched by Micawber, and in due time that wonderful man cleared his own reputation and that of Mr. Wickfield by denouncing Uriah and proving his guilt. He last appears as the model prisoner, No. 27, at a Middlesex gaol, awaiting transportation for life for fraud against the Bank. *Copperfield*, 15–17, 19, 25, 26, 35, 36, 39, 42, 49, 52, 54, 61.

Mrs. Heep, his mother, was a skilful teacher of the art of hypocrisy, "Ury, be 'umble," was her constant maxim and advice. 17, 39, 42, 52, 54, 61.

**"HELM A WEATHER."** Part of a song from *The Tar for All Weathers*. *Mutual Friend*, II, 7.

**HELVES, CAPTAIN.** A guest of the Tauntons on the Steam Excursion. He was full of wonderful stories of his own prowess in India and elsewhere, but sadly disappointed the Tauntons by his defection to the Briggs' faction. *Boz, Tales, Excursion*.

**HENDON.** "That was a good place, not far off, and out of most people's way," reasoned Bill Sikes to himself, during his flight from justice. "But when he got there

all the people he met—the very children at
the doors—seemed to view him with suspicion." *Twist*, 48.

**HENLEY.** " When we lived at Henley,
Barnes's gander was stole by tinkers," re-
marked Mr. F's Aunt (*Dorrit*, I, 13). The
Angler's Inn where Eugene Wrayburn was
taken after Headstone's murderous attack
was probably the Red Lion, Henley (*See*
Angler's Inn), and Plashwater Weir Mill
Lock was probably Hurley Lock, about
six miles down river from Henley. *Mutual
Friend*, IV, 1, 7, 15.

**HENRIETTA.** The young lady with whom
Tom the pavement artist " walked " for a
while. " As a friend I am willing to walk
with you on the understanding that softer
sentiments may flow. We walked." *Somebody's Luggage*.

**HENRY.** 1. " A cousin of Maria Lobbs
. . . who seemed to keep Maria Lobbs all
to himself." *Pickwick*, 17.
2. A pawnbroker's assistant " with curly
black hair, diamond ring, and double silver
watchguard." *Boz, Scenes*, 23.

**HERBERT, MR.** A member of the House
of Commons, who protested against Lord
George Gordon sitting in the House wearing
a blue cockade. *Barnaby*, 73.

**HERSCHEL, JOHN.** First cousin of John,
the lessee of the Haunted House. He and
his wife, " a charming creature," were
among the guests invited to solve the
mystery of the ghost. *Haunted House*.

**HESSIAN BOOTS.** These were high boots,
reaching almost to the knees, with a shaped
top frequently ornamented with a tassel.
*Pickwick*, 10.

**HEXAM.** Jesse or Gaffer Hexam was a
" nightbird " of the Thames, who made a
living by searching the turbid waters for
corpses, which he robbed before handing
over to the police. It was he who found the
supposed corpse of John Harmon, of whose
murder he was accused by his quondam
partner, Rogue Riderhood. The party
which went to arrest him, however, found
him drowned near his own boat. *Mutual
Friend*, I, 1, 3, 6, 12–14 ; II, 16.

Lizzie Hexam, the Gaffer's daughter, was
a dark girl of nineteen or twenty, who un-
willingly rowed his boat, and brought up her
young brother, Charlie, on whom she expended a wealth of love and care. On her
father's death she became acquainted with
Eugene Wrayburn, who took an interest in
her and had her educated. On refusing
Bradley Headstone's passionate offer of
marriage she was indignantly repudiated by
her brother, who desired the match for the
sake of his own " respectability." To escape
Headstone, Lizzie hid herself in the country.
Eugene Wrayburn found out where she was
living and followed her, being himself
followed by the schoolmaster, who tried to
murder him. Eugene was saved by Lizzie,

who tended his bedside lovingly. As soon
as he was strong enough to speak they were
married. I, 1, 3, 6, 13 ; II, 1, 2, 5, 6, 11,
14–16 ; III, 1, 2, 8, 9, 11 ; IV, 5–7, 9–11,
16, 17.

Charlie Hexam, Lizzie's young brother,
was a selfish, conceited lad, obsessed with
the ambition of becoming respectable. To
this end he worked hard at school, becoming
a pupil teacher, and tried to persuade Lizzie
to marry Headstone. On her refusal, Charlie
cast her aside, forgetting the weary years
she had nursed him and cared for him ; when
he discovered Bradley Headstone's attack
on Wrayburn, young Hexam, with equal
callousness, disowned his friend, fearful lest
his " respectability " should be damaged by
association with a murderer. He eventually
became assistant master at another school,
with the prospect of becoming headmaster.
I, 3, 6 ; II, 1, 6, 11, 14, 15 ; IV, 7.

**HEYLING, GEORGE.** The subject of the
Old Man's tale about the Queer Client. He
was cast into prison for debt by his wife's
father, and while there his wife and child
died. On inheriting a fortune from his
own father, Heyling devoted his whole life
to wreaking vengeance on the man who
had caused him so much misery. *Pickwick*,
21.

**HICKS, SEPTIMUS.** One of Mrs. Tibbs's
boarders, " a tallish, white-faced young man,
with spectacles, and a black ribbon round his
neck." " He was fond of lugging into
conversation all sorts of quotations from *Don
Juan*." He married Miss Matilda Maplesone,
whom he eventually deserted. *Boz, Tales,
Boarding House*.

**HICKSON.** 1. Subscriber of one guinea
to the Indigent Orphans' Friends' Benevolent Institution. *Boz, Scenes*, 19.
2. Guests of the Gattletons at their
theatrical entertainment. *Boz, Tales, Porter*.

**HIGDEN, BETTY.** " An active old woman,
with a bright dark eye, and a resolute face,
yet quite a tender creature." Though
nearly eighty, she kept a " minding school "
and a mangle, operated by Sloppy, one of
her lads. Mrs. Boffin desired to adopt
Betty's great grandson, Johnny, but the
child died and his loss broke old Betty's
heart. Her one dread was to go into the
workhouse, and she started out to earn her
living by peddling needlework. At last, still
terrified by the thought of the poor-house,
she sank dying by the roadside, and expired
in the arms of Lizzie Hexam. *Mutual
Friend*, I, 16 ; II, 9, 10, 14 ; III, 8, 9.

**HIGHGATE.** Dickens had a personal and
sad connection with this place, for there are
buried his parents and his infant daughter,
Dora Annie. He was writing *Copperfield*
when his child died, and the place finds
considerable mention in that book. Mrs.
Steerforth's house, according to Mr. Walter
Dexter, was Church House, South Grove

(*Copperfield*, 20, 29, 32), and in another part of the town lived Dr. Strong after he left Canterbury (36, 42, 51). On the Highgate Road were the cottages of David and Miss Trotwood (36). Mr. Pickwick conducted invaluable researches in Highgate (*Pickwick*, 1). The famous Highgate Archway, carrying Hornsey Lane across Archway Road, built in 1813, was replaced by the present viaduct in 1900. Noah Claypole and Charlotte passed beneath it when tramping into London (*Twist*, 42). There was a toll-gate at the Archway, and there Inspector Bucket first found a trace of the missing Lady Dedlock (*Bleak House*, 57). Bill Sikes strode up Highgate Hill (*Twist*, 48) in his wild flight from justice.

**HIGH HOLBORN.** This is the name given to that portion of Holborn lying west of Holborn Bars and reaching to Drury Lane. *See* Holborn.

**HIGHLOWS.** These were laced boots, reaching to the ankle, practically identical with the modern ankle boots.

**HILL, MRS. SEYMOUR.** Probable original of Miss Mowcher. (*q.v.*)

**HILTON.** Master of Ceremonies at the ball given by the Misses Crumpton at Minerva House. *Boz, Tales, Sentiment.*

**HOBLER, MR.** Francis Hobler, mentioned several times in *Boz* as a great cracker of jokes, was a solicitor and, for over fifty years, principal clerk at the Mansion House Police Court. He retired in 1843. *Boz, Our Parish*, 1 ; *Scenes*, 17.

**HOCKLEY-IN-THE-HOLE.** This was one of the worst regions of London at a time when London possessed its worst slums. It ran from Windmill Hill, leading to the right out of Leather Lane, and curved round to Townsend Lane, leading into Clerkenwell Green. In 1774 its name was changed to Ray Street, and in 1856–57 the whole district was transformed by the making of Clerkenwell Road and Rosebery Avenue. The Artful Dodger led Oliver Twist through this district when bringing him to London. *Twist*, 8.

**HOGARTH, MARY.** The original of so many of Dickens's heroines was his wife's next youngest sister, who frequently stayed with the newly married couple. According to Forster, " by sweetness of nature even more than by graces of person she had made herself the ideal of his life " when she died, in 1837, at the age of seventeen. His grief at her death not only so upset Dickens at the time that he was unable to proceed with *Pickwick*, of which no number appeared in June, 1837, but tinged practically the whole of his subsequent life. Mary Hogarth furnished the original for Kate Nickleby, Rose Maylie, Madeleine Bray, Emma Haredale, Mary Graham, Florence Dombey, Agnes Wickfield, Ada Clare and Lucy Manette.

**HOGHTEN TOWERS.** " A house centuries old . . . a mile or so from the road between Preston and Blackpool." This was where George Silverman was sent " to be purified." *George Silverman.*

**HOLBORN.** This great thoroughfare finds such constant mention in Dickens that only the principal references can be dealt with in any detail. The street has undergone several changes since the period of the novels. Before the making of New Oxford Street in 1847, the east-west thoroughfare led through High Holborn, Broad Street and High Street to the junction of Oxford Street and Tottenham Court Road, the district to the right, now traversed by New Oxford Street, being the famous Rookery of St. Giles. At its other extremity, Holborn descended by a steep hill into Farringdon Street, opposite Snow Hill. The viaduct from the present Holborn Circus to Newgate Street was built in 1867. In addition to these great changes, the making of Southampton Row and Kingsway, early in the present century, destroyed Kingsgate Street, while a monument to mid-Victorian bad taste covers the site of old Furnival's Inn. Holborn was the scene of great excitement during the Gordon Riots (*Barnaby*, 50, 66, 68), when Mr. Langdale's distillery was burned down. Job Trotter ran up Holborn to summon Perker when Mr. Pickwick decided to leave the Fleet (*Pickwick*, 47), and Bill Sikes hurried little Oliver Twist up the hill on their way westward (*Twist*, 21). Esther Summerson's first introduction to " a London particular " was when Guppy took her and the cousins by Holborn to Thavies Inn (*Bleak House*, 4). In a stable yard in High Holborn Plornish negotiated with Tip Dorrit's creditor (*Dorrit*, I, 12). But the associations of the street with *Chuzzlewit* surpass all others. First and foremost, Mrs. Gamp lived in Kingsgate Street, High Holborn, and it was in search of her that Mr. Pecksniff rattled in a hackney cab over Holborn stones (19). Later, Mrs. Gamp took on the case of Lewsome, in the Bull, Holborn (25, 29), while it was to the breathless interest of a hackney coach-stand in High Holborn that Betsey Prig stowed a huge twopenny salad in her pocket (49).

**HOLBORN COURT, GRAY'S INN.** The name of this court was changed to South Square in 1829. Mr. Phunky lived there (*Pickwick*, 31), and on the top story of No. 2 were the chambers to which Traddles took his bride. *Copperfield*, 59.

**HOLIDAY ROMANCE.** This story was specially written for an American magazine, *Our Young Folks*, appearing Jan.–May, 1868, being published simultaneously in *All the Year Round*. It consists of four stories, supposed to be written by two boys and two girls ; the boys recounting the adventures of William Tinkling and of Captain Boldheart ; the girls telling the fairy tale of

Princess Alicia, and the story, with a moral for the grown-ups, of the country where parents obey their children.

**HOLLOWAY.** As late as the 60's Holloway was something of a rural suburb, " divided from London by fields and trees." Mr. Wilfer's home, however, was approached from Battle Bridge (King's Cross) by a wilderness of dustheaps and waste land. *Mutual Friend*, I, 4.

**HOLLY TREE, THE.** This story appeared in the Christmas Number of *Household Words*, 1855. It relates the story of a young man, Charley, who supposing himself jilted, is on the way to America when he is snowed up in the Holly Tree Inn. There he becomes friendly with Cobbs, the Boots, who relates the story of two children's elopement. In the end Charley's supposed rival appears, on his way to Gretna Green with the cousin of the girl whom Charley loved. Mr. B. W. Matz considers that the Holly Tree was meant for the George Inn, Greta Bridge.

**HOLYWELL STREET.** This old street, long the resort of second-hand booksellers and old clothes dealers (*Boz, Scenes*, 6), ran parallel with the Strand on the north side, between the churches of St. Clement Danes and St. Mary-le-Strand. The whole neighbourhood was demolished in widening the Strand and making Aldwych, 1899–1905.

**HOMINY, MRS.** An American " philosopher and authoress," who had travelled abroad, sending home letters to her daughter signed, " The Mother of the Modern Gracchi." *Chuzzlewit*, 22, 23, 34.

**HONEY, LAURA.** (1816–43.) This was a very talented and popular actress, who made a great success at the Adelphi in 1833. *Sketches of Gentlemen* (*Theatrical*).

**HONEYTHUNDER, REV. LUKE.** A hypocritical philanthropist of the brow-beating type, married to Mrs. Crisparkle's sister and guardian of the Landless twins. Like all men of his breed he was ready to believe the worst of his fellow-men, and consequently renounced all responsibility for Neville Landless when the lad was suspected of Edwin Drood's murder. *Drood*, 6, 7, 17.

**HOPE.** The name of one of Miss Flite's captive birds. *Bleak House*, 14.

**HOPKINS.** 1. Captain Hopkins, a debtor in the King's Bench Prison "in the last extremity of shabbiness." *Copperfield*, 11.

2. Jack Hopkins, a student friend of Bob Sawyer, and narrator of a remarkable story of a child who swallowed a necklace. *Pickwick*, 32.

3. Candidate for the office of beadle. *Boz, Our Parish*, 4.

4. The bashful young gentleman whose sister, Harriet, was very ill. *Sketches of Gentlemen*.

5. Matthew Hopkins, the witch-finder, flourished from 1644–47, during which time he hunted out and destroyed many supposed witches in East Anglia. In 1647 he was himself accused of witchcraft and was hanged. *Humphrey*.

6. Vulture Hopkins was one of Mr. Boffin's pet misers. *Mutual Friend*, III, 15.

**HOP POLE INN, TEWKESBURY.** On their journey to Birmingham, Mr. Pickwick, Ben Allen and Bob Sawyer stopped to dine at this inn. It is still the best inn in the town, and unchanged since that historic journey. *Pickwick*, 50.

**HORN COFFEE HOUSE.** This is now the Horn Tavern, 29 Knightrider Street. Mr. Pickwick sent thither for a supply of wine with which to entertain his friends in the Fleet. *Pickwick*, 44.

**HORNER, MR.** Mentioned as " of Colosseum fame," this gentleman was the projector of that building for which he painted the remarkable panorama of London, exhibited from 1829 until 1854. The venture ruined him. *See* Colosseum. *Boz, Scenes*, 12.

**HORNSEY.** This was another of the scenes of Mr. Pickwick's "unwearied researches " (*Pickwick*, 1). Betsy Trotwood's worthless husband was born at Hornsey and was buried in the parish churchyard. *Copperfield*, 54.

**HORSEGUARDS.** One of Mr. Merdle's guests. *Dorrit*, I, 21.

**HORSE GUARDS, THE.** " Shorn of his graceful limbs," Sim Tappertit was established by Gabriel Varden as a shoeblack under an archway near the Horse Guards (*Barnaby*, 82). According to the Gentleman in Small Clothes, the planet Venus had business in the Horse Guards (*Nickleby*, 41). The striking of the clock there warned Mark Tapley that it was time for Martin and Mary to separate after their stolen meeting in St. James's Park (*Chuzzlewit*, 14). Then, as now, the mounted guard stood at the entrance, and Peggotty took Mr. Dick to see them. *Copperfield*, 35.

**HORSEMONGER LANE.** Opposite the junction of Borough Road and Newington Causeway is Union Street, formerly called Horsemonger Lane, on the southern side of which was Horsemonger Lane Gaol, closed in 1877, the site being turned into a recreation ground. At this gaol the Mannings (*q.v.*) were executed in 1849, and Dickens, who witnessed the scene, wrote a letter to *The Times*, which had much to do with the abolition of public executions. At 5 Horsemonger Lane was Mrs. Chivery's "snug tobacco business." *Dorrit*, I, 18, 22.

**HORTENSE.** Lady Dedlock's maid, " a Frenchwoman of two and thirty . . . who would be handsome but for a certain feline mouth." After five years in Lady Dedlock's service she became jealous of Rosa and was dismissed. Having gained an inkling of her late mistress's secret she tried to extract money from Tulkinghorn, and failing to do so, murdered him. Although Hortense did her utmost to throw suspicion on Lady Dedlock, Inspector Bucket and his wife succeeded in proving her guilt and she was duly arrested. The original of Hortense was Mrs. Manning (*q.v.*). *Bleak House*, 12, 18, 22, 23, 42, 53, 54.

**HORTON, PRISCILLA.** This popular actress was better known in later days as Mrs. German Reed. She and her husband were much in vogue for their amusing dramatic entertainments which were long a feature of London life. *Sketches of Gentlemen* (*Theatrical*).

**HOSIER LANE,** up which Bill Sikes led Oliver Twist, runs out of West Smithfield into King Street, opposite St. Bartholomew's Hospital. *Twist*, 21.

**HOWLER, REV. MELCHISEDEK.** Mrs. MacStinger's spiritual adviser, and the officiating minister at her wedding to Jack Bunsby. *Dombey*, 15, 32, 60.

**HUBBLE.** The village wheelwright and friend of the Gargery family. "His legs were so extraordinarily wide apart that in my short days I always saw some miles of open country between them when I met him coming up the lane." *Expectations*, 4, 5, 35.

**"HUE AND CRY."** This was the paper which deeply absorbed the attention of Fagin (*Twist*, 15). The *Hue and Cry* and *Police Gazette* was a popular paper among the lower classes. In the British Museum are Nos. 461–634, dated Jan. 17, 1818–Dec. 29, 1827, after which date the name was changed to *The Police Gazette* or *Hue and Cry*, No. 1 of which appeared January 18, 1828. The last number in the British Museum Collection is dated November 12, 1834.

**HUGGIN LANE.** This runs from Wood Street, Cheapside, to Gutter Lane, at the corner of which is the Goldsmith's Arms, where there is little doubt the Pickwick Club was wont to meet. The church in which Uncommercial Traveller and Angelica took shelter from a shower (*Uncommercial* 9) was probably St. Michael's, Wood Street, which has an entrance in Huggin Lane.

**HUGH OR MAYPOLE HUGH.** Ostler at the Maypole Inn and a wild, lawless creature who cared for nobody but Barnaby Rudge. Recognising in him a useful tool, Gashford enlisted him among the ranks of rioters, of whom he soon became a ringleader. He had long wanted to possess Dolly Varden, and the riots delivered her into his hands, but she was rescued and Hugh was captured. Gabriel Varden discovered that Hugh was the illegitimate son of Sir John Chester and appealed to the baronet to use his influence to save him, but Chester refused, and in due course Hugh was hanged. *Barnaby*, 10–13, 17, 20–3, 25, 28, 29, 34, 35, 37–40, 44, 48–50, 52–5, 59, 60, 63–5, 67–9, 74–7, 79.

**HUGHES, REVS. HUGH AND STEPHEN ROOCE.** Clergymen in the neighbouring parishes of Penrhos and Llanallgo, who ministered to the people shipwrecked on the *Royal Charter*, homeward bound from Melbourne to Liverpool, which foundered on October 26, 1859. The account of the disaster given in *Uncommercial*, 2, is singularly accurate.

**HULKS, THE.** These were ship prisons, moored in the river, and elsewhere, upon which convicts were confined. The principal hulks off Woolwich were the *Warrior*, an old 74-gun ship, which accommodated 480 convicts employed in the dockyard, and the *Justitia*, whose inmates worked in the arsenal. The men lived in gangs of 15–20, each gang occupying separate compartments, and the communication between the convicts was the source of much evil. *Expectations*, 2.

**HUMM, ANTHONY.** President of the Brick Lane Branch of the United Grand Junction Ebenezer Temperance Association, "a converted fireman, now a schoolmaster and occasionally an itinerant preacher." It has been suggested that the original of Humm was a Mr. G. J. King, who died in 1875. *Pickwick*, 33.

**HUMMUMS HOTEL, COVENT GARDEN.** This is at the corner of Russell Street, and the south-east corner of the Garden. The present building dates from 1892, when it was erected on the site of the hotel where the Finches of the Grove used to meet, and where Pip put up when warned by Wemmick to avoid his own chambers in the Temple. *Expectations*, 34, 45.

**HUMPHREY, MASTER.** "A miss-shapen, deformed, old man," who gathered a circle of friends about him. His clock became the medium for relating the stories of *Barnaby Rudge* and *Old Curiosity Shop*. Master Humphrey was the younger brother of Nell's grandfather. *See* Master Humphrey's Clock.

**HUNGERFORD MARKET** stood on the site now occupied by Charing Cross Station, and had existed from the end of the seventeenth century, though the original market had dwindled and the buildings had fallen into great decay early in the nineteenth century. New buildings were opened in 1833, after the design of Fowler, the architect of Covent Garden Market, and a brisk trade in fish and vegetables was carried on, but the market was a commercial failure and was pulled down to give place to the station in 1862. It was, therefore, the old market with which Dickens's childhood was connected. Through the market were Hungerford Bridge and Hungerford Stairs, by which stood Warren's Blacking Warehouse, where Dickens spent his boyhood's purgatory. There was then, of course, no embankment. At a chandler's shop in the old market lodgings were found for Mr. Dick (*Copperfield*, 35), while from Hungerford Stairs the Micawbers set out for the vessel which was to take them to Australia. 57.

**HUNT.** 1. Captain Boldwig's head gardener. *Pickwick*, 19.

2. Leigh Hunt was the original of Harold Skimpole. (*q.v.*)

**HUNTED DOWN.** This story, for which Dickens received the unusually high payment of £1000, was written specially for the *New York Ledger*, in which it appeared, Aug.-Sept., 1859. It was republished the following year in *All the Year Round*, August 4 and 11. The story was based upon T. G. Wainewright, the murderer. *See* Chuzzlewit, Jonas.

**HUNTER.** 1. Mrs. Leo Hunter, of The Den, Eatanswill, was the famous poetess who wrote the *Ode to an Expiring Fog*, repeated so touchingly to Mr. Pickwick by her husband. *Pickwick*, 15.

2. Horace Hunter was the successful wooer of Miss Emily Brown, and one of the parties to The Great Winglebury Duel. *Boz, Tales, Winglebury.*

3. Mr. Fogle Hunter, a gentleman connected with the Swell Mob. *Mudfog Papers.*

**HUTLEY, JEM,** otherwise known as Dismal Jemmy. A brother of Job Trotter and a down-at-heel actor whom Mr. Pickwick met at Rochester. He read aloud to the Pickwickians "The Stroller's Tale." *Pickwick*, 3, 5, 53.

**HYDE PARK.** Dickens lived in the neighbourhood of the park at several periods. In 1865 he was at 16 Somers Place; the following year at 6 Southwick Place, Hyde Park Square; and in January, 1870, at 5 Hyde Park Place, facing Marble Arch. Oliver Twist and Bill Sikes passed Hyde Park Corner on their weary tramp to Chertsey (*Twist*, 21), and Nancy went to see Rose Maylie at an hotel near by. 39.

**HYPOLITE.** A soldier billetted at the Perfumer's shop, which he offered to mind " while the fair perfumeress stepped out to speak to a neighbour." *Somebody's Luggage.*

# I

**"I BELIEVED YOU TRUE."** Dick Swiveller's apostrophe to the faithless Sophy Wackles, was from one of Moore's songs, beginning :—

> Mary, I believed thee true,
> And I was blessed in thus believing ;
> But now I mourn that e'er I knew
> A girl so fair and so deceiving.
> *Curiosity Shop*, 8.

**"I BELIEVE YOU, MY BO-O-OY."** For many years this was an extremely popular catch phrase. It originated with Paul Bedford, the famous comedian of the 40's and 50's. *Copperfield*, 22.

**"IF I KNOW'D A DONKEY."** This was a parody on a comic coster song, beginning :—

> If I had a donkey wot wouldn't go,
> D'ye think I'd wallop him ? No, no, no.
> But gentle means I'd try, d'ye see,
> Because I hate all cruelty:

The song was really a satire against Humanity Martin (*q.v.*), who is mentioned in it. *Curiosity Shop*, 27.

**"IF YOU'LL COME TO THE BOWER."** Wegg's adaptation of Moore's song, beginning :—

> Will you come to the Bow'r I have shaded for you ?
> Our bed shall be roses all spangled with dew.
> *Mutual Friend*, IV, 3.

**IKEY.** 1. The factotum of Solomon Jacobs, the Cursitor Street bailiff who imprisoned Mr. Watkins Tottle. *Boz, Tales, Tottle.*

2. The stable boy at the inn near the Haunted House, who was responsible for the ghostly phenomena which gave the house its reputation. *Haunted House.*

**"I'LL TELL THEE HOW THE MAIDEN WEPT."** This is, except for Wegg's polite additions, substantially the second verse of the " Light Guitar " (*q.v.*). *Mutual Friend*, I, 15.

**ILLUSTRATORS.** The original illustrators were : George Cruikshank : *Boz, Twist, Humphrey* (1 sketch). R. Seymour : *Pickwick* (7 plates). R. W. Buss : *Pickwick* (2 plates in 3 parts). " Phiz " (H. K. Browne) : remainder of *Pickwick, Nickleby, Humphrey* (part), *Chuzzlewit, Dombey, Copperfield, Bleak House, Dorrit, Two Cities.* G. Cattermole : *Humphrey* (part). D. Maclise : *Humphrey* (1 sketch), title and frontispiece to *Chimes, Cricket on the Hearth* and *Battle of Life.* John Leech : *Christmas Carol*, part of *Chimes, Battle of Life* and of *Haunted Man.* R. Doyle : part of *Chimes* and *Battle of Life.* Clarkson Stanfield : part of *Chimes, Battle of Life* and *Haunted Man.* Marcus Stone : *Haunted Man* (part), *Expectations, Mutual Friend.* S. Luke Fildes : *Drood.* Among the many illustrations to subsequent editions the best known are those of Fred Barnard.

**"I'M A FRIAR."** This is O'Keefe's song, set to music by Reeve, beginning, " I'm a Friar of Orders Grey." *Boz, Characters*, 8.

**INDIA HOUSE.** The old headquarters of the East India Company stood at the corner of Leadenhall Street and Lime Street. On the dissolution of " John Company " in 1858, the house became empty, and in 1862 was pulled down. *Uncommercial*, 3.

**INEXHAUSTIBLE, THE.** The Rokesmith baby. *Mutual Friend*, IV, 12.

**INFANT BONDS OF JOY.** A children's society patronised by Mrs. Pardiggle, of which the members were pledged never to use tobacco in any form. *Bleak House*, 8.

**INFANT PHENOMENON, THE.** The stage name of Miss Ninetta Crummles. (*q.v.*)

**INFORMER.** Before the complete organisation of the police and detective forces a thriving trade used to be driven by a certain class of persons who went about giving information (for which they were paid) against those who committed minor illegal acts. Mr. Pickwick was mistaken for such an one (*Pickwick*, 2), and Noah Claypole set up in the business after the dispersal of Fagin's gang. *Twist*, 53.

**"IN HURRY POST HASTE FOR A LICENCE."** Jungle was quoting from Kane O'Hara's version of Fielding's play of *Tom Thumb*, Act II, Scene 5. *Pickwick*, 10.

**INN.** The principal unnamed inns are the following : 1. The inn on the Marlborough Downs, where Tom Smart met his adventure. Mr. F. G. Kitton considers that the original of this was the inn which once existed at Shepherd's Shore ; other claimants are the Marquis of Ailesbury Arms, Clatford ; the Catherine Wheel, and the Kennet Inn, both at Beckhampton. *Pickwick*, 14.

2. The famous Salisbury Inn where John Westlock entertained Tom Pinch and Martin Chuzzlewit. The White Hart, and the Angel both claim to be the prototype. *Chuzzlewit*, 12.

3. The spacious inn where Bucket and Esther Summerson changed horses while searching for Lady Dedlock. *Bleak House*, 57.

4. The various inns remembered by the traveller at the Holly Tree.

5. The roadside inn where Nicholas and Smike encountered Mr. Crummles. This has been identified as the Coach and Horses at Petersfield. *Nickleby*, 22.

6. The little inn at Canterbury where the Micawbers put up. This was probably the Sun Inn. *Copperfield*, 17.

**INNS OF COURT.** A general term for the law inns, i.e. Gray's Inn, Lincoln's Inn, the Inner and the Middle Temple. These legal societies possess the exclusive right of calling persons to the Bar. *Barnaby*, 67. *Humphrey. Boz, Scenes*, 1.

**INSOLVENT DEBTORS' COURT.** This was in Portugal Street, and was a court where insolvent debtors could appeal for relief from their imprisonment by proving their utter destitution, among other things, that their clothes and personal belongings did not amount to £20 in value. With the alteration of the debtors' laws the court building was turned into the Bankruptcy Court ; then became the Westminster County Court, and was finally demolished in 1909. *Pickwick*, 41, 43, 55. *Copperfield*, 11.

**INSPECTOR, THE.** Also known as the Night Inspector ; he was in charge of the Thames police station, to which the supposed body of John Harmon was taken. He took the case in hand and later went to arrest Rokesmith. *Mutual Friend*, I, 3 12–14 ; IV, 12, 16.

**"INTRIGUE."** The two first plays mentioned by Crummles were well-known stock pieces very popular in their time. *Intrigue* was a farce, *Ways and Means* a comedy by Colman, Junior. The *Mortal Struggle* would appear to have been a melodrama of the deepest dye. *Nickleby*, 23.

**IPSWICH.** Dickens's personal association with Ipswich, dated from 1835, when he was

sent there to report election speeches. He stayed at the Great White Horse (*q.v.*) and gained an intimate acquaintance with the town. He subsequently visited Ipswich on a reading tour in 1861. It has been claimed that Ipswich was the original of Eatanswill. In any case the place was later described without any attempt at disguise, and will be forever associated with the lady in curl papers and Mr. Nupkins. The courtyard where Sam Weller met Job Trotter and the green gate leading to the back of Mr. Nupkins' house are locally pointed out in the vicinity of St. Clement's Church (*Pickwick*, 22–4). In Ipswich Market Place, " opposite the corn chandler's shop,"Dr. Marigold met the Suffolk young woman whom he married. *Dr. Marigold*.

**IRON BRIDGE.** Southwark Bridge, which was at one time popularly known as the Iron Bridge, was a favourite walk of Little Dorrit (I, 9, 18). It was built in 1818 and consisted of three arches of cast iron, the middle one having a span of 240 ft. The Iron Bridge was replaced by the present structure, opened in 1921.

**IRREPRESSIBLE, THE.** The term commonly applied to Lavinia Wilfer. (*q.v.*)

**ISAAC.** The sheriff's officer who took Mrs. Bardell to the Fleet Prison. *Pickwick*, 46.

**"I SAW THY SHOW."** A parody on Moore's, " I saw thy form in youthful prime." *Curiosity Shop*, 27.

**ISLINGTON.** " Merry Islington," as Tom Pinch liked to call it, was on the northern outskirts of London in the first half of the last century. The Angel, for over two centuries a tavern but now a tea shop, was the most important feature of the place as all traffic to and from the north passed by its door. At different times Joe Willett and Barnaby Rudge passed through Islington, leaving London (*Barnaby*, 31, 68). The Artful Dodger brought Oliver into London past the Angel (*Twist*, 8), while later Mr. Brownlow took Oliver out to his home in Pentonville by the same route (12). Messrs. Potter and Smithers, after Making a Night of It, determined to return to their homes in Islington (*Boz, Characters*, 11). Upon settling in London, Tom Pinch went to Islington at random, and there settled with pretty Ruth (*Chuzzlewit*, 36, 37). Mr. Morfin lived in Islington (*Dombey*, 13). The Peacock Inn, where Nicholas's coach stopped on the way to Yorkshire (*Nickleby*, 5), and which is also mentioned in *The Holly Tree*, was further up the street. On their several journeys John Browdie (*Nickleby*, 39) and Esther Summerson, accompanied by Bucket (*Bleak House*, 59), came into London past Islington in the early hours of the morning. Finally, it should not be forgotten that Mrs. Lirriper first began to let lodgings in the neighbourhood. *Lirriper's Lodgings*.

**IS SHE HIS WIFE? OR SOMETHING SINGULAR.** This farce was produced at the St. James's Theatre, Monday, March 6, 1837. Soon after their marriage Mr. Lovetown becomes inattentive to his wife, and she pretends to flirt with a bachelor neighbour, Tapkins, who thinks she is not Lovetown's wife. This gives rise to a great imbroglio, increased by Lovetown flirting with Mrs. Limbury and rendering her little husband dreadfully jealous.

**IVINS.** The popular pronunciation of the name of Miss Jemima Evans. (*q.v.*)

**"I WISH YOU TO SEE IT."** This is an extraordinary perversion of "Drink to me only with thine eyes, and I will pledge with mine." *Mutual Friend*, III, 14.

**IZZARD.** One of the committee which welcomed Mr. Elijah Pogram. *Chuzzlewit*, 34.

# J

**JACK.** 1. The prisoner charged with ill-treating a woman, who died in hospital. *Boz, Characters*, 6.

2. The Lord Mayor, who had come from Hull as a poor boy, and made his fortune in London. *Humphrey.*

3. Mrs. Lupin's man. *Chuzzlewit*, 36.

4. One of the policemen who arrested Jonas Chuzzlewit. *Chuzzlewit*, 51.

5. Riverside character at the public-house where Pip and Magwitch put up in the attempt to smuggle the latter from the country. *Expectations*, 54.

6. A suicide from Waterloo Bridge. *Reprinted, Down with Tide.*

7. The typical sailor described in *Uncommercial*, 5, 20.

**JACKMAN, MAJOR JAMES.** Mrs. Lirriper's lodger, who occupied the parlours and "was punctual in all respects except one." He was a good-hearted man and became joint guardian of little Jemmy Lirriper. *Lirriper's Lodgings and Legacy.*

**"JACK'S DELIGHT."** This is from the first verse of Dibdin's "Lovely Nan." *Jack's Delight is his Lovely Nan* was a popular drama by W. H. Bland, produced at the Pavilion, Whitechapel, in 1835. *Copperfield*, 11 ; *Uncommercial*, 5.

**JACKSON.** 1. Dodson and Fogg's chief clerk, who served the writs on the Pickwickians, and was later detailed to effect the arrest of Mrs. Bardell. *Pickwick*, 20, 31, 46.

2. Young Jackson, of the firm of Barbox Brothers, whose experiences are related in *Mugby Junction.* He had worked his way up in the office until he had become the sole member of the firm which he then dissolved.

3. A former turnkey at the Marshalsea Prison. *Dorrit*, I, 19.

4. An acquaintance of Cousin Feenix, who kept a boxing establishment in Bond Street. *Dombey*, 61.

5. Inspector Bucket's imaginary informant of Lady Dedlock's visit to the brickmaker's. *Bleak House*, 57.

6. Friends of the Plausible Couple. *Sketches of Couples.*

**JACKSONINI.** The clown at the Cloisterham Christmas pantomime. *Drood*, 14.

**JACOBS, SOLOMON.** The bailiff from whose house in Cursitor Street Gabriel Parsons rescued Mr. Watkins Tottle. *Boz, Tales, Tottle.*

**JACOB'S ISLAND.** This is near St. Saviour's Dock, Bermondsey, and has been much improved since the days when *Twist* was written. Much of its slums were demolished in 1883 when a large block of workmen's dwellings was erected. The site of the old island is now traversed by Jacob Street. According to Mr. Dexter (*The London of Dickens*), Toby Crackit's house was "situated at the back of what is now No. 18 Eckell Street." *Twist*, 50.

**JACQUES.** A general name adopted by certain members of the Revolutionary committee, of which Defarge was a leader. There are five Jacques specially mentioned. *Two Cities*, I, 5 ; II, 8, 9, 15, 16, 21–3 ; III, 5, 9, 12, 14, 15.

**JAGGERS.** The Old Bailey lawyer who was employed by Magwitch to pay Pip his allowance while enjoying his Great Expectations. Jaggers was also Miss Havisham's solicitor. He had a large criminal practice, and among his clients was a woman named Molly, whose acquittal for murder he secured, taking her into his service and handing over her child to Miss Havisham to adopt. That child was Estella, the daughter of Molly and Magwitch. In his cautious way Jaggers was a good friend to Pip, and did his best to secure Magwitch's acquittal when finally arrested. *Expectations*, 11, 18, 20, 24, 26, 29, 30, 36, 40, 48, 49, 51, 55, 56.

**JAIRING'S HOTEL.** The establishment "for families and gentlemen" in high repute among the Midland counties, where the Grazinglands put up during their stay in London. *Uncommercial*, 6.

**JAMES.** 1. The servant who waited at table in Mrs. Tibbs's boarding house. *Boz, Tales, Boarding House.*

2. Mr. Brook Dingwall's servant. *Boz, Tales, Sentiment.*

3. Henry James, was commander of the barque *Defiance*, which reported the loss of the *Son and Heir. Dombey*, 32.

4. Butler of the Bayham Badgers. *Bleak House*, 13.

**JANE.** 1. The waitress at Bellamy's. *Boz, Scenes*, 18.

2. Aunt Jane and her family were guests at the Christmas party, described in *Boz, Characters*, 2.

3. A young lady encountered by the Tuggs's at Ramsgate library. *Boz, Tales, Tuggs's.*

4. Sister of the old lord's fiancée, who admired Kate Nickleby. *Nickleby*, 18.

5. Aunt Jane, one of Wegg's fictitious

patrons. *See* Miss Elizabeth. *Mutual Friend*, I, 5; II, 7, 10; III, 6, 7; IV, 3, 14.

6. Various maidservants: Kitterbell's (*Boz, Tales, Christening*); Wardle's (*Pickwick*, 5); Mrs. Potts's (*Pickwick*, 13); Pecksniff's (*Chuzzlewit*, 31); Miss Wozenham's (*Lirriper's Lodgings*); Mrs. Orange's (*Holiday Romance*).

**JANET.** Miss Betsy Trotwood's maidservant at her cottage near Dover. She was greatly averse from matrimony, but finally married a tavern-keeper. *Copperfield*, 13, 14, 23, 39, 43, 60.

**JARBER.** The character in *A House to Let*, who read the story of *Going into Society*.

**JARGON.** One of Miss Flite's captive birds. *Bleak House*, 14.

**JARLEY, MRS.** The proprietor of a travelling waxworks with whom Little Nell took refuge. She was a kind-hearted woman, who proved a real friend to the wandering couple, engaging Little Nell to act as showwoman. She eventually married her driver, George. Of her waxworks she remarked, "It's calm and classical. No low beatings and knockings about like your precious Punches, but always the same with a constantly unchanging air of coldness and gentility. . . . I won't go so far as to say I have seen waxworks quite like life, but I've certainly seen some life that was exactly like waxwork." *Curiosity Shop*, 26–9, 31, 32, 47, 73.

**JARNDYCE, JOHN.** The owner of Bleak House and a party in the great lawsuit. He adopted Esther Summerson when she was a child, and later engaged her as a companion to his cousins Ada Clare and Richard Carstone who, by permission of the Lord Chancellor, were allowed to live with him. Hating the lawsuit he did his utmost to keep Richard out of its clutches, but failed. He fell in love with Esther, and although nearly sixty years of age asked her to marry him. Out of gratitude she consented, but Jarndyce soon discovered that she and Woodcourt loved one another, and finally he set them up together in a new Bleak House in the north, devoting himself to the care of the widowed Ada and her child. When he felt out of humour John Jarndyce would say, "The wind's in the east," and retire to his "Growlery." Jarndyce had two great friends, Boythorn and the worthless Harold Skimpole. *Bleak House*, 1, 3, 6, 8, 9, 13–15, 17, 18, 23, 24, 30, 31, 35–7, 39, 43–5, 47, 50–2, 56, 57, 60–2, 64, 65, 67.

**JARNDYCE AND JARNDYCE.** The interminable lawsuit arising out of a will which had dragged succeeding generations into the miserable suspense of a Chancery suit. "In the question how the trusts under that will were to be administered, the fortune left by the will" was entirely dissipated in costs. Tom Jarndyce blew out his brains in despair; Richard Carstone wore himself to death in the same cause, and when finally a new will was found which settled the whole case, the whole of the fortune had been eaten up in lawyers' fees. Such interminable Chancery suits were no rare things when *Bleak House* was written to expose them. The case on which Jarndyce and Jarndyce was founded was probably Jennens v. Jennens, which related to property in Acton, Suffolk, belonging to an intestate miser who died in 1798. The case was only concluded some time in the 80's.

**JARVIE.** This was the old term applied to a hackney coachman. The origin of the term is unknown, though many fanciful suggestions have been made.

**JARVIS.** A clerk in the offices of Wilding and Co. *No Thoroughfare*.

**JASPER, JOHN.** The uncle of Edwin Drood and lay precentor at Cloisterham Cathedral. He was a secret opium taker, making periodical visits to the East End of London for his debauches. Although apparently deeply attached to his nephew, he had long cherished a consuming passion for Edwin's fiancée, Rosa Bud, and the suggestion of the story is that this passion was sufficient incentive to make him get rid of young Drood. His obvious attempts to saddle Neville Landless with the responsibility of the disappearance further this view, and at the point where the novel stops, Jasper is being closely watched by Datchery and others. *Drood*, 1, 2, 4–10, 12–20, 23.

**JEDDLER.** The family who furnish the principal characters in *The Battle of Life*. Dr. Jeddler, the father, was a philosopher who looked upon the world as a gigantic practical joke. He had two daughters, Grace and Marion, the latter being engaged to marry Alfred Heathfield. She discovered, however, that Grace loved him with all her heart, and inspired by a noble self-sacrifice, Marion disappeared just before Alfred's return from a long journey. Everything seemed to point to her having run away with Michael Warden, but in reality she took refuge with her Aunt Martha, a woman who had seen trouble herself. In course of time Grace and Alfred Heathfield were married, then Marion returned and cleared her name, eventually marrying Michael Warden.

**JELLYBY.** Mrs. Jellyby was a woman with a mission, unhappily not that of looking after her numerous family. While she devoted her whole attention to the colonisation of Borrioboola-Gha, on the Niger, her household got into utter confusion, her husband became bankrupt and her children savages. On the failure of the African scheme she turned her attention to the Rights of Women. *Bleak House*, 4–6, 14, 23, 30, 38, 50, 67.

Caddy or Caroline, her eldest daughter, was at first her amanuensis. She married Prince Turveydrop, the dancing master, and left the uncongenial atmosphere of her home. After much hard work she and Prince built up a good connection, and in the intervals of her work Caddy devoted herself to her little deaf and dumb daughter. 4, 5, 14, 17, 23, 30, 38, 50, 65, 67.

Peepy Jellyby was Caddy's little brother, always getting into mischief, but a favourite of Esther Summerson. 4, 5, 14, 23, 30, 38, 50, 67.

**JEM.** 1. A friend of the girl imprisoned in Newgate. *Boz, Scenes,* 25.

2. Solomon Jacob's boy. *Boz, Tales, Tottle.*

3. One of the men on Mr. Wardle's farm. *Pickwick,* 28.

**JEMIMA.** Polly Toodle's sister, who took charge of the family while she was at the Dombeys. *Dombey,* 2, 6.

**JEMMY, DISMAL.** *See* Hutley.

**JENKINS.** 1. Miss Jenkins was the accomplished pianist in the Gattleton's orchestra. *Boz, Tales, Porter.*

2. Sir Mulberry Hawk's servant. *Nickleby,* 50.

3. A friend of the contradictory couple. *Sketches of Couples.*

**JENKINSON.** One of the Circumlocution Office messengers. *Dorrit,* I, 10.

**JENNENS v. JENNENS.** Original lawsuit of Jarndyce and Jarndyce. (*q.v.*)

**JENNINGS.** 1. A robe-maker and friend of Mr. John Dounce. *Boz, Characters,* 7.

2. Nicholas Tulrumble's secretary. *Tulrumble.*

3. A pupil at Dotheboys Hall. *Nickleby,* 7.

4. A pupil at Nun's House. *Drood,* 9.

**JENNY.** The brickmaker's wife, whose infant died during one of Mrs. Pardiggle's visits. She reappears several times during the story, finally exchanging her cloak with Lady Dedlock in order that the latter might elude her pursuers. *Bleak House,* 8, 22, 31, 35, 46, 57, 59.

**JERRY.** A travelling showman with a troupe of performing dogs, whom Little Nell and her Grandfather encountered at the Jolly Sandboys Inn. *Curiosity Shop,* 18, 19, 37.

**JERUSALEM BUILDINGS.** Here were situated the shop and house of the Tetterby's where the poor student lodged. The original of Jerusalem Chambers may have been Jerusalem Court or Jerusalem Passage, both in Clerkenwell. *Haunted Man.*

**JERUSALEM COFFEE HOUSE.** This resort of Jeremiah Flintwinch was in Cowper's Court, between Change Alley and Birchin Lane. It was frequented by India and Australia merchants. *Dorrit,* I, 29.

**JEWBY.** One of Snagsby's clients. *Bleak House,* 10.

**JILKINS.** The physician who successfully treated Our Bore with mutton chops and sherry. *Reprinted, Our Bore.*

**JINGLE, ALFRED.** A strolling player who rescued Mr. Pickwick from the irate cabman

outside the Golden Cross Hotel. He accompanied the Pickwickians to Rochester, where his effrontery at the Bull ball got the whole party into hot water. Introduced by Mr. Pickwick to the Wardles, he induced Miss Rachel to elope with him, and was bought off by her brother for £120. Mr. Pickwick next met him at Eatanswill, masquerading as Captain Fitz Marshall, and followed him to Bury St. Edmunds and to Ipswich, where he exposed him at the house of Mr. Nupkins. Eventually Mr. Pickwick encountered Jingle and his friend and servant, Job Trotter, in the Fleet. Having learned a lesson from misfortune, both rascals turned over a new leaf and were sent at Mr. Pickwick's expense to start life anew in Demerara. The character of Jingle is said to have been founded upon a certain Potter, a fellow-clerk in Ellis and Blackmore's law office. *Pickwick,* 2, 3, 7–10, 15, 16, 18, 20, 22, 23, 25, 42, 45, 47, 53, 57.

**JINIWIN, MRS.** Mrs. Quilp's mother, "known to be laudably shrewish in her disposition," and constantly egging on her daughter to rebellion, though herself terrified of her son-in-law. It was made a condition, on Mrs. Quilp's second marriage, that Mrs. Jiniwin should not form one of the household. *Curiosity Shop,* 4, 5, 23, 49, 50, 73.

**JINKINS.** 1. The senior boarder at Mrs. Todgers's and a gentleman of a fashionable turn, "being a regular frequenter of the Park on Sundays." He was the especial object of Mr. Moddle's animosity. *Chuzzlewit,* 8–11, 32, 54.

2. A drunken customer of the pawnbroker's shop. *Boz, Scenes,* 23.

3. The suitor of the widow innkeeper on Marlborough Downs, who was cut out by Tom Smart. *Pickwick,* 14.

**JINKINSON.** A barber friend of Sam Weller, who found relief on his death-bed in shaving his children's heads. *Humphrey.*

**JINKS.** Mr. Nupkins's unpaid, half-fed clerk who, by virtue of having spent three years in a country attorney's office, supplied the Ipswich bench with all its law. *Pickwick,* 24, 25.

**JIP.** Dora Spenlow's pet, who always barked at David Copperfield. When they were married he lived in his own little pagoda-like kennel, finally dying of old age at David's feet, just as Dora died upstairs. *Copperfield,* 26, 33, 36–8, 41–4, 48, 52, 53.

**JO.** The crossing sweeper and street Arab who was Captain Hawdon's last friend and mourner. His total ignorance of everything made him a pitiable object at the inquest, and exposed him to the unedifying cant of Chadband. Tulkinghorn, the solicitor, having learned that Jo had shown Lady Dedlock the haunts of Captain Hawdon, caused him to be hounded from place to place, and during the course of his wanderings he was befriended by Esther Summerson at Bleak

House. On that occasion he communicated smallpox to Charley, and through her to Esther Summerson. He finally died, tended by Allan Woodcourt, in George's Shooting Gallery. All Jo's life and experiences of the world were summed up in the words of the police, who continually told him to "move on." *Bleak House*, 11, 16, 19, 22, 25, 31, 46, 47, 57.

**JOBBA.** A member of the Mudfog Association, who invented a forcing machine for bringing joint - stock railway shares prematurely to a premium.

**JOBLING.** 1. Dr. John Jobling was the physician who attended Anthony Chuzzlewit and had charge of Lewsome when the latter was ill at the Bull, Holborn. He had a comfortable City practice and became medical officer to the Anglo-Bengalee, though far too clever to be more than a paid servant of the Company. "Perhaps he could shake his head, rub his hands, or warm himself before a fire, better than any man alive." *Chuzzlewit*, 19, 25, 27, 28, 38, 41, 42.

2. Tony Jobling was Guppy's greatest friend and a law writer, who occupied Hawdon's rooms over Krook's shop. He and Guppy were to have obtained the papers relating to Hawdon on the night of Krook's death. He accompanied Guppy when the latter made his final proposal to Esther. For financial reasons Jobling usually passed under the name of Weevle. *Bleak House*, 7, 20, 32, 33, 39, 64.

**JOBSON.** A family of Mormon emigrants. *Uncommercial*, 20.

**JOBY.** A one-eyed tramp, also answering to the name of Greenwood. *Haunted House.*

**JODD.** A member of the welcoming committee who waited on Elijah Pogram. *Chuzzlewit*, 34.

**JODDLEBY.** An aristocratic connection of the Barnacles. *Dorrit*, I, 17.

**JOE.** 1. Mr. Wardle's fat page boy, who was always either eating or sleeping, except on the memorable occasion when he spied Tupman making love to Miss Rachel and communicated the fact to old Mrs. Wardle. *Pickwick*, 4–9, 28, 53, 54, 56.

2. A manservant at the hotel where Rose Maylie stayed near Hyde Park. *Twist*, 39.

3. A labourer at the Docks. *Dombey*, 6.

4. Guard of the Dover coach. *Two Cities*, I, 2.

5. The dealer in old clothes to whom Scrooge's laundress sold his effects. *Christmas Carol.*

6. The driver of the Cloisterham bus. *Drood*, 6, 15, 20.

**JOEY, CAPTAIN.** A bottle - nosed customer of the Six Jolly Fellowship Porters, apt to drink more than his allowance. *Mutual Friend*, I, 6 ; III, 3.

**JOGG, MISS.** An artist's model. *Bleak House*, 29.

**JOHN.** 1. The clown who formed the subject of the Stroller's Tale. *Pickwick*, 3.

2. An out-of-work labourer. *Dombey*, 24.

3. The poetical young gentleman. *Sketches of Gentlemen.*

4. Narrator of the story entitled *The Haunted House.*

5. Host at the Christmas Party. *Reprinted, Poor Relation's Story.*

6. An out-of-work boilermaker. *Uncommercial*, 30.

7. Various servants : Mr. Lovetown's (*Is She His Wife ?*) ; at the house where the brokers take possession (*Boz, Our Parish*, 5) ; Malderston's man (*Boz, Tales, Sparkins*) ; Gabriel Parson's butler (*Boz, Tales, Tottle*) ; Emma Fielding's servant (*Sketches of Couples*) ; waiter at the St. James's Arms (*Strange Gentleman*) ; waiter at the Saracen's Head, Towcester (*Pickwick*, 51).

**JOHNNY.** Betty Higden's great grandchild, whom the Boffins wished to adopt in memory of John Rokesmith. Before the scheme could be carried out, however, little Johnny died in the Children's Hospital, talking of the Boofer Lady, his name for Bella Wilfer. *Mutual Friend*, I, 16 ; II, 9, 10.

**JOHNSON.** 1. One of Dr. Blimber's pupils, who nearly choked himself at dinner. *Dombey*, 12, 14, 41.

2. The name adopted by Nicholas Nickleby when he was acting with the Crummles. *Nickleby*, 16.

3. Tom, "man with a cork leg, from White's," a friend of Cousin Feenix. *Dombey*, 41.

4. John, a scatterbrain who eloped to Gretna Green with Mary Wilson. *Strange Gentleman.*

**JOLLSON, MRS.** Mrs. MacStinger's predecessor at No. 9, Brig Place. *Dombey*, 39.

**"JOLLY ! "** Mark Tapley's great philosophy of life was to be Jolly under the most adverse circumstances. When he was too far gone with fever to speak, he scratched "Jolly" on a slate to let Martin know he was coming out strong. *Chuzzlewit*, 5, 7, 13–15, 17, 21–3, 33–5, 43, 48, 51–3.

**JOLLY SANDBOYS, THE.** "A small roadside inn of pretty ancient date," where various wandering showmen congregated before the races. Little Nell and her Grandfather were put up there at the recommendation of Codlin and Short. *Curiosity Shop*, 18.

**"JOLLY YOUNG WATERMAN."** One of Dibdin's songs, adapted by Brother Mordlin to the tune of the Old Hundredth ! *Pickwick*, 33.

**JOLTERED, SIR WILLIAM.** President of the Zoology section of the Mudfog Association.

**JONATHAN.** One of the habitual customers of the Six Jolly Fellowship Porters. *Mutual Friend*, I, 6 ; III, 3.

**JONES.** 1. A witty barrister's clerk, friend of Mr. John Dounce. *Boz, Characters*, 7.

2. A guest at Octavius Budden's. *Boz, Tales, Minns.*

3. Mary, a girl of nineteen, whom Dennis "worked off" for stealing a piece of cloth. *Barnaby*, 37.

4. Master Jones was David Copperfield's boyish rival in the love of Miss Shepherd. *Copperfield*, 18.

5. George, one of the regulars at the Six Jolly Fellowship Porters. *Mutual Friend*, I, 6 ; III, 3.

6. An employé of Blaze and Sparkle, the fashionable jewellers. *Bleak House*, 58.

**JONES, WILLIAM.** Original of Creakle. (*q.v.*)

**JONES, SPRUGGINS AND SMITH.** The cheap linendraper's shop in Tottenham Court Road, where the Malderton's discovered that Horatio Sparkins was really plain Mr. Smith. *Boz, Tales, Sparkins.*

**JOPER, BILLY.** One of Cousin Feenix's club friends—"man with a glass in his eye." *Dombey*, 41.

**JORAM.** Assistant to Omer, the Yarmouth undertaker, and eventually a partner in the business. He married Minnie, Omer's pretty daughter. *Copperfield*, 9, 21, 23, 30, 32, 51, 56.

**JORGAN, CAPTAIN SILAS.** A New Englander, from Salem, who found Hugh Raybrock's message on an island and helped to clear up the mystery of his disappearance. *Message from the Sea.* .

**JORKINS.** Mr. Spenlow's partner, "a mild man of a heavy temperament, whose place in the business was to keep himself in the background, and be constantly exhibited by name as the most obdurate and ruthless of men." He was thus made responsible for all Spenlow's hardness. *Copperfield*, 23, 29, 33, 35, 38, 39.

**JOSEPH.** 1. "The much respected head waiter of the Slamjam Coffee House, London, E.C." *Somebody's Luggage.*

2. A charity child found shaking mats in a City church, and making love to another charity child named Celia. *Uncommercial*, 21.

**JOWL, JOE.** One of the gambling gang who assembled at The Valiant Soldier publichouse. Having fleeced Nell's Grandfather, Jowl tried to persuade him to rob Mrs. Jarley. *Curiosity Shop*, 29, 42, 73.

**JOY.** 1. A London carpenter with whom John put up when he went to London to see about his patent. *Reprinted, Poor Man's Patent.*

2. One of Miss Flite's captive birds. *Bleak House*, 14.

**JULIA.** The lady beloved by the bachelor who writes *The Ghost of Art. Reprinted Pieces.*

**JULLIEN, M.** The reference in *Reprinted, Bill Sticking* is to M. Jullien, a well-known writer of dance music and conductor of an orchestra, who advertised freely in the 40's, 50's and 60's. In 1843 he held a series of promenade concerts in Covent Garden Theatre, and the following year gave the first masked ball held in England in recent times. In 1851 he was engaged to provide the orchestra for the Queen's Court Ball.

**JUPE, CECILIA OR SISSY.** The daughter of Signor Jupe, a clown in Sleary's circus, who finding himself getting too old for his work disappeared, leaving Sissy destitute. She was adopted by Gradgrind and proved the good angel of his house, softening the harsh influence of his eternal facts. When Louisa fled from the attentions of Harthouse, Sissy went to the latter and persuaded him to leave the district. She and Rachel were walking together when they discovered Stephen Blackpool, dying in the Old Hell Shaft, and she accompanied Gradgrind and Louisa on the search for Tom, finding him at last with her old friends the Slearys. *Hard Times*, I, 2, 4–9, 14, 15 ; II, 9 ; III, 1–9.

**JURYMAN.** The narrator of the first of the *Two Ghost Stories*, entitled, *The Trial for Murder.*

# K

**KAGS.** A convict who had returned from transportation and was in hiding at Toby Crackit's house on Jacob's Island when Sikes took refuge there. *Twist*, 50.

**KATE.** 1. Wife of the debtor in Solomon Jacobs's lock-up in Cursitor Street. *Boz, Tales, Tottle.*

2. The arch, impudent-looking, bewitching little cousin of Maria Lobbs. *Pickwick*, 17.

3. An orphan child who visited the Skettles while Florence was staying there. *Dombey*, 24.

**KEDGICK, CAPTAIN.** The landlord of the National Hotel in the town whence Martin and Mark took boat for Eden. He arranged levees for Martin, and for Elijah Pogram when the latter passed through his town. *Chuzzlewit*, 22, 34.

**KENGE, "CONVERSATION."** A solicitor of the firm of Kenge and Carboy, " portly and important," and employed by Mr. John Jarndyce to watch his interests in the great suit. He arranged for the adoption of Esther Summerson, and it was at his office that Richard Carstone was articled and devoted himself to the study of Jarndyce and Jarndyce. Kenge and Carboy's office was in Old Square, Lincoln's Inn, probably at No. 13, since rebuilt. *Bleak House*, 3, 4, 13, 17, 18, 20, 24, 62, 65.

**KENILWORTH.** Dickens stayed at this beautiful place in company with H. K. Browne in the autumn of 1838, his visit probably prompting him to make it the scene of the outing in which Mr. Dombey finally decided to make Edith Granger his wife. *Dombey*, 27.

**KENNET, ALDERMAN.** Lord Mayor in *Barnaby.* *See* Lord Mayor.

**KENNINGTON.** Mr. Vholes and "his three raw-visaged, lank and buttoned-up daughters" lived in an earthy cottage at Kennington (*Bleak House*, 39). One of little Jemmy Lirriper's youthful escapades was getting lost and being found by the police at Kennington. *Lirriper's Lodgings.*

**KENSINGTON.** The unfortunate victim of principle, whose death by crumpets was so graphically narrated by Sam Weller, resided at Kensington (*Pickwick*, 44). Prince Turveydrop taught dancing in a school there (*Bleak House*, 14). Gabriel Parsons and his sweetheart had secret meetings in the Gardens (*Boz, Tales, Tottle*). Kensington Turnpike, mentioned in *Pickwick*, 35, was a little to the west of Gore House, which stood on the site now occupied by the Albert Hall. Kensington Gravel Pits (*Nickleby*, 28) were in the Bayswater Road, where Clanricarde Gardens now starts.

**KENTISH TOWN.** Mrs. Kidgerbury, occasional charwoman of the Copperfield household was supposed to be the oldest inhabitant of this district. *Copperfield*, 44.

**KENT ROAD.** After being robbed on the outset of his journey to Dover, David Copperfield made his way down New Kent Road and stopped to rest "at a terrace with a piece of water before it." This was at the County Terrace, now opposite Rodney Place. The piece of water no longer exists. *Copperfield*, 13.

**KENT STREET.** Now called Tabard Street, this was the main thoroughfare to Dover prior to the making of the Old Kent Road early in the nineteenth century. It was the old road along which the Canterbury pilgrims passed, hence its new name. *Uncommercial Traveller* mentions it as one of the worst kept parts of London (13).

**KENWIGS.** A turner in ivory who lodged in the same house as Newman Noggs, near Golden Square, and by virtue of occupying a suite of two rooms was "looked on as a person of some consideration on the premises." His wife, Mrs. Susan, being "of a very genteel family, having an uncle who collected a water rate," engaged Nicholas Nickleby to teach her three eldest daughters French. Mrs. Kenwigs found four pints of malt liquor a day hardly able to sustain her in her grief at her Uncle Lillyvick's marriage to Henrietta Petowker, but when he returned to the bosom of his family, he settled his money on the Kenwigs children. *Nickleby*, 14–16, 25, 36, 52.

**KETCH, PROFESSOR JOHN.** A member of the Mudfog Association, who exhibited a skull purporting to be that of Mr. Greenacre.

**KETTLE, LA FAYETTE.** Secretary of the Watertoast Institution, whom Martin and Mark met while travelling west. In his presumptuous ignorance and unabashed vulgarity Kettle combines all the characteristics of that class of American Dickens pilloried so unmercifully. *Chuzzlewit*, 21, 22.

**KIBBLE, JACOB.** A fellow-passenger of John Harmon on his voyage back from the Cape. He gave evidence at the inquest on the supposed body of Harmon. *Mutual Friend*, I, 3 ; II, 13 ; IV, 12.

**KIDDERMINSTER.** A lad who assisted E. W. B. Childers in his equestrian feats in Sleary's Circus. *Hard Times*, I, 6 ; III, 7.

**KIDGERBURY, MRS.** A woman employed by the Copperfields, but "too feeble to execute her conceptions of the art" of charing. *Copperfield*, 44.

**KIMMEENS, KITTY.** One of Miss Pupford's pupils, who was taken by the Traveller to see *Tom Tiddler*.

**KINCH, HORACE.** A man who suffered from dry rot, which had carried him inside the walls of the King's Bench Prison, and out of them with his feet foremost. *Uncommercial*, 13.

**KINDHEART, MR.** A friend of the Uncommercial Traveller, whom he met in an Italian City. *Uncommercial*, 26.

**KING.** 1. Christian George, was a negro who betrayed the colonists on Silver Store Island to the pirates. *English Prisoners.*

2. Tom King was a character in W. T. Moncrieff's farce, Monsieur Tonson. He described himself as "a jolly dog" who worried to distraction M. Morbleu, a French barber of Seven Dials, by repeated enquiries for a Mr. Thompson. *Boz, Scenes*, 5.

**KING DEATH.** A once popular song, by Barry Cornwall, set to music by von Neukomm. The first verse was :—

> King Death was a rare old fellow,
> He sat where no Sun could shine,
> And he lifted his hand so yellow,
> And poured out his coal-black wine ;
> Hurrah for the coal-black wine.
>
> *Bleak House*, 33.

**KING'S BENCH PRISON.** This debtor's prison stood, until its demolition in 1869, at the junction of Newington Causeway and Borough Road, on the site now occupied by Queen's Buildings. It was the last debtor's prison to be used, and the last prisoner left it in 1860. The original building, dating from 1755, was burned down by the Gordon rioters in 1780 (*Barnaby*, 67). Mr. Micawber was incarcerated in the King's Bench while David was living with them (*Copperfield*, 11). Walter Bray and his daughter lived in the rules of the prison (*Nickleby*, 46, 47, 51). Permission to live in the rules, which covered an area comprised in a circle of about three miles in circumference, was obtained by money payments. For perpetual living in the rules prisoners were charged ten guineas for the first £100 and five guineas for each succeeding £100 of the debt for which they were in custody. Liberty for three days was purchased by 4s. 2d. for the first day and 3s. 10d. for each of the two following days. The prison contained 224 rooms, and sometimes as many as 500 prisoners. There is some description of the prison and its effect on inmates in *Uncommercial*, 13.

**KING'S BENCH WALK.** This shady old portion of the Temple is associated with Sydney Carton, who walked up and down it before commencing his labour with Stryver. *Two Cities*, II, 5.

**KINGSGATE STREET, HIGH HOLBORN.** The street in which lived Mrs. Gamp, " at a bird fancier's, next door but one to the celebrated mutton pie shop, and directly opposite to the original cats' meat warehouse." The whole street was demolished and absorbed into Southampton Row and the buildings on its eastern side, early in the present century. *Chuzzlewit*, 19, 26, 29, 49.

**KING'S HEAD INN, BARNARD CASTLE.** It was at this inn that Dickens and H. K. Browne stayed on their visit to the Yorkshire schools in 1838. Opposite the inn was a clockmaker named Humphrey, who thus gave the title to Humphrey's Clock. Newman Noggs commented on the excellent quality of the ale to be had there. *Nickleby*, 7.

**KING'S SCHOOL, CANTERBURY.** Original of Dr. Strong's school. *See* Canterbury.

**KING'S THEATRE.** This was at the corner of Tottenham Street and Charlotte Street, Tottenham Court Road, on the site now occupied by the Scala Theatre. On Queen Victoria's accession it became the Queen's Theatre, changing its name to The Prince of Wales's Theatre in 1865. *Boz, Characters*, 9.

**KINGSTON.** One of Mr. Dombey's friends, a Bank Director, boasted deprecatingly of his " little place " at Kingston (*Dombey*, 36). Betty Higden was well known as she peddled her simple goods through the town (*Mutual Friend*, III, 8). Magwitch was once in jail there (*Expectations*, 42). In Mr. Pickwick's tale about John Podgers the people of Kingston expressed great alarm on account of certain witchcrafts practised in their town. *Humphrey*.

**KIRBY'S WONDERFUL MUSEUM.** The full title of this book which gave Mr. Boffin so much pleasure was *The Wonderful and Scientific Museum or Magazine of Remarkable Characters, including all the Curiosities of Nature and Art.* Six vols., 1803–20. A subsequent edition substituted Eccentric for Scientific. *Mutual Friend*, III, 6.

**KITT, MISS.** The " girl in pink " to whom David paid attentions on the Norwood picnic when Dora was monopolised by " Red Whisker." *Copperfield*, 33.

**KITTEN.** The Deputy Commissioner on Silver Store Island, " a small, youngish, bald, botanical gentleman." *English Prisoners*.

**KITTERBELL, CHARLES.** The nephew who invited Nicodemus Dumps to the christening of his infant son, Frederick Charles William. A large party was gathered at their house at 14 Great Russell Street,

and Dumps, who had lost the christening cup on his way thither, was able to cast a profound gloom on all the guests. Mrs. Jemima Kitterbell, the wife, was " one of those young women who almost invariably recall to one's mind the idea of a cold fillet of veal." *Boz, Tales, Christening*.

**KLEM.** Caretakers in the Uncommercial Traveller's lodgings, who seem to have " a dejected consciousness that they are not justified in appearing on the surface of the earth. They come out of some hole when London empties itself, and go in again when it fills." *Uncommercial*, 16.

**KNAG, MISS.** Madame Mantalini's forewoman and " a bustling overdressed female . . . who still aimed at youth, although she had shot beyond it years ago." At first she was friendly with Kate Nickleby and her mother, taking them to see her melancholy brother, Mortimer, who kept a circulating library near Tottenham Court Road, but she became jealous of Kate's beauty and finally was her direst foe. Miss Knag eventually took over Madame Mantalini's business to save it from the inroads of Mantalini. *Nickleby*, 10, 17–21, 44.

**KNIFE-SWALLOWER.** *See* African Knife Swallower.

**KNIGHT BELL, MR.** A member of the Mudfog Association, who exhibited a wax preparation of the interior of a gentleman who had swallowed a door-key.

**KNOTT, NEWMAN.** Original of Newman Noggs. (*q.v.*)

**KOELDWITHOUT, BARON.** Family name of the Baron of Grogzwig, whose story was told by the merryfaced gentleman when the Yorkshire coach broke down. *Nickleby*, 6.

**KROOK.** The drunken rag and bone dealer, commonly known as the Lord Chancellor, who lived near Lincoln's Inn (in Chichester Rents). Nemo, the law writer, and Miss Flite were his lodgers, the former's rooms being later occupied by Jobling. Krook amassed a huge quantity of stuff, among which were some papers relating to Captain Hawdon, which he promised to give to Guppy. On the night when he was to fulfil his promise, however, he mysteriously vanished through spontaneous combustion, leaving no remains but what seemed to be " the cinder of a small, charred log of wood sprinkled with white ashes." It later transpired that Krook was Mrs. Smallweed's only brother, and that harpy family swooped on his house, discovered the missing Jarndyce will and other papers with which they tried to blackmail Sir Leicester Dedlock. The possibility of spontaneous combustion in human beings has been finally disproved. *Bleak House*, 5, 10, 11, 14, 20, 32, 33.

**KUTANKUMAGEN.** A Russian member (from Moscow) of the Mudfog Association.

**KWAKLEY.** A member of the Mudfog Association.

**L**

**LA CREEVY, MISS.** A miniature painter with whom the Nicklebys lodged on first coming to London. She was their only friend and stood by them in all their vicissitudes, helping Kate and putting up with Mrs. Nickleby's whims and fancies. Little Miss La Creevy, introduced as "a mincing young lady of fifty" is one of the brightest characters in *Nickleby*. Her invincible good spirits and kindliness made her a fit wife for old Tim Linkinwater, whom she eventually married. She had a brother, John, with whom she went to stay in the country. A Miss Rose Emma Drummond and Dickens's aunt, Janet Barrow, have been suggested as originals for the miniature painter. Her house was indentified as No. 11, Strand. *Nickleby*, 3, 5, 10, 11, 20, 27, 31–3, 35, 38, 49, 61, 63, 65.

**LAD LANE.** This was the name given to what is now part of Gresham Street, lying between Wood Street and Milk Street. There was an important coach booking office there, the Swan with Two Necks, now a railway collecting depot. The danger of mail coaches rushing out of Lad Lane on their way to St. Martin's-le-Grand was commented upon by the passer-by in *Dorrit*, I, 13.

**LADLE, JOEY.** The head cellarman of Wilding and Co., "a slow and ponderous man of the drayman order of human architecture." He became Marguerite's devoted servant and accompanied her to Switzerland, helping to rescue Vendale from the chasm on the "Simpleton." *No Thoroughfare*.

**LADY JANE.** The large grey cat which seemed Krook's attendant sprite. *Bleak House*, 5, 10, 11, 14, 20, 32, 33.

**LAGNIER.** One of the names adopted by Rigaud. (*q.v.*)

**LAING, ALLAN STEWART.** Original of Fang, the magistrate. (*q.v.*)

**LAMBERT.** 1. Miss Lambert was one of the partners of the bashful young gentleman. *Sketches of Gentlemen*.

2. Daniel Lambert (1770–1809) was the famous fat man who for the last four years of his life exhibited himself in London and elsewhere. At the time of his death he weighed well over fifty-two stone. *Nickleby*, 37.

**LAMBETH.** Among the slums of Lambeth, Peg Sliderskew hid herself after robbing old Arthur Gride, and thither went Squeers to find her and recover the stolen document (*Nickleby*, 57). In the Kennington Park Road, just south of Brook Street, is Walcot Square, where Mr. Guppy had taken the house of which he invited Esther to be mistress. *Bleak House*, 64.

"**LAMBS** could not forgive nor worms forget," words uttered by Mrs. Gamp in a violent outburst of feeling. *Chuzzlewit*, 49.

**LAMERT, DR.** The second husband of Dickens's aunt, and an army surgeon who sat for the portrait of Dr. Slammer (*q.v.*). For his son James, *see* Murdstone and Grinby.

**LAMMLE, ALFRED AND SOPHRONIA.** Friends of the Veneerings and scheming adventurers who deceived each other into marriage, each pretending to be a person of means. They then joined forces to prey upon their friends. Mrs. Lammle retained some vestige of good feeling, however, and at the last moment saved Georgiana Podsnap, whom they had designed to marry Fledgeby, from such a dreadful fate. They tried to obtain a footing in the Boffin household, but their schemes were seen through and they were finally dismissed by Boffin with a note for £100, with which they left the country. *Mutual Friend*, I, 2, 10, 11 ; II, 4, 5, 16 ; III, 1, 5, 12, 14, 17 ; IV, 2, 8.

**LAMPS.** A porter at Mugby Junction and the father of Phoebe, the crippled girl, whose life he tried to make happier by his own unvarying cheerfulness and unselfishness. His greatest self-denial was composing and singing comic songs for her benefit. *Mugby Junction*.

**LANCASTER.** On his Lazy Tour with Wilkie Collins, Dickens visited Lancaster in September, 1857, staying at the King's Arms, kept by Mr. Sly. The old inn was pulled down in 1879, and the present commercial hotel erected on its site. Dr. Marigold had opened on the square near this hotel when he came across the giant Pickelson, who told him of Sophy's lover.

**LANDLESS, NEVILLE AND HELENA.** Twin brother and sister who were sent to Cloisterham by their guardian, Mr. Honeythunder, the boy to be coached by Mr. Crisparkle, the girl to be one of Miss Twinkleton's pupils. They had been born in Ceylon and were impetuous in their actions and strong in their feelings. Neville was soon attracted by Rosa Bud and largely through Jasper's instigation quarrelled with Edwin Drood. When the latter disappeared, Jasper threw suspicion on Neville, and though no definite charge could be made, the lad was unable to clear his name and went to hide himself in London, followed by his sister. They were living in Staple Inn when Rosa fled to London, and where the book finishes the presumption is that Helena is falling in love with Crisparkle, who had gone to see his old pupil in retirement. *Drood*, 6–10, 12–17, 19–22.

**LANDOR, WALTER SAVAGE.** Original of Boythorn. (*q.v.*)

**LANE, MISS.** The harassed governess to the Borum family. *Nickleby*, 24.

**LANGDALE, MR.** The distiller and vinter, an actual character, whose premises were sacked and burned by the Gordon rioters. He gave Mr. Haredale shelter during the fury of the riots, until the attention of the crowd was turned to his own premises. Thomas Langdale's distillery was between Barnard's Inn and Fetter Lane, into the latter being the side entrance by which they made their escape. *Barnaby,* 13, 61, 66–8.

**LANGLEY.** Madame Bouclet's English tenant, whose name was mistaken by her for M. L'Anglais, the Englishman. He adopted Bebelle, the little orphan girl. *Somebody's Luggage.*

**LANREAN.** The Devonshire village in which Captain Silas Jorgan found the Raybrocks and communicated to them the *Message from the Sea.*

**LANT STREET.** "A little distance after you've passed Saint George's Church, turns out of the High Street on the right-hand side of the way." Thus Bob Sawyer to Mr. Pickwick, and his directions still hold good. The High Street end has been altered, but down the street many of the old houses yet remain. During his dreadful probation for life in the blacking warehouse (1822–3), while his father was still a prisoner in the Marshalsea, Dickens had a poor lodging in this street at the house of an insolvent court agent who sat for the portrait of the Garlands. In the back attic once occupied by himself, Dickens placed Bob Sawyer, changing his own kind landlady, however, for the redoubtable Mrs. Raddle. *Pickwick,* 30, 32.

**LARKEY BOY, THE.** A prizefighter who gave the Game Chicken a bad beating. *Dombey,* 44.

**LARKINS.** 1. Jem, an amateur actor, under the name of Horatio St. Julien, whose line was "genteel comedy." *Boz, Scenes,* 13.
2. The eldest Miss Larkins, "maybe about thirty," inspired the youthful David Copperfield "with a passion beyond all bounds," but eventually married Mr. Chestle, the hop grower. *Copperfield,* 18.

**LATIN GRAMMAR MASTER.** Captain Boldheart's dire enemy. *Holiday Romance.*

**LAURIE, SIR PETER.** Original of Alderman Cute. (*q.v.*)

**LAZARUS, ABRAHAM.** A Jew whom Mr. Jaggers was engaged to prosecute on a charge of stealing plate. *Expectations,* 20.

**LEADENHALL MARKET.** Near the market was the Blue Boar, where Sam Weller indited his valentine to Mary. The nearest Blue Boar (*q.v.*) was in Aldgate, a few doors up from Leadenhall Street, and it is supposed that the Green Dragon, in Bull's Head passage, was the scene of Sam's literary efforts (*Pickwick,* 33). Tim Linkinwater argued for a town residence from the fact that he could buy new-laid eggs any morning in Leadenhall Market (*Nickleby,* 40). Captain Cuttle engaged a lady from there to perform the household work of the Wooden Midshipman and a watchman to put up and take down the shutters every day (*Dombey,*

39, 56). Lastly, the Bill Stickers' procession "turned into Leadenhall Market and halted at a public-house." *Reprinted, Bill Sticking.*

**LEADENHALL STREET.** The instrument shop of Sol Gills, No. 157 Leadenhall Street, outside which once hung the Wooden Midshipman, belonged to Messrs. Norie and Wilson, who have since removed to 156 Minories. Bradley Headstone and his pupil made their way through the street when going to meet Lizzie coming from St. Mary Axe. Just across Gracechurch Street, in Cornhill, is the Church of St. Peter, where on the same evening Bradley Headstone made his final passionate appeal to Lizzie (*Mutual Friend,* II, 15). Captain Ravender was walking down Leadenhall Street when he was offered the command of the *Golden Mary.*

**LEAMINGTON.** In the late autumn of 1838 Dickens and H. K. Browne visited this town and put up at Copps's Royal Hotel, later patronised by Mr. Dombey and Major Bagstock. At Leamington Joey B. introduced his friend Dombey to Mrs. Skewton and her daughter, and thus helped change the whole of the worthy merchant's subsequent life. *Dombey,* 20, 21, 26, 27.

**LEATH, ANGELA.** The girl beloved by Charley, the bashful man who was on his way to America, thinking that she had given him up for Edwin, when he was snowed up in the *Holly Tree Inn.*

**LEATHER BOTTLE INN, COBHAM.** This is a famous Dickens's shrine, and the parlour where Mr. Tupman regaled his wounded soul with "roast fowl, bacon, ale and etceteras" is much as he left it, although the walls are adorned with a number of interesting Pickwick pictures, autographs and other personalia. *Pickwick,* 11.

**LEATHER LANE.** Originally running up from Holborn by the east side of Furnival's Inn, now situated between the Prudential offices and Messrs. Gamage's shop, Leather Lane was practically opposite Barnard's Inn, and hence formed an easy escape for Barnaby and Hugh from the drunken crowd who burned Langdale's distillery. *Barnaby,* 68.

**LEAVER.** 1. Mr. and Mrs. Leaver were the Loving Young Couple.
2. A member of the Mudfog Association.

**LEDBRAIN, MR. X.** A statistical member of the Mudfog Association who read a curious paper on the relative numbers of human legs and chair legs.

**LEDROOK, MISS.** One of the Crummles company and the friend of Miss Snevellicci. "Of a romantic turn," she was one of Henrietta Petowker's bridesmaids. *Nickleby,* 23–5, 30.

**LEEFORD, EDWIN.** This was the betrayer of Oliver Twist's mother, Agnes Fleming, and the father of Edward Leeford, called throughout the story Monks (*q.v.*). His will, leaving his money to Agnes and her child, was suppressed by his widow, the mother of Monks. *Twist*, 51.

**LEICESTER SQUARE.** This was known as Leicester Fields until about 1800. Saville House, which stood approximately on the site now occupied by the Empire Music-hall, belonged to Sir George Saville, who introduced the Catholic Relief Bill which occasioned the Gordon Riots, hence the plots to burn the mansion (*Barnaby*, 56). Saville House was later occupied by various exhibitions, including that of Miss Linwood (*q.v.*), and was burned down in 1865. George's Shooting Gallery was somewhere between Leicester Square and the Haymarket, possibly in Whitcomb Street (*Bleak House*, 21, 26). No. 10 Green Street, leading from the Square to Charing Cross Road (formerly Castle Street), was said to have been the original Old Curiosity Shop.

**LEITH WALK, EDINBURGH.** Here was the coachyard where the Bagman's Uncle had the vision of the old mail coach (*Pickwick*, 49). This yard belonged to a Mr. Croall, whose family, at one time, owned all the Edinburgh cabs.

**LEMON, MRS.** One of Mrs. Orange's friends, " who kept a preparatory establishment." *Holiday Romance*.

**LENVILLE, MR. AND MRS. THOMAS.** Members of the Crummles company. The husband was jealous of Nicholas Nickleby and, egged on by Folair, sent him a ridiculous challenge to which Nicholas replied by knocking him down in the presence of the company. *Nickleby*, 23, 24, 29.

**LEOPOLD, PRINCE.** This model of fashion was Queen Victoria's uncle and the husband of the shortlived Princess Charlotte, daughter of George IV. In 1831 he became King of the Belgians, and was the grandfather of the present king, Albert. When a young man Leopold lived in England and cut a dash in society. *Boz, Tales, Sparkins*.

**"LET US GO RING FANCY'S KNELL."** From the song, " Tell me where is Fancy Bred," in *Merchant of Venice*, III, 2. It should be, " let us all," etc. The song has various settings, that by Bishop being the best known. *Curiosity Shop*, 21.

**LEWSOME.** A young physician who was persuaded by Jonas Chuzzlewit to give him the poison with which he intended to hasten his father's death. His part in the attempted crime preyed on his mind, and while lying ill at the Bull, attended by Mrs. Gamp, he let out certain words which roused her suspicions. Later he confessed to the crime he thought he had committed. *Chuzzlewit*, 25, 29, 48, 49, 51.

**LICENSED VICTUALLER, MR.** The landlord of a house of entertainment for merchant seamen. *Uncommercial*, 5.

**LIFE.** One of Miss Flite's captive birds. *Bleak House*, 14.

**"LIGHT GUITAR."** This was an exceedingly popular song by John Barnett, sung by Madame Vestris. *Boz, Tales, Boarding House*. See, " I'll tell thee."

**LIGHTWOOD, MORTIMER.** A barrister and the intimate friend of Eugene Wrayburn. Too indolent to work up a practice, his only client was Mr. Boffin, in connection with whose affairs Lightwood played a part in all that concerned the Harmon mystery. He was a diner at the Veneerings, where he usually recounted the various phases the strange case underwent. At last, disgusted with Society, as exemplified in the Veneerings and Lady Tippins, and moved to better things by what he saw in the Harmons and Boffins, Lightwood determined to follow his friend Eugene's example and turn to and do something in earnest. Mortimer Lightwood's chambers in the Temple were in the buildings pulled down in 1861, on the site of which Goldsmith's Buildings were erected later. *Mutual Friend*, I, 2–4, 8, 10, 12–14, 16 ; II, 6, 8, 12, 14, 16 ; III, 4, 10, 11, 17 ; IV, 9–12, 16, 17.

**LIGNUM VITAE.** The nickname given to Matthew Bagnet. (*q.v.*)

**LILIAN.** The niece of William Fern, whom he brought up to London in his search for work. *Chimes*.

**LILLERTON, MISS.** " A lady of very prim appearance and remarkably inanimate," who was staying with the Parsons' when Gabriel decided that she should marry his friend Tottle. When Watkins came to make his declaration, however, he discovered that she was already engaged to Mr. Timson, the parson. *Boz, Tales, Tottle*.

**LILLYVICK, MR.** Mrs. Kenwigs's uncle and a man of importance as being the collector of water rates. He was much courted by the family on account of the property he was to leave, but to their disgust married Miss Henrietta Petowker, the Drury Lane actress. After leading him a dance, however, she eloped with a halfpay captain, and Mr. Lillyvick returned to his adoring relatives, " turning off " forever the woman who had played him so false. The reconciliation so affected Mr. Kenwigs that he cried, " This is an event at which 'Evins itself looks down." *Nickleby*, 14–16, 25, 30, 36, 48, 52.

**LIMBKINS, MR.** Chairman of the Board of Guardians in the parish where Oliver was born. *Twist*, 2, 3, 7.

**LIMBURY, MR. AND MRS. PETER.** Two of the characters in *Is She His Wife ?*

**LIMEHOUSE.** In his childhood Dickens had a personal connection with this district as his uncle and his godfather both lived there, the latter, Mr. Huffman, being a well-to-do mastmaker and rigger. The Six Jolly Fellowship Porters, presided over by Miss Abbey Potterson, was probably the Grapes Inn, 7 Narrow Street, which runs along the water side from Butcher Row to Limehouse Dock (*Mutual Friend*, I, 3, 6). In Limehouse Hole, near-by, lived Rogue Riderhood and the Hexams (II, 12), and near Limehouse Church John Harmon fell into his soliloquy after his visit to Pleasant Riderhood's shop (13). On his Amateur Beat, Uncommercial Traveller found himself at the Lead Mills, which he describes in Chapter XIII. Finally, near Limehouse Hole, Captain Cuttle came across Jack Bunsby, being led a victim to the altar by Mrs. MacStinger. (*Dombey*, 60.)

**LINCOLN'S INN.** This is one of the oldest inns of court, and with its old squares and the Fields, full of Dickens associations. Much of *Bleak House* is centred round the old inn which, with the exception of the New Hall, built in 1843–45, presents much the same appearance as it has done any time these last two hundred years. The Court of Chancery was formerly held in the old Hall before the erection of the new Law Courts in 1874, and it is in this court that *Bleak House* opens. Kenge and Carboy's offices were in Old Square, probably No. 13, since rebuilt (*Bleak House*, 20), as also were the chambers of Serjeant Snubbin (*Pickwick*, 31). In 1827 Dickens was a clerk in Mr. Molloy's offices, 8 New Square. Out of New Square a passage leads into Chichester Rents, where Krook, the rag dealer, lived.

**LINCOLN'S INN FIELDS.** On the western side of the Fields is No. 58, the house of John Forster, the biographer of Dickens and one of his most intimate friends. This house was assigned to Mr. Tulkinghorn (*Bleak House*, 10). Miss Trotwood had lodgings in a private hotel in the Fields, where the fire precautions satisfied her. *Copperfield*, 23.

**LINDERWOOD.** The officer commanding the Marines on the *Christopher Columbus* sloop. He was taken ashore sick and played no part in the subsequent adventures. *English Prisoners.*

**LINK.** This was a torch made of tow dipped in pitch and bound on a short pole. Links were carried by linkboys, who lighted foot passengers or sedan chairs before there was any proper system of street lighting. Link extinguishers are still to be seen by the doors of some of the older London houses. *Pickwick*, 36.

**LINKINWATER, TIM.** The old, confidential clerk of the Brothers Cheeryble, who had kept their books for forty-four years, during the whole of which time he had never slept out of the back attic over the offices. Nicholas was engaged to help and relieve him in his duties, and actually succeeded in winning the old fellow's approbation. The twins took him into partnership, and he proved a loyal friend to the Nicklebys, eventually marrying their good little friend, Miss La Creevy. Tim had a sister, a chubby old lady and his exact counterpart, who was

a guest of the Cheerybles at all their festivities. Tim Linkinwater had his original in an old and valued clerk of the Grant Brothers. *Nickleby*, 35, 37, 40, 43, 46, 48, 49, 55, 59–61, 63, 65.

**LINSEED, DUKE OF.** One of Mr. Boffin's correspondents asking for a subscription to the Family Party fund. *Mutual Friend*, I, 17.

**LINWOOD'S EXHIBITION.** Called by David Copperfield "a mausoleum of needle-work," for nearly fifty years this was one of the sights of London. It consisted of about 100 copies of pictures by old and modern masters, executed in needlework by Miss Mary Linwood (1755–1845). She worked with stitches of different lengths on a specially prepared fabric and superintended the dyeing of her own wools. Her last work, "The Judgment of Cain," took her ten years to execute. The Linwood Galleries were in Saville House, Leicester Square, which was burned down in 1865. The Empire Music-hall now stands on its site. *Copperfield*, 33. *Reprinted, Plated Article.*

**LINX, MISS.** One of Miss Pupford's pupils. *Tom Tiddler.*

**LION.** Henry Gowan's dog, mysteriously poisoned by Rigaud. *Dorrit*, I, 17, 34; II, 6, 7.

**LIRRIPER, MRS. EMMA.** The widow and lodging-house keeper of Norfolk Street, Strand, whose reminiscences make such delightful reading. On her husband's death she inherited nothing but debts, and accordingly set to and started a lodging house, gradually clearing off his obligations. Among her boarders was Major Jackman, and between them they adopted a little boy, Jemmy Lirriper. Mrs. Lirriper is one of the best characters of the kind ever drawn. Mention must also be made of Joshua Lirriper, her husband's brother, who was a doctor of some science, "though of what it would be hard to say, unless liquor." *Mrs. Lirriper's Lodgings and Legacy.*

**LISSON GROVE.** The first omnibus to run in London started from the Yorkshire Stingo public-house, in the New Road (now Marylebone Road), opposite Lisson Grove, on the morning of July 4, 1829. *See* Omnibus. *Boz, Scenes*, 17.

**LIST, ISAAC.** One of the party of gamblers who inveigled Nell's Grandfather into an attempt to steal. List and Jowl were in league with Groves, of the Valiant Soldier, but their party was eventually broken up by the detection of Fred Trent. *Curiosity Shop*, 29, 30, 42, 73.

**"LISTEN TO THE WATERFALL."** This is from a glee, "Here in cool grot," by the Earl of Mornington (father of the Duke of Wellington). *Bleak House*, 32.

**LISTON, JOHN.** This actor, whose private manners were known to the theatrical young gentlemen, had a great reputation as a comedian in his day. He was at Covent

Garden, 1808–22 ; Drury Lane, 1823, and subsequently at the Olympic. He died in 1846. *Sketches of Gentlemen (Theatrical)*.

**LITERARY LADIES, THE TWO.** The name applied to themselves by Miss Codger and Miss Toppit when they interviewed Elijah Pogram. *Chuzzlewit*, 34.

**LITTIMER.** The servant of James Steerforth, who helped to make the arrangements for his master's elopement with Little Em'ly. He brought back the story of the couple's wanderings abroad and told how Steerforth had wished to pass Em'ly over to him when he tired of her. A perfect example of the smug, hypocritical villain, Littimer is last seen in prison, in the cell adjacent to Uriah Heep, awaiting transportation for robbing his master. He had been apprehended through the agency of Miss Mowcher. *Copperfield*, 21–3, 28, 31, 32, 46, 61.

**LITTLE BRITAIN.** The office of Mr. Jaggers, the Old Bailey lawyer, was situated in this street. *Expectations*, 20.

**LITTLE COLLEGE STREET, CAMDEN TOWN.** In this street, which runs parallel to Great College Street and is now called College Place, lived Mrs. Roylance, the original of Mrs. Pipchin. Dickens boarded with her when his father went to the Marshalsea in 1822. Mr. E. G. Kitton·thinks it probable that Mrs. Roylance's house was No. 37, which was demolished in 1890 when the street was rebuilt.

**LITTLE DORRIT.** This novel was first christened *Nobody's Fault*, the final name only being given just before the publication of the first monthly number, Christmas, 1855. The last appeared in June, 1857. It was illustrated by H. K. Browne. The novel is an indictment of the system of imprisonment for debt and of the dilatoriness of government departments.

*Principal Characters.* The Dorrit family ; Arthur Clennam, his self-righteous mother and her clerk, Jeremiah Flintwinch ; the Meagles family, and their connections by marriage, Henry and Mrs. Gowan ; Rigaud, the murderer and blackmailer ; Cavaletto, an Italian ; the Plornishes ; Flora Finching, her father Casby and his clerk, Pancks ; Mrs. General, the Dorrit chaperone ; the parvenus Merdles ; Daniel Doyce, the inventor.

Arthur Clennam, returning from China, meets with a chilly reception from his mother, but sees at her house Little Dorrit, in whom and whose family he immediately takes an interest, going to see old William Dorrit, who has been so long in the Marshalsea that he has become known as its Father. In his endeavours to unravel the Dorrit affairs, Clennam makes a fruitless appeal for information to the Circumlocution Office, and then tries old Patriarch Casby, the father of his boyhood's sweetheart, now Flora Finching. Clennam has, meanwhile, just saved himself from falling in love with

Pet Meagles, who marries Henry Gowan, an aristocratic wastrel. Pancks, Casby's clerk, has also interested himself in the Dorrits and succeeds in proving their right to a large fortune. Having come into his money, William Dorrit takes his whole family abroad, Fanny and Amy under the chaperonage of the frigid Mrs. General. Fanny marries her old admirer, Edmund Sparkler, the son of Mrs. Merdle, wife of the wonderful financier. William Dorrit, who has developed into a pompous old man, is persuaded to embark his money in one of Merdle's great schemes. Happily for him he dies before it is all lost in the crash succeeding Merdle's suicide. Clennam and Pancks also lose all their money in this scheme, and Clennam is cast into the Marshalsea, where he is visited by Little Dorrit, whom he marries on leaving the prison. Throughout the story runs the series of dark events centring round Mrs. Clennam and a suppressed codicil of her husband's will, and its discovery by the villain Rigaud, who uses it to blackmail her.

**LITTLE EM'LY.** Peggotty's niece. *See* Em'ly, Little.

**LITTLE GOSLING STREET.** According to Mrs. Finching, she and Mr. F. settled down to married life, after their honeymoon, in No. 30 Little Gosling Street, London Docks, where " Gout flying upwards soared with Mr. F. to another sphere." There was never any street of this name. *Dorrit*, I, 24.

**LITTLE NELL.** The heroine of *Curiosity Shop*. *See* Nell, Little.

**LITTLE RUSSELL STREET.** The Albion Hotel in this street was a great resort of theatricals, and thither went Messrs. Potter and Smithers to " make a night of it." *Boz, Characters*, 11.

**LITTLE SWILLS.** The comedian at the Sol's Arms. *See* Swills.

**" LITTLE TAFFLIN."** This is a song from Storace's opera of *Three and the Deuce*, beginning :—

> Should e'er the fortune be my lot
> To be made a wealthy bride.
>              *Copperfield*, 28.

**LITTLEWOOD, MISS.** Original of Miss Flite. (*q.v.*)

**LIVELY.** A receiver of stolen goods in Field Lane. *Twist*, 26.

**LIVERPOOL.** Dickens's associations with Liverpool began in 1842, when he sailed thence for the U.S.A. Two years later he presided at a meeting in the Mechanic's Institution. In 1847 he acted there, with his amateur company, in *Every Man in His Humour*, and subsequently visited the city on reading tours, the last of which concluded with a banquet held in the St. George's Hall, April 10, 1869. The city is chiefly mentioned in connection with embarkation therefrom ; Lummy Ned (*Chuzzlewit*, 13) ; Tip Dorrit (*Dorrit*, I, 7) ; Richard Carstone (*Bleak House*, 24) ; Tom Gradgrind (*Hard Times*, III, 7) ; Captain Jorgan (*Message* *from Sea)* ; Charley (*Holly Tree*) ; Captain Ravender (*Golden Mary*). A vivid description of the conditions in which mercantile seamen lived in Liverpool is given in *Uncommercial*, 5.

**LIVING SKELETON.** Claude Ambroise Seurat, the " Living Skeleton " or " Anatomic Vivante," was exhibited in 1825 at the Chinese Gallery in Pall Mall. Although 5 ft. 7 in. in height, he only weighed 77¾ lb. Seurat set the fashion in " living Skellintons," of which every country fair soon had its specimen. *Pickwick*, 15. *Boz, Scenes*, 12.

**LIZ.** A brickmaker's wife and the friend of Jenny, whom she comforted after the loss of her baby, allowing Jenny to bring up one of her own children in its place. *Bleak House*, 8, 22, 31, 46, 57.

**LLANALLGO.** On October 26, 1859, the *Royal Charter*, Melbourne to Liverpool, foundered off this hamlet, which is near Moelfra, on the Isle of Anglesey. *Uncommercial*, 2.

**LOBBS, OLD.** A wealthy saddler and the father of Maria Lobbs, the beloved of Nathaniel Pipkin, whose ill-starred courtship was narrated in Mr. Pickwick's tale of the Parish Clerk. *Pickwick*, 17.

**LOBLEY.** Mr. Tartar's man and an old sailor who looked after his boat on the river. *Drood*, 22.

**LOBSKINI, SIGNOR.** The singing master at the Misses Crumpton's academy in Minerva House. *Boz, Tales, Sentiment*.

**LOGGINS.** An amateur actor, under the name of Beverley, who played *Macbeth* in the private theatre. *Boz, Scenes*, 13.

**LOMBARD STREET.** At No. 2 lived Maria Beadnell, the Dora of Dickens's early manhood, whose father was employed in the bank of Smith, Payne and Smith, upon whom, incidentally, Mr. Weller, Senior, was given a cheque for £530 (*Pickwick*, 55). Until 1829 the G.P.O. was in this street, commemorated by Post Office Court. George Yard, on the left-hand side, leads to the George and Vulture (*Pickwick*, 26). Mr. Dorrit accompanied Merdle to his bank in " the golden Street of the Lombards " (*Dorrit*, II, 16), while the offices of Barbox Brothers (*Mugby Junction*) were situated in or near the street. The Uncommercial Traveller (21), passing by there on a Sunday, pleased himself with the thought of all the money lying behind the closed doors of the banks.

**LONDON BRIDGE.** The present bridge was only opened for traffic August 1, 1831 ; some of our references, therefore, are to the older bridge, which was demolished in the following year. This old bridge had stood for many centuries and, until 1758, bore a number of wooden structures, shops, etc. It was some distance to the east of the present bridge, being a direct continuation of Fish Street Hill. It was thus the old bridge which was connected with David Copperfield's childhood (*Copperfield*, 5, 11) ; and was referred to in *Pickwick*, 32 ; *Boz, Tales, Tuggs* ; *Barnaby*, 5, 8, 16, 43, 49 and *Humphrey*. At each end of the new bridge are stairs to the water. Nancy had what proved to be her fatal interview with Rose Maylie and Mr. Brownlow on the stairs on the Surrey side (*Twist*, 46), while from those on the opposite shore Jonas Chuzzlewit sank his bundle of bloody clothes (*Chuzzlewit*, 51). From London Bridge or Steam Packet Wharf, on the City side of the Bridge, Mrs. Gamp and Mrs. Harris went to see the Ankworks Package (*Chuzzlewit*, 40), and the former is referred to in *Boz, Scenes*, 10, written in 1835. Finally Gaffer Hexam is introduced floating on the Thames, between Southwark and London Bridges (*Mutual Friend*, I, 1).

**LONDON BRIDGE STATION.** The terminus of the South Eastern Railway is referred to in *Reprinted, A Flight*. The two stations were built on the site of St. Thomas's Hospital, and were opened about 1851. There was then no continuation to Cannon Street.

**LONDON COFFEE HOUSE.** This well-known tavern was situated on the upper part of Ludgate Hill, then called Ludgate Street, next to the church of St. Martin. The house was closed in 1867, but was subsequently re-opened as a tavern, and is now (1924) one of Messrs. Short's establishments. On his return to England Arthur Clennam put up there, and spent a wretched Sunday evening watching the passers-by hurrying through the rain. *Dorrit*, I, 3.

**LONDON TAVERN, THE.** This was situated in Bishopsgate Street Within, on the site now occupied by the Royal Bank of Scotland, and was much used for public meetings similar to that of the United Metropolitan Improved Hot Muffin and Crumpet Baking and Punctual Delivery Company (*Nickleby*, 2). The jury which sat on The Trial for Murder (*Two Ghost Stories*) were housed in the London Tavern.

**" LONE, LORN CREETUR."** When in low spirits Mrs. Gummidge would moan, " I'm a lone, lorn creetur and everythink goes contrairy with me." *Copperfield*, 3, 30.

**LONG ACRE.** This is mentioned as one of the resorts of the Shabby Genteel (*Boz, Characters*, 10). By consuming, but not paying for, a meal fetched from a Long Acre eating-house, Dick Swiveller was obliged to mark off the street as one of those thoroughfares henceforward closed to him. *Curiosity Shop*, 8.

**LONG EERS, THE HON. AND REV.** A member of the Mudfog Association.

**LONGFORD, EDMUND.** A student of the Institution, who was nursed by Milly Tetterby, who only knew him under his assumed name of Denham. Coming under

Redlaw's evil spell he repudiated Milly, but came to his right senses at last. *Haunted Man.*

**LONG-LEGGED YOUNG MAN, THE.** A youth who robbed David of his trunk and money as he was starting for Dover. *Copperfield*, 12.

**LONG'S HOTEL, BOND STREET.** This was at the corner of Clifford Street and Bond Street, and was a fashionable hotel, such as would be frequented by Cousin Feenix. *Dombey*, 31.

**LONG VOYAGE, THE.** These "recollections of various incidents of travel" appeared in *Household Words*, December 31, 1853, and were republished in *Reprinted Pieces*, 1858.

**LORD CHANCELLOR.** 1. The judge who gave his permission for Mr. John Jarndyce to take charge of Ada Clare and Richard Carstone. *Bleak House*, 1, 3, 24.

2. Krook, the rag and bone merchant, was called jocularly the Lord Chancellor. *Bleak House*, 5.

**LORD MAYOR.** 1. The grossly incompetent Lord Mayor in the year of the Gordon Riots was Alderman Kennet, who had been a waiter, but made his money as a vintner. When asked why he did not summon the *posse comitatus* when the riots broke out, Kennet replied that he did not know where the fellow lived. *Barnaby*, 61, 65.

2. Mr. Toddyhigh's friend, a member of the Patten Maker's Company. *Humphrey.*

**LORD WARDEN HOTEL, DOVER.** Dickens stayed here in 1861, when it was run by Mr. and Mrs. Birmingham, of whom he speaks in *Uncommercial*, 17. It is now one of the Gordon Hotels.

**LORRY, JARVIS.** The confidential clerk in Tellson's bank who was concerned in bringing Dr. Manette back to life and freedom. He was a diplomatic, kindly old gentleman, who proved an invaluable friend to the Manettes in England. When the Revolution broke out he hastened to France to look after the interests of the Bank. There he assisted Lucy and Darnay, and after Carton's sacrifice brought them safely back to England. *Two Cities*, I, 2-6 ; II, 2-4, 6, 12, 16-21, 24 ; III, 2-6, 8, 9, 11-13.

**LOSBERNE, MR.** A surgeon, usually called The Doctor, and a close friend of the Maylies. When summoned to look after Oliver, who had been shot in the attempted burglary, Losberne succeeded in diverting the suspicions of the Bow Street runners. After the marriage of Rose to Harry, Losberne settled down near them, having given his practice to his assistant. *Twist*, 29-36, 41, 49, 51, 53.

**LOTTERIES, STATE.** Until their abolition in 1826 these lotteries were a source of considerable revenue to the Government. They were held to raise money for special objects

and offered large prizes, such as the £25,000 of which Chops the Dwarf won a half (*Going into Society*). Bills announcing the lotteries were circulated very extensively. *Reprinted, Bill Sticking.*

**LOUIS.** 1. A murderer in the Swiss Inn. *Holly Tree.*

2. The Uncommercial Traveller's foreign servant. (7).

**LOUISA.** The wife in The Cool Couple. *Sketches of Couples.*

**"LOVELY PEG."** Captain Cuttle's refrain was probably like many others of his literary recollections, somewhat confused. There are several songs about " Peg," and one about "Lovely Polly," by C. Dibdin, which was probably what he had in mind. *Dombey*, 32.

**LOVETOWN, MR. AND MRS.** The newly married couple in *Is She His Wife ?* who weary of one another, but by each arousing the other's jealousy re-establish their intimacy and affection.

**LOWESTOFT.** David was taken to this pleasant seaside town by Mr. Murdstone, who there perpetrated the Brooks of Sheffield joke. *Copperfield*, 2.

**LOWFIELD, MISS.** A young lady rather smitten with Mr. Caveton, the throwing-off young gentleman. *Sketches of Gentlemen.*

**LOWTEN.** Mr. Perker's clerk, "a puffy-faced young man," who shone in the convivial society of the Magpie and Stump. The class of law clerk represented by Lowten, Guppy, Jackson, etc., is now practically extinct, having given place to a better educated if less amusing race of men. *Pickwick*, 20, 31, 34, 40, 47, 53, 54.

**LOYAL DEVASSEUR, M.** Landlord of the inn at *Our French Watering Place.* *Reprinted Pieces.*

**LUCAS, JAMES.** Original of Mopes the hermit (*q.v.*). *See also* Tom Tiddler.

**LUCAS, SOLOMON.** The Eatanswill fancy dress dealer whose wardrobe was "extensive, not strictly classical, perhaps, not quite new, nor did it contain any one garment made precisely after the fashion of any age or time, but everything was spangled, and what can be pretty than spangles ?" *Pickwick*, 15.

**LUCY.** The long lost lover of the peevish bachelor. *Sketches of Couples (Old Couple).*

**LUDGATE HILL.** Until the widening of the thoroughfare in 1864, only the lower part, from Old Bailey to Farringdon Street, was called Ludgate Hill, the upper part being known as Ludgate Street. It was when crossing to St. Paul's Churchyard that David and Miss Trotwood were accosted by the latter's husband (*Copperfield*, 23). On his unlucky journey back from Miss La Creevy, which ended in his capture by Squeers, Smike dawdled up Ludgate Hill (*Nickleby*, 38). From the windows of the London Coffee House (*q.v.*) Arthur watched the dripping wayfarers. *Dorrit*, I, 3.

**LUD HUDIBRAS, KING.** The father of Prince Bladud and King of Britain, according to the story related in *Pickwick*, 36.

**LUFFEY.** A redoubtable batsman of the Dingley Dell Cricket Club. *Pickwick*, 7.

**LUKIN.** One of Mrs. Nickleby's early suitors. *Nickleby*, 41.

**LUMBEY, DR.** Mrs. Kenwigs's medical man, who expressed the opinion that a family of six was not half enough. *Nickleby*, 36.

**LUMMY NED.** The musical guard of the Light Salisbury coach, who emigrated to America. *Chuzzlewit*, 13.

**LUPIN, MRS.** Landlady of the Blue Dragon, " broad, buxom, comfortable and good looking . . . with a bright black eye and jet-black hair." She was a great admirer of Mr. Pecksniff, though her confidence was shaken when he got rid of Tom Pinch, and when Old Martin asked her to protect Mary Graham. When Martin and Mark Tapley returned from America they received a hearty welcome from Mrs. Lupin, none the less warm that she and Mark had long liked one another. In due course they were married, and the sign of the Blue Dragon was changed to The Jolly Tapley. *Chuzzlewit*, 3–5, 7, 31, 35–7, 43, 44, 48, 52, 53.

**LYING AWAKE.** This sketch appeared in *Household Words* for October 30, 1852, and was collected in *Reprinted Pieces*, 1858. It describes the succession of thoughts which may pass through a man's mind when unable to sleep.

**LYON'S INN.** This was one of the small law inns and was situated in Newcastle Street, between Holywell Street and Wych Street. It was demolished in 1863, and the Globe and Opera Comique Theatres were erected on its site. In this inn Mr. Testator had the curious adventure with the furniture which is recounted in *Uncommercial*, 14.

# M

**MACASSAR OIL.** In the days of luxuriant whiskers and curled hair this vegetable oil was largely employed, the preparation sold by Rowland, of Hatton Garden, being perhaps the most popular. *Boz, Tales, Tuggs.*

**MACEY, MR. AND MRS.** Miss Maryon's married sister and her husband, living on Silver Store Island. *English Prisoners.*

**MACKIN, MRS.** A slipshod customer at the pawnshop. *Boz, Scenes*, 23.

**MACKLIN, MRS.** The suburban resident, at No. 4, who screamed " Muffins." *Boz, Scenes*, 2.

**MACMANUS.** A midshipman on the *Halsewell. Reprinted, Long Voyage.*

**MACSTINGER, MRS.** Captain Cuttle's landlady at 9 Brig Place, India Docks. This redoubtable woman kept Captain Cuttle in a state of terrified subjection. When he took up his quarters at the Wooden Midshipman the Captain made a furtive escape from Brig Place, leaving his goods behind, and for many months lived in terror of Mrs. MacStinger discovering his whereabouts. When she did, Captain Bunsby was happily present and succeeded in taking her away, although this act of friendship was to his own cost, for the last that is seen of either is when Mrs. MacStinger is leading the Captain to the altar. Her children, Alexander, Juliana and Charles, are worthy of notice. *Dombey*, 9, 15, 17, 23, 25, 32, 39, 56, 60.

**MADDOX, JOHN.** Rose's sweetheart in *The Village Coquettes.*

**MADGERS, WINIFRED.** One of Mrs. Lirriper's maids, " a Plymouth sister," who married a Plymouth Brother, and afterwards called with Plymouth Twins. *Lirriper's Legacy.*

**MADMAN, THE.** The Narrator of the terrible story recounted in the Dingley Dell clergyman's manuscript. *Pickwick*, 11.

**MADNESS.** One of Miss Flite's captive birds. *Bleak House*, 14.

**MAGG.** A member of *Our Vestry. Reprinted Pieces.*

**MAGGY.** The granddaughter of Little Dorrit's old nurse, Mrs. Bangham, and a half-witted creature of twenty-eight, who called Amy Little Mother. The great event of her life had been when she was an inmate of a hospital, and if Maggy wanted to express her approval of anything, she would call it " hospitally." She was eventually employed by Mrs. Plornish, and is last seen at Little Dorrit's wedding. *Dorrit*, I, 9, 14, 20, 22, 24, 31, 32, 35 ; II, 4, 13, 29, 33, 34.

**MAGNUS, PETER.** A red-haired, inquisitive man who accompanied Mr. Pickwick to Ipswich, whither he was going to make a proposal of marriage to Miss Witherfield. Mr. Pickwick's unfortunate adventure in that lady's bedroom and the confusion of both parties when subsequently introduced by Mr. Magnus, threw him into such a rage that Miss Witherfield denounced an impending duel between the parties to Nupkins, the Mayor, and had the Pickwickians arrested. It may be noted as a *lapsus calami* that Magnus's spectacles at first called blue are later said to be green. *Pickwick*, 22, 24.

**MAGOG.** One of the Guildhall giants. *See* Gog.

**MAGPIE AND STUMP.** This rendezvous of Mr. Lowten and other choice spirits was probably either the George IV or the Old Black Jack, both of which were taverns in Portsmouth Street, Lincoln's Inn Fields. They were both demolished in 1896, though the former was rebuilt. *Pickwick*, 20, 21.

**MAGSMAN, TOBY OR ROBERT.** A showman who once occupied the House to Let and related the story of *Going into Society.*

**MAGWITCH, ABEL.** The convict whom Pip befriended on the Marshes when he had escaped from the hulks. After the recapture of himself and his enemy, Compeyson, he was transported to Australia, and there made a fortune which, through the agency of Jaggers, he devoted to Pip's education, with Great Expectations for the future. Returning to London at the risk of his life, death being the punishment for returned convicts, he took the name of Provis and for a while was concealed by Pip and Herbert Pocket. As they were trying to smuggle him out of the country he was arrested on information supplied by Compeyson. In the fight which ensued Magwitch drowned his lifelong enemy. He was tried and sentenced to death, but died in hospital, unaware that all his fortune had fallen to the Crown. Before his death Pip told him that Estella was his daughter. *Expectations*, 1, 3, 5, 39–43, 46, 54–6.

**MAIDEN LANE, HOLLOWAY.** About 1870 the name of this road was changed to its present name of York Road. It formerly ran through a wilderness of dustheaps and refuse, "inhabited by proprietors of donkey carts, boilers of horseflesh, makers of tiles and sifters of cinders " (*Boz, Scenes*, 20). Mr. Boffin gave the address of the Bower as "up Maiden Lane, Battle Bridge." *Mutual Friend*, I, 5.

**MAIDSTONE.** It is very probable that this old county town was the original of Muggleton, to the description of which it answers fairly well. This view is confirmed by its vicinity to Sandling, which is almost certainly the original of Dingley Dell. *See* Dingley Dell and Muggleton.

**MAILS.** An abbreviation often used for mail coaches. *See* Coach.

**MALDERTON.** A City man and his family, who lived at Oak Lodge, Camberwell, where they entertained the élite of the local society and tried to marry off the two girls, Marianne and Teresa. Among their genteel friends was Mr. Horatio Sparkins, who, however, turned out to be merely Mr. Samuel Smith, a draper's assistant. *Boz, Tales, Sparkins*.

**MALDON, JACK.** Mrs. Strong's idle, good-for-nothing cousin, who had been continually befriended and started in life by the old doctor. Maldon was in love with Mrs. Strong and played the villain's part in the somewhat unconvincing drama of estrangement between the doctor and his wife. *Copperfield*, 16, 19, 36, 42, 45, 64.

**MALLARD.** Serjeant Snubbin's elderly clerk, who "presented imposing indications of the extensive and lucrative practice of his master." *Pickwick*, 31, 34.

**MALLETT.** A member of the Mudfog Association.

**MALLOWFORD, LORD.** A former client of Arthur Gride, who was burnt to death in his bed. *Nickleby*, 51.

**MALTA.** The elder Bagnet girl, so called from her parents having been stationed there when she was born. *Bleak House*, 26.

**MANCHESTER.** Possible original of Coketown. (*q.v.*)

**MANCHESTER BUILDINGS.** This was a block of chambers, largely occupied by members of Parliament, which opened out of Cannon Row, Westminster, and stretched down to the river. The buildings were pulled down in the 60's and the Westminster Underground Station built on part of the site. Mr. Gregsbury lived there (*Nickleby*, 16) and they are also mentioned in *Boz, Scenes*, 18.

**MANETTE.** Dr. Alexandre Manette was a physician of Beauvais, who, after eighteen years in the Bastille, was released and taken to London, where, living with his daughter Lucie, he regained the faculties of which his long incarceration had bereft him. After Lucie's marriage to Darnay and the latter's subsequent imprisonment by the Revolutionists, Dr. Manette went to Paris and, as an old Bastille sufferer, was enabled to procure Darnay's liberation. But in the early days of his imprisonment Manette had written a statement of his wrongs, and this had been discovered upon the destruction of the Bastille. This statement incriminated the St. Evremonde family, of which Darnay was the representative, and on the strength of it Darnay was condemned to death. After Carton's sacrifice Dr. Manette accompanied the Darnay's to England, where he practised as a physician. Dr. Manette's House was probably 10 Carlisle Street, Soho. The neighbouring Rose Street was rechristened Manette Street in honour of the Doctor. *Two Cities*, I, 3–6 ; II, 2–4, 6, 9, 10, 16–21 ; III, 2–7, 9–13.

Lucie, the daughter of Dr. Manette, was taken by Jarvis Lorry to Paris to meet her long-imprisoned father, whom she had thought dead. While living in London Lucie married Darnay and followed him to Paris when she heard of his imprisonment. Ever since he had met her at Darnay's trial in London, Sydney Carton had loved Lucie with a self-denying love which realised that he was not good enough for her. Hastening to Paris when he heard of her trouble, he took advantage of his resemblance to her husband to substitute himself in Darnay's place, and for love of her went gladly to the guillotine. Lucie and her husband settled afterwards in London. Lucie Manette was the last of the Mary Hogarth heroines. I, 4–6 ; II, 2–6, 9–13, 16–18, 20, 21, 24 ; III, 2–7, 9, 11–13, 15.

**MAN FROM SHROPSHIRE.** The name usually given to Gridley. (*q.v.*)

**MANGLE.** The apparatus to which Mr. Mantalini referred as making his life one demd horrid grind was by no means the easy running domestic appliance now in common use. The old-fashioned box mangle was a bulky affair, consisting of a heavily weighted box resting upon wooden rollers. The article to be mangled was placed between these rollers and a long polished board. Considerable exertion was required to move the box backward and forward by means of a barrel from which a cord passed to either end. There were various improved patterns, one of which was Baker's Patent, made by Richard Baker of Cripplegate. *Nickleby*, 64. *Boz, Tales, Boarding House. Pickwick*, 15, 34. *Mutual Friend*, I, 16.

**MANGNALL.** A very common schoolbook in the early nineteenth century was *Historical and Miscellaneous Questions for the Use of Young People*. It appeared in 1800 and was written by Richmal Mangnall (1769–1820), principal of Crofton Hall School, near Wakefield, Yorks. *Tom Tiddler*.

**MANN, MRS.** The woman with whom Oliver Twist and sundry other childish unfortunates were " farmed " by the parochial authorities for sevenpence halfpenny a week. As Mrs. Mann kept the greater part of this sum for her own use, the condition of the children may be imagined. *Twist*, 2, 17.

**MANNERS, JULIA.** " A buxom, richly dressed female of about forty," who eloped by mistake with Alexander Trott, but duly married him at Gretna Green. *Boz, Tales, Winglebury*.

**MANNING.** 1. Sir Geoffrey, the proprietor of the shooting near Bury St. Edmunds, where Wardle and the Pickwickians had the " cold punch " outing. *Pickwick*, 18, 19.

2. The two Mannings were murderers whose trial was one of the chief *causes célèbres* of the nineteenth century. She was a Frenchwoman, and with the knowledge of her husband carried on an intrigue with one Patrick O'Connor. Deciding to murder him for his money they invited him to a dinner of roast goose, shot him on his arrival in the house, threw the corpse into a hole beneath the kitchen floor, and continued their meal off roast goose with the utmost composure. Dickens was present at their execution, witnessed by 50,000 people, outside Horsemonger Lane Gaol, November 13, 1849, and wrote a tremendous letter to *The Times* denouncing the barbarity of such sights. *See* Hortense.

**MANOR FARM.** The fine old home of the Wardles at Dingley Dell has been almost certainly identified as Cob-Tree Hall, an Elizabethan house in the neighbourhood of Sandling. *See* Dingley Dell.

**MANSEL, MISS.** One of the *Halsewell's* passengers. *Reprinted, Long Voyage*.

**MANSFIELD, LORD.** This peer was Lord Chief Justice at the time of the Gordon Riots, and his support of the Catholic Relief Bill made him an object of the rioters' especial hatred. They burned his house in Bloomsbury and fully intended to destroy his country mansion at Ken Wood. Lord Mansfield retired from the bench in 1788 and died March 20, 1793, aged 88. *Barnaby*, 66, 67.

**MANSION HOUSE.** The official residence of the Lord Mayor of London was built in 1739–53, and has given its name to the immediate neighbourhood. At half-past eleven o'clock on a pouring Friday morning Mr. Nicodemus Dumps departed from the Mansion House in the Admiral Napier omnibus, bound for the Kitterbells (*Boz, Tales, Christening*). Kit Nubbles was taken to the Mansion House police court (*Curiosity Shop*, 60), while the same place was the scene of Mr. Hobler's witicisms with the driver of the red cab at the expense of the unfortunate fare. *Boz, Scenes*, 17.

**MANTALINI, MR. AND MRS. ALFRED.** He was a curiously likeable blackguard, who " had married on his whiskers ; upon which property he had previously subsisted for some years." Originally named Muntle, upon his marriage to a fashionable dressmaker he had changed it to Mantalini. A good-for-nothing spendthrift, he kept his wife infatuated with him by dexterous flattery and comparison with a Countess and other high folk whom he had thrown over for her. He succeeded in wheedling all her money out of her, until she went bankrupt. Mantalini last appears toiling at a mangle for a laundress who had paid £2 14s. to release him from prison (*Nickleby*, 10, 17, 21, 34, 44, 64). Madame Mantalini, the dressmaker who had fallen a victim to Mr. Muntle's whiskers, was a vain, elderly woman who worked her employees to death, but squandered her money on her husband. The couple had got into Ralph Nickleby's hands, and he induced her to give Kate employment. Eventually, ruined and with her eyes opened to her husband's character, she handed over the business to Miss Knag, her forewoman. It has been suggested, on slender authority, that the Mantalini establishment was at 10 Wigmore Street. 10, 17, 18, 21, 34, 35, 44.

**MANTUA MAKER.** Originally a maker of " manteaux," the term was usually employed for what is now called a dressmaker. *Pickwick*, 32.

**MAPLESONE.** Mrs. Matilda and her daughters, Julia and Matilda, were among Mrs. Tibbs's first boarders. They had done the rounds of the watering places for four seasons, but had not succeeded in getting establishments of their own. Events happened at Mrs. Tibbs's however ; Julia married Mr. Simpson, but eloped with a half-pay officer six weeks after marriage ; Matilda became Mrs. Septimus Hicks, and was deserted by her husband ; Mrs. Maplesone was to have married (but didn't) Mr. Calton. *Tales, Boz, Boarding House*.

**MARCHIONESS, THE.** The small, slipshod drudge at Bevis Marks, whom Dick

Swiveller discovered looking through the keyhole. She was bullied and underfed by Sally Brass, but Dick made a friend of her, taught her how to play cribbage and called her the Marchioness. When Dick was dismissed from the Brasses and taken ill with a fever, the Marchioness ran away from Bevis Marks and nursed him. The conversations she had heard between the Brass couple were sufficient to procure their downfall and prove the innocence of Kit Nubbles. Dick Swiveller sent the Marchioness to school, under the name of Sophronia Sphynx, and eventually married her. *Curiosity Shop*, 34–6, 51, 57, 58, 64–6, 73.

**MARGARET.** 1. Aunt Margaret, who suffered from the disgrace of having married a poor man. *Boz, Characters*, 2.

2. Mr. Winkle Senior's pretty housemaid. *Pickwick*, 50.

**MARGATE.** Although so often in the vicinity, Dickens seldom went to Margate, there being only two recorded visits to the town, in 1844 and 1847. One of the earliest steamboat services from London was to Margate (*Boz, Scenes*, 10. *Tom Tiddler*). It was a resort of young clerks madly in love (*Bleak House*, 19); though the Tuggses complained that nobody but tradespeople went there (*Boz, Tales, Tuggs's*). Young Abel Garland's only dissipation in life had been a visit to Margate with Mr. Tomkinley, his schoolmaster. *Curiosity Shop*, 14.

**"MARGIN, LEAVING A."** A rather dangerous feature in Pip's scheme of account keeping. *Expectations*, 34.

**MARIGOLD, DOCTOR.** A Cheap Jack who tells the story of Doctor Marigold's Prescriptions. He adopted a deaf and dumb girl, whom he had educated. She married another deaf mute and went to India, leaving Doctor Marigold lonely and forlorn. One day she returned, bringing her little daughter with her, and to Marigold's delight, the child could talk.

**MARKER, MRS.** A client of the registry office who wanted a cook. "Five servants kept. No man. No followers." *Nickleby*, 16.

**MARKHAM.** A friend of Steerforth and one of David's guests at his bachelor dinner. Markham always referred to himself indefinitely as "a man." *Copperfield*, 24.

**MARKLEHAM, MRS.** The mother of Mrs. Strong and a scheming lady whom the schoolboys used to call The Old Soldier. By her tactlessness and selfishness she did much to widen the breach between her daughter and the good old Doctor. *Copperfield*, 16, 19, 36, 42, 45, 64.

**MARKS, WILL.** John Podgers's nephew, and a wild, roving young man and the hero of Mr. Pickwick's tale. *Humphrey*.

**MARLBOROUGH DOWNS.** It is, according to Mr. F. G. Kitton, probable that Dickens put up in the inn he describes on the Marlborough Downs on the occasion of one of his early reporting visits, about 1835. It was probably the hostelry which once existed at Shepherd's Shore. *Pickwick*, 14. *See also* article Inn.

**MARLEY, JACOB.** Scrooge's late partner and his ghostly visitor on Christmas Eve. "Marley was dead to begin with. There is no doubt whatever about that. Old Marley was as dead as a door nail." Nevertheless, his ghost warned Scrooge of what would befall him unless he mended his ways, showing him a vision of fettered, miserable ghosts like himself. *Christmas Carol*.

**MAROON, CAPTAIN.** Tip Dorrit's creditor, a horsy gentleman "with tight drab legs." *Dorrit*, I, 12.

**MARQUIS OF GRANBY, DORKING.** This inn, the scene of Mr. Tony Weller's married life and of his struggles with Mr. Stiggins, has never been identified. In 1897 Mr. Robert Allbut announced that he had found the original "Markis" at the corner of High Street and Chequer Court, but the general opinion follows that of Mr. Matz in identifying it with the old King's Arms. *Pickwick*, 10, 27, 52.

**MARSEILLES.** This was the port at which Arthur Clennam and the Meagles were quarantined and where Rigaud and Cavaletto were imprisoned at the opening of *Dorrit*, I, 1, 2. Herbert Pocket was on a business visit there when Magwitch revealed himself to Pip. *Expectations*, 39.

**MARSHALL.** 1. Mary was betrothed to Dick Doubledick, but gave him up on account of his wild ways. When he was taken into Brussels she went to nurse him, and he recovered consciousness to find her his wife. *Seven Poor Travellers*.

2. Miss Marshall was a friend of the Censorious Young Gentleman. *Sketches of Gentlemen*.

**MARSHALSEA PRISON.** There is often some confusion with regard to this prison, for it was moved in 1811 from the block between Newcomen Street and Mermaid Court (opposite Union Street) to farther down the Borough High Street, adjacent to St. George's Church. This second building, which was the scene of all the Dickens's incidents, ceased to be used in 1849, portions of it were demolished shortly afterwards, and only part of the wall now remains, marked by a tablet in St. George's Churchyard and traceable in Angel Court. Dickens's father was imprisoned in the Marshalsea, and thither the lad went to see him and gained that knowledge of the place and its manners which he afterwards embodied in *Dorrit*, the greater part of the first volume of which deals with life in the prison. The place is also mentioned in *Pickwick*, 21.

**MARSHES, THE.** "The dark, flat wilderness" which made such an impression on

Pip's young mind was the stretch of marshes which lies between Cooling and the Thames. *Expectations*, 1.

**MARSH GATE, LAMBETH.** This squalid neighbourhood is mentioned in *Boz, Scenes*, 2, 3.

**MARSH MILL.** Original of the Paper Mill (*q.v.*), where Lizzie Hexam worked.

**MARTHA.** 1. Mrs. Gabriel Parsons's parlourmaid. *Boz, Tales, Tottle*.

2. A decrepit, old workhouse inmate who attended the confinement of Agnes Fleming. *Twist*, 23, 24, 51.

3. The daughter of John, the riverside labourer to whom Florence Dombey spoke. *Dombey*, 24.

**MARTIGNY.** This Swiss town was the scene of Mr. Dorrit's encounter with Mrs. Merdle and Mr. Sparkler, who were occupying the apartments engaged by him. *Dorrit*, II, 3.

**MARTIN.** 1. " Mr. Martin of coster-monger notoriety " was Richard Martin (1754–1834), called Humanity Martin, one of the principal founders of the Society for the Prevention of Cruelty to Animals (1824). *Boz, Scenes*, 7.

2. Miss Amelia, the Mistaken Milliner, who thought she could sing, but was " booed " off the stage. *Boz, Characters*, 8.

3. Betsey Martin, a charwoman converted to temperance, who attributed the fact of having only one eye to her mother's having drunk stout. *Pickwick*, 33.

4. The young lady at the bar of Christopher's hotel. *Somebody's Luggage*.

5. Dear friends of Mr. Mincin. *Sketches of Gentlemen* (*Very Friendly*).

6. Jack, the Bagman's Uncle, " one of the merriest, pleasantest fellows that ever lived." *Pickwick*, 49.

7. Tom, a butcher imprisoned in the Fleet. *Pickwick*, 42.

8. Miss Allen's groom, a surly, silent man. *Pickwick*, 39, 48.

9. Captain Martin, a prisoner in the Marshalsea. *Dorrit*, I, 19.

**MARTIN, BETTY.** " All my eye and Betty Martin." *See* Betty Martin.

**MARTIN CHUZZLEWIT.** *The Life and Adventures of Martin Chuzzlewit* was begun in November, 1842, and the first number appeared in the following January. It came out in twenty monthly parts, the last appearing in July, 1844, when it was published in book form, with illustrations by H. K. Browne.

*Principal Characters.* Seth Pecksniff, and his two daughters; Tom Pinch and his sister Ruth; Martin Chuzzlewit, Senior, and his ward, Mary Graham; Martin Chuzzlewit, Junior, and his friend Mark Tapley; Jonas Chuzzlewit; Mrs. Gamp and Betsey Prig; Montague Tigg; John Westlock; Old Chuffey; Bailey, Junior; Mrs. Todgers; sundry Americans.

The story opens with the hypocrite architect Pecksniff, who takes in Martin, Junior, after his quarrel with his grandfather. The cause of the quarrel was Mary Graham, a pretty girl adopted by old Martin, with whom the younger man has fallen in love. At old Martin's instigation Pecksniff turns his new pupil away, and in desperation the young man goes to America, accompanied by " jolly " Mark Tapley. Old Martin then goes to live with Pecksniff and by degrees appears to fall under that man's influence, even to the extent of favouring his designs of marrying Mary Graham. In the meantime, Pecksniff marries his daughter, Mercy, to her boorish cousin, Jonas Chuzzlewit. Jonas becomes involved in a bogus insurance concern, run by a rare adventurer, Montague Tigg, who gains certain knowledge that Jonas had tried to poison his father, old Anthony. Desperate at having his secret known, Jonas murders Tigg and hides the body in a wood. While these events have been happening in England, young Martin and Mark Tapley have had sad experiences in America, where they lose all their money and are obliged to return home penniless. Pecksniff carries his wooing of Mary Graham to such a pitch that even his faithful admirer and pupil, Tom Pinch, has his eyes opened. Pinch leaves the house and goes to London, where he finds work with a mysterious employer and sets up housekeeping with his sister Ruth, with whom John Westlock promptly falls in love. Jonas Chuzzlewit is arrested and commits suicide, and then the day of reckoning comes in which old Martin pays off his long score with the hypocrite Pecksniff, reunites Mary Graham and young Martin, and blesses the matches of John Westlock and Ruth, of Mark Tapley and Mrs. Lupin, the landlady, and turns out to be Tom Pinch's employer. Only one person is unmarried and that is Charity Pecksniff, whose lover levants on the wedding morning. Throughout the book appear at intervals some of the most wonderful of all the Dickens's characters: Mrs. Gamp; Betsey Prig; Mr. Mould, the undertaker; Bailey, the perfect Cockney lad; and the American grotesques, such as Pogram; Mrs. Hominy; Chollop.

**MARTON.** The village schoolmaster who took pity on Little Nell and her Grandfather and enabled them to settle in the village, where they ended their days. *Curiosity Shop*, 24–6, 45, 46, 52–4, 71, 73.

**MARWOOD, ALICE.** The daughter of " Good Mrs. Brown " and James Carker's cast-off mistress, who had been transported for theft. On her return she was instrumental in setting Mr. Dombey on the track of his fugitive wife and treacherous manager. In the end she died, cared for by Harriet Carker, who had long been her only friend. *Dombey*, 33, **34**, 40, 46, 52, 53, 58.

**MARY, THE PRETTY HOUSEMAID.**
She first appeared as housemaid at Mr.
Nupkins's house, where she and Sam Weller
fell in love at sight.  Sam sent her a valentine,
but they did not meet again until he went to
Clifton on Mr. Winkle's love errand.  Mary
was largely instrumental in bringing the
lovers together, and after their marriage
entered Mrs. Winkle's service.  She and Sam
willingly waited for two years after Mr.
Pickwick settled in Dulwich, but on the
death of the housekeeper, Mary was installed in her place on condition that she
married Sam forthwith.  The character was
founded on Mary Weller, one of Dickens's
nurses, who later became Mrs. Mary Gibson
of Mount Row, Ordnance Place, Chatham.
She died in 1888, aged 84.  *Pickwick*, 25, 33,
39, 47, 52, 54, 56, 57.

**MARY.**  1. A quarrelsome lady at Seven
Dials.  *Boz, Scenes*, 5.

2. A young lady at Greenwich Fair.  *Boz,
Scenes*, 12.

3. A spectator of the aeronauts at Vauxhall.  *Boz, Scenes*, 14.

4. A gin-shop barmaid.  *Boz, Scenes*, 22.

5. The daughter of Old John, the inventor.  *Poor Man's Patent.*

6. Daughter of the dying drunkard.  *Boz,
Tales*, 12.

7. Maid servants at : Wardle's house
(*Pickwick*, 5); the Peacock, Eatanswill
(*Pickwick*, 14).

**MARY ANN.**  One of the young ladies
attending a lottery in the Margate Library.
*Boz, Tales, Tuggs's.*

**MARY ANNE.**  1. Wemmick's little maid
of all work.  *Expectations*, 25, 45.

2. Miss Peecher's favourite pupil, who
prefaced all her remarks by holding up her
hand.  *Mutual Friend*, II, 1, 11 ; IV, 7.

**MARYON.**  Captain Maryon commanded
the sloop *Christopher Columbus*, which proceeded to Silver Store Island.  He was taken
ashore sick on the island, where he died.
His sister, Miss Marion Maryon, played a
brave part in the struggles with the pirates,
and was dearly loved by Gill Davis, who tells
the story.  Eventually she married Captain
Carton.  *English Prisoners.*

**MASH.**  A character in *Sandford and
Merton.  Uncommercial*, 33.

**MASTER HUMPHREY'S CLOCK.**  This
was started, April 4th, 1840, as a threepenny
weekly, of which each number was to
contain short papers, with occasional correspondence, and a continuous story.  These
were to be welded into a whole by means of
Master Humphrey, who was to be the
founder of a club, the members of which
would place MSS. in the case of his old
grandfather clock.  The work ran into 88
parts, though the machinery of Master
Humphrey and the club, including the
Wellers, whose introduction revived the
public's flagging interest in the paper, was

dropped after a time, and *Curiosity Shop*
and *Barnaby* were allowed to run their
course uninterrupted by extraneous matter.

**MATHEWS, CHARLES.**  (1803–78.)  This
was the son of a famous actor, and was
himself an actor and theatrical manager of
repute.  He was at Drury Lane and Haymarket.  Mathews married Madame Vestris,
the leading figure on the London boards at
that time.  *Sketches of Gentlemen (Theatrical).*

**MATINTER, MISSES.**  Visitors at Bath,
" single and singular."  *Pickwick*, 35.

**MATTHEWS.**  Mr. Gregsbury's page boy,
" who looked as if he had slept underground
from infancy."  *Nickleby*, 16.

**MAUNDERS.**  The proprietor of a variety
show who kept in his cottage at Spa Fields
eight male and female dwarfs, waited on by
giants who were too old for exhibiting
purposes.  *Curiosity Shop*, 19.

**MAWLS AND MAXBY.**  Pupils at *Our
School.  Reprinted Pieces.*

**MAXEY, CAROLINE.**  One of Mrs. Lirriper's servants who suffered from a violent
temper.  *Lirriper's Lodgings.*

**MAXWELL, MRS.**  A guest at the Kitterbell christening party.  *Boz, Tales, Christening.*

**MAYDAY.**  A friend of the Uncommercial
Traveller, who gave gloomy birthday parties.
*Uncommercial*, 19.

**MAYLIE.**  Mrs. Maylie, the mother of
Harry, was the kind-hearted woman who
adopted Rose Maylie and befriended Oliver
Twist, when he fell into her hands after the
attempted burglary of her house in Chertsey.
This house has been identified in Pycroft
Road.  *Twist*, 29–35, 41, 51, 53.

Harry Maylie, her son, had been destined
for public life, but chose the Church, obtaining a quiet rural living after he married
Rose.  34–6, 49, 51, 53.

Rose Maylie was a beautiful girl of seventeen, who had been discovered, when a child,
in the hands of some poor people, and had
been brought up by Mrs. Maylie as her
niece.  She and Mr. Brownlow interested
themselves in Nancy, and it was largely
due to the girl's surreptitious interview with
them, overheard by Claypole, that she was
murdered by Sikes.  It afterwards transpired that Rose was the sister of Agnes
Fleming, and the victim of the cruelty of
" Monks " and his mother, who had hoped
that her identity would never come to light.
Rose married Harry Maylie, and took her
adopted mother to live with them in the
country parsonage.  28–36, 39–41, 46, 51, 53.

**MAYNE, SIR RICHARD.**  On the institution of the Police Force in 1829 this
gentleman became a Joint Commissioner
with Colonel Rowan, and in 1850 became
Chief Commissioner.  It was he that practically organised and formed the Force.  He
died in office, 1868.  *Uncommercial*, 6.

**MAYPOLE INN.**  The picturesque original
of this magnificent old inn is the King's Head

at Chigwell, at one time a favourite resort of Dickens. *Barnaby*, 1–3, 10–13, 19, 20, 25, 29–31, 33–7, 54–6, 82.

**"MAY WE NEVER WANT A FRIEND."** Captain Cuttle was quoting, not Solomon, but J. Davy's song, sung by Incledon, the refrain of which ran :—

And my motto, though simple, means more than it says,
May we ne'er need a friend or a bottle to give him.
         *Dombey*, 15 ; *Curiosity*, 56.

**M'CHOAKUMCHILD.** The schoolmaster employed by Mr. Gradgrind to instil FACTS into the children of Coketown. *Hard Times*, I, 1, 2, 9, 14.

**MEAGLES, MR. AND MRS.** A kindly old couple who were fond of travel, though heartily despising the Allongers and Marshongers, as Mr. Meagles called the French. They introduced Arthur Clennam to Doyce and continually performed acts of kindness to them both. Years previously they had adopted a girl from the Foundling. Tattycoram, as they called her, ran away to Miss Wade for a time, and Meagles searched for her high and low, but she returned of her own accord to the worthy old couple. Their great grief was the marriage of Pet to Henry Gowan, whose selfish worthlessness they fully realised. Meagles and Doyce eventually released Arthur Clennam from the Marshalsea. *Dorrit*, I, 2, 10, 12, 16, 17, 23, 26–8, 33, 34 ; II, 7–9, 11, 33, 34.

" Pet " or Minnie Meagles, their daughter, was a pretty girl with whom Arthur Clennam would have fallen in love, had he permitted himself. As it was she married Henry Gowan, who took her abroad for a while. He proved but an indifferent husband and held his wife's parents in the utmost contempt, having no further communication with them than was necessary to receiving the allowance they made his wife. I, 2, 16, 17, 26, 28, 34 ; II, 1, 3–9, 11, 28, 33.

**MEALY POTATOES.** Nickname of one of David's companions in the warehouse of Murdstone and Grinby. *Copperfield*, 11, 12.

**MECHI.** A widely advertised firm of fancy goods manufacturers and retailers, of 4 Leadenhall Street. Mechi's Elegances for Presents and Use was a phrase which found its way into every magazine and newspaper. It may be remarked that Mechi's catalogue appeared in the advertisements bound up in Parts 19 and 20 of *Pickwick*. *Reprinted, Bill Sticking.*

**MEDWAY, THE.** Mr. Pickwick was surveying this Kentish river from Rochester Bridge when he fell into conversation with Dismal Jemmy (*Pickwick*, 5). The Micawbers considered that something might turn up in the Medway Coal Trade, so they went to Canterbury, " as Mr. Micawber very properly said, the first step to be taken . . . was to come and see the Medway " (*Copperfield*, 17). Chatham Dockyard on the Medway is described in *Uncommercial*, 24.

**MEEK, GEORGE.** The husband of Mrs. Meek ; the father of Augustus George, and the son-in-law of Mrs. Bigby. In this triple rôle Mr. Meek led a miserable life, especially when Augustus George made his first appearance in the family. *Reprinted, Mrs. Meek.*

**MEEK MAN, THE.** One of Mr. Podsnap's guests who dared to differ in opinion from his host. *Mutual Friend*, I, 11.

**MEGGISSON'S.** A Liverpool lodging house for the reception and delusion of Mercantile Jack. *Uncommercial*, 5.

**MELCHISEDECH.** A solicitor in Clifford's Inn to whom Trooper George was referred by Mr. Tulkinghorn for the adjustment of his money difficulties. *Bleak House*, 47.

**'MELIA.** The good-natured maid at Dr. Blimber's school. *Dombey*, 12, 14.

**MELL, CHARLES.** The "gaunt, sallow" assistant at Salem House who met David Copperfield on his first coming to London, and took the lad to see his mother in an almshouse. David unfortunately told this to Steerforth, who used his knowledge to procure Mell's dismissal from the school. The master subsequently went to Australia, where he fell in with the Micawbers. The original of Mell was probably a Mr. Taylor, English Master at Wellington House Academy. *Copperfield*, 5–7, 63.

**MELLOWS, J.** The landlord of the Dolphin's Head, the old coaching establishment ruined by the advent of the railway. *Uncommercial*, 22.

**MELTHAM.** The clever actuary who, under the guise of Beckwith and Major Banks, succeeded in unmasking the villainy of Julius Slinkton. *Hunted Down.*

**MELVILLESON, MISS M.** The singer at the Sol's Arms who had, despite her name, been married eighteen months. According to Mrs. Perkins her baby was clandestinely conveyed to the Sol's Arms every night to receive its natural nourishment. *Bleak House*, 32, 33, 39.

**MEMORIAL, THE.** This was the document Mr. Dick continually worked at with the idea of memorialising the Lord Chancellor about his affairs. He had been " for upwards of ten years endeavouring to keep King Charles the First out of it," but invariably failed, for try as he would, some reference of the execution of that monarch would creep into the document. *Copperfield*, 14.

**MEMORY.** This was the nickname applied by Stryver to his hack worker, Sydney Carton. *Two Cities*, II, 5.

**MENDICANT'S BRIDE, THE.** The grandiloquent term applied by Mrs. Wilfer to her daughter Bella after her marriage to Rokesmith. *Mutual Friend*, IV, 5.

**"MEN OF PROMETHEUS."** Beethoven's only ballet, " Prometheus " was originally known by the longer title. It was produced in 1801. *Boz, Tales, Porter.*

**MERCANTILE JACK.** The typical merchant seaman who forms the subject of *Uncommercial*, 5.

**MERCURY.** Sir Leicester Dedlock's footman. *Bleak House*, 16, 48, 53.

**MERCY.** The nurse who told the Uncommercial Traveller gruesome stories when he was a child. *Uncommercial*, 15.

**MERDLE, MR.** A financier and banker, who " was in everything good from banking to building." A member of Parliament and apparently possessed of immense wealth, he entertained lavishly. Attracted by his dazzling financial schemes, which had even received the benediction of the Circumlocution Office, Arthur Clennam, the Dorrits and many others invested their entire fortunes with him, only to meet their ruin when the crash came. One evening Merdle committed suicide in a Turkish Bath establishment, and within a few days it transpired that the powerful financier had been the greatest forger and thief that ever cheated the gallows.

The prototype of Merdle was John Sadleir, an Irish M.P., who founded the Tipperary Joint Stock Bank, was chairman of the London and County Joint Stock Bank from 1848 to 1856, and a prominent follower of Lord John Russell. Having embezzled some £200,000 of the Tipperary Bank funds, he forged various deeds to conceal the deficiency and on the eve of discovery committed suicide on Hampstead Heath, February, 1856. The catastrophe ruined hundreds of small clerks and farmers in the south of Ireland and was, in the words of *The Times*, " a national calamity." *Dorrit*, I, 21, 33 ; II, 5–7, 12–16, 18, 24, 25, 28.

**Mrs. Merdle,** wife of the financier, had been the widow of a colonel, and was the mother of Edmund Sparkler. She was a great Society lady and, although she had formerly looked askance at the Dorrits in their poverty, when she met them as wealthy people in Italy she was glad to settle the match between Fanny and her son. I, 20, 21, 33 ; II, 3, 5–7, 12, 14, 15, 18, 19, 24, 25, 33.

**MERITON, HENRY.** Second mate of the Halsewell. *Reprinted, Long Voyage.*

**MERRYLEGS.** Signor Jupe's performing dog. Sometime after the clown had disappeared from the circus, Merrylegs made his way back to Sleary, then at Chester, and died at his feet. *Hard Times*, I, 3, 5–7, 9 ; III, 8.

**MERRYWEATHER'S LIVES.** The book from which Mr. Boffin derived so much satisfaction was *The Lives and Anecdotes of Misers*, published in 1850. *Mutual Friend*, III, 6.

**MERRYWINKLE, MR. AND MRS.** The Couple who Coddle Themselves. *Sketches of Couples.*

**MESHECK, AARON.** A Jew criminal whom Serjeant Dornton tracked down by means of his carpet bag. *Reprinted, Detective Police.*

**MESROUR.** The name given to Miss Griffin's servant, Tabby, by the youngsters who formed the Seraglio. *Haunted House.*

**MESSAGE FROM THE SEA.** This story in five chapters, of which Dickens wrote the first two and the last, appeared as an extra Christmas number of *All the Year Round*, 1860.

**MICAWBER, WILKINS.** Introduced as the agent of Murdstone and Grinby, to whose house David Copperfield was sent as a lodger, Micawber passes through the novel as a gigantic, marvellous personification of impecuniosity, optimism, despair and gaiety —of what Mr. Chesterton calls the " preposterous and sublime victory of the human spirit over circumstances." After imprisonment for debt in the Marshalsea he went to Plymouth, hoping that something would turn up in the excise line. He then drifted to the Medway to look at the coal trade, was back in London with Traddles as his lodger, went to Canterbury, where he entered the office of Wickfield and Heep, and there succeeded in unmasking Uriah and setting to right all the wrongs committed by that villain in Mr. Wickfield's name. In gratitude for this Miss Trotwood and his friends paid all Micawber's debts and sent him out to Australia, where he became the principal man at the settlement of Port Middlebay. The character was drawn from Dickens's own father, whose superiority over misfortunes is thus admirably delineated.

**Mrs. Emma Micawber** was the worthy wife of such a man, sharing his optimism, convinced of his abilities and resolved never to desert him, however much such a course might be advised by her relatives. *Copperfield*, 11, 12, 17, 27, 28, 34, 36, 39, 42, 49, 52, 54, 55, 57, 60, 63.

**MICHAEL.** 1. The Poor Relation, who tells his story in *Reprinted Pieces*.

2. A rogue in the St. Giles Rookery. *Reprinted, Inspector Field.*

**MIDSHIPMAN, THE WOODEN.** *See* Wooden Midshipman.

**MIFF, MRS.** The wheezy little pewopener at the church where Mr. Dombey and, later, his daughter Florence, were married. *Dombey*, 31, 57.

**MIGGOTT, MRS.** The laundress of Mr. Parkle's chambers in Gray's Inn Square. *Uncommercial*, 14.

**MIGGS, MISS.** The slender and shrewish young lady who acted as maid of all work to Mrs. Varden, played up to all her mistress's whims and fancies, and very effectively set her and her husband at loggerheads. Setting her cap at Sim Tappertit, or " Simmuns " as she called him, she followed him when he went a-rioting, hoping to win his heart from Dolly Varden. When the Riots were over, Miggs made her way back to the

Vardens, only to find that she was no longer wanted, as Mrs. Varden had realised the evil part she had played in the house. Miggs thereupon became a turnkey at the Bridewell, and died at her post some thirty years later. *Barnaby*, 7, 9, 13, 18, 19, 22, 27, 31, 36, 39, 41, 51, 63, 70, 71, 80, 82.

**MIKE.** A client of Jaggers, the Old Bailey lawyer. *Expectations*, 20, 51.

**MILE END.** The Turnpike, which occasioned Mr. Weller Senior's philosophical remarks when driving Mr. Pickwick down to Ipswich, was at the corner of the Cambridge Road, the spot being still known as Mile End Gate (*Pickwick*, 22). Mrs. Jellyby had Borrioboolan business there. *Bleak House*, 14.

**MILES.** 1. Bob, a London pickpocket. *Reprinted, Inspector Field.*

2. Owen, one of Master Humphrey's friends, "not of quick apprehension, and not without some amusing prejudices." *Humphrey.*

3. Original of Tope. (*q.v.*)

**"MILESTONES."** "There's milestones on the Dover Road" was one of Mr. F.'s aunt's most cryptic sayings. *Dorrit*, I, 23.

**MILKWASH, MR.** The poetical young gentleman. *Sketches of Gentlemen.*

**MILLBANK.** The road by the riverside along Millbank is now called the Grosvenor Road, and has completely changed in appearance since David Copperfield and Peggotty followed Martha Endell to the old ferry, where she paused, contemplating suicide (*Copperfield*, 47). This was at the end of Horseferry Road, where Lambeth Bridge now replaces the ferry. The Tate Gallery occupies the site of the Penitentiary, where Mr. Bill Barker lodged (*Boz, Scenes*, 17). At the N.W. corner of Dean Stanley Street (formerly Church Street), and Smith Square stands a large house, occupying the site of Jenny Wren's old home (*Mutual Friend*, II, 1), the "very hideous church" being that of St. John Evangelist.

**MILLER.** 1. A hardheaded old gentleman who was a guest at Dingley Dell. *Pickwick*, 6, 28.

2. Mrs. Jane Ann Miller, the sister of Mrs. Wilding, who adopted on her behalf the child from the Foundling. *No Thoroughfare.*

**MILLER, JOE.** In 1739 a book was brought out by John Mottley, the dramatist, purporting to be the collected jokes and sayings of Joe Miller, the comedian (1684–1738), who was an entirely illiterate man. This collection, entitled *Joe Miller's Jests*, or the *Wit's Vade Mecum*, had a great vogue, went through numberless editions and retained its popularity down to the early days of the last century. *Christmas Carol. Chuzzlewit*, 22.

**MILLER AND HIS MEN.** This was a two-act drama which maintained the greatest popularity for many years. It first appeared

about 1822, and was still a stock piece in the 50's. Kelmar was the father of the heroine. *Reprinted, Christmas Tree.*

**MILLERS.** One of Mrs. Matthew Pocket's nursemaids. *Expectations*, 22, 23.

**MILLS, JULIA.** The bosom friend of Dora Spenlow and a sentimental girl of twenty, who did much to keep the young lovers together. She revelled in despair, "but was still able to take a calm interest in the unblighted hopes and loves of youth." Julia went, at last, to India and returned thence the peevish wife of a growling old Scotch Crœsus (*Copperfield*, 33, 37–9, 42, 48, 64). A Miss Julia Mills is mentioned as writing comments on the pages of novels in the library of *Our English Watering Place. Reprinted Pieces.*

**MILVEY, REV. FRANK.** A curate, "expensively educated and wretchedly paid," to whom the Boffins referred when they wanted to adopt a child. He and his cheery little wife, Margaretta, told them of Betty Higden, and long afterwards, when that stout old heart had stopped, Milvey went to the country to bury her. Later he married Eugene Wrayburn and Lizzie Hexam. *Mutual Friend*, I, 9, 16; II, 10; III, 9; IV, 11.

**MIM.** The ferocious showman from whom Dr. Marigold bought little Sophy for half a dozen pair of braces.

**MINCIN.** The very friendly young gentleman. *Sketches of Gentlemen.*

**MINCING LANE.** This very prosaic centre of the tea trade is forever hallowed by the visits of Bella Wilfer to R. W., who occupied a stool in the office of Chickesey, Veneering and Stobbles. This was in all probability the little office next to Dunster Court, the fourth house from the corner of Fenchurch Street. *Mutual Friend*, II, 8; III, 16.

**MINDERS.** These were the children given to old Betty Higden to mind while their parents were working. The minding school was a humble forerunner of the modern creche. *Mutual Friend*, I, 16.

**MINNS, AUGUSTUS.** The hero of Dickens's first published tale. He was a retiring old bachelor who was persuaded by his boisterous cousin, Octavius Budden, to visit him at Stamford Hill. His misadventures on the way thither and his agony at finding himself the guest of the day are feelingly described in *Boz, Tales, Minns.*

**MISSIS, OUR.** The head of the Mugby Junction Refreshment Room. She paid a visit to similar establishments in France and came back with horrific tales of how they actually tried to cater for the passengers in those unenlightened parts.

**MISTY, MESSRS. X AND XX.** Members of the Mudfog Association.

**MITH, SERJEANT.** The London police officer who told the Butcher's Story in *Reprinted, Detective Police.* This is an obvious disguise for Detective-Sergeant M. Smith, well known in the early 50's.

**MITHERS, LADY.** A client of the volatile Miss Mowcher. *Copperfield*, 22.

**MITRE INN.** This inn, associated with the childhood of Charley, was the Mitre and Clarence Hotel at Chatham (*Holly Tree*). The landlord of the Mitre was a friend of Dickens's father, and as a child young Charles and his sister used to sing at evening parties held there. F. G. Kitton's *Dickens's Country*.

**MITTON, MARY ANNE.** Suggested original of Amy Dorrit (*q.v.*). Her father, Thomas Mitton, was the original of Wemmick. (*q.v.*)

**MITTS, MRS.** An inmate of Titbull's Almshouses, who caused a sensation by marrying a Greenwich pensioner with one arm. *Uncommercial*, 27.

**MIVINS.** One of the inmates of the room where Mr. Pickwick spent his first night in the Fleet Prison. *Pickwick*, 41, 42, 44.

**MIZZLER, MARQUIS OF.** One of Mr. Chuckster's aristocratic acquaintances. *Curiosity Shop*, 40.

**MOBBS.** A pupil at Dotheboys Hall, who could not eat fat. *Nickleby*, 8.

**MODDLE, AUGUSTUS.** Also known as the Youngest Gentleman in Company, he was a boarder at Todgers's when he fell in love with Mercy Pecksniff. His hopeless affection for her is rather pathetic, and he passed his days weeping for "Her Who is Another's." Taking advantage of his broken spirit, Charity inveigled him into an engagement, but on the eve of the wedding he departed for America. "I will not reproach, for I have wronged you. May the Furniture make some amends." *Chuzzlewit*, 9-11, 32, 37, 46, 54.

**MODEL, THE.** The model who sat for many popular pictures, who was encountered on a river steamboat. *Reprinted, Ghost of Art.*

**MOGLEY.** One of Mrs. Nickleby's early suitors. *Nickleby*, 41.

**MOLLY.** A strange looking woman of forty whom Jaggers employed as his housekeeper, having obtained her acquittal on a murder charge. She turned out to be Magwitch's wife and the mother of Estella. *Expectations*, 24, 26, 48.

**MONFLATHERS, MISS.** Headmistress of a school taken to view Mrs. Jarley's Waxworks, that eminent lady having for the occasion altered the face of Grimaldi the clown to represent Mr. Lindley Murray, the grammarian. Miss Monflathers was very superior and took the opportunity of reproaching Little Nell publicly for being such a wicked child as to be a "waxworks girl." *Curiosity Shop*, 29, 31, 32.

**MONKS.** This was the name assumed by Edward Leeford, Oliver Twist's half-brother. Having connived with his mother to destroy his father's will, leaving most of the property to Oliver, Leeford robbed and deserted her, making his way to London with no object but to harm Oliver Twist. He bribed Mrs. Corney and Bumble to destroy certain evidence of the boy's identity, and persuaded Fagin to make Oliver a thief and outcast. The plot was discovered through Nancy, however, and Monks, as he called himself, was brought to book by Mr. Brownlow and obliged to disgorge some of the property. Monks finally went to America, where he ended his days in gaol. *Twist*, 26, 33, 34, 37-40, 46, 49, 51, 53.

**MONMOUTH STREET.** This "only true and real emporium of second-hand wearing apparel" ran out of St. Andrew Street, parallel to New Compton Street, and was absorbed into Shaftesbury Avenue when the latter was made in 1885. *Boz, Scenes*, 6.

**MONTAGUE.** 1. The name assumed by Montague Tigg in the days of his prosperity. See Tigg, Montague.

2. Miss Julia, soloist at the concert where Miss Martin made her debut. *Boz, Characters*, 8.

**MONTAGUE PLACE.** In this street, leading from Russell Square past the new north front of the British Museum, lived Mr. Perker. *Pickwick*, 47.

**MONTAGUE SQUARE.** This square is approached from Gloucester Place through Upper George Street. "Mr. Jorkins lived by himself in a house near Montague Square." *Copperfield*, 35.

**MONTARGIS, DOG OF.** In the fourteenth century a certain Aubrey de Montdidier was murdered in the forest of Bondy, near Montargis, by Robert Macaire. Aubrey's dog hunted down the murderer; the Emperor, Charles V, ordered Macaire to fight the beast, who pinned him to the earth until he made a full confession. This story furnished the plot of several very popular melodramas in the 30's and 40's. *Reprinted, Our School. Christmas Tree.*

**MONUMENT.** Our chief association with this landmark is that of Todgers's, which was "in a kind of paved yard" near by, which has never been identified (*Chuzzlewit*, 8-10, 13, 32, 37, 54). Messrs. Peddle and Pool, the Dorrit solicitors, had their offices in Monument Yard (*Dorrit*, I, 36). Old John Willett's idea of cheap amusement in London was to "go to the top of the Monument and sit there" (*Barnaby*, 13), though the custodian told Tom Pinch it was worth twice the entrance money to stay at the bottom (*Chuzzlewit*, 37). The Poor Relation and Little Frank used to go and look at the outside of the Monument. *Reprinted, Poor Relations Story.*

**MONUMENT OF FRENCH FOLLY.** This paper appeared in the March 8 issue of *Household Words*, 1851, and was collected in *Reprinted Pieces*, 1858. It is an indictment of the British methods of slaughtering cattle, comparing them with those of the French abattoirs.

**MOON.** Our Bore's physician, who said "kidneys." *Reprinted, Our Bore.*

**MOONEY.** The intelligent beadle summoned when the tragedies occurred at Krook's shop. *Bleak House*, 11, 33.

**MOPES.** The hermit on *Tom Tiddler's Ground*, a loathsome creature who delighted in the notoriety he gained by a life of filth and wretchedness. The character was founded on James Lucas, the so-called Hertfordshire Hermit, a well-educated man who became unbalanced on the death of his mother. He lived in the condition described in *Tom Tiddler*. Lucas died in 1874, and his house was destroyed in 1893.

**MORDLIN, BROTHER.** The musical member of the Brick Lane Ebenezer Temperance Association, who adapted Dibdin's "Jolly Young Waterman" to the tune of the "Old Hundredth." *Pickwick*, 33.

**"MORE!"** "Please, Sir, I want more!" The tremendous words with which Oliver Twist staggered the workhouse and the whole Board of Guardians. *Twist*, 2.

**MORFIN, MR.** Assistant manager in the office of Dombey and Son, "a cheerful-looking, hazel-eyed bachelor," who was an enthusiastic amateur musician. He knew enough of the business to appreciate the relative worth of the Carker Brothers, and was John's staunch friend. Eventually he married Harriet Carker. *Dombey*, 13, 33, 53, 58, 62.

**MORGAN, BECKY.** An old woman who had been buried by David, the gravedigger. *Curiosity Shop*, 54.

**MORGAN AP KERRIG.** One of the Woodcourt ancestors, whose deeds were related in the Mewlinnwillinwodd of Crumlinwallinwer. *Bleak House*, 17, 30.

**"MORRIS."** This was an old slang expression, meaning to move on, to go away, to disappear. *Twist*, 8. *Hard Times*, III, 8.

**MORTAIR.** A member of the Mudfog Association.

**MORTIMER.** 1. A friend of the Cool Couple. *Sketches of Couples.*

2. For financial reasons Mr. Micawber assumed the name of Mortimer while living at Camden Town. *Copperfield*, 34.

**MOSCHELES, IGNAZ.** (1794–1870.) A famous Bohemian composer and pianist who taught and gave concerts in London between 1820 and 1846, though he occasionally appeared after then, his last performance being in 1865. *Boz, Tales, Sentiment.*

**MOSES AND SON.** An outfitting firm of 157, Minories, whose advertisements, in rhyme and otherwise, were known far and wide in the 40's, 50's and 60's. *Reprinted, Bill Sticking.*

**MOTHER OF THE MODERN GRACCHI.** The imposing name with which Mrs. Hominy signed her letters from Europe. *Chuzzlewit*, 22.

**MOULD, MR. AND MRS.** The undertaker, in the neighbourhood of Cheapside, who carried out the funeral of Anthony Chuzzlewit and was a patron of Mrs. Gamp. He owned a good business and only undertook "a walking one of two, with the plain wood and a tin plate" on condition that the beadle followed in his cocked hat. *Chuzzlewit*, 19, 25, 29, 38.

**MOUNT PLEASANT.** On the City side of the Parcels Post Office (built in 1900 on the site of Coldbath Fields Prison) is Mount Pleasant, where lived Grandfather Smallweed and his promising grandchildren. *Bleak House*, 21.

**MOURNING COACH-HORSE INN.** The house of call for undertakers, somewhere in the City, where Mr. Nadgett made inquiries of Tacker concerning Anthony Chuzzelwit's funeral. *Chuzzlewit*, 38.

**"MOVING ON."** The one duty which Society imposed upon Jo, the crossing sweeper, was that he should "Move On," and most of his short and wretched life was spent in "Moving On" at the orders of the police. *Bleak House*, 19.

**MOWCHER, MISS.** A dwarf manicurist, masseuse, etc., who attended Steerforth and kept him amused by chattering about her fashionable clients. She was heartbroken at hearing of his elopement with Little Em'ly, and long afterwards was instrumental in effecting the arrest of Littimer. "Ain't I volatile?" was her constant expression. The original of the character probably was a Mrs. Seymour Hill. *Copperfield*, 22, 32, 61.

**M.R.F.** Initials, representing My Respected Father, by which Eugene Wrayburn referred to his parent. *Mutual Friend*, I, 12; IV, 6, 16.

**MR. F.'S AUNT.** Flora Finching's legacy. *See* Aunt, Mr. F.'s.

**MRS. LIRRIPER'S LODGINGS AND LEGACY.** These very charming stories appeared in the Christmas numbers of *All the Year Round*, 1863 and 1864. They attained great popularity at the time and have remained favourites among Dickens's minor writings. In the *Lodgings* Mrs. Lirriper relates some of her experiences as a London lodging-house keeper, and tells the tale of Mrs. Edson and the child she left to be adopted by Mrs. Lirriper and Major Jackman. The Legacy takes up the story some years later, and describes the death of Mrs. Edson's runaway husband.

**"MUCH LINEN, LACE, ETC."** From *Don Juan*, Canto I, Stanza 143. *Boz, Tales, Boarding House.*

**MUDBERRY, MRS.** A friend of Mrs. Sanders "which kept a mangle." *Pickwick*, 34.

**MUDDLEBRANES, MR.** A member of the Zoology Section of the Mudfog Association.

**MUDFOG.** This was the scene of Nicholas Tulumble's public life and of the first meeting of the Mudfog Association. It is the first disguise used by Dickens for the town of Chatham.

**MUDFOG PAPERS.** The Full Report of the First Meeting of the Mudfog Association for the Advancement of Everything was published in *Bentley's Miscellany* for October, 1837 ; that of the Second meeting in the September number of 1838. These papers were written as a satire on the annual conferences of the British Association for the Advancement of Science, which had been founded in 1831 by Sir David Brewster and others.

**MUDGE, JONAS.** Secretary of the Brick Lane Ebenezer Temperance Association, and " an enthusiastic and disinterested vessel who sold tea to the members." *Pickwick*, 33.

**MUFF, PROFESSOR.** A member of the Mudfog Association and advocate of the infinitesimal doses system.

**MUGBY JUNCTION.** This was the title of the extra Christmas number of *All the Year Round* for 1866. For this number Dickens contributed the story of "Barbox Brothers" and the sketch "The Boy at Mugby." The latter is a remarkable satire on the English system of station refreshment rooms. Mugby Junction is probably a thin disguise for Rugby Junction.

**MUGGLETON.** Many and heated have been the discussions regarding the identity of this place. Faversham, Town Malling and Tenterden have all been suggested, and a good claim was put forward for Gravesend, but the general opinion of modern Dickensians is that Maidstone was the town Dickens had in his mind. *Pickwick*, 7.

**MUGGS, SIR ALFRED.** A gentleman who recommended Miss Crumpton's academy. *Boz, Tales, Sentiment.*

**MULL, PROFESSOR.** A member of the Mudfog Association.

**MULLINS, JACK.** A customer at the Six Jolly Fellowship Porters. *Mutual Friend*, I, 6.

**MULLION, JOHN.** One of the crew of the *Golden Mary*.

**MULLIT, PROFESSOR.** Professor of education and author of some powerful pamphlets under the name of " Suturb," or Brutus reversed. *Chuzzlewit*, 16.

**MUNTLE.** The real name of Mr. Mantalini. (*q.v.*)

**MURDERER, CAPTAIN.** A character in one of the nurse's stories. *Uncommercial*, 15.

**MURDSTONE, EDWARD.** Mrs. Clara Copperfield's second husband and a handsome man who easily obtained the mastery over his timid wife. With the assistance of his sister he introduced a " firm " regime into the household and set himself to master young David. After a struggle with the boy he sent him to Salem House School, and later,

having killed his wife by the rigour of his discipline, he consigned the lad to the horrors of the warehouse. Murdstone made a formal offer to take David from Miss Trotwood, when he had made his way thither. He later married again and blighted another life by his harshness. *Copperfield*, 2–4, 8–10, 14, 17, 33, 59.

Jane Murdstone was a fitting sister for such a brother. She seconded him in his plan of making Clara Copperfield " firm," and had much to do in worrying the poor girl to death. David came across her again when she was chaperoning Dora Spenlow. 4, 8–10, 12, 14, 17, 26, 33, 38, 59.

**MURDSTONE AND GRINBY.** The firm of wine merchants to whose warehouse David Copperfield was consigned as a lad. The original was Warren's Blacking Manufactory, at 30 Hungerford Stairs, where Dickens himself worked as a boy. The facts as related by Forster are that James Lamert, son of Dr. Lamert, his aunt's second husband, had entered a kind of partnership with a Jonathan Warren, who claimed to have invented the original Blacking recipe which had made the fame of Warren's, 30 Strand. They opened at 30, Hungerford Stairs, and later removed to the corner of Bedford Street and Chandos Street, Strand. The Dickens family were then in one of their financial straits, and James offered to find work for Charles, then a child of ten. The offer was accepted and he entered the warehouse to work under conditions that to any child, let alone a boy of his temperament, would have been hellish. After two years of this life his father quarrelled with Lamert and young Charles was taken away. *Copperfield*, 11, 12.

**MURGATROYD.** The undertaker who frequented the company at the Green Dragon, Westminster. *Robert Bolton*.

**MUSIC HALL.** This is a development of the old Harmonic Meeting. (*q.v.*)

**MUTANHED, LORD.** A foppish, foolish young nobleman who visited Bath while Mr. Pickwick was there. *Pickwick*, 35, 36.

**MUTTON HILL.** More generally known as Mutton Lane, this was the old name of that portion of Vine Street which ran from Hatton Garden to Clerkenwell Green. The back entrance to Mr. Fang's police court, whither Oliver Twist was taken, was " beneath a low archway out of Mutton Hill." *Twist*, 11.

**MUTUEL, MONSIEUR.** A friend of Madame Bouclet. *Somebody's Luggage*.

**MUZZLE.** Mr. Nupkins's footman, " with a long body and short legs," who was engaged to marry the cook, and deeply resented Job Trotter's aspiration to that honour. *Pickwick*, 24, 25, 39.

**" MY BOAT IS ON THE SHORE."** This is a song by Byron, set to music by Bishop :
My boat is on the shore and my bark is on the sea.
But before I go, Tom Moore, here's a double health to thee.
*Copperfield*, 54 ; *Curiosity Shop*, 8 ; *Going into Society*.

**"MY FEELINGS I SMOTHER."** The conclusion of the second verse of " We met—'twas in a crowd," words and music by T. H. Bayley, is :—

The world may think me gay, for my feelings I smother.
Oh, thou hast been the cause of this anguish, my mother !
*Curiosity Shop*, 36.

# N

**NADGETT.** The inquiry agent employed by the Anglo-Bengalee Assurance Company. Detailed by Montague Tigg to investigate the antecedents of Jonas Chuzzlewit, he pieced together the evidence of Jonas's attempt to poison his father, and communicated his information to Tigg. When the latter accompanied Jonas to Salisbury, Nadgett was watching Jonas's house, and saw him return alone and set out again, dressed as a countryman to commit the murder. Finally, fishing from the Thames the bundle of bloodstained clothes Jonas had cast into the river, Nadgett was able to prove his guilt. *Chuzzlewit*, 27–9, 38, 40, 41, 47, 48, 50, 51.

**NAMBY.** The sheriff's officer, of Bell Alley, Coleman Street, who arrested Mr. Pickwick. *Pickwick*, 40.

**NAMELESSTON.** The seaside resort where the Uncommercial Traveller was served with the worst dinner in his experience. *Uncommercial*, 32.

**NAN.** Typical of the harpies who fatten on the merchant seamen. The name is taken from Dibdin's song of " Lovely Nan "—" Jack's delight is his lovely Nan." *Uncommercial*, 5.

**NANCY.** A girl in Fagin's gang of pickpockets who befriended Oliver Twist. At great personal risk she communicated with Rose Maylie and told her about the lad, being largely responsible for his eventual identification. She had another interview with Rose, accompanied by Brownlow, on the steps of London Bridge, when they tried to persuade her to leave Sikes and hand over Fagin to justice. She refused to do this, but the conversation had been overheard by Fagin's spy, Claypole, and as a result the Jew told Sikes that the girl was untrue. In a fit of rage Sikes murdered her. *Twist*, 9, 13, 15, 16, 18–20, 26, 39, 40, 44–7.

**NANDY, JOHN EDWARD.** Mrs. Plornish's father, " a poor little reedy piping old gentleman . . . who had seldom been able to make his way and had retired of his own accord to the Workhouse." He was a great admirer of Mr. Dorrit when in the Marshalsea, and was much patronised by that individual. *Dorrit*, I, 31 ; II, 4, 13, 26, 27.

**NAPLES.** James Steerforth deserted Little Em'ly at Naples, and thither Daniel Peggotty hastened in a fruitless endeavour to find her. *Copperfield*, 46, 50.

**NATHAN.** " A red-headed, red-whiskered Jew," who acted as dresser in a private theatre. *Boz, Scenes*, 13.

**NATIVE, THE.** Major Bagstock's Indian servant, supposed to be a prince in his own country, but now the butt of all the major's ill-humoured brutality. *Dombey*, 7, 10, 20, 24, 26, 29, 58, 59.

**NECKETT.** The bailiff's man employed by Coavins to arrest Skimpole. On his death he left three orphan children, Charlotte, Emma and Tom, who were all cared for and set up in life by Mr. Jarndyce, the eldest, called Charley, becoming Esther Summerson's maid. *See* Charley. *Bleak House*, 6, 15, 23, 67.

**NED.** A chimney sweep who kept a small boy on purpose for breaking into houses. *Twist*, 19.

**NEDDY.** One of the Fleet turnkeys, a friend of Mr. Tom Roker. *Pickwick*, 42–4.

**NEESHAWTS, DR.** A member of the Mudfog Association.

**NELL, LITTLE.** The principal character in *Curiosity Shop*, whose full name was Nellie Trent. She was the granddaughter of the old man who kept the shop, and when they fell into Quilp's power she contrived to fly with him into the country. There they wandered on, encountering strange characters on the roads, such as Codlin and Short, Mrs. Jarley and others, eventually coming to rest at a quiet village (Tong, Shropshire), where they obtained employment. The anxiety of looking after the old man and keeping him from gambling, the hardships they encountered during their wanderings, and the unnatural excitement of their life proved, however, too much for the child's strength. She gradually declined and died, being buried in the village churchyard just before their friends from London had traced their whereabouts. The death of Little Nell was, at one time, considered a masterpiece of Dickens's pathos ; she was one of his favourite creations, and in the description of her death bed he lived over again the grief he had experienced on the death of her prototype, Mary Hogarth. Two among the many routes suggested for Nellie's journey to Tong are given in Hopkins and Read's *Dickens Atlas* (Spurr and Swift) based on researches by Mr. W. T. Tyrrell. The first and most probable is : London, Watford, Rickmansworth, Wendover, Aylesbury, Buckingham, Brackley, Banbury, Warwick, Coventry, Birmingham, Wolverhampton, Tong. The other is : London, Brentford, Uxbridge, High Wycombe, Deddington, Banbury, Southam, Coventry and thence as above. The journey from Tong to Shrewsbury and back is a debated point. *Curiosity Shop*, 1–3, 5–7, 9–13, 15–19, 21, 24–32, 40, 42–6, 52–5, 71, 72.

**NEMO.** The name adopted by Captain Hawdon when working as a law-writer. *See* Hawdon.

**NETTINGALL, MISSES.** Principals of the girls' school at Canterbury, where David's early love, Miss Shepherd, was a pupil. *Copperfield,* 18.

**NEUCHATEL.** In this Swiss town were the offices of Defresnier and Co. and of Maitre Voigt, the clever lawyer. *No Thoroughfare.*

**NEW CHURCH.** Although consecrated in 1723 St. Mary-le-Strand was known as the New Church until about 1840. *Boz, Characters,* 1.

**NEWCOME, CLEMENCY.** The Jeddlers' maid, a lively, cheerful, plump woman of about thirty, whose philosophy of life was founded on the inscriptions on her thimble and nutmeg grater—"Forget and Forgive," "Do as you would be done by." Dismissed after Marion's disappearance, Clemency married Benjamin Britain, and they set up in the Nutmeg Grater Inn, where she still had scope for her kindly nature and generous ways of life. *Battle of Life.*

**NEWGATE MARKET.** This was situated in the quadrangle between Paternoster Row, Ivy Lane, Newgate Street and Warwick Lane, now called Paternoster Square. Until the opening of the Central Meat Market, Smithfield, in 1855, Newgate Market was the principal wholesale and retail meat market. It was finally closed in 1861. Grandpa toddled round there to buy the Christmas turkey (*Boz, Characters,* 2). Peepy Jellyby wandered thither and was brought back by a policeman. *Bleak House,* 5.

**NEWGATE PRISON.** The old prison, destroyed in 1780, was one of the best in England, having been reconstructed only a couple of years before the attack by the Gordon Rioters. The burning of this old gaol is well described in *Barnaby,* 58, 61, 63, 64, 66, 67. The prison was rebuilt in 1782, and from the following year until 1868 public executions took place outside it. The gaol was reconstructed in 1857, ceased to be a place of detention in 1880, and was demolished in 1903–4, the Central Criminal Court being built on its site. A visit to Newgate is graphically described in *Boz, Scenes,* 25. Oliver's visit to Fagin in the condemned cell is narrated in *Twist,* 52. The exterior of the prison is described in *Nickleby,* 4; the interior in *Expectations,* 32.

**NEWGATE STREET.** It was in this street that Sam Weller recounted the sad story of the inventor of a "patent never-leaving-off sassage steam ingine" (*Pickwick* 31). Estella and Pip drove along it on their way to Richmond. *Expectations,* 33.

**NEWINGTON BUTTS.** This stretch of the main road south of the Elephant and Castle was, as late as the 40's, a pleasant and convenient residential neighbourhood. Thither Mr. Gobler and Mrs. Bloss retired after marriage. *Boz, Tales, Boarding House.*

**NEW INN.** A Chancery Inn, opening out of Wych Street, Strand. It was demolished in the course of making Aldwych at the beginning of the present century. *Pickwick,* 20. *Uncommercial,* 14.

**NEWMAN STREET.** For long this was a centre of artists, musicians and dancing masters (*Boz, Characters,* 9). Mr. Turveydrop's Academy was probably at No. 26, nearly opposite East Castle Street. *Bleak House,* 14, 23, 30.

**NEW OXFORD STREET.** This was opened for traffic in 1847, making a direct line between Holborn and Oxford Street. *See* Holborn. It traversed the slum known as the Rookery of St. Giles, and, according to *Reprinted, Inspector Field,* made houseless a number of the wretched inhabitants of that wretched region.

**NEW POLICE.** The Metropolitan Police Force was only organised in 1829, and was naturally, for some years afterwards, known as the New Police Force. *Boz, Characters,* 1.

**NEWPORT MARKET.** This was situated near the junction of Castle Street (now approximately Charing Cross Road) and Newport Street. It was merely a narrow avenue of butcher's shops, and disappeared in the making of Charing Cross Road and Shaftesbury Avenue, 1885–87. *Reprinted, Detective Police.*

**NEW RIVER HEAD.** This is just off Rosebery Avenue, and is a large reservoir filled by the water of the New River. Uriah Heep had lodgings thereby. *Copperfield,* 25.

**NEW ROAD, THE,** was the name given, until 1857, to the thoroughfare from the Angel, Islington, to Lisson Grove, now known in its different sections as Pentonville Road, Euston Road, and Marylebone Road. It was made about 1750, and for many years ran through fields. *Boz, Characters,* 5. *Nickleby,* 21.

**NEW THERMOPYLAE.** The next " city " to Eden and the home of Mrs. Hominy's married daughter. *Chuzzlewit,* 22, 23.

**NEW YORK.** Martin Chuzzlewit and Mark Tapley landed there from England and put up at the Pawkins boarding house. *Chuzzlewit,* 16.

**NEW YORK ROWDY JOURNAL.** The spicy and vigorous newspaper conducted by Colonel Diver with the able assistance of Jefferson Brick. *Chuzzlewit,* 16.

**NICHOLAS.** The head waiter at Bellamy's coffee house, adjoining the Houses of Parliament. *Boz, Scenes,* 18.

**NICHOLAS NICKLEBY.** Dickens began this novel February 6, 1838, and finished it while staying at the Albion Hotel, Broadstairs, about September 20, 1839. It was published in twenty monthly parts, with illustrations by Phiz, the first number appearing in April, 1838. In his preface to the volume form of the novel, 1839, Dickens explained that one of his principal objects was to expose the Yorkshire schools and their scandalous ill-treatment and neglect of the children committed to their care. To obtain material for this he had taken H. K. Browne with him to Yorkshire early in 1838, and they had visited several schools to obtain the impressions embodied in the story.

*Principal Characters.* Nicholas Nickleby, his mother and sister Kate; Ralph, his uncle, a heartless usurer; Newman Noggs, Ralph's clerk; Squeers, a brutal Yorkshire schoolmaster; Crummles, a touring actor; Mantalini, an amusing rogue who lived on his wife, a fashionable costumier; Sir Mulberry Hawk and Lord Verisopht, a dissolute couple who pester Kate with their attentions; the Cheeryble brothers, benevolent City merchants; Madeleine Bray, a beautiful girl whom Nicholas rescues from a forced marriage with the miser, Arthur Gride; Smike, a half-witted lad.

On the death of her husband Mrs. Nickleby brings her children to London and casts herself on the mercy of her brother-in-law, Ralph. Ralph sends Nicholas to Yorkshire as assistant to Squeers, the ignorant bully of Dotheboys Hall, and obtains employment for Kate with Madame Mantalini, a West-End dressmaker. Disgusted with Squeers's brutality, Nicholas leaves with Smike, after giving the schoolmaster a sound beating. They meet with Crummles's touring company and act with them at Portsmouth, but Nicholas is recalled by Newman Noggs in time to protect his sister Kate from the molestation of Sir Mulberry Hawk, whom he thrashes. Nicholas is looking for work when he meets the Cheerybles, who take him into their employ, and enable him to make a home for his mother and Kate. Nicholas then meets Madeleine Bray, whose father is a prisoner for debt, Ralph Nickleby and Gride being the detaining creditors. The latter, who knows that Madeleine is entitled to a large sum of money, offers to set Bray free in exchange for the hand of his daughter, but Nicholas, who has fallen in love with the girl, frustrates this scheme; the plots of Ralph and Gride are brought to light, and Ralph commits suicide to avoid exposure and ruin. Nicholas marries Madeleine, while Kate becomes the bride of Frank Cheeryble, nephew of the kindly twins.

**NICKITS.** The former owner of Bounderby's country estate, whose improvidence and ill-fortune had obliged him to fly the country. *Hard Times,* II, 7.

**NICKLEBY.** Mrs. Nickleby, mother of Nicholas and Kate, was " a well meaning woman enough, but weak, withal," whose remarkable irrelevance, extraordinary reminiscences and amusing vanity, together with her " conquest " of the lunatic Gentleman in Small Clothes, form one of the most delightful features of the book. The character of Mrs. Nickleby was largely founded upon that of Dickens's mother. *Nickleby,* 1, 3, 5, 10, 11, 17–21, 26–8, 31–3, 35, 37, 38, 40, 41, 43, 45, 49, 55, 61, 63, 65.

Nicholas is the hero of the novel, under which heading his adventures are described. The character was founded on Dickens's brother-in-law, Henry Burnett, a music teacher at Manchester. 1, 3–9, 12, 13, 15, 16, 20, 22, 23–5, 29, 30, 32, 33, 35–8, 40, 42, 43, 45, 46, 48, 49, 51–5, 58, 61, 63–5.

Kate, Nicholas's sister, was a beautiful girl and one of the most natural of the Mary Hogarth heroines. She was apprenticed to Madame Mantalini, but her good looks soon aroused the jealousy and animosity of Miss Knag, the forewoman. Ralph made use of her beauty to ensnare Lord Verisopht yet deeper into his toils, but she attracted the notice of Sir Mulberry Hawk, who made her life miserable with his evil attentions. Rescued from this situation by her brother, she retired with her mother to the cottage at Bow, and in due course married Frank Cheeryble, the nephew of the family's benefactors. 1, 3, 5, 8, 10, 17–21, 26–8, 31–3, 35, 37, 38, 40, 41, 43, 45, 49, 55, 58, 61, 63–5.

Ralph Nickleby, the uncle of Kate and Nicholas, was a hard moneylender, who lived in Golden Square. He had many people in his clutches, among them the Mantalinis, with whom he placed Kate, and Squeers, upon whom he planted Nicholas. Between him and the lad, however, an implacable animosity arose, and turn where he would, the old man found his evil schemes thwarted by the younger, assisted by his own clerk, Newman Noggs. Ralph's final defeat by Nicholas was over an attempt to cozen Madeleine Bray into a marriage with the usurer, Arthur Gride. This was thwarted, and shortly afterwards Ralph was summoned to the Cheerybles, where they revealed to him the fact that his only son, whose very existence had been hitherto unknown, had been Nicholas's friend, Smike, who was now dead. Overwhelmed by the accumulation of disasters, Ralph shut himself up in his own house and hanged himself. 1–5, 8, 10, 19, 20, 26, 28, 31, 33, 34, 38, 44, 45, 47, 51–4, 56, 59, 60, 62.

**NICOLL.** Messrs. Nicoll, clothiers and outfitters of 114–120 Regent Street, advertised very widely during the 40's and 50's. *Reprinted, Bill Sticking.*

**NIGHT INSPECTOR, THE.** The police inspector in charge of the Harmon case. *See* Inspector.

**NINER, MISS MARGARET.** Niece of Julius Slinkton, and sister of the girl, beloved of Meltham, whom he had already poisoned. Margaret's life was saved by Meltham and Sampson, and she married Sampson's nephew. *Hunted Down.*

**NIPPER, SUSAN.** The maid and devoted friend of Florence Dombey. With a sharp tongue and a ready resentment of the slights put upon her young mistress, Susan championed her cause even into the presence of Mr. Dombey himself, thereby occasioning her own dismissal. She last appeared as the sensible and affectionate wife of Toots. *Dombey*, 3, 5, 6, 9, 12, 14–16, 18, 19, 22, 23, 28, 31, 32, 43, 44, 56, 57, 60–2.

**NISBETT, MRS. LOUISA.** A well-known comedienne at Drury Lane and The Queen's Theatre. She died in 1858. *Sketches of Gentlemen (Theatrical).*

**NIXON.** 1. Patrons of the Indigent Orphans Institution. *Boz, Scenes,* 19.

2. Guests of the Gattletons. *Boz, Tales, Porter.*

3. The domestic young gentleman. *Sketches of Gentlemen.*

4. The Nixon to whom Sam Weller likened his father (*Pickwick,* 43) was the so-called Cheshire prophet, whose works were popular in the early nineteenth century.

**NOAKES.** 1. Percy, a law student and the promoter of the Steam Excursion. He was " smart, spoffish and eight-and-twenty," and very popular with the ladies. *Boz, Tales, Excursion.*

2. Mrs., landlady of the St. James's Arms. *Strange Gentleman.*

3. A member of the Mudfog Association.

**NOBLE SAVAGE, THE.** This paper, a counterblast to the various attempts to hold the savage up as a model of all the simple virtues, first appeared in *Household Words,* June 11, 1853, and was reissued in *Reprinted Pieces,* 1858.

**NOBODY'S STORY.** This sketch appeared in the Christmas number of *Household Words,* 1853, and was included in *Reprinted Pieces,* 1858. The narrator was " one of an immense family, all of whose sons and daughters gained their daily bread by daily work."

**NOCKEMORF.** Bob Sawyer's predecessor in the surgeon's practice at Bristol. *Pickwick,* 38.

**NODDY.** A guest at Bob Sawyer's party in Lant Street, " a scorbutic youth, in a long stock." *Pickwick,* 32.

**NOGGS, NEWMAN.** Ralph Nickleby's down-at-heel clerk who had once kept his hounds in the north of England, but, having fallen into the hands of moneylenders, was reduced to drudgery. Aware of his employer's evil designs, Noggs warned Nicholas to take care of his sister Kate and, at last, by careful spying on Ralph, was able to give Nicholas and the Cheerybles sufficient information to bring about the usurer's final exposure. The original of Newman Noggs was a certain Newman Knott, a broken-down farmer from the neighbourhood of Barnard Castle, whom Dickens knew as a hanger-on and occasional clerk to Ellis and Blackmore, the solicitors of Gray's Inn. *Nickleby,* 2–5, 7, 11, 14–16, 22, 26, 28, 29, 31–4, 40, 44, 47, 51, 52, 56, 57, 59, 63, 65.

**NOGO, PROFESSOR.** One of the medical members of the Mudfog Association.

**NOLAND, SIR THOMAS.** A friend of Mr. Flamwell. *Boz, Tales, Sparkins.*

**" NO MALICE TO DREAD."** Mr. Wegg was misquoting verse 3 of Hamilton's " My Ain Fireside " :—

Nae falsehood to dread, nae malice to fear,
But truth to delight me, and friendship to cheer ;
O' a' roads to happiness ever were tried,
There's nane half sae sure as ane's ain fireside.
My ain fireside, my ain fireside,
O sweet is the blink o' my ain fireside.
*Mutual Friend,* III, 6.

**NORAH.** Harry Walmer's little sweetheart, with whom he ran away to make a match at Gretna Green. *Holly Tree.*

**NORFOLK ISLAND.** This Pacific Island was, for many years, a penal settlement. *Reprinted, Begging Letter Writer.*

**NORFOLK STREET, STRAND.** This street has been rebuilt from end to end since Mrs. Lirriper and Miss Wozenham kept their respective boarding houses in it.

**NORMANDY.** The rogue with whom Chops the Dwarf went into Society. He had acted as a bonnet, had a genteel appearance and ended by squandering Chops's money and bolting with the plate. *Going into Society.*

**NORRIS FAMILY.** Friends of Mr. Bevan in New York, and toadies who looked with scorn upon Martin Chuzzlewit when they heard he had come over from Europe in the steerage. *Chuzzlewit,* 17, 33.

**NORTHUMBERLAND HOUSE.** This was the town mansion of the Dukes of Northumberland, and stood at the south-west corner of the Strand, on the site now occupied by the Grand Hotel and Northumberland Avenue. It was demolished in 1874 to make room for the Avenue. Over the entrance was a large lion, famed throughout London, which was removed to Syon House, Isleworth. *Boz, Scenes,* 4 ; *Tales, Sparkins.*

**NORTON, SQUIRE.** The villain of *The Village Coquettes,* who vainly tried to seduce Lucy Benson.

**NORWICH.** Little Miss Mowcher, in the course of her country rounds was visiting Norwich when she heard of Steerforth's elopement with Em'ly (*Copperfield,* 32). Bazzard, Mr. Grewgious's angular clerk came from the neighbourhood of that city (*Drood,* 9). The claims of Norwich to be the original of Eatanswill are very slight.

**NORWOOD.** Until comparatively recent years this was a delightful wooded district, a favourite residence of well-to-do City merchants, with pleasant villas of the type belonging to Gabriel Parsons (*Boz, Tales, Tottle*) and James Carker (*Dombey,* 33, 42). It was at Mr. Spenlow's house at Norwood that David first saw Dora, and from that moment loved her to distraction. *Copperfield,* 26, 33.

**NORWOOD FORTUNE TELLER.** " The Norwood Gipsy Fortune Teller, containing the art of telling fortunes by cards, signification of moles, etc.," was published about 1835. *Reprinted, Out of Season.*

**NORWOOD GYPSY, THE.** This old woman, whose picture was not only reproduced on the covers of dream books, but formed the sign of The Queen of Gypsies Inn on Gypsy Hill, was Margaret Finch, who died in 1760 at the reputed age of 109 years. *Uncommercial*, 5.

**"NOTE OF."** "When found make a note of," was a common saying of Captain Cuttle. *Dombey*, 19, 23, 32, 39, 56.

**NO THOROUGHFARE.** This story, which appeared in the Christmas number of *All the Year Round*, 1867, was written in collaboration with Wilkie Collins. The only parts written exclusively by Dickens were the Overture and Act III. Collins wrote Act I and assisted Dickens in writing Acts I and IV.

**"NOW'S THE DAY."** From " Scots wha hae." *Copperfield*, 54.

**NO ZOO, LORD.** A reputed ancestor of the Chuzzlewit family. *Chuzzlewit*, 1.

**NUBBLES, KIT.** Shop boy at the Old Curiosity Shop and the devoted slave of Little Nell. After his discharge and the disappearance of the old man and his daughter, Kit entered the service of Mr. Garland, his duty being to look after the pony Whisker. At the instigation of his inveterate enemy, Quilp, Kit was accused of theft by the Brasses, but thanks to the Marchioness his name was cleared, and eventually he married Barbara, the Garlands' maid. *Curiosity Shop*, 1, 3, 6, 9–11, 13, 14, 20–2, 38–41, 48, 51, 56–65, 68–73.

Mrs. Nubbles, Kit's mother, was a laundress with a leaning towards the ministrations of the Little Bethel. 10, 13, 20–2, 39–41, 47, 48, 61, 63.

**"NUMBER ONE,"** St. Paul's Churchyard, was the widely advertised address of Messrs. Dakin and Co., coffee merchants. *Reprinted, Bill Sticking*.

**NUMBER TWENTY,** Coffee Room Flight. The debtor in the Fleet, imprisoned for nine pounds, who, after seventeen years' confinement, ventured out into Fleet Market, but found himself happier under lock and key. *Pickwick*, 41.

**NUPKINS, GEORGE.** The Mayor of Ipswich and a consequential man, destitute of the slightest sense of humour. The Pickwickians were taken before him as disturbers of the peace, and would have been treated with ludicrously summary justice had not Mr. Pickwick been able to unmask the villainy of FitzMarshall, alias Jingle, and thus save the Nupkins family from disgrace. Mrs. Nupkins and her daughter, Henrietta, exhibit a striking example of how a great man is treated in his own home. *Pickwick*, 24, 25, 34.

**NUTMEG GRATER INN.** The roadside tavern kept by Benjamin Britain and Clemency Newcome. It received its name from the inscription on Clemency's nutmeg grater, which bore the inscription—" Do as you would be done by." *Battle of Life*.

## O

**OAKUM HEAD.** Leader of the refractory inmates of Wapping Workhouse. *Uncommercial*, 3.

**OBELISK, THE.** This was one of the landmarks of South London and stood in the centre of St. George's Circus. The strange unsightly clock tower which replaced it in 1907 is locally known as the Obelisk, although the original now stands in the grounds of Bethlehem Hospital, facing St. George's Cathedral. It was formerly in the rules of the King's Bench Prison (*Pickwick*, 43. *Nickleby*, 46). When running away to Dover, David Copperfield came across the long-legged young man with an empty donkey cart, who robbed him of box and money, standing near the Obelisk (*Copperfield*, 12). The anonymous pavement artist lived near the Obelisk, " more generally called the Obstacle." *Somebody's Luggage*.

**OBENREIZER, JULES.** A wine merchant's agent in London and a business acquaintance of Wilding and Co. Having misappropriated some of his employer's money, and foreseeing that Vendale would discover his crime, he accompanied the latter to Switzerland and attempted to murder him in an Alpine pass. He later discovered Vendale's identity with the missing Foundling orphan. After the exposure of his crime Obenreizer was killed on the Alps by a falling glacier. Marguerite, his beautiful niece, was the girl who saved Vendale from death, and later became his bride. *No Thoroughfare*.

**O'BLEARY, FREDERICK.** One of Mrs. Tibbs's boarders, a perfectly wild Irishman who hoped to better his fortunes by marrying Mrs. Bloss. *Boz, Tales, Boarding House*.

**O'BRIEN.** A sentimental passenger on the Gravesend packet. *Boz, Scenes*, 10.

**ODD GIRL, THE.** One of the maids taken to the *Haunted House*.

**O'DONOVAN.** A dweller in the St. Giles's Rookery. *Reprinted, Inspector Field*.

**OFFLEY'S.** This was a well-known tavern at 23 Henrietta Street, Covent Garden. *Boz, Characters*, 7.

**"OFF SHE GOES."** A popular country dance by George Macfarren (1788–1843), father of the well-known Sir G. A. Macfarren. *Boz, Tales, Excursion*.

**"OH! LADY FAIR,"** sung by Mr. Wopsle and the Hubbles, was a ballad for three voices by Moore, 1802. *Expectations*, 13.

**"OH! POWERS OF HEAVEN."** From *Don Juan*, Canto IV, Stanza 35. *Boz, Tales, Boarding House*.

**OLD BAILEY.** The name of the street running from Ludgate Hill to Newgate Street, but frequently applied to the Old Bailey Court, now the Central Criminal Court. The Court House in which Charles

Darnay was tried (*Two Cities*, II, 2) was destroyed a few months later in the Gordon Riots. It was rebuilt, and in 1809 was enlarged, but it was demolished with Newgate, which it adjoined, in 1904–5. The Court, with its procedure, is described in *Boz, Scenes*, 24 ; *Two Ghost Stories, Trial for Murder* ; *Curiosity Shop*, 63 (Kit Nubbles) ; *Expectations*, 48 (Magwitch) ; *Twist*, 52 (Fagin).

**OLD BLACK JACK INN.** *See* Magpie and Stump.

**OLD CLEM.** Several similar blacksmith's songs have been traced, but the original of the song has not been discovered ; probably Dickens wrote it himself. *Expectations*, 12.

**OLD CURIOSITY SHOP, THE.** This novel appeared in *Master Humphrey's Clock*, the first chapter being in Part IV, April 25, 1840, and the book concluding in the following January. It was a great success and attained wide popularity, Little Nell's death being, at the time, considered a masterpiece of pathos.

*Principal Characters.* Nellie Trent, her old Grandfather, and her brother Fred ; Quilp, the evil dwarf ; Sampson and Sarah Brass, shady attorneys ; Dick Swiveller ; the Garlands and their servants, Kit Nubbles and Barbara ; the Marchioness, Brass's maid ; the Single Gentleman ; Codlin, Short, Mrs. Jarley, characters Nellie and her Grandfather meet in their wanderings.

Little Nell is introduced as living with her Grandfather in the Old Curiosity Shop. The old man gambles, in the hope of making a fortune for the child, but falls into the hands of Quilp. To escape his clutches, Nell and her Grandfather take flight, and wander many miles and for many days, finally making their way to Shropshire. (For their route, *see* article Nell.) On the road they meet some remarkable characters—the Punch and Judy showmen, Mrs. Jarley of the Waxworks, and some gamblers who do their utmost to drag the old man still deeper into the mire. At last they settle in a village (Tong), but the journey has been too much for Nell and she dies, soon to be followed to the grave by her old Grandfather. Meanwhile the old man's brother has been searching for them, only to discover their whereabouts too late to save their lives. A secondary plot centres round Kit Nubbles, who is hated by Quilp. A conspiracy is hatched between the dwarf and the Brasses to convict Kit of theft. This is foiled and the Brasses are disgraced, while Quilp meets his end by drowning. Throughout the story stalks the magnificent figure of Dick Swiveller, needy and poetic to the last, when he marries the Marchioness.

**OLD CURIOSITY SHOP.** Various places have claimed to be the original Curiosity Shop. If Dickens had any particular premises in his mind it was probably No. 10, Green Street, Leicester Square, since demolished. Another reasonable claimant was No. 24 Fetter Lane, demolished in 1891. The widely advertised " Old Curiosity Shop, immortalised by Charles Dickens " in Portsmouth Street, though an ancient enough house, has no connection whatever with Little Nell's home.

**OLD GRAVEL LANE.** *See* Baker's Trap.

**OLD GREEN COPPER ROPE WALK.** This, like the other directions for finding Mrs. Whimple's House on Mill Pond Bank, was fictitious. *Expectations*, 46.

**OLD HELL SHAFT.** The abandoned mine shaft down which Stephen Blackpool fell. *Hard Times*, III, 6.

**OLD KENT ROAD.** Down this main road to Greenwich and Kent, David Copperfield made his way on foot, there disposing of his waistcoat at a little second-hand shop (*Copperfield*, 13). The Asylum for the Deaf and Dumb, to which Dr. Marigold took Sophy, was about half a mile beyond the Bricklayers' Arms Station, at one time a terminus of the Chatham and Dover Railway.

**OLD MINT.** The Mint, a low district opposite St. George's Church, Southwark, was for many years an asylum of fraudulent debtors and criminals. It was so called from a mint having been established there in the sixteenth century. Mint Street perpetuates the site. *Reprinted, Inspector Field*.

**OLD ROYAL HOTEL, BIRMINGHAM.** In Mr. Pickwick's time this was a fine old three-storied Georgian house, but it has since then been rebuilt and modernised. Dickens was a frequent visitor there. *Pickwick*, 50.

**OLD SOLDIER, THE.** The name given by the schoolboys to Mrs. Markleham, Dr. Strong's mother-in-law. *Copperfield*, 16.

**OLD SQUARE, LINCOLN'S INN.** This is the first square through the archway from Chancery Lane. Kenge and Carboy's offices were situated at No. 13, since demolished. *Bleak House*, 20.

**OLD STREET ROAD.** This was the name formerly given to the eastern end of Old Street, from City Road to Shoreditch Church. At No. 302 lived Mrs. Guppy " in an independent though unassuming manner." *Bleak House*, 9, 20.

**OLD 'UN, THE.** Mr. Peggotty's way of referring to the deceased Mr. Gummidge. " She's been thinking of the old 'un," he would say, in explanation of the widow's lowness of spirits. *Copperfield*, 3.

**OLIVER TWIST, ADVENTURES OF.** Dickens's second novel was published in Bentley's *Miscellany*, January 1837 to March, 1839, and with its conclusion the author handed over his editorship of the *Miscellany* to Harrison Ainsworth. *Oliver Twist* was a violent attack on the abuses of the poor law, and the exposure of the workhouse system had a very salutary effect.

*Principal Characters.* Oliver Twist ;

Bumble, the beadle; Fagin, the master thief, with his accomplices the Artful Dodger, Charley Bates and Noah Claypole; Bill Sikes, the burglar, and his mistress, Nancy; Mr. Brownlow, Mrs. Maylie and Dr. Losberne, Oliver's protectors; Monks; Mrs. Corney.

Born in a workhouse, and ill-treated by all who have anything to do with him, Oliver is at last apprenticed to Sowerberry the undertaker, but runs away to London, where he falls into the hands of Fagin, who tries to make him a pickpocket. Arrested for a theft committed by the Artful Dodger, Oliver is taken before Fang, the brutal magistrate, but is discharged on the evidence of the Bookstall Keeper and taken home by Mr. Brownlow. He is kidnapped by Fagin's gang, however, and taken by Sikes to assist in breaking into Mrs. Maylie's house. Oliver is shot during the alarm this occasions, and is cared for by the Maylies. Fagin and Monks, Oliver's wicked brother, discover his whereabouts and lay a plot to recapture him, but this is revealed to Rose Maylie by Nancy, Sikes' mistress. Fagin learns of Nancy's betrayal and tells Sikes, who, in a fit of rage, murders her. He flies from justice, but accidentally hangs himself while escaping from his pursuers. Fagin's gang is broken up and he, the arch-villain, is hanged. Oliver then comes into his own, and is adopted by Mr. Brownlow. Bumble and his wife, the former Mrs. Corney, are disgraced for the part they played in concealing the facts of Oliver's birth, and end their days as paupers in the workhouse over which they once ruled.

**OLYMPIC THEATRE.** This old theatre was in Wych Street, Strand. The first building, opened in 1806, was burned down in 1849, a new theatre being opened the same year, and continuing in popularity until the demolition of the street early in the present century. Madame Vestris was manager at the time of writing *Sketches of Gentlemen* (*Theatrical*).

**OMER, MR.** Draper, tailor and undertaker of Yarmouth, who arranged for the funeral of Mrs. Copperfield. Whenever he went to Yarmouth David visited him, and it was he who employed Little Em'ly before she ran away with Steerforth. Omer's pretty daughter, Minnie, married Joram, his foreman and successor in the business. *Copperfield*, 9, 21, 23, 30–2, 51.

**OMNIBUS.** The first omnibus service in London was started by John Shillibeer on July 4, 1829, and ran from the "Yorkshire Stingo," Lisson Grove, to the Bank, at a fare of one shilling. The vehicles were drawn by three horses and carried twenty-two inside passengers, but they were soon superseded by smaller buses, holding twelve inside passengers. The London General Omnibus Company was founded in 1856. The old-time conductor, or "cad," was usually a keen business man and wholly

unscrupulous in his manner of getting passengers. He stood on a step at the back of the bus, a door being closed on the passengers when the vehicle was in motion, and forced into the bus a far greater number than it could comfortably hold. Early omnibus travelling is described in *Boz, Scenes*, 16. *Tales, Christening.*

**ON DUTY WITH INSPECTOR FIELD.** This account of a walk with the famous police inspector was printed in *Household Words*, June 14, 1851, and republished in *Reprinted Pieces*, 1858. It gives an excellent idea of the London slums at that period.

**ONE POUND NOTES.** Banks were allowed to issue notes for small amounts until 1826, when a law forbade the issue of notes of less value than £5 and restricted these to certain provincial banks. *Expectations*, 10.

**ONOWENEVER, MRS.** The mother of an early love of the Uncommercial Traveller (19). The name is taken from the song, "Oh no, we never mention her"; words by T. H. Bayley, music by Bishop. *See* From Sport to Sport.

**OPERA COLONNADE.** This was a colonnade on the west of the King's Theatre, or Italian Opera House, Haymarket, which stood on the site now occupied by His Majesty's Theatre and the Carlton Hotel. The old theatre was demolished in 1893, but the Royal Opera Arcade perpetuates the existence of the Opera Colonnade, which was full of shops, coffee houses and restaurants. *Nickleby*, 2. *Bleak House*, 14.

**ORANGE, MRS.** One of Mrs. Lemon's friends. *Holiday Romance.*

**ORFLING, THE.** Mrs. Micawber's maid. *See* Clickett.

**ORLICK, DOLGE.** Joe Gargery's journeyman blacksmith, a bad character and Pip's inveterate enemy. He had a grudge against Pip's sister and attacked her so violently that she never recovered. After this Orlick was employed by Miss Havisham, and got into the hands of Compeyson, who employed him to waylay Pip and murder him. The scheme would have succeeded had not Herbert Pocket and others arrived on the scene. *Expectations*, 15–17, 29, 30, 53.

**ORSON.** A wild man of the forest, brought up by a bear, as narrated in the old romance of Valentine and Orson. *Boz, Tales, Boarding House.*

**OSBORNE'S HOTEL, ADELPHI.** This is now called the Adelphi Hotel, but is otherwise almost unchanged from the days when the closing scenes of *Pickwick* were enacted within its doors (*Pickwick*, 54, 56, 57). The hotel was opened in 1777 as the Adelphi New Tavern and Coffee House, and was patronised by many famous people. Mrs. Edson stayed there before she took lodgings at Mrs. Lirriper's house. *Lirriper's Lodgings.*

**OUR BORE.** This and the three following sketches appeared in *Household Words* on the dates here given, and were republished in *Reprinted Pieces*, 1858. *Our Bore*, October 9, 1852.

**OUR ENGLISH WATERING PLACE,** August 2, 1851.

**OUR FRENCH WATERING PLACE,** November 4, 1854.

**OUR HONOURABLE FRIEND,** July 31, 1852.

**OUR MUTUAL FRIEND.** This, Dickens's last completed novel, was published in monthly parts, May, 1864, to November, 1865. It was illustrated by Marcus Stone. The application of the title, which has been much criticised on the score of grammar, will be found in *Book I*, 9, 15.

*Principal Characters.* Mr. and Mrs. Boffin, inheritors of the Dustman's wealth; John Harmon, supposed to be dead, who appears as Rokesmith; the Wilfer family; the Veneerings, with their circle of friends; Lizzie Hexam, her brother Charlie and her friend Jenny Wren; Eugene Wrayburn and Bradley Headstone, both in love with Lizzie; Riderhood, a rogue; Betty Higden; Silas Wegg, the wonderful impostor and his friend Venus.

The rather complicated plot of this novel centres primarily around John Harmon, the son of a rich dust contractor, who is left a fortune provided he marries Bella Wilfer. On his way home from abroad John Harmon disappears, supposedly murdered. In reality he adopts the name of Rokesmith, enters Boffin's service as secretary, is recognised by that worthy old couple and with their aid wooes and wins Bella for his wife, she being yet in ignorance of his identity, which is not revealed until he is arrested on a charge of his own murder. Before Rokesmith's appearance Mr. Boffin had got into the hands of the impostor Wegg, who discovers a will of old Harmon which, as he supposes, will disinherit Boffin, whom he forthwith begins to blackmail. His schemes are exposed by Venus, however, and he is disgraced. A separate plot is that of the courtship of Lizzie Hexam by Eugene Wrayburn, a trifler who is not himself sure whether he means to marry her. He has a rival in Bradley Headstone, passionately in love with Lizzie. Headstone tries to murder Wrayburn; Lizzie saves him, nurses him through his illness and marries him, while Headstone, desperate at his failure and threatened with exposure by Rogue Riderhood, ends his own life, and that of Riderhood, by drowning. Yet a third interest in the book centres in the Veneerings and their friends, including the adventurers Mr. and Mrs. Lammle, the ponderous Podsnap, and the impossible Fascination Fledgeby. In reality unconnected with the story, but actually some of the most important characters in the book are the Wilfers, the cherubic R.W.; his majestic and remarkable wife; the irre-

pressible Lavvy and her unfortunate admirer, George Sampson.

**OUR SCHOOL.** This and the three following sketches appeared in *Household Words* on the dates here given, and were republished in *Reprinted Pieces*, 1858. *Our School*, October 11, 1851.

**OUR VESTRY,** August 28, 1852.

**OUT OF THE SEASON,** June 28, 1856.

**OUT OF TOWN,** September 29, 1855.

**" OVERHAUL YOUR CATECHISM."** Advice from Captain Cuttle. *Dombey*, 4, 23.

**OVERS, JOHN.** One of the misers by whose lives Mr. Boffin affected to profit. *Mutual Friend*, III, 5.

**OVER THE LEFT.** This gesture of incredulity or disbelief was formerly in common use among a certain class. Ingenious and fanciful classic derivations have been found for it. *Pickwick*, 42.

**OVERTON, JOSEPH.** Mayor of Great Winglebury, and a man of the world (*Boz, Tales, Winglebury*). The same character appears as Owen Overton in *The Strange Gentleman*.

**OWEN, JOHN.** One of Mr. Marton's pupils. *Curiosity Shop*, 52.

**OXFORD MARKET.** This was on the northern side of Oxford Street between Great Titchfield Street and Great Portland Street, on the site still called Market Place. It was closed in 1876 and the site sold for building purposes. It was Towlinson's ambition to set up business there as a serious greengrocer. *Dombey*, 18.

**OXFORD STREET.** This thoroughfare was formerly known as the Oxford Road. Dickens was, however, mistaken in saying that " there were few buildings then (1780) north of the Oxford Road," as practically the whole area between that road and the New Road (Marylebone Road) was occupied by houses (*Two Cities*, II, 6). Mr. Gabriel Parsons walked up and down the sunny side of Oxford Street in tight boots for a week in the hope of meeting his fiancée (*Boz, Tales, Tottle*). It was at the western end, facing Hyde Park, that Mr. Micawber had a fancy to live (*Copperfield*, 28), while John Jarndyce and his wards lodged over an upholsterer's shop there (*Bleak House*, 13). Mrs. Nickleby's mother, turning into Oxford Street one day, collided with her hairdresser escaping from a bear, or vice versa (*Nickleby*, 35). While trying to find Miss Wade, Clennam and Meagles " rode to the top of Oxford Street . . . and dived in " among the side streets of that stately neighbourhood. *Dorrit*, I, 27.

**P**

**PACKER.** 1. A client of Snagsby. *Bleak House*, 10.

2. Tom, a marine who fought with Gill Davis against the pirates. *English Prisoners.*

**PACKLEMERTON, JASPER.** A murderer who figured in Mrs. Jarley's waxworks. *Curiosity Shop*, 28.

**PALL MALL.** In this aristocratic street were the lodgings of Mr. Tigg Montague (*Chuzzlewit*, 27, 28, 38); there also lived Chops the Dwarf, spending his money on *Going into Society*. In the window of his Pall Mall Club, Twenlow spent a whole day canvassing for his friend Veneering (*Mutual*, II, 3). Other references are *Boz*, *Tales*, *Winglebury*, *Golden Mary*, *Uncommercial*, 16.

**PANCKS.** Christopher Casby's rent collector and agent, a " short, dark man who snorted and sniffed and puffed and blew like a labouring steam engine." The instrument of Casby's griping avarice, he took the blame for the Patriarch's meanness and screwed the tenants down for their rents. He discovered and established the Dorrits' right to their fortune, and eventually hoped to make his own in one of Merdle's schemes, which ended by ruining him. He had the final satisfaction of showing Casby up in his true colours and clipping the Patriarchial locks in the presence of his tenants. *Dorrit*, I, 12, 13, 23–5, 27, 29, 32, 35; II, 9, 11, 13, 20, 22, 26, 28, 30, 32, 34.

**PANCRAS ROAD.** This runs up between King's Cross and St. Pancras Stations, though neither existed when Miss J'mima Ivins and her young man met their friends there (*Boz*, *Characters*, 4). Some distance up on the right is old St. Pancras Church, where Jerry Cruncher dug up the supposed coffin of Roger Cly (*Two Cities*, II, 14), while further still is the Workhouse, almost facing the wall of the Veterinary College, which Heyling passed when tracking down the object of his hatred. *Pickwick*, 21.

**PANGLOSS.** A Government official prepared to demonstrate " that we live in the best of all possible official worlds." *Uncommercial*, 8.

**PANKY, MISS.** One of Mrs. Pipchin's boarders, " who was shampooed every morning and seemed in danger of being rubbed away altogether." *Dombey*, 8, 11, 59.

**PAPER BUILDINGS.** These pleasant chambers, the back of which looks over the Temple Gardens, date from 1848, the old Paper Buildings, where Sir John Chester lived (*Barnaby*, 15), having been destroyed ten years previously by a fire caused by a convivial Templar, who, returning to his chambers after a good dinner, tried to extinguish a lighted candle by putting it under his bed.

**PAPER MILL.** The mill at which Lizzie Hexam worked and near which Eugene Wrayburn was attacked by Headstone, was the Marsh Mill, Henley. *Mutual Friend*, IV, 6.

**PARAGON, MARY ANNE.** The Copperfields' first servant, whose nature " was represented as being feebly expressed in her name." *Copperfield*, 44.

**PARDIGGLE, MRS. AND FAMILY.** Obtrusive and violent philanthropists, friends of Mrs. Jellyby, and neighbours of John Jarndyce. The boys were forced against their will to subscribe all their money to charities, while little Alfred, the youngest, aged five, was pledged never through life to use tobacco in any form. *Bleak House*, 8, 15, 30.

**PARIS.** Most of the action of *Two Cities* takes place in revolutionary Paris, which is admirably described in that book. Other references are to Lady Dedlock's visits there (*Bleak House*, 2, 12); Mr. Dorrit's and Father Meagles's passage through the city (*Dorrit*, II, 18, 33); the Dombey honeymoon (*Dombey*, 35) and the journey thither by the south-eastern express (*Reprinted*, *A Flight*).

**PARKER.** 1. Mrs. Johnson Parker was the mother of seven extremely fine girls, all unmarried. *Boz*, *Our Parish*, 6.
2. Uncle Parker was the name given by Silas Wegg to one of the inhabitants of the corner house. See Elizabeth, Miss. *Mutual Friend*, I, 5 ; II, 7, 10 ; III, 6, 7 ; IV, 3, 14.
3. A London constable. *Reprinted*, *Inspector Field*.

**PARKES, PHIL.** A ranger in Epping Forest and one of old John Willett's cronies. *Barnaby*, 1, 11, 30, 33, 54, 56, 82.

**PARKINS.** 1. A mysterious friend of Our Bore. *Reprinted Pieces*.
2. Mrs., a laundress in chambers in the Temple. *Reprinted*, *Ghost of Art*.

**PARKLE.** A barrister who lived in Gray's Inn Square. *Uncommercial*, 14.

**PARKSOP, BROTHER.** Grandfather of *George Silverman*.

**PARLIAMENT, HOUSES OF.** The old Houses of Parliament were a number of disconnected buildings, practically on the site of the present New Palace of Westminster. The House of Commons had used the St. Stephen's Hall from 1547 ; the Lords sat in the Court of Requests in Old Palace Yard after 1800. The entire Houses, with the exception of Westminster Hall, were burned down in 1834, and the present building was erected in its place. The Lords moved in in 1847, the Commons three years later.

**PARSONS.** 1. Gabriel, the friend of Watkins Tottle, who paid off Tottle's debts on condition that he married Miss Lillerton. *Boz*, *Tales*, *Tottle*.
2. Miss Letitia, was a pupil of the Misses Crumpton. *Boz*, *Tales*, *Sentiment*.
3. A tall lady acquainted with the Contradictory Couple. *Sketches of Couples*.

**PARVIS, OLD ARSON.** A storekeeper in New York, who originally came from Lanrean. *Message from Sea*.

**PASSNIDGE.** A friend of Mr. Murdstone, whom David saw at Lowestoft. *Copperfield*, 2.

**PATENT THEATRES.** Drury Lane and Covent Garden were the two patent theatres in London, i.e. held by letters patent, the others being licensed. *Boz, Characters*, 8.

**PATRIARCHS, LAST OF THE.** *See* Christopher Casby.

**PATTEN.** This almost obsolete form of footwear consisted of a wooden sole, secured to the foot by a strap over the instep and mounted on on oval iron ring, raising it a couple of inches or so above the ground. Pattens were, of course, used for working on wet floors. As clogs (without the iron ring) they are still in use in the north of England.

**PATTY.** Sister of John, the tenant of the *Haunted House.*

**PAUL'S CHAIN.** This was a passage from St. Paul's Churchyard into Doctors' Commons. Its site is now covered by warehouses, but it was the next turning eastward to Dean's Court. *Boz, Scenes*, 8.

**PAVILIONSTONE.** A disguise for Folkestone, taking its origin from the Pavilion Hotel, then (1855) as now, the principal hotel in the lower town. The upper town was hardly in existence. *Reprinted, Out of Town.*

**PAWKINS, MAJOR.** Husband of the lady who kept the boarding house where Martin Chuzzlewit put up in New York. "He was a bold speculator—in plainer words, he had a most distinguished genius for swindling." *Chuzzlewit*, 16.

**PAYNE, DOCTOR.** A surgeon of the 43rd Regiment and a fire-eating friend of little Doctor Slammer. *Pickwick*, 2, 3.

**PEACE.** One of Miss Flite's captive birds. *Bleak House*, 14.

**PEACOAT.** A Thames policeman. *Reprinted, Down with the Tide.*

**PEACOCK.** 1. The Islington inn, a short way up the High Street, formerly the main coaching road to the North, became the stopping place for the York coaches in 1829, replacing the old Queen's Head Inn. There the hearty-looking gentleman, who told the story of the Baron of Grogzwig, joined Nicholas on the coach top (*Nickleby*, 5). Charley, of the *Holly Tree*, found everyone drinking purl there when he started North.

2. The Peacock, Eatanswill, where Messrs. Snodgrass and Tupman put up, was probably the Swan Inn, Sudbury. *Pickwick*, 13, 14.

**PEAK.** Sir John Chester's manservant who, after his death, decamped with all his portable effects, setting up for himself as a gentleman. *Barnaby*, 23, 24, 32, 75, 82.

**PEAL OF BELLS.** The village alehouse where Mr. Traveller put up. This was the White Hart, Stevenage. *Tom Tiddler.*

**PEBBLESON NEPHEW.** Founders of Wilding and Co.'s wine business. *No Thoroughfare.*

**PECKHAM.** This was long a country suburb, and to reach the Rye by coach would doubtless take Dick Swiveller some good while (*Curiosity Shop*, 56). Walter Gay went to a weekly boarding school there; while Mr. Feeder intended making the home of his two maiden aunts at Peckham the centre of his investigations of the dark mysteries of London (*Dombey*, 4, 14). Mrs. Swidger was once taken off her balance at Peckham Fair (*Haunted Man*). How patriotic Peckham picked a peck of pickled poetry is described in *Uncommercial*, 35.

**PECKSNIFF.** Seth Pecksniff, architect and surveyor, was a cousin of old Martin Chuzzlewit, and one of the most remarkable hypocrites in fiction. In the hope of inheriting some of old Martin's money he first made friends with and then repudiated young Martin. He secured Jonas Chuzzlewit as a husband for his younger daughter, and then took old Martin, who affected senility, into his house, hoping to strengthen his hold on the old man by marrying his protégé Mary Graham. On his scheme being discovered by Tom Pinch, hitherto Pecksniff's most devoted slave and admirer, Tom was turned from the house, and when young Martin, home from America, appealed once again for his grandfather's friendship, Pecksniff turned him away. At last his villainy was unmasked by old Martin, his wealth was lost in the downfall of Jonas and Montague Tigg, and his last appearance is as a begging letter writer. Various originals have been suggested for Pecksniff. Some have seen in it a caricature of Sir Robert Peel; Pugin, who built St. Mary's Grange, on the Salisbury Southampton Road, which is almost certainly Pecksniff's house, is another candidate; while others have suggested Samuel Carter Hall (1800–89), who founded and edited the *Art Journal*, and with his wife produced over five hundred books. *Chuzzlewit*, 2–6, 8–12, 14, 18–20, 24, 30, 31, 35, 38, 43, 44, 47, 52, 54.

Charity Pecksniff was a striking contrast to her father, bitter and sharp tongued, a shrew of the first order. Disappointed in her hopes of marrying Jonas, she eventually went to London and there caught the weak-minded and sentimental Moddle, to whom she became engaged. On the eve of the wedding, however, Moddle disappeared, preferring the uncertainties of Tasmania to the certain misery of life with Charity. 2, 4–6, 8–12, 18, 20, 24, 30–2, 37, 44, 46, 54.

Mercy, Pecksniff's younger daughter, first appears as an empty-headed, silly girl, not altogether free from the family taint of hypocrisy. From sheer vanity she married her cousin, Jonas Chuzzlewit, who from the first began to treat her badly and finally broke her spirit. After his suicide Mercy, refined and improved by troubles, was taken care of by old Martin. 2, 4–6, 8–12, 18, 20, 24, 26, 28, 30, 32, 37, 40, 46, 47, 51, 54,

**PEDDLE AND POOL.** Mr. Dorrit's solicitors. *Dorrit*, I, 36.

**PEDRO.** A member of Jerry's troupe of performing dogs. *Curiosity Shop*, 18.

**PEECHER, MISS EMMA.** Mistress of the girls' section in Bradley Headstone's school. She was in love with Bradley and kept a watchful, interested eye on all his doings. *Mutual Friend*, II, 1, 11 ; III, 11 ; IV, 7, 15.

**PEEL, SIR ROBERT.** Suggested original of Pecksniff. (*q.v.*)

**PEEPY, HON. MISS.** " The beauty of her day " and a former visitor to *Our Watering Place. Reprinted Pieces.*

**PEERYBINGLE, JOHN AND MARY.** A carrier and his wife (usually called Dot), who were instrumental in bringing together Edward Plummer and May Fielding. Dot was the good angel of the story, and a charming little, good-humoured, kindly personage. *Cricket on the Hearth.*

**PEFFER.** Mr. Snagsby's deceased partner and uncle of Mrs. Snagsby. *Bleak House*, 10.

**PEGASUS ARMS.** This was the public-house where the Sleary Troupe made their headquarters. The inscription is to be found on the Malt Shovel Inn, Chatham Hill. *Hard Times*, I, 6.

**PEGG.** A Liverpool crimp, also known as Waterhouse. *Uncommercial*, 5.

**PEGGOTTY.** Daniel Peggotty, the brother of David Copperfield's nurse, was a fisherman who lived on Yarmouth beach in a boat which had been converted into a house. There he brought up his nephew, Ham, and his niece, Little Em'ly, and gave a home to his partner's widow, Mrs. Gummidge. His affections were bound up in Little Em'ly, and when she eloped with Steerforth, Daniel set out to find her and bring her back. For months he continued his search, traversing most parts of the Continent, and ever and anon returning to London, where at last, by the aid of Martha Endell, he found her. He thereupon took her, Martha and Mrs. Gummidge to Australia, where they throve amid new surroundings. *Copperfield*, 2, 3, 7, 10, 17, 21, 22, 30-2, 40, 46, 47, 50, 51, 55, 57, 63.

Clara Peggotty, generally known as Peggotty, was Mrs. Copperfield's servant and David's devoted nurse. When her mistress was being married to Murdstone, Peggotty took David to her brother's house at Yarmouth ; after the marriage she was Mrs. Copperfield's only friend. Discharged on her mistress's death, Peggotty married Barkis, the carrier who had always been " willin'," and after his death she went to live with David and his aunt, with whom she remained to the end. Clara Peggotty, like Mary the Housemaid (*q.v.*), was founded on Dickens's own nurse, Mary Weller. 1-5, 8-10, 12, 13, 17, 19-23, 28, 30-5, 37, 43, 51, 55, 57, 59, 63, 64.

Ham Peggotty, Daniel's nephew and the betrothed husband of Little Em'ly, was heartbroken at her desertion, but lived on at Yarmouth, where he was eventually drowned while swimming out with a life-line to the wrecked vessel in which Steerforth met his end. 1-3, 7, 10, 21, 22, 30-2, 40, 46, 51, 55, 56, 63.

**PEGGY.** 1. A housemaid. *Going into Society.*

2. Lord Chamberlain to King Watkins I. *Holiday Romance.*

**PEGLER, MRS.** A quiet respectable old countrywoman, friendly with Stephen Blackpool and Rachel, who proved to be the mother of Josiah Bounderby, kept in the background by him so that he could vaunt his fictitious origin from the gutter. *Hard Times*, I, 12 ; II, 6, 8 ; III, 5, 9.

**PEGWELL BAY.** A visit to Pegwell, to the south of Ramsgate, makes a pleasant little excursion as performed by the Tuggs's and their friends. Pegwell is still noted for its " srimps." *Boz, Tales, Tuggs's.*

**PELERINE.** A lady's long cape with ends coming down to a point in front. *Pickwick*, 46.

**PELL, SOLOMON.** An attorney in the Insolvent Court, employed by various friends of Mr. Tony Weller when in financial difficulties. He undertook the business of Sam's voluntary imprisonment with Mr. Pickwick, and finally proved Mrs. Weller's will. Pell, who vaunted his friendship with a late Lord Chancellor, belonged to a race of rather shady ill-educated lawyers now extinct. *Pickwick*, 43, 47, 55.

**PELTIROGUS, HORATIO.** According to Mrs. Nickleby a possible suitor for Kate's hand. *Nickleby*, 55.

**PEN.** Although steel pens were introduced widely by Joseph Gillott between 1820-30, quill pens were in general use until well into the middle of the last century. Turkey and goose quills were the best, crow quills being employed for drawing fine lines. The great disadvantage of quill pens was the necessity of frequently cutting fresh points, for which a certain knack was required (*Nickleby*, 9). The hard-nibbed pen Sam Weller purchased for writing his valentine may either have been a steel nib, or a quill rendered hard and durable by means of a horn or tortoise-shell tip. *Pickwick*, 33.

**PENITENTIARY.** The building mentioned as being passed on the way home, by river, from the Red'us, was the Millbank penitentiary, where now stands the Tate Gallery. *Boz, Scenes*, 10.

**PENREWEN.** An old inhabitant of Lanrean. *Message from Sea.*

**PENTONVILLE.** This was formerly a pleasant residential suburb, inhabited by well-to-do people of the Brownlow class (*Twist*, 12), and comfortable City clerks like Mr. Dumps (*Boz, Tales, Christening*). On the rare occasions he was allowed to go home,

Mr. Pickwick's first cab horse lived in "Pentonwil" (*Pickwick*, 2). Mr. Rugg's Agency, at which Pancks lodged, was there (*Dorrit*, I, 13, 25), while Mr. Guppy lived in Penton Place, leading from Pentonville Road to King's Cross Road (*Bleak House*, 9). At the Crown Tavern, Miss Ivins and her friend partook of shrub. *Boz, Characters*, 4.

**PEPLOW, MRS.** One of the dwellers in the street described in *Boz, Scenes*, 2.

**PEPPER.** Pip's page boy, also called the Avenger, dressed "with a blue coat, canary waistcoat, white cravat, creamy breeches and top boots. . . . I had to find him a little to do and a great deal to eat." *Expectations*, 27, 30, 34.

**PEPS, DR. PARKER.** Mrs. Dombey's doctor, "of immense reputation for assisting at the increase of great families." *Dombey*, 1, 16.

**PERCEVAL, SPENCER** (1762–1812) was a prominent statesman who became Prime Minister in 1809. He was assassinated in the lobby of the Commons by a mad bankrupt, May 11, 1812. *Pickwick*, 25.

**PERCH, MR. AND MRS.** The messenger at the offices of Dombey and Son, and his wife, the mother of an ever-increasing family. Perch was a gossipy little fellow, in constant apprehension for his wife's state of health ; she was a little busybody who came up from their home in Balls Pond to the Dombey kitchen for each of its functions. *Dombey*, 13, 17, 18, 22, 23, 31, 35, 46, 51, 53, 58, 59.

**PERCY, LORD ALGERNON.** In command of the Northumberland Militia at London during the Gordon Riots. *Barnaby*, 67.

**PERILS OF CERTAIN ENGLISH PRISONERS.** This was the Christmas number of *Household Words*, 1857, and was in three chapters, of which the first and last only were by Dickens.

**PERKER, MR.** The solicitor of Gray's Inn employed by Mr. Wardle and Mr. Pickwick. He squared Jingle in the matter of the elopement with Miss Rachel, and next appears as Blue agent at the Eatanswill election. A kindly, business-like little man, he took charge of Mr. Pickwick's interest in the Bardell case, and made the final arrangements for his release from the Fleet. The character was probably founded on that of Mr. Ellis, a partner of the firm of Ellis and Blackmore, in whose office Dickens was employed in 1827–8. *Pickwick*, 10, 13, 20, 26, 31, 33–5, 40, 45–7, 53, 54.

**PERKINS.** 1. A lady, living near the Sol's Arms, who, with her friend and neighbour, Mrs. Piper, took a keen interest in the thrilling events which occurred in Krook's house. *Bleak House*, 11, 20, 32, 33, 39.

2. A lady who was expecting the professional assistance of Mrs. Gamp. *Chuzzlewit*, 19.

3. General dealer in the neighbourhood of the *Haunted House*.

**PERKINSOP, MARY ANNE.** One of Mrs. Lirriper's maids, "worth her weight in gold." *Lirriper's Lodgings*.

**PESSELL.** A member of the medical section of the Mudfog Association.

**PET.** Name usually given to Minnie Meagles. (*q.v.*)

**PETER, LORD.** An imbecile peer to whom Miss Julia Manners was engaged and for whom she mistook Alexander Trott when it came to an elopement. *Boz, Tales, Winglebury*.

**PETERSFIELD.** See Inn (5).

**PETERSHAM COAT.** This was a greatcoat made of a heavy rough-napped woollen cloth, and so named after Lord Petersham. It was in great vogue in the 30's and 40's. *Boz, Scenes*, 15.

**PETOWKER, HENRIETTA.** An inferior actress, of the Theatre Royal, Drury Lane, and a friend of Mrs. Kenwigs. She joined the Crummles Company, being accompanied to Portsmouth by Lillyvick, the water rate collector, who was infatuated with her and married her. After a short time, tired of her ponderous husband, she ran away with a half-pay captain, and was formally "cut off" for ever by Mr. Lillyvick. *Nickleby*, 14–16, 25, 30, 36, 48, 52.

**PETTIFER, TOM.** Captain Jorgan's steward, in the lining of whose hat were found the papers that finally cleared up the mystery connected with *A Message from the Sea*.

**PHENOMENON, THE INFANT.** Stage name of Ninetta Crummles. (*q.v.*)

**PHIB.** Miss Squeers's name for her maid Phoebe. *Nickleby*, 12.

**PHIBBS.** A cheapside haberdasher unintentionally connected with the Grimwood murder. *Reprinted, Detective Anecdotes*.

**PHIL.** The morose, but kindly janitor at *Our School. Reprinted Pieces*.

**PHILLIPS.** A constable at the Mansion House. *Barnaby*, 61.

**PHIZ.** The name by which H. K. Browne signed his illustrations. *See* Browne, H. K.

**PHOEBE.** Crippled daughter of Lamps, the porter at Mugby Junction. She supported herself by lacemaking and teaching a few small children, but her invincible contentedness and gentleness so acted on Young Jackson, of Barbox Brothers, that his whole outlook on life was changed. *Mugby Junction*.

**PHOENIX FIRE OFFICE.** This insurance company was established by London sugar bakers in 1782. Mrs. Tibbs was insured in it. *Boz, Tales, Boarding House*.

**PHUNKY, MR.** Serjeant Snubbin's junior in the Bardell-Pickwick case, "an infant barrister" of little more than eight years standing. *Pickwick*, 31, 34.

**PHYSICIAN.** One of the Merdle guests, called in eventually, at the time of the financier's suicide. *Dorrit*, I, 21 ; II, 12, 25.

**PICCADILLY.** Considerable changes have taken place in this street during the last century. Piccadilly Circus (formerly known as Regent's Circus) has been greatly enlarged; the Piccadilly Hotel occupies the site of the famous St. James's Hall (1858–1905); the Egyptian Hall, near St. James's Street was demolished in 1905; the Ritz Hotel stands on the site of the old White Horse Cellar Coaching Inn. The narrator of the Trial for Murder (*Two Ghost Stories*) had chambers near the corner of Piccadilly and St. James's Street, and had the psychic experience of seeing the murderer and his victim passing through the crowds in Piccadilly. Casual references to the street are *Barnaby*, 67; *Copperfield*, 28; *Nickleby*, 64; *Mutual Friend*, I, 10; *Somebody's Luggage*.

**PICKLES.** The fishmonger in whose shop King Watkins met the Fairy Grandmarina. *Holiday Romance.*

**PICKLESON.** A giant exhibited by Mim under the name of Rinaldo di Velasco. Through him Dr. Marigold obtained his adopted daughter Sophy.

**PICKWICK, MOSES.** This once well-known coach proprietor, whose name Sam saw on the Bath coach, was the grandson of Eleazer Pickwick, the founder of the business. Moses developed it and took over several inns, of which the principal was the White Hart, Bath. There is no doubt he furnished the surname for Mr. Samuel Pickwick. *Pickwick*, 35.

**PICKWICK, SAMUEL.** Founder and General Chairman of the Pickwick Club, a retired merchant and a man of considerable independent means. The most famous of the Dickens characters—perhaps of English fiction—Pickwick developed during the course of the book from an eccentric old fellow, little more than a general butt, to a benevolent, jolly, genial old gentleman, loved and respected by all (including the reader) who come into contact with him. His adventures are briefly summed up in the article on the book. Pickwick also appears in *Humphrey*, mainly for the purpose of introducing the story of John Podgers. There have been many surmises as to the original of Pickwick. The name was taken from Moses Pickwick; his personal appearance from John Foster, a friend of Chapman, the publisher; the character was doubtless a creation. *Pickwick*, 1–28, 30–2, 34–7, 39–48, 50–4, 56, 57.

**PICKWICK CLUB.** The prospectus of Pickwick talks of "The Pickwick Club, so renowned in the annals of Huggin Lane," where it probably met in the Goldsmiths' Arms. Mr. Pickwick was General Chairman; Mr. Joseph Smiggers, Perpetual Vice-President. The original idea of the club is told in the preface to *Pickwick*.

**PICKWICK PAPERS.** The origin of "The Posthumous papers of the Pickwick Club" is told in the preface to that book. It was issued in twenty monthly shilling parts, the first appearing in March, 1836, Parts 19 and 20 (bound together) in October, 1837. Parts 1 and 2 contained each four plates by Seymour; Part 3, two plates by R. W. Buss; the remainder of the book being illustrated by H. K. Browne (Phiz). In the bound volume (1837) Buss's illustrations were replaced by two of Browne's.

Ingenious chronologies have been made of *Pickwick*. That Dickens did not set to work with a calendar before him is, however, evident from the outset, as he makes his party travel to Rochester, where a ball was being held the evening of their arrival, on May 13, 1827, which was a Sunday.

*Principal Characters.* Messrs. Pickwick, Tupman, Snodgrass and Winkle, of the Club; Sam Weller and his father; Jingle and his servant, Job Trotter; the Wardle family; Mrs. Bardell and her cronies; Perker, the lawyer; Bob Sawyer and Ben Allen, medical students; Ben's sister Arabella; Dowler and his wife; Mr. and Mrs. Pott.

There is no real plot to *Pickwick*. Mr. Pickwick and his three friends set out on their travels and meet Jingle, who gets them into a scrape in Rochester, turning up again when they are staying with their newly made friends the Wardles. There he cuts out Tracy Tupman in his courtship of Miss Rachel Wardle, and elopes with that lady to London. Pickwick and Wardle pursue the couple to the White Hart, Borough, where Perker squares the adventurer, while Mr. Pickwick meets Sam Weller, whom he shortly after engages as a servant. Owing to a misunderstanding, Mrs. Bardell thinks that Mr. Pickwick has proposed to her. The rascally attorneys, Dodson and Fogg, persuade her to commence an action for breach of promise. In the meantime Mr. Pickwick and his friends have gone to Eatanswill for the election, and there Mr. Pickwick sees Jingle again and is led by that gentleman on wild-goose chases to Bury St. Edmunds and to Ipswich. There Mr. Pickwick goes by mistake into a lady's bedroom in the Great White Horse, and encounters his adventures with Nupkins, the magistrate. The breach of promise case comes on, Mrs. Bardell wins and is awarded £750 damages, which Mr. Pickwick flatly refuses to pay. Before he can be committed to prison he goes with his friends to Bath, where further great adventures take place, chief of which is Winkle's misadventure with Mrs. Dowler, and his discovery of Arabella Allen. On his return Mr. Pickwick goes to the Fleet Prison, where he remains for three months, attended by Sam Weller. Eventually the imprisonment of Mrs. Bardell by her own lawyers induces Mr. Pickwick to pay the costs of the case, and he emerges from prison to help settle all the young people in the book, finally retiring himself to Dulwich.

**PIDGER.** A former suitor of Miss Lavinia Spenlow, by virtue of whom she posed as an authority on matters of the heart. *Copperfield*, 41, 43.

**PIEMAN.** This is an extinct London street trade. The piemen sold meat and fruit pies, goods, and cried, " Pies, all 'ot ! eel, beef or mutton pies ! Penny pies, all 'ot ! " It was a favourite custom of the street urchins to " toss the pieman " for his pies. He never tossed, but always called to the customer. In 1851 Horace Mayhew reckoned there were at most fifty piemen left in London. They were mostly out-of-work bakers, and, like Mr. Brooks, they made their own pies. *Boz, Scenes,* 1. *Pickwick,* 2, 22, 31. *Bleak House,* 11.

**PIERCE, CAPTAIN.** Commander of the East Indiaman *Halsewell*. *Reprinted, Long Voyage.*

**PIFF, MISS.** One of the young ladies in the refreshment room at *Mugby Junction*.

**PIG AND TINDERBOX INN.** An inn at Mudfog, where members of the Association put up.

**PIGEON, THOMAS.** An alias of Tally Ho Thompson. (*q.v.*)

**"PILJIAN'S PROJISS."** Mrs. Gamp's description of life—"This Piljian's Projiss of a mortal wale." *Chuzzlewit,* 25.

**PILKINS, DR.** Family practitioner of the Dombeys. *Dombey,* 1, 8.

**PINCH.** Tom Pinch was the devoted admirer and assistant of Mr. Pecksniff, a gentle, kindly, sweet-tempered, ungainly fellow, quite blind to his patron's hypocrisy and cant. He played the organ at the village church and there fell in love with Mary Graham, whose persecution by Pecksniff first opened Tom's eyes to that individual's true character. Discharged by Pecksniff, Pinch went to London, set up housekeeping with his sister Ruth, and obtained employment from a mysterious patron in the Temple, afterwards discovered to be old Martin Chuzzlewit. Meanwhile his great friend, John Westlock, had fallen in love with Ruth, and after their marriage Tom went to live with them. *Chuzzlewit,* 2, 5–7, 9, 12–14, 20, 24, 30, 31, 33, 36, 37, 39, 40, 41, 43, 45, 46, 48, 50, 52–4.

Ruth Pinch, Tom's pretty little sister, was a downtrodden governess whom he rescued from her drudgery and took to keep his house when he went up to London. She and John Westlock soon fell in love, and he proposed to her in the picturesque surroundings of Fountain Court, where they went to meet Tom from his work. 6, 9, 36, 37, 39, 40, 45, 46, 48, 50, 52–4.

**PINNOCK.** William Pinnock (1782–1843) was a well-known producer of school books, chief among which was a series of eighty-three Catechisms on all kinds of subjects. *Tom Tiddler.*

**PIP.** 1. A theatrical friend of Mr. Tigg Montague. *Chuzzlewit,* 28.

2. The name by which Philip Pirrip (*q.v.*) was always known.

**PIPCHIN, MRS.** Proprietor of the children's boarding house at Brighton, where Paul and Florence Dombey were sent. She was an ill-favoured, ill-conditioned old lady, whose husband had broken his heart in pumping water out of the Peruvian mines. She kept the children and her niece, Berinthia, in awe, and when Mr. Dombey wanted a housekeeper he chose her as being the most capable of managing his houseful of servants. The original of Mrs. Pipchin was Mrs. Roylance, the landlady in Little College Street with whom Dickens lived while his father was in the Marshalsea. *Dombey,* 8, 10–12, 14, 16, 40, 42–4, 47, 51, 59.

**PIPER.** 1. Mrs. Anastasia, friend of Mrs. Perkins, and a witness at the inquest on Nemo. *Bleak House,* 11, 20, 32, 33, 39.

2. Professor, a member of the committee which interviewed Elijah Pogram. *Chuzzlewit,* 34.

**PIPKIN.** 1. Nathaniel, the parish clerk in love with Maria Lobbs. *Pickwick,* 17.

2. Mr. Pipkin, M.R.C.S., was a medical member of the Mudfog Association.

**PIPSON, MISS.** One of Miss Griffin's pupils. *Haunted House.*

**PIRRIP, PHILIP,** generally known as Pip. The narrator and chief character of *Great Expectations,* under which heading the principal incidents of his life are detailed.

**PITCHER.** One of Squeers's victims at Dotheboys Hall. *Nickleby,* 7.

**PITT.** 1. Mr. Pitt, whose name was sometimes given to Bailey Junior, was William Pitt the Younger (1759–1806), who became Prime Minister at the age of twenty-four and organised European action against the French Revolution. *Chuzzlewit,* 9.

2. Jane, the kindly wardrobe woman at the school, who married Old Cheeseman. *Reprinted, Schoolboy's Story.*

**P.J.T. 1747.** The interpretation of this inscription of Mr. Grewgious's chambers in Staple Inn is " President James Taylor. 1747." This gentleman was, in that year, President of the Society of Antients of Staple Inn. *Drood,* 11.

**PLASHWATER WEIR MILL LOCK.** The scene of Bradley Headstone's fatal struggle with Rogue Riderhood was probably Hurley Lock, about six miles down river from Henley. *Mutual Friend,* IV, 1, 7, 15.

**PLATED ARTICLE, A.** This description of pottery making appeared in *Household Words,* 1852, and was republished in *Reprinted Pieces,* 1858.

**PLORNISH, THOMAS AND SALLY.** A plasterer and his wife who lived in Bleeding Heart Yard. Plornish had made the acquaintance of the Dorrit in the Marshalsea, and had done small kindnesses for them.

In return he was helped by Arthur Clennam, who sent the Italian Cavaletto to live with them. Mrs. Plornish constituted herself interpreter to John Baptist, and her jargon of broken English, " Me ope you leg well soon," was considered " but a very short remove indeed from speaking Italian." When Clennam was imprisoned in the Marshalsea the Plornishes visited and nursed him in his sickness. It may be noted as a *lapsus calami* that Mrs. Plornish is called Mary in II, 27. *Dorrit*, I, 6, 9, 12, 23–5, 31, 36; II, 4, 13, 26, 27, 29, 32, 33.

**PLUCK.** One of Sir Mulberry Hawk's toadies. With his friend Pyke he set himself to play on Mrs. Nickleby's vanity in order to find out for Sir Mulberry the whereabouts of Kate. *Nickleby*, 19, 27, 28, 38, 50.

**PLUMMER.** Caleb, the father of Edward and Bertha, was a poor toymaker in the service of Gruff and Tackleton. He tried to hide their poverty from his blind daughter, Bertha, who thought they lived in a comfortable house and that Tackleton, Caleb's miserly master, was a kindly patron. Edward, the son, coming back from the Golden South Americas, found his fiancée, May Fielding, about to marry Tackleton, but with Dot Perrybingle's help, won her for his own bride. *Cricket on the Hearth.*

**PLUNDER.** One of Miss Flite's captive birds. *Bleak House*, 14.

**PLYMOUTH.** Mrs. Micawber's family lived in Plymouth, and thither went Mr. Micawber to see what would turn up in the Excise line (*Copperfield*, 12). It was on board the *Crippler*, when she lay in Plymouth water, that Captain Swosser fell in love with the future Mrs. Dingo and Mrs. Bayham Badger. *Bleak House*, 13.

**POCKET.** Herbert, eldest son of Matthew Pocket, was Pip's friend and companion in London. They lived together at Barnard's Inn and at the Temple. Pip secured a partnership for his friend in the firm of Clarriker and Co., and this enabled Herbert to marry pretty little Clara Barley, daughter of the grumpy old ship's purser, and take her abroad. Herbert Pocket is one of the most natural young men Dickens drew. *Expectations*, 11, 21–8, 30, 31, 34, 36, 38–43, 45–7, 50–5, 58.

Matthew, Herbert's father, was the only one of Miss Havisham's relatives who did not dangle round her for the sake of her money. As a result she left him " a cool four thousand " in her will. 22–4, 33, 39, 49, 57.

Mrs. Belinda, wife of Matthew, and a " highly ornamental but perfectly helpless and useless lady," who committed the care of her young children, Alick, Jane, Joe and Fanny, to the care of maids. 22, 23, 33.

Sarah Pocket was a perfect example of the toady. Miss Havisham left her £25 per annum " to buy pills." 11, 15, 17, 19, 29.

**POCKET BREACHES.** The borough for which Veneering was elected parliamentary representative " by the spontaneous thingummies of the incorruptible whatdoyoucallums." *Mutual Friend*, II, 3.

**PODDER.** One of the stand-bys of the All Muggleton Cricket Club. *Pickwick*, 7.

**PODGERS, JOHN.** A citizen of Windsor and one of the principal characters in Mr. Pickwick's Tale. *Humphrey.*

**PODSNAP, JOHN.** A solid, pig-headed British business man, in the marine insurance line, " who always knew what Providence meant, while it was very remarkable that what Providence meant was invariably what Mr. Podsnap meant." He was a constant guest of the Veneerings, where he laid down the law with a " peculiar flourish of his right arm " . . . in clearing the world of its most difficult problems by saying, " I don't want to know about it ; I don't choose to discuss it ; I don't admit it ! " This attitude has given rise to the term Podsnappery. The original of this character, in its pompous, self-sufficient complacency, is supposed to have been Dickens's friend and biographer, Forster. *Mutual Friend*, I, 2, 10, 11, 17 ; II, 3–5 ; III, 1, 17 ; IV, 17.

Georgiana Podsnap, his only daughter, was usually referred to as " the young person." The question about everything was would it bring a blush into the cheek of the young person. She was a kind, weak little creature, who nearly fell a victim to the Lammle scheme of marrying her to Fledgeby. I, 11, 17 ; II, 4, 5, 16 ; III, 1, 17 ; IV, 2.

**POGRAM, ELIJAH.** A member of Congress and the impersonation of all that was bombastic and ridiculous in the American character. Martin met him on his return from Eden, shortly after Pogram had uttered his defiance to the world at large to compete with America. *Chuzzlewit*, 34.

**POLKA, THE ORIGINAL.** The *Opera Polka* by Jullien, published about 1845, has two Polish peasants on the cover, as described in *Reprinted, Out of the Season.*

**POLLY.** The waitress at the Slap Bang eating house, patronised by Smallweed and Guppy. *Bleak House*, 20.

**" POLLY PUT THE KETTLE ON."** This was one of the sentences of Grip the raven. It is the name of an old country dance. *Barnaby*, 17.

**POLREATH, DAVID.** An old resident of Lanrean. *Message from the Sea.*

**POLYGON, THE.** This was the name given to a block of houses which formerly occupied the centre of Clarendon Square, Somers Town. They were replaced by workman's dwellings in 1891. The Dickens family lodged there in 1827–8, and there he placed the home of Mr. Skimpole. *Bleak House*, 43.

**PONTO.** Jingle's remarkably intelligent sporting dog. *Pickwick*, 2.

**POODLES.** A dog in the East London Children's hospital. *Uncommercial*, 30, 34.

**POOR MAN'S TALE OF A PATENT.** A satire on the red-tape difficulties placed in the way of a poor inventor, which appeared in *Household Words*, October 19, 1850. It was republished in *Reprinted Pieces*, 1858.

**POOR RELATION'S STORY.** This was Dickens's contribution to the Christmas Number of *Household Words*, 1852. It was reissued in *Reprinted Pieces*, 1858.

**POPLAR.** The home of Captain Ravender, commander of the *Golden Mary*.

**PORDAGE, COMMISSIONER.** The self-important, incapable official on Silver Store Island, who spoke of himself as " the Government." *English Prisoners.*

**PORKENHAM.** The rival family to the Nupkinses in the society of Ipswich. *Pickwick*, 25.

**PORTER, MRS. JOSEPH.** A busybody in Clapham, who made up her mind to spoil the amateur theatrical party given by her neighbours, the Gattletons. To this end she enlisted the services of their uncle, Tom Balderstone, whose ill-timed knowledge of Shakespeare ruined the whole entertainment. *Boz, Tales, Porter.*

**PORTERS.** An early aspirant to Miss Twinkleton's hand, called by her " Foolish Mr. Porters." *Drood*, 3.

**PORTER'S KNOT.** The porters at Covent Garden and other markets carried their baskets by means of a kind of double shoulder pad, from which a loop passed round the forehead. The whole contrivance was not unlike a horse collar in appearance.

**PORTLAND PLACE.** This was the home of the rather extensive Tapkins family (*Mutual Friend*, I, 17). Somewhere between this place and Bryanstone Square was Mr. Dombey's house. *Dombey*, 3.

**PORTMAN SQUARE.** In or near this Square was the sombre house in a shady angle where Mr. Podsnap lived. *Mutual Friend*, I, 11.

**PORT MIDDLEBAY.** The Australian home of the Peggotty and Micawber families. *Copperfield*, 63.

**PORTSMOUTH.** In this town, at 1 Mile End Terrace, Portsea, now 393, Commercial Road, Portsmouth, Charles Dickens was born, February 7, 1812. The house is now a Dickens Museum. When he was a few months old the family moved to No. 16 Hawke Street, whence they left for London in 1814. In 1838 Dickens went to Portsmouth for material for *Nickleby*, and Chapters 22–5, 29, 30 recount Nicholas's adventures with the Crummles company, then at the Portsmouth Theatre. This latter stood at the corner of High Street and the present Alexandra Road, on the site now occupied by the Cambridge Barracks. Parallel with High Street is St. Thomas's Street, where, at No. 78, the Crummles

lodged with Mr. Bulph. Near by is the Hard, where Nicholas himself put up with Smike. When he landed from Australia Magwitch wrote from Portsmouth under the name of Provis, to Wemmick. *Expectations*, 39.

**PORTUGAL STREET.** Here stood the Insolvent Debtors' Court, latterly the Westminster County Court, until its demolition in 1909. The Horse and Groom public-house, which formerly stood near the Court, was the scene of Mr. Pell's business transactions with his coachmen clients. *Pickwick*, 43.

**POST CHAISE.** A vehicle used for fast travelling. *See* Chaise.

**POST PAID.** Before the introduction of postage stamps in 1841 the cost of transporting a letter could either be paid by the sender in advance or by the recipient on delivery. This system was abolished with the advent of the penny post. *Chuzzlewit*, 13.

**POTKINS, WILLIAM.** Waiter at the Blue Boar. *Expectations*, 58.

**POTT, MR.** The bombastic, ponderous, self-important editor of the *Eatanswill Gazette*, with whom Messrs. Pickwick and Winkle lodged. Enraged at an anonymous communication regarding his wife and the latter gentleman, Pott created a great scene, which ended rather tamely, as he lived in terror of Mrs. Pott, who finally separated from him. Pott's last appearance is at the Saracen's Head, Towcester, where he engaged in fisticuffs with his opponent Slurk, of the *Eatanswill Independent*. Lord Brougham has been suggested as the original of Pott. *Pickwick*, 13–15, 18, 51.

**POTTER.** 1. Thomas, a boisterous City clerk, friend of Mr. Smithers, with whom he made a night of it. *Boz, Characters*, 11.

2. Original of Alfred Jingle. (*q.v.*)

**POTTERSON, MISS ABBEY.** Hostess of the Six Jolly Fellowship Porters, where she reigned supreme, keeping it a respectable house in a rough district. She befriended Lizzie Hexam and gave shelter to Rogue Riderhood when he was drawn half-drowned from the river. *Mutual Friend*, I, 6, 13 ; III, 2, 3 ; IV, 12, 16.

Her brother, Job, was steward on the vessel by which John Harmon returned to England, and was called upon to identify Rokesmith as the missing man. I, 3 ; II, 13 ; IV, 12.

**POUCH, MRS. JOE.** A soldier's widow whom Mrs. Bagnet wished Trooper George to marry. *Bleak House*, 27.

**POUNCERBY, SQUIRE.** Guarantor for a tramp. *Uncommercial*, 5.

**POUND, THE.** Formerly almost every village had an enclosure, called the pound, in which any stray animal was confined until redeemed by its owner, who was charged a fine and expenses. *Pickwick*, 19.

**POWLERS.** Connections of Mrs. Sparsit's late husband. " The Powlers were an ancient stock who could trace themselves so exceedingly far back that . . . they sometimes lost themselves." *Hard Times*, I, 7 ; II, 1.

**PRATCHETT, MRS.** Head chambermaid at the hotel where Christopher waited. Her husband's address was The Bush, Australia. *Somebody's Luggage.*

**PRATT, PARLEY.** A prominent Mormon missionary in Europe and one of the leaders of the Latter Day Saints. *Uncommercial*, 20.

**PRECEDENT.** One of Miss Flite's captive birds. *Bleak House*, 14.

**PRENTICE KNIGHTS.** A society, presided over by Simon Tappertit, which later changed its name to the United Bulldogs. *Barnaby*, 8.

**PRESTON.** Dickens stayed here, at the Bull Hotel, in 1854, and later assigned the town as the birthplace of *George Silverman*.

**PRICE.** 1. Matilda, the pretty Yorkshire girl who took a mischievous delight in egging on Nicholas to make love to Fanny Squeers. She married honest John Browdie, and took Fanny with her as a travelling bridesmaid to London. *Nickleby*, 9, 12, 39, 42, 43, 45, 64.

2. A prisoner for debt in Namby's lock-up. *Pickwick*, 40.

**PRIG, BETSEY.** A nurse at Bartholomew's and professional friend of Mrs. Gamp, whom she somewhat resembled, though " her voice was deeper and more like a man's ; she had also a beard." Her temper and speech were marked by some asperity. She nursed Lewsome turn and turn about with Mrs. Gamp, and was to have taken a hand with Chuffey when the famous battle royal took place between the two friends. A reference to Mrs. Harris elicited the remark from Mrs. Prig, " I don't believe there's no sich a person." Whereupon Mrs. Gamp denounced her as a " bage creetur " and cast her off for ever. *Chuzzlewit*, 25, 29, 46, 49, 51.

**PRINCE BULL.** An allegory on the Crimean War which appeared in *Household Words*, February 17, 1855, and in *Reprinted Pieces*, 1858.

**PRINCESS'S PLACE.** No indication is given of the neighbourhood in which this semi-genteel residence of Miss Tox and Major Bagstock was situated. *Dombey*, 7, 20, 29.

**PRISCILLA.** Mrs. Jellyby's maid, rather given to drinking. *Bleak House*, 4, 5.

**PROCTOR.** This was the name given to solicitors attached to the Ecclesiastical, Admiralty and Probate Courts at Doctors' Commons. The dissolution of Doctors' Commons in 1857 and the enablement of an ordinary solicitor to perform all a proctor's duties did away with the distinction.

**PRODGIT, MRS.** The monthly nurse who helped Mrs. Bigby to upset the Meek household. *Reprinted, Mrs. Meek.*

**PROFILE MACHINE.** This instrument which, according to Sam Weller, " finished

a portrait and put the frame and glass on complete, with a hook at the end to hang it up by, and all in two minutes and a quarter," was adapted from a contrivance invented in 1806 by Charles Schmalcalder. It consisted of a long rod, one end of which was finely tapered, while the other held a sharp, pointed blade. The rod was universally pivoted a few inches from the blade end, and was so placed against sheets of paper mounted on a board that any motion of the rod caused the blade to cut the paper. The sitter took his place at the pointer end of the rod, facing at right angles to it. Beginning with the throat, the operator followed the sitter's profile with the pointer, and the movement of the rod, thus transmitted to the blade end, cut out as many silhouettes as there were sheets of paper beneath the blade. Mr. Van Noorden gives a diagram of this machine in the invaluable Topical Edition of the Pickwick Papers (Chapman and Hall). There were several types of these " profeel macheens," and they formed a great attraction at country fairs and markets, where silhouettes were cut and mounted almost as promptly as described by Sam. *Pickwick*, 33.

**PROSEE.** 1. An eminent counsel. *Pickwick*, 47.

2. A member of the Mudfog Association.

**PROSS, MISS.** Lucie Manette's companion, a wild-looking woman, who inspired Mr. Lorry with a kind of terror, but was the soul of faithfulness and loyalty. She accompanied Lucie to Paris, where she met her brother, Solomon, acting as a spy or prison sheep for the Revolutionary government, under the name of Barsad. After Lucie and her husband escaped, Miss Pross and Jerry Cruncher encountered Madame Defarge. The two women came to grips and Madame Defarge was killed by a shot from her own pistol, the concussion of which deafened Miss Pross for life. *Two Cities*, I, 4 ; II, 6, 17–21 ; III, 2, 3, 6–8, 11, 14.

Solomon Pross, her brother, was a thoroughly bad character, who had robbed his sister, been an informer in England and drifted over to Paris, where he became a spy. Sydney Carton used the man's association with the prison to ensure his own entry and exchange of clothes with Darnay. Like his friend Roger Cly, Pross eventually found his way to the guillotine. II, 3, 6, 16 ; III, 8, 9, 11, 13–15.

**PROTESTANT MANUAL.** This stand-by of Mrs. Varden was *The Protestant Manual of Christian Devotions, composed of instructions, offices and forms of prayer in a plain, rational and scriptural method.* It was published in 1750. *Barnaby*, 4.

**"PROTICIPATE."** " Seek not to proticipate," was Mrs. Gamp's advice when consulted on the probable size of Mrs. Harris's family. " Take 'em as they come and as they go." *Chuzzlewit*, 40.

**PROVIS.** The name assumed by Magwitch when he came to England. *See* Magwitch.

**PRUFFLE.** Butler of the scientific gentleman at Clifton. *Pickwick*, 39.

**"PRUNES AND PRISM."** Mrs. General's formula for producing a ladylike composure of the lips was to repeat the words. " Papa, potatoes, poultry, prunes and prism—prunes and prism." *Dorrit*, II, 5, 7, 15, 19.

**PUBLIC-HOUSE.** 1. The public-house opposite the Insolvent Court, Portugal Street, patronised by Pell was probably the Horse and Groom. *Pickwick*, 43.

2. The house where David took his glass of Genuine Stunning was the Red Lion at the corner of Parliament Street and Cannon Row. The house was rebuilt in 1899. *Copperfield*, 11.

3. In his flight from justice Bill Sikes took refuge in a small public-house in Hatfield. This was the Eight Bells, at the foot of the main street. *Twist*, 48.

**PUBLIC LIFE OF MR. TULRUMBLE.** This early skit on civic powers and the town of Chatham (Mudfog) was published in *Bentley's Miscellany*, January, 1837, and was afterwards incorporated in the *Mudfog Papers*.

**PUBSEY AND CO.** The usurer's business, with offices in St. Mary Axe, which was run by Mr. Riah as a blind for Fledgeby. *Mutual Friend*, II, 5 ; III, 1, 2, 13 ; IV, 8, 9.

**PUCKLER MOSKAU, COUNT.** Original of Count Smorltork. (*q.v.*)

**PUFFER, PRINCESS.** The name given to the old hag who kept the East End opium shop frequented by John Jasper. She overheard some of his wanderings, implicating him in the Drood mystery, and went to Cloisterham to watch or blackmail him. The original is supposed to have been a woman known as Lascar Sal, of Limehouse. *Drood*, 1, 14, 23.

**PUGIN, A. W. N.** *See* Pecksniff.

**PUGSTYLES.** One of Mr. Gregsbury's constituents, who headed the deputation asking that gentleman to resign. *Nickleby*, 16.

**PUMBLECHOOK, UNCLE.** Joe Gargery's uncle and a power in the family on account of his wealth and importance. He was a ponderous hypocrite who, on Pip's coming into his Expectations, pretended to be the origin of his fortune, though he cringed and grovelled before the lad. When Pip returned, poor and without prospects, Uncle Pumblechook's pity and patronising air became insufferable. He was a crude specimen of the type of hypocrite of which Pecksniff was the finished article. *Expectations*, 4–9, 12, 13, 15, 19, 35, 58.

**PUMPKINSKULL, PROF.** A weighty member of the Mudfog Association.

**PUPFORD, MISS EUPHEMIA.** Principal of the Lilliputian College. *Tom Tiddler.*

**PUPKER, SIR MATTHEW.** Chairman of the United Metropolitan Improved Hot Muffin and Crumpet Baking and Punctua Delivery Company. *Nickleby*, 2.

**PURBECK ISLAND.** On the rocks near Seacombe, on the Isle, the East Indiaman *Halsewell* was driven ashore. *Reprinted, Long Voyage.*

**PURBLIND.** A member of the Mudfog Association.

**PURDAY, CAPTAIN.** An old half-pay naval officer who made himself a nuisance at vestry meetings. *Boz, Our Parish*, 2, 4.

**PURL.** This was once a very popular beverage. The following is an old and good recipe for concocting it : Warm 1 pint of ale with ½-pint of milk and add some sugar and a wineglassful of gin, brandy or rum.

**"PUT IT DOWN A WE, MY LORD."** Tony Weller's injunctions to the judge as to spelling the family name. *Pickwick*, 34, 55.

**PUTNEY** was little more than a riverside village when the Misses Spenlow lived there. Thither David went, accompanied by Traddles, to ask their permission to call on Dora, and there, presumably in the parish church of St. Mary, the youthful couple were married (*Copperfield*, 41–3). Arthur Clennam strolled over Putney Heath on his way to visit the Meagles. *Dorrit*, I, 16.

**PYEGRAVE, CHARLEY.** One of Miss Mowcher's clients. *Copperfield*, 22.

**PYKE.** One of the toadies of Sir Mulberry Hawk. *See* Pluck.

## Q

**QUADRANT, THE.** This is the name applied to the curve in Regent Street, between Piccadilly Circus and Vigo Street. The arcades on either side, demolished in 1848, were the resort of " precocious puppyism " and " gay old boys." *Boz, Characters*, 1, 7.

**QUALE.** A philanthropic friend of Mrs. Jellyby " with large shining knobs for temples," who wanted to marry Caddy Jellyby. *Bleak House*, 4, 5, 15, 30.

**QUANKO SAMBA.** The bowler in one of Jingle's West Indian cricket matches, who was killed by the heat. " Bowled on, on my account—bowled off, on his own—died." *Pickwick*, 7.

**QUARLL, PHILIP.** The hero of a story called *The Hermit*, published in 1727, author unknown. It is an imitation of Robinson Crusoe, the hero having an ape instead of man Friday. *Chuzzlewit*, 5, 36. *Reprinted, Christmas Tree.*

**QUEBEC.** The youngest Bagnet girl, so called from having been born there. *Bleak House*, 26.

**"QUEEN OF MY SOUL."** The Gentleman in Small Clothes was quoting an Anacreontique of Moore's, beginning, " Friend of my soul ! This goblet sip." *Nickleby*, 41.

**QUEEN SQUARE.** 1. Bloomsbury. This can be approached through a passage from

Southampton Row, while Guilford Street enters it on the north. Richard Carstone was established near there by Mr. Jarndyce in " a neat little furnished lodging in a quiet old house." *Bleak House*, 18.

2. Westminster. This occupied the site now covered by Queen Anne's Mansions. The Westminster Police Court was situated in it. *Reprinted, Bill Sticking.*

3. The house of Angelo Cyrus Bantam, master of ceremonies at Bath, was at No. 12 Queen Square, in that city. Near by was Mr. Harris's greengrocer's shop, now the Beaufort Arms, where the " swarry " was held. *Pickwick*, 35, 37.

**QUEER CLIENT, THE.** The subject of a story related by Jack Bamber at the Magpie and Stump. *Pickwick*, 21.

**QUEERSPECK, PROFESSOR.** A member of the Mudfog Association who exhibited a model of a portable railway.

**QUICKEAR.** One of the police in the neighbourhood of the Liverpool Docks. *Uncommercial*, 5.

**QUILP, DANIEL.** The diabolical, malignant dwarf who lent money to Nell's Grandfather and from whom the couple fled. He is a sort of evil spirit which pervades the story, ill-treating his wife, hatching conspiracies with the Brasses, leading Dick Swiveller into temptation and trying to ruin Kit Nubbles's character. Latterly he lived in a ramshackle hut on his wharf, attended by a lad of somewhat kindred spirit, Tom Scott. While making an attempt to fly thence, when tracked down by the police, he fell into the river and was drowned. Quilp's wharf was on the Surrey side, probably the old Butler's wharf below Tower Bridge, at the end of Thomas Street, now Curlew Street. His house has been identified variously as No. 6 Tower Dock, and No. 2 Tower Hill, both now demolished. *Curiosity Shop*, 3–6, 9, 11–13, 21, 23, 27, 33, 41, 48–51, 60, 62, 64, 66, 67, 73.

Mrs. Betsy Quilp, Daniel's wife and daughter of Mrs. Jiniwin, was a pretty little timid creature, terrified of her bullying husband and furtively kind to Little Nell. On her husband's death she inherited his wealth and married a man of her own choice. 3–6, 13, 21, 23, 49, 50, 67, 73.

**QUINCH, MRS.** The oldest inmate of Titbull's Almshouses. *Uncommercial*, 27.

**QUINION, MR.** Murdstone and Grinby's manager, to whose care David was committed when he entered the warehouse. A kind enough man, he was unable to do much for the lad, beyond handing him over to Mr. Micawber. *Copperfield*, 2, 10–12.

# R

**RACHAEL.** 1. The faithful friend of Stephen Blackpool, who was unable to marry her as he could not be freed from his own drunken wife. Rachael championed his cause when Stephen was accused of theft ; she looked after the dissolute drab who wrecked his home, and when Stephen did not appear to clear his name, it was Rachael who divined that something had happened, and, with Sissy Jupe, found him lying down the Old Hell Shaft. *Hard Times*, I, 10–13 ; II, 4, 6 ; III, 4–7, 9.

2. Mrs. Rachel was the name of Esther Summerson's nurse before she married Chadband. (*q.v.*)

**RADDLE, MRS. MARY ANN.** Sister of Mrs. Cluppins and landlady of Bob Sawyer's rooms in Lant Street. She was a fierce little woman who led her husband a dog's life. *Pickwick*, 32, 46.

**RADFOOT, GEORGE.** Third mate on the vessel which brought John Harmon home, and singularly like him in appearance. He drugged and robbed Harmon, but met his own death at the time, his body being found by Hexam and identified as that of Harmon. *Mutual Friend*, II, 12, 13.

**RAGS.** One of Miss Flite's captive birds. *Bleak House*, 14.

**RAILWAY SIGNALS.** *See* Signal Lights.

**RAINBIRD, ALICE.** The schoolgirl bride of Bob Redforth, who wrote the romance of the Princess Alicia and the Fairy Grandmarina. *Holiday Romance.*

**RAINBOW TAVERN, FLEET STREET.** This former resort of " old boys " is one of the oldest taverns in London, though the interior has been rebuilt. It was the second coffee house started in London, and dates from 1656. *Boz, Characters*, 7.

**RAIRYGANOO, SALLY.** One of Mrs. Lirriper's maids, strongly suspected of an Irish ancestry. *Lirriper's Legacy.*

**RAM CHOWDAR.** An Oriental potentate who formed the subject of Captain Helves's unfinished story. *Boz, Tales, Excursion.*

**RAMES, WILLIAM.** Second mate of the *Golden Mary*, whom Steadiman left in command of the shipwrecked survivors. *Golden Mary.*

**" RAM-PAGE."** Mrs. Gargery's condition when arming herself with Tickler " She made a grab at Tickler and she Rampaged out . . . she's on the Ram-page." *Expectations*, 2.

**RAMPART, SIR CHARLES.** Commanding officer of Mr. Tibbs's volunteer regiment. *Boz, Tales, Boarding House.*

**RAMSEY.** " A seedy-looking customer," against whom Dodson and Fogg issued a writ. *Pickwick*, 20.

**RAMSGATE.** Considered by the Tuggses " just the place of all others," Ramsgate has been popular with Londoners ever since steamboats began to run there, shortly after 1816. The Tuggs' adventures there are described in *Boz, Tales, Tuggs's.* Mrs. Parsons's mother was at Ramsgate when her daughter got married. *Boz, Tales, Tottle.*

**RAPPERS.** At one time a popular name for Spiritualists or spirit rappers. *Holly Tree.*

**RARX, MR.** One of the passengers on the *Golden Mary*, who lost his reason during the spell in the long boat.

**RATCATCHER'S DAUGHTER.** This was a song, very popular about 1846, beginning :—

> In Westminster not long ago
> There lived a ratcatcher's daughter.

The catchy air to which this was set was adapted to various dances. *Reprinted, Out of Season.*

**RATCLIFF.** Described in 1831 as a large hamlet, it was even then a fairly rough quarter, frequented by such as Nancy, who had been living there before she went to Field Lane (*Twist*, 13). The Highway, now called St. George's Street, is described in *Boz, Scenes*, 21, and by the *Uncommercial Traveller*, 30, who passed through the neighbourhood many years later. The Cautious Clara was lying hard by Ratcliff when Florence was taken to consult with Bunsby. *Dombey*, 23.

**RAVENDER, WILLIAM GEORGE.** Captain of the *Golden Mary*, who died of privation in the Long Boat.

**RAYBROCK.** Mrs. Raybrock was Post-mistress of Steepways Village. She had two sons, Alfred, a fisherman, and Hugh, a sailor, who was supposed to have been lost at sea, but whose message was brought to England by Captain Jorgan, who was able to clear up the misunderstandings and troubles by the *Message from the Sea.*

**RAYMOND, COUSIN.** Husband of Camilla, and one of the toadies who hung around Miss Havisham. *Expectations*, 11, 25.

**RAYMOND AND AGNES.** This was a well-known two-act drama which appeared about 1825. *Holly Tree.*

**READING.** Miss Donny's school, at Green-leaf House, was in Reading. *Bleak House*, 3.

**RECRUITING SERGEANT.** The roy-stering soldier with whom Joe Willett enlisted. *Barnaby*, 31, 58.

**REDBURN, JACK.** Master Humphrey's intimate friend and one of the original members of his circle. The worthy old man left Jack and the Deaf Gentleman all his goods and a handsome legacy upon which the two old fellows lived for the remainder of their lives. *Humphrey.*

**REDFORTH, BOB.** William Tinkling's cousin, and husband of Miss Alice Rainbird (aged seven). He relates a stirring pirate yarn in the *Holiday Romance.*

**RED-HEADED MAN, THE.** The sceptical keeper of the roadside public-house where the Pickwickians sought help with their restive steeds. *Pickwick*, 5.

**REDLAW.** The chemist and scientific lecturer whose musings on Christmas Eve conjured a spectre which robbed him of all memory of the past, with its happinesses and sorrows. This dangerous gift, full of incalculable mischief, he communicated to others, and only the goodness of Milly Swidger brought Redlaw and his victims to their senses again. *Haunted Man.*

**"RED RUFFIAN, RETIRE."** This was probably a fictitious song title. *Boz, Characters*, 8.

**RED 'US.** The Red House was a familiar Cockney resort until 1850. It was a riverside public-house, situated in Battersea, prac-tically on the site now occupied by the Victoria Bridge. Pigeon shooting was carried on in the grounds, and the house was a favourite winning post for boat races. *Boz, Scenes*, 10.

**REGENT'S CANAL.** Desperate after his unsuccessful wooing of Miss Lillerton, Watkins Tottle ended his woes with his life in the Regent's Canal. *Boz, Tales, Tottle.*

**REGENT STREET.** This was cut through and built in 1813–20, being originally intended as a thoroughfare between Carlton House and Regent's Park. The upper end practically followed the line of Swallow Street, a few yards of which yet remain. Regent Street, and especially the Quadrant (*q.v.*), was a favourite resort of dandies of all kinds (*Boz, Characters*, 1, 7 ; *Tales, Boarding House*). Lord Frederick Verisopht had a handsome suite of apartments in this street. *Nickleby*, 10, 26.

**REPRINTED PIECES.** Thirty-one sketches from *Household Words* were published under this title in the Library Edition of Dickens, issued by Chapman and Hall, with Bradbury and Evans, in 1858. In this work they are dealt with under their respective titles.

**REST.** One of Miss Flite's captive birds. *Bleak House*, 14.

**RESURRECTION MEN.** Also known as body snatchers, these "honest tradesmen," to use Jerry Cruncher's euphemism, dis-interred recently buried bodies with the object of selling them to surgeons and medical students for purposes of dissection. Between 1760 and 1840 the practice was very common in Britain, so common that several persons saved themselves the trouble of digging by killing the subjects themselves, e.g. Bishop and Williams, Burke and Hare. *Two Cities*, II, 14.

**REVALENTA ARABICA.** A much adver-tised quack food for nervousness, dyspepsia, etc. *Reprinted, Bill Sticking.*

**REVOLUTION OF JULY.** This event, of which Mr. Jingle had such a prophetic glimpse, occurred in Paris, July 27–30, 1830. There was some stiff street fighting, in which over 600 civilians were killed ; Charles X was forced to fly to England and Louis Philippe reigned in his stead. *Pickwick*, 2.

**REYNOLDS, MISS.** One of Miss Twinkle-ton's pupils. *Drood*, 9.

**RIAH.** An old Jew employed by Fledgeby to conduct his moneylending business in St. Mary Axe under the name of Pubsey and Co. Although almost unnaturally nobleminded, he was obliged to carry out Fledgeby's harshest orders and bear the blame upon his own shoulders, in the character of a typical, grasping Jew. Riah befriended Lizzie Hexam, for whom he obtained work in the country. Finally he left Fledgeby's service and made his home with Jenny Wren, the crippled doll's dressmaker. *Mutual Friend*, II, 5, 15 ; III, 1–3, 10, 12, 13 ; IV, 9, 16.

**RICHARD.** 1. Meg Veck's handsome young sweetheart. *Chimes.*

2. The waiter at the Saracen's head. *Nickleby*, 4.

**RICHARDS.** The name assigned, in the Dombey household, to Polly Toodle. (*q.v.*)

**RICHARDSON'S SHOW.** The travelling theatrical show described in *Boz, Scenes*, 12, was well known in the 30's and 40's at all the fairs in the south of England, especially at the two great London fairs of Greenwich and Camberwell.

**RICH FOLKS AND CAMELS.** " Rich folks may ride on camels, but it an't so easy for 'em to see out of a needle's eye. That is my comfort, and I hope I knows it." One of Mrs. Gamp's philosophical consolations. *Chuzzlewit*, 25.

**RICHMOND.** When his friends married and Mr. Pickwick settled at Dulwich, Tracy Tupman made his home at Richmond (*Pickwick*, 57). In a " staid old house " near the Green lived Mrs. Brandley and her daughter, the couple with whom Estella was sent to stay (*Expectations*, 33, 38).

**RICKITTS, MISS.** One of the pupils at Nuns' House. *Drood*, 13.

**RIDERHOOD.** Roger, better known as Rogue, was formerly Gaffer Hexam's partner, and tried to lay on him the blame of the Harmon murder in the hope of getting the reward. He was himself, however, implicated in the murderous attack, and Harmon succeeded in getting his confession of the fact to help Lizzie Hexam clear her father's memory. After an almost miraculous escape from drowning, Rogue took work as a lock-keeper on the Thames, and thus became aware of Bradley Headstone's attack on Wrayburn. Using his knowledge as a means of blackmail, Riderhood at last goaded the schoolmaster to a struggle, in which the latter dragged the Rogue into the lock, where both were drowned. *Mutual Friend*, I, 1, 6, 12–14 ; II, 12, 13, 16 ; III, 2, 3, 8, 11 ; IV, 1, 7, 15.

Pleasant Riderhood, the Rogue's daughter, kept a small unlicensed pawnbroker's shop. She was the lady who had such an aversion to Mr. Venus's business, though she subsequently conquered it and became his wife. *Mutual Friend*, I, 7 ; II, 12 ; III, 3, 7 ; IV, 14.

**RIGAUD.** Otherwise known as Blandois and Lagnier, was a blackmailer and murderer. He first appeared in prison at Marseilles, later attaching himself to the Gowans while travelling in Switzerland and Italy. Obtaining possession of the papers implicating Mrs. Clennam in the suppression of her uncle's will, Rigaud tried to blackmail her by threats of exposure. In this he did not succeed, but negotiations were going on when he met his end in the collapse of her house. *Dorrit*, I, 11, 29, 30 ; II, 1, 3, 6, 7, 9, 10, 17, 20, 22, 23, 28, 30, 31, 33.

**RINALDO DI VELASCO.** Professional name of the giant Pickleson. (*q.v.*)

**ROBERT, UNCLE.** Aunt Jane's husband and a guest at the Christmas Party. *Boz, Characters*, 2.

**ROBINS, GEORGE.** A very floury, eloquent auctioneer of the 40's and 50's, whose salerooms were in Covent Garden. He used to issue most remarkable poetical catalogues. Robins was employed to dispose of Strawberry Hill and its contents. *Boz, Tales, Boarding House.*

**ROBINSON.** 1. Mrs. Tibbs's maidservant. *Boz, Tales, Boarding House.*

2. A witty clerk in the Dombey counting-house. *Dombey*, 51.

3. The fashionable gentleman who married the youngest Miss Willis. *Boz, Our Parish*, 3.

**ROB THE GRINDER.** Polly Toodles's eldest son, also called Biler, and educated at the school of the Charitable Grinders, hence his name. He was a mean, sneaking lad, stealing when he got the chance, and addicted to bad company. He was placed by James Carker as a spy over Sol Gills and Captain Cuttle, then acted as Carker's groom and gave away the secret of where his master and Edith Dombey were to meet. He was finally taken in hand by the gentle Miss Tox. *Dombey*, 2, 5, 6, 20, 22, 23, 25, 31, 32, 38, 39, 42, 46, 52, 59.

**ROCHESTER.** This ancient city was connected with the earliest and last days of Dickens, and is so full of associations that only the most important can be dealt with here. The city also figures as the unnamed town of *Expectations*, Cloisterham and Winglebury. Rochester was the first stopping place of the Pickwickians, who put up at the Bull Inn, situated in the High Street, being warned by Jingle against going to Wright's, originally the Crown. The bridge over the Medway on which Mr. Pickwick leaned has been replaced long since by an iron erection (*Pickwick*, 2–4). Watts's Charity in the High Street still remains (*Seven Poor Travellers*), while in the same street is the magnificent old house allotted to Uncle Pumblechook (*Expectations*, 8) and Mr. Sapsea (*Drood*, 4). Almost opposite, at the corner of Eastgate, is Eastgate House, the original of the Nuns' House, kept by Miss Twinkleton (*Drood*, 3). In Crow Lane is Restoration House which, as Satis House, figures as the mysterious home of Miss Havisham. *Expectations*, 8.

**ROCKINGHAM CASTLE.** Original of Chesney Wold. (*q.v.*)

**RODOLPH, MR. AND MRS. JENNINGS.** Singers at the White Conduit House Tavern, and friends of the journeyman painter. *Boz, Characters*, 8.

**ROGERS.** 1. The bar parlour orator. *Boz, Characters*, 5.

2. A London constable. *Reprinted, Inspector Field.*

3. Johnny, an inmate of the workhouse. *Reprinted, Workhouse.*

4. Third mate of the *Halsewell* East Indiaman. *Reprinted, Long Voyage.*

5. A former friend of Mrs. Nickleby. *Nickleby*, 37.

6. Mrs. Bardell's lodger, very genteel. *Pickwick*, 46.

**ROKER, TOM.** The turnkey who arranged Mr. Pickwick's accommodation at the Fleet Prison. *Pickwick*, 40–4.

**ROKESMITH, JOHN.** Name assumed by John Harmon after his supposed murder. See Harmon, John.

**ROLLAND.** Signing clerk for Defresnier et Cie. *No Thoroughfare.*

**ROLLS YARD.** This opened out of Chancery Lane through Rolls Passage, opposite Chichester Rents, and there Mr. Snagsby used to wander, enjoying the calm of the summer evenings. *Bleak House*, 10, 19.

**ROOKERY, THE.** 1. Among the slums of London there was probably none to equal the Rookery of St. Giles, now happily wiped off the face of the earth. It is admirably described in *Reprinted, Inspector Field, Boz, Scenes*, 22. The Rookery was mostly swept away in the making of New Oxford Street, 1844–7, which was cut right through the foul alleys and tumbledown houses which lay to the north of High Street and Broad Street.

2. The name was given by Mr. Copperfield, much to the indignation of Miss Betsey Trotwood, to the house at Blunderstone. "Calls a house a Rookery when there's not a rook near it." It was either the Rectory or the Hall at Blundeston. *Copperfield*, 1.

**ROSA.** The "dark-eyed, shy village beauty," whom Mrs. Rouncewell took to train in service. Her beauty and manners attracted the attention of Lady Dedlock, who made Rosa her confidential maid, thereby incurring the fatal anger of Hortense. Young Watt Rouncewell fell in love with Rosa who, after a struggle, left the Dedlocks and eventually married him. *Bleak House*, 7, 12, 16, 18, 28, 40, 41, 48, 63.

**ROSE.** 1. The surgeon's fiancée. *Boz, Tales, Black Veil.*

2. Cousin to Lucy Benson, and one of the *Village Coquettes.*

**ROSS.** 1. Frank, one of Gabriel Parson's friends. *Boz, Tales, Tottle.*

2. Captain Ross (later Sir John) returned from his voyage in search of the north-west passage in October, 1833, after great adventures in which his boat, the *Victory*, was abandoned. The following month, December 4, an "authenticated drama" of his voyage, in which occurred an Indian ballet, terrific broad-sword fighting and the popular song of Cork Legs, was produced at the Pavilion Theatre, Whitechapel. Early in 1834 a mild version of this, ostensibly of an instructive nature was presented at Vauxhall Gardens. *Boz, Tales, Boarding House; Sparkins.*

**ROTUNDA, THE.** This was the large music room, later called the Grecian Saloon, at the Eagle Tavern, City Road. *Boz, Characters*, 4.

**ROUNCEWELL.** Mrs. Rouncewell was the Dedlock's housekeeper at Chesney Wold, "a fine old lady, handsome and stately." Her heart always mourned over her scapegrace son, who had gone to be a soldier, and thanks to Mrs. Bagnet she found him again, as Trooper George. *Bleak House*, 7, 12, 16, 26, 28, 34, 40, 52, 55, 56, 58, 63, 66.

Her eldest son was a successful ironmaster, whose son Watt fell in love with Rosa, Lady Dedlock's maid. 7, 12, 18, 28, 40, 48, 63.

George Rouncewell was the younger son, who ran away for a soldier. *See* George.

**ROVER.** A young rake in O'Keefe's play, *Wild Oats*. He thinks vice is "naughty, but yet nice." *Nickleby*, 23.

**ROWLAND'S OIL.** *See* Macassar.

**ROYAL CHARTER.** A vessel bound from Melbourne to Liverpool, which was wrecked off Llanallgo, Anglesey, October 26, 1859. *Uncommercial*, 2.

**ROYAL EXCHANGE.** The old Exchange, associated with *Boz* and the earlier novels, faced Cornhill. It was built after the Great Fire (1666), and was itself burned down, January 10, 1838. With the erection of the new building, opened in 1844, Cornhill was widened, Freeman's Court and other alleys disappeared, and the space before the Mansion House was considerably enlarged. *Boz, Tales, Sparkins; Christmas Carol; Nickleby*, 41; *Dombey*, 5, 56; *Expectations*, 22; *Chuzzlewit*, 8, 27, 36; *Dorrit*, I, 29.

**ROYAL GEORGE HOTEL, DOVER.** This was the inn where Mr. Lorry put up, being shown into the Concord room. The original was probably the King's Head Hotel. *Two Cities*, I, 4.

**ROYLANCE, MRS.** Original of Mrs. Pipchin (*q.v.*). *See also* Great College Street.

**RUDGE.** Barnaby Rudge was the wild, half-witted lad from whom the novel takes its name. With his raven, Grip, he wandered about the roads between Chigwell and London. On the outbreak of the Gordon Riots, Barnaby left his broken-hearted mother and, joining his friend Hugh of the Maypole, took a prominent part in some of the leading incidents. He was arrested and sentenced to death, but was reprieved through the endeavours of Gabriel Varden, finally settling in the country and refusing ever to see London again. *Barnaby*, 3–6, 10–12, 17, 24, 25, 42, 45–50, 52, 53, 57, 58, 60, 62, 65, 68, 69, 73, 76, 77, 79, 82.

Mary Rudge, Barnaby's mother, was the supposed widow of Rudge, the Haredale's steward. She was worried and driven from place to place in her frantic endeavours to get away and hide from her murderer-husband, being constantly helped and be-friended by Gabriel Varden. When the Riots were over and her son restored to her they settled on the Maypole farm. 4–6, 10, 16, 17, 24–6, 42, 45–50, 57, 62, 69, 73, 76, 79, 82.

Rudge, the steward who murdered his master, Reuben Haredale, passes in sinister fashion through the book. Supposed to have been murdered with his master, he lived a hunted life, every now and again pestering his wife for money she could ill-afford to give him. He was caught by Geoffrey Haredale on the scene of the murder, his guilt was proved, he was taken to Newgate and put in a cell with his son. He was eventually hanged. 1–3, 5, 6, 16–18, 26, 33, 45, 46, 55, 56, 61, 62, 65, 68, 69, 73, 76.

**RUGG.** Pancks's landlord and a general agent and accountant. He helped trace out the Dorrit fortune, and was employed by Clennam to look after his affairs when he was imprisoned for debt in the Marshalsea (*Dorrit*, I, 25, 32, 35, 36 ; II, 26, 28, 32, 34). His daughter, Miss Anastasia Rugg, had acquired a little property by means of a successful breach of promise action against a middle-aged baker named Hawkins. I, 25 ; II, 26, 28.

**RUIN.** One of Miss Flite's captive birds. *Bleak House*, 14.

**RULES.** The rules of the debtors' prisons were certain areas surrounding the prisons where, on payment of fees, prisoners were allowed to live. The practice originated as a remedy to overcrowding, but it was done away with in 1835. *Boz, Scenes*, 21. *Nickleby*, 46.

**RUMMUN, PROF.** A member of the Mudfog Association.

**RUMTY.** The name given by fellow clerks to R. Wilfer. (*q.v.*)

**RUSHLIGHT.** A form of tallow candle with a wick made of the pith of a rush. It gave a very feeble, glimmering light.

**RUSSELL SQUARE.** This was formerly a favourite residence of well-to-do merchants. *Boz, Characters*, 1.

**RUSSIAN PRINCE, THE.** One of Miss Mowcher's clients. *Copperfield*, 22.

# S

**SACKVILLE STREET.** Mr. Lammle as a bachelor had lived in this fashionable and central street off Piccadilly; as a married man he put up with it until some more palatial place could be found. *Mutual Friend*, I, 10 ; II, 4 ; III, 17.

**SADLER'S WELLS THEATRE.** Before the making of Rosebery Avenue, Sadler's Wells Theatre was approached from the St. John's Street Road. It has a long and interesting history, was associated with Grimaldi the clown, 1819–28, with T. P. Cooke, in *Black-Eyed Susan*, 1832, and with Samuel Phelps, 1844–62. It is now a cinema. *Boz, Scenes*, 13 ; *Twist*, 8.

**SADLEIR, JOHN.** Original of Merdle. (*q.v.*)

**SAFFRON HILL.** Before the alterations caused in that vicinity by the construction of Holborn Viaduct (1867), Saffron Hill was the continuation of Field Lane beyond Charles Street, and ran only as far as Ray Street, now approximately Clerkenwell Road. The district is closely associated with Fagin and his nest of thieves (*Twist*, 8, 15, 26). Phil Squod worked the Hill as part of his beat. *Bleak House*, 26.

**SAGGERS, MISS.** An elderly inmate of Titbull's Almshouses. *Uncommercial*, 27.

**ST. ALBANS.** Dickens was a frequent visitor to this ancient city, in the vicinity of which he placed Bleak House (which was probably at the top of Gombard's Road), and some of the scenes of that novel. Bill Sikes was making his way thither when his courage failed him and he turned back to London to meet his death (*Twist*, 48). Other references are *Copperfield*, 24 ; *Uncommercial*, 11.

**ST. ANDREW'S, HOLBORN.** This church was on the level of Holborn Hill, and is chiefly mentioned on account of its clock (*Twist*, 21 ; *Copperfield*, 25 ; *Bleak House*, 10). The father of the Bill-sticking king was engineer, beadle and billsticker of St. Andrew's parish in 1780. *Reprinted, Bill Sticking*.

**SAINT ANTOINE.** The poor quarter of Paris, near the Bastille, where the Revolutionary agitation arose and was carried into action. Most of the Parisian scenes of *Two Cities* are in that quarter.

**ST. BARTHOLOMEW'S HOSPITAL.** Mr. Jack Hopkins was a student at Bart's (*Pickwick*, 32), while Mrs. Betsey Prig appears to have been a casual nurse there (*Chuzzlewit*, 25, 49). After his accident, John Baptist Cavaletto was taken to the hospital, where he was tended by a skilful surgeon. *Dorrit*, I, 13.

**ST. CLEMENT DANES.** In this church Mrs. Lirriper was married and later had her own sitting, with genteel company and her own hassock. *Lirriper's Lodgings*.

**ST. CLEMENT'S, IPSWICH.** Sam Weller met Job Trotter outside Mr. Nupkins's green gate in a kind of courtyard of venerable appearance near St. Clement's. Local tradition points out the identical gate adjoining the churchyard, close to Church Street. *Pickwick*, 23, 25.

**ST. DUNSTAN'S, FLEET STREET.** The old church, replaced by the present structure in 1831, jutted out into Fleet Street and was a dangerous block to the traffic. Its clock was one of the sights of London, having a large gilt dial overhanging the street, surmounted by two wooden figures, each of which struck the hours on a bell, at the same time moving its head. This clock was removed to the Marquis of Hertford's house in Regent's Park, now St. Dunstan's Institute for the Blind. David Copperfield and his aunt watched the giants strike noon (*Copperfield*, 23) as in former days Hugh of the Maypole had done (*Barnaby*, 40). Beneath the tower of the present church Trotty Veck had his porter's stand, and the bells in the church tower are those immortalised in the *Chimes*.

**ST. EVREMONDE.** The family name of Charles Darnay. The marquis, Charles's uncle, trampled the child of a Parisian labourer beneath his carriage wheels and drove on, careless of what he had done. In revenge the father followed him to the country and there stabbed him. In the trial of Charles Darnay before the Revolutionary tribunal, it transpired that Dr. Manette's long imprisonment was due to having offended the St. Evremonde family. *Two Cities*, II, 7–9 ; III, 10.

**ST. GEORGE'S CHURCH.** 1. St. George's Southwark, adjoining the Marshalsea, was the church where Little Dorrit was christened; on the steps of which she waited with Maggie one night ; and where she was married. *Dorrit*, I, 6, 14 ; II, 34.

2. The church of this name at Camberwell, built in 1830, has been mentioned as the possible scene of Wemmick's wedding. *Expectations*, 55.

3. At St. George's, Hart Street, Bloomsbury, was christened Frederick Charles William Kitterbell. *Boz, Tales, Christening*.

**ST. GEORGE'S FIELDS.** The name was somewhat vaguely applied to the district centring round the Obelisk, and comprised roughly the area between (the present) Newington Causeway, Gravel Lane, Charlotte Street, Lambeth Marsh, Westminster Bridge Road and St. George's Road. The open fields, which were somewhat of a marsh, were rallying places for the Gordon Rioters (*Barnaby*, 48). As the place was built over its proximity to the Borough prisons kept it a low neighbourhood, frequented by people of the Solomon Pell type (*Pickwick*, 43) and dwellers in the rules of the King's Bench Prison. *Nickleby*, 46.

**ST. GEORGE'S GALLERY.** This stood at the beginning of Knightsbridge, almost on the site now occupied by the Hyde Park Corner Tube Station. It was built in 1842 for Dunn's Chinese Collection, and was sometimes known as the Chinese Gallery. *Reprinted, Noble Savage*.

**ST. GHASTLY GRIM.** A descriptive name for St. Olave's in Hart Street, where Samuel Pepys and his wife are buried. *Uncommercial*, 21.

**ST. GILES.** This church was formerly in the heart of that notorious slumland, which included the Rookery and Seven Dials. The neighbourhood with its gin shops and poverty is described in *Boz, Scenes*, 5, 22 ; *Reprinted, Inspector Field* ; *Uncommercial*, 10. Sampson and Sally Brass are last seen in this sink of humanity. *Curiosity Shop*, 73.

**ST. JAMES'S, PICCADILLY.** Here were married Alfred Lammle and Sophronia Akershem. *Mutual Friend*, I, 10.

**ST. JAMES'S PARK.** Walking along this park one evening Ralph Nickleby was caught in a thunderstorm, and while sheltering was accosted by his old accomplice, Brooker (*Nickleby*, 44). Here, too, Martin took his final farewell of Mary Graham before going to America (*Chuzzlewit*, 14). Clennam, Meagles and Daniel Doyce unburdened themselves in the Park after leaving the Circumlocution Office (*Dorrit*, I, 10). It was darkly whispered that Sally Brass had enlisted in the Guards and been seen in a sentry-box in St. James's Park. *Curiosity Shop*, 73.

**ST. JAMES'S SQUARE.** This square has changed little since Bailey Junior drove round it at a gallop (*Chuzzlewit*, 27). Here Twemlow used to meditate as to his actual status in the number of Veneering's friends (*Mutual*, I, 2). There was formerly a pond in the centre of the square, into which the Gordon Rioters threw valuables (*Barnaby*, 70) as well as the keys of Newgate, which were not found until many years later.

**ST. JAMES'S STREET.** Near the corner of this street and Piccadilly were the chambers occupied by the narrator of the Trial for Murder (*Two Ghost Stories*) ; in an hotel further down Mr. Josiah Bounderby was staying when Mrs. Sparsit hastened to acquaint him with Louisa's elopement. *Hard Times*, III, 3.

**ST. JAMES'S THEATRE.** This was the house at which most of Dickens's early plays were produced. It was opened in 1835, and the season of 1836 began (Sept. 29) with the *Strange Gentleman*, followed on December 9 by *The Village Coquettes, Is She His Wife?* being produced March 6 of the following year. From 1841–52 it was leased by Mitchell for a series of French plays, acted by the stars of the Paris stage. *Reprinted, A Flight*.

**ST. JOHN'S ROAD.** Now known throughout its length as St. John's Street, this thoroughfare was formerly called St. John's Street Road from Islington to the corner of Perceval Street, and St. John's Street, thence to Smithfield. Oliver and the Artful Dodger made their way to Field Lane along this street. *Twist*, 8, 42.

**ST. JULIEN, HORATIO.** The stage name of Mr. Jem Larkins. *Boz, Scenes*, 13.

**ST. LUKE'S WORKHOUSE.** This, the home of the " Orfling," stood at the corner of Shepherdess Walk and City Road. *Copperfield*, 11.

**ST. MARTIN'S-IN-THE-FIELDS.** Before the making of Trafalgar Square, 1829–41, St. Martin's Lane ran as a narrow thoroughfare in front of the church. On the steps of the portico David Copperfield ran across Peggotty during his search for Em'ly (*Copperfield*, 40), and a horrible experience on these same steps is related in *Uncommercial*, 13. Behind the church was a courtyard, demolished in the making of Adelaide Place, where little David found a special currant pudding shop. *Copperfield*, 11.

**ST. MARY AXE** is now full of modern offices, and the premises of Pubsey and Co., are no longer discernible. *Mutual Friend*, II, 5 ; III, 1.

**ST. PANCRAS.** The old church, in the yard of which Roger Cly was supposedly buried, is in the Pancras Road, some distance to the back of the railway station. It was almost entirely rebuilt in 1848 (*Two Cities*, II, 14 ; III, 8). New St. Pancras, the familiar building in Euston Road, was built in 1819–22. Its clock gave the time to Mrs. Tibbs and the *Boarding House*. *Boz, Tales*.

**ST. PAUL'S.** Needless to remark, the casual references to the cathedral are innumerable. The principal are *Barnaby*, 22 ; *Nickleby*, 3, 39, 45 ; *Boz, Scenes*, 3 ; *Copperfield*, 4, 33 ; *Expectations*, 20 ; *Chuzzlewit*, 38 ; *Humphrey* ; *Mutual Friend*, III, 1, 10 ; *Dombey*, 48 ; *Dorrit*, I, 3 ; II, 34 ; *Twist*, 18 ; *Bleak House*, 19. Paul's Churchyard, out of which opened Doctors' Commons, was the scene of Miss Trotwood's meeting with her husband (*Copperfield*, 23). Other references are *Barnaby*, 37 ; *Mutual Friend*, I, 8.

**ST. PETER'S.** This church, in Cornhill, was the scene of Bradley Headstone's passionate pleading with Lizzie Hexam to be his wife. *Mutual Friend*, II, 15.

**SALCY, FAMILY P.** A company of French actors in the French-Flemish country. *Uncommercial*, 25.

**SALEM HOUSE.** The school, kept by Creakle, where David was first educated and made the acquaintance of Steerforth and Traddles. The site, near Blackheath, is unknown, but the original of the school was Wellington House Academy, at the corner of Hampstead Road and Granby Street, where Dickens was a pupil from 1824–6. This was kept by a William Jones (Creakle) and figures as *Our School* (*Reprinted*). Portion of the house has been demolished for railway construction, but the greater part still remains. *Copperfield*, 5–7, 9, 13.

**SALISBURY.** This peaceful Wiltshire city is hallowed by memories of Tom Pinch. The cathedral and market-place are carefully described, while the famous old inn where John Westlock entertained Tom and young Martin was probably the White Hart, St. John's Street, still the best in the city. *Chuzzlewit*, 2, 5, 12, 36, 44.

**SALISBURY ARMS.** The Hatfield Inn patronised by Mr. Lirriper and his brother. It is now a private house. *Lirriper's Lodgings*.

**SALLY.** 1. Niece of Uncle Bill. *Boz, Scenes*, 9.

2. The workhouse inmate who assisted at the birth of Oliver Twist and robbed his dead mother. *Twist*, 1, 23, 24.

3. Compeyson's wife. *Expectations*, 42.

**SALWANNERS.** John Willett's rendering of Savannas. " At the defence of the Salwanners, in America, where the war is," became a favourite saying of his, and his last words were, " I'm a going, Joseph, to the Salwanners." *Barnaby*, 72, 82.

**SAM.** 1. Mr. Pecksniff's stableman. *Chuzzlewit*, 5.

2. The cabman with whom Mr. Pickwick had a " row " at the Golden Cross Hotel. *Pickwick*, 2.

**SAMPSON.** 1. The insurance manager who relates the story of *Hunted Down*.

2. George, the young man who hung round Lavinia Wilfer, having lost his chance of getting Bella. A remarkable youth, sat upon by everybody, especially by Mrs. Wilfer, his attitude of respect mixed with indignation towards that lady, and of hopeless devotion to Lavinia, made him a fitting member of the Wilfer circle. *Mutual Friend*, I, 4, 9 ; II, 14 ; III, 4, 16 ; IV, 5, 16.

**SAMSON.** The chief executioner during the French Revolution. Some spurious memoirs were later published under his name. *Two Cities*, III, 9.

**SANDERS, MRS. SUSANNAH.** Mrs. Bardell's particular friend, who gave evidence at the trial, remarking that Mr. S. had often called her a " duck," but never " tomata sauce." *Pickwick*, 26, 34, 46.

**SANDFORD AND MERTON.** This well-known children's book, by Thomas Day, appeared in 1783–9. It plays off selfish Tommy Merton against Harry Sandford, the model of all a boy should be. *Uncommercial*, 33.

**SANDLING.** *See* Dingley Dell ; Manor Farm ; Wardle.

**SAPSEA, THOMAS.** The bombastic auctioneer at Cloisterham, who dressed at the Dean and introduced something of an ecclesiastical manner into his auction sales. He married Miss Brobity, a schoolmistress, who was so overcome with the honour of his proposal that she could only murmur, in reply, "Oh Thou." After her death, Sapsea erected a monument with the following egregious inscription :—

Ethelinda,
Reverential Wife of
MR. THOMAS SAPSEA,
Auctioneer, Valuer, Estate Agent, &c.,
Of this city,
Whose knowledge of the World,
Though somewhat extensive,
Never brought him acquainted with
A Spirit
More capable of
Looking up to him.
STRANGER, PAUSE
And ask thyself the Question,
CANST THOU DO LIKEWISE?
If not,
WITH A BLUSH RETIRE.

Sapsea's House was the magnificent old timbered house in Rochester High Street. *Drood*, 4, 6, 12, 14–16, 18.

**SARACEN'S HEAD.** 1. The well-known coaching house stood at the top of Snow Hill, adjoining St. Sepulchre's Church. It was one of the finest examples of the old London inn, but was pulled down in 1868. The building (now offices) lower down the hill, embellished with a bust of Dickens and several reliefs, has no connection whatever with the old inn. The Saracen's Head was Squeers's headquarters in London, where he collected his pupils and started for Yorkshire ; there, too, the Browdies put up on their honeymoon. *Nickleby*, 4, 39, 42, 43.

2. The Towcester Inn, where Mr. Pickwick, Ben Allen, Bob Sawyer and Sam Weller put up on their return journey from Birmingham. "Everything looked (as everything always does, in all decent English inns) as if the travellers had been expected, and their comforts prepared, for days beforehand." There they met Mr. Pott, editor of the *Eatanswill Gazette*, between whom and Slurk, of the rival *Independent*, who arrived later in the evening, a terrific battle took place. The Saracen's Head changed its name in 1831 to the Pomfret Arms, but otherwise shows little sign of the century which has elapsed since those heroic doings. *Pickwick*, 51.

**SARAH.** 1. A jealous lady of Seven Dials. *Boz, Scenes*, 5.

2. Maidservants of the Old Lady (*Boz, Our Parish*, 2) ; Westgate House. *Pickwick*, 16.

**SATIS HOUSE.** The original of Miss Havisham's mysterious dwelling was Restoration House, Crow Lane, Rochester. This is a fine Tudor mansion, taking its name from the fact of Charles II having slept there on his triumphal return to London. *Expectations*, 8, 9, 11–13, 15, 19, 29, 38, 44, 49, 59.

**SAUNDERS.** A visitor of the Couple who Dote on Their Children. *Sketches of Couples*.

**SAVANNAH.** The defence of Savannah, at which Joe Willett lost his arm, was in the American War of Independence. Savannah was captured by the British, December 20, 1778, and was subsequently besieged by a combined force of Americans and French. *Barnaby*, 72.

**SAWYER, BOB.** A medical student at Guy's Hospital, and Ben Allen's boon companion. He lived at Mrs. Raddle's, in Lant Street, where he held a bachelor's party which would have proved a success had not his landlady taken umbrage at the non-payment of her rent. Having passed his medical examination, Bob bought the practice of Nockemorf, at Bristol. It had been arranged between the friends that he should marry Ben Allen's sister Arabella. Having been forestalled in this by Mr. Winkle, Bob accompanied his friend and Mr. Pickwick to Birmingham to reconcile Winkle, Senior, to the match. Finally, having passed through the *Gazette*, Bob and his friend went to Bengal and started life afresh. *Pickwick*, 30, 32, 38, 39, 47, 48, 50–2, 57.

**SAWYER.** A baker who was murdered by his son. *Bolton*.

**SAXBY, LONG.** A friend of Cousin Feenix—"Six foot ten." *Dombey*, 51.

**SCADDER, ZEPHANIAH.** The real estate swindler who induced Martin Chuzzlewit to embark his whole capital in purchasing land in the flourishing city of Eden, which turned out to be a malarial swamp. Scadder was one of a type of rascal common in America when the development of the country was proceeding apace. *Chuzzlewit*, 21.

**SCADGERS, LADY.** Mrs. Sparsit's great aunt, bedridden for fourteen years. *Hard Times*, I, 7 ; II, 8 ; III, 9.

**SCALEY.** The bailiff sent in possession at Madame Mantalini's. *Nickleby*, 21.

**SCARBOROUGH.** At this seaside resort Meltham, disguised as a Major Banks, watched Slinkton with his niece and intended victim, Margaret Niner. *Hunted Down*.

**SCHOOLBOY'S STORY, THE.** This pleasant little sketch appeared in the Christmas number of *Household Words*, 1853, and in *Reprinted Pieces*, 1858. It tells of Old Cheeseman, sent to Coventry by the school, but befriended by Jane Pitt, the wardrobe woman, whom he marries.

**SCHUTZ.** One of the *Halsewell's* passengers. *Reprinted, Long Voyage*.

**SCIENTIFIC GENTLEMAN, THE.** An elderly gentleman at Clifton, who drew remarkable scientific deductions from his observation of the flashing of Mr. Pickwick's lantern. *Pickwick*, 39.

**SCOTLAND YARD.** This originally consisted of Great, Middle and Little or Inner Scotland Yard, extending in all from Northumberland House to Whitehall Place. The locality before the establishment of the Metropolitan Police Force there, in 1829, is well described in *Boz, Scenes*, 4. The whole site has been altered beyond recognition.

**SCOTT, TOM.** An impish lad employed at Quilp's wharf. He was full of extraordinary contortions and antics which, after Quilp's death, he put to practical use by going on the stage as an Italian tumbler. *Curiosity Shop*, 4–6, 11, 13, 49–51, 67, 73.

**SCREW, THE.** The vessel in which Martin and Mark Tapley crossed to, and returned from, America. *Chuzzlewit*, 15–17, 34, 35.

**SCREWZER, TOMMY.** A friend of Cousin Feenix—"man of an extremely bilious habit." *Dombey*, 61.

**SCROGGINS, GILES.** The ballad of Giles Scroggins's Ghost related the dream of a young country girl whose lover died just before their marriage. It began :—

Giles Scroggins courted Molly Brown,
    Fol de riddle, lol de riddle, lido,
The fairest wench in all the town.
                                *Haunted House.*

**SCROO.** A member of the Mudfog Association.

**SCROOGE, EBENEZER.** "A squeezing, grasping, scraping, clutching, covetous old sinner," the surviving partner of the firm of Scrooge and Marley. His dream adventures and consequent conversion form the subject of *Christmas Carol.* (*q.v.*)

**SCUTTLEWIG, DUKE OF.** An intimate friend of the Egotistical Young Couple. *Sketches of Couples.*

**SEAMSTRESS, THE.** A young girl with whom Sydney Carton travelled in the tumbril to the guillotine. *Two Cities*, III, 13, 15.

**SEARLE'S YARD.** This boat-building yard, in the days of *Boz, Scenes*, 10, was by Westminster Bridge, on the shore now covered by the Albert Embankment and St. Thomas's Hospital.

**SEDAN CHAIR.** An enclosed arm-chair carried between two poles passed through rings on either side. The door was in front, and the top was usually hinged, originally for the convenience of ladies wearing the high headdresses of Georgian times. Sedan chairs lingered in the country for some time after they had disappeared from the London streets. *Pickwick*, 24, 35, 36.

**"SEE FROM OCEAN RISING."** This once popular duet was taken from Mazzinghi's opera, *Paul and Virginia. Boz, Tales, Excursion; Dorrit*, I, 13.

**SENS.** "A pretty little town with a great two-towered cathedral," where Mrs. Lirriper, Major Jackman and little Jemmy went to see Edson on his death bed, and receive *Mrs. Lirriper's Legacy.*

**SERAPHINA.** Heroine of little Jemmy Lirriper's tale. *Lirriper's Lodgings.*

**SERJEANT'S INN.** There were two Serjeant's Inns : one still exists behind a modern frontage, in Fleet Street ; the other was four houses up Chancery Lane, on the right hand side. It was closed in 1877 and demolished soon afterwards. The former ceased to be an inn of court in 1730, hence it was to the vanished building that Perker and Mr. Pickwick repaired before the latter

was committed to the Fleet (*Pickwick*, 40). It is also mentioned in *Bleak House*, 19.

**SETTING MOON, COMMERCIAL ROAD.** This public-house was the scene of Serjeant Mith's arrest of the Butcher. *Reprinted, Detective Police.*

**SEVEN DIALS.** Though the spot with its seven converging streets still remains, easiest approached up St. Martin's Lane and Great St. Andrew Street, it has been cleansed and made comparatively respectable since the days of *Boz, Scenes*, 5. The alterations consequent on the cutting of Shaftesbury Avenue, 1885, and the general improvement of housing conditions, have helped to clear up what was one of London's worst slums. It was near Seven Dials that Mr. Mantalini was last seen, working at the mangle. *Nickleby*, 64.

**SEVEN POOR TRAVELLERS.** This very delightful story, centring round the Watts's Charity and incorporating the tale of Richard Doubledick, appeared as the Christmas number of *Household Words*, 1854.

**SEXTON.** 1. The old sexton at the village where Nell and her Grandfather made their home. *Curiosity Shop*, 53–5, 70, 72.

2. The old man at St. George's, Southwark, who was proud of showing Little Dorrit's name in the register. *Dorrit*, I, 14 ; II, 35.

3. The two men connected with the christening of Little Paul Dombey, and the marriage of Florence. *Dombey*, 5, 57.

**SEYMOUR, ROBERT.** (1800–36.) This artist had already made his reputation for comic drawings when Messrs. Chapman and Hall asked Dickens to provide the letterpress for some sporting plates which Seymour was to do. Thus originated *Pickwick*. Seymour had, however, only provided plates for the first two numbers when he shot himself, April 20, 1836.

**SHADWELL.** Lying up at a wharf near Shadwell Church was the Amazon emigrant ship with its 800 Mormons, whom the *Uncommercial Traveller* visited (20). It was in Shadwell that Dickens obtained material for the opium den scenes in *Drood*, 1, 23.

**SHANKLIN.** Dickens spent part of June, 1849, in this pleasant seaside town, and subsequently placed the scene of the Lammle's mutual disillusionment on Shanklin sands. *Mutual Friend*, I, 10.

**SHARP, MR.** Principal assistant master at Salem House School. *Copperfield*, 6, 7, 9.

**SHARPEYE.** An efficient member of the Liverpool Police Force. *Uncommercial*, 5.

**SHAW, WILLIAM.** Original of Wackford Squeers. (*q.v.*)

**SHEEPSKIN.** One of Miss Flite's captive birds. *Bleak House*, 14.

**SHEPHERD, MISS.** A boarder at Miss Nettingall's school, " a little girl in a spencer with a round face and curly flaxen hair," who was the first to win David's heart. *Copperfield*, 18.

**SHEPHERD, THE.** "A great fat chap in black . . . smilin' avay like clockwork." One of Mrs. Weller's spiritual advisers. *Pickwick*, 22, 27.

**SHEPHERDSON.** The butcher thief, whose arrest formed the subject of Serjeant Mith's story. *Reprinted, Detective Police.*

**SHEPHERD'S SHORE.** *See* Inn (1); Marlborough Downs.

**"SHE SHALL WALK."** A Swivellerian version of the song by Susanna Blamire, beginning :—

And ye shall walk in silk attire and siller ha'e to spare,
Gin ye'll consent to be my bride, nor think on Donald
mair.        *Curiosity Shop*, 66.

**"SHE'S LIKE THE RED, RED ROSE."** Dick Swiveller's adaptation of Burns's "My love is like a red, red rose." *Curiosity Shop*, 8.

**SHINY VILLIAM.** Deputy hostler at the Rochester Bull. *Pickwick*, 5.

**SHIP, THE.** The riverside public-house where Pip and his friends put up while hiding from the police was the Ship and Lobster Inn, less than a mile down river from Gravesend. *Expectations*, 54.

**SHIP TAVERN, CHANCERY LANE.** *See* Sol's Arms.

**"SHIVERY SHAKEY."** This is part of the chorus of a very popular comic song of 1851, called "The Man who couldn't get Warm," words by J. Beuler, music by J. Clinton. It is about an Indian merchant who came to England and ate so many ice creams that "he gave his corpus such a chill" that he cried—

Shiver and Shakery, O, O, O,
Criminy Crikey! Isn't it cold?
Woo, woo, woo, oo, oo,
Behold the Man that couldn't get Warm.
       *Dr. Marigold.*

**SHOE LANE.** The northern end of this was originally in Holborn Hill, running along one side of Fleet Market, and was the next turning up from Farringdon Street. The Lane was straightened at that end with the rebuilding consequent on the construction of the Viaduct. *Boz, Scenes*, 16.

**SHOOTER'S HILL.** This hill, on the main London–Dover road, was the place where Jerry Cruncher caught up the mail coach, with Mr. Lorry aboard, and delivered his mysterious message (*Two Cities*, I, 2). On retiring from the box Mr. Tony Weller took up his residence at an excellent public-house near by (*Pickwick*, 57); Master Harry Walmer's father lived in "The Elmses," also in that neighbourhood. *Holly Tree.*

**SHORT,** also called Trotters, his real name being Harris, was one of the Punch and Judy showmen with whom Nell and her Grandfather travelled for a while. He was a cheery, kindly fellow, a direct contrast to his misanthropic, selfish partner, Codlin. *Curiosity Shop*, 16–19, 37, 73.

**SHOT TOWER.** The Patent Shot Tower, standing just above Waterloo Bridge, was built by Messrs. Watts in 1789. *Boz, Scenes*, 4.

**SHREWSBURY.** Though only mentioned once by name, Sydney Carton and Stryver having been educated at Shrewsbury School (*Two Cities*, II, 5), the city is referred to again, according to F. G. Kitton, as "a large town . . . in the streets were a number of old houses built of a kind of earth or plaster, crossed and recrossed . . . with black beams" (*Curiosity Shop*, 46). Modern Dickensians throw considerable doubt on this theory that Nell and her Grandfather went so far. *See* Nell.

**SHRUB.** This was a favourite drink, compounded of some fruit juice, e.g. blackcurrant, boiled with sugar and added to hot rum.

**SIGNAL LIGHTS.** The "railway shutting a green eye and opening a red one " has been the subject of much enquiry and of many ingenious theories. The simplest and most obvious explanation, however, is the correct one. It was a mistake, a slip of the pen. This is a classic instance among railway experts of how one of the most careful of writers can make a glaring mistake. At no time and on no line was red ever an all-clear signal. *Mutual Friend*, III, 9.

**SIGNALMAN, THE.** The victim of a railway accident, narrated in *Two Ghost Stories*.

**SIKES, BILL.** A desperate, surly, villainous housebreaker, working in conjunction with Fagin's gang, but the terror of even that cunning Jew. He has not a single redeeming character, but from first to last is the incarnation of brutality and ignorance. At Fagin's suggestion Sikes attempted to break into Mrs. Maylie's house at Chertsey, taking Oliver Twist with him for the purpose of slipping through a window. The plan miscarried, however, and Oliver was finally rescued from the thieves' clutches. Meanwhile, Fagin's suspicions had been aroused concerning Nancy, Bill's mistress. He set a watch upon her, discovered her communication with Rose Maylie and Mr. Brownlow, and told Bill Sikes that the girl was a traitress. Without any hesitation, Sikes returned to his home, bade Nancy get out of bed, and, deaf to her appeals for mercy, beat her brains out with the butt of his pistol. Flying from the scene of murder, after wandering about the country as far as Hatfield, he returned to a thieves' den on Jacob's Island, where, as the crowd was surging round to capture him, he accidentally hanged himself in trying to escape. *Twist*, 13, 15, 16, 19–22, 25, 28, 39, 44, 47, 48, 50.

**SILENT SYSTEM.** This was a system in practice at Coldbath Fields Prison which enforced absolute silence on all the prisoners, even communication by signs being forbidden. It was introduced December 29, 1834, mainly with the object of stopping the contamination of first offenders by association and intercourse with old criminals. Hard labour on the "wheel" or treadmill was also enforced. *Boz, Scenes,* 17.

**SILVERMAN, GEORGE.** The narrator of the Explanation was an orphan lad, brought up by religious fanatics. He obtained scholarships and succeeded in being ordained. Presented to a living by Lady Fareways, he acted as tutor to her daughter Adelina, but falling in love with the girl, by an act of self-sacrifice, turned her affection in the direction of Granville Wharton, another of his pupils. Eventually he married the young couple, and for this was dismissed by Lady Fareway and compelled to resign his living.

**SILVER STORE ISLAND.** The opening scene of the exciting adventures of *Certain English Prisoners.*

**SILVER STREET.** This was the former name of Beak Street, at the corner of which and Upper James Street is the Crown (rebuilt since then), where Newman Noggs was known. *Nickleby,* 7.

**SIMMERY, FRANK.** The smart friend with whom Mr. Wilkins Flasher exchanged bets. *Pickwick,* 55.

**SIMMONDS, MISS.** One of Madame Mantalini's young ladies. *Nickleby,* 17.

**SIMMONS.** 1. Beadle of *Our Parish,* who over-exerted himself in conveying an intoxicated lady to the workhouse strong room. "Intelligence was conveyed to the board one evening that Simmons had died, and left his respects." *Boz, Our Parish,* 1, 4.

2. Mrs. Henrietta, a friend of Mrs. Quilp. *Curiosity Shop,* 4.

3. William or Bill, driver of the van which carried Martin Chuzzlewit to London. *Chuzzlewit,* 13.

**SIMON.** Servant of the bullying squire who turned the Rudges from his door. *Barnaby,* 47.

**SIMPSON.** 1. The "leg" upon whom Mr. Pickwick was chummed in the Fleet. *Pickwick,* 42.

2. One of Mrs. Tibbs's first boarders, who married Julia Maplesone, and was deserted by her six weeks after marriage, he being by that time in the Fleet prison. *Boz, Tales, Boarding House.*

3. "Vauxhall Simpson" was master of ceremonies at those gardens in the 30's, and made them very attractive with brilliant lighting and excellent amusements. He had once been a sailor, serving with the Duke of Clarence, later William IV. *Boz, Scenes,* 14.

**SIMSON.** A guest of Mr. Percy Noakes on the *Steam Excursion. Boz, Tales.*

**"SINCE LAWS WERE MADE."** A quotation from the *Beggar's Opera,* cited in full by Bar in *Dorrit,* II, 12. *See also Curiosity Shop,* 66.

**SINGLE GENTLEMAN, THE.** Brother of Little Nell's Grandfather and, as appears at the end of the book, Master Humphrey himself. Throughout the story the Single Gentleman, from his lodgings with the Brasses, attempted to trace the fugitives, at last finding their hiding-place, only to discover that Nell was dead. *Curiosity Shop,* 34–8, 40, 41, 47, 48, 50, 56, 57, 59, 62, 66, 69–73.

**SIX JOLLY FELLOWSHIP PORTERS.** The waterside tavern over which Miss Abbey Potterson presided so autocratically. It was probably the Grape's Inn, 76 Narrow Street, Limehouse, between Limehouse Basin and the river. *Mutual Friend,* I, 6, 13 ; III, 2, 3 ; IV, 12, 16.

**SKETCHES BY BOZ.** This collection of short pieces contains the earliest of Dickens's work. It is undoubtedly the most valuable from the antiquarian's point of view, containing references and descriptions of life in the 30's to be found nowhere else. The sketches were collected and issued in volume form, with illustrations by Cruikshank, in 1836. The sketches were reprinted from *The Monthly Magazine, Evening Chronicle, Bell's Life, Morning Chronicle, Library of Fiction.* The name of "Boz" was first used in signing the second part of the *Boarding House,* which came out in the *Monthly Magazine* for August, 1834. The first of Dickens's published works was *Mr. Minns and his Cousin,* which originally appeared as *A Dinner in Poplar Walk* in the *Monthly Magazine* for December, 1833.

**SKETTLES, SIR BARNET.** Father of one of Dr. Blimber's pupils, and a pompous but kindly gentleman with whom Florence went to stay while her father was in Leamington. Sir Barnet was in the House of Commons, and it was supposed that when he *did* catch the Speaker's eye (which he had been expected to do for three or four years) he would rather touch up the Radicals. He eventually obtained a diplomatic appointment. *Dombey,* 14, 18, 23, 24, 28, 60.

**SKEWTON, HON. MRS.** Edith Dombey's mother, a vain, scheming woman, usually known as Cleopatra from her portrait having been painted in that character. She was successful in securing the wealthy Dombey for a son-in-law, and though protesting to be all heart was in reality little more than mere paint. The original of Mrs. Skewton was a Mrs. Campbell, well known at Leamington as Cleopatra. *Dombey,* 21, 26–8, 30, 31, 35–7, 40, 41.

**SKIFFINS, MISS.** A lady "of a wooden appearance . . . but apparently a good sort of fellow," who married Wemmick. "Hallo ! Here's Miss Skiffins, let's have a wedding." *Expectations,* 37, 55.

**SKIMPIN.** Sergeant Buzfuz's junior at the Bardell-Pickwick trial. *Pickwick,* 34.

**SKIMPOLE, HAROLD.** A friend of John Jarndyce who, under the guise of an innocent ignorance of business and money matters, passed through life sponging on his friends. He was constantly being arrested for debt, and as often being cleared by the generosity of Jarndyce. He was, nevertheless, a delightful companion, musical and artistic, and carried off his selfishness with the most naïve air in the world. For a time he lived on Richard Carstone, thus occasioning a final difference with Jarndyce, whom, in a posthumously published diary he stigmatised as the incarnation of selfishness. He had three girls, Arethusa, Laura and Kitty, whom he called his Beauty, Sentiment and Comedy daughters, and gaily described himself as the youngest child of them all. The portrait of Skimpole was drawn from Leigh Hunt, and occasioned much bitterness. The heartless extract from the diary was taken from an incident connected with R. B. Haydon. *Bleak House*, 6, 8, 9, 15, 18, 31, 37, 43, 44, 57, 61.

**SLACKBRIDGE.** The Socialist orator at Coketown, who succeeded in driving Stephen Blackpool from the place. *Hard Times*, II, 4 ; III, 4.

**SLADDERY.** Proprietor of a fashionable London bookshop and lending library. *Bleak House*, 2, 58.

**SLAMJAM COFFEE HOUSE.** The establishment of which Joseph was head waiter. *Somebody's Luggage.*

**SLAMMER, DOCTOR.** The fiery little surgeon to the 98th Regiment, whom Jingle cut out at the Rochester ball. Jingle was wearing Mr. Winkle's coat, and to his horror, the latter was next morning challenged by Slammer to fight a duel, of the cause of which he knew nothing. Fatal consequences were averted by Slammer's discovery of his mistake. The original of Slammer was Dr. Lamert, Dickens's aunt's second husband, and the father of James Lamert of Warren's Blacking Warehouse. *See* Murdstone and Grinby. *Pickwick*, 2, 3.

**SLANG, LORD.** A friend of the Egotistical Young Couple. *Sketches of Couples.*

**SLASHER.** A remarkably skilful surgeon at St. Bartholomew's hospital, whose performances were described by Mr. Jack Hopkins. *Pickwick*, 32.

**SLAUGHTER, LIEUTENANT.** A fire-eating friend of Captain Waters. *Boz, Tales, Tuggs's.*

**SLEARY.** A circus proprietor with " a voice like the efforts of a broken old pair of bellows." He was a kind and good-hearted fellow, who protected Sissy Jupe after her father's desertion, and later gave shelter to young Tom Gradgrind when he was in trouble, eventually helping the young vagabond to make his escape from the country. His daughter, Josephine, married E. W. B. Childers. *Hard Times*, I, 3, 6 ; III, 7, 8.

**SLIDERSKEW, PEG.** Arthur Gride's housekeeper, a horrible old hag fit for such a household. On the day he was to have

been married she stole a box of valuable papers. Squeers was employed by Ralph Nickleby to track her down and recover the document relating to Madeleine Bray, but just as he secured the paper it was wrested from him by Frank Cheeryble. For her share in the proceedings Peg was transported and never returned. *Nickleby*, 51, 53, 54, 56, 57, 59, 65.

**SLINGO.** A horse-dealer with whom Top Dorrit found employment. *Dorrit*, I, 7.

**SLINKTON, JULIUS.** A murderer and swindler of insurance companies, whose plots were unearthed by Meltham the Actuary. This character, like Jonas Chuzzlewit, was founded on Thomas Griffiths Wainewright. *Hunted Down.*

**SLITHERS.** Master Humphrey's barber, or, as he preferred to call it, hairdresser. *Humphrey.*

**SLIVERSTONE.** A type of egotistical couple. *Sketches of Couples.*

**SLOPPY.** A foundling who had been cared for by Betty Higden and grew up to turn the mangle for her. He also had a gift for reading police reports in different voices, and was thus enabled to disguise himself as a dustman and keep an eye on Wegg when the mounds were being cleared. He was eventually trained as a cabinet-maker at Mr. Boffin's expense, and became a possible suitor for the hand of Jenny Wren. *Mutual Friend*, I, 16 ; II, 9, 10, 14 ; III, 9 ; IV, 3, 14, 16.

**SLOUT.** Master of the workhouse where Oliver Twist was born and Bumble's predecessor in that office. *Twist*, 27.

**SLOWBOY, TILLY.** Dot Peerybingle's maid. *Cricket on the Hearth.*

**SLUDBERRY, THOMAS.** Party in a Doctors' Commons case, having been cited for using the words, " You be blowed " to one Michael Bumple at a vestry meeting. For this he was excommunicated for a fortnight. *Boz, Scenes*, 8.

**SLUFFEN.** An eloquent master sweep of Adam and Eve Court. *Boz, Scenes*, 20.

**SLUG, MR.** A member of the Mudfog Association.

**SLUM.** A poetical friend of Mrs. Jarley, very shabby in appearance, who made a living by adapting famous poems to suit the business needs of his clients. Typical of his efforts was :—

> If I know'd a donkey wot wouldn't go
> To see Mrs. Jarley's wax-work show.
> Do you think I'd acknowledge him ?
> Oh, no, no !
> Then run to Jarley's.

Slum was probably founded on a character in Warren's Blacking Warehouse (*Curiosity Shop*, 28, 47). *See* " If I had a donkey."

**SLUMKEY, HON. SAMUEL.** The successful Parliamentary candidate, in the Blue interest, for the borough of Eatanswill. *Pickwick*, 13.

**SLUMMERY.** A clever painter, friend of the Plausible Couple. *Sketches of Couples.*

**SLUMMINTOWKENS.** Members of the Nupkins's social circle at Ipswich. *Pickwick*, 25.

**SLURK.** Editor of the *Eatanswill Independent*, and a deadly opponent of Mr. Pott, with whom he had a stand-up fight at the Saracen's Head, Towcaster. *Pickwick*, 51.

**SLYME, CHEVY.** A down-at-heels connection of the Chuzzlewit family, who, like the rest, hurried to the scene of old Martin's illness on the chance of what he could pick up. A mean, dissipated creature, he had, according to his friend Tigg, the peculiarity of being always round the corner. He finally appeared as a police officer, sent to arrest Jonas. *Chuzzlewit*, 4, 7, 51.

**SMALDER GIRLS, THE.** Friends of Cousin Feenix, seen at Brighton. *Dombey*, 41.

**SMALL-CLOTHES.** These were close-fitting knee-breeches, and were frequently called simply " smalls."

**SMALLWEED.** Old Joshua Smallweed was a paralysed old usurer, who got Trooper George into his clutches and thus extracted from him the Hawdon paper for which Mr. Tulkinghorn was so desirous. On the death of his wife's brother Krook, old Smallweed took possession of his effects and discovered the letters compromising Lady Dedlock. He tried to use their contents to blackmail Sir Leicester, but was outwitted by Bucket. One of the features of the old villain's life was his constant bickering with his imbecile wife, at whom he would throw cushions or other handy missiles, usually calling her a brimstone chatterer or words of like endearment. His granddaughter, Judy, a worthy specimen of the breed, kept house for the old couple. *Bleak House*, 21, 26, 27, 33, 34, 39, 54, 62.

Bart Smallweed, Judy's twin brother, was a credit to the family, precocious and grasping. At first he was a great admirer of Guppy, but a coolness rose between them on account of Guppy's secrecy during his investigations into the Hawdon mystery. *Bleak House*, 20, 21, 32, 33, 39.

**SMANGLE.** An inmate of the room where Mr. Pickwick spent his first night in the Fleet Prison. " There was a rakish, vagabond smartness, a kind of boastful rascality about the whole man, that was worth a mine of gold." *Pickwick*, 41, 42, 44.

**SMART, TOM.** Hero of the Bagman's Story. With the aid of an old arm-chair he outwitted a designing rascal named Jinkins, who wanted to marry the buxom widow proprietor of an inn on the Marlborough Down. *Pickwick*, 14.

**SMAUKER, JOHN.** Mr. Bantam's footman and a pillar of the society of Bath menservants. He introduced Sam to other choice spirits in livery at the " leg o' mutton swarry." *Pickwick*, 35, 37.

**SMIF, PUTNAM.** The soulful shop assistant who wrote to Martin Chuzzlewit under the name of America Junior. *Chuzzlewit*, 22.

**SMIFSER.** One of Mrs. Nickleby's many suitors. *Nickleby*, 41.

**SMIGGERS, JOSEPH.** Perpetual Vice-President of the Pickwick Club. *Pickwick*, 1.

**SMIKE.** The half-witted victim of Squeers's brutality, whom Nicholas Nickleby rescued from Dotheboys Hall. He followed Nicholas with dog-like devotion to London and thence to Portsmouth, where Crummles was taken with his appearance and gave him the melancholy parts to play. Returning with Nicholas to London, he shared the fortunes of the family. Once he was recaptured by Squeers, but was delivered by John Browdie. Partly through years of suffering and partly because of a hopeless love for Kate, Smike pined away, and finally died in the country. After his death it transpired that he had been Ralph Nickleby's son, put to school in Yorkshire by Brooker. *Nickleby*, 7, 8, 12, 13, 15, 16, 20, 22, 23, 25, 29, 30, 32, 33, 35, 37–40, 42, 45, 46, 49, 55, 58–60, 65.

**" SMILE."** Mrs. Fezziwig appeared " as one vast, substantial smile." *Christmas Carol*.

**SMITH.** 1. A member of Parliament. *Boz, Scenes*, 18.
2. Subscriber to the Indigent Orphans' Friends' Fund. *Boz, Scenes*, 19.
3. A City clerk, described at length in *Boz, Characters*, 1.
4. Samuel, the unromantic but real name of Horatio Sparkins. *Boz, Tales, Sparkins*.
5. A member of the Mudfog Association.

**SMITHERS.** 1. Robert, the roaring city clerk who made a night of it with his friend Potter. *Boz, Characters*, 11.
2. Miss Emily, the belle of Minerva House. *Boz, Tales, Sentiment*.
3. Miss, one of the boarders at Westgate House. *Pickwick*, 16.

**SMITHFIELD.** This was formerly a market for live cattle and horses, presenting a scene of confusion and filth well described in *Twist*, 16, 21, 42 ; *Expectations*, 20 ; *Monument of French Folly*. In 1855 the market was moved to Caledonian Road, and the Central Meat Market was built on its site, 1867–8. The following references, therefore, apply to the old cattle market. *Barnaby*, 18 ; *Dorrit*, I, 13 ; *Nickleby*, 4.

**SMITHWICK AND WATERSBY.** The firm which owned the *Golden Mary*.

**SMITHIE.** A family connected with the Dockyard and patrons of the Rochester Ball. *Pickwick*, 2.

**SMITH SQUARE.** Walking up Dean Stanley Street (formerly Church Street) from Millbank, on the left hand corner as one enters Smith Square, was the house in which Lizzie Hexam lived for a while with

Jenny Wren. The centre of the square is occupied by "the very hideous" church of St. John Evangelist. *Mutual Friend*, II, 1.

**SMIVEY, CHICKEN.** Name given by Tigg for Martin Chuzzlewit when the latter was pawning his watch. *Chuzzlewit*, 13.

**SMORLTORK, COUNT.** A foreign visitor at The Den, Eatanswill. He was writing a great work on England, and was spending three weeks in the country gathering material. The original was Count Puckler Moskau, who produced a book with almost as little excuse. *Pickwick*, 15.

**SMOUCH.** An assistant to Namby the sheriff, who accompanied his master when arresting Mr. Pickwick. *Pickwick*, 40.

**SMUGGINS.** A singer in the comic line at the Harmonic Meeting, described in *Boz, Scenes*, 2.

**SNAGSBY.** The kindly law stationer who, to his amazement and consternation, found himself involved in some of the Dedlock mysteries on account of having employed Hawdon as a law writer. He was a staunch friend to Jo, although much badgered by his shrewish wife and the hypocritical Chadband, who gained a footing in the house. Mrs. Snagsby's curiosity and suspicion developed into little less than a mania, and only when she was undeceived by Bucket did she exonerate her husband from various undefined charges. *Bleak House*, 10, 11, 19, 20, 22, 25, 32, 33, 42, 47, 54, 59.

**SNAP, BETSY.** Uncle Chill's "hard-favoured, yellow" old housekeeper. *Reprinted, Poor Relation's Story.*

**SNAWLEY.** "A sleek, fat-nosed man," and a mean hypocrite who disposed of his two stepsons by placing them with Squeers. He later became intimate with the schoolmaster, and was employed by Ralph Nickleby to pose as Smike's father for the purpose of getting the lad away from Nicholas. After the failure of this scheme Snawley took fright and eventually revealed the whole conspiracy, thus hastening the disgrace of Ralph and Squeers. *Nickleby*, 4, 38, 39, 45, 56, 59.

**SNEVELLICCI, MISS.** One of the leading ladies in Crummles's Company. She was greatly taken with Nicholas Nickleby and vainly tried to draw him into a flirtation, but was eventually happily married to an affluent young tallow chandler. Mr. Snevellicci, her father, was a pompous actor of the heavy type, and an ardent devotee of Bacchus. *Nickleby*, 23–5, 29, 30, 48.

**SNEWKES.** A visitor of the Kenwigs, paying court to Mrs. Kenwigs's sister. *Nickleby*, 14.

**SNICKS, MR.** One of Mr. Perker's guests, secretary of the Life Office. *Pickwick*, 47.

**SNIFF, MRS.** A waitress at Mugby Junction Refreshment Room, "always looking another way from you when you look at her." Her husband, also employed at the

refreshment rooms, in charge of the sawdust department, was disgustingly servile towards the public. *Mugby*.

**SNIGGS.** Mr. Tulrumble's predecessor as Mayor of Mudfog. *Tulrumble*.

**SNIGSWORTH, LORD.** Twemlow's high and mighty cousin, the subject of much discussion in the Veneering circle. *Mutual Friend*, I, 2, 10 ; II, 3, 5, 16 ; III, 13.

**SNIPE, HON. WILMOT.** An ensign in the 97th, present at the Rochester Ball. *Pickwick*, 2.

**SNITCHEY, JONATHAN.** Partner of the solicitor's firm of Snitchey and Craggs. He was a keen business man, sharp and kindly, who had charge of the affairs of Dr. Jeddler and Michael Warden. Snitchey was the talking partner of the firm, which he always referred to as "self and Craggs," or, when the latter was dead, "self and Craggs, deceased." *Battle of Life.*

**SNIVEY, SIR HOOKHAM.** A member of the Mudfog Association.

**SNOBB, HON. MR.** A guest at Ralph Nickleby's dinner party. *Nickleby*, 19.

**SNOBBY.** Chuckster's contemptuous nickname for Kit Nubbles. *Curiosity Shop*, 14.

**SNOBEE.** An unsuccessful parliamentary candidate. *Boz, Characters*, 5.

**SNODGRASS, AUGUSTUS.** A member of the Pickwick Club, one of Mr. Pickwick's companions in his travels, and a poetical young gentleman. He played but a minor part in the adventures the party encountered, falling in love with Emily Wardle at an early stage of the proceedings and more or less pining for her until the end of the book, where, after a series of secret meetings, assisted by Arabella, Wardle gave his blessing to the match. They married and lived happy ever after on a farm near Dingley Dell. *Pickwick*, 1–9, 11–15, 18, 19, 22, 24–6, 28, 30–2, 34, 35, 44, 47, 54, 57.

**SNORE, PROF.** A member of the Mudfog Association.

**SNORFLERER, DOWAGER LADY.** A friend of the egotistical Young Couple. *Sketches of Couples.*

**SNORRIDGE BOTTOM.** The place "between Chatham and Maidstone," where Gill Davis was employed as a lad to frighten birds. *English Prisoners.*

**SNOW, TOM.** The negro steward of the *Golden Mary.*

**SNOW HILL.** This now deserted street was formerly one of the busiest thoroughfares in London, forming part of the main east to west route via Holborn, which then sloped down Holborn Hill into Farringdon Street, opposite Snow Hill. The winding nature of Snow Hill, however, made it awkward for the increasing volume of traffic, and in 1802 a street, called Skinner Street, was cut through, making a direct line between Holborn and Newgate Street. This was in turn demolished with the making of the Viaduct in 1867, when Snow Hill was entirely rebuilt. At the upper end was the Saracen's Head (*q.v.*). Among the references to Snow Hill are the following : *Barnaby*, 67 ; *Nickleby*, 3, 4, 42 ; *Twist*, 26 ; *Dorrit*, I, 13 ; *Boz*, *Tales*, *Christening*.

**SNUBBIN, SERJEANT.** Counsel for Mr. Pickwick in the trial for breach of promise. His common-sense interpretation of Mr. Pickwick's suspicious behaviour and compromising messages stood no chance against the florid eloquence of Serjeant Buzfuz. The original of Serjeant Snubbin was probably Serjeant Arabin, a noted counsel of the time. *Pickwick*, 31, 34.

**SNUFFIM, SIR TUMLEY.** Mrs. Wittitterley's doctor. *Nickleby*, 28, 33.

**SNUFFLETOFFLE, Q. J.** A member of the Mudfog Association.

**SNUPHANUPH, DOWAGER LADY.** " A fat old lady," with whom Mr. Pickwick played whist at Bath. *Pickwick*, 35, 36.

**" SOARING HUMAN BOY."** One of Chadband's hypocritical remarks to Jo, the crossing sweeper :—

> O running stream of sparkling joy
> To be a soaring human boy !
> *Bleak House*, 19.

**SOEMUP, DR.** President of the medical section of the Mudfog Association.

**SOHO SQUARE.** Except that it is, perhaps, less residential, this square has changed little since the day when Caddy Jellyby waited there by appointment for Esther Summerson (*Bleak House*, 23). It may be remarked that Caddy was sitting in the gardens. This must have been a slip of the pen, as the gardens were already railed in by 1835, and many attempts had been made to throw them open to the public. Jules Obenreizer lived near the square (*No Thoroughfare*), while at No. 10 Carlisle Street, near by, lived Dr. Manette. *Two Cities*, II, 6, 13.

**" SOLDIER TIRED, THE."** This is Dr. Arne's " The Soldier Tired of War's Alarms." *Boz*, *Characters*, 4.

**SOL'S ARMS.** This public-house, the scene of Little Swills's musical triumphs, was the Old Ship Tavern, which once stood at the corner of Chichester Rents and Chancery Lane. *Bleak House*, 11, 20, 32, 33.

**SOMEBODY'S LUGGAGE.** This Christmas Tale appeared in *All the Year Round*, 1862. Purporting to be MSS. found in a some unclaimed luggage, it contains two delightful stories. It was said that Dickens received a letter from the country identifying the luggage, from the inventory given, and enclosing £2 16s. 6d., the amount of the bill.

**SOMERSET HOUSE.** Dickens's father and uncle were both at one time clerks in Somerset House, which was then, as now, the home of various Government offices. It will be remembered that Mr. Minns had a good position there. *Boz*, *Tales*, *Minns*.

**SOMERS TOWN.** This is the name given to the area between the Euston, Pancras and Hampstead Roads. It was formerly largely occupied by foreigners, and as late as the 30's was a kind of colony apart from the growing suburbs of London. The Dickens family at one time lived in the Polygon (*q.v.*). Somers Town was a favourite residence of City clerks (*Boz*, *Scenes*, 1 ; *Pickwick*, 20). Near by lived Mr. Snawley, with whom Squeers went to lodge. *Nicholas*, 38, 39, 59.

**SOPHIA.** 1. Ruth Pinch's pupil, daughter of the brass and copper founder at Camberwell. *Chuzzlewit*, 9, 36.

2. One of the Matthew Pocket's maids. *Expectations*, 23.

**SOPHONISBA.** A lady apostrophised by Jarber. *Going into Society*.

**SOPHY.** 1. Dr. Marigold's adopted daughter, deaf and dumb, whom he bought from Mim, the travelling showman. He had her educated and took her about with him until she married a deaf mute like herself and went to India. Thence she returned with her little daughter, who could speak. *Dr. Marigold*.

2. Willing Sophy was one of Mrs. Lirriper's maids. *Lirriper's Lodgings*.

**SOUTHAMPTON STREET.** In this short street, leading from High Holborn to Bloomsbury Square, was Billickin's, probably at No. 20, by the Arching which formerly led to " Mewses." *Drood*, 22.

**SOUTHCOTE, MR.** An ingenious *Begging Letter Writer. Reprinted Pieces*.

**SOUTHWARK BRIDGE.** Under its old name of the Iron Bridge (*q.v.*) this is referred to in *Dorrit*. Between this and London Bridge Gaffer Hexam is introduced as plying his dreadful calling (*Mutual Friend*, I, 1), while the bridge is also referred to in *Reprinted, Down with the Tide*.

**SOWERBERRY.** The undertaker who secured the services of Oliver Twist from the parish authorities. Finding the lad useful in the business, he treated him fairly well, thereby incurring the anger of Noah Claypole, his other assistant. As a result Noah and Oliver fought, and Sowerberry was summoned by his vixenish wife to thrash Oliver, who ran away that same night. *Twist*, 4–7, 27, 51.

**SOWNDS.** The pompous beadle at the church where the Dombey functions took place. *Dombey*, 5, 31, 57.

**SOWSTER.** The Oldcastle beadle " with a very red nose which he attributed to early rising." *Mudfog*.

**SPA FIELDS.** Until the early years of the nineteenth century the district round Exmouth and Rosoman Streets, known as Spa Fields, was an open space, much frequented by showmen who there made their winter quarters. Old Maunders was one of these, having in his cottage the eight dwarfs served by eight giants, too old for exhibition, described in *Curiosity Shop*, 19.

**SPANIARDS, HAMPSTEAD.** This famous inn, with its adjacent tea gardens, has altered but little since Mrs. Bardell and her friends, escorted by the luckless Mr. Raddle, went there for the tea party, so unfortunately disturbed by the arrival of Mr. Jackson. *Pickwick*, 46.

**SPARKINS, HORATIO.** A stylish young man who imposed himself on the Malderton family. They thought him a man of fashion and fortune, but finally discovered him serving in a small draper's shop in the Tottenham Court Road—his real name being Samuel Smith. *Boz, Tales, Sparkins.*

**SPARKLER, EDMUND.** Mrs. Merdle's son by her first marriage, an aristocratic, foolish young man who succumbed to the charms of Fanny Dorrit, when she was a ballet dancer. At the time Fanny was bought off by Mrs. Merdle, but when they all met again later, the Dorrits being then people of wealth, Edmund renewed his courtship and they were married. He soon after became a lord of the Circumlocution Office. He was blindly devoted to his domineering wife, but had the good trait of recognising the worth of his sister-in-law, Amy. *Dorrit*, I, 20, 21, 33 ; II, 3, 5–7, 11, 12, 14–16, 18, 24, 33.

**SPARKS, TOM.** Boots at the St. James's Arms. *Strange Gentleman.*

**SPARSIT, MRS.** Josiah Bounderby's housekeeper, a lady of extremely aristocratic connections, but none the less anxious to ally herself to the vulgar and wealthy Bounderby. On his marriage with Louisa Gradgrind, Mrs. Sparsit made it her business to cause dissension, setting Bounderby against his wife and spying upon Young Tom. She hurried to London with the false news of Louisa's elopement, but when she brought to light the existence of Bounderby's respectable mother, Mrs. Pegler, she was ignominiously dismissed. *Hard Times*, I, 7, 11, 16 ; II, 1, 3, 6, 8–11 ; III, 3, 5, 9.

**SPATTER, JOHN.** Clerk, later partner, of Michael, the Poor Relation. *Reprinted Pieces.*

**SPECIAL CONSTABLE.** Before the establishment of the Police Force, law and order were preserved in country towns by one or two constables, genus Grummer, who, when required, requisitioned the services of such loyal townsmen as they required. No better description of the system and its working can be required than that afforded by *Pickwick*, 24, 25.

**SPECKS, JOE.** The Dullborough doctor and husband of Lucy Green, the sweetheart of the Uncommercial Traveller's childhood. *Uncommercial*, 12.

**SPENCER.** A short overcoat or jacket without skirts. The garment was named after Earl Spencer (1758–1834), who in-

vented or introduced it about the end of the eighteenth century.

**SPENLOW.** Dora Spenlow was the daughter of the proctor to whom David Copperfield was articled. David's meeting and courtship of this delightful and charming girl cannot be " summarised." After her father's sudden death she went to her aunts, Lavinia and Clarissa, at Putney, there David visited as her fiancé and in due course they were married. When she and David set up house he tried to teach her the practical things of life, but Dora could only be his " child-wife," beloved by Miss Trotwood, Agnes and all who knew her, but quite unable to manage a home. At last, after how short a married life, she faded and died. The original of Dora was Dickens's first love, Maria Beadnell (*q.v.*). *Copperfield*, 26, 28, 29, 33–9, 41–5, 48–53, 62.

Francis Spenlow, Dora's father, was a proctor of the firm of Spenlow and Jorkins, of Doctors' Commons. David was articled to him and visited his Norwood home, where he met Dora. After his aunt's reverses David asked to be released, but Spenlow, as was his wont, referred to the implacability and hardness of Jorkins, and refused the request. He died suddenly, leaving no will. Spenlow and Jorkins has become a phrase for business partnerships where one partner performs any unpleasant business with the excuse that it is the other partner's fault. He was founded on George Beadnell, Maria's father. 23, 26, 29, 33, 35, 38.

**SPHYNX, SOPHRONIA.** The name given by Dick Swiveller to the Marchioness. (*q.v.*)

**SPIGWIFFIN'S WHARF.** It was near here, between Billingsgate and the Custom House, that Ralph Nickleby sent his sister and niece to " a large, dingy old house . . . with a wharf behind opening on the Thames." There was a Wiggins' Quay thereabouts which may have suggested the name. *Nickleby*, 11, 26.

**SPIKER, MR. AND MRS. HENRY.** Friends of the Waterbrooks and very tremendous people. Mrs. Spiker, christened by David " Hamlet's Aunt," delivered some striking remarks on the subject of Blood. *Copperfield*, 25.

**SPILLER AND SPOKER.** The artists who executed the portrait and bust of Mr. Pecksniff. *Chuzzlewit*, 5.

**SPINACH.** One of Miss Flite's captive birds. *Bleak House*, 14.

**SPONG.** Original of Wardle. (*q.v.*)

**SPONGING HOUSE.** In the old days of imprisonment for debt, the sheriff's officer usually kept a house or tavern, where he accommodated his prisoners for twenty-four hours before they were put into prison. This gave their friends a chance to release them, as in the case of Watkins Tottle (*Boz, Tales, Tottle*). The sponging house charges, which were little short of robbery, had to be defrayed at the time by the prisoner. The best-known sponging house was Sloman's, No. 2 Cursitor Street, probably the original of Coavinses Castle. *Bleak House*, 15.

**SPOTTLETOE, MR. AND MRS.** Relatives of the Chuzzlewit family who hastened into the country on the news of Old Martin's illness. They appeared again for Charity Pecksniff's wedding, which never came off. *Chuzzlewit*, 4, 54.

**SPRODGKIN, MRS. SALLY.** An exacting member of Mr. Milvey's parish, constantly needing, at untimely moments, spiritual counsel on Who begat Whom, or similar subjects. *Mutual Friend*, IV, 11.

**SPRUGGINS, THOMAS.** A candidate for the office of beadle. *Boz, Our Parish*, 4.

**SPYERS, JEM.** The police officer who arrested Conkey Chickweed, the fraudulent publican. *Twist*, 31.

**SQUEERS.** Wackford Squeers was proprietor of Dotheboys Hall, one of the establishments for which, at that time, Yorkshire was notorious. He accepted boys who for various reasons were not wanted by their relatives, and kept them indefinitely, teaching them nothing, underfeeding them disgracefully and treating them abominably in every way. Nicholas went to him as an assistant master, but protesting at his brutality, gave him a sound thrashing and left. On next coming to London, Squeers placed himself at Ralph Nickleby's disposal to get his revenge on Nicholas. The conspiracy these two hatched was brought to nothing, however, by the defection of Snawley, with whom Squeers was living. Squeers was spying on Peg Sliderskew for the purpose of recovering Arthur Gride's stolen papers when he was taken by Frank Cheeryble. He soon found himself in prison, and in due time was transported. The original of Squeers was William Shaw, of Bowes. Although there were many Squeers among the Yorkshire schoolmasters, Shaw himself was not so bad as his portrait, and the writer has been assured that real injustice was done by depicting him in so brutal a light. *Nickleby*, 3–9, 13, 15, 34, 38, 39, 42, 44, 45, 56, 57, 59, 60, 64, 65.

Mrs. Squeers was a worthy mate for such a husband. When the news of his transportation was received in Yorkshire the school broke up excitedly, and John Browdie only arrived in time to save her and her children from the fury of the half-starved boys. 7–9, 13, 15, 34, 64.

Fanny, their spiteful, vixenish daughter, was enraged at Nicholas's indifference to her attractions. She accompanied her friend Tilda Price as travelling bridesmaid to London, but there quarrelled with her finally. (9, 12, 13, 15, 39, 42, 64.) Her brother, Wackford Junior, a greasy little urchin, fattened on the misfortunes of the other boys, was taken to London as an example of the generous dietary of Dotheboys Hall. 8, 9, 13, 15, 34, 38, 39, 42, 64.

**SQUIRES, OLYMPIA.** A sweetheart of the Uncommercial Traveller's childhood. (19.)

**SQUOD, PHIL.** Trooper George's assistant at the shooting gallery, a little one-sided man who had originally been an itinerant tinker. George took him to live at Chesney Wold. *Bleak House*, 21, 24, 26, 34, 47, 66.

**STABLES, HON. BOB.** A connection of the Dedlock family, well versed in all to do with horses. *Bleak House*, 2, 28, 40, 58.

**STAGG.** The blind ruffian who kept a subterranean drinking shop, frequented by Sim Tappertit and other Prentice Knights. He took up with the murderer Rudge and helped him bleed Mrs. Rudge for money. He was eventually shot when the ringleaders of the riots were captured through Dennis's treachery. *Barnaby*, 8, 18, 45, 46, 62, 69.

**STAGGS'S GARDENS.** Here was situated the home of the Toodles before the London and Birmingham Railway (later the L.N.W. Rly.) built their terminus at Euston and goods yards in " Camberling town." Staggs's Gardens is a fictitious name, but the description of it during and after the construction of the railway would suit most of the locality at that time. *Dombey*, 6, 15.

**STALKER.** 1. A smart Detective-Inspector. The original was Ins. Walker, of Bow Street. *Reprinted, Detective Police*.

2. A thief of St. Giles. *Reprinted, Inspector Field*.

**STAMFORD HILL.** Here, at Amelia Cottage, Poplar Walk, lived Mr. Octavius Budden. *Boz, Tales, Minns*.

**STANHOPE.** This was a light two- or four-wheeled carriage without a cover or hood.

**STANLEY, LORD.** (1799–1869.) Afterwards the fourteenth Earl of Derby, he was a prominent politician in the 30's and 40's, being an ardent supporter of the Reform Bill of 1832. He was three times Prime Minister, 1852, 1858 and 1866. *Boz, Scenes*, 18.

**STAPLE, MR.** An adherent of the Dingley Dell Cricket Club, who made the speech at the dinner after the great match with Muggleton. *Pickwick*, 7.

**STAPLE INN.** This old Chancery inn, the exterior of which is a prominent landmark in Holborn, contains two courtyards, in which Mr. Snagsby loved to walk in summer time and observe how countrified the sparrows and leaves were (*Bleak House*, 10). Mr. Grewgious lived in a house in the second quadrangle. His house still presents "in black and white on its ugly portal the mysterious inscription : "

P

J　　T

1747

This stands for President James Taylor, President of the Society of Antients of Staple Inn in 1747. It is of interest to note that Dr. Johnson was living in the same house in 1759, and there wrote *Rasselas*. Lieutenant Tartar's rooms and those occupied by the Landless twins were in an adjacent building visible from Mr. Grewgious's chambers. *Drood*, 11, 17, 20, 21, 22.

**STARELEIGH, MR. JUSTICE.** The judge who tried the Bardell-Pickwick case, " so fat that he seemed all face and waistcoat." The original of this irascible little justice was Sir Stephen Gazelee, who, though an excellent lawyer, made himself ridiculous by his behaviour on the bench. The portrait was at once recognised, and Sir Stephen's retirement soon afterwards was expedited, if not caused, by the ridicule he suffered. *Pickwick*, 34.

**STARLING.** 1. Alfred, one of the guests at the *Haunted House*.
2. Mrs., a widow friend of the Loving Couple. *Sketches of Couples*.

**STARTOP.** One of Matthew Pocket's pupils and a friend of Pip and Herbert, whom he introduced to the Finches of the Grove. He was taken into their confidence regarding Magwitch and helped row the boat in which they hoped to smuggle the convict to the foreign-going steamer. *Expectations*, 23, 25, 26, 34, 52–4.

**STEADIMAN, JOHN.** Chief mate of the *Golden Mary* and in command of the survivors after the death of Captain Ravender.

**STEAMBOATS, THAMES.** From the 40's until comparatively recent times there was a regular steamer service on the river. There were wharves at every bridge and at many intermediate points, and frequent services, at fares from one penny upwards, between them. These steamers afforded a quick and easy means of transit between places situated near the river.

**STEELE, TOM.** A Dublin man who lost his life at Waterloo Bridge. *Reprinted, Down with the Tide*.

**STEEPWAY.** The village where Mrs. Raybrock was postmistress and where her family lived. *Message from the Sea*.

**STEERFORTH.** James Steerforth was head boy at Salem House and the hero of David Copperfield's boyhood. Even then he was domineering, but was the school favourite. When David was a young man he ran across Steerforth again and fell under his influence. In a fatal moment David took him to Yarmouth, where his engaging manner soon endeared him to the simple fisher folk. Then came the tragedy of Steerforth's elopement with Little Em'ly. From the story told later by his servant Littimer, he took her abroad, but tired of her after a while and wished to pass her on to Littimer. Nothing was heard of him until one day at Yarmouth, in the midst of a terrific storm, David perceived him on a shipwrecked vessel, and later, one of the bodies washed up was that of James Steerforth. It was laid

alongside that of the man he had so much wronged, Ham Peggotty, who had lost his life in a vain endeavour to save those on board. The original of Steerforth, so far as his heroic boyhood is concerned, was George Stroughill, one of Dickens's early schoolfellows. *Copperfield*, 5–7, 9, 19–26, 28, 29, 31, 32, 46, 50, 55, 56.

Mrs. Steerforth, the mother of James, was a proud, handsome woman whose life was bound up in her son. When Peggotty interviewed her after Little Em'ly's disappearance, she took up the attitude that the only harm done was her son's degradation by consorting with one so low. She was eventually estranged from her boy, and partially lost her reason, never realising his death. *Copperfield*, 20, 21, 24, 29, 32, 36, 46, 56, 64.

**STETTA, VIOLETTA.** An opera singer who figured among Mr. Chuckster's muddy anecdotes. *Curiosity Shop*, 40.

**STEVENS, BILLY.** A workhouse inmate. *Reprinted, Walk in a Workhouse*.

**STIGGINS, MR.**, otherwise known as " the red-nosed man," or the deputy shepherd, was a drunken ranter who, in the name of religion, lived on the foolishness of " a parcel of silly women." Mrs. Weller's snug bar at the Marquis of Granby made her an especial object of his attentions. By artful scheming old Weller exposed his drunkenness at the Brick Lane Temperance Meeting, but not until Mrs. Weller's death was he able to get his own back by kicking Stiggins out of the house and ducking him in the horse-trough. *Pickwick*, 22, 27, 33, 43, 45, 52.

**STILTSTALKING, LORD LANCASTER.** A guest at Mrs. Gowan's and one of a great and powerful family. *Dorrit*, I, 10, 26.

**STOCK.** This was a kind of cravat, usually a band of some stiff material covered with black silk. It was worn with or without a collar. Stiff leather stocks formed part of the Army uniform until after the Crimean War. *Expectations*, 5.

**STOKES, MARTIN.** A small farmer acquainted with *The Village Coquettes*.

**STORR AND MORTIMER.** A firm of fashionable Bond Street jewellers, now represented by Messrs. Hunt and Roskell. *Dorrit*, I, 21; *Reprinted, Bill Sticking*.

**STRAND.** No part of London is so frequently mentioned as the Strand, which has undergone many changes since the beginning of the Dickens novels. Temple Bar went in 1878, the Law Courts have been built (1879–82), the street has been widened with the demolition of Holywell Street and the making of Aldwych (1899–1905), Exeter Hall has gone (1907), the street has been widened at places further along, Charing Cross Station has been built (1863), and Trafalgar Square made (1829–41). The Strand has many associations with Dickens himself, from the early days when he wandered up to it from Hungerford

Stairs, to the times when he walked along it to his editorial offices in Wellington Street. Trafalgar Square has absorbed the site of the Golden Cross Hotel (*q.v.*) of *Pickwick*, *Boz* and *Copperfield*. Miss La Creevy lived at a house which has been identified as No. 11 (*Nickleby*, 3, 5). The following are the principal casual references to people passing up or down the street. *Boz*, *Characters*, 1; *Tales*, 10; *Pickwick*, 28; *Copperfield*, 11, 24, 35, 40; *Chuzzlewit*, 13, 48; *Barnaby*, 15, 66; *Two Cities*, II, 14; *Bleak House*, 19; *Curiosity Shop*, 8; *Mutual Friend*, III, 2; *Dorrit*, II, 9; *Lirriper's Lodgings*, *Somebody's Luggage*, *Reprinted*, *Poor Man's Patent* and *Detective Police*, *Uncommercial*, 34.

**STRAND LANE.** At the foot of this lane, by the side of Somerset House, were Strand Lane Stairs, whence Mr. Percy Noakes hired a row-boat to take him to the *Endeavour* (*Boz*, *Tales*, *Excursion*). In Strand Lane is the Roman bath where David Copperfield used to have his cold plunge before going to Hampstead. *Copperfield*, 35.

**STRANGE GENTLEMAN, THE.** This dramatised version of The Great Winglebury Duel was produced at the St. James's Theatre, September 29, 1836, and had a run of a little over two months.

**STRAUDENHEIM.** A Strassburg shop-keeper. *Uncommercial*, 7.

**STRAW, SERJEANT.** One of the *Detective Police*, *Reprinted Pieces*.

**STREAKER.** The housemaid in the *Haunted House*, who produced "the largest and most transparent tears I ever met with."

**"STREW THEN, OH STREW."** From Moore's "Holy be the Pilgrim's Sleep." *Curiosity Shop*, 65.

**STRONG, DR.** The Canterbury school-master to whom David was sent by Miss Trot-wood. He was an amiable old man, engrossed in writing a colossal dictionary which he could never possibly finish. He had married a young wife, Annie, and rather improbable complications and misunderstandings arose about her and her cousin, Jack Maldon. Thanks to Mr. Dick's tact all was satisfactorily settled in the end. During the story the Doctor moved from Canterbury to Highgate, where David worked for him. The Doctor's house at Canterbury has been identified as No. 1 Lady Wootton's Green; the school was King's School, in the Cathedral precincts, on the west side of Green Court. *Copperfield*, 16–19, 35, 36, 39, 42, 45, 62, 64.

**STROUGHILL, GEORGE.** Original of James Steerforth (*q.v.*). His sister, Lucy, was the original of Lucy Atherfield. (*q.v.*)

**STRUGGLES.** A member of the Dingley Dell Cricket Team. *Pickwick*, 7.

**STRYVER, MR.** The barrister who defended Darnay in his trial for treason. Much of his success was due to his friend, Sydney Carton, who, too dilatory to work up a practice for himself, "devilled" for Stryver and worked up his cases—Memory, Stryver called him. At one time Stryver thought he would marry Lucie Manette, and was surprised to hear that she would not marry *him*. *Two Cities*, II, 3–5, 11–13, 21–4.

**STUBBS.** 1. Mrs., Percy Noakes's laundress. *Boz*, *Tales*, *Excursion*.

2. Lawrence Boythorn's pony. *Bleak House*, 36.

**STUMPS, BILL.** According to Mr. Blotton the original sculptor of the inscription discovered by Mr. Pickwick at Cobham :—

**BILST**
**UM**
**PSHI**
**S. M.**
**ARK**

This was maliciously deciphered by Mr. Blotton as "Bill Stumps, His Mark." *Pickwick*, 11.

**STYLES.** A member of the Mudfog Association.

**SUDBURY.** This was undoubtedly the original of Eatanswill (*q.v.*), the Rose and Crown Inn (burned down in 1922) being the Eatanswill Town Arms. Mr. Gabriel Parsons had an exciting adventure, unfortunately never related, while travelling from Sudbury to Bury St. Edmunds. *Boz*, *Tales*, *Tottle*.

**SUFFOLK BANTAM.** A prizefighter whose meeting with the Middlesex Dumpling was prohibited by Mr. Nupkins. *Pickwick*, 24.

**SULLIWIN.** 1. A charlady of Seven Dials. *Boz*, *Scenes*, 5.

2. One of the rowers in a Thames race. *Boz*, *Scenes*, 10.

**SUMMERSON, ESTHER.** Heroine and part narrator of the story of Bleak House. She was brought up as an orphan by her aunt, Miss Barbary, her origin being shrouded in mystery. On her aunt's death she was adopted by Mr. John Jarndyce, who had her educated and finally took her to manage his own home and be a companion for his ward, Ada Clare. She was the narrator of the pleasant and human side of *Bleak House*, in which her friendship with Caddy Jellyby, the attentions shown her by Guppy, her illness, her secret love of Allan Woodcourt, her consent to become John Jarndyce's wife, and his final magnanimity in handing her over to Allan, are all pleasantly and unaffectedly recounted. During the story it transpires that she is the illegitimate daughter of Captain Hawdon and Lady Dedlock, before the latter's marriage. The original of Esther Summerson was probably Miss Esther Elton, daughter of a friend of Dickens. She married a Mr. Nash, and died as late as 1903. *Bleak House*, 3–6, 8, 9, 13–15, 17–19, 23, 24, 29–31, 35–8, 43–7, 50–2, 55–7, 59–65, 67.

**SUNBURY.** Bill Sikes and Oliver passed through Sunbury at seven o'clock in the evening on their way to Shepperton. *Twist,* 21.

**SUN COURT.** On his way to serve the subpœnas on Mr. Pickwick's friends, Mr. Jackson is represented as going " direct to Sun Court, and walking straight into the George and Vulture." This was a slip of the pen, Sun Court being on the opposite side of Cornhill to St. Michael's Alley and some distance further up the street. *Pickwick,* 31.

**SUN INN, CANTERBURY.** *See* Canterbury, also Inn (6).

**SUPERINTENDENT.** The officer of the Liverpool Police who conducted the Uncommercial Traveller round the haunts of Mercantile Jack. *Uncommercial,* 5.

**SURREY CANAL.** This is now known as the Grand Surrey Canal, running from Greenland Dock to the Camberwell Road, and is familiar to all railway travellers from London Bridge Station, being crossed outside New Cross Station. *Uncommercial Traveller* (6) commented on the number of people blown into it.

**SURREY THEATRE.** This was probably the theatre at which Frederick Dorrit played the clarionet and Fanny danced (*Dorrit,* I, 7, 20). Forster relates that he and Dickens went to the Surrey Theatre in December, 1838, and saw a mangled version of *Oliver Twist,* during which, " in the middle of the first scene, Dickens laid himself down on the floor in a corner of the box and never rose from it until the drop scene fell." The theatre in which this happened was burned down in 1868, and the present building is its successor.

**SURTOUT.** This was a long coat worn, as its name implies, over all the other garments. It had voluminous skirts and was the ancestor of the frock coat.

**SUSAN.** Mrs. Mann's maid. *Twist,* 17.

**SWALLOW.** 1. One of Mrs. Jellyby's correspondents. *Bleak House,* 4.
2. The owner of a chaise at Greta Bridge. *Nickleby,* 13.

**SWALLOW STREET.** Before the making of Regent Street (1813–20) the main thoroughfare from Piccadilly to Oxford Street was up Swallow Street, the lower part of which still remains. The new street was laid out practically on the line of Swallow Street. *Barnaby,* 37.

**SWEEDLEPIPE, POLL.** Mrs. Gamp's landlord at Kingsgate Street, High Holborn, where he kept a bird-fancier's shop and did easy shaving. One of his clients was Bailey Junior, between whom and Poll a great friendship arose. At the time of Bailey's reported death, Poll was nearly demented with grief, but he finally appeared with Bailey as his future partner, and was adjured by old Martin to take better care of Mrs. Gamp. *Chuzzlewit,* 19, 26, 29, 38, 49, 52.

**SWEENEY, MRS.** A laundress in Gray's Inn. *Uncommercial,* 14.

**SWEET WILLIAM.** A card-sharper and conjurer encountered by Little Nell and her father at the Jolly Sandboys. *Curiosity Shop,* 19.

**SWIDGER, MILLY.** Wife of William Swidger, gatekeeper at the college, and the sweet-tempered, kindly woman whose nobleness of heart kept her immune from the baneful influence of the Haunted Man. Her whole family were affected by Redlaw; George, her husband's brother, died with an oath on his lips, while Philip, her husband's father, and William, her husband, were only saved by Milly's goodness. *Haunted Man.*

**SWILLENHAUSEN, BARON VON.** Father-in-law of the Baron of Grogzwig. *Nickleby,* 6.

**SWILLS, LITTLE.** A comic singer at the Sol's Arms, typical of the fourth-rate entertainers at the smaller Harmonic Meetings. *Bleak House,* 11, 19, 32, 33, 39.

**SWIVELLER, DICK.** Introduced as a rather shady friend of Fred Trent, Dick develops in the story into one of the great Dickens creations, the embodiment of grandiloquent optimism. Persuaded by Trent to wait to marry Little Nell for the sake of the old Grandfather's money, he gave up Sophy Wackles, who to Dick's disgust forthwith married a man named Cheggs. For his own purposes Quilp then made friends with Dick and got him employment with the Brasses. There Dick encountered the Marchioness, as he called their little half-starved servant, and became aware of the Brasses' villainy. Overtaken with a bad fever, Dick was nursed through it by the Marchioness, who enabled him to expose the conspiracy against Kit Nubbles, hatched by Brass and Quilp. About the same time Dick inherited a small annuity from his aunt and settled down to a respectable life, sending the Marchioness to school and eventually marrying her. One of the most remarkable features about Dick Swiveller's conversation was the number of quotations from current songs. Most of these have been traced, and are inserted in this *Encyclopædia* under their respective headings. *Curiosity Shop,* 2, 3, 7, 8, 13, 21, 23, 33–8, 48, 50, 56–66, 73.

**SWOSHLE, MRS. HENRY GEORGE.** One of the Tapkins family, callers on Mr. and Mrs. Boffin. *Mutual Friend,* I, 17.

**SWOSSER, CAPTAIN.** Mrs. Bayham Badger's first husband, an officer in the Navy. *Bleak House,* 13.

**SYLVIA.** A daughter at the farm where *George Silverman* was sent to stay as a lad.

**SYMOND'S INN.** This was on the east side of Chancery Lane near Breams' Buildings. It was neither an Inn of Court nor of Chancery, but contained mostly private offices, such as that of Mr. Vholes. *Bleak House,* 39, 51.

# T

**TABBLEWICK, MRS.** A beautiful woman, friendly with the Plausible Young Couple. *Sketches of Couples.*

**TABBY.** A maid of all work at Miss Griffin's school, the Mesrour of the Seraglio. *Haunted House.*

**TACKER.** Chief mourner and general assistant of Mould, the undertaker. " From constant blowing in the fat atmosphere of funerals he had run to seed." *Chuzzlewit,* 19, 25, 38.

**TACKLETON.** Sole representative of the firm of Gruff and Tackleton, toy merchants. He was Caleb Plummer's employer, a harsh, griping, mirthless man, to whom May Fielding had become engaged during Edward Plummer's absence in America. She was saved from marrying him, however, while Bertha Plummer's ideas of Tackleton's generosity were finally dispelled by hard facts. *Cricket on the Hearth.*

**TADGER, BROTHER.** A prominent member of the Brick Lane Ebenezer Temperance Association, who was knocked down the entrance ladder by the drunken Stiggins. *Pickwick,* 33.

**TALE OF TWO CITIES, A.** This novel appeared in *All the Year Round,* beginning in the first number of that weekly, April 30, 1859, and concluding in the issue for November 26. It was also published in the familiar green-covered monthly parts. The complete volume was published by Chapman and Hall, with illustrations by Phiz, at the close of the year.

*Principal Characters.* Dr. Manette, a Bastille prisoner and his daughter, Lucie; Charles Darnay, an emigré; Sydney Carton, a briefless barrister; Jarvis Lorry, clerk of Tellson and Co.; Jerry Cruncher, bank messenger and Resurrection Man; John Barsad, a spy; Miss Pross, Lucie's companion; the Defarges, Revolutionary leaders; various Revolutionaries.

The story opens with Jarvis Lorry's journey to Paris to bring back the liberated Bastille prisoner, Dr. Manette, who has lost his reason during his solitary confinement, but gradually regains it. The next incident is the Old Bailey trial of Charles Darnay, a Frenchman who has relinquished his title and nobility, on a charge of high treason. Partly owing to the skilful use made by his counsel of his extraordinary resemblance to Sydney Carton, Darnay is acquitted. After the trial Darnay, his counsel Stryver and Carton all visit the Manettes and try to gain Lucie's hand, but Darnay is the favoured one and they are duly married. At the earnest request of his French steward, Darnay goes over to Paris when the Revolutionary fury is at its height. He is arrested as a ci-devant noble, and after much agitation is condemned to death. Sydney Carton also goes to Paris. The great love he still

bears Lucie awakens in him a great resolve. He secures his entrance to the prison, and making use of his resemblance to Darnay, manages to get him smuggled out while he himself remains. Carton's plan succeeds, Darnay gets away with his family to England, but Carton ascends the guillotine, content at having done one good thing before his death. Side by side with this English part of the story is the narrative of events at Paris, centring round the grim Madame Defarge, implacably knitting her records of men and people.

**TALFOURD, JUSTICE.** Original of Traddles. (*q.v.*)

**TAMAROO.** An ancient female who acted as Bailey Junior's successor at Todgers's. The name, given in joke by the boarders, was from an old Winchester School song, beginning :—

Ben was a hackney coachman rare,
　"Jarvey! Jarvey! Here I am your honour."
Crikey, how he used to swear,
　Tamaroo!
How he'd swear and how he'd drive
Number three hundred and sixty-five!
　　　　　　　*Chuzzlewit,* 32, 54.

**TANCREDI.** An opera by Rossini, produced in England in 1820. *Boz, Scenes,* 14.

**TANGLE.** An eminent counsel in Jarndyce and Jarndyce. *Bleak House,* 1.

**TAPE.** Prince Bull's prim and tyrannical godmother. *Reprinted, Prince Bull.*

**TAPKINS.** 1. The name of a very extensive family who called on the Boffins. *Mutual Friend,* I, 17.

2. Felix, the gay bachelor who flirted with Mrs. Lovetown. *Is She His Wife?*

**TAPLEY, MARK.** Hostler at the Blue Dragon, Martin Chuzzlewit's friend and companion, and the apostle of good spirits and optimism. Mark's great ambition was to be jolly under the most depressing circumstances, and finding himself too comfortable to put this into practice while at the Blue Dragon, he went to London and then accompanied Martin to America. There his invincible good spirits under the worst conditions taught Martin a much needed lesson, and thanks to Mark he came back an altered man. After their return they helped in the final downfall of Pecksniff, and Mark married his old landlady, Mrs. Lupin, returning to the Blue Dragon, which was to be renamed The Jolly Tapley. *Chuzzlewit,* 5, 7, 13–15, 17, 21–3, 33–5, 43, 48, 51–4.

**TAPLIN, HARRY.** A comic singer at the White Conduit House. *Boz, Characters,* 8.

**TAPPERTIT, SIMON.** Gabriel Varden's apprentice, a bombastic youth with pretensions to winning Dolly Varden, and wholly indifferent to the blandishments of his old fellow-servant, Miggs. He was leader of the Prentice Knights, a secret society organised to restore apprentices their lost liberties and privileges, and on the outbreak of the Gordon Riots became a sort of ringleader, hoping thereby to win Dolly for his bride. During the suppression of the riots, however, Sim was badly wounded, his slender legs, so long his pride, were cru hed, and he was forced to pass the rest of his life as a shoeblack. *Barnaby*, 4, 7–9, 18, 19, 22, 24, 27, 31, 36, 39, 48–54, 59, 60, 62, 63, 70, 71, 82.

**TAPPLETON, LIEUT.** Dr. Slammer's friend and the bearer of his challenge to Winkle. *Pickwick*, 2, 3.

**TARE AND TRET.** A commercial term for the allowances which have to be made in weighing goods. *Chuzzlewit*, 19.

**TARTAR.** An old schoolfellow of Crisparkle and a neighbour of Neville Landless in Staple Inn. He was very attracted by Rosa Bud, and the impression, where the story breaks off, is that he will play a more important part and probably marry her. *Drood*, 17, 21, 22.

**TARTER, BOB.** First boy at the school, who wrote a parody on Old Cheeseman. *Reprinted, Schoolboys' Story*.

**TATHAM, MRS.** A customer at the pawnbroker's shop. *Boz, Scenes*, 23.

**TATT, MR.** An amateur detective friend of Inspector Field. *Reprinted, Detective Anecdotes*.

**TATTYCORAM.** The girl adopted by the Meagles from the Foundling Hospital to be Pet's maid. She had been given the name of Harriet Beadle, but Mr. Meagles rightly considered Beadle an impossible name for a girl. Of an intensely jealous and passionate nature, she was constantly flying into paroxysms of temper, on which occasions Mr. Meagles would bid her count twenty-five, thus allowing her a chance for calm reflection. At last Tattycoram ran away to Miss Wade, who fostered the spirit of rebellion in her. After a while she returned to the Meagles' household, however, bringing with her the iron box which Rigaud had stolen from the Clennams and had passed to Miss Wade for safe keeping. *Dorrit*, I, 2, 16, 27, 28; II, 9, 10, 20, 21, 33.

**TAUNTON, VALE OF.** This is the Vale of Taunton Dene, famous for its cider. Mrs. Nickleby, as a girl, used to visit the Hawkins's of that part (*Nickleby*, 35); while one of Mr. Vholes's objects in life was to provide honourably for his father, who lived there. *Bleak House*, 37, 39.

**TAUNTON.** 1. Mrs., with her daughters, Emily and Sophia, were the friends invited by Percy Noakes for the Steam Excursion. The whole family were bitter rivals and enemies of the Briggses. *Boz, Tales, Excursion.*

2. Captain Taunton was Dick Doubledick's officer and friend on whose advice he applied himself to his career and became a valiant soldier. Dick carried the news of her son's death to old Mrs. Taunton, his mother. *Seven Poor Travellers.*

**TAVISTOCK STREET, COVENT GARDEN.** This street is now entirely devoted to offices and warehouses, but it was residential in the days when Mr. Minns occupied a first floor there. *Boz, Tales, Minns.*

**TAXED CART.** This was a two-wheeled open vehicle drawn by one horse, and was generally used for purposes of trade. A smaller tax was paid on it than on other vehicles. *Pickwick*, 40.

**TAYLOR.** 1. A shining light in the Mormon church. *Uncommercial*, 20.

2. Jemmy, of Southwark, was one of the misers in whose lives Mr. Boffin affected an interest. *Mutual Friend*, III, 6.

3. Harriette Taylor was considered in her time as a rival of Madame Vestris; this actress made her name at Covent Garden and later joined Macready. She died in 1874. *Sketches of Young Gentlemen (Theatrical).*

**TELLSON'S BANK.** The bank of which Mr. Lorry was a confidential servant, with an extensive French connection. This was Child's Bank, whose offices are at No. 1 Fleet Street, formerly next to Temple Bar. The old building was replaced by the present in 1878. *Two Cities*, I, 2–4; II, 1, 12, 14, 21, 24; III, 2.

**TEMPLE, THE.** Associations with this old part of legal London are many, and though each Court is dealt with separately, the references to the Temple are here briefly recapitulated. Sir John Chester's chambers were in Paper Buildings (*Barnaby*, 15, 75); near which, also, were those of Stryver (*Two Cities*, II, 5). The public offices for the issue of writs, etc., is described in *Pickwick*, 31. Some of the most charming chapters of *Chuzzlewit* relate Tom Pinch's installation in his mysterious librarian's job in the Temple, Ruth's visits to fetch him and the ever-memorable courtship of John Westlock and Ruth in Fountain Court (*Chuzzlewit*, 39, 40, 43, 50, 53). Mortimer Lightwood's chambers were on the site of the present Goldsmith's buildings, by the church (*Mutual Friend*, I, 8, 12; II, 6; IV, 9, 10). Pip and Herbert Pocket shared rooms in Garden Court (*Expectations*, 39). Charley, the narrator of the *Holly Tree*, lived in the Temple, as also did Mr. Slinkton, the villain of *Hunted Down*, and the bachelor who saw the *Ghost of Art* (*Reprinted*).

**TEMPLE BAR.** "That leaden-headed old obstruction," as the old City landmark is called in *Bleak House*, was one of the features of London in olden days. It was built in 1670–2, marking the western boundary of the City. In 1878–9 it was removed and was for sale as rubbish when bought by Sir H. B. Meux and erected as the entrance to Theobald's Park, 1888. The site is now marked by the extraordinary street obstruction, known as the Griffin, erected in 1880 at a cost of over £10,000. The following are the principal references to the old Bar: *Two Cities*, I, 12; II, 12, 24; *Barnaby*, 8; *Boz, Tales, Steam Excursion; Bleak House,*

1, 19; *Mutual Friend*, III, 2; IV, 10; *Copperfield*, 46; *Dorrit*, II, 17; *Humphrey, Reprinted, Two Ghost Stories, Poor Man's Patent.*

**TEMPLE STAIRS.** These were at the foot of Middle Temple Lane. Pip and his friends used to take boat from the stairs when training for the rescue of Magwitch (*Expectations*, 46, 47), and there, also, Tartar kept his skiff. *Drood*, 22.

**" TEREWTH."** Mr. Chadband waxed very eloquent, perhaps from knowing so little about it, on " the light of Terewth." *Bleak House*, 25.

**TESTATOR, MR.** The tenant of a set of chambers in Lyons's Inn, who set himself up with furniture found in a cellar. *Uncommercial*, 14.

**TETTERBY, ADOLPHUS.** A struggling newsvendor who, with his wife and family, lived in Jerusalem Buildings. They were affected by the spirit of evil spread abroad by Redlaw, but like the rest, returned to their natural selves, thanks to Milly Swidger's good influence. *Haunted Man.*

**TEWKESBURY.** Mr. Pickwick, Ben Allen and Bob Sawyer passed through here on their way to Birmingham, dining at the Hop Pole (*q.v.*). *Pickwick*, 50.

**THAMES, BOATS ON.** Before the introduction of steam, when omnibuses were slow and uncertain, and when there were fewer bridges, one of the quickest means of transport between east and west was by the river. Watermen plied small row-boats between the many stairs which ran down to the water's edge before the Embankments were made (*Boz, Tales, Excursion*). The Thames watermen were notorious for their boisterous wit and coarse manners. It was a curious traditional custom on the river that when any two boats passed each other the boatmen, and often the occupants, should salute one another, though the best of friends or perfect strangers, in the vilest language they could summon for the purpose.

**THAMES STREET.** This long street runs practically from Blackfriars to the Tower, and formerly contained a few tumbledown private houses similar to that occupied by Mrs. Clennam (*Dorrit*, I, 3; II, 31) and by Mrs. Nickleby (*Nickleby*, 11). Florence Dombey, in the strange clothes supplied her by Good Mrs. Brown, strayed somewhere down Thames Street before she asked her way home. *Dombey*, 6.

**THAVIES INN.** This former inn of Chancery now opens out of St. Andrew's Street, near Holborn Circus. In the days when the Jellyby family lived there it was entered through an archway opening from Holborn Hill. Some of the old houses, with the area railings in which Peepy caught his head, are practically unaltered. *Bleak House*, 4, 23.

**" THEN FAREWELL, MY TRIM-BUILT WHERRY."** The words attributed to Mr.

Wegg's father were really from the first verse of Dibdin's song beginning as above. *Mutual Friend*, I, 15.

**THEOPHILE, CORPORAL.** The protector of Bebelle before she was adopted by Mr. Langley. *Somebody's Luggage.*

**THICKNESSE.** The baker friend of *Robert Bolton.*

**THIGSBERRY, DUKE OF.** The subject of one of Chuckster's spicy anecdotes. *Curiosity Shop*, 40.

**THIRSTY WOMAN OF TUTBURY.** Mrs. Nickleby was doubtlessly thinking of the Fasting Woman of Tutbury. This was Anne Moore, who claimed to have fasted for twenty-six days. After a rigid examination of her claims by Sir Oswald Mosely and Legh Richmond, Anne was proved and confessed herself an impostor. *Nickleby*, 49.

**THOM.** An advocate and practiser of homeopathy. *Mudfog.*

**THOMAS.** 1. The pavement artist who tells his story in *Somebody's Luggage.*

2. The pastrycook who catered for the Gattleton's Theatrical Party. *Boz, Tales, Porter.*

3. Various servants:—Mr. Knag's boy (*Nickleby*, 18); waiter on the gentleman who killed himself by eating crumpets on principle (*Pickwick*, 44); Sir Leicester Dedlock's groom (*Bleak House*, 40); waiter at the Winglebury Arms (*Boz, Tales, Winglebury*).

**THOMPSON.** 1. Bill, an actor at the Victoria Theatre. *Boz, Scenes*, 2.

2. A dweller in Seven Dials. *Boz, Scenes*, 5.

3. Harry, a friend of the Waters. *Boz, Tales, Tuggs's.*

4. Miss, a friend of the Domestic Young Gentleman. *Sketches of Gentlemen.*

5. A member of Parliament. *Boz, Scenes*, 18.

6. Tally Ho Thompson, a famous horse stealer. *Reprinted, Detective Police.*

**" THOUGH SEAS BETWEEN US."** From the third verse of " Auld Lang Syne." *Copperfield*, 63.

**THREADNEEDLE STREET.** In a courtyard somewhere off to the right of this street were the offices of Cheeryble Brothers. *Nickleby*, 35, 37.

**THREE CRIPPLES INN.** The filthy tavern in Little Saffron Hill, frequented by Bill Sikes and other members of Fagin's gang. *Twist*, 26, 42.

**THREE DETECTIVE ANECDOTES.** These stories, the substance of which is fact, were published in *Household Words*, September 14, 1850, and collected in *Reprinted Pieces*, 1858. Inspector Wield is, of course, the thinnest of all disguises for Inspector Field.

**THREE JOLLY BARGEMEN INN.** The village inn where Joe took his recreation and where Pip received the mysterious gift of money from the convict's friend. The original of the Bargemen was probably the

Horseshoe and Castle Inn at Cooling. *Expectations*, 10.

**"THROWN ON THE WIDE WORLD."** The actual words of the ballad, adapted by Mr. Wegg, were :—

Thrown on the wide world, doomed to wander and roam,
  Bereft of his parents, bereft of his home,
A stranger to pleasure, to comfort and joy,
  Behold little Edmund, the poor peasant boy.
        *Mutual Friend*, I, 15 ; *Bleak House*, 31.

**THURTELL, JOHN.** A gambler and cheat who murdered a man named Weare, to whom he had lost a large sum of money. Thurtell was hanged at Hertford, January 9, 1824. *Sketches of Gentlemen (Out and Out)*.

**TIBBS, MRS.** The bustling little woman who kept the boarding house in Great Coram Street, in which occurred the adventures related in *Boz, Tales, Boarding House*. Her husband was a miserable nonentity, reduced to a mere polisher of boots.

**TICKET PORTER.** This was a licensed messenger, much in use before the days of frequent posts, telephones or telegraphs, who bore a badge or ticket with the number of his licence stamped upon it. He also wore a little white apron as a kind of official uniform. The best illustration of a ticket porter is Trotty Veck in *The Chimes*. See also *Nickleby*, 37.

**TICKIT, MRS.** Housekeeper and cook to the Meagles family. *Dorrit*, I, 16, 34 ; II, 9, 33.

**TICKLE.** A member of the Mudfog Association.

**TICKLER.** The pliant cane with which Mrs. Joe Gargery maintained discipline. *Expectations*, 2.

**TIDDYPOT.** A vestryman who held that water was not a necessity of life. *Reprinted, Our Vestry*.

**"TIDE, GOING OUT WITH THE."** When Barkis lay dying, Peggotty explained to David that along the coast people always died as the tide went out. *Copperfield*, 30.

**TIFFEY.** Spenlow and Jorkins's principal clerk. *Copperfield*, 23, 26, 33, 35, 38.

**TIGER.** A servant in livery, frequently a boy of the Bailey Junior type. *Boz, Tales, Winglebury*.

**TIGG, MONTAGUE.** A choice example of the impudent, successful adventurer. His first appearance was as the friend and hanger-on of Chevy Slyme, the seedy connection of the Chuzzlewits. Even then, at the nadir of human respectability, Tigg carried it off with a rakish air. Later he turned up as Tigg Montague, the flash promoter of a bogus Assurance Company— the Anglo-Bengalee—founded on no capital and with no assets. In this position his colossal impudence demands a sort of admiration, especially at the manner in which he beat the surly and suspicious Jonas Chuzzlewit at his own game. Making use of the knowledge of Jonas's past, Tigg forced him to co-operate in luring Peck-sniff into their toils. They went down to Salisbury to do so, but Jonas was desperate at the thought of Tigg's knowledge of his secret, and murdered him in a wood near Pecksniff's house. *Chuzzlewit*, 4, 7, 12, 13, 27, 38, 40–2, 44, 47, 49, 51, 52.

**TIGGIN AND WELP.** The firm for which the Bagman's Uncle travelled—" in the printed calico and waistcoat piece line." *Pickwick*, 49.

**TILTED WAGON INN.** The roadside tavern near Cloisterham, where Neville Landless took his breakfast on setting out for his walking tour. *Drood*, 15.

**TIMBERED, MR.** A prominent member of the Mudfog Association.

**TIMBERRY, SNITTLE.** Chairman at the farewell dinner to the Vincent Crummleses before their departure for America. *Nickleby*, 48.

**TIMKINS.** A candidate for the dignity of beadle. *Boz, Our Parish*, 4.

**TIMOUR THE TARTAR.** This was a popular two-act drama which maintained its popularity on the provincial boards for many years. *Nickleby*, 22.

**TIMPSON.** A coach owner of Dullborough, knocked out of business by Pickfords. *Uncommercial*, 12.

**TIMSON, REV. CHARLES.** A friend of Gabriel Parsons and the successful aspirant to Miss Lillerton's hand and fortune. *Boz, Tales, Tottle*.

**TINKER.** 1. The ferocious-looking ruffian who tried to rob David Copperfield on the Dover Road. *Copperfield*, 13.

2. The philosophical tinker whom Mr. Traveller met on *Tom Tiddler's Ground*.

**TINKLER.** Mr. Dorrit's valet, always suspected of treating his master with disrespect. *Dorrit*, II, 3, 5, 15, 19.

**TINKLING, WILLIAM.** The editor, aged eight, of the *Holiday Romance*.

**TINY TIM.** The cripple child of Bob Cratchit. (*q.v.*)

**TIPKINS.** Promoter of a case in Doctors' Commons. *Copperfield*, 29.

**TIPKISSON.** A contumelious saddler, and a constituent of *Our Honourable Friend. Reprinted Pieces*.

**TIPP.** A carman in the employ of Murdstone and Grinby. *Copperfield*, 11, 12.

**TIPPIN, MRS. AND FAMILY.** Performers at the Ramsgate library. *Boz, Tales, Tuggs's*.

**TIPPINS, LADY.** A garrulous, vain old woman, " relict of the late Sir Thomas Tippins, knighted in mistake for somebody else." She was a prominent figure at all the Veneering functions, and voiced the opinion of Society. *Mutual Friend*, I, 2, 3, 10, 17 ; II, 3, 16 ; III, 17 ; IV, 17.

**TIPSLARK.** An early suitor of Mrs. Nickleby. *Nickleby*, 41.

**TISHER, MRS.** Miss Twinkleton's companion at Nuns' House, " a deferential widow with a suppressed voice . . . which leads one to infer that she has seen better days." *Drood*, 5, 7, 9, 13, 19.

**TITBULL'S ALMSHOUSES.** A London almshouse, founded by Samuel Titbull, deceased in 1723, for nine poor women and six poor men, and visited by the *Uncommercial Traveller*, 27. This was probably the Vintners' Almshouses, between the Cambridge and Cleveland Roads, Mile End Road.

**TITTLEBAT.** Commonly known as a stickleback. *Pickwick*, 1.

**TIX, TOM.** A bailiff put in possession at Madame Mantalini's showrooms. *Nickleby*, 21.

**TOBY.** Gabriel Varden's beer mug. *Barnaby*, 4.

**TODDLES AND PODDLES.** Two of Betty Higden's minders, who "came across the floor . . . as if they were traversing an extremely difficult road." *Mutual Friend*, I, 16.

**TODD'S YOUNG MAN.** The baker's fascinating assistant. *Boz, Scenes*, 1.

**TODDYHIGH, JOE.** A poor friend of the Lord Mayor's boyhood, who went to claim his assistance and, falling asleep in the Guildhall, overheard the story related by the giant Magog. *Humphrey*.

**TODGERS, MRS. M.** Proprietor of the commercial boarding-house near the Monument, where Mr. Pecksniff took his daughters to stay. She was a kindly soul, much harassed in the matter of gravy and in keeping her boarders contented. After Mercy's marriage to Jonas Chuzzlewit, Mrs. Todgers proved her only friend in London and gave her shelter when the tragedy reached its climax. She also made a home for Charity, and it was in the boarding-house that the guests were assembled for the wedding which never came off. *Chuzzlewit*, 8–11, 30, 32, 37, 46, 52, 54.

**TOLLIMGLOWER, LADY.** A friend of Mrs. Wardle's girlhood days. *Pickwick*, 28, 57.

**TOM.** 1. Mr. Wardle's coachman. *Pickwick*, 4, 9.

2. Driver of the Dover coach. *Two Cities*, I, 2.

3. A prisoner in Newgate. *Expectations*, 32.

4. Driver of the train which killed the signalman. *Two Ghost Stories*.

5. Clerk at the registry office, subsequently thrashed by Frank Cheeryble. *Nickleby*, 16, 43.

6. A number of purely casual characters : *Boz, Scenes*, 7, 10, 18 ; *Tales, Black Veil, Winglebury, Porter, Tottle, Drunkard; Pickwick*, 11, 31 ; *Chuzzlewit*, 19 ; *Holly Tree; Holiday Romance*.

**TOM-ALL-ALONES.** The dreadful slum, composed of streets of ruined houses abandoned in a Chancery suit, where Jo the crossing sweeper lived, was typical of the hideous areas which at that time polluted parts of London. Field Lane and the Rookery of St. Giles have been suggested as originals, but Tom-All-Alones was probably the ruined district which once centred about Drury Lane, Russell Court (now York Street) and the burial ground of St. Mary-le-Strand, closed and grassed over in 1885, and since then absorbed into the new district formed by the making of Aldwych. *Bleak House*, 16, 22, 46.

**TOMKINLEY.** The schoolmaster with whom Abel Garland went for a week-end to Margate. *Curiosity Shop*, 14.

**TOMKINS.** 1. Alfred, an artistic clerk in a winehouse, one of Mrs. Tibbs's boarders. *Boz, Tales, Boarding House.*

2. Miss, the head mistress of Westgate House seminary. *Pickwick*, 16.

3. One of the boys at Dotheboys Hall. *Nickleby*, 13.

4. The lover and eventually husband of Miss Fanny Wilson. *Strange Gentleman.*

**TOMLINSON, MISS.** Rochester postmistress and society leader of the tradesfolk at the Bull ball. *Pickwick*, 2.

**TOMMY.** 1. A greengrocer who argued with the parlour orator. *Boz, Characters*, 5.

2. Waterman at the coach stand at St. Martin's-le-Grand. *Pickwick*, 2.

**TOMPION CLOCK.** This clock, still standing in the Pump Room at Bath, is by the famous London clockmaker, Thomas Tompion (1640–1713). *Pickwick*, 36.

**TOMPKINS.** A subscriber to the Indigent Orphans' Friend's Fund. *Boz, Scenes*, 19.

**TOM TIDDLER'S GROUND.** This story appeared in the Christmas number of *All the Year Round*, 1861. Of its seven chapters, Dickens only wrote the first and two last, centring his story round James Lucas, the Hertfordshire hermit, whom he had seen earlier in the year.

**TONG.** This village, three miles E. of Shifnal, Shropshire, was acknowledged by Dickens to be the scene of Little Nell's death. The church is one of the finest in the county, but nineteenth-century restorers have left their usual marks. A " Little Nell's Cottage " is pointed out at Tong, but it has no claims whatever to the title. *Curiosity Shop*, 46, 51–5.

**TOOBY.** The unrecognised poet of *Our Town's* newspaper. *Expectations*, 28.

**TOODLE, POLLY.** Foster-mother of little Paul Dombey, and known in the Dombey household as Richards. She was dismissed for returning to see her own family and taking Paul " into haunts and society which are not to be thought of without a shudder." After Mr. Dombey's second marriage, Polly became friendly with Miss Tox and was summoned by Captain Cuttle to look after the Wooden Midshipman, where Florence had taken refuge. Polly's husband was a stoker and later the driver of a railway engine.

Their eldest son was Rob the Grinder (*q.v.*). The original of Polly Toodle was possibly Mrs. Hayes, of Manchester, servant to Dickens's sister, Mrs. Burnett. *Dombey*, 2, 3, 5–7, 15, 16, 20, 22, 38, 56, 59.

**TOORELL, DR.** A medical member of the Mudfog Association.

**TOOTING.** Guster, the Snagsby's maid, came from a sort of orphanage at Tooting. In *The Paradise at Tooting* (one of Dickens's Miscellaneous Papers collected by Mr. Matz), Drouet's Child Farm at Tooting was exposed, and it is also mentioned in *Reprinted, Walk in a Workhouse*, and this was probably the original of Guster's first home. *Bleak House*, 10, 25.

**TOOTLE, TOM.** A customer at the Six Jolly Fellowship Porters. *Mutual Friend*, III, 2.

**TOOTS, MR. P.** Dr. Blimber's oldest pupil, who, " when he began to have whiskers, left off having brains." The embodiment of kindness, and the more likeable for his weakness of mind, Toots is one of the most attractive characters of Dombey. Overwhelmed with love for Florence, he became her devoted slave, and after his emancipation from Blimber's spent his whole time trying to serve her. A curious and cordial friendship sprang up between him and Captain Cuttle, and when Walter returned, to claim Florence's love, after some anguish, Toots accepted the inevitable. Finally he married Susan Nipper, who proved the best wife he could possibly have and of whom he was immensely proud. "It's of no consequence," was Toot's constant saying, even when his suit was rejected by Florence ! *Dombey*, 11, 12, 14, 18, 22, 28, 31, 32, 39, 41, 44, 48, 50, 56, 57, 60, 62.

**TOOZELLEM, HON. CLEMENTINA.** A connection of the Stiltstalkings. *Dorrit*, I, 17.

**TOPE.** The verger of Cloisterham Cathedral, in whose house John Jasper lodged. Tope's grammar was the source of much reproof from Crisparkle. When he settled at Cloisterham, the mysterious Datchery took rooms with Mrs. Tope, and was thus able to watch Jasper. The original of Tope was a man named Miles, who worked in Rochester cathedral for seventy-five years. *Drood*, 2, 6, 12, 14, 16, 18, 23.

**TOPPER.** A guest of Fred at the Christmas dinner, where Old Scrooge made his debut as an altered man. *Christmas Carol*.

**TOPPIT, MISS.** One of the two literary ladies introduced to Elijah Pogram. *Chuzzlewit*, 34.

**TOP SAWYER.** Long, two-handled saws were usually worked over a pit, one man being above, and the other at the bottom of the pit. The latter got all the sawdust in his eyes, the former worked in comfort, directed proceedings and was altogether a more important man. *Nickleby*, 34.

**T'OTHER GOVERNOR.** Rogue Riderhood's name for Eugene Wrayburn; "T'Otherest Governor" being Bradley Headstone. *Mutual Friend*, III, 11.

**TOTT, ISABELLA.** The full name of Mrs. Belltot. (*q.v.*)

**TOTTENHAM COURT ROAD.** New shops have sprung up the whole length of this street within the past century, but it was already a kind of centre for drapery shops when Mrs. Malderton took her daughters to Messrs. Jones, Spruggins and Smiths, where Mr. Horatio Sparkins was found under his own name (*Boz, Tales, Sparkins*). A hackney coach wedding-party in this street is described in *Boz, Scenes*, 7; Meux's Brewery, the ruins of which are still (1924) in Streatham Street, stood next the Horseshoe Tavern, and is mentioned in *Boz, Scenes*, 22. Before the making of New Oxford Street the Brewery overlooked the Rookery of St. Giles. Mr. Mortimer Knagg's library was in this street. *Nickleby*, 18.

**TOTTLE, WATKINS.** The timorous old bachelor who was urged by his friend, Gabriel Parsons, to pay court to Miss Lillerton. Gabriel was obliged to pay his debts and extract him from a sponging house, but when Tottle finally proposed to Miss Lillerton he discovered that he had been forestalled by the Rev. Charles Timson. *Boz, Tales, Tottle*.

**"TOUGH, SIR, TOUGH, AND DEVILISH SLY."** One of Major Bagstock's constant appreciations of Joey B. *Dombey*, 7.

**TOUGHY.** A nickname of Jo, the crossing sweeper.

**TOWCESTER.** Mr. Pickwick, Ben Allen and Bob Sawyer stopped here on their return from Birmingham. *See* Saracen's Head.

**TOWER HILL.** This is chiefly notable as the residence of Mr. Quilp, whose reputed house, at No. 2, was demolished some while back (*Curiosity Shop*, 4). Next door was the " Crooked Billet," where Joe Willett enlisted (*Barnaby*, 31). Bella Wilfer waited in the gardens opposite Trinity House, on Tower Hill, while her father was being fitted with a new suit preparatory to taking her to Greenwich. *Mutual Friend*, II, 8.

**TOWLINSON, THOMAS.** Mr. Dombey's footman, later married to Mary Anne and established as a grocer in Oxford Market. *Dombey*, 5, 17, 18, 20, 27, 28, 31, 35, 44, 51, 59.

**TOWN ARMS, EATANSWILL.** The headquarter of the Blue party in the much contested election. It was probably the Rose and Crown, Sudbury, which was burned down in 1922. *Pickwick*, 13.

**TOX, MISS LUCRETIA.** Mrs. Chick's bosom friend, and a kindly old spinster who lived opposite Major Bagstock in Princess Place. Having entertained secret hopes of becoming the second Mrs. Dombey, Miss Tox was so overcome with disappointment at his second marriage that her secret was discovered by Mrs. Chick, who disowned her from that hour. The only one of his friends who did not turn from him in his hour of need, Miss Tox secretly ministered to Mr. Dombey, and remained his friend to the last. She is last seen trying to make something of Rob the Grinder. *Dombey*, 1, 2, 5–8, 10, 14, 16, 18, 20, 29, 31, 36, 38, 51, 59, 62.

**TOZER.** One of Dr. Blimber's pupils. *Dombey*, 12, 14, 41, 60.

**TPSCHOFFSKI, MAJOR.** Professional name of Chops, the dwarf. (*q.v.*)

**TRABB.** The obsequious tailor who fitted Pip with his first suit of clothes when he first knew of his *Great Expectations*, 19, 35.

**TRABB'S BOY.** An impudent urchin who ridiculed Pip's airs and affectations, but was one of the first to save him from the hands of Orlick. *Expectations*, 19, 30, 53.

**TRADDLES, THOMAS.** David Copperfield's old schoolfellow and intimate friend. One of the boys at Salem House, where he spent most of his time in drawing skeletons in schoolbooks, Traddles next appeared as a young law student whom David met at Mr. Waterbrook's. He was engaged to " the dearest girl in the world," but at that time saw little chance of marrying her, even upon a Britannia metal footing. He was lodging with the Micawbers, and was later that worthy man's adviser and assistant in the unmasking of Uriah Heep. Traddles was best man at David's wedding to Dora, and his constant friend and counsellor in all the difficulties which beset him. Finally Traddles married his Sophy, succeeded at the Bar and is last seen, surrounded with his wife's sisters, a prosperous lawyer about to be made a judge. Traddles's original was Justice Talfourd, for whom Dickens had the greatest affection and to whom he dedicated the volume edition of *Pickwick*. *Copperfield*, 5–7, 9, 13, 25, 27, 28, 34, 36, 38, 41, 43, 44, 48, 49, 52, 54, 57, 59, 61, 62, 64.

**TRAFALGAR SQUARE.** Work was begun in laying out this square in 1829. Portion of the Strand, including the old Golden Cross Hotel, was demolished, some dirty courts were cleared and the original square in front of the Royal Mews (the site of the National Gallery) was enlarged, the whole work taking some twelve years to complete; Nelson's Column with its statue in November, 1843, and the lions put in position in 1868. From the first Trafalgar Square was looked at askance by Londoners, and in *Reprinted, Bill Sticking*, Dickens expressed the general doubt as to whether it was an improvement. *See also Uncommercial*, 23.

**TRAMPFOOT.** A member of the Liverpool Police. *Uncommercial*, 5.

**TRANSPORTATION.** This was an old system of punishment, by which criminals were taken to some penal settlement in the colonies for a period of years or for life. The first convicts to be sent to Botany Bay, New South Wales, landed in January, 1788. Transportation thither ceased in 1840, convicts being sent thenceforward to Tasmania. By the Penal Servitude Act of 1853 transportation was abolished.

**TRAVELLER, MR.** The narrator of *Tom Tiddler's Ground*.

**TRAVELLERS' TWOPENNY.** The common lodging house where Durdles's impish friend acted as Deputy. The original was the White Duck public-house, later known as Kitt's Lodging House, in the Maidstone Road, Rochester. *Drood*, 5.

**TREASURY.** One of the magnate friends of Mr. Merdle. *Dorrit*, I, 21 ; II, 16.

**TREDGEAR, JOHN.** An old inhabitant of Lanrean. *Message from Sea*.

**TREGARTHEN, KITTY.** Alfred Raybrock's sweetheart and daughter of one of Dringworth's clerks, who had been implicated in the dishonesty of Lawrence Clissold. Her father's name was cleared by *The Message from the Sea*.

**TRENT, FREDERICK.** Little Nell's brother, and a gambling wastrel and profligate. Originally a friend of Dick Swiveller, it was his intention to marry his sister to that volatile gentleman. Later, after the disappearance of Nell and her Grandfather, young Trent became a member of a gang of gamblers, ending his life in Paris. *Curiosity Shop*, 2, 3, 7, 8, 21, 23, 34, 50, 73.

**TRENT, NELLY.** *See* Little Nell.

**TRESHAM.** The husband of Beatrice, the woman whom Young Jackson had loved and lost. By means of their little child, Polly, he was taken to their home and was in time to help them in the poverty and trouble caused by Tresham's illness. *Mugby Junction*.

**" TRICKS."** One of the phrases constantly on the lips of little Jenny Wren, the doll's dressmaker, when referring to people she did not like, was, " I know their tricks and their manners." *Mutual Friend*, II, 2.

**TRIMMERS.** A philanthropic friend of the Cheerybles. *Nickleby*, 35.

**TRINITY HOUSE.** In the garden near by (Trinity Square), Bella Wilfer waited for R. W. while he bought himself suitable clothes to take her to Greenwich. *Mutual Friend*, II, 8.

**TRINKLE.** The Cheapside upholsterer, one of whose gloves was found in Eliza Grimwood's room after the murder. *Reprinted, Detective Anecdotes*.

**TROTT, ALEXANDER.** A young tailor anxious to marry Emily Brown, but deterred from doing so by Horace Hunter's challenge. After a series of mistakes he found himself in a carriage with Miss Julia Manners, and ended by taking her to Gretna Green. In the *Strange Gentleman* the same character is called Walker Trott. *Boz, Tales, Winglebury*.

**TROTTER, JOB.** The manservant and friend of Jingle, and a worthy confederate in his rascalities. With his lachrymose contrition Job was cunning enough to deceive Sam Weller twice, but after their meeting in the Fleet Prison, Sam forgave him, and Job turned into a trusty messenger for Mr. Pickwick. Faithful to Jingle to the last, Job accompanied him to the West Indies. *Pickwick*, 16, 20, 23, 25, 42, 45–7, 53, 57.

**TROTTERS.** Nickname of Short. (*q.v.*)

**TROTTLE.** One of the unconnected characters in *Going into Society*.

**TROTWOOD, MISS BETSEY.** David Copperfield's great-aunt, a strong-minded but lovable woman. She was present at David's birth, and was so intensely annoyed and indignant that he was not a girl that she left the house in high dudgeon. When David ran away from Murdstone and Grinby's he tramped to Dover, where she lived, and claimed her protection. This she readily afforded him, and by the advice of her protegée, Mr. Dick, gave him a good education. Eventually she set him up in life, and when her own fortune was, as she imagined, dissipated by Mr. Wickfield, went to London to live with her lad. A constant and true friend to Dora, David's childwife, Miss Trotwood's hopes and desires were realised when, after his widowhood, David married Agnes Wickfield. At intervals throughout the story her scapegrace husband appears darkly, pestering her for money and eventually dying in a hospital. She was a remarkable figure of a masculine woman, keeping the donkeys from the green before her house, defying Jane Murdstone and helping in the overthrow of Uriah Heep. The original of Miss Trotwood was probably a Miss Strong, who lived at Broadstairs in the house in Victoria Parade now called Dickens House. *Copperfield*, 1, 12–15, 17, 19, 23, 34, 35, 37–45, 47–9, 51–5, 57, 59, 60, 62–4. For her husband the references are 1, 17, 23, 47, 54.

**TROUSER STRAPS.** On their first introduction, during the Regency, trousers were worn very tight, being kept stretched by a strap passing under the instep. *Boz, Characters*, 10.

**TRUCK.** A member of the Mudfog Association.

**TRUEFITT.** The well-known hairdresser's, now Walter Truefitt, Ltd., of 1 New Bond Street. *Uncommercial*, 6.

**TRUNDLE.** Wardle's son-in-law, whose marriage with Isabella Wardle gave occasion to one of the pleasantest chapters in *Pickwick*. Despite the number of occasions on which he is mentioned, there is no recorded speech of Trundell throughout the whole book. *Pickwick*, 4, 6, 8, 11, 16–19, 28, 57.

**TUCKLE.** A stout and noisy footman, one of the select party at the leg of mutton swarry. *Pickwick*, 37.

**TUGBY.** Porter to Sir Joseph Bowley, and afterwards Mrs. Chickenstalker's husband and business partner. *Chimes*.

**TUGGS.** The family whose adventures form the subject of a tale in *Boz*. Joseph, the father, came into money through winning a lawsuit; the family thereupon retired and celebrated their accession to gentility by going to Ramsgate, where they became the dupes of a couple of adventurers; Cymon, the son, being lured into a "platonic" friendship with Mrs. Captain Waters. *Boz, Tales, Tuggs's*.

**TULKINGHORN, MR.** Family lawyer to the Dedlocks and most of the aristocratic families in England. He made it his business to find out the mystery of Lady Dedlock's past. Making use of Snagsby, Jo, Trooper George and Mademoiselle Hortense, he at last found out the truth and interviewed Lady Dedlock. Almost immediately afterwards Tulkinghorn was murdered in his own house, and suspicion, which fell in turn on Trooper George and Lady Dedlock, was at last set at rest by Bucket's arrest of Hortense, who considered that Tulkinghorn had not paid her sufficiently for her information. Tulkinghorn's house was that actually occupied by John Forster, and now turned into offices, 58 Lincoln's Inn Fields. *Bleak House*, 2, 7, 10–12, 16, 22, 24, 25, 27, 29, 33, 34, 36, 39–42, 47–9, 52, 54.

**TULRUMBLE, NICHOLAS.** The vulgar coal merchant who, on being elected Mayor of Mudfog, decided to treat the town to an inaugural show, like the Lord Mayor's show in London. *Tulrumble*.

**TUNBRIDGE WELLS.** Both the references to this watering place are of a romantic nature. Mr. Finching proposed to Flora " once in a hackney coach, once in a boat, once in a pew, once on a donkey at Tunbridge Wells and the rest on his knees " (*Dorrit*, I, 24). A chubby old gentleman went up to Miss Pupford on the Promenade and, according to Miss Linx, squeezed her hand, murmuring, " Cruel Euphemia, ever thine." *Tom Tiddler*.

**TUNGAY.** The brutal one-legged man who acted as porter and factotum at Salem House. *Copperfield*, 5–7.

**TUPMAN, TRACY.** One of Mr. Pickwick's companions, and although somewhat elderly, a very susceptible gentleman. He accompanied Jingle to the Rochester ball, and was the first to make the acquaintance of the Wardles, where he conquered the heart of Miss Rachel, but lost her through the unscrupulous machinations of Jingle. After that episode Tupman took little further part in the doings of the book, and is left in retirement at Richmond, where he posed as a gay bachelor, much admired by the elderly ladies. *Pickwick*, 1–9, 11–15, 18, 19, 22, 24–6, 28, 30–2, 34, 35, 40, 44, 47, 57.

**TUPPLE.** The life and soul of the New Year's party. *Boz, Characters,* 3.

**TURK.** A bloodhound kept by John in *The Haunted House.*

**TURNPIKE.** The maintenance of the highroads formerly depended on tolls collected at the various turnpike gates. In the middle of the last century the development of county and other local authorities placed the roads in their hands, a system of rates was arranged and, with the exception of a few small bridges, every road and bridge is now open to traffic. The tolls over the London bridges were abolished in 1878–79.

**TURNSTILE.** The neighbourhood of this turning from Holborn into Lincoln's Inn was formerly a great place for tailors. *Boz, Characters,* 9.

**" TURN UP."** With invincible optimism Mr. and Mrs. Micawber were always " waiting for something to turn up." *Copperfield,* 11, 12, 17, 27, 28, 36, 52, 54.

**TURVEYDROP, PRINCE.** The dancing master whom Caddy Jellyby married was named after the Prince Regent, much admired by his father as a model of deportment. Prince was a cheerful, hardworking soul, who supported his father in all that old man's monstrous vanity and laziness ; with Caddy's help he built up a good connection. His father, the Model of Deportment, was a selfish creature, one of the relics of the shallow foolish days of the Regency. The academy, where his son worked so hard, has been identified as 26 Newman Street, Oxford Street. *Bleak House,* 14, 23, 30, 38, 50, 67.

**TUSSAUD, MADAME.** These famous waxworks were brought to England by Madame Tussaud in 1802. After touring the country they were established at the Baker Street Bazaar in 1833, whence they were removed to the present galleries in 1884. *Reprinted, Bill Sticking.*

**" 'TWAS EVER THUS."** This quotation is from the " Fire Worshippers," in Moore's *Lalla Rookh.* The actual lines are :—

> Oh ! Ever thus, from childhood's hour
> I've seen my fondest hopes decay ;
> I never loved a tree or flower,
> But 'twas the first to fade away.
> I never nursed a dear gazelle,
> To glad me with its soft black eye,
> But when it came to know me well,
> And love me, it was sure to die.

*Curiosity Shop,* 56 ; *Copperfield,* 38 ; *Mutual Friend,* IV, 16.

**TWEMLOW, MELVIN.** A harmless little gentleman, the only individual deserving that title, who was one of Veneering's constant guests. He owed his popularity to being the cousin of Lord Snigsworth. Mrs. Lammle confided in him and used him to rescue Georgiana Podsnap from her husband's clutches. *Mutual Friend,* I, 2, 10, 17 ; II, 3, 16 ; III, 13, 17 ; IV, 16, 17.

**TWICKENHAM.** Dickens lived here for a while in 1838 at 4 Ailsa Park Villas. In the

meadows opposite Twickenham by the riverside Sir Mulberry Hawk and Lord Verisopht fought their fatal duel (*Nickleby,* 50). The Meagles's house was " a charming place on the road by the river," and thither Arthur Clennam often went visiting. *Dorrit,* I, 16, 17, 26, 28.

**TWIGGER, EDWARD.** Better known as Bottle-nosed Ned, he was a drunken character at Mudfog, whom Tulrumble persuaded to dress up in armour for his Mayoral procession. *Tulrumble.*

**TWINKLETON, MISS.** Principal of the Nun's House School at Cloisterham, and a charmingly prim old maid. She was fond of Rosa Bud, whom she joined in London after the girl had run away from Jasper's attentions. Mr. Grewgious settled Rosa and Miss Twinkleton at the redoubtable Billickins, who declared instant war on the schoolmistress. *Drood,* 3, 6, 7, 9, 13, 19, 20, 22.

**TWIST, OLIVER.** The chief character in the novel of that name under which heading his adventures are briefly outlined. *Twist,* 1–22, 24–6, 28–36, 38, 40, 41, 49, 51–3.

**TWO GHOST STORIES.** These short stories, entitled *The Trial for Murder* and *The Signal Man,* appeared in the extra Christmas Numbers of *All the Year Round* for 1865 and 1866 respectively. The former was one of Dr. Marigold's prescriptions, and was labelled, " To be taken with a grain of salt."

**TWOPENNY POST.** Before the introduction of the penny postage there was a twopenny post within the City, with extension for a small extra charge to towns and suburbs within a radius of about ten miles. There were six collections and deliveries daily, and the two main offices for collection were the G.P.O. (until 1829 in Lombard Street) and Gerrard Street, Soho. Up to 5 p.m. letters were handed in at the various sub-post offices, and from 5 p.m. until 6 p.m. the twopenny postman went round the streets, sometimes on horseback, ringing a bell, receiving any letters and charging an extra penny for his trouble. His uniform was " a scarlet cloth coat with blue lapels and lining, blue cloth waistcoat and a hat with a gold band." *Boz, Tales, Boarding House ; Pickwick,* 2, 30 ; *Sketches of Gentlemen* (*Military*).

**TYBURN.** The brass triangle in Bayswater Road, opposite Edgware Road, does not mark the site of the gallows mentioned in *Two Cities,* II, 2, and *Barnaby, Preface.* The old gallows, commemorated by the triangle, were moved in 1759 to make way for a turnpike toll-house, and were re-erected to one side, on a spot now covered by a house at the south-east corner of Connaught Square.

# U

**" 'UMBLE, I'M VERY."** The battle cry and watchword of the Heep family. *Copperfield*, 16, 17, 25, 35, 39, 42, 52, 61.

**UNCOMMERCIAL TRAVELLER.** This is a delightful series of essays and short sketches which appeared at various times in *All the Year Round*. The first seventeen were collected and published by Chapman and Hall in 1860 ; a second edition, in which were included eleven more papers, appeared in 1868, and six New Uncommercial Samples were added the following year. The whole collection is now usually bound together. It need scarcely be remarked that the sketches are records of actual events and travels.

**UNDERY.** The solicitor and friend of John, who made one of the party assembled to lay the ghost of the *Haunted House*.

**UNITED BULLDOGS, THE.** This was the name adopted by Sim Tappertit's secret society of Prentice Knights when it allied itself to the Protestant party and joined the Gordon Rioters. *Barnaby*, 36.

**UNITED GRAND JUNCTION EBENEZER TEMPERANCE ASSOCIATION.** A full and circumstantial report of the meeting of the Brick Lane branch of this worthy assembly is given in *Pickwick*, 33.

**UNITED METROPOLITAN IMPROVED HOT MUFFIN AND CRUMPET BAKING AND PUNCTUAL DELIVERY COMPANY.** A concern of which Ralph Nickleby was a director. *Nickleby*, 2.

**UPWITCH, RICHARD.** Greengrocer and common juryman, impanelled in the jury which tried the case of Bardell v. Pickwick. *Pickwick*, 34.

**UXBRIDGE.** On December 23, 1864, Dr. Marigold finished up his country round at Uxbridge, clean sold out, and made his way to London to spend his Christmas, and, as it transpired, to meet his Sophy.

# V

**VALE, SAM.** *See* Weller, Samuel.

**VALENTINE.** Captain de la Cour's orderly, " sole housemaid, valet, cook, steward and nurse in the family." *Somebody's Luggage.*

**VALENTINE AND ORSON.** Twin brothers and heroes of an ancient romance. They were born in a forest, Orson was suckled and reared by a bear, while Valentine was brought up in a king's palace. Orson was eventually reclaimed from a life of savagery by his polished brother. *Reprinted, Child's Story.*

**VALIANT SOLDIER INN.** This was the public-house kept by Jem Groves. Nell and her Grandfather were sheltering there when the old man was lured into gambling by the gang of swindlers whom " honest Jem Groves " encouraged. *Curiosity Shop,* 29.

**VARDEN.** Gabriel Varden was a jolly, honest locksmith, a constant friend to Mrs. Rudge and a stalwart upholder of law and

order when the riots broke out. His life was made wretched by the religious meagrims of his wife, who was aided and abetted by her malicious maid, Miggs. When the riots broke out in all their fury, however, Mrs. Varden appreciated the value of her husband and turned over a new leaf, as a preliminary refusing to take Miggs back into the household. *Barnaby*, 2–7, 13, 19, 21, 22, 26, 27, 36, 41, 42, 51, 63, 64, 71, 72, 74–6, 79, 80, 82.

Dolly Varden was Gabriel's pretty daughter, loved by Joe Willett and the object of Sim Tappertit's adoration. Dolly was her father's only friend in the gloom cast in their household by Mrs. Varden and Miggs. She was the foster sister and close friend of Emma Haredale, between whom and Edward Chester she contrived to maintain communication. In a fit of coquetry she let Joe Willett enlist as a soldier, much to Sim Tappertit's satisfaction. When the riots broke out Dolly and Emma fell into the hands of the rioters, both Maypole Hugh and Sim Tappertit having set their hearts on obtaining Dolly. The dispersal of the rioters and the timely arrival of Joe and Edward saved the girls, however, and not long afterwards Dolly became Joe's happy bride. Dolly Varden was founded largely upon Maria Beadnell, the description of her face tallying almost exactly with portraits of that young lady. 4, 7, 13, 19–23, 27, 28, 31, 41, 59, 70–2, 78, 80, 82.

**VAUXHALL BRIDGE.** The present structure, opened in 1906, replaced the first bridge, opened in 1816, which spanned the river at this spot. After his rejection by Lizzie Hexam, Bradley Headstone and his young friend were crossing the bridge on their way home when they encountered Eugene Wrayburn (*Mutual Friend*, II, 1). Thomas, the pavement artist, and his Henrietta were " enjoying the cool breezes wafted over Vauxhall Bridge " when she made the fatal decision to go to Piccadilly. *Somebody's Luggage.*

**VAUXHALL GARDENS.** These once popular and famous pleasure gardens were just across Vauxhall Bridge, on the left-hand side of Upper Kennington Lane. The site is now covered with small streets, the area being approximately that contained by Goding Street, Leopold Street and Tyers Street. In its latter days Vauxhall became rather a rowdy resort. Many famous balloon ascents were made from the Gardens, which were finally closed July 25, 1859. The gardens are well described in *Boz, Scenes*, 14.

**VECK, TOBY or TROTTY.** The cheery, diligent little ticket porter who fell asleep on New Year's Eve and had the visions which form the story of *The Chimes*. The church beneath whose tower he had his pitch was St. Dunstan's, Fleet Street.

**VENDALE, GEORGE.** Partner and eventually sole representative of Wilding and Co., wine merchants. After Wilding's death, following the discovery of the mistake which had taken place in his adoption, Vendale carried on the business, and paid court to Marguerite Obenreizer. He accompanied Jules Obenreizer to Switzerland, having been summoned thither to detect a fraud which Obenreizer had perpetrated, but when they were in a dangerous mountain pass Obenreizer threw him over a precipice and left him for dead. He was, however, saved by Marguerite, and eventually it transpired that Vendale himself was the missing orphan and heir to the Wilding business. *No Thoroughfare.*

**VENEERING, HAMILTON AND ANASTASIA.** A showy couple, " a trifle sticky " from being so bran-new, who entertained a large circle of guests on any and every occasion. Veneering bought himself a seat for the rotten borough of Pocket Breaches, but he and his wife take little part in the story, though their dinner table was a great place for hearing the voice of Society. *Mutual Friend*, I, 2, 10, 11, 17; II, 3, 16; III, 17; IV, 17.

**VENGEANCE, THE.** One of Madame Defarge's friends, the wife of a grocer, and was one of the most prominent furies of the Revolution, who evinced a ghastly interest in the daily spectacle of the guillotine, to which she herself finally found her way. *Two Cities*, II, 22; III, 3, 5, 9, 10, 12, 14, 15.

**VENICE.** This was the first place to which the Dorrits, with their new-found fortune, repaired on the Continent; thither went Mr. Sparkler to pay his court to Fanny. *Dorrit*, II, 4–7.

**VENNING, MRS.** One of the residents on Silver Store Island. *English Prisoners.*

**VENTRILOQUIST, THE.** Companion of the Face Maker in the French-Flemish fair. *Uncommercial*, 25.

**VENUS, MR.** Taxidermist and general practitioner in bones, "human and various." He made Wegg's acquaintance through having bought that gentleman's amputated leg. At Wegg's suggestion Venus entered into the plot to blackmail Boffin, but at an early stage repented and let Mr. Boffin into the secret of what was going on. Venus's life was darkened by his hopeless love for Pleasant Riderhood, who objected strongly to his business. "I do not wish to regard myself, nor to be regarded in that bony light " were the fatal words by which his hopes were blighted. In the end, however, she changed her opinion and married him. The original of Venus was a J. Willis, of 42 St. Andrew Street, Seven Dials. *Mutual Friend*, I, 7; II, 7; III, 6, 7, 14; IV, 3, 14.

**VERISOPHT, LORD FREDERICK.** One of Sir Mulberry Hawk's dupes, a wealthy young nobleman whose whole life was wrecked by his debauched mentor. He protested against Hawk's designs on Kate and

his treatment of Nicholas, a quarrel arose, followed by a duel, and the young peer was killed " by the hand which he had loaded with gifts and clasped a thousand times." *Nickleby*, 19, 26–8, 32, 38, 44, 50.

**VHOLES, MR.** Richard Carstone's solicitor and adviser in the Jarndyce case. Professing the utmost uprightness and integrity, prating about his good name and those dependent on him, Vholes undoubtedly dragged Richard yet deeper into the toils of the law and poisoned his mind against his friend John Jarndyce and all who would have helped him. *Bleak House*, 37, 39, 43, 45, 51, 60, 62, 65.

**VICTORIA THEATRE.** This was the name, since corrupted to Old Vic., given in 1833 to the Cobourg Theatre (*q.v.*). *Boz, Scenes*, 2.

**VICTUALLER, MR. LICENSED.** Proprietor of a place of entertainment for mercantile seamen in Liverpool. *Uncommercial*, 5.

**VILLAGE COQUETTES, THE.** This comic opera, the music of which was by John Hullah, was produced at the St. James's Theatre on December 6, 1836. Despite the good company by which it was presented, it had a run of fifteen nights only. The story deals with two pretty village girls who coquette with the squire and his friend but resist their too ardent advances and finally marry the lads of their choice.

**VILLAM.** Hostler at the Bull Inn, Whitechapel. *Pickwick*, 22.

**VINTNERS' ALMSHOUSES.** *See* Titbull's Almshouses.

**VOIGT, MAÎTRE.** The chief notary of Neuchatel, who was largely instrumental in unmasking the villainy of Jules Obenreizer. He had a wonderful clock safe which Obenreizer manipulated for his own ends and learned the secret of Vendale's identity. *No Thoroughfare.*

**VOLUNTEER CORPS.** During the Napoleonic Wars many volunteer corps were raised throughout the country. It was to one of these that Mr. Tibbs had belonged. *Boz, Tales, Boarding House.*

**VUFFIN.** A travelling showman, proprietor of a giant and a limbless lady whom Nell and her Grandfather met on their wanderings. *Curiosity Shop*, 19.

# W

**WACKLES, MISS SOPHY.** Dick Swiveller's first love, " a fresh, good humoured, buxom girl of twenty " who, with her sisters Jane and Melissa, kept a small day school. Intending to follow Fred Trent's advice, and marry Little Nell, when she was old enough, Dick threw over Sophy Wackles and had the mortification of seeing her married to a market gardener named Cheggs. *Curiosity Shop*, 7, 8, 21, 50, 58.

**WADE, MISS.** A curious, discontented woman who urged Tattycoram to run away from the Meagles, although after a time the girl came to her senses and returned to them. Miss Wade was implicated in Rigaud's theft of Mrs. Clennam's papers. Her full story is told in Book II, Chapter 21. *Dorrit*, I, 2, 16, 27, 28 ; II, 9, 20, 21, 33.

**WAFERS** were used before the invention of envelopes or gummed edges. The letter, written on one side only of the paper, was folded over and stuck together with a wafer, which was simply a small disk of dried paste, usually made of flour, water and gum. The wafer was moistened, placed between the two parts to be stuck together, and the whole was then usually sealed or pressed together with a stamp.

**WAGHORN, MR.** A member of the Mudfog Association.

**WAINEWRIGHT, T. G.** Original of Jonas Chuzzlewit and Julius Slinkton.

**WAKEFIELD.** A family who arrived late for the *Steam Excursion*. *Boz, Tales.*

**WAKLEY, THOMAS.** (1795–1862.) A surgeon, and founder of the *Lancet*, Wakley was best known in his time as the coroner for West Middlesex, an office he occupied from 1839 until his death. *Uncommercial*, 18.

**WALCOT SQUARE.** This opens out of the Kennington Road (second turning on the left from Lambeth Road) and is little changed since Mr. Guppy laid " the 'ouse in Walcot Square, the business and myself, before Miss Summerson for her acceptance." *Bleak House*, 64.

**WALDENGARVER.** The stage name of Mr. Wopsle. (*q.v.*)

**"WALKER."** This was formerly a popular expression of incredulity. It was an abbreviation of Hookey Walker, said to be the nickname of a certain eagle-nosed old clerk in a Cheapside warehouse, named John Walker. One story says that he was responsible for the output of work, and when this fell below the standard would tell his employers all kinds of stories to account for the fact. His tales were, however, disbelieved, and the expression Hookey Walker became current to describe a story not worthy of credit.

**WALKER.** 1. A resident at No. 5, in the suburban street. *Boz, Scenes, 2.*

2. Auditor of the Indigent Orphans' Friends. *Boz, Scenes, 19.*

3. A horse-dealer from Islington, imprisoned for debt. *Boz, Tales, Tottle.*

4. Mick, one of the boys at Murdstone and Grinby's. *Copperfield, 11, 12.*

5. H., a convert to teetotalism, whose edifying story was told in the Brick Lane report. *Pickwick, 33.*

**WALK IN A WORKHOUSE, A.** This sketch appeared in *Household Words*, May 25, 1850, and was republished in *Reprinted Pieces*, 1858. It gives a rather gloomy picture of a Metropolitan workhouse of the time.

**WALMER, HARRY.** The young gentleman, aged eight, whose elopement with

Norah formed the subject of Boots' tale in the *Holly Tree*.

**WALTER, EDWARD M'NEVILLE.** Name under which Theodosius Butler wrote his *Considerations on the Policy of Removing the Duty on Beeswax*. *Boz, Tales, Sentiment.*

**WALTERS.** 1. Charley, an inmate of the workhouse. *Reprinted, Walk in a Workhouse.*

2. Lieutenant Walters was the name invariably given by Toots to Walter Gay. *Dombey, 50.*

**WALWORTH.** This is no longer the quiet suburban retreat which Wemmick found favourable to romance and generous sentiments, and the situation of the Castle is not known (*Expectations*, 24, 25, 37, 45, 48). The back part of Walworth, " a dreary waste," was the scene of the young doctor's mysterious adventure (*Boz, Tales, Black Veil*), and there Mr. Tibbs retired after separation from his wife (*Boz, Tales, Boarding House*). The high winds of Walworth are described in *Uncommercial*, 6.

**WANDSWORTH.** Part of the piece of waste land by the railway line, upon which Dr. Marigold pitched his carts, is still used by caravans, and can be seen from the L.B. & S.C. Railway, a short distance on the up line from Clapham Junction Station. *Marigold.*

**WANT.** One of Miss Flite's captive birds. *Bleak House*, 14.

**WAPPING.** This neighbourhood and its workhouse is described in *Uncommercial*, 3, Mr. Baker's Trap being the Old Gravel Lane Bridge between the London and East Docks.

**WARDEN.** 1. Michael, the ne'er-do-well squire in Dr. Jeddler's village, with whom Marion Jeddler was supposed to have eloped. His affairs were pulled round by Snitchey and Craggs, and he did eventually marry Marion. *Battle of Life.*

2. William, the subject of *Boz, Tales, Drunkard.*

**WARDLE.** Mr. Wardle was a jolly old English yeoman farmer, bluff and hearty, and never so happy as when he had his house full. The Pickwickians made his acquaintance at the Chatham review, and were thereafter frequent visitors at Manor Farm, Dingley Dell. His Christmas festivities, his shooting parties, his simple openheartedness make Wardle one of the most refreshing characters in the book. He and his old mother, rather querulous, but full of affection, are supposed to be founded on Mr. Spong and his mother, occupants of Cob Tree Hall, Sandling. *Pickwick*, 4–10, 16–19, 28, 30, 54, 57.

Miss Rachel, Wardle's elderly spinster sister, inspired a tender passion in the breast of Mr. Tupman. Her small fortune, however, aroused the cupidity of Jingle, who, trading on her jealousy and vanity, persuaded her to elope with him. They were pursued to London, where Jingle readily gave up Miss

Rachel in exchange for Wardle's cheque for £120. 4, 6–11, 18, 25.

Isabella and Emily were Wardle's pretty daughters. Isabella married Trundle, the wedding being the occasion of much jollity and not a little flirting; Emily and Snodgrass were secretly in love throughout the story, becoming openly engaged when Mr. Pickwick came out of the Fleet. They married and settled down near Dingley Dell. 4, 6–9, 11, 14, 18, 28, 30, 54, 56, 57.

**WARMING PAN.** Before the introduction of hot bottles, beds were warmed by means of live coals placed in a brass-covered receptacle at the end of a stick. The warming pan, as this was called, was pushed up and down between the sheets until they were thoroughly aired and warm. *Pickwick,* 34.

**WARREN, THE.** This was the Haredale mansion near Chigwell, the scene of Reuben Haredale's murder, and after its sack by the Gordon Rioters, of his murderer's arrest. *Barnaby,* 1, 20, 55, 56.

**WARREN'S BLACKING.** Dickens's old associations with one of the Warren's Blacking firms (*see* Murdstone and Grinby), possibly occasioned the various references in the novels. Characteristic advertisements of those days were parodies and adaptations of popular songs and poems, and Warren's were famous for such jingles. *Curiosity Shop,* 28; *Boz, Scenes,* 5; *Pickwick,* 33.

**WARWICK.** The scene of a pleasant day's outing by Mr. Dombey and his guests, when Mrs. Skewton waxed particularly enthusiastic about the Castle and its reminiscences of ancient days (*Dombey,* 27). In the autumn of 1838 Dickens and Browne made the trip there together.

**WARWICK, THE EARL OF.** A pickpocket encountered in the Rookery of St. Giles. *Reprinted, Inspector Field.*

**WASTE.** One of Miss Flite's captive birds. *Bleak House,* 14.

**WATCHMAN.** Before the institution of the police force a number of decrepit old men were employed as watchmen in London and other towns, their duty being to patrol the streets at night, call out the time and state of the weather, and keep an eye on property. Watchmen or "Charlies," as they were commonly called, were the recognised butt of practical jokers, the height of humour being to upset the old fellows as they sat dozing in their boxes. Police superseded the London watchmen in 1829, but they lingered on in the country for some time. *Pickwick,* 36.

**WATERBROOK, MR. AND MRS.** The London friends with whom Agnes Wickfield stayed in Ely Place. He was a pompous, self-satisfied solicitor, with great notions of gentility; "Other things are all very well in their way, but give me Blood." *Copperfield,* 24, 25, 27.

**WATERLOO BRIDGE.** The first stone of the Strand Bridge was laid October 11, 1811, and under its new name of Waterloo Bridge it was opened June 18, 1817. From the beginning its arches have sheltered the homeless, and one of its early patrons must have been Sam Weller, who saw many strange and heartrending sights there (*Pickwick,* 16). If the arches sheltered the homeless, the bridge itself seemed to present a dreadful attraction for the desperate, many a poor wretch having cast himself from it in despair. *Boz, Tales, Drunkard; Reprinted, Down with the Tide.*

**WATERLOO ROAD.** The scene of the murder of Eliza Grimwood, as related by Inspector Wield (*Reprinted, Three Detective Anecdotes*). While walking along this road with his friend Click, Thomas, the pavement artist, expatiated on his sorrows. *Somebody's Luggage.*

**WATERLOO STATION.** This was the railway station from which Lizzie Hexam's friends set off with Frank Milvey for her bedside wedding. Bradley Headstone was waiting in the station, and there learned how fruitless had been his crime. The original station, where these events happened, was built in 1846 and originally consisted of two platforms only, for arrival and departure. *Mutual Friend,* IV, 11.

**WATERMAN.** Hackney coach stands and cab ranks were each supplied with a licensed waterman, whose duty it was to water the horses and see that the drivers accepted fares in rotation. A typical waterman is described in *Boz, Scenes,* 7 and *Pickwick,* 2.

**WATERMEN.** The name commonly given to Thames boatmen. *See* Thames.

**WATERS, CAPTAIN.** The gallant captain and his fascinating wife, Belinda, were fellow-passengers with the Tuggses on the Ramsgate boat. The susceptible Cymon fell a victim to Belinda's charms, his protestations of platonic love were not believed, and the friendship cost the Tuggs family fifteen hundred pounds. *Boz, Tales, Tuggs's.*

**WATERTOAST SYMPATHISERS.** An American association sympathising with an Irish patriot—not from admiration of him, but from jealousy of England. *Chuzzlewit,* 21, 22.

**WATKINS.** Kate Nickleby's godfather, not to be confounded with the Watkins who kept the Old Boar. *Nickleby,* 18.

**WATKINS THE FIRST.** The father of Princess Alicia. *Holiday Romance.*

**WATSON.** 1. The Misses, friends of the Very Friendly Young Gentleman. *Sketches of Gentlemen.*

2. Robert, original of Gashford. (*q.v.*)

**WATTS'S CHARITY.** This is a gabled building in Rochester High Street, fully described, together with the particulars of the Charity, in *Seven Poor Travellers.*

**WATTY.** One of Mr. Perker's clients, " a pestering bankrupt." *Pickwick*, 31.

**"'WE,' SPELL IT WITH A."** How the Wellers spelled their name. *Pickwick*, 34, 55.

**WEAK-EYED YOUNG MAN, THE.** Dr. Blimber's footman, the special object of Mrs. Pipchin's wrath. *Dombey*, 11, 12, 14.

**WEDGINGTON, MR. AND MRS. B.** Variety artists at the seaside resort. *Reprinted, Out of the Season.*

**WEEDLE, ANASTASIA.** A Mormon emigrant to Salt Lake City. *Uncommercial*, 20.

**"WEEP FOR THE HOUR."** Mr. Wegg's adaptation was from Moore's poem, " Eveleen's Bower," which begins :—

> Oh ! weep for the hour
> When to Eveleen's bower
> The Lord of the Valley with false vows came.
> *Mutual Friend,* I, 15.

**WEEVLE.** This was the name adopted, while under a cloud, by Guppy's friend Jobling. *Bleak House*, 20.

**WEGG, SILAS.** A rascally, old, one-legged ballad monger, who kept a stall near Cavendish Square and exhibited a board with the inscription :—

> Errands gone
> On with fl
> Delity By
> Ladies and Gentlemen
> I remain
> Your humble Servt.
> Silas Wegg.

He was engaged by Mr. Boffin to initiate him into the mysteries of literature by reading out *The Decline and Fall Off the Rooshan Empire*, in which he was assisted by draughts of gin and water " to meller the organ." For his readings Wegg charged half a crown a night, poetry extra on account of "its weakening effect on the mind," but agreed to lapse into verse occasionally, in the light of a friend. He was eventually installed in Boffin's Bower, and while poking about the Mounds discovered a will of Old Harmon, of later date than that already proved, and leaving all the property to the Crown. By means of this document Wegg attempted to blackmail Boffin, but Venus, whom he had taken into partnership in the " friendly move " to bleed Boffin, informed that gentleman of Wegg's plot, and assisted at that impostor's final downfall.

The original of Silas Wegg was a well-known character who for many years kept a ballad and gingerbread stall near Cavendish Square. *Mutual Friend*, I, 5, 7, 15, 17 ; II, 7, 10 ; III, 6, 7, 14 ; IV, 3, 14.

**WELBECK STREET.** Lord George Gordon's house, whither he rode on his triumphal entry to London, was No. 64, entirely altered since his time. *Barnaby*, 37.

**WELLER.** Samuel, Mr. Pickwick's man-servant. One of the best-known characters of Dickens, Sam is the embodiment of Cockney wit, resourcefulness and trust-worthiness. He was boots at the White

Hart, Borough, when engaged by Mr. Pickwick as his personal attendant, and thenceforward was that worthy man's inseparable companion and often his counsellor. His evidence at the trial was amusing and highly damaging to Dodson and Fogg. When Mr. Pickwick settled down as a prisoner in the Fleet, Sam arranged for his own imprisonment so that he could still attend his master. In the final pairing off of the various lovers Sam took a prominent part, assisted therein by Mary, the Pretty Housemaid, whom he had met at Mr. Nupkins' house in Ipswich. When Mr. Pickwick settled at Dulwich, Sam remained by his side, finally marrying Mary, who was appointed housekeeper. In *Humphrey* he reappears, with his little son Tony. Among the many suggested originals of Sam Weller the most probable is Sam Vale, who played the character of Simon Spatterdash in Beazeley's *Boarding House* at the Surrey Theatre in 1822. *Pickwick*, 10, 12, 13, 15, 16, 18–20, 22–8, 30, 31, 33–5, 37–48, 50–2, 55–7. A list of Wellerisms is given at the end of this book.

Mr. Tony Weller, Sam's father, was a stage coachman and " a rayther stout gen'l'm'n of eight-and-fifty." Almost as great a character as Sam, old Tony Weller represents the extinct race of coachmen at their prime. Always susceptible to ladies, he married a widow for his second wife and lived to consider himself a warning to all men against the evils of matrimony. With the aid of Sam he got his revenge on the pious fraud who had sponged on his wife, and some time after her death retired from the road with a comfortable competence, residing in a public-house on Shooter's Hill. He reappeared with Sam in *Humphrey*, very proud of his grandson and namesake. 10, 13, 16, 20, 22, 23, 27, 33, 34, 43, 45, 52, 55–7.

Tony Weller's second wife, Mrs. Susan Weller, was relict of a Mr. Clarke and hostess of the Marquis of Granby, Dorking. Her wooing by Mr. Weller is narrated in *Pickwick*, 10 ; after their marriage she got into the hands of the canting drunkard, Stiggins, and though a good enough woman in her way, led her husband a miserable life. On her deathbed, however, she saw her mistake and expressed her sorrow, leaving Mr. Weller all her property, excepting a small legacy to Sam. 10, 16, 20, 22, 23, 27, 33, 43, 45, 52, 55.

**WELLER, MARY.** Original of Mary the Pretty Housemaid and of Clara Peggotty.

**WELLINGTON STREET.** This street was cut through from Bow Street, across the Strand, to the new bridge in 1829–30. The first editorial offices of *Household Words* faced the Lyceum Theatre, at No. 16 (demolished in the construction of Aldwych, 1903). They were later moved to the present No. 26 (formerly No. 11). *Reprinted, Detective Police.*

**"WE MET."** T. H. Bayley's song, "We met—'twas in a crowd." *Boz, Tales, Christening.* See also "My Feelings."

**WEMMICK, JOHN.** Chief clerk to Mr. Jaggers, the Old Bailey attorney. Businesslike and unsentimental in the Little Britain offices, Wemmick was a kindhearted fellow at home in Walworth with his old father, known as the Aged, and it was as the Walworth Wemmick that he assisted Pip to obtain a partnership for Herbert Pocket and to attempt the smuggling away of Magwitch. In his curious dry way Wemmick invited Pip one day to his Castle at Walworth, and took him for a walk. "Halloa, here's a church," he said. "Let's go in." Then, "Here's Miss Skiffins, let's have a wedding." The original of Wemmick was Thomas Mitton, a solicitor, Dickens's old schoolfellow and lifelong friend. *Expectations,* 20, 21, 24, 25, 32, 36, 37, 45, 48, 51, 55.

**WEST, DAME.** Grandmother of Harry, the clever scholar. *Curiosity Shop,* 25.

**WESTGATE HOUSE.** This was the girls' school at Bury St. Edmunds, where Job Trotter sent Mr. Pickwick on a wild-goose chase after Jingle. There have been various surmises as to the original of this, but it is generally supposed to have been Southgate House. *Pickwick,* 16.

**WESTLOCK, JOHN.** A former pupil of Pecksniff and Tom Pinch's staunch friend. While living with Pecksniff he had discovered his true character, and it was with delight that John welcomed Tom's severance from that hypocrite's service. Westlock was a friend of Lewsome, and saw that he was taken care of when ill. The arrival of Ruth Pinch sealed John's fate, and after a delightful courtship and proposal in Fountain Court they were duly engaged and married, on the condition that Tom was always to live with them. *Chuzzlewit,* 2, 12, 25, 29, 36, 37, 39, 40, 45, 48–53.

**WESTMINSTER ABBEY.** Here Charles Dickens was buried, Tuesday, June 14, 1870. The stone above his grave, in the Poets' Corner, bears the simple inscription :—

CHARLES DICKENS,
Born February the Seventh, 1812;
Died June the Ninth, 1870.

Herbert Pocket took Pip to the Abbey the morning of his first Sunday in London (*Expectations,* 22). Martha Endell hurried past it on her way to the river, where she sought to destroy herself (*Copperfield,* 47). It is also mentioned in *Uncommercial,* 13.

**WESTMINSTER BRIDGE.** The original stone bridge, built in 1739–50, was replaced by the present iron structure in 1862. It was, therefore, over the former that Barnaby Rudge and his mother saw the crowds of Gordon demonstrators marching to St. George's Fields (*Barnaby,* 47). Close by the old bridge on the Surrey side was Searle's Yard (*Boz, Scenes,* 10). Charles Hexam and

Bradley Headstone crossed the new bridge on their way to see Lizzie in Smith Square (*Mutual Friend,* I, 1), while in one of his night walks *Uncommercial Traveller* (13) speculated on the Houses of Parliament while crossing from the Surrey side.

**WESTMINSTER HALL.** The old houses of Parliament were clustered irregularly between Westminster Hall and the river, and there took place the angry scenes which preceded the Gordon Riots (*Barnaby,* 42, 43). At the north-west angle of the hall, in Old Palace Yard, was the Exchequer Coffee House, given as an address by Julius Handford, alias Harmon (*Mutual Friend,* I, 3). Adjoining the Hall on the west, where now is a sunken green and the statue of Oliver Cromwell, were the old law courts. Here the Jarndyce case dragged its weary way to extinction (*Bleak House,* 19, 24, 65). These courts were closed and demolished when the new courts were made in the Strand, 1883.

**WESTWOOD.** Sir Mulberry Hawk's second in the fatal duel with Lord Frederick Verisopht. *Nickleby,* 50.

**WHARTON, GRANVILLE.** George Silverman's pupil whom he married to Adelina Fareway.

**WHEEZY, PROF.** A member of the Mudfog Association.

**"WHEN FOUND MAKE A NOTE OF."** Captain Cuttle's advice. *Dombey,* 19, 23, 32, 39, 56.

**"WHEN HE WHO ADORES THEE."** One of Moore's best known Irish Melodies. *Curiosity Shop,* 35.

**"WHEN THE HEART OF A MAN."** A song from the "Beggar's Opera," quoted correctly by Mr. Wegg (substituting "Venus" for "a woman") in *Mutual Friend,* III, 14. See also *Curiosity Shop,* 8.

**WHIFF, MISS.** A young lady in Mugby Refreshment Room.

**WHIFFERS.** A member of the fraternity of Bath footmen, obliged to leave his place because he had been required to eat cold meat. *Pickwick,* 37.

**WHIFFIN.** The town crier of Eatanswill. *Pickwick,* 13.

**WHIFFLER, MR. AND MRS.** The Couple who Dote upon their Children. *Sketches of Couples.*

**WHILKS, MRS.** A prospective client of Mrs. Gamp. *Chuzzlewit,* 19.

**WHIMPLE.** The landlady of the house where Old Bill Barley and his daughter lodged. *Expectations,* 46.

**WHISKER.** Mr. Garland's restive pony, the pride of Kit Nubbles's life. *Curiosity Shop,* 14, 20–2, 38, 40, 57, 65, 68, 73.

**WHITE.** 1. A super in the amateur theatrical company. *Boz, Scenes,* 13.

2. A riotous young gas fitter. *Boz, Characters,* 9.

3. The policeman on duty in Gray's Inn Road. *Reprinted, Inspector Field.*

4. Betsey, a Liverpool harpy, battening on Mercantile Jack. *Uncommercial*, 5.

5. One of Mrs. Lemon's pupils. *Holiday Romance.*

**WHITECHAPEL.** There were several coaching houses in the Whitechapel Road. The Black Lion, where Joe Willet suffered such ignominy, has disappeared with the exception of the yard, at the back of No. 75 (*Barnaby*, 4, 37). The Bull Inn, whence Mr. Weller drove Mr. Pickwick and Mr. Peter Magnus to Ipswich, was demolished in 1868, its site being now occupied by Aldgate Avenue, just beyond the Metropolitan Station (*Pickwick*, 20, 22). On the same side of the road, citywards, was the Blue Boar where David Copperfield alighted on his first arrival in London (*Copperfield*, 5). In the neighbourhood of Whitechapel was the house to which Oliver was conveyed after he had been kidnapped from Mr. Brownlow (*Twist*, 19). The *Uncommercial Traveller* passed through the district several times (3, 10, 34) and mused on the neighbourhood.

**WHITE CONDUIT HOUSE.** This was on the right-hand side going up Penton Street, the site being now covered by the block of buildings between Albert Street and Denmark Road. It was a tavern with grounds and for many years a favourite Cockney resort, until, towards the 30's, it became so disreputable that it was closed and demolished, 1849. *Boz, Scenes*, 20 ; *Characters*, 8.

**WHITECROSS STREET.** The debtors' prison was on the left-hand side going from Fore Street, on the site now occupied by the Midland Railway Goods Offices. It was one of the strictest prisons, used more as a place of punishment for contempt than for detention. It was opened in 1815, and the building was demolished in 1870. *Pickwick*, 40.

**WHITEFRIARS.** Now in the heart of newspaper world, this was anciently Alsatia, and one of the most disreputable parts of London. In one of its slums lived the Drunkard, whose pitiful story is told in the last of *Boz's Tales*. Jerry Cruncher lived in Hanging Sword Alley, also in Whitefriars (*Two Cities*, II, 1). At the Whitefriars gate of the Temple Pip received his warning from Wemmick, not to go home. *Expectations*, 44.

**WHITEHALL.** "Fine place—little window—somebody else's head off there—eh, sir ? " Thus Mr. Jingle summed up the palace and its history (*Pickwick*, 2). At Whitehall, probably outside the Metropolitan Police Office, then at 4 Whitehall Place, John Harmon saw the placard announcing the discovery of his own body under suspicious circumstances. *Mutual Friend*, II, 13.

**WHITE HART INN.** 1. The house at Bath where Mr. Pickwick and his friends put up. This inn, which belonged to the coach proprietor Moses Pickwick, was closed in 1864, the Grand Pump Room Hotel being subsequently built on its site. *Pickwick*, 35.

2. The White Hart, Borough, was the inn to which Jingle took Miss Rachel Wardle and where Sam Weller was employed as boots. White Hart Yard, in Borough High Street, opposite Southwark Street, is all that remains of the old inn which was demolished in 1889. *Pickwick*, 10.

**WHITE HORSE CELLAR.** This was the starting place of the West of England coaches. The old house stood at the corner of Piccadilly and Arlington Street, now covered by part of the Ritz Hotel, and from there Mr. Pickwick and his friends started for Bath (*Pickwick*, 35). It was at the "Whytorseller" that Esther Summerson arrived from Reading to be met by the susceptible Mr. Guppy (*Bleak House*, 3, 9). The house was later moved to the other side of Piccadilly, and this, in turn was replaced in 1884 by Hatchett's Restaurant.

**"WHITE SAND AND GREY SAND."** A very ancient round : " White sand and grey sand, who'll buy my white sand, who'll buy my grey sand." *Dorrit*, I, 32.

**"WHO RAN TO CATCH ME."** This was a favourite and much parodied nursery song by Anne Taylor. *Curiosity Shop*, 38.

**WICKAM, MRS.** Paul Dombey's nurse in succession to Polly Toodle. She was a doleful person, " always ready to pity herself, or to be pitied, or to pity someone else." *Dombey*, 8, 9, 11, 12, 18, 58.

**WICKFIELD.** Mr. Wickfield was the Canterbury lawyer who managed Miss Trotwood's affairs and with whom David lived while at school. Although with no thought in the world but for the welfare of his daughter Agnes, he gave way to drink and fell into the hands of his clerk Uriah Heep, who became partner in the business. In Mr. Wickfield's name Uriah defrauded many people of their money, but his villainy was detected and brought to light by Micawber and Mr. Wickfield's name cleared. His house at Canterbury has been identified as 71 St. Dunstan's Street. *Copperfield*, 15–7, 19, 25, 35, 39, 42, 52, 54, 60.

Agnes Wickfield was the friend and " sister " of David Copperfield's youth, whom he called his good angel. Like most angelic beings, Agnes was a rather dull and wearisomely good young woman. From early days she loved David, but when he married Dora she proved a staunch friend of the " child wife," who, on her deathbed, made the extraordinary request that only Agnes should fill her vacant place as David's wife, which all came to pass in due course. Agnes was pestered by the attentions of Uriah Heep, who used his malign influence with old Mr. Wickfield to favour his suit. Agnes Wickfield, justly summed up by Mr. Edwin Pugh as " the apotheosis of the female prig and bore," was one of the Mary Hogarth heroines. *Copperfield*, 15–19, 23–6, 28, 34–6, 39, 42, 43, 49, 52–4, 57, 58, 60, 62–4.

**WICKS.** A clerk in the offices of Dodson and Fogg. *Pickwick*, 20.

**"WIDDERS."** The principal observations of Mr. Tony Weller on this subject were the following :—

Be wery careful o' widders all your life, specially if they've kept a public-house (*Pickwick*, 20). If ever you're attacked with the gout, Sir, jist you marry a widder as has got a good loud woice with a decent notion of usin' it, and you'll never have the gout agin (20). Widders are 'ceptions to ev'ry rule. I *have* heerd how many ord'nary women one widder's equal to in pint o' comin' over you. I think its five and twenty (23). I was a goin' down to Birmingham by the rail, and I wos locked up in a close carriage vith a living widder. Alone we wos ; the widder and me wos alone ; and I believe it was only because we *wos* alone, and there was no clergyman in the conweyance that that 'ere widder didn't marry me afore ve reached the half-way station. *Humphrey.*

**WIDGER, MR. AND MRS. BOBTAIL.** The Plausible Young Couple. *Sketches of Couples.*

**WIDOWS.** See "Widders."

**WIELD, INSPECTOR CHARLES.** An officer of the London Detective Police. A thin disguise for Inspector Field (*q.v.*). *Reprinted, Detective Police.*

**WIG, WELSH.** This was a kind of close-fitting worsted cap. *Dombey*, 4 ; *Christmas Carol.*

**WIGS.** One of Miss Flite's captive birds. *Bleak House*, 14.

**WIGSBY.** 1. A member of the Mudfog Association.

2. An active and loquacious member of *Our Vestry. Reprinted Pieces.*

**WILDING, WALTER.** Head of Wilding and Co., wine merchants, and a foundling. He had been adopted from the Foundling Hospital by Mrs. Wilding, brought up by her and established in business. After her death it transpired that a mistake had been made at the Foundling, that he was not the child whom she had intended to adopt. Wilding died while attempting to unravel the intricacies and discover the true facts of the case, which form the subject of *No Thoroughfare.*

**WILDSPARK, TOM.** A coachman tried for manslaughter, but "got off vith a alleybi." *Pickwick*, 33.

**WILFER.** Bella Wilfer was the beautiful girl destined by old Harmon's will to marry his son John. She was a rather capricious but altogether charming girl, greatly mortified at being a widow without ever having been married, owing to John Harmon's supposed death. Bella was adopted by the Boffins, and for a while lost her head, though always realising her mercinariness. When wooed by John Rokesmith she indignantly refused so humble a match, but her better nature

was aroused at seeing his apparent ill-treatment by Boffin, sympathy became love and she ran away and married him, not being told the secret of his identity until some time later. A delightful feature of Bella's character was her love for her henpecked father. This most charming and natural of Dickens's girls was founded upon Maria Beadnell. *Mutual Friend*, I, 4, 9, 16, 17 ; II, 8–10, 13, 14 ; III, 4, 5, 7, 9, 15, 16 ; IV, 4, 5, 11–13, 16.

Reginald Wilfer, called by his wife R. W. and in his office Rumty, was a long-suffering little man whose life may be summed up in his own words, "What might have been is not what is." He had, however, a staunch friend in his daughter Bella, upon whom, in turn, he exerted a good influence. I, 4 ; II, 8, 14 ; III, 4, 16 ; IV, 4, 5, 16.

Mrs. Wilfer is one of the most tremendous of Dickens's characters, indescribable in her stateliness and grandiloquence. Beyond being invariably disagreeable and posing as the ill-used victim of everybody and everything, she played but little part in the story. She was "much given to tying up her head in a pocket handkerchief knotted under the chin. This headgear, in conjunction with a pair of gloves worn within doors, she seemed to consider as at once a kind of armour against misfortune—and as a species of full dress." It is surmised that the original of Mrs. Wilfer was partly founded on Dickens's mother, Mrs. John Dickens. I, 4, 9, 16 ; II, 8 ; III, 4, 16 ; IV, 5, 16.

Lavinia, or Lavvy Wilfer, was Bella's younger sister, and her nickname of the Irrepressible summed up this young lady's character admirably. She had no particular affection for anybody, laughed at her mother, sneered at her father, was jealous of Bella, and expended her ill-humour on George Sampson, her unfortunate adorer. I, 4, 9 ; II, 8 ; III, 4, 16 ; IV, 5, 16.

**WILKINS.** 1. Samuel, Miss Jemima Ivins's young man. *Boz, Characters*, 4.

2. One of Captain Boldwig's gardeners. *Pickwick*, 19.

3. A prospective client of Mrs. Gamp. *Chuzzlewit*, 49.

4. Scrooge's fellow apprentice. *Christmas Carol.*

5. A resident of Chichester, cited by the Very Friendly Young Gentleman. *Sketches of Gentlemen.*

**WILLETT.** Joe Willett, son of old John, was a likely young fellow, head over ears in love with Dolly Varden. He was treated as a child by his father and the silly old men of the Maypole, until at last, running away to London and making a final but vain appeal for Dolly's love, he enlisted. After some years he returned in time to save Dolly from the Rioters, and this time she did not forbid his lovemaking. Joe had lost an arm in the defence of the Savannah, and this, more than anything else, helped to reconcile him to his old father. *Barnaby*, 1–4, 13, 14, 19, 21, 22, 24, 29–31, 33, 41, 58, 59, 67, 71, 72, 78, 80, 82.

John Willett was the wooden-headed, obstinate and dogmatic old landlord of the Maypole Inn, Chigwell. By treating his son as a child he drove the lad into the Army. He narrowly escaped with his life when the Gordon Rioters passed the Maypole on their way to sack the Warren, but he was pulled round by his old cronies, who had the utmost veneration for his sagacity. On Joe's return, with one arm lost "in the defence of the Salwanners," old John was overcome with admiration of his prowess, and his last words were, " I'm a going, Joseph, to the Salwanners." 1–3, 10–14, 19, 21, 29, 30, 33–5, 54–6, 72, 78, 82.

**WILLIAM.** 1. The waiter at the Yarmouth Hotel who ate David's dinner and drank his ale on his first trip to London. *Copperfield*, 5.

2. The coachman who drove David to London from Canterbury. *Copperfield*, 19.

3. Waiter at the Saracens' Head. *Nickleby*, 5.

4. Sir Mulberry Hawk's groom. *Nickleby*, 32.

5. A visitor at Astley's. *Boz, Scenes*, 11.

**WILLIAMS.** 1. William, one of the customers at the Six Jolly Fellowship Porters. *Mutual Friend*, I, 6 ; III, 3.

2. A police constable in Ratcliff Highway. *Reprinted, Inspector Field.*

3. A murderer. *See* Bishop and Williams.

4. Caleb, the hero of a strong but somewhat morbid novel of the same name, written by William Godwin, 1794. *Boz, Scenes*, 20.

**WILLIAMSON, MRS.** Landlady of the Winglebury Arms. *Boz, Tales, Winglebury.*

**WILLING MIND TAVERN.** Daniel Peggotty's house of call. *Copperfield*, 3.

**WILLIS.** 1. The Misses Willis, four sisters, were the subjects of much discussion in *Boz, Our Parish*, 3.

2. A vulgar prisoner in the Cursitor Street sponging house. *Boz, Tales, Tottle.*

**" WILL WATCH THE SMUGGLER."** This was a ballad by John Davy, beginning :

One morn when the wind from the northward blew keenly,
While sullenly roared the big waves of the main,
A famed smuggler, Will Watch, kissed his Sue, then serenely
Took helm and to sea boldly steered out again.
*Reprinted, Out of Season.*

**WILLY.** The dead brother of Little Nell's friend. *Curiosity Shop*, 55.

**WILSON.** 1. A constable at the houses of Parliament. *Boz, Scenes*, 18.

2. A member of the Old Street Suburban Representative Discovery Society. *Boz, Characters*, 5.

3. Caroline, a pupil at Minerva House, the ugliest girl in Hammersmith, or out of it. *Boz, Tales, Sentiment.*

4. The gentleman who played Iago at the Gattletons' amateur theatricals. *Boz, Tales, Porter.*

5. Fanny and Mary, characters in *The Strange Gentleman.*

**WILSON'S CHARACTERS.** The book purchased by Boffin was Henry Wilson's " Wonderful Characters, comprising memoirs and anecdotes of the most remarkable persons of every age and nation." London, 1821. *Mutual Friend*, III, 6.

**WINDOW TAX.** This was a house tax, originally levied upon all windows, but subsequently upon all above six in number. It was repealed in 1851, the house tax being then graded according to rent. *Boz, Characters*, 5 ; *Reprinted, Begging Letter Writer.*

**" WIND'S IN THE EAST, THE."** John Jarndyce's way of saying that things were not going smoothly. *Bleak House*, 6, 8, 14.

**WINDSOR.** The home of John Podgers and the scene of some of the exciting adventures narrated by Mr. Pickwick in *Humphrey*. Esther Summerson's first unhappy home with her aunt, Miss Barbary, was at Windsor (*Bleak House*, 3). On the way thither *Dr. Marigold* began to teach little deaf and dumb Sophy her letters.

**WINDSOR TERRACE, CITY ROAD.** This is the second turning on the right past St. Luke's Workhouse, going up the City Road. No house now has " a great brass plate on which was engraved ' Mrs. Micawber's Boarding Establishment for Young Ladies,' " but the street is little changed otherwise from the days when David lodged with that remarkable couple. *Copperfield*, 11.

**WINKLE.** Nathaniel Winkle was one of Mr. Pickwick's companions in his journeys, and the more or less comic character of the party. His ambitions to be a sportsman led him into all sorts of scrapes, but his most sporting adventure was a runaway match with pretty little Arabella Allen. Having obtained his father's forgiveness for his rash marriage he settled down " presenting all the external appearance of a civilised Christian ever afterwards." *Pickwick*, 1–9, 11–15, 18, 19, 22, 24–6, 28, 30–2, 34–9, 44, 47, 48, 50, 51, 53, 54, 56, 57.

Mr. Winkle, Senior, was a prosperous wharfinger in Birmingham. When Mr. Pickwick, accompanied by Bob Sawyer and Ben Allen, went to acquaint him with his son's marriage, they met with a cold welcome, but the old gentleman went to London to see his daughter-in-law for himself, and became quite reconciled to the match. Mr. Winkle's house in Birmingham, identified as being in Easy Row, was demolished in 1913. *Pickwick*, 47, 50, 53, 56, 57.

**WINKS.** Deputy at the Travellers' Twopenny at Cloisterham. *See* Deputy. *Drood*, 23.

**WISBOTTLE, MR.** One of Mrs. Tibbs's boarders, of a musical turn and an aristocratic taste. " He knew the peerage by heart and could tell off-hand where any illustrious personage lived." *Boz, Tales, Boarding House.*

**WISK, MISS.** Mr. Quale's fiancée, a lady with a mission. *Bleak House*, 30.

**WITCHEM, SERGEANT.** One of the *Detective Police*. Obviously a disguise for Sergeant Jonathan Whitcher, a well known detective of the 40's and 50's. *Reprinted Pieces*.

**WITHERDEN, MR.** The notary to whom Abel Garland was articled. He was a close friend of the Garlands and assisted the Single Gentleman in tracing out Little Nell and her Grandfather. With the information supplied by the Marchioness Mr. Witherden was enabled to unmask the villainy of the Brasses and Quilp. *Curiosity Shop*, 14, 20, 38, 40, 41, 60, 63, 65, 66, 73.

**WITHERFIELD, MISS.** The middle-aged lady in curl papers whose bedroom Mr. Pickwick inadvertently entered. The morning following this misadventure Mr. Peter Magnus introduced her to Mr. Pickwick as his affianced bride. The confusion of each party aroused his most violent suspicion; he threatened Mr. Pickwick dreadfully but vaguely, whereupon Miss Witherfield hurried to Nupkins the Mayor and gave information of an intended duel. *Pickwick*, 22, 24, 34.

**WITHERS.** Mrs. Skewton's wan page, constantly pushing her about in a chair. *Dombey*, 21, 26, 27, 30, 37, 40.

**WITTITTERLEY, HENRY AND JULIA.** The soulful lady and her devoted husband with whom Kate Nickleby was employed as companion. All went well until Mrs. Wittitterley became jealous of the attentions Kate received from Sir Mulberry Hawk; she was then dismissed. *Nickleby*, 21, 27, 28, 33.

**WIZZLE.** A member of the Steam Excursion party. *Boz, Tales, Excursion*.

**WOBBLER, MR.** Clerk in the Circumlocution Office. *Dorrit*, I, 10.

**WOLF, MR.** A guest at Tigg Montague's dinner to Jonas Chuzzlewit. Wolf was a literary character of a particularly offensive type. *Chuzzlewit*, 28.

**WOOD, JEMMY.** One of the misers in whom Mr. Boffin pretended to take an interest. *Mutual Friend*, III, 6.

**WOODCOURT, ALLAN.** A young surgeon, first called in to certify the death of Nemo the law-writer. Before going as a ship's doctor to India he fell in love with Esther Summerson. On his return he became Richard Carstone's friend and adviser, attended poor Jo's last moments and played an active part in the story. Eventually Mr. Jarndyce bade Esther marry him and set them up in a practice in the north of England. Allan's mother, old Mrs. Woodcourt, a kindly old lady but intensely proud of her Welsh and Scottish ancestry, at first felt that Esther was not well enough connected to be her daughter-in-law. But she soon grew to love the girl. *Bleak House*, 11, 13, 14, 17, 30, 35, 45-7, 50-2, 59-61, 64, 65, 67.

**WOODEN MIDSHIPMAN, THE LITTLE.** This was the sign outside old Sol Gills's instrument shop. This originally stood above the shop of Messrs. Norie and Wilson, 157 Leadenhall Street. The Midshipman was subsequently moved with the business to 156 Minories, where it may still be seen inside the shop. *Dombey*, 4; *Uncommercial*, 3.

**WOODENSCONCE, MR.** A member of the Mudfog Association.

**" WOODPECKER TAPPING."** This is from a once popular song by Moore, set to music by M. Kelly, beginning, " I knew by the smoke that so gracefully curled." The last two lines of the second verse are :—

Every leaf was at rest and I heard not a sound
But the woodpecker tapping the hollow beech tree.
*Boz, Tales, Boarding House ; Chuzzlewit*, 25 ;
*Copperfield*, 36 ; *Dorrit*, I, 35.

**WOOD SAWYER, THE.** A man outside the prison of La Force who used to talk with Lucie when she went to see her husband. *Two Cities*, III, 5, 9, 13.

**WOOD'S HOTEL.** *See* Furnival's Inn.

**WOOD STREET.** The Cross Keys Hotel, the house for the Rochester coaches (*Expectations*, 20, 32), was on the site now occupied by Nos. 129-30. The speed at which the mail coaches used to dash through the street is mentioned in *Dorrit*, I, 13.

**WOOLFORD, MISS.** One of the horseriders at Astley's. *Boz, Scenes*, 11.

**WOOLWICH.** Name of the Bagnet boy. *See* Bagnet.

**WOPSLE, MR.** Parish clerk and a friend of the Gargery family. He had great leanings to the Church, but ultimately turned to the stage and having thrown up his job, left the village and went on the London boards, taking the name of Waldengarver. Pip and Herbert went to see him as Hamlet, but his success was not commensurate with his ambitions and he eventually became a mere super. *Expectations*, 4–7, 10, 13, 15, 18, 31, 47.

**WORDS.** One of Miss Flite's captive birds. *Bleak House*, 14.

**WOSKY, DR.** Mrs. Bloss's obsequious medical man. *Boz, Tales, Boarding House*.

**WOZENHAM, MISS.** Mrs. Lirriper's rival lodging-house keeper in Norfolk Street, Strand. When she was about to be sold up, Mrs. Lirriper stepped in and saved her, thus making a lifelong friend. *Lirriper's Lodgings and Legacy*.

**WRAYBURN, EUGENE.** Mortimer Lightwood's intimate friend, a briefless, indolent barrister. From aimless curiosity he interested himself in the Harmon case and thus met Lizzie Hexam, to whom he was immediately attracted. Much against her brother's will Lizzie allowed Eugene to have her educated, but when she realised her own love for him, and the blind jealousy which made Bradley Headstone his enemy, she disappeared. Eugene discovered her whereabouts through Jenny Wren's drunken father, followed her to her hiding-place up the river and was there attacked by Bradley Headstone. Lizzie saved his life and nursed him through the illness which followed, eventually marrying him upon his sick-bed as soon as he recovered consciousness. His final determination was to work and uphold his wife in the face of Society. *Mutual Friend*, I, 2, 3, 8, 10, 12–14; II, 1, 2, 6, 11, 14–16; III, 1, 9, 10, 11, 17; IV, 1, 6, 7, 9–11, 16.

**WRECK OF THE "GOLDEN MARY."** This story appeared in the Christmas number of *Household Words*, 1856. It is a simply told narrative of the experiences of a shipwrecked party exposed for many days in open boats.

**WREN, JENNY.** The name adopted by Fanny Cleaver, the crippled dolls' dressmaker, who proved such a staunch friend to Lizzie Hexam. A hard working girl, she supported her drunken father, called by Wrayburn Mr. Dolls, to whom she always referred as her bad child. It was through a letter to Jenny, intercepted by Mr. Dolls, that Eugene obtained Lizzie's address in the country. After Mr. Doll's death, Jenny found a protector in Riah, the Jew. She was fetched to Eugene Wrayburn's bedside, where she guessed his wish to make Lizzie his wife. Jenny is last seen with Sloppy as a constant visitor, from which suitable inferences may be drawn. *Mutual Friend*, II, 1, 2, 5, 11, 15; III, 2, 3, 10, 13; IV, 8–10, 16.

**WRIGHT'S INN, ROCHESTER.** Described by Jingle as "Wright's, next house," this was originally known as the Crown, but was rechristened Wright's by one of its proprietors of that name. The house was rebuilt in 1864. It also reappears as the Crozier, where Datchery put up at Cloisterham. *Pickwick*, 2; *Drood*, 18.

**WRYMUG, MRS.** One of the clients of the general agency office, seeking a cook—three serious footmen employed. *Nickleby*, 16.

**WUGSBY, MRS. COLONEL.** One of the ancient, whist-like ladies, in the Bath Assembly Room. *Pickwick*, 35, 36.

# Y

**YARMOUTH.** This seaside town, which figures so largely in *Copperfield*, was visited by Dickens in 1848, when he stayed at the Royal Hotel with John Leech and Mark Lemon. Peggotty's house, made from a boat, was on the Denes, but it had no particular prototype, Mr. F. G. Kitton effectually disposing of the theory that the inverted bricked-up boat, found in 1879, was the original. *Copperfield*, 3, 5, 8, 9, 10, 21, 22, 30, 51, 55.

**YATES, FRED.** (1797–1892.) In his prime this actor was famous in Shakespearean parts. For many years he was manager at the Adelphi. *Sketches of Gentlemen* (*Theatrical*).

**YAWLER.** An old schoolfellow of Traddles at Salem House, who assisted him at the beginning of his legal career. *Copperfield*, 27.

**"YET LOVED I."** Dick Swiveller's remarkable adaptation is from the old song "Alice Gray," words by W. Mee, music by Mrs. P. Millard. The first verse ends :—

Yet lov'd I as man never lov'd, a love without decay,
Oh! my heart, my heart is breaking for the love of Alice Gray. *Curiosity Shop*, 50.

**YORK.** The somewhat melancholy story of the Five Sisters of York was related by the grey-haired gentleman to the passengers of the broken-down coach (*Nickleby*, 6). Young John Chivery went thither in search of a clue in the establishment of the Dorrit fortune. *Dorrit*, I, 25.

**YORK STREET.** *See* Tom-All-Alone's.

**YOUNG, BRIGHAM.** The successor to Joe Smith as head of the Mormons, and the moving spirit in the establishment of that "religion" in Salt Lake City. He made polygamy compulsory, himself possessing over twenty wives, and was active in encouraging conversions and immigration of converts to Utah. *Uncommercial*, 20.

**YOUNG, CHARLES.** (1777–1856.) This actor was of great repute in his day, being the leading tragedian in the interim between Kemble and Kean. *Sketches of Gentlemen* (*Theatrical*).

**YOUNG BLIGHT.** The office boy employed by Mortimer Lightwood to look after the clients who never arrived. *Mutual Friend*, I, 8, 12; III, 17; IV, 9, 16.

**YOUNGEST GENTLEMAN IN COMPANY.** *See* Augustus Moddle.

**YOUNG PERSON, THE.** "A certain institution in Mr. Podsnap's mind . . . embodied in Miss Podsnap, his daughter. . . . The question about everything was, would it bring a blush to the cheeks of the young person ? " *Mutual Friend*, I, 11.

**YOUTH.** One of Miss Flite's captive birds. *Bleak House*, 14.

# Z

**ZAMBULLO, DON CLEOPHAS.** The person to whom the sights of Madrid were revealed in Le Sage's *Le Diable Boiteux*. *Curiosity Shop*, 33.

**ZAMIEL.** "A tall, grave, melancholy Frenchman," passenger on the express train to Paris. *Reprinted, A Flight*.

**ZEPHYR.** A drunken prisoner in the Fleet, in whose room Mr. Pickwick spent his first night. *Pickwick*, 41, 42.

**ZULU KAFFIRS.** The exhibition of Zulus which occasioned the writing of *Our Noble Savage* (*Reprinted Pieces*), opened at St. George's Gallery, May 16, 1853, and attracted great attention. The native party consisted of 11 men and 1 woman with her infant. The chief was named Moxos, and his second in command was the witch doctor Umlow. They were brought over by A. T. Caldecott and performed amid realistic scenery, with actual Zulu huts, etc.

# FAMILIAR SAYINGS

*A collection of the phrases and whimsicalities by which the most famous of the Dickens characters are best known.*

**AUNT, MR. F.'s.** "There's milestones on the Dover Road." *Dorrit*, I, 23.

**BAGNET.** "Discipline must be maintained." *Bleak House*, 27, 34, 52, 66.

**BAGSTOCK.** "He's tough, sir, tough, and devilish sly." *Dombey*, 7, 10, 26.

**BARKIS** is willin'. *Copperfield*, 5, 8, 21, 30.

**BLIMBER, MRS.** If she could have known Cicero she would have died contented. *Dombey*, 11, 24, 60.

**BUMBLE.** "The law is a ass—a idiot." *Twist*, 51.

**BUNSBY, CAPTAIN.** "The bearings of this observation lays in the application on it." *Dombey*, 23, 39.

**CARTON, SYDNEY.** "It is a far, far better thing that I do than I have ever done ; it is a far, far better rest that I go to than I have ever known." *Two Cities*, III, 15.

**CHADBAND.** "Terewth, the lamp of heaven." *Bleak House*, 25.

**CHICK, MRS.** "Make an effort." *Dombey*, 1, 18, 29, 58.

**CIRCUMLOCUTION OFFICE.** How not to do it. *Dorrit*, I, 10, 34 ; II, 8.

**CRUNCHER.** Jerry calls himself an honest tradesman and complains bitterly of his wife's constant "flopping." *Two Cities*, II, 1, 14 ; III, 8, 14.

**CRUPP, MRS.** "I'm a mother myself." *Copperfield*, 26, 34.

She also remarked, when David took rooms with her, "Thank heaven she had now found some 'un she could care for." 23, 26.

**CUTTLE, CAPTAIN.** "Overhaul your catechism." *Dombey*, 4, 23.

"When found make a note of." 19, 23, 32, 39, 56.

"Put it back half an hour every morning and about another quarter towards the arternoon, and it's a watch that'll do you credit." 19, 48.

"Cap'en Cuttle is my name and England is my nation, this here is my dwelling-place and blessed be creation—Job." 32.

"Any just cause or impediment why two persons should not be jined together in the house of bondage." 50, 56.

**DICK, MR.** He cannot keep Charles the First and his head out of the Memorial. *Copperfield*, 14, 17, 36, 60.

**DOMBEY, PAUL.** Little Paul wonders what the waves are always saying. *Dombey*, 8, 12, 16.

**GAMP, MRS.** *See* page 175.

**GENERAL, MRS.** "Papa, potatoes, poultry, prunes and prism—prunes and prism." *Dorrit*, II, 5, 7, 15, 19.

**GENTLEMAN IN SMALL CLOTHES.** "All is gas and gaiters." *Nickleby*, 49.

**GRIP, THE RAVEN.** "Polly put the kettle on and we'll all have tea." *Barnaby*, 17, 25, 47, 57, 81.

**GUMMIDGE, MRS.** "I'm a lone, lorn creetur, and everythink goes contrairy with me." *Copperfield*, 3, 30.

**GUPPY.** "There are chords in the human mind." *Bleak House*, 20.

**HEEP, URIAH.** He and his family believe in being "'umble." *Copperfield*, 16, 17, 25, 35, 39, 42, 52, 61.

**HUNTER, MRS. LEO.** Her receptions are "feasts of reason and flows of soul" enlivened by the recitation of her "Ode to an Expiring Frog." *Pickwick*, 15.

**JARNDYCE, MR. JOHN.** He feels the wind in the East when things are not as they should be. *Bleak House*, 6, 8, 14, 67.

**JO.** He is always being told to "move on." *Bleak House*, 19, 31, 46, 47.

**JOE, THE FAT BOY.** "I wants to make your flesh creep !" *Pickwick*, 8.

**LILLYVICK, MR.** "The plug of life is dry, and but the mud is left." *Nickleby*, 52.

**MANTALINI, MR.** He calls his wife "my essential juice of pineapple." *Nickleby*, 34.

"The two countesses had no outlines at all, and the dowager's was a dem'd outline." 34.

"I am always turning the mangle ; I am perpetually turning, like a dem'd old horse in a demnition mill. My life is one dem'd horrid grind." 64.

**MICAWBER, WILKINS.** He is always waiting for something to turn up.

*Copperfield*, 11, 12, 17, 27, 28, 36, 52, 54.

His wife says : " I will never desert Mr. Micawber." 12, 17, 28, 36, 57.

" Annual income twenty pounds, annual expenditure nineteen, nineteen six, result happiness. Annual income twenty pounds, annual expenditure twenty pounds and sixpence, result misery." 12.

**MODDLE, AUGUSTUS.** This melancholy youth was wont to speak of Mercy Chuzzlewit as " She who is Another's." *Chuzzlewit*, 32, 46, 54.

**PECKSNIFF, SETH.** " Let us be merry ! " Here he took a captain's biscuit. *Chuzzlewit*, 4.

" Those fabulous animals (pagan I regret to say) who used to sing in the water," said Mr. Pecksniff, referring to sirens. 4.

**PEGGOTTY, DANIEL.** " She's been thinkin' of the old 'un," was his explanation of Mrs. Gummidge's low spirits. *Copperfield*, 3, 51.

**PLORNISH, MRS.** " Me ope you leg well soon " was this lady's very near approach to speaking Italian. *Dorrit*, I, 25 ; II, 13.

**PRIG, BETSEY.** " I don't believe there's no sich a person," were her blasphemous words regarding Mrs. Harris. *Chuzzlewit*, 49.

**SIMMONS.** Intelligence was conveyed to the Board one evening that Simmons, the Beadle, had died and left his respects. *Boz, Our Parish*, 4.

**SKEWTON, MRS.** " One might be induced to cross one's arms and say like those wicked Turks that there's no what's-his-name but Thingmummy and what-you-may-call-it is his prophet." *Dombey*, 27.

**SLURK, MR.** " Ungrammatical twaddler ! " was the taunt hurled by the editor of the *Eatanswill Independent* in the teeth of his rival, Pott. *Pickwick*, 51.

**SMALLWEED, GRANDFATHER.** " You're a brimstone chatterer," was a favourite mode of addressing his wife. *Bleak House*, 21, 33.

**SQUEERS.** " This is the right shop for morals," he said of Dotheboys Hall. *Nickleby*, 4.

" She's a rum 'un, is Natur ! Natur is more easier conceived than described. Oh what a blessed thing, sir, to be in a state of natur ! " 45.

" The pigs is well, the cows is well, and the boys is bobbish." Extract from a letter of Mrs. Squeers. 57.

**TAPLEY, MARK.** Under the most trying circumstances he persists in being " Jolly ! " *Chuzzlewit*, 5, 7, 13–15, 17, 21–3, 33–5, 43, 48, 51–4.

**TOOTS.** " It's of no consequence." *Dombey*, 18, 22, 28, 32, 41, 44, 50, 56.

**TROTWOOD, MISS.** " Janet, donkeys ! "— call to hostilities against intruders on her green. *Copperfield*, 13, 14.

**TWIST, OLIVER.** " Please, sir, I want some more ! " *Twist*, 2.

**VENUS, MR.** " ' I do not wish to regard myself, nor yet to be regarded in that bony light,' " were the words which rankled in his mind when his love was rejected by Pleasant Riderhood. *Mutual Friend*, I, 7 ; II, 7 ; III, 7 ; IV, 14.

" Bones warious. Skulls warious. . . . Say human warious." I, 7.

**WEGG.** " When a person comes to grind off poetry night after night, it is but right he should expect to be paid for its weakening effect on the brain." *Mutual Friend*," I, 5.

" I generally read on gin and water ; it mellers the organ, sir." I, 5.

" With the single exception of the salary I renounce the whole and total sitiwation." IV, 3.

**WELLER, SAM.** " There ain't a magistrate goin' as don't commit himself twice as often as he commits other people." *Pickwick*, 25.

" If my eyes wos a pair o' patent double-million magnifyin' gas microscopes of hextra power." 34.

" The have-his-carcase, next to the perpetual motion is one of the blessedest things as wos ever made." 43.

" French beans, taters, tart and tidiness." 51.

**WELLER, TONY.** " Put it down a ' we,' my lord, put it down a ' we.' " *Pickwick*, 34.

For his remarks on Widders, see that article.

**WEMMICK.** " Get hold of portable property." *Expectations*, 24, 25, 32, 36.

" Halloa, here's a church . . . let's have a wedding." 55.

**WILFER, R.** "Ah me, what might have been is not what is." *Mutual Friend*, I, 4.

**WILFER, MRS.** " When I use the term attractions, I do so with the qualification that I do not mean it in any way whatever." *Mutual Friend*, I, 16.

# WELLERISMS

*Arranged alphabetically from " Pickwick Papers."*

Allow me to express a hope as you won't reduce me to ex-tremities, as the nobleman said to the fractious pennywinkle ven he vouldn't come out of his shell by means of a pin, and he conseqvently began to be afeerd that he should be obliged to crack him in the parlour door. 38.

Anythin' for a quiet life, as the man said wen he took the sitivation at the lighthouse. 43.

Avay vith melincholly, as the little boy said ven his school missis died. 44.

Business first, pleasure arterwards, as King Richard the Third said wen he stabbed the t'other king in the Tower, afore he smothered the babbies. 25.

Fall on, as the English said to the French when they fixed bagginets. 19.

Fine weather for them as is well wropped up, as the Polar bear said to himself, ven he was practising his skating. 30.

He's the wictim o' connubiality, as Blue Beard's domestic chaplain said, vith a tear of pity, ven he buried him. 20.

Hooroar for the principle, as the money-lender said ven he wouldn't renew the bill. 35.

If this don't beat cockfightin' nothin' never vill, as the lord mayor said ven the chief secretary o' state proposed his missis's health arter dinner. 39.

If you knowed who was near, I rayther think you'd change your note, as the hawk remarked to himself with a cheerful laugh ven he heerd the robin redbreast a-singin' round the corner. 47.

If you walley my precious life don't upset me, as the gen'l'm'n said to the driver wen they was a-carryin' him to Tyburn. 19.

I hope our acquaintance may be a long 'un, as the gen'l'm'n said to the fi'pun'note. 25.

I'm a prisoner. Con-fined, as the lady said. 44.

I only assisted natur, as the doctor said to the boy's mother arter he'd bled him to death. 47.

It wos to be—and wos, as the old lady said arter she'd married the footman. 52.

It's a great deal more in your way than mine, as the gen'l'm'n on the right side o' the garden vall said to the man on the wrong 'un, ven the mad bull wos a comin' up the lane. 37.

It's over and can't be helped, as they always says in Turkey, ven they cuts the wrong man's head off. 23.

It's unekal, as my father used to say wen his grog worn't made half-and-half, and that's the fault on it. 41.

No one else'll do, as the Devil's private secretary said ven he fetched avay Doctor Faustus. 15.

Nothin' less than a nat'ral conwulsion, as the young gen'l'm'n observed ven he was took with fits. 37.

Now we look compact and comfortable, as the father said ven he cut his little boy's head off to cure him o' squintin'. 28.

Out vith it, as the father said to the child wen he swallowed a farden. 28.

Proud o' the title, as the Living Skellinton said, ven they show'd him. 15.

Quite enough to get, as the soldier said ven they ordered him three hundred and fifty lashes. 34.

Rayther a change for the worse, as the gen'l'm'n said wen he got two doubtful shillin's and sixpenn'orth o' pocket pieces for a good half-crown. 45.

Reg'lar rotation, as Jack Ketch said, wen he tied the men up. 10.

Sorry to do anythin' as may cause an interruption to such wery pleasant pro-ceedin's, as the king said wen he dissolved the parliament. 48.

Take adwice, sir, as the doctor said. 51.

Take the privilidge of the day, as the gen'l'm'n in difficulties did, ven he walked out of a Sunday. 33.

There's nothin' so refreshin' as sleep, as the servant girl said afore she drank the egg-cupful of laudanum. 16.

The wery best intentions, as the gen'l'm'n said ven he run away from his wife 'cos she seemed unhappy with him. 27.

This is rayther too rich, as the young lady said wen she remonstrated with the pastry-cook, arter he'd sold her a pork pie as had got nothin' but fat inside. 38.

Ve make no extra charge for the settin' down, as the king remarked wen he blowed up his ministers. 45.

Vich I calls addin' insult to injury, as the parrot said ven they not only took him from his native land, but made him talk the English langwidge arterwards. 35.

Wery sorry to 'casion any personal inconwenience, ma'am, as the housebreaker said to the old lady when he put her on the fire. 26.

What the devil do you want with me, as the man said wen he see the ghost. 10.

Wotever is, is right, as the young nobleman sweetly remarked wen they put him down in the pension-list 'cos his mother's uncle's wife's grandfather vunce lit the king's pipe with a portable tinderbox. 51.

You're a comin' it a great deal too strong, as the mailcoachman said to the snowstorm, ven it overtook him. 42.

# WISDOM FROM MRS. GAMP

*Gathered from the pages of "Martin Chuzzlewit."*

"Mrs. Harris," I says, "leave the bottle on the chimley piece, and don't ask me to take none, but let me put my lips to it when I'm so dispoged." 19, 46, 52.

Some people may be Rooshans, and others may be Prooshans; they are so born and will please themselves. Them which is of other naturs thinks different. 19.

This Piljian's Projiss of a mortal wale. 25.

I'm but a poor woman, and I earns my living hard; therefore I *do* require it, which I make confession, to be brought reg'lar and draw'd mild. 25.

Rich folks may ride on camels, but it an't so easy for 'em to see out of a needle's eye. That is my comfort, and I hope I knows it. 25.

What a blessed thing it is—living in a wale—to be contented. 25.

Gamp is my name and Gamp my natur. 26.

"Sairey," says Mrs. Harris, "sech is life. Vich likeways is the hend of all things." 29.

The families I've had, if all was know'd and credit done where credit's doo, would take a week to christen at St. Polge's fontin. 29.

The torters of the Imposition shouldn't make me own I did. 29.

The Ankworks Package . . . and I wish it was in Jonadge's belly, I do. 40.

"Sairey," says Mrs. Harris, in an awful way, "tell me what is my indiwidgle number." "No, Mrs. Harris," I says to her, "Excuge me, if you please . . . Seek not to proticipate, but take 'em as they come and as they go.'" 40.

Bless the babe and save the mother is my mortar; but I makes so free as add to that, Don't try no impogician with the Nuss, for she will not abear it. 40.

Bite a person's thumbs or turn their fingers the wrong way and they comes to (from a faint) wonderful. 46.

He was born into a wale and he lived in a wale and he must take the consequences of sech a sitiwation. 49.

Mrs. Harris's constant words in sickness is and will be, "Send for Sairey." 49.

"Sairey," said Mrs. Harris, "you are gold as has passed the furnage." 49.

The words Betsey Prig spoke of Mrs. Harris, lambs could not forgive nor worms forget. 49.

A pleasant evenin' though warm, which we must expect when cowcumbers is three for twopence. 51.

PLATE I

THE OXFORD AND OPPOSITION STAGE COACHES RACING AT HYDE PARK CORNER
(*After W Flavell*)

PLATE II

The Angel, Bury St. Edmunds.   While staying here Mr. Pickwick and Sam Weller
fell victims to the wiles of Job Trotter (*see p. 3*)

The Great White Horse, Ipswich, where Mr. Pickwick met his adventure with the
middle-aged lady in yellow curl papers (*see p. 73*)

## SUFFOLK INNS WITH PICKWICK TRADITIONS

(*Photos. T. W. Tyrrell*)

PLATE III

Rockingham Castle, Northamptonshire, from which was drawn the description of Chesney Wold, the ancient seat of the Dedlocks (*see p.* 33)

The Rookery of St. Giles, demolished in the making of New Oxford Street, was one of the worst London Slums, and a prototype of Tom-All-Alones (*see p.* 134)

## CONTRASTS FROM BLEAK HOUSE

(*Photo. T. W. Tyrrell*)

PLATE IV

Cob Tree Hall, Sandling, the original of Manor Farm, Dingley Dell, showing a corner of the garden where Mr. Tupman wooed the fair Rachel (*see p.* 50)

Lant Street, Borough, where Bob Sawyer entertained Mr. Pickwick in his rooms at Mrs. Raddles's. Dickens lodged here as a lad (*see p.* 95)

## HOMES OF MR. PICKWICK'S FRIENDS

(*Photos. T. W. Tyrrell*)

PLATE V

Daniel Grant, the original of Brother Charles (*see p. 33*)

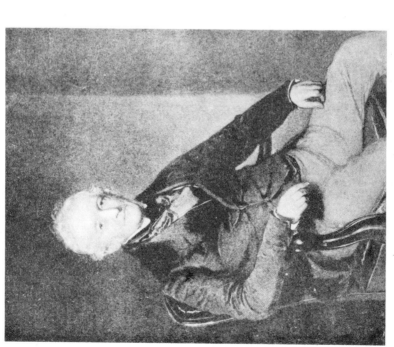

William Grant, the original of Brother Ned

PORTRAITS OF THE CHEERYBLE TWINS IN REAL LIFE

PLATE VI

Mrs. Crupp's residence, York House,
Buckingham Street, where David set up
in bachelor state (*see p.* 25)

141 Bayham Street, Camden Town, one
of the Dickens' homes and the house
of Mr. Micawber (*see p.* 28)

Blundeston Rectory, the original of The Rookery at Blunderstone, where David
was born (*see p.* 19)

DAVID COPPERFIELD IN LONDON AND SUFFOLK

(*Photos. T. W. Tyrrell*)

PLATE VII

W. S. Landor, Lawrence Boythorn
(see p. 22)

Mrs. Winter, née Maria Beadnell, Flora Finching
(see p. 10)

PORTRAITS OF SOME ORIGINALS

S. Carter Hall, Mr. Pecksniff
(see p. 122)

PLATE VIII

The Guildhall, London, and the old Law Court, seen on the right, where the Bardell-Pickwick trial took place. From an engraving dated 1828, the year of the trial (*see p.* 76)

The Market Place, Sudbury, Suffolk, generally accepted as the town upon which Dickens founded his description of Eatanswill. From a contemporary engraving (*see p.* 56)

## SCENES ASSOCIATED WITH MR. PICKWICK

*(Photo. Charles Emeny, Sudbury)* ·

PLATE IX

The King's Head, Chigwell, immortalised as the Maypole Inn, of Barnaby Rudge.
It is little changed since the days of old John Willett (*see p.* 106)

The Bull, Rochester, at which Mr. Pickwick and his friends began their adventures.
It is also called the Winglebury Arms in Boz, and the Blue Boar in Great
Expectations (*see p.* 26)

## TWO FAMOUS DICKENSIAN INNS

*(Photos. T. W. Tyrrell)*

PLATE X

The George Inn, Amesbury, suggested original of the Blue
Dragon (*see p.* 18)

ORIGINALS OF INNS MENTIONED IN MARTIN CHUZZLEWIT AND OUR MUTUAL FRIEND

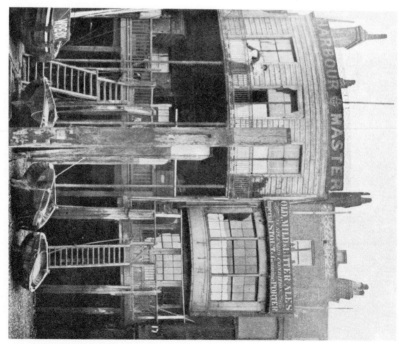

The Grapes Inn, Limehouse, original of the Six Jolly
Fellowship Porters (*see p.* 141)

*(Photos, T. W. Tyrell)*

PLATE XI

The younger sister of his wife, this girl exercised a great influence on Dickens, and her death, at the age of seventeen, prostrated him with grief. Mary Hogarth was the original of Little Nell, Kate Nickleby, Madeleine Bray, Rose Maylie, Emma Haredale, Mary Graham, Florence Dombey, Agnes Wickfield, Ada Clare and Lucie Manette

## MARY HOGARTH, ORIGINAL OF MOST OF DICKENS'S HEROINES

*(From an oil painting by H. K. Browne)*

PLATE XII

The Leather Bottle, Cobham, where Mr. Tupman retired to soothe his wounded heart after the loss of Miss Rachel Wardle (*see p.* 95)

The Saracen's Head (now the Pomfret Arms), Towcester, was the scene of the battle royal between Messrs. Pott and Slurk (*see p.* 138)

## TWO INNS UNCHANGED SINCE PICKWICKIAN DAYS

*(Photos. T. W. Tyrrell and Gravesend Brewery, Ltd.)*

PLATE XIII

Interior of the Dorrits' garret in the Marshalsea Prison, from a sepia sketch made shortly before its demolition (*see p.* 104)

The old Surrey Theatre, where Frederick Dorrit played the clarionet (*see p.* 150). In the foreground is a hackney coach (*see p.* 76)

## ASSOCIATIONS WITH LITTLE DORRIT

PLATE XIV

Serjeant Bompas, Serjeant Buzfuz

Leigh Hunt, Harold Skimpole

Sir Stephen Gazelee, Justice Stareleigh

John Forster, John Podsnap and Dowler

Justice Talfourd, Thomas Traddles

PORTRAITS OF SOME ORIGINALS

PLATE XV

Bow Street and a posse of Bow Street Runners, commonly known as Robin Redbreasts, who constituted the police force before 1829 (*see p.* 21)

Old Bailey and Newgate on the occasion of a public execution. It was before such a crowd as this that Fagin was hanged (*see pp.* 114 *and* 117)

## THE TERROR OF THE LAW

PLATE XVI

Eastgate House, called in Edwin Drood " The Nun's House," where Miss Twinkleton
kept her school (*see p.* 133)

Restoration House, the Satis House of Great Expectations, where Miss Havisham
passed her mysterious existence

### LANDMARKS IN ROCHESTER

(*Photos. T. W. Tyrrell*)

PLATE XVII

The old Theatre, where Nicholas and Smike enjoyed their brief theatrical career
on the stage in the Vincent Crummles Company

The Common Hard, where Nicholas and his friend lodged " at a tobacconist's
shop," now known as " The Old Curiosity Shop"

### PORTSMOUTH AND ITS NICKLEBY ASSOCIATIONS

*(Photos. T. W. Tyrrell)*

PLATE XVIII

General view of the town and the old bridge, as they appeared at the time of the Pickwickians' visit. From a drawing by G. H. Shepherd, 1828

The High Street, showing the fine old house associated with Mr. Sapsea, the auctioneer, and Uncle Pumblechook, the seedsman

### THE ANCIENT CITY OF ROCHESTER
(*Photo. T W. Tyrrell*)

PLATE XIX

John Dickens, who had many of the characteristics portrayed
in Wilkins Micawber

Elizabeth Dickens, whose different aspects are seen in
Mrs. Nickleby and Mrs Wilfer

THE PARENTS OF CHARLES DICKENS

PLATE XX

Inspector Field, who also appears as
Inspector Bucket (*see p.* 61)

Sir Peter Laurie, Alderman Cute in
The Chimes (*see p.* 46)

Lord Brougham, Mr. Pott of the
Eatanswill Gazette (*see p.* 128)

PORTRAITS OF SOME ORIGINALS

PLATE XXI

"Dotheboys Hall" at Bowes, near Greta Bridge. This was the school kept by William Shaw, forever immortalised as Wackford Squeers (*see p. 54*)

The King's Head Inn, Barnard Castle, recommended by Newman Noggs and the house where Dickens stayed when collecting material (*see p. 93*)

## NICHOLAS NICKLEBY IN YORKSHIRE

*(Photos. T. W. Tyrrell)*

PLATE XXII

The old Golden Cross, Charing Cross, as it appeared in Pickwickian days before Trafalgar Square was made. Opposite is Northumberland House (*see p.* 70)

The Fleet Prison, seen from the Racquet Ground. Mr. Pickwick's room was on the second floor of the main building (*see p.* 62)

SCENES OF VANISHED LONDON

PLATE XXIII

Interior of Tong parish church, before its restoration, where the tired child passed so many happy hours at the close of her life *(see p. 155)*

WHERE LITTLE NELL ENDED HER WANDERINGS

PLATE XXIV

The Wooden Midshipman
(*see p.* 169)

The old shop kept by Sol Gills, 157 Leadenhall
Street, with the sign of the Wooden Midshipman over the door (*see p.* 95)

Chichester House, Chichester Terrace, Brighton, identified on the authority ot
Harrison Ainsworth as the original of Dr. Blimber's (*see p.* 18)

DEALINGS WITH DOMBEY AND SON

(*Photos. and information from T. W. Tyrrell*)